T0355599

AFTER THE NAZIS

OTHER BOOKS BY MICHAEL H. KATER

Das "Ahnenerbe" der SS 1935–1945: Ein Beitrag zur Kulturpolitik des Dritten Reiches (1974)

Studentenschaft und Rechtsradikalismus in Deutschland, 1918–1933: Eine sozialgeschichtliche Studie zur Bildungskrise in der Weimarer Republik (1975)

The Nazi Party: A Social Profile of Members and Leaders, 1919–1945 (1983)

Doctors Under Hitler (1989)

Different Drummers: Jazz in the Culture of Nazi Germany (1992)

The Twisted Muse: Musicians and Their Music in the Third Reich (1997)

Composers of the Nazi Era: Eight Portraits (2000)

Hitler Youth (2004)

Never Sang for Hitler: The Life and Times of Lotte Lehmann, 1888–1976 (2008)

Weimar: From Enlightenment to the Present (2014)

Culture in Nazi Germany (2019)

After the Nazis

The Story of Culture in West Germany

Michael H. Kater

YALE UNIVERSITY PRESS
NEW HAVEN AND LONDON

For information about this and other Yale University Press publications, please contact:
U.S. Office: sales.press@yale.edu   yalebooks.com
Europe Office: sales@yaleup.co.uk   yalebooks.co.uk

Set in Adobe Caslon Pro regular by IDSUK (DataConnection) Ltd
Printed in Great Britain by TJ Books, Padstow, Cornwall

Library of Congress Control Number: 2023938731

ISBN 978-0-300-25924-7

A catalogue record for this book is available from the British Library.

10 9 8 7 6 5 4 3 2 1

I dedicate this book to my wife Barbara and my first-born daughter Eva, a historian of Canada. Eva arrived in 1972, during the rewriting of my dissertation on the SS for publication. Barbara had been with me since the beginning of my doctoral studies in Heidelberg, in 1961, supporting me against often seemingly insurmountable odds. During my last three books, with Yale University Press, she has been a pillar of support.
This photograph shows us in Heidelberg, in 1963.

Contents

Illustrations

13. Hans Werner Henze, 1957. Photo by Keystone / Hulton Archive / Getty Images.
14. Karlheinz Stockhausen, 1994. Kathinka Pasveer, CC BY-SA 3.0.
15. Alexander Kluge, 1983. Gorup de Besanez, CC BY-SA 4.0.
16. Hark Bohm, Rainer Werner Fassbinder, Bernhard Wiki, and Rudolf Augstein, 1971. United Archives GmbH / Alamy.
17. *The Pack (Das Rudel)*, by Joseph Beuys, 1969. bpk / Museumslandschaft Hessen Kassel © DACS 2023.
18. Werner Höfer at the Frankfurt Book Fair, 1978. Bundesarchiv_B_145_Bild-F051796-0017.
19. Rudi Dutschke leading demonstrators in West Berlin, 1968. Kunz Wolfgang / Alamy.
20. Peter Zadek, *c.* 1977. Interfoto / Alamy.
21. Rolf Hochhuth with Erwin Piscator during rehearsals of *Der Stellvertreter* in West Berlin, 1973. Keystone Press / Alamy.
22. Thorwald Proll, Horst Söhnlein, Andreas Baader, and Gudrun Ensslin on trial, 1968. dpa picture alliance / Alamy.
23. Holger Meins, 1974. ZUMA Press, Inc. / Alamy.
24. Ulrike Meinhof and Gudrun Ensslin in prison, 1975. Photo by Keystone / Getty Images.
25. Hanns Martin Schleyer, 1976. Sueddeutsche Zeitung Photo / Alamy.
26. *Confrontation 1*, by Gerhard Richter, 1988. © Gerhard Richter 2023 (0077).
27. *Ganz unten*, by Günter Wallraff, 1988. © Verlag Kiepenheuer & Witsch GmbH & Co. KG, Cologne, Germany.
28. Ernst Nolte, 2006. Photo by Martin Lengemann / ullstein bild via Getty Images.
29. A scene from Edgar Reitz's *Heimat*, 1984. Photo 12 / Alamy Stock Photo.
30. A scene from Hans-Jürgen Syberberg's *Hitler: Ein Film aus Deutschland*, 1977, DVD cover from 30th anniversary edition. © Filmgalerie 451.
31. Volker Schlöndorff and Margarethe von Trotta. Sueddeutsche Zeitung Photo / Alamy Stock Photo.
32. Anselm Kiefer, 2011. dpa picture alliance archive / Alamy.

Abbreviations

AFN	American Forces Network
APA	author's private archive
ARD	Arbeitsgemeinschaft der öffentlich-rechtlichen Rundfunkanstalten der Bundesrepublik Deutschland (= First Channel, Public Television, Germany)
BAB	Bundesarchiv Berlin
BBC	British Broadcasting Corporation
BFN	British Forces Network
CCC	Central Cinema Compagnie-Film GmbH
CDU	Christlich Demokratische Union (Christian Democratic Union)
CIA	Central Intelligence Agency
CM	Carl-Orff-Zentrum München
CSR	Czecho-Slovak Republic
CSU	Christlich Soziale Union (Christian Social Union)
DAZ	*Deutsche Allgemeine Zeitung*
DEFA	Deutsche Film-Aktiengesellschaft
DKP	Deutsche Kommunistische Partei (German Communist Party)
DP	Displaced Person

DR	*Das Reich*
DS	*Der Spiegel*
DW	*Die Welt*
DZ	*Die Zeit*
FAZ	*Frankfurter Allgemeine Zeitung*
FDP	Freie Demokratische Partei Deutschlands (Free Democratic Party of Germany)
FLN	Front de Liberation Nationale (National Liberation Front)
FM	frequency modulation
FR	*Frankfurter Rundschau*
FRG	Federal Republic of Germany
FSK	Freiwillige Selbstkontrolle (Voluntary Self-Control)
FU	Freie Universität [Berlin] (Free University [Berlin])
FZ	*Frankfurter Zeitung*
GDR	German Democratic Republic
Gestapo	Geheime Staatspolizei (secret police)
GSG	Grenzschutzgruppe (border patrol)
IfZ	Institut für Zeitgeschichte München
KGB	Komitet Gosudarstvennoy Bezopasnosti (secret police)
KPD	Kommunistische Partei Deutschlands (Communist Party of Germany)
NATO	North Atlantic Treaty Organization
NAW	National Archives Washington
NBC	National Broadcasting Company
NDR	Norddeutscher Rundfunk (North German Radio)
NGF	New German Film
NPD	Nationaldemokratische Partei Deutschlands (National Democratic Party of Germany)
NSDAP	Nationalsozialistische Deutsche Arbeiterpartei (Nazi Party)
NWDR	Nordwestdeutscher Rundfunk (Northwest German Radio)
NY	*The New Yorker*
NYRB	*The New York Review of Books*
NYT	*The New York Times*
OMGUS	Office of Military Government of the United States for Germany

PEN	Poets, Essayists, Novelists (=PEN International)
POW	Prisoner of war
RAF	Rote Armee Fraktion (Red Army Faction)
RIAS	Rundfunk im amerikanischen Sektor (Radio in the American Sector)
SA	Sturm-Abteilungen (storm troopers)
SD	Sicherheitsdienst (security service of the SS)
SDS	Sozialistischer Deutscher Studentenbund (Socialist German Student League)
SED	Sozialistische Einheitspartei Deutschlands (Socialist Unity Party of Germany)
SF	Südfunk [Stuttgart] (Radio Stuttgart)
SFB	Sender Freies Berlin (Radio Free Berlin)
SPD	Sozialdemokratische Partei Deutschlands (Social Democratic Party of Germany)
SS	Schutzstaffel
Stasi	Staatssicherheit (state security)
SWF	Südwestfunk [Baden-Baden] (Southwest Radio)
SZ	*Süddeutsche Zeitung*
taz	*tageszeitung* (Berlin)
UCLA	University of California at Los Angeles
Ufa	Universum Film Aktiengesellschaft
UKW	Ultrakurzwelle (ultra-shortwave=FM wave band)
UNESCO	*United Nations Educational, Scientific and Cultural Organization*
USSR	Union of Soviet Socialist Republics
WDR	Westdeutscher Rundfunk (West German Radio)
YMCA	Young Men's Christian Association
YUA	York University Archives and Special Collections, Toronto
ZDF	Zweites Deutsches Fernsehen (=regional TV)

Introduction

G ROWING UP IN Krefeld, West Germany, in the early 1950s, I was
fascinated by the cultural offerings in that mid-size Rhenish town.
As a young teenager, my parents took me to art exhibitions with
pictures I had difficulty making sense of, there were concerts of the classics
and recitals, and a choir, in which I sang. I also took piano lessons from two
renowned teachers, former stage performers. On my bicycle route home
from the Humanistische Gymnasium, where I studied Greek, Latin, and
English, I used to stop at the Mennenöh bookstore on Rheinstrasse, where
the latest literature was on offer. I spent much time there sampling the latest
books (I loved the smell), but they also had two magazines in English,
Reader's Digest and *Popular Mechanics*, which fascinated me. Eventually I
read the first of these in a German translation, but longed to understand its
contents in the English original. Germany then was on the brink of important cultural changes, including an embracing of foreign impulses, but of
course I could not recognize any of that at the time. Nor could I know of the
difficulties a cultural renaissance would encounter, this having begun in the
late 1940s.

This book is an attempt to deal with these changes seventy years later as
well as subsequent developments. Its story is loosely tied to the hypothesis that
the relative success of the Federal Republic of Germany (FRG) after 1945 was,
to an important extent, the consequence of a fertile interdependence of politics

and culture. This manifested itself significantly. Insofar as that democracy had to be rebuilt under the Western Allies' supervision, freedom of cultural expression was a precondition. In everyday praxis, active engagement with culture, in antithesis to Nazism, would prompt good government, meaning representative democracy. For true culture to form and continue to grow, democracy and its institutions had to offer foundational support. Culture creators sought such freedom and such support, and through their productions worked to establish good government – representative democracy. Democracy's post-war exponents, in politics and the arts, were predominantly found on the ideological left in opposition to Nazism. Conversely, the more right-wing and authoritarian were the political trends, the more the arts were liable to suffer – shades of the Third Reich.

This is the last in a trilogy of books on German culture in modern times that I have written. The first volume, *Weimar: From Enlightenment to the Present*, deals with the town of Weimar, the cradle of culture under Goethe and Schiller during the Enlightenment, from 1770 into the twenty-first century. It shows that the apotheosis of its history was under those two poets; thereafter was decline. It was published in 2014. The second book, of 2019, is *Culture in Nazi Germany*. It tells of culture's compromises and agony under Hitler and his Nazi followers, with passages on resisters, emigrants, and survivors.

I happened upon the first project when in the early 1990s I visited Weimar, taking a break from research in Munich on the history of German music and composers. While there, I remembered an ancestor who, in family lore, was supposed to have been a savant in Goethe's, and later Schiller's, circle. His name was Johann Michael Heintze, and I found the house he had lived in with his family very near the Church of St Peter and Paul on today's Herderplatz, where he had regularly preached. In the early years of the new millennium, I decided to probe this more thoroughly and attempt a Weimar history. It turned out that Heintze, although not a personal friend, had served under Goethe's ministry at the end of the eighteenth century, not only as main pastor but also as overseer of the Weimar duchy's educational system and rector of its Wilhelm-Ernst Gymnasium, where he taught Greek and Latin (family members apparently spoke those languages at the dinner table). His superior in the Weimar administration and personal friend was Johann Gottfried von Herder, who conducted a funeral sermon at the time of his death in October 1790. I later found it reprinted in a family chronicle.

Heintze's brief biography in my Weimar book introduced a personal factor that resurfaced when I began research for the third volume on West German culture, because Helmut Roloff, an uncle of mine and one of Heintze's direct descendants, was found to have played an interesting role as a musician, both during the Third Reich and as co-founder of New Music endeavors thereafter. As I proceeded to write the current volume, I remembered, from my own childhood this or that episode (such as meeting Roloff on a stage in 1943), which, as I thought, could serve as evidence just as well as other episodes that I found for documentation in printed sources. Hence, I kept up the practice of weaving in reminiscences, up to and including some encounters as late as the 1980s. And although I conceived this book as an academic historian, the musician in me made brief appearances as well.

To write an encyclopedic history of culture in the FRG from 1945 to 1990, or a textbook, would be well-nigh impossible today, not least because important archival resources will not be available for a very long time, but also because as an historian one is still too close to that era. Therefore, much of the story is based on biographies, memoirs, some timely scholarly analyses such as in musicology, filmography and German literature, together with contemporaneous newspaper and magazine articles and reviews, as well as reproductions of artifacts, sound recordings, and films. In addition, published letters and diaries are referred to.

There are, thus far, few comprehensive histories of West Germany and even fewer FRG histories covering the period after 1990, much less chronicles of culture. From the 1980s, there are two volumes on culture in West and East Germany, by Jost Hermand, but their texts are not supported by documentary evidence. As one reflects on culture in the years from 1945 to 1990, one tends to perceive mostly highlights, perhaps a certain exhibit at the Kassel documenta exposition of modern art; a concert of Pierre Boulez conducting his own music in Berlin; a critical film by Rainer Werner Fassbinder; an idiosyncratic character from a novel by Günter Grass or Heinrich Böll – Oskar Matzerath perhaps, from *The Tin Drum*, or Katharina Blum from Böll's morality piece mirroring the 1970s fear of left-radical terrorism; or, on a theatrical stage, Padre Riccardo Fontana from Rolf Hochhuth's anti-papal drama *The Deputy*. For this reason, other than chronologically and, rudimentarily, by genre, narrative and reflection in this book do not unfold systematically, but rather more impressionistically, as in a succession of untitled vignettes.

Since there were main protagonists putting their stamps on events, those men and women are mentioned repeatedly, rather than the twenty-five or fifty others who together accomplished not even half of what each one of those did. In the area of literature, they are Heinrich Böll, Günter Grass, and Martin Walser, joined by the major critics Marcel Reich-Ranicki and Joachim Kaiser. Hans Magnus Enzensberger's loquacious commentary was omnipresent. In musical progressive circles, Hans Werner Henze and Karlheinz Stockhausen are most often encountered, and in the visual arts the seminal painters and masters of Happening Joseph Beuys, Gerhard Richter, and Anselm Kiefer. Pace-setting films in those decades were made by Rainer Werner Fassbinder, Alexander Kluge, and Volker Schlöndorff, and in journalism, Rudolf Augstein, Marion Gräfin Dönhoff, and Henri Nannen surpassed everyone else. Peter Zadek, joined sometimes by Peter Palitzsch and Claus Peymann, was the outstanding director in the republic's theaters.

These personalities often determined the fate of the cultural organizations I have chosen to focus on. In literature this was the Gruppe 47 – until 1967, when it died, in music the Darmstadt New Music course festival, and in the visual arts the Kassel documenta. The fate of those was varied, and the documenta are currently experiencing an existential crisis that may be understood only through precursors in the 1960s or 1970s. Happily, this does not seem to be an indicator for the entire course of German culture from 1945 to the present, and will be for future historians to assess. Be this as it may, the personalities as much as the groups they inhabited all stood in some critical relationship to National Socialism and the Third Reich, so that their creations were touched – the closer they were to 1945, the stronger tended to be the impact. They either suffered from Nazism or were, to some degree, complicit – sometimes even both – and so they reacted, with characteristic cultural output. In their work also, the fate of the Jews under Hitler became an increasing concern, memorializing Auschwitz being a key issue. Was it not possible, as Theodor W. Adorno famously said, to compose poetry after Auschwitz? Whatever that case may be, to the extent that culture creators after 1945 repudiated what had been Nazism, they were liable to embrace manifestations of democracy; often, their criticism extended to West German politics and society. In cases where this did not happen, democracy appeared at risk.

I have many people to thank for helping me to write and publish these books. The first two volumes of the trilogy, on Weimar and the Third Reich, were chaperoned expertly by Heather McCallum at Yale University Press in London, and she remained the patron saint while this last book was written, and edited with perspicacity by Joanna Godfrey, to whose guidance it owes much. Other professionals at the press were Rachael Lonsdale, Meg Pettit, and Katie Urquhart. At York University in Toronto, Dean of Research and Graduate Studies Ravi de Costa ensured that I received continued institutional financing, for which I thank him. In the university's interlibrary-loan department, Samantha McWilliams and Sandra Snell provided me reliably with out-of-town literature, as they have done for many years. Even given York University's growing resources, no book in German history could be written without them.

Here at home in Oakville, my wife Barbara, with her own background in German Studies, art, and photography, carefully looked at almost every sentence I wrote and always discussed major issues in context with me. She saved me from making serious mistakes. Several chapters were read at various stages by Albrecht Riethmüller (Berlin), Roland Pahlitzsch (Karlskrona), Jürgen W. Falter (Mainz), William E. Seidelman (Jerusalem), and Barney McClure (Ukiah). They answered specific questions and judged the validity of some of my tentative conclusions, and I benefited much. Sherri Jones, George R. Kater, Hartmut Lehmann, Christian Streit, and Hans R. Vaget also contributed to the writing process in several ways. My gratitude extends to them all.

CHAPTER ONE

◆ ◆ ◆

Out of Ruins (1945–1950)

O N TUESDAY, MAY 1, 1945, I was drying a small collection of Hitler stamps on the windowsill of my grandfather's house in a small village near Bremen in North Germany. I had been staying with my grandfather, a Lutheran minister, for some weeks with my younger brother and my mother, having escaped bombing raids on a days-long train ride from Zittau, in south-east Saxony, with my father still serving in the Wehrmacht. As I learned later, we had passed through Dresden two weeks before that fateful British firebomb attack of February 13–15, during which at least 25,000 people perished. There was an air raid as we hunkered down in a railroad underpass in Magdeburg. The last few months in Zittau had been quiet, with only a few raids. I had been going to school almost until we left. All of seven years old, I had been looking forward to joining the Hitler Youth like the older neighborhood boys whom I played with and whom I admired. They told me I could be in a tank racing down the street and running people down. That prospect excited and scared me at the same time. Hitler's portrait – a lithograph, black on white – hung in our dining room. Sitting underneath it, I loved listening to the march music on the radio, drumming to it on the tabletop. In the North German village, life continued peacefully, except for a squat British airman in a blue uniform who after bombing Bremen, parachuted onto the meadows behind our house. They took this enemy away, and I did not know what they did with him; I did not ask. On that Tuesday, May 1, as I was drying my stamps, the beloved march music in the radio was suddenly interrupted and a man's voice somberly announced: "Our Führer Adolf Hitler has just fallen in the defense of Berlin. Heil Hitler!" And then sounded the national anthem, "Deutschland, Deutschland über alles!" I was left bewildered.

A few weeks later, the Third Reich ceased to exist after German capitulation to the victors – effective May 8, 1945. To replace the Nazi government, an Allied Control Council was established, of Great Britain, France, the United States, and the Soviet Union. For each, an occupation zone was created, the Soviets holding the region east of the Elbe. Berlin, too, was divided into four sectors. An immediate task was to liquidate the Nazi system, demobilize German society, transform the German economy to peacetime production, and, carefully, transfer basic administrative functions to the Germans. A trial of major Nazi leaders commenced at Nuremberg on November 20, before an inter-Allied tribunal.[1]

Political parties were authorized in all occupation zones by the end of 1945. In the three Western zones, German self-government was instituted at local and regional levels. Regional elections in the American zone, for example, brought the Christian Democratic Union (CDU) to victory, followed by the Social Democratic Party (SPD). There were similar results in the British and French zones. In the Eastern zone by April 1946, where the Soviets had maintained much tighter control, Social Democrats and Communists merged into a Communist-led Socialist Unity Party (SED), which was to govern East Germany as a client to Soviet leadership until the late 1980s.[2]

In early December 1946 an agreement was signed for an economic union of the American and British zones of occupation (Bizonia; in April 1948, with the French zone joining, this became Trizonia). Half a year later a German economic council was set up to direct bizonal economic reconstruction. By this time a rift had appeared between the West and the Soviet Union. The British and Americans opposed a large Soviet reparations demand, from current German production, because it would impede the establishment of German economic self-sufficiency. This disagreement would exacerbate the Cold War between East and West, which was already sweltering because of Soviet power designs in the western hemisphere.[3] By April 1, 1948, the Soviets were interfering with traffic between western

2

Germany and Berlin. After the Western Powers had introduced the stable Deutsche Mark, ushering in rapid economic recovery, the Soviets completely stopped road and rail movements between Berlin and the West. This led to a Western, large-scale air lift of vital supplies by the Americans to Berlin airports. At the height of this, one hundred freight planes were constantly in the air, twenty-four hours a day, "veritably endless chains in the three corridors between Berlin and the West."[4]

The Soviet blockade ended in May 1949, the same month the Federal Republic of Germany (FRG) was established. Its government was to be guided by a new Basic Law, adopting many ingredients of the past Weimar constitution, but also trying to avoid some of its pitfalls, such as inordinate powers granted to a president.[5] In August general elections were held for the Bundestag, the new West German federal parliament's lower house, which gave the CDU (and its Bavarian sister party Christian Social Union – CSU) a small lead over the Socialists, with the mid-center Free Democratic Party (FDP) holding the balance. Theodor Heuss, a Free Democrat, was elected president, and Konrad Adenauer, a Christian Democrat, chancellor of the FRG, with Bonn as its provisional capital. On September 21, an Allied Occupation Statute came into force. The functions of military government, still superseding the new West German administration in Bonn, were transferred to an Allied High Commission. This meant more independence for the Germans. Bent on rejuvenating West Germany as an ally in the ongoing confrontation with the Soviet Union, this commission made economic concessions to West Germany, especially funds from the newly instituted American Marshall Plan. This helped to end the last rationing restrictions in January 1950 and spurred per capita growth. By September 1950, accelerated by urgency resulting from the divisive Korean War, the status of West Germany experienced a rapid change from that of an enemy to that of a future ally of the Western Powers.[6]

◆ ◆ ◆

One of the first tasks of the Allies in all four occupation zones was to establish mechanisms for the creation of denazified German administrations to lift the country out of chaos and move it forward in democracy. Local and regional institutions were to be staffed with reliable non-Nazis who would resuscitate the economy, revert to democratic education of German citizens and their children, and, last but not least, create cultural incentives conducive to democracy. The Soviets relatively quickly punished those whom they considered to have been important Nazi bigwigs while installing lesser Nazis willing to repent in positions of some authority.[7] For the Western Allies, it was difficult to identify men and women who had not been National Socialists and thus could be trusted with the rebirth of democracy. In western Germany, in the pace-setting American zone of Bremen, Hesse, Württemberg-Baden, and Bavaria, the Nationalsozialistische Deutsche Arbeiterpartei (National Socialist German Workers' Party, NSDAP) was dissolved and approximately 200,000 persons deemed to be hard-core Nazis, such as members of the Schutzstaffel (SS), Gestapo, and political leaders, were arrested. Well into 1946, former functionaries of the public service and the national economy were taken into custody. Until the beginning of 1947, the British and French authorities followed suit.[8] In the American zone, Germans had to fill out a questionnaire to supply 131 answers as to their wartime activities and Nazi sympathies – much derided and resented by whoever was affected.[9] Job assignments depended on the answers, so systemic lies were a foregone conclusion. Moreover, Germans were able to appeal Allied decisions against them, and in 1946 the Americans handed the ever more complicated process of denazification to German authorities. The British had been more lenient, let alone the French, who tended to judge rather more arbitrarily.[10] What favored the Germans all along was that they knew the Allies needed expertise, for instance in education or in construction; hence as early as 1946 they were profiting from this, because not every guilty person could be dismissed from a position or, worse, detained in an internment camp.[11]

Those camps were meant for die-hard Nazis who spent months or years there, a total of 250,000 men and some women in 1945, but fewer in the following years as the denazification processes were becoming less effective, especially as several were taken over by Germans in 1946.[12] By 1948, most camps had been dissolved. The internees were assigned to forced labor and hard conditions, which bred a sense of resentment and caused many to reinforce their belief in National Socialism.[13] When I was allowed to visit a friend of my mother's in Hanover in 1948, her husband, a former SS medical officer just returned from a British internment camp, put me and his children in a car. He took us to the railway station and pointed to some miserable-looking, badly dressed people hurrying to and fro. "See, those are Jews," he said to us, "filthy vermin. Unfortunately, we did not remove enough of them." He was entirely unrepentant.

To speed denazification, the Allies organized court procedures, jointly and in their respective zones of occupation. In preparation for those, the Allies kept suspected Nazis in special detention centers, some of which, such as the British one at Bad Nenndorf some distance west of Hanover, used torture in interrogations reminiscent of the Nazi era.[14] The Nuremberg War Trials, to serve justice to twenty-two prominent Nazi leaders and eight organizations, took place from November 1945 to October 1946.[15] In addition, successive trials were conducted against specified military, professional, and economic groups. For example, Otto Ohlendorf, a forty-year-old economist, was tried and executed as leader of Einsatzgruppe D. At his funeral in June 1951, over a thousand sympathizers saluted with the Hitler greeting.[16] After a British trial at Lüneburg in autumn 1945, the attractive twenty-two-year-old Irma Grese, who had aspired to be a film star, was hanged for her role as a guard in Auschwitz. A former mistress of the notorious doctor Josef Mengele, she was later used by Rolf Hochhuth as the basis for the character of Helga in his 1963 stage play *Der Stellvertreter* (*The Deputy*).[17]

German authorities took over denazification proceedings in the American zone in 1946, and by 1947 also in the British and French zones. They created *Spruchkammern*, or inquisition courts, staffed by 20,000 personnel. These frequently failed in their purpose, not only because the courts were overloaded and tricked by clever defendants, but also because the jurors were often sympathetic to the Nazi cause. Despite this, suspect defendants were often assumed to be guilty; they were tried on the basis of the earlier questionnaires and had to adduce proof of innocence. To do so, they conjured pieces of paper signed by friends or neighbors to the effect that they had not been Nazis, had been duped, or were actually victims of Nazi rule.[18]

From the arts world, the appearance of Munich composer Werner Egk before local courts serves as an example. During the Third Reich, this Classical Modernist, whose music was influenced by Stravinsky, had been employed as a section leader in Goebbels's Reich culture chamber. He had composed in support of Nazi cultural policy, such as background music for the Hitler Youth film *Jungens* (*Lads*, 1941). He had been decorated by the Nazis and profited by having been allowed to perform his compositions many times in Occupied Paris. The courts accepted without scrutiny several stories that Egk was able, with the help of friends and colleagues, to tell them in his defense. These culminated in the falsehood that he had engaged in resistance to the Nazi regime from Paris, Berlin, and Austrian territory, and as a result he was cleared of all charges in October 1947. Classified as "non-affected," he resumed work as a composer in Munich, and by 1950 had been appointed as director of the Berlin Hochschule für Musik.[19]

At the end of this denazification process in February 1950 approximately 900,000 Germans had been cleared, and their economic and political progress in the country could no longer be blocked.[20] To them must be added scores of Germans who were never registered by either the Allied or German authorities for denazification, who had lied on the questionnaires, or, having returned from a prisoner of war (POW) camp or being born after 1919, were exempt. And even for formally guilty people the new West German government issued an amnesty law on December 31, 1949, which affected all those who were subject to penalties under six months. This was augmented by parliament-sanctioned statutes of limitations on May 8, 1950.[21]

As a consequence of ineptitude or leniency, entire segments of West German society, its administration, economic, educational, and cultural institutions were, in effect, "renazified." In May 1951 the Bonn Bundestag interpreted Article 131 of the Basic Law to mean that former members of the Nazi bureaucracy who had been suspended in the first rush after May 1945 had to be reinstated professionally, with full rights and pensions.[22] And so among the 402 delegates of that first Bonn parliament, fifty-three were former members of the Nazi Party.[23] Already in one of his earliest cabinet sessions in 1949, Chancellor Adenauer had proposed that one might as well ignore the Nazis and start from scratch.[24] Many jurists and the overwhelming majority of journalists were able to return to their jobs after going through the motions of denazification, as early as 1947.[25] Hence, at the beginning of the republic, about one-quarter of the staff of French-supervised Südwestfunk radio station (SWF) in Baden-Baden had been in the NSDAP, the Sturmabteilung (SA), or the SS.[26]

Apart from formal denazification, the Western Allies faced the task of re-educating the Germans in the spirit of civil liberty and democracy. Toward this end, culture could be instrumentalized. Ideally, as they realized early, the Germans themselves should participate in this, but German culture as it had existed until May 1945 was tainted. In fact, on May 12, 1945, General Dwight Eisenhower, in his capacity as supreme commander of the Allied Expeditionary Forces, had denounced the propaganda ministry and prohibited Germans from any public cultural pursuits.[27] Instead, the Germans would have to relearn cultural activity under Western tutelage. But since this would be a longer process, the Allies tried, at first, to introduce German consumers to cultural products of their own.

This could be done with books in translation or even in the original, although those would influence only a small number of educated German elite. The Americans took the lead by authorizing for the market American novels in translation, for instance Ernest Hemingway's *For Whom the Bell Tolls*. Hemingway's books would influence throngs of young German writers such as Siegfried Lenz, who were at a loss for style and content.[28] Yet another means of cultural propaganda was providing German theaters with Western plays in translation – by Eugene O'Neill, John Steinbeck, and Jean-Paul Sartre. In broadcasting, RIAS (Rundfunk im amerikanischen Sektor, or Radio in the American Sector), an exclusively American creation in West Berlin, performed Thornton Wilder's *Our Town* as a radio play.[29]

That some of these efforts were motivated by commerce rather than altruism was shown in the film industry, particularly in a contest between the Americans and the British. Hollywood was bent on selling as many feature films to German movie audiences as possible. In November 1949, for instance, John Ford's Western *My Darling Clementine* was shown under the German title *Faustrecht der Prärie* at Berlin's Neue Scala theater. To make it sell, *Die Neue Zeitung*, another American media creation, gave it a superb review: "Wonderful landscape shots and cool guys make an exciting film," and the rating of "excellent."[30] In 1950, on a visit to relatives in Hamburg, I saw in one of the largest movie houses a Technicolor film with Ann Sheridan and Cary Grant entitled *I Was a Male War Bride*, which I found silly, not least because Grant's character Captain Rochard was wearing a female nurse's outfit.[31] Whereas by this time 70 percent of all feature films in the American zone were from Hollywood, there were far fewer of them shown in the British zone, because the filmmakers in London resented American predominance. On the other hand, they themselves did not have enough suitable movies to show the Germans, so recourse had to be taken to older German period flicks that were not deemed objectionable.[32]

In 1946 the American government founded America Houses in large cities such as Frankfurt and Munich, to assist in the distribution of American culture and dissemination of ideas about the American way of life. These *Amerikahäuser* had libraries with American literature and sponsored visiting American speakers, and they also supported music recitals, although American music especially from composers such as Aaron Copland and Virgil Thomson was accepted by German ears only reluctantly.[33] Younger Germans were more receptive to jazz, even though U.S. zonal administrators, inevitably white men, harbored scruples regarding the spread of what they regarded as inferior music. But jazz was also played on the American Forces Network (AFN), less so on the British BFN, and live in many soldiers' clubs, for this is what GIs wanted to listen and dance to, and through their German girlfriends much of this music was passed on to a larger German population, primarily those from the middle and upper classes, who soon became jazz fans.[34]

For a new beginning for West German culture creators and media, the Allies decreed licensing procedures as early as 1945, and these remained in place until September 21, 1949. But in their attempts to decide who was to be censored and what was to be allowed, the Allies were unsure, because they lacked knowledge and were uncoordinated. Hence the British dithered during summer 1946, trying to determine the future of theater Intendant Heinz Hilpert, who had worked at the Deutsches Theater in Berlin under Goebbels and now, after a sojourn in Switzerland, was trying to land another job in the divided city. After questions of whether he was "politically suitable," he was refused permission for Berlin, eventually receiving a mid-level post in provincial Göttingen.[35] On other issues the Allies were equally uncertain, one factor being that communication between them was inconsistent. When a German literary circle in Hamburg wished to organize a "Poets' Week," British censors wanted affirmation, as late as March 1947, that writer Hans Carossa, art critic Paul Fechter, and actor Mathias Wieman were "politically unobjectionable."[36] They did not know that Carossa had headed Goebbels's international writers' union, a rival to the PEN Club, that Fechter had written pro-Nazi essays, and that Wieman had played in the 1941 film *Ich klage an* (*I Accuse*), through which Third Reich leaders wished to mollify the public regarding forced "euthanasia."[37]

It was comparatively easy to censor music and art because here Nazi content, even if it was salient, was scarce and, once detected, easily acted upon.

Paintings could be removed from public places and artists prohibited from selling or exhibiting; and composers (and musicians) kept from public office and employment, with existing creations indicted. Conversely and proactively, music events could be promoted and the founding of galleries subsidized. One composer thus accepted in the long run was Carl Orff in Munich, who had prospered in the Third Reich without joining Nazi organizations.[38] With considerably more conviction, the Americans supported Orff's Munich colleague Karl Amadeus Hartmann, who had recused himself during the Third Reich and now established a "Musica Viva" series featuring hitherto neglected modern composers' works, including his own. Hartmann was also appointed dramaturge at the Bavarian Staatstheater as early as September 1945.[39] The British authorized public concerts in large towns such as Hanover and Essen, as well as the British sector of Berlin, early in 1945, with performances of music by composers prohibited by the Nazis being made mandatory.[40] The French, meanwhile, saw to it that their composer Arthur Honegger of the group *Les Six* received a listen.[41]

In Berlin, under the British, artists opened the Galerie Gerd Rosen on August 9, 1945, the first venue to show formerly condemned modern art. Several other galleries in the West followed suit, in Stuttgart or Karlsruhe, with art exhibitions to follow. When new art journals were founded and art academies hired new faculty, all had to be vetted by the occupation authorities. In 1946 a large comprehensive art exhibition opened in Dresden under Soviet auspices.[42]

For theater and other media supervision, three émigrés returned to the Western zones. In the British zone, it was the twenty-seven-year-old Friedrich Arzt, originally an actor from Vienna, who fought for the British in World War II and came back under the name John Olden to take charge. For the French it was novelist Alfred Döblin of *Berlin Alexanderplatz* fame, who had emigrated, via Paris, to the United States, and now represented the French in Baden-Baden. For the Americans it was Thomas Mann's son Golo, who had studied with the philosopher Karl Jaspers in Heidelberg before landing in New York as a half-Jewish fugitive from Hitler. Mann now relocated to Frankfurt.[43]

Whereas the Americans decreed that "pieces with militaristic, anti-democratic, Nazi content" were not to be staged, the British held more generally that "National Socialist drama" had to be avoided. This would exclude tendentious pieces of the Nazi era, such as those penned by Richard Billinger or Curt Langenbeck.[44] The most frequently performed work considered to be safe, with wide popular appeal, was Hugo von Hofmannsthal's *Jedermann* (*Everyman*), the moralist play by a poet who, as a "non-Aryan," had been off-limits in the Third Reich. It was staged in Stuttgart on August 4, 1945, by Albert Kehm, who had opposed the National Socialists as early as 1933 and been retired. Kehm was one of the few men the Americans had found – and this of course was the crux – who were both politically uncontaminated and experts in their fields.[45] Sometimes theater launches appeared as curious as the men who were placed on their stages: in Krefeld the British decided to license a municipal theater largely because they wanted to provide entertainment for their troops, and in Nuremberg the Americans employed Curt Max Richter, a show master whose specialty was jokes about the U.S. Forces.[46]

New German films were, like the visual arts and music, not so difficult to control as long as licensing mechanisms were in effect. The Soviets, who had no interest in selling (Russian-language) films to the Germans in their zone and instead expressed a genuine desire for the anti-fascist refashioning of the people under their control, were the first to issue permits to a new film company called DEFA, which on October 15, 1946, came out with the first post-war German film, entitled *Die Mörder sind unter uns* (*The Murderers are Among Us*). It showed how a former Wehrmacht officer and a young woman liberated from a concentration camp overcame initial difficulties of post-war survival and, after confronting an unconverted Nazi, found love. The British, eager like the Americans to sell films in Germany, licensed the Camera Film Company run by director Helmut Käutner in May 1946, who produced the second such movie on June 13, 1947, showing an Opel car that had seven moving stories to tell from the Third Reich.[47] The French followed in August 1947 with a comedy, *Herzdame* (*Queen of Hearts*), produced by Artur Brauner, a Polish-Jewish survivor of the Holocaust, founder of the new production company CCC Film. It featured Third Reich veteran actors Hans Nielsen and Lisa Lesco. It was only on December 8, 1947 that the Americans ramped up, significantly behind the three other Allies, sponsoring the movie *Und über uns der Himmel* (*And the Heavens Above Us*), in which Ufa idol Hans Albers, for the newly licensed Objectiv-Film, portrayed a Wehrmacht returnee, willing, against all odds, to help in the rebuilding of Berlin. Almost certainly, both the British and the Americans had been under pressure from their own film industries to delay the German licensing as long as possible, in order to sell their own, German-synchronized, films.[48] Altogether, from 1946 to 1950, the Germans mostly under Allied censorship were able to produce a respectable 114 feature films, competing against 240 British, 300 French, and 340 American imports.[49]

American commercial self-interest was the reason why the film-control officer who was to oversee all new production in the American zone, Erich Pommer, was dispatched by Washington only in July 1946. Pommer was the ultimate professional in filmmaking. The son of Jewish parents from Hildesheim, he had produced legendary pre-war German films, such as *Das Cabinet des Dr. Caligari* (*The Cabinet of Dr. Caligari*) in 1920 and *Der blaue Engel* (*The Blue Angel*) in 1930. By 1939 he had found a permanent home in Hollywood. For the Office of Military Government of the United States for Germany (OMGUS) from 1946 to 1948, he produced twenty-eight films. In his last year, as U.S. licensing was to be withdrawn, he helped to establish, on the basis of Hollywood's reactionary Hays system, new censorship rulings for German control boards, *Freiwillige Selbstkontrolle* (FSK, or Voluntary Self-Control), which laid the foundation for future narrow self-censorship by the German film industry, in conjunction with the strict morality concepts upheld by successively conservative Bonn cabinets.[50] The first film it tested was *Intimitäten* (*Intimacy*) in July 1949, begun under the Nazis but finished only after the war. While the Americans had already approved it in 1947, the FSK forbade it for youngsters under sixteen.[51]

Radio and the press were important as instruments of cultural re-education because the spoken and written word could most immediately formulate comprehensible messages. Goebbels had known that well, and for this reason the Nazi propaganda ministry's broadcasting system had to be completely eradicated. With this in mind, the Allies proceeded to found their own stations in 1945–6. The Americans in particular, the British less so and also the French arbitrarily insisted that the new German broadcasters be apolitical, decentralized, and noncommercial.[52] As it was decreed by the U.S. Information Services Control Command for the new Radio Stuttgart in July 1945, for example, the aim was "to stamp out every vestige of Nazism and Militarism" to effect the "re-education of the German people." This was to occur in an American "control capacity," with the co-optation of German associates who were "absolutely reliable."[53]

Radio Stuttgart, which began broadcasting in May 1945, sought to employ 100 percent reliable anti-Nazis, preferably former resistance fighters (who inevitably tended to possess less broadcasting expertise), to bring to their listeners modern music, literature, and radio plays previously condemned by the Nazis. Those might have been authored by the Jewish Viennese Arthur Schnitzler, for instance, but could include some adapted from Oscar Wilde's or George Bernard Shaw's writings. There was to be plenty from the Voice of America, and pro-Nazi pronouncements or a critical stance towards the United States were explicitly forbidden. The Americans set up three subsequent regional stations, in Bremen, Frankfurt, and Munich, while the British followed with Nordwestdeutscher Rundfunk (NWDR) for their entire zone of occupation (in area the largest in the occupied West), in Hamburg and Cologne in September 1945. The French established Südwestfunk in Baden-Baden on March 31, 1946.[54] For the Eastern zone, the Soviets had been the first to take over the old, Goebbels-led, Berliner Rundfunk on Masurenallee in Berlin-Charlottenburg, in May 1945.[55]

RIAS in West Berlin was an American station never intended to be handed over to the Germans; it had been established firmly by the fall of 1946. Assuredly, this had been because of the strong Soviet presence in the former Nazi capital, and the Americans' exclusive hold on that station became a mainstay of their power after 1947, when the Cold War had broken out.[56] As the months wore on, German workers in all the Allied stations increased in number to the extent that the Occupying Powers relinquished their control. But it was only in 1955, when the FRG had acquired full sovereignty, that all Allied-supervised radio stations except RIAS were entrusted fully to German hands.[57]

If Nazi radio had to be eliminated by the Allies, this held equally true for the Nazi press. The Allies thought it "so rotten in its structure, so thoroughly impregnated with Nazism, and so completely subservient to the Propaganda Ministry, that it had to be rooted out, and re-created from the bottom up."[58] Eager to hire suitable journalists who, just as in the case of broadcasting, could be guided in the reshaping of many newspapers that would re-educate Germans, the Americans once again assumed the lead in searching for undisputed experts, with the British not quite emulating them, and the French, cynically pragmatic, in third place.[59]

As they had done with RIAS, the Americans funded their own print medium to serve as a model for subsequent German creations. This was *Die Neue Zeitung*, based in Berlin. Stylistically of very high quality, it was led by Hans Habe, a Jew originally from Hungary but returning to Europe from America, like Golo Mann, in a U.S. military uniform. He was assisted by Hans Wallenberg, a Berlin-born Jew, and the children's books author Erich Kästner, originally a Weimar democrat who had saved himself in Nazi Germany through compromise, writing essays in Goebbels's flagship organ *Das Reich* and scripts for Nazi feature films.[60] *Die Neue Zeitung* attracted excellent staff: Hildegard Hamm-Brücher, with a Jewish grandparent and possessing a doctorate in chemistry, Karl Jaspers, the Heidelberg philosopher who was married to a Jew, and Walter Jens, a new light on the German literary scene. The paper was as democratic as its contributions were impressive, and the Americans retained it until 1955, much beyond the end of newspaper licensing in September 1949, when the number of newly founded German newspapers had jumped from an initial 150 to almost 550.[61] The Americans also stood behind the creation of *Frankfurter Rundschau* (*FR*) led by Social Democrats.[62] And in Munich, *Süddeutsche Zeitung* (*SZ*) was licensed, to be edited by a former Nazi prisoner and a half-Jewish journalist. It, too, was of superior quality, leaning to the left, and becoming an authoritative daily newspaper with a super-regional appeal.[63] The Americans encouraged democratic deportment, but they brooked neither critique nor opposition. In summer 1945 formerly Communist writers Alfred Andersch and Hans Werner Richter, who were ex-U.S. POWs, had been permitted to issue *Der Ruf* (*The Call*); however, when that weekly became critical of American occupation policy, their license was revoked.[64]

The British wisely insisted that papers in their purview should separate news from commentary, in order to keep party politics out of their pages. Thus they sponsored *Aachener Nachrichten*, which, on June 27, 1945, became the first of many local newspapers they were to support.[65] In Hamburg, they tried their hand at *Die Welt* in the manner of *Die Neue Zeitung* – designed to be an exclusively British-interest platform. But its initial staff turned out to be not particularly liberal-democratic and therefore not credible.[66] When they founded *Die Zeit*, also in Hamburg, its leading group of journalists contained questionable right-wingers but, fortunately, also Gerd Bucerius, who was unassailably democratic, and the redoubtable Marion Gräfin Dönhoff, originally from an East-Elbian estate.[67] By January 1947 British authorities had authorized *Der Spiegel*, a weekly journal based on *Time* magazine and inspired by maverick journalist Rudolf Augstein, a twenty-two-year-old former Wehrmacht lieutenant from a Hanoverian Catholic, anti-Nazi family.[68] Meanwhile the French had neglected to establish either a daily or a weekly paper that would make a mark for itself as an anti-fascist medium and stay around to put its imprint on the developing German democracy.

◆ ◆ ◆

"Ruin stood beside ruin, and behind the ruin there was a chaotic mass of rubble." Thus Alfred Döblin remembered the town of Pforzheim on the edge of the Black Forest, as he had visited it in 1945. Pforzheim had been almost totally destroyed.[69] Most German towns and cities had been bombed to bits by the Allies or damaged by artillery; in Cologne only three hundred houses had been left standing. Out of 760,000 former citizens, only 32,000 remained, huddled together on the left bank of the Rhine. In Berlin in 1946–7, the police routinely had to check ruins where people were still living: during that fatefully cold winter around fifty of them froze to death each day, and in January 1947 two hundred Berliners killed themselves. In Hamburg 224 citizens died of lung disease in January 1947, a figure that doubled in February.[70]

Civilians who had survived the bombings walked around in odd clothing – whatever could be found, out of style, ill-fitting, often Wehrmacht uniforms newly dyed.[71] Barter replaced currency, as the old Reichsmark was useless. Quickly the new sought-after standard of currency became the cigarette, especially an American one from the GIs. Black markets were illegal and often, therefore, on the fly or situated out of the way, yet ubiquitous in all of Germany. Here the heirloom porcelain of city dwellers was exchanged for butter brought by farmers from the countryside; schnapps changed hands for potatoes. Many children could be seen frequenting the black markets, because they were able to run away fast and could not be charged. The markets were dangerous as they could be raided by displaced persons or dissolved without warning by Allied military or German policemen. By this skewed economy the already distressed social order was upset even further as mothers were turned into thieves and young sons and daughters became delinquents.[72]

But bartering helped only a fortunate few and never for a long time; the minimum calories an average person should receive, 2,200 per day, were seldom distributed in the first two post-war years, particularly in urban areas. In Munich in 1945 food was rationed at a level below 1,000 calories per day per person; in the British zone it was at 1,500 calories. Hence at the end of that year, only 12 percent of all children in Cologne, for example, weighed what they should have.[73] To make ends meet, curious provisions were consumed, including dandelions, and new, strange recipes made the rounds – such as how to make liverwurst from flour and marjoram spice, and a kind of coffee cake from acorns.[74] These problems were compounded when Wehrmacht prisoners started to come home from Allied POW camps, and Germans who had been driven out of Silesia, Mecklenburg, Pomerania, and West and East Prussia started trekking in, often on horse-drawn wagons, some 12 million of them by 1949.[75]

What were the ramifications of such disorder for culture and its inventors? Apart from the physical and psychological causes of interruptions for theater, concert hall, gallery, printing press, and cinema activities since the end of April 1945, artists and writers were hampered well into 1948 by difficulties in rebuilding. Once they had the will and ability to resume their role as un-encumbered creators of culture, recourse had to be taken to improvisation and subterfuge. Hence in summer 1945 gallerists and artists in Berlin employed the mechanisms of the novel black market to install new large window panes in a bombed-out shop at the corner of Kurfürstendamm and Uhlandstrasse to found the Galerie Rosen, bartering vodka and cigarettes.[76] In Krefeld a wooden hall, where theater had been improvised until the lumber was stolen by citizens for firewood, had to be repaired before stage performances could resume.[77] In virtually all theaters, inveterate audiences attended, during the dreadful winters from 1945 to 1947 in thick coats and wrapped in blankets, while musicians were given small heaters.[78] Actors and musicians always went hungry, so that extra ration cards were issued for a Darmstadt New Music festival as late as 1948, while in Munich during that year musicians and actors had to cease performing because, undernourished, they were too weak.[79]

In those years immediately after the war, when consumer goods were hard to get, Germans were spending their Reichsmarks on cultural events and buying (or bartering for) books, because those were comparatively cheap. That changed when currency reform was introduced in April 1948. Now the new Deutsche Mark was needed to purchase staples that were, all of a sudden, available again on shelves – new clothes, bicycles, and cooking gear, all newly manufactured. These items took precedence, so that no household funds were left over for theater, concerts, and sometimes even movies. Theater and opera stages were affected by this shift in particular, because their productions were always expensive, what with new costumes needing to be purchased and artists customarily commanding higher wages. Hence most theaters during 1948–9 lost visitors, and at many staff had to make do with lower pay. Many performing artists were dismissed and theaters closed.[80] In the art world, too, the creators of paintings and gallery proprietors suffered. In cities such as Berlin artists often continued to trade portraits for services or foodstuffs. Countless creative men and women could not maintain their studios anymore and left the arts.[81]

Individual artists had to cope. The young publisher Wolf Jobst Siedler remembers carpets and valuable china being traded on the black market in Berlin; he watched the painter Werner Heldt going from table to table in a cellar bar peddling portraits for bottles of wine.[82] Young journalist Carola Stern and her mother scavenged and stole goods in and around Berlin – "food ration stamps from a forsaken administrative building, a gray soldier's blanket from a Canadian jeep, fruits from farmers' gardens, begging from house to house."[83] Music students Hans Werner Henze and Karlheinz Stockhausen played piano gigs in clubs and for dance studios when not freezing in their cubbyholes trying to compose. To sustain himself, Stockhausen collected cigarette butts, twisted them into new smokes, and exchanged them on the black market for butter.[84] In her very early twenties, actress Hildegard Knef began her stage career under Boleslaw Barlog in Berlin, where the audience was asked to bring to the performance nails for the fixing of decorations. She then played in the film *Die Mörder sind unter uns* a young woman who was suffering the same deprivations as Knef did in real life.[85]

Like Knef's in that film, Heinrich Böll's life was one of poverty. Having returned from the war and a brief stay in American captivity in spring 1945, the aspiring writer eked out a living for himself and his wife as an occasional clerk and by giving private lessons in his native city of Cologne. Sometimes he sold a script to the NWDR radio station. They suffered from hunger and cold, so he gathered planks from ruins and coals from the cellars of broken houses. "I never had any compunction about stealing," he said later. As late as summer 1948 he was still suffering, lacking groceries and also craving cigarettes and alcohol, both of which he had become addicted to during the war. In 1953, in one of his first novels, *Und sagte kein einziges Wort* (*And Never Said a Word*), he described such indigence by characterizing Fred Bogner, who lives in Cologne with his wife Käte and their two children, but struggles to acclimatize to family life. He has to roam the streets, sleeping in parks or churches, soliciting small change from acquaintances here and foraging for hot street food there. He never pays when using the tram and meets his wife in run-down hotels for intimate encounters. The couple is permanently on the edge of divorce.[86]

In his novel Böll portrayed Fred Bogner as one of those men who had returned from the war, beaten in body and soul. There were waves of German soldiers coming back from Allied camps, beginning in 1945, when the Americans released over 2 million men, followed by the British. Mass transports of prisoners came from Soviet camps starting in 1946, and it was especially those German men pouring in from the East who were under-nourished and unfit for work.[87] The men suffered from dystrophy and sexual impotence, languishing at home where their wives often despised them for having lost the war, not having defended them against rape by Soviet or French soldiers, or not finding appropriate employment in the post-war world.[88] Helma Sanders-Brahms fashioned her character Hans after the model of the weak World War II returnee in her 1980 film *Deutschland bleiche Mutter* (*Germany Pale Mother*), and in *Rosen für den Staatsanwalt* (*Roses for the Prosecutor*) (1959) Walter Giller plays an ex-soldier who sells card tricks on the streets.[89] German men are "too soft, they are not men anymore," said a waitress to playwright Carl Zuckmayer in 1946, adding that she would no longer touch them.[90] Only men who actually managed to secure a livelihood for themselves and their family counted for something and thus were not in danger of losing their self-esteem.[91] And then there were the wounded. The journalist Bernt Engelmann heartrendingly describes a Düsseldorf used-car dealer with missing legs, wheeling around on a wooden board with casters attached.[92] Many others were blind, without arms, or hobbling on crutches.

Back home, those broken men were confronted by assertive wives, who had had to manage by themselves throughout the years of the war and after. They had raised children and looked after households. When their husbands had come home on furlough, they were often alienated, going as far as suspecting their spouses of adultery, as shown in Sanders-Brahms's film. In 1950 Gerd Gaiser made this a subject of his novel *Eine Stimme hebt an* (*There Was a Voice*), in which the hero, an ex-Wehrmacht officer, finds himself deceived by his wife after his return from the war front.[93] Toward the end of the war, many of these women fled eastern to western Germany with their children (as did my mother with her two pre-teen sons) and re-integrated themselves socially until their men came home, if they ever did.[94] They were the first to take a hand in the physical rebuilding of the country, with the Trümmerfrau, the lady of the ruins who picks up and cleans rubble bricks (as Lene in the film *Deutschland bleiche Mutter* does in Berlin), becoming an iconic symbol of German reconstruction.[95] They also ran businesses, as Böll demonstrated in his novel *Haus ohne Hüter* (*House without Guardians*) of 1954, in which Berna is the successful butcher's wife, leaving her husband in the shadows.[96]

On the other hand, showing their strength, after the war many wives did their best to assist their emasculated ex-Wehrmacht men in attempted comebacks, whether they despised them or not. The prostitute Marina is doing this for the married veteran officer Alexander in the movie *Die Sünderin* (*The Sinner*) of 1951, to the point where she sells herself for money to finance an operation to cure his blindness.[97] In *Rosen für den Staatsanwalt* Lissy Flemming supports her boyfriend, the unsuccessful playing-cards peddler Rudi Kleinschmidt, economically, and encourages him to resume a sexual relationship with her. But many men remained suspicious, especially because they were aware of Russians or Central Asians having raped their wives or fiancées and they were witnessing, and often could not prevent, sexual liaisons between girls or women and occupation soldiers, chiefly in the West.

There were several reasons why German women, unmarried girls and war widows, but also wives of soldiers still not home, were agreeing to relationships with occupation soldiers, especially American GIs. One was, undeniably, the attractiveness of well-nourished and comparably affluent young men. The aura of the victor was a winning proposition for these soldiers.

As Hildegard Knef observed about the GIs, one of whom she was later to marry, they were "taut soldiers with tight bottoms and fixed bayonets."[98] But apart from sex and emotional warmth, occupation soldiers also had goods to offer, such as nylon stockings, chocolate and cigarettes, and upscale restaurant meals in casinos. They had cars and enjoyed themselves in posh clubs with liquor and exciting new music such as swing.[99] This was often played by Black musicians, most of them soldiers, who had German girlfriends of their own. German men in particular became outraged once young women would agree to enter into intimate relationships with Black GIs.[100]

After the war there existed a demographic imbalance, in that women vastly outnumbered men and the divorce rate was rising precipitously until, again, a marriage boom set in. In such environments children suffered, especially where fathers neglected their familial duties, and thus the seeds were sown for a crucial generational conflict later.[101] Not least, this had an impact on the personalities and possibly the works of certain artists. The 1960s student revolutionary Ulrich Enzensberger, later a writer, laments the questionable authority of the loser-fathers, and painter Anselm Kiefer told novelist Karl Ove Knausgaard that he had wanted his returned, authoritarian father "to die," as his mother had reduced him "to nothing."[102]

◆ ◆ ◆

The question whether any of these men experienced a sense of guilt for what had happened in the recent past was brought to the fore by the Heidelberg philosopher Karl Jaspers when in 1946 he published a small book with the title *Die Schuldfrage* (*The Question of Guilt*). In it, he repudiated the allegation of "collective guilt" of the entire German people for the Third Reich that had been set forth by certain among the Allies, driven initially by politicians – Henry Morgenthau Jr. in the United States and Lord Robert Vansittart in England. To the extent that Germans became aware of this charge, the large majority of them rejected it.[103] As far as Jaspers was concerned, he was willing to apply the concept of collective guilt to the comparatively small group of active National Socialists who had been directly responsible for crimes under Hitler, as the men currently being tried at Nuremberg were. Beyond that, Jaspers advocated individual admissions of criminal, political, moral, and metaphysical guilt, as well as an acknowledgment of shame, of "collective affectedness."[104]

But how was such shame to be expressed, and by whom? Jaspers did not specify, nor did he expressly mention by far the greatest crime the Nazis had committed, namely the genocide of European Jews.[105] The fact that by 1947, during the incipient Cold War, the Western Allies were calling for the allegiance of western Germans made any discussion of German guilt difficult, whether philosophical or theological.[106] Most Germans felt that they were blameless and harbored sentiments of "collective innocence."[107] They themselves, they thought, had been victims of Nazism; had been wronged by the Allies.

The alleged victims of Nazism comprised a larger group that adduced suffering as civilians or as simple cogs in the Third Reich machinery, and a smaller one that had actively done the bidding of the Hitler clique. Civilians claimed damages by Allied bombing raids, military hardships, deprivations during war, the loss of loved ones at the fronts, and, most lately, Soviet brutality and forced evacuations from the East.[108] When the British man of letters Stephen Spender mentioned to a German woman, in summer 1945, that he felt pity for the various European nations occupied by the Nazi Wehrmacht, she answered: "I suppose they are all badly off, but it is always poor Germany who suffers most."[109] The Jewish actor Fritz Kortner, recently returned to Germany from the United States, received the impression that most Berliners persisted with the claim that "no suffering was as large as theirs."[110]

Many Germans felt that the Western armies as well as the Soviet one had inflicted an unjust victory on their fatherland and introduced undue hardship, causing material and psychological suffering. The division of Germany into four zones of occupation was the visible manifestation of this. They rejected the message that all Allies wanted to convey, that they were liberators from a totalitarian dictatorship rather than enforcers of a new order. Instead it was widely believed that American, British, and French troops had arrived to exploit Germany and feast on her resources; and, as they had already done in the 1920s, that they wished to enforce patterns of democratic governance that were alien to the German soul.[111]

Anti-Semitic sentiment remained after the fall of the Nazi regime. Some Germans equated themselves with Jewish victims outright.[112] Others believed anti-Semitic conspiracy theories that suggested the Jews were behind Allied occupation policy, resulting encumbrances, and, especially, what were perceived as malicious denazification procedures.[113] Others again, as the visiting Hannah Arendt, a former student of Jaspers, found out, set off any Nazi crimes perpetrated on the Jews against injustices done to the Germans, such as bombing raids or forced flights from the European East.[114] In the imagination of certain Nazis revenge was taking over where the victors saw just punishment. For example, the psychiatrist Alexander Mitscherlich treated a former SS sergeant who had done time in an Allied internment camp. He was convinced that Jews among the staff had been scheming to gang up against him and others there who had served as guards in concentration camps.[115]

Germans also had mixed feelings about the Nuremberg Trials. Three sentiments predominated. The great majority approved of that reckoning as a righteous course affecting the most guilty. Many deplored the fact that Hitler and Goebbels had committed suicide in the chancellery bunker, as had Hermann Göring in his cell, to escape justice. But there were those who used the trials as a means to extinguish their own sense of responsibility for what had happened; once one could point to the men in the docks, this was where the guilty were. This mood accorded with the sentiment of those who had enthusiastically served Hitler but now felt betrayed. Finally, there were diehards, many of them unreconstructed Nazis, who claimed that the Allies had imposed victors' justice on Germany, irrespective of either side's responsibility. The Allies – here was that compensatory argument again – were held to be just as guilty on account of their bombings, their own killings of civilians on the ground, and, not least, their abuse of German women. Seen from this angle, the occupation of western Germany by three victors' armies was merely an extension not of an equitable, but a one-sided and therefore unfair treatment of Germany after 1945.[116]

The two Christian Churches concurred in such an interpretation. By emphasizing German victimhood, they welcomed returning soldiers and harshly indicted the Allies' policies of denazification. In June 1945, Cardinal Michael Faulhaber of Munich, who had already rejected the Weimar Republic, warmly welcomed repatriated POWs and thanked them for their "unspeakable achievement and suffering."[117] He and Protestant bishop Hans Meiser protested to OMGUS over mass dismissals of Nazis from the public service and industry, as well as over a blanket denunciation of SS members. In 1948 the Protestant Church issued the Stuttgart Declaration of Guilt, which admitted German responsibility for starting the war, yet erroneously identified the German clergy as the most resolute resistance fighters against the Third Reich. In reality, more than a quarter of the clergy had joined the Nazi Party even before Hitler had come to power in 1933.[118]

What was taking place in Dr. Mitscherlich's office was not just a falsification of facts by way of an inversion, but a separation of the self from reality. Many Germans, as a coping mechanism, decided to remove themselves from the phenomenon of the Third Reich by claiming that it was something different from what they themselves had stood for, that it was an evil that had overcome them – an inevitable fate beyond their control. They had become enchained victims of a demonized entity from which there had been no escape. By denying National Socialism for themselves *ex post facto*, these Germans were able to claim that they had never been Nazis, even if the opposite was true.[119] "No one had ever been a Nazi," Peter Viertel, son of the exiled playwright Berthold Viertel, wrote home to his mother Salka in Los Angeles, as he was sampling people's opinions for the American Office of Strategic Services in 1945.[120] Journalist Martha Gellhorn, Ernest Hemingway's third wife, and Corporal Klaus Mann, the Nobel laureate's eldest son – he for the U.S. Army journal *Stars and Stripes* – recorded similar utterances.[121] And as late as December 1949 the one-time émigré music critic Theodor W. Adorno wrote to the Viertels' neighbor Thomas Mann that so far he had not seen a Nazi, only men and women who believed they had not been Nazis, and therefore "totally suppress it."[122]

This martyrological self-indulgence, which lasted well into the 1950s, was endorsed by many German pronouncements of an official, scholarly, or artistic nature, beginning with the novelist Ernst Wiechert who in a speech of 1945 characterized the Nazi state as "an empire of anti-Christ," thereby disconnecting Christian believers such as himself from perceived wickedness.[123] Soon afterwards Friedrich Meinecke, the doyen of German historians in Berlin, declared the Third Reich to have been an accident of history, followed by his colleague in Freiburg, Professor Gerhard Ritter, who decreed that Hitlerism was "something fundamentally new," an aberration, a kind of seizure.[124] The highly influential author Erich Kästner pointed to "this other Germany" and differentiated between "victims and hangmen," as he counted himself among the former.[125] Publicly, lord mayor Otto Ziebill of Nuremberg in 1947 compared his home town to a "sick and impoverished woman who had once been healthy and beautiful."[126] What historian Hans Mommsen has termed an illicit elision "from the continuity of German history" was practiced again, and from an exulted position, by Federal President Theodor Heuss when he, also in Nuremberg, lamented in 1952 that the name of this defenseless town had been stained by most recent events – its party rallies, the Nuremberg race laws, and, lastly, by the Nuremberg Trials.[127]

But there were other Germans, unreconstructed National Socialists, such as the SS physician I met in Hanover. They experienced nothing less than profound satisfaction over what Hitler had accomplished, including, as far as they knew about it or were complicit in its execution, the genocide of Jews. This huge group took in men and women released from American or British trials and internment camps, but also the legions that were routinely denazified, if only nominally, such as Werner Egk. They included the 37 percent of respondents who replied to American demographers in 1946 that the annihilation of Jews, Poles and other "non-Aryans" had been necessary "for the security of Germany." As late as the mid-1950s, 42 percent of all Germans thought Hitler to have been one of the greatest German statesmen, had he not started the war.[128] In light of these figures the assurances of masses of people that they had not known about concentration camps and atrocities committed by the Gestapo and SS appear not to be credible.[129] Ralf Dahrendorf stated, in 1968, that Germans may not have been aware of the details, but they certainly knew of those instruments of terror.[130]

I can substantiate this from my own experience. In 1943, when I was six, I was in a Zittau pharmacy. There I overheard my mother talking to the pharmacist in a hushed voice. She was saying "So they came for the Kohns as well now?" while the man in the white coat nodded gravely. Today I do not correctly remember the precise details, but they were people in our neighborhood whose name I thought I recognized. The conversation was ominous and remained stuck in my mind, for I knew the two adults had been talking about something sinister. Twenty years later, when writing my doctoral dissertation on the SS in Heidelberg, a woman in her forties who lived above my flat told me that her husband had been an SS guard at Auschwitz. Whenever he came home on furlough, he had the worst of nights. Unable to sleep, he sought to unburden his conscience to his wife. Therefore she must have known, as well as any person she might have chosen to confide in.[131]

◆ ◆ ◆

In the years from 1945 to 1950, many Nazis, genuine or nominal, returned to the world of arts and letters, as they returned to government or the retail trade. Beyond hard-core believers and hangers-on with party backgrounds there were also many who had not necessarily been card-carrying Nazi Party members, but had worked in branches of the wider culture networks within Goebbels's propaganda apparatus. Now, as in those other areas of human endeavor, experienced persons, people familiar with practical routines, were needed to turn the cranks of production and creation once more, in order for life to go on. Overall, many women were not qualified, and even if they were, they were disparaged as men were recovering their power. Because many able men had disappeared, any male who was remotely suitable was encouraged to reintegrate into a society that was meant by the Allies to continue. This hugely favored the untainted, but also favored the tainted. Among the latter in the arts, there were committed collaborators such as the filmmaker Veit Harlan, and those who had merely found it opportune to work for the Nazi regime, such as the novelist Hans Carossa. Novelists were self-employed, and perhaps they could rely on a readership from years ago. But those who needed to be hired, such as orchestra conductors, would have to find their way to the new cultural mainstream. The Nazi Generalmusikdirektor of the Munich Philharmonic Oswald Kabasta was dismissed from his post and subsequently killed himself, but he was the exception.[132]

The most famous German conductors who had worked in the Third Reich faced obstacles on their return to the concert halls, but because they were thought to be indispensable, they were eventually successful, even if their denazification lasted years. During a formal defense in September 1945, Wilhelm Furtwängler declared that no one in the German music scene had fought as persistently against the Nazis as he had. Nevertheless, it took until summer 1951 for him to be able to reopen the Bayreuth Wagner Festival.[133] Herbert von Karajan, initially banned from conducting in the Western zones of Germany, worked in occupied Austria, largely by suppressing knowledge of his Nazi Party membership, then in Switzerland and Italy, until he was able to conduct at Bayreuth in 1950, in the Wagnerian Festspielhaus (and a year later he conducted Wagner there along with the equally compromised Hans Knappertsbusch).[134] Lesser conductors fared varyingly. Clemens Krauss, a

Richard Strauss specialist and Hitler's favorite opera conductor, also had to take the detour via Austria before he was able to work again in Bamberg and Bayreuth, but not in tenured posts. He died in 1954 on a tour of Mexico.[135] Robert Heger, who in 1936 had premiered his own mediocre opera, *Der verlorene Sohn* (*The Lost Son*), about the German loss of Alsace to France in 1919, had conducted in Nazi Occupied Poland. Because of ignorance and confusion on the part of the controlling Americans he was installed as a Staatskapellmeister at the Bavarian Staatsoper in Munich, serving, in addition, as president of the Munich Musikhochschule until 1954.[136] Heger's colleague Hans Rosbaud also did surprisingly well. Although a follower of Arnold Schoenberg and originally not National Socialist-inclined, he had allowed himself to be appointed in Occupied France in a similar position to Heger in Poland – the French were to be won over by Germany's extraordinary cultural overtures. Despite Allied qualms, Rosbaud received employment as Generalmusikdirektor in Munich as early as 1945 under the Americans, and in 1948, under the more permissive French, was welcomed as director of the new Südwestfunk orchestra in Baden-Baden.[137]

Composers who were able to teach in conservatoires and at festivals featuring lecture series were also in demand. Bruno Stürmer of Kassel, who had taught music to the Hitler Youth and, winning awards, composed in praise of the Third Reich, in 1947 managed to be hired as an instructor at the New Music festival in Darmstadt, commenced during 1946.[138] A parallel appointment at Darmstadt to that of Stürmer's was that of composer and church musician Wolfgang Fortner, who, while in Heidelberg, had also led Hitler Youth choirs.[139] But unlike Stürmer, Fortner took an active interest in dodecaphony, pioneered by Schoenberg, even composing and teaching in that mode at around this time.

Elisabeth Schwarzkopf may stand for the many instrumentalists and singers who had compromised themselves under Hitler. Schwarzkopf was born in 1915; she died a Dame of the British Empire in Switzerland in August 2006. She had volunteered as a Nazi student leader in Berlin during the late 1930s, became a Nazi Party member in 1940, and entertained SS troops in 1942. While ill with tuberculosis in 1943–4, she was cared for by a medical specialist in the Tatra Mountains, in Nazi-controlled Slovakia. This specialist was Dr. Hugo Jury, who subsequently became her lover – he was an SS-Obergruppenführer and Gauleiter of Niederdonau as well as a connoisseur of high culture. After Jury had committed suicide on May 8, 1945, Schwarzkopf made her way musically via Vienna, London, and Milan, remaining silent on her Third Reich connections. She partnered with the Vienna-based British impresario and record producer Walter Legge and eventually, on her way to world fame, became a British subject.[140]

During her early post-war performances, Schwarzkopf was on stage with many actors, dramaturges and directors who had also had a Third Reich past. A good many of those now resurfaced on West German film screens and in the playhouses but, especially if they were younger, they probably eagerly embraced the new era, recognizing it as a vast improvement over totalitarian dictatorship. This might have been the case with artists such as Heidemarie Hatheyer, who had starred as the incurable multiple-sclerosis patient mercy-killed by her husband in the 1941 pro-"euthanasia" film *Ich klage an* (*I Accuse*). Hatheyer, who at twenty-eight was still youthful, appeared on theatrical stages in Munich and Nuremberg as early as 1946, but, because of censorship by the Americans, in new (and forgettable) German films only after 1948.[141] Also into this category of the converted would fall Wolfgang Staudte, who had assumed a minor role in the notorious 1940 anti-Semitic propaganda film *Jud Süss* (*Jew Sweet*), but who, six years later, became the director of the very first post-war German film, *Die Mörder sind unter uns*, an utterly convincing anti-Nazi morality play.[142]

Infinitely more questionable was Kristina Söderbaum, the wife of Veit Harlan and star in most of his Nazi-themed films who, because she had been banned from filmmaking after 1945, took to the stage all over Germany. Beyond recommending caution, the Americans apparently saw nothing wrong with such live performances, after Söderbaum had appeared in the drama *Augen der Liebe* (*Eyes of Love*), by the Viennese Jew Edmund Wolf, in the Nuremberg municipal theater in early 1949. After displaced persons had protested against the performance, the supervising OMGUS official Murray D. van Wagoner expressed concern not over the actress's appearance, but a possible recurrence of demonstrations.[143]

Third Reich filmmakers also returned, several with obviously democratic intentions. One of them was Helmut Käutner, who had scripted and filmed *Auf Wiedersehen, Franziska* (*Good Bye, Franziska*) in 1941, a movie about a young housewife encouraging her husband to willingly accept his war service on behalf of Hitler's regime. The film had been a message to all German wives to endure their husbands' absence in war and remain at the home front chaste and true, while husbands were expected to lead an adventurous life, martially and sexually.[144] So unlike Staudte, Käutner was already well known when he was licensed by the British to make *In jenen Tagen* (*In Those Days*) in 1947 in Berlin; like Staudte's movie, this turned out to be a lesson in humanity.[145] Käutner may be believed when he stated that in producing that film he wanted to make an effort "to finally come to grips with reality."[146]

The situation was less clear in the case of Wolfgang Liebeneiner. He had been a frequent guest of Goebbels, a Führer-anointed professor and director of an official film academy. This school, apart from acting, also taught a course, "The Shadow of the Jews over the World." Liebeneiner had been the director and cowriter of *Ich klage an*;[147] but he, too, adapted. No sooner had he received work permission in the fall of 1945 than he began planning for a stage production of Wolfgang Borchert's drama *Draussen vor der Tür* (*The Man Outside*) at the Hamburg Kammerspiele two years later. His film *Liebe 47* (*Love '47*) of 1949, based on that play, was a financial disaster, but established him anew, and credible, in movies.[148]

Germany's most famous and arguably most able stage personality, Gustaf Gründgens, exemplifies the complexities inherent in the return of former Nazi-sanctioned culture elites. As an early intimate of Klaus and Erika Mann, he was a typical creature of the Weimar republican era and himself a republican. But Gründgens then became the reluctant favorite of Hermann Göring, and as such not only much benefited from Nazi patronage personally, but also did his share to conflate traditional German culture with a Nazi catechism. After 1945 many thought that even if he had secretly believed otherwise, he had disqualified himself and should not have been welcomed back to the German stage.

But reality was different. At first arrested by the Soviets and imprisoned near Berlin, he was, in spring 1946, allowed to join the Deutsches Theater in the Eastern sector. In 1947 he was able to move to the Schauspielhaus in Düsseldorf, where he delivered, once more, record-breaking theater. As before, he favored the classics, Shakespeare, Schiller, and Goethe (his signature role was Mephistopheles from *Faust*), but he also turned to more modern authors such as T.S. Eliot and Christopher Fry. In 1955 he relocated to the Deutsches Schauspielhaus in Hamburg, along with Düsseldorf the premier German playhouse. Yet altogether he had to endure no fewer than four denazification procedures, and in 1945 there were protests when British admirers of his planned a guest performance in London.[149] If realized, this would have been a provocation and an insult, remarked the English theater director Peter Zadek decades later, himself the son of Berlin expatriate Jews.[150]

The tally is sobering. In the years after 1945 there were altogether 192 men and women active in the German movie business who had been script-writers or directors under Hitler's regime, including the compromised artists Harlan, Thea von Harbou, and Karl Ritter.[151] In theater 65 percent of all directors, of a total of 427 who were employed from 1945 to 1948, had flourished in the Third Reich.[152]

As has already been observed, scores of journalists sympathetic to the Nazi cause or doing its bidding filled positions in the newly established newspaper editorial offices and joined the copywriters' ranks. Why was this so? One probable answer is that in the Allies' view newspapers, in as much as they were under censorship, were thought to be the most effective medium of political and ideological control, because almost everybody would have access to them. Therefore staff writers were hired more hurriedly and after fewer checkups than, say, actors for film and stage. Moreover, many people could pretend to be journalists when in fact they were not, whereas actors would be discovered more quickly if they were mere pretenders. Fewer checkups, however, would compromise the Allies.

Thus the art critics Carl Linfert and Bruno E. Werner had no difficulty reconnecting. In September 1940 Linfert had written in the *Frankfurter Zeitung* (*FZ*) that the "moral aim" of the film *Jud Süss* had been to show the Jews as the proponents of evil incarnate, in particular to demonstrate the creepy insinuations of assimilated Westernized Jews, who at the core had remained eastern Jews.[153] Linfert then joined the Berlin *Kurier* in the French zone of Berlin, knowing that those occupiers would let him pass without scrutiny. Keeping busy as a local art critic, he made it from there to the NWDR, where, in Cologne, he took over the night program in 1949.[154] The *Deutsche Allgemeine Zeitung* (*DAZ*) journalist Werner had lauded Hitler in 1937 for having announced "a purge against the elements of cultural decomposition" on the occasion of the degenerate art exhibition in Munich in July.[155] But already in 1945–6 he was able to assume the post of culture-section chief at the NWDR station in Hamburg, and from 1947 to 1952 he was in charge of the arts-and-letters section at America's democratic showcase *Die Neue Zeitung*.[156] Subsequently, Werner was a much sought-after art and theater critic.[157]

The new *Frankfurter Allgemeine Zeitung* (*FAZ*) under American supervision welcomed several journalists from the Third Reich such as Heinz Höpfl, who was hired as a specialist for the English desk. When he had been an editor at the official Nazi daily *Völkischer Beobachter*, this member of the NSDAP and SA had called Churchill a "criminal" with a "corrupted brain." In 1941 he had identified "international Jewry" as "inspirator of the world coalition against the German people." Nonetheless, in 1953 Höpfl was posted as the *FAZ*'s correspondent to London.[158] His colleague Karl Korn in 1940 had stated in *Das Reich* that the "alien race" of the Jews was "revengeful," was lusting after "blond women," and was "totally cynical . . . servile to the point of masochism."[159] When Korn expounded on "Jewish greed for power and Jewish hatred," he was servicing National Socialist clichés.[160] But come 1949, Korn was appointed at the *FAZ* as one of its publishers. Over the years, he came to hold such sway in press circles that Joachim Kaiser, a certified democrat at *Süddeutsche Zeitung*, did not dare to offer his colleague anything but effusive praise – "a great feuilletonist" – on his seventy-fifth birthday in 1983.[161]

When Theodor Heuss re-entered the press world, some could question his past. He had been a co-founder of the left-of-center Deutsche Demokratische Partei (German Democratic Party) in 1918, but as a member of the right-leaning Deutsche Staatspartei (German State Party), Heuss voted for Hitler's Enabling Law in the Reichstag on March 24, 1933.[162] Although personally Heuss disliked Hitler, he became a contributor to papers such as *DAZ* and *FZ*.[163] As such, he defended the foreign-political ambitions of the Nazi regime more than interior policy, starting with denouncements of the Versailles Treaty (1919) and hailing the Anschluss of Austria in spring 1938.[164] From the beginning of the war he identified the resettlement of Germans from the European East as a "great venture of historic proportions" and insisted on the "leadership entitlement of the Germans." He was on the staff of *Die Hilfe*, which in 1940 printed, framed on the first page, compliments to Hitler on his fifty-first birthday: "It is wholly unimportant whether we live, but it is of importance that our Volk, that Germany may live . . . Congratulations."[165]

Heuss, during the war a regular contributor to *Das Reich* as well as other Nazi papers, was chosen by the U.S. occupiers to publish the daily newspaper *Rhein-Neckar-Zeitung* after the war, with its offices in Heidelberg, the location of U.S. headquarters. The Americans allowed him to be appointed minister of culture for Württemberg and, in 1949, president of the newly created FRG.[166]

The closer creative individuals were tied to institutions, the easier it was to control them politically – by granting or withholding employment. In the case of freewheeling artists such as painters or novelists, this was harder. If assured of an income, they could continue to spread Nazi-friendly ideas through the visual arts or their books, once a gallery, clients, or a publisher were found and there was a sympathetic audience. The most prominent example of a Nazi artist who became eminently successful after the war and did not repent his former stance is that of sculptor Arno Breker, who managed to receive commissions from industry and politicians for portraiture, including Konrad Adenauer. But the great majority of Nazi painters lost their cachet and possibly their livelihoods, although mainstays of political reaction remained, such as the Akademie der Bildenden Künste (Academy of Fine Arts) in Munich – until 1945 the hub of Nazi art in the Reich.[167]

In book publishing, there were many authors who had been prominent from 1918 to 1945, not all of whom were dyed-in-the wool Nazis, and who were read again by a conservative-minded German public both in the original and through post-war publications. To them belonged Gottfried Benn, Ernst Jünger, and Hans Carossa, among whom the two first-mentioned had had on-and-off relationships with Nazism.[168] Three more seriously committed Nazis among them were Agnes Miegel and Ina Seidel, who had specialized in internalized feelings and themes tied to the homeland à la "Blut und Boden" ("Blood and Soil") and Hans Grimm, who had concentrated on German colonial and imperialist chimeras. The fact that they found post-war publishers reflects, again, on the porousness of Allied cultural controls, for book publishing was one of the more neglected areas of post-1945 regulation, complicated by inconsistent paper distribution.[169] Right-wing publishers were able to thrive from the late 1940s, when Allied licensing was cut, until well beyond the 1960s; among the most extreme houses on the old or neo-Nazi fringe was Druffel Verlag in Leoni on Lake Starnberg, to name only one.[170]

Ina Seidel had been the doyenne of Nazi novelists; in her personal life she demonstrated the viability of a union between upper-middle-class Protestant values and National Socialist beliefs. The daughter of a physician, she was married to a Lutheran minister and, along with her husband, a staunch believer in Hitler. During the Third Reich she had excelled with paeans to the Führer, blessing in verse the columns of uniformed men that paraded beneath his gaze and encouraging everyone to lower their heads to him in heart-felt devotion.[171] After 1945 she resumed publishing novellas and essays. She announced an "accounting" with National Socialism in the 1950s, which then turned out to be the novel *Michaela*, a trivialization of the Nazi period.[172] She died in 1974, a member of the West Berlin Akademie der Künste, at the age of eighty-nine, still vastly popular in center to center-right circles.

Agnes Miegel had always sung of her homeland East Prussia; she had excelled as a bard for the Hitler Youth. Her reverence for Hitler was boundless; she praised him as East Prussia's protector and rhymed that he and the German people could never be separated in a joint devotion "for our German land."[173] After 1945 Miegel became the official patroness of all unreconstructed Nazis who had been forced to flee from the East, and she was able to publish prolifically again after the suspension of censorship upon the republic's founding in 1949 – dramas and collections of poetry, novellas and memoirs.[174]

Hans Grimm (1875–1959), "folkish-nationalist and racist," argued for an expansion of German Lebensraum as early as 1926 and especially during the Third Reich.[175] In works Grimm published after 1945, his unabated devotion to Hitler shone through and, among other things, he presented accounts of alleged falsehoods by the post-war Allies, such as that 6 million Jews had been murdered: "The list of forgeries, piled one on top of the other, could be extended over many pages." As early as 1949 Grimm established the "Lippoldsberger Dichtertage" on the Weser River, where he presided over readings by other former Nazi greats.[176]

◆ ◆ ◆

The fact that after 1945 German-Jewish émigrés to non-Nazi-occupied countries did not, as a rule, return to western Germany may have been grounded in their knowledge that anti-Semitism had not died out in the country. Just as shame, or the absence thereof, for Nazism on the part of Germans influenced the rebirth of culture, so too did their conception of Jews and an acknowledgment of their fate before and after 1945. The continuance of anti-Semitism in immediate post-war western Germany was largely bound up with the situation of Displaced Persons (DPs), from eastern Europe.

An OMGUS survey of December 1946 showed that about one-fifth of Germans asked were firm anti-Semites. This proportion had increased slightly by 1949.[177] Anti-Semitism was fed by two sources. One was the pre-established image of the Jews as aliens who were forever forbidden to enter the, racially defined, pure German Volk. The extreme consequences of this view had been physical extermination in the Holocaust, accepted by the most radical of Nazis. After the war, the uncomfortable memory of this was again turned against the Jews, as in the parlance of hatred: "The Jews are responsible for Auschwitz," or, a corollary of this, "The Germans will never forgive the Jews for Auschwitz."[178]

Secondly, some Germans resented concentration-camp survivors seeking a new home for themselves. Most often, those were displaced persons lodged in special camps and trying to secure a livelihood, which exposed them to the gaze of the surrounding citizens. The anti-Jewish feelings were in contradistinction to an early official German opinion, which held that ever since the defeat of the Nazi regime anti-Semitism was negligible. In his first address as chancellor on September 10, 1949, Adenauer, rather than mentioning Germany's paramount duty to make restitution to the Jewish people, spoke of the need to assist German victims of war, namely the refugees and the bombed-out.[179] In line with this, President Heuss told a representative of Associated Press in December that "real anti-Semitism" did not exist in Germany anymore. Whom should it target? Competition between Jews and non-Jews had ceased, and there were no other reasons for envy. Any "National Socialist confusion" in confounded German heads was harmless.[180]

After May 1945, just 40,000 German Jews, at most, were counted in Germany, within the pre-aggression, pre-war borders of 1937. This was not even one-tenth of the 1933 Jewish population.[181] By about 1947, approximately a million eastern European displaced persons were staying in camps on German soil organized by the United Nations. Between 200,000 and

250,000 of those were Jews – from Poland, the former Baltic states of Estonia, Latvia, and Lithuania, and intermittent fugitives to the Soviet Union.[182] Fearing a forced return to the Soviet orbit, their overriding concern was to emigrate to the British mandate of Palestine, but a large proportion also wished to go to the United States. This fear was shared to an even larger extent by the non-Jewish camp inmates, who often had been collaborators of the Nazis – Latvian Waffen-SS or Ukrainian Trawniki-trained concentration camp guards. Whereas at first the Jews were housed together with the non-Jews, eventually they came to be cared for in separate camps, such as Landsberg in Bavaria.

Jews in the camps were frequently unsuccessful in both their attempts to move to Palestine and their efforts to be sponsored by U.S. citizens to enter America. Both actions were prevented on principle by the two powers holding them in Germany – the Americans, who, citing their harsh immigration law of 1924, pressured London to allow Jews to sail for Palestine, and the British, who resisted this, wanting the Jews, with Washington's help, either to go to America or return to their (eastern European) countries of birth. Against these heavy odds, the camp Jews did manage slowly to leave Germany for either Palestine, which became Israel in 1948, and the United States and other Western nations, so that by 1948 the DP problem could largely be considered solved.[183] By this time only about 23,000 German Jews remained as registered members of Jewish communities in what was to become the FRG.[184]

In relation to the DPs, a number of factors caused expressions of continued or renewed anti-Semitism among Germans. Generally, Germans resented all displaced persons, whether they were Jews or other eastern Europeans. DP violence against the civilian population caused much concern.[185] Further, Germans suspected dishonesty by DPs in black-market dealings, in which they ruled.[186] And they were worried about aesthetics and hygienics, for often DPs in ragged outfits, but also long black kaftans and wide-brimmed hats, with sidelocks and beards, were thought to be the bearers of disease and the cause of epidemics. As Richard Bessel has rightly called attention to, these men and women had previously been classified as "vermin," which was, of course, a Nazi racial category. Here deep-seated pre-1933 prejudices were reinforced by new misconstructions.[187] Moreover, indicative of a general anti-Jewish sentiment in the land – sometimes fatal for the Jewish DPs affected – was the attitude of officials and bureaucrats at municipal, regional-government, and judicial levels. All German officials below the highest levels referred to DPs and Jews in discriminatory, racist jargon.[188] In engagements with assumed smugglers or black-market offenders, the German police employed excess force, sometimes killing their quarry needlessly.[189] German lawyers, judges, and magistrates, many of whom had been in Nazi formations and had only nominally been denazified, disadvantaged Jews, for instance by not recognizing marriages that had been ministered by rabbis.[190]

The German civilian population did not bother to ascertain the validity of many complaints made against DPs, in particular whether the Jews among them were at fault. After all, the non-Jewish DPs had a much larger inclination towards violence, many having served in the SS. As theater director Fritz Kortner found out, the Germans were just as likely to benefit from black markets as any DP. In a Bavarian pub serving as a black market he encountered an eastern Jew, gesticulating towards his partner, an old Nazi.[191]

Resulting acts of anti-Semitism by Germans were manifold. Private citizens expressed disgust about Jews, as they had seen them in ragged queues being marched from recently closed concentration camps. Newspapers such as the Berlin *Tagesspiegel* – breaching regulations – announced in December 1945 that "once again, the 'Jewish problem' had to be solved." Typical was the devastation of Jewish cemeteries. In Munich, kosher butcheries were stoned. Merchants everywhere refused to sell to Jewish customers. Municipal administrations, such as the one in the Richard Wagner town of Bayreuth, disadvantaged Jews by curtailing milk deliveries. In plain sight of the public, Jews were insulted on public transportation. Sometimes a public-school class would break into anti-Jewish chant.[192]

With the memory of past National Socialist experiences and within the post-war context of devastation, personal loss, and faint hope for redemption, German émigré Jews hesitated to return. It is true that Konrad Adenauer, who had spent time in Nazi captivity, invited former Jewish acquaintances to come back while still lord mayor of Cologne, as early as April 1945.[193] Eventually some did, to serve the new chancellor's politics: Richard Löwenthal and Ernst Fraenkel, the political scientists, or Herbert Weichmann, later lord mayor of Hamburg.[194] Rudolf Katz, once a lawyer in Hamburg, came back as minister of justice in Schleswig-Holstein; tragically, he proceeded to employ old Nazi lawyers in the hope of breaking down their suspicion against returnees.[195] For on the whole, there was a strong psychological barrier between those who had stayed at home and *all* émigrés, who tended to be stigmatized with accusations of cowardice and desertion, as was the Social Democratic politician Willy Brandt, who had hidden in Scandinavia and was maligned, by Adenauer himself, as illegitimately born.[196] In line with German feelings of denial about the Nazi past, there was no serious attempt to understand the motives of those émigrés, charged Alexander and Margarete Mitscherlich, and there never was an official invitation by representatives of the new German government to any of the refugees, much less an apology.[197]

In the ranks of the culture class, anti-Semitism had been as virulent as in any sector of German society. Therefore artists and men and women of letters, most of them Jewish, hesitated to return. The former Bauhaus designer László Moholy-Nagy remained in Chicago, his student Marcel Breuer at Harvard. The (non-Jewish) painter Max Ernst and the pianist Rudolf Serkin stayed in New York. So did the composer Kurt Weill and the actress Elisabeth Bergner, who made a brief appearance on German stages only in 1954. Among many who had come to America, the German-Jewish circle around Los Angeles was particularly notable, including, among others, the writer Lion Feuchtwanger, the actress and screenwriter Salka Viertel, and the composer Arnold Schoenberg. Their rich American legacy meant a huge cultural and intellectual loss for Germany.[198]

The most prominent denizen of the Los Angeles diaspora was Nobel laureate Thomas Mann, whose wife Katia was Jewish. He had assumed a position of moral authority for those Germans who had deeply resented the Hitler regime, but there were not enough of those in the cultural domain to persuade him to return. After visiting Germany during the Goethe memorial year of 1949, when he defended emigration and a pro-democracy stance in his speeches, Mann decided to settle permanently in Zurich three years later.[199] Mann's children Erika, Klaus, and Golo chose somewhat different paths. His oldest daughter Erika repeatedly visited Germany, but in 1952 she too moved to Zurich. Klaus, after his service in the U.S. Army, failed in permanently resettling in Germany, which contributed to his suicide in Cannes in 1949.[200] Only Golo Mann managed reintegration into German society, when, after his service for OMGUS in Frankfurt, he became a political scientist at Stuttgart Technical University in 1960.[201]

Golo Mann published popular histories of seventeenth-century Germany. Therefore, in the cultural establishment of the new FRG, he was more fortunate than other returnees in the arts and letters. One particularly sad case is that of Alfred Döblin, the once-celebrated author, who, in a similar capacity to Golo Mann, had served the French occupation forces in Baden-Baden as a book censor. He was harsh on authors who had flirted with Nazism, such as Ernst Jünger and Gottfried Benn. While there, he tried to found a literary review, for which he wished to recruit writers from the realm. However, because he was a Jew collaborating with the French, he was met with outbursts of hatred and the project folded. Later, in 1947, he traveled to Berlin, hoping for more rapport from among the revived intellectual elite in the city he had, earlier, in his novel *Berlin Alexanderplatz*, described so well. But he made the mistake of emphasizing the occupational functions of the foreign power he was serving: "The man who entered through the door," rued the former resistance fighter Günther Weisenborn, who had almost lost his head in 1942, "wore Döblin's face, but it was a French major in uniform." Because Döblin would not be accepted by his former confrères, he turned his back on Germany again and left, once more, for Paris. Still attached to Germany and a victim of Parkinson's disease, he died in a hospital near Freiburg in 1957, a virtually forgotten man.[202]

The most famous artist to return to Germany was the actor and theater director Fritz Kortner. During the Weimar Republic Kortner, born Nathan Kohn in 1892 in Vienna, had excelled through the virtuosity of his performances, he was legendary for his portrayals of Shylock and Richard III. In exile in the United States, playing Hollywood bit parts, his professional life had been less than stellar, and he and his wife, actress Johanna Hofer, were correspondingly unhappy.[203] Kortner cast anchor again in Munich, where at the Kammerspiele in February 1949 he staged *Donauwellen* (*Danube Waves*), a satirical comedy he himself had authored. It was to show the opportunism of mean, mediocre, average Nazis who had passed through the denazification machinery effortlessly. Predictably, it was a flop.[204] Then, in December 1950, he returned to Berlin to produce Schiller's *Don Carlos*, in which the actors playing soldiers aimed their guns at the audience, which incensed the public. While Kortner's objective had been to project polemics against former Nazis, whom he suspected everywhere, this made him even less welcome. Meanwhile the director, notoriously difficult to work with, was subjected to anti-Semitic slurs by former colleagues who had endured the Nazi period, especially by the older Jürgen Fehling, who was wary of Kortner's re-emergence.[205] During these months Kortner also managed to make *Der Ruf* (*The Last Illusion*), a film with a script he again had written. It was about Professor Mauthner, a Jewish philosophy professor who returns from California to post-Nazi Germany to find his way back, and who resigns and dies. Kortner's own wife Johanna Hofer was cast in the role of Lisa, Mauthner's wife. The symbolism could not have been starker. This was a maudlin attempt to rework the recent past, set up to mirror Kortner's own, at that time rather pathetic, career. But it was also a comment on an underground network of deep-rooted prejudices many Germans were still beholden to, judging by their negative, dismissive reactions.[206]

◆　◆　◆

After 1945, several factors combined to facilitate a revivification of the arts. This occurred after the realization that culture in the Third Reich had been immorally abused and aesthetically had lost the dynamics of invention. To cultural chauvinists, this admission amounted to a national disaster: culture had been a key German export ever since the late eighteenth century. Germans had got into the habit of viewing their country as "culturally, the highest-standing nation on earth," with the mission of "blessing the entire world," as Adelheid von Saldern has put it. Albrecht Riethmüller explains that in particular this had held true for "the nimbus of classical music," exemplified by conductor Wilhelm Furtwängler, where international consensus had always been unshaken that the Germans could not be surpassed.[207]

A number of conditions had to be fulfilled in order for new culture to arise and prosper. Old art had to be denationalized and high degrees of internationalization had to be achieved, to allow new influences to enter and guarantee transnational connectedness. Moreover, in style and content experimentation was to be encouraged, and the new culture had to be discursive rather than static and self-contained.

Thus went the prescription, but in reality there were hurdles to be overcome. In theater, for example, where at least half of the stages had been destroyed, the output was problematic.[208] The deeper in the provinces the theaters, the more they preferred provincial fare. "The public likes the well-known chestnuts of yesterday," wrote the chronicler of small-town Neuss.[209]

Under those directors who had emerged intact from the Third Reich, at least nominally, classical pieces such as *Iphigenie auf Tauris* (*Iphigenia in Tauris*, by Euripides) and modern dramas such as *Jedermann* (*Everyman*, by the Austrian Hugo von Hofmannsthal) were featured, next to the obligatory foreign ones; they served escapist purposes and cossetted bad consciences. Into that group also fell *Nathan der Weise* (*Nathan the Wise*) by Lessing, *Don Carlos* and *Die Räuber* (*The Robbers*) by Schiller, and *Romeo and Juliet* by Shakespeare. Some stages performed boulevard pieces, fairy tales, and comedies.[210] What lessons could post-war Germans draw from these? Few, it seemed. In fact, some classic plays were used to perpetuate the current aura of victimhood, urging citizens to dissociate themselves from past travails. When Shakespeare's *Macbeth* was given as the opening drama at the Munich Kammerspiele in October 1945, the program text likened the murderous king to Hitler and demonized a jurisdiction from which the blameless audience had only recently been salvaged.[211]

There were three modern dramas performed, none of which was reflective about Germans' responsibility for dictatorship and aggressive warfare in the manner Jaspers had suggested. One, *Die Illegalen* (*The Illegals*), was by Günther Weisenborn, who had worked for the Berlin Red Orchestra cell (Schulze-Boysen group) that had spied for the Soviet Union and who had miraculously survived to talk about it. It was premiered in Berlin in 1946. Having submitted to Communists – from one totalitarian system to another – was not something that endeared this author to the German public. He was soon forgotten.[212]

Another play about the war, *Des Teufels General* (*The Devil's General*), was by Carl Zuckmayer, whose mother was Jewish. But it could not really qualify as post-war drama because it had been written during the author's wartime exile in Vermont. After the war he returned to work in the American zone as an authority on culture for OMGUS and later settled in Switzerland.[213] Zuckmayer's Luftwaffe general Harras feels anything but shame over the Third Reich, but commands the audience's respect and admiration for personally choosing suicide after having bungled some of Göring's strategic orders. It suggests that the evil Harras had to face was not of his own making but an unavoidable consequence of fate. If there had been any guilt at all, Harras atoned for it. He is a jolly, likeable fellow; he lives for flying, women, and drink; he dies for honor. In the end the audience was given to understand that there had been "decent" soldiers in Hitler's Wehrmacht, even heroes who were on the opposite side of Hitler's regime; by identifying with such figures, ordinary Germans were removed from it as well. How strongly Germans agreed with this denialist theme is shown by the fact that the play was performed more than 3,000 times from December 1946 to 1950 and was made into a popular film as well.[214]

In Wolfgang Borchert's drama *Draussen vor der Tür* three motifs converged. One was that of the returned sergeant Beckmann who, emasculated and tired of life, is spurned by women. Back in Hamburg, his wife is with another man, and a new girl who comes his way will not stay with him; she too prefers someone else. "I cannot get up," Beckmann says as he is lying in the Elbe sand, an obvious sexual reference.[215] The second theme is that of hunger, which was pervasive in 1945.[216] The third theme is of victimhood in general. It is the war that has rendered Beckmann so unfortunate, and as he visits the colonel, his former commander at the Russian front, at his home and wants to hand over to him his own burden of responsibility (rather than continuing to shoulder it himself), he is cast out. The ending suggests that Beckmann sees no way out other than taking his own life by drowning himself in the Elbe. There is no doubt that Borchert himself felt this way. He had returned to Germany as a twenty-six-year-old soldier, after 600 kilometers on foot, with a liver ailment that killed him one day before his play was premiered in Hamburg on November 21, 1947.[217] It, too, became a film, in 1949.[218]

Political theater as a critical genre was missing on German stages well into the 1950s. One reason for this was the absence of Bertolt Brecht, shunned as an exile and a Communist. In October 1948, after the Cold War had commenced and ideological differences between the Western and Eastern zones had been accentuated, Brecht returned via Switzerland. But, significantly, he went to East Berlin, where he resumed his dramaturgical stance at the Berliner Ensemble, fashioned by the German Democratic Republic (GDR) ministry of culture especially for him.[219] In western Germany, they performed his *Threepenny Opera* (1928) without stringency, more like a fairy tale.[220] However, as occurred in Munich, they also produced pieces by Hans Rehberg, a former protégé of Goebbels, who had managed to secure his whitewash in a German court.[221] Apart from Kortner, there were very few Jews who came back to the German stage, and if so, only in subordinate positions, as did Fritz Wisten in Berlin, after having worked for the Nazi-monitored Jüdischer Kulturbund (Jewish Culture League).[222] In the absence of fresh impulses, German responsibility for National Socialism and the war was not dealt with, much less viewed with guilt, with little attention paid to the genocide of Jews.

As theater stages were reconstructed after 1945 relatively quickly, so too did the number of cinemas increase. In the Western zones, 1,150 movie houses had been left by the end of 1945; there were 2,125 in 1946, 2,975 in 1948, and 3,962 in 1950. The number of moviegoers increased from 300 million to just over 487 million in the same time span.[223] There was only one film produced in all four zones in 1946, but seventy-six in the West alone by 1950.[224] Not least to escape from the drabness of everyday life, Germans flocked to the silver screen (as they flocked, at higher social levels, to the theater); obviously, they wished to be entertained. But whether they were motivated to learn a lesson, as the Allies were hoping, was questionable. In 1947 Gustav Zimmermann, a spokesman for the movie-theater industry, remarked that "film should not primarily be intended to discuss problems of the day, or to prompt us to search eternally for their causes or the guilty party."[225]

Under Allied license, the Germans produced so-called rubble films, set in cities' ruins and peopled by deprived and forsaken Germans. They turned out not nearly as popular with audiences as the other movies that were being offered – lighter German fare and Allied imports.[226] This was because these films were rather demanding, challenging the viewers to reflect critically on the most recent past and their place in it. Although they certainly tried, the scriptwriters and directors, who almost without exception had worked in the movie business during the Nazi regime and had experienced a, more or less sincere, change of heart, did not wholly succeed with every effort. Aesthetically, there were interesting nuances, as in *Die Mörder sind unter uns*, which with its Expressionist scenes reminded connoisseurs of *Dr. Caligari*, or *In jenen Tagen*, which in part was reminiscent of Fritz Lang's *Metropolis* (1927).[227] But the moral compass they purported to show more often than not was askew – even though the directors were able to get one or two salient points across, they missed out on others.

This was apparent from the start, from *Die Mörder sind unter uns* of 1946. Its director Wolfgang Staudte chose as his main actors Hildegard

Knef and Ernst Wilhelm Borchert. In Berlin, the teenager Knef had survived the last days of fighting as the mistress of the last chief of the Nazi movie industry, the adulterous SS officer Ewald von Demandowsky, executed by the Soviets in October 1946; Borchert had been a member of the SA. But now both Knef and Borchert concurred with Staudte's moral mission to alert viewers to the continued presence of Nazis in their midst – the main theme of the movie. However, they neglected to show that every German bore some share of the responsibility for Nazi crimes, not just Brückner, the former front commander in the film, presented as a Wehrmacht executioner of innocent civilians now posing as paterfamilias. By rendering Knef's character, Susanne Walmer, and Borchert's, Dr. Hans Mertens, innocent, Staudte endorsed that ubiquitous new German sentiment of victimhood and encouraged collective amnesia. This judgment could be seen to apply more to Mertens, who had been present at Brückner's shooting of Polish hostages without voicing a protest, than Walmer, who was said to have been liberated from a concentration camp (although her radiant looks belied it).[228] It could have been worse: when Staudte had asked Carl Raddatz, who had starred in the Nazi propaganda film *Wunschkonzert* (*Request Concert*, 1940), to play Brückner, he declined saying that he did not wish to participate in a movie "where Germans come off so badly."[229]

Next to this, Helmut Käutner's *In jenen Tagen* of 1947 was arguably the most significant of the rubble films. It showed scenes from the Third Reich itself, with much rubble in the last of seven segments. Mostly, German victims of the Third Reich are portrayed here – a businessman who is impelled to flee abroad in January 1933, a composer of modern music, the wife and mother of resistance fighters, a soldier at the Eastern Front, and an unwed young mother. The one Jew, the proprietor of a picture-frame shop, portrayed by Jewish survivor Ida Ehre, is visualized in a somewhat unfavorable, stereotypically anti-Semitic light, as her husband, an "Aryan," accuses her of always having pushed for business's sake, always wanting more than the neighbors. The film pursued the fate of individuals without relating them to a larger canvas, and it merely exposed hints of the pervasive malevolence – in one shot, rather than the SS officer, just the SS license plate of his car is seen. Like his colleagues, Käutner sketched time itself as an anonymous power, against which every human soul was rendered helpless. Humanity continued to exist during the criminal dictatorship, he insisted, but over this he forgot to demonstrate the inhumanity caused by the collective of everyone concerned, even before January 30, 1933, which marks the beginning of this touching narrative.[230]

Wolfgang Borchert's disturbing drama *Draussen vor der Tür*, before it had appeared on stage and in the cinemas, was produced as a radio play and broadcast by NWDR Hamburg on February 13, 1947, before Borchert himself had returned from the war.[231] It bears repeating here that radio was reconstituted by the Western Allies as an antidote to Goebbels's oppressive propaganda apparatus, and for that reason decentralized and endowed with broad pro-democracy program guidelines by the authorities. Among the new broadcasters, the NWDR, initially under British leadership, developed over time as the most progressive, with its Cologne branch becoming a hotbed of artistic experimentation. By contrast, Munich's station was slow to adopt new standards, which could have been the result of the initially tight but gradually receding U.S. tutelage there, yet Munich's culture had never historically been at the center of the avant-garde, something both Richard Strauss and Carl Orff had deplored.[232] The other progressive station turned out to be the SWF in Baden-Baden under the French, partly because of that administration's overall more laissez-faire stance, but also, undeniably, because of French cultural traditions since Napoleon that begged for emulation. Altogether, radio attracted a few ideologically reliable and intellectually brilliant Germans as intendants and program directors. Outstanding was, for instance, Axel Eggebrecht, who as a former Communist had suffered incarceration, and Ernst Schnabel, a friend of Käutner, who had been a Kriegsmarine officer but demonstrably not a Nazi. Both men became active for the NWDR in Hamburg.[233]

Two reasons why new German broadcast ventures turned out to be successful were the extended use of audio-tape equipment (perfected by the Nazis in the 1940s) and the establishment of a frequency modulation (Ultrakurzwelle, UKW) band in May 1950.[234] Moreover, Germans turned increasingly to radio during years when theater stages and cinemas had still to be rebuilt, which did not happen overnight.

The radio play, or Hörspiel, became a characteristic feature of weekly broadcasting on account of a number of factors. It had been invented in the Weimar Republic, in 1923, when radio could be said to be a republican institution par excellence within the available media spectrum.[235] As such, although radio itself was adapted, the Hörspiel fell out of favor with Nazi broadcasters, who used other audible methods to indoctrinate the masses. Brecht, Walter Benjamin, and Günter Eich had all written radio plays; Döblin had adapted his novel *Berlin Alexanderplatz* for radio in 1930.[236] Now Eich was returning – after service in the Wehrmacht – as a Hörspiel author, contributing to make this medium a hallmark of the new republic. He was destined, in fact, to become the most performed Hörspiel author of the early 1950s. Another factor was that radio plays lent themselves to the use of techniques specific to audio broadcasting, producing sounds that on a stage or in film could not be heard or would be superseded by peripheral noises, such as whispering, lightning, or stroking – even kissing. Those made for challenging experimentation – a hallmark of the new era. Finally, because of the adaptability of tape recorders radio plays did not have to be trans-mitted live anymore but could be recorded at any time and then preserved.[237] The overall effect was astounding. In 1949, 47 percent of all West German listeners declared themselves to be fans of the Hörspiel.[238] Around that time, when I was a young teenager, I listened to Anna Seghers's novel *Das siebte Kreuz* (*The Seventh Cross*), fashioned into a Hörspiel. I was mesmer-ized by the story of resistance fighters hunted down by the Nazis one by one.[239] When I later read the book, the excitement had evaporated.

Former collaborators with the Nazi regime were often obvious in the new press and prone to influencing content, despite foreign-license sover-eignty. A telling example is *Die Welt*, printed in Hamburg under the British since early 1946. Although the daily newspaper was viewed as excessively pro-English by the German public, its initial editor was Hans Zehrer, not a bona-fide National Socialist but former editor of the proto-fascist *Die Tat*. Many critics considered that journal to have played an enabling role for Hitler within the pre-1933 intelligentsia, especially among the young elite. The reason Zehrer had subsequently exiled himself to the island of Sylt during the regime was that he had criticized Hitler for not having taken power through an outright coup in 1932–3, rather than going through the motions of legality. In April 1933, Zehrer had publicly condemned the alleged "Golden International of Jewry, Money and Trade and called for the removal of Jewish influence from the key institutions of the nation," writes Richard J. Evans. Zehrer's presence at the helm of *Die Welt* became so egre-gious that in pronouncedly Social Democratic Hamburg he was forced to abdicate his position in March 1946.[240] He would surface again later under

Die Welt's new right-wing owner Axel Springer; this had not been an auspicious beginning for the metropolitan broadsheet.

Also in Hamburg under the British, things looked even more ominous after the founding of *Die Zeit*. Today a liberal bastion, this paper was then, above all, a testimony to the ineffectualness of the entire denazification process, as it consistently questioned that process's validity. Its first chief editor, Richard Tüngel, decried the Allied war trials as illegitimate and argued for the rights of former Nazis in the new republic. In a Christmas contribution in December 1946, he compared the Israelite Jews under the Emperor Augustus's occupation with post-war Germans. "Germany too is occupied today," he wrote. "In many regards we are worse off. We do not have enough living space, we are freezing and are suffering from hunger."[241] If ever there was an assertion of (self-imagined) victimhood, this stood as a prime example. Then there was Hans-Georg von Studnitz, a noted anti-Semite who had worked in Ribbentrop's foreign ministry. In 1941 he had published an article entitled "The Jew Roosevelt" in a Berlin daily, in which he suggested that the president's advisers' ancestors had once crossed the Red Sea. Von Studnitz's specialty became polemics against Robert Kempner, a Jewish assistant chief counsel for the American judiciary team at the Nuremberg Trials. In the midst of this alt-Nazi group, how the liberal-minded Bucerius as chief licensee and Marion Gräfin Dönhoff as a forward-looking if less experienced editor were able to hold their own is truly noteworthy.[242]

The one new paper that could have appeared as a cleaned-up replica of a Nazi sheet was the well-endowed *FAZ*, not only because of its seat in the Main metropolis, but also by virtue of its main editors. Key men in the editorial group of 1949 hailed from the offices of its seeming precursor *FZ*; before 1933, they had represented right-of-center viewpoints and this remained the case after 1945. Erich Welter and Erich Dombrowski appeared as old reactionaries in new clothing; the path of Karl Korn into the *FAZ* has already been traced. Founding co-editor Paul Sethe as chief editor of the *FZ* since 1934 had changed from a right-liberal to a Nazi mouthpiece. He celebrated the march into Austria in spring 1938, and later compared Hitler to Caesar. Alongside his aforementioned colleagues, Sethe's assumption of head-office duties in the newly formed *FAZ* dates from November 1, 1949.[243]

In a discussion of the most important weekly magazines after the war, two oscillating characters enter the scene: Henri Nannen and Rudolf Augstein. First Nannen. He managed to have a journal licensed by the British on August 1, 1948, which he called *Der Stern*. From an ideological perspective, its content turned out to be beyond reproach. Somehow, however, Nannen was an unlikely character to have been tasked with this pursuit. Born in 1913, there were factors that predisposed him to opposing the Nazi regime. His father, a Social Democratic postal worker, was dismissed from his job in 1934. Henri himself had a Jewish girlfriend who was persecuted until forced to emigrate, with her family, to Palestine in 1938. And yet Nannen, by then a journalist specializing in contemporary-art criticism, had already allowed himself to be seconded to play a small part in Leni Riefenstahl's 1936 propaganda film about the Olympics. Tall, blond, blue-eyed, and with a cleft chin, he was handsome beyond description – picture-book "Aryan" looks. He also worked for a Nazi art journal. In that capacity he wrote about the "heroic earnestness" and "victorious pathos" engulfing the swearing-in of SS recruits, and later held that "the rejuvenation of German Man is the Führer's work." In 1976 Nannen claimed he had penned such sentences in order to benefit his father, who had been left without a pension. During the war, however, as a member of a propaganda company with organizational ties to the SS, Nannen wrote in a letter home about "the gunning down of thousands of Jews." He should have known, for he was allegedly responsible for the content of leaflets transported to the enemy's lines in 1944. They charged, among other lies, that Jews had been responsible for starting the war. Easily denazified after 1945, Nannen received his license for print-media production from the same group of British-Jewish officers who had helped launch *Die Welt* and would help launch *Der Spiegel*: John Chaloner, Henry Ormond, and Harry Bohrer. Notwithstanding Nannen's checkered past, *Der Stern* became West Germany's largest and most enlightened of several illustrated weeklies established well into the early 1950s. Hans Weidemann, his SS superior from the 1944 Italian Front, became one of its leading employees.[244]

The father of Rudolf Augstein (b. 1923), although against the Nazis, was an anti-Semite. Nonetheless, before Rudolf volunteered for the Wehrmacht in 1944, they both assisted a Jewish family emigrating in 1936. But later, wanting to become a journalist, he published essays in *Das Reich*. Later still, he witnessed the grinding-down of a comrade on the exercise field; the

45

comrade died. Yet undaunted, Augstein opted for an officer's career – the easiest way to survive, he thought – and emerged from the war as lieutenant, after little action at the front.

An ideal candidate, Augstein was in 1947 quickly entrusted, by the Chaloner team, with the founding of a new weekly magazine eventually called *Der Spiegel.* It was immediately committed to democratic values and a mandate to deliver the most news to the most people in the most palatable manner, employing the latest possible advances in photojournalism. Indeed, the magazine was instantly successful, its print volume climbing from 20,000 in the fall of 1947 to 65,000 in 1948, 85,000 in 1949, and 100,000 a year later.[245]

In Augstein's quest to publish the most eye-catching and up-to-date news, he resorted to methods bordering on yellow journalism. Early on, this included a hankering for Nazi sources in a way that tended to endanger *Der Spiegel's* integrity. A case in point was that of Rudolf Diels, Göring's first Gestapo chief, from 1933 to 1934, when Himmler had him removed after the Röhm Putsch. Augstein began to serialize Diels's Third Reich memoirs in the May 1949 issue of his journal, and this went through a further eight episodes until early July. In his first instalment, entitled "Hitler's Court," Diehls's opening sentence was: "Göring personified heroes in permanence." He then proceeded to describe the Luftwaffe boss's entourage as generous and good-humored, "free from the molestations of the party and SS." One salacious tidbit mentioned further on is that he had supplied Göring with details about Alfred Rosenberg's Jewish mistress, Liselotte Kohlrausch, so that Hitler's official ideologue could be held in check for life.[246]

The memoir was mostly inside-Nazi gossip, with Diels glossing over his own role in having brought the Nazis to power and having transformed Prussia's pre-existing political police into the Nazi-style Gestapo. Diels had not, as he claimed, "worked against the coming of the National Socialists" before January 1933. In fact, he had helped to facilitate Reich Chancellor Franz von Papen's takeover of Prussia in July 1932, which was a stepping stone to the Third Reich. He also neglected to mention that it had been on his watch that the first suspects had been arrested after the burning of the Reichstag on February 27, 1933, many of whom were thrown into the basement of the Columbia-Haus headquarters of the SA in Berlin and tortured.[247] If *Der Spiegel* later acquired a reputation for crass sensationalism, and even mendacity, the seeds were sown in its earliest years.

In 1943, I was dressed up, handed a huge bunch of yellow flowers, and taken to the Zittau concert hall. Here my uncle, Helmut Roloff from Berlin, was giving a piano recital. I believe he played Schumann. After the concert, nervous as I was, I had to clamber up some stairs to the stage and hand the flowers to the pianist, who rewarded me with a big smile. There was much applause. Little did the audience know whom they had just applauded. For, as I learned after the war, the thirty-year-old Roloff had been released from a death cell in Berlin only weeks before. The previous year he had been accused of being a member of the Red Orchestra spying on behalf of the Soviet Union, for having hidden a radio transmitter under his Steinway grand. Roloff had been interrogated under torture by the Gestapo and accused of high treason, but he claimed his friends had come to his place only to listen to music. He had paid no attention to the transmitter. Because he kept repeating this false legend and the Schulze-Boysen cell did not betray him, even under torture, he was eventually released and continued touring.[248] In the latter half of the 1940s, Roloff was one of several pianists who taught and performed at the Darmstadt New Music summer courses. Roloff, who had become fascinated by twentieth-century music, was joined there at the piano by Udo Dammert, known to have been a Nazi, and in the choir department by Bruno Stürmer, the former Hitler Youth instructor.[249]

Modern contemporary music did not come to the Darmstadt event immediately, and on almost all platforms of musical performance in the land it was anathema. To the extent that Nazi-tainted musicians were allowed to reconnect with the German music scene, they shunned the experiment. When Franz Paul Decker in Krefeld attempted to present a mix of formerly forbidden composers such as Hindemith and Schoenberg, he was scolded by the critics, for "the public hardly wished to hear the new music."[250] Karl Amadeus Hartmann in Munich with his novel "Musica Viva" series had the same experience.[251] Munich's audience preferred the well-tried standard fare of yesteryear in opera and in the concert hall: Mozart's Symphony No. 40, much Richard Strauss, Siegmund von Hausegger, and yes, Munich's own Classical Modernists Carl Orff and Werner Egk. Mozart's *Magic Flute* was as popular as Beethoven's *Fidelio*, to which some ascribed a make-amends character, because it was seen as an anti-concentration camp opera – a judgment that incensed Klaus Pringsheim, the music-critic brother-in-law of Thomas Mann.[252] Nuremberg clung to much the same repertoire in opera and concert, but also – as was true in Munich and elsewhere – a surfeit of operetta. The redoubtable mainstays, compositions by Bach and Beethoven, or Haydn's *Creation*, predominated (in April 1945 Strauss, the regnant traditionalist, in a letter to conductor Karl Böhm, praised German music from Haydn via Carl Maria von Weber and Richard Wagner as "the highest peaks" of development to the current day).[253] Here there was really no difference from a Third Reich program, except that in operetta, high-middlebrow fare, the once beloved Jewish pieces, such as those by Leo Fall or Oscar Straus, could be played again. In addition, the Jewish Mendelssohn's and Mahler's works now were often performed.[254] Next to Munich and Nuremberg, in music throughout Germany from 1945 to 1950, the repertoire was pedestrian.[255] Specifically in opera, the most frequently performed composers of a German "Klassische Moderne" apart from Egk and Orff were Paul Hindemith, Boris Blacher, and Gottfried von Einem – a respectable group, but cravenly tracing the traditional; and there was little by non-Germans.[256]

Although Hartmann favored music by those German and other Moderns in his series, his own compositions were arguably the least progressive of the group. His fame rested mostly on the works he had created before 1945, while officially spurned by the Nazis. Some of these he reset, and he also composed eight symphonies, and works for small ensembles, solo piano, and voice. Works to accompany *Macbeth* on stage, *Undine* after Jean Giraudoux, and a fugue for percussion orchestra remained unfinished. All these stayed within the conventional tonal constraints of what might be called "culinary modernism," to paraphrase Brecht. If at all, it was Hartmann's pre-1945 œuvre that tended to be in demand in the temples of music, not his postwar work.[257] Although he was revered by musical newcomers such as Hans Werner Henze, Hartmann could hardly serve as a stimulus in new composition.[258]

Next to Orff's, Hartmann was contemptuous of music by Werner Egk, whom he thought to be "someone with absolutely no artistic qualities."[259] Egk had asked him – vainly – for a whitewash at his denazification trial. Besides, in Hartmann's widow's recollection, Egk "always introduced notes into his compositions that were supposed to sound modern."[260] But surely Hartmann had Orff unfairly judged! Orff continued to ride on the crests of success he had enjoyed with his signature oratorio *Carmina Burana* and after 1945 had follow-up works performed to much acclaim – music theater pieces *Die Bernauerin* (1944–5) and *Astutuli* (1946–7); *Antigonae* was completed in 1949. Skeletonized instrumentation, pronounced percussion, and rhythmic exaltations remained the hallmarks of his style.[261] Among insiders, however, Orff suffered from the aura of Nazi collaboration.

Egk's post-war music was also characterized, as before, by strong percussion and angular rhythm, but his melodic and harmonic instrumentation was richer, more colorful, and more generous than Orff's. Indeed, like Orff, Egk fancied himself a modernizer. And yet Theodor Adorno satirized Egk's *Sonata for Piano for Two Hands* that Schott's had published in 1948, dubbing it "Egkomion" in a letter to Thomas Mann. The novelist was amused, calling the music critic's comment "a most earnest joke."[262] Clearly, both Adorno and Mann, who knew their Schoenberg and their Alban Berg, chuckled over the pretense of modernity that was apparent. For like Orff's or Hartmann's scores, Egk's music was virtuously tonal, still very disciplined in rhythm and harmonic form. Whatever his artistic standing at that time, either as composer or conductor, unlike Orff, Egk was not able to appear in public because of his long-pending denazification trial, which was unresolved until October 1947. During this period he wrote music for his ballet *Abraxas*, financed by the Baden-Baden SWF under the permissive French, an instrumental version of which he was able to conduct there in December. By 1950 Egk had assumed something of a contradictory position in the German music scene: among true Modernists he tended to be slighted as old-school, while entrenched conservatives, many of those in Munich, thought him distastefully avant-garde.[263]

As he was already in German modern-music circles everywhere, Hindemith became the top player at the new Darmstadt summer school, which doubled as a festival, in 1946, followed by Schoenberg. Darmstadt was one of many German music venues where, beginning in 1945, Hindemith was on demand as yet another token of cultural restitution. His case was the closest the Germans came to accepting an emigrant potentially wanting to return with enthusiasm, because they were able to dwell on his Germanness (rather than Jewishness) and rejoice in the knowledge that Hindemith in the 1920s had been experimental enough to be classified as avant-garde, yet had settled for conventional tonality as an executor of the neo-Baroque style at which he was regarded, in 1945, as a mature craftsman.[264] The fact that Hindemith had left Germany in 1938 not as a political emigrant but as someone who could not shape his own artistic future in the Reich was conveniently not considered by his acolytes: in September 1933 he had informed the already exiled composer Ernst Toch that the regime had asked him to cooperate and he "had not declined."[265] Now, in late 1945, his music was regarded as proof of the continuum of German culture from pre-Nazi times to the present, with Hitler's regime detached. For his contemporaries he served as a great exonerator, remarked Henze in 1980 – his music could be performed as if National Socialism had never happened, and the Germans were relieved of guilt.[266]

As an auspicious new beginning, Hindemith's late opera *Mathis der Maler* finally had its German premiere in Stuttgart in December 1946 and he became the Great Praeceptor for a whole new generation of German musicians. "Hindemith is the grand creative younger musician of our time," crowed Heidelberg's *Rhein-Neckar-Zeitung* in October 1946. It called his music "simply overwhelming"; he could be shown to be inseparably tied to "the tradition of Western and especially of German music."[267] Indeed, the entire first run of courses of the Darmstadt festival during the summer of 1946 was dominated by his work, as neoclassicism became the standard that neophyte German musicians now wished to be judged by. His prevalence persisted into 1947 (although he was never present in the flesh), when the influential music critic Fred Hamel, a circumspect Nazi survivor, gave a laudatory Hindemith lecture at that year's event.[268]

But in 1947 some of the more experimental among the younger composers at the festival were beginning to harbor doubts. Henze was on the brink of rejecting Hindemith.[269] In 1948 at Darmstadt, when there was renewed talk about Schoenberg – who already in the early 1920s had gone farther musically than Hindemith would ever do thereafter – there were "muffled reactions" against the Frankfurt-Hanau-born composer, who, to leave no doubt, reiterated what he had proclaimed in 1937 in his *Unterweisung im Tonsatz*, that "music had to remain tonally circumscribed."[270] In 1949 Henze openly polemicized against Hindemith, claiming for himself the right to practice "polytonal harmony or even twelve-tone techniques."[271] In Darmstadt during that year, when Hindemith was told that a great many of his younger colleagues thought of his compositions as outmoded, he snorted that theirs were "new goat crap."[272] That summer, the influential electronic composer Herbert Eimert sanctioned Hindemith's ostracism by vocally taking a stand for Schoenberg.[273] Eventually, even though he proved somewhat more successful on the concert stage, the

U.S. resident Hindemith could not countenance moving either to Darmstadt or his nearby birthplace, but in 1953 changed from Yale to the University of Zurich as a teaching venue, preferring, like Thomas Mann, the Swiss environs that had welcomed him before.[274]

The year 1949 marked a sea change not only in government and politics for the new republic, but also in the German music world. The last Romantics, Richard Strauss and Hans Pfitzner, died that year. Darmstadt festival officials corresponded with Schoenberg about a possible return to Germany, certainly to teach, which subsequently could not be realized, not least because of the composer's failing health – he died two years later.[275] Hindemith's music was subdued. Contrary to John Mauceri, who claims in his largely undocumented recent survey of modern music that Schoenberg was "summarily discarded by the European avant-garde," his music became all the rage in Darmstadt at the end of the decade.[276] And in 1949 Bernd Alois Zimmermann, a thirty-one-year-old former student of the Cologne conservatory who was interested in Eimert and Schoenberg's work, attended the summer courses for the first time.[277] He and Karlheinz Stockhausen would become the heralds of New Music in Germany in the 1950s.

Similar to post-1945 filmmakers, visual artists and their impresarios also showed a predilection for a pictorial rendition of the new German disposition. And as in some films, the emphasis was on German victimhood, German suffering, and German innocence. There were three approaches to the visual arts in 1945 and immediately after. The first pretended there had never been a serious interruption of creative processes during the Hitler regime and proceeded to show Expressionist art. In the absence of contemporary artists of that genre and not seeing any of the emigrants returning, resort was taken to exhibiting the works of well-known masters of yesterday. This was the purpose of the 1946 Dresden exhibition. Paintings by Expressionist artists such as Karl Schmidt-Rottluff, Ernst Ludwig Kirchner, and Paul Klee were on display.[278] These showings were designed to signal to a German audience that Expressionism had not been degenerate as formerly charged, that the Third Reich had merely been a blip, and that time was moving on.[279] Exhibitions under similar auspices, all mirroring reactive rather than proactive sentiments, were staged locally everywhere, in Berlin at the Galerie Rosen, at the Kestner-Gesellschaft in Hanover, and the Schäzlerpalais in Augsburg. Duisburg showed work by the sculptor Wilhelm

Lehmbruck, long deceased, Neuss showed Alfred Cossmann's, and Munich the "Blaue Reiter" painter Franz Marc's.[280]

Significantly, the audience on the whole, most certainly still influenced by Nazi aesthetics, resented the modernity of the established Expressionists, as it had few ideas what to do with art at this particular point in time, avant-garde or not. Indeed, as Döblin observed in Berlin, artists and impresarios themselves did not agree about the place and purpose of art in the current circumstances and debated this as a problem, as did the musicians and their students in early sessions at the Darmstadt summer-course festival.[281]

The second approach originated among surviving artists of the representational Expressionist school who were again active in Germany, chief among them Karl Hofer, whose paintings had been included at the Nazi exhibition of "degenerate art" in July 1937. The philosophy behind their post-1945 work was that it could be used to show a reaction to the horrors of the more recent past by creating strong figurative images. Such a practice was rejected by another group of painters, led by Willi Baumeister, who as a third approach championed abstraction. They believed that through an engagement in abstraction a protest could be lodged against Nazi dictates of the past, which had insisted on representationalism in contemporary art and sculpture to the exclusion of the abstract form. Now "abstract art was essentially conceived as expression of the new political order," judged the sociologist of art Gerhard Grohs.[282] These artists did not all strictly work in the abstract, as Baumeister did, but also engaged in semi-representational shapes, as did Heinz Trökes, who was a noted exponent of Surrealism. Nonetheless, Hofer protested their practices by calling Klee a "painting poet" and Wassily Kandinsky a "space decorator" who merely produced "dead-colored kitsch," recalled Günter Grass, then a graphics student at the Berlin academy where Hofer taught.[283]

Regardless of their style, artists from these two groups invoked motifs of finger-pointing, repudiation, or self-rehabilitation, as far as retrospectives on the Third Reich were concerned, to rationalize their own past experience. For this, *Das Gleichnis von den Blinden*, a Brueghelesque painting by Karl Schwesig of 1947, is paradigmatic, featuring five blind men characterized as Allied soldiers leading each other and following another blind man who, with a swastika armband, has plunged into a brook. This is to be interpreted to mean that not only the Allies were duped by fate, but also the

Nazified German people: the whole thing was a natural catastrophe.[284] Karl Hofer's painting of *The Blind Ones* (1948) displays a similar theme, of four (German) men and women helplessly delivered into the unknown.[285] Willi Geiger's portrait *The General Staff* (1947) pointed more fingers, clearly holding the three skeletons wearing Wehrmacht uniforms and planning aggressive warfare responsible.[286] Hofer's *Cain and Abel* of 1946 delineated even more clearly guilt and innocence, as the evil Cain is about to slay his helpless brother – exemplifying Nazis and their callow people.[287] In Wilhelm Lachnit's *The Death of Dresden* (1945) a mother sits trapped in the ruins of her house, her face in one hand, while the other holds her son, his arms draped over her lap. Skeletal limbs lurk in the background.[288] And in a painting of more contemporary relevance, yet again pronouncing German victimhood, Erwin Oehl depicted a war cripple in front of ruins, followed by a strumpet in an ecstatic, lurid strut, fondled by a lecherous GI. The work is entitled *Fraternization*.[289]

Toward the end of the 1940s, the group around Baumeister consolidated to form what was meant to be a movement, specifically to attract younger artists. The ZEN 49 clique became conspicuous in Munich. One aim was to work along lines of continuity originating with Kandinsky and Klee; its credo was abstract art, a repudiation of anything representational. But only a few of its younger adherents made some impact on the future art scene, not least through international connections, in contrast to the national isolation characterizing most of the 1940s artists.[290] Baumeister died in 1955; ZEN 49 survived a bit longer. Overall, the post-1945 artists were a static rather than dynamic group, close to senescence, caught in partial paralysis and used up. They were war-damaged. Some had been born in the nineteenth century; all of them were active already before 1933. Defying sterility, really just one man stood out – Ewald Mataré at the Kunstakademie in Düsseldorf, born in 1887 and a former student of the German Impressionist Lovis Corinth. In 1947, he became the teacher of Joseph Beuys.

Just as a majority of post-war Germans kept admiring conventional paintings and sculpture produced before 1945, so too did most Germans continue to prefer reading literature of that period, as traditional stylistically as they were critically unreflective of contemporary issues in content. In many, the Nazi trend toward "Blood and Soil" again predominated, or racist allusions persisted; the glorification of Social Darwinist struggle or war endured. Works by Gottfried Benn, the Jünger brothers, Ernst Wiechert, Hans Carossa, and Ina Seidel fell into that category.[291]

Among the few authors who had been around during the Third Reich but wished to escape from that dingy literary practice and do something new was Günter Eich. Born in 1907, he was a freewheeling though not well-known author, having served in the war from 1939 to 1945. After his return from a U.S. POW camp he continued earning his living mostly as a Hörspiel author. Next to radio plays, he concentrated on poetry, using only simple words essential for comprehension. This was meant as a protest against past and hollow, bloated Nazi jargon, and regarded as being in tune with the basic mode of post-war living in sparse, reduced environs. Eich's poem *Inventur* (*Inventory*) became a classic: "This is my cap / this is my coat / here my razor / in the linen bag / ... / In the bread bag are / a pair of woolen socks / and some things which / I tell no one." In the laconic vernacular of resignation, this was a list of things, the fundamental requisites of a survivor, as which he saw himself.[292]

As the Swiss essayist Urs Widmer has explained, a new, sober language was employed here for enumeration and registration. It began from scratch, doing away with embroidery and false emotionalisms such as were common among nationalists or Nazis.[293] Adhering to these principles in prose, the newly emerging spirit was Heinrich Böll. Born in 1917, he, too, had written sporadically before being inducted into the Wehrmacht in 1939 and serving till the war's end. After 1945, Böll believed that his own matter-of-fact way of writing suited a changed scenario, what with Germany being "destroyed, from the inside, at the outside," with "the inner destruction almost more serious."[294]

Böll published a few novellas and short stories at the end of the 1940s that established him as a writer of note to be watched. They are all strongly autobiographical. In *Der Zug war pünktlich* (*The Train Was On Time*) of 1949 he tells the story of the young soldier Andreas who travels on a Wehrmacht train from the Ruhr through Saxony and Silesia to the Eastern Front in Galicia. Andreas, extraordinarily sensitive, can hardly bear the uncouth manners of his comrades who are interested only in food, drink, and sex. In a small Galician town the group of four decamp and, after a sumptuous dinner, visit a brothel. Andreas meets up with Olina, a former music student, but instead of sleeping with her she plays the piano for him and they talk music. The reader is given to understand that they fall in love, but also that Olina is there to spy on Wehrmacht soldiers for the Polish partisan group she belongs to. At the end they get into a car along with other soldiers and are blown up. Andreas reappears in short stories collectively entitled *Die Verwundung* (*On Being Wounded*), as he is in retreat from the Hungarian front back home. The (this time somewhat less sensitive) protagonist is in sympathy with the native population he encounters during a slow ride home, and expresses compassion with his (sometimes severely) wounded comrades on the train.

Böll's capacity for empathy with German war victims, including himself, is strong and runs like a thread through these stories. These victims are helpless cogs in the machinery of war; they are used and abused. They suffer, often silently, and accept a fate they had not wished for but have no control over. Far from being censorious of the author, the prominent literature critic Marcel Reich-Ranicki writes poignantly that "the young Böll does not demonstrate how humans make war, but what war does to humans."[295]

Hence, if Reich-Ranicki's judgment were to prevail, Böll's interpretation of victimhood was the equivalent of that offered by the painters Oehl and Lachnit, who laid no blame on Germans. But Böll did go further than those painters, for in *Zug* he caricatures a Wehrmacht lieutenant ("this stupid pig") and applauds the Polish partisan Olina, and Andreas even prays, "especially for the Czernowitz Jews and for the Lemberg Jews," obviously knowing what fate awaits them under Nazi occupation (as did the journalist Henri Nannen).[296] In *Verwundung* (*Wound*), where it is said that no one is allowed "to start a war," there is a story, in clipped style and therefore even more effective, about a Pole taken by the Germans for a Jew and being shot, along with other Jews, into a pit – that was Einsatzgruppen genocide, a subject hardly to be encountered anywhere at this time in German arts, be it film, novel, or painting.[297]

Böll's insights might have been expected from politically motivated anti-Nazis; in his case it was deep-seated Catholic belief that was the wellspring of his thinking. Strong anti-Nazi convictions were the source of action for the ex-Communist Hans Werner Richter, born in 1908 and forced to serve in the Wehrmacht, who had been taken prisoner by the Americans in 1943. Released in 1946, it was he who, together with a fellow ex-POW, Alfred Andersch, had founded the U.S.-sponsored journal *Der Ruf* in the same year.

Dead-set against former and current Nazis, but also conscious of his being German, Richter disliked patronizing American tutelage and thought denazification to be "a farce," which of course it largely was.[298] After his first journal failed he planned for a second one, to be called *Der Skorpion*. This too the Americans eventually objected to, but before this happened Richter, joined by Andersch, met with fellow writers in Bannwaldsee in September 1947, in the Bavarian Allgäu region, to discuss this and future prospects. He had asked them to bring along stuff they had written to be read and discussed; perhaps something would come of it. This turned out to be the first meeting of Gruppe 47.

Here Wolfdietrich Schnurre read his story *Das Begräbnis* (*The Funeral*); it was in curt Berlin jargon, similar to the style of Eich, who would be invited later. From the beginning it was clear that this was Richter's very own affair; he had personally invited the first group of writers and would do so again in the future – no one could invite himself. The informal format of the first meeting of seventeen writers served as a template for all those that followed. There was a semicircle facing Richter and a guest was invited to speak for twenty minutes or so; thereafter came rounds of criticism. This was often harsh and hurt personal feelings, which was difficult to bear because Richter allowed for no rebuttal. When Andersch read from new writings early on, he was judged so severely that he never showed up again. The first meeting also offered a pattern for social engagement: fish caught in a nearby lake were consumed, no mean achievement in times bereft of foodstuffs, wine was handed around, there was swimming in the lake, and conversations thrived.[299]

Reich-Ranicki, with his customary mixture of invective and charm, has called Richter a "lovable dilettante" who "improvised frivolously."[300] But in fact Richter was closer to genius because he was able to attract, in the beginning about twice a year, like-minded writers simply by sending them a postcard – changing venues all over Germany. They came because, like him, they were not apolitical and denialist, they were worn front survivors, committedly anti-fascist and pacifist; they wanted to prevent "a repetition of what had happened, and at the same time wished to plant the cornerstone for a new democratic Germany, for a better future, for a new literature mindful of its responsibility for the political and collective social development."[301] The ritualistic criticism was cruel but necessary, because under the

Nazis this had not existed and now discourse and debate were once more possible. (Later, when Richter read from his own works, such as the World War II novel in progress, *Die Geschlagenen – The Beaten Ones –* he was booed out and never tried his luck again.)[302] For the same reason experimental new forms of writing were now welcomed, "Gertrude Stein and Ernest Hemingway, invisible, were virtually present."[303]

The next informal meeting of the group occurred in Herrlingen near Ulm in November, and its anti-Nazi character there was accentuated by the presence of Ulm's Inge Scholl, the surviving older sister of Hans and Sophie Scholl of the White Rose resistance group, who had been executed in 1943. A third meeting took place in Jugenheim near Mainz in April 1948. This time its attendees were introduced to the public, and the liberal *Süddeutsche Zeitung* dedicated a favorable review to them. When in October 1949 foreign guests were invited to Utting on Lake Ammer south of Munich, an important criterion of anti-Nazi conduct had been realized – international connectedness and cooperation. Richter's get-togethers attained more gravitas after the introduction of a Gruppe 47 Prize, financed by progressive publishers. At the May 1950 meeting in Inzigkofen, Württemberg, Günter Eich was the first to receive the award.[304]

◆ ◆ ◆

Fighting progress, forces of reaction attempted to control the German postwar cultural scene. They had their origins in an aura of Cultural Pessimism during the Weimar Republic, fortified by racialist nationalism in the Third Reich, and fed by the undulating mood of recalcitrance and denial pervading all strata of society in the late 1940s. At the base was the philosophy of, among others, Paul Krannhals, who abhorred Modernism. At the end of the 1920s Krannhals was a newspaper editor who, along with other archconservatives such as Winifred Wagner, joined Alfred Rosenberg's circle. There they sought to influence cultural developments from within the Nazi Party along reactionary lines, tempered by an extreme racism.[305] Around that time Krannhals published his two-volume magnum opus, *Das organische Weltbild* (*The Organic World View*), where he held, with references to Albrecht Dürer and Goethe, that German culture was organically anchored in the medieval past. Carried away by hubris, he championed stasis rather than mobility in German culture, whose unique qualities he confidentially proclaimed.[306]

The art historian Hans Sedlmayr followed his path. A professor of art history in Vienna in 1936, he supported – illegally in the Austrian Republic – the National Socialists, became a secret party member, and two years later greeted the Anschluss enthusiastically. Dismissed from his Vienna chair in 1945, Sedlmayr was in waiting for a new position when he proceeded to polemicize against modern art similar to Krannhals, because he saw it re-emerging in the group around Baumeister in Munich.[307] In his book *Verlust der Mitte* (*Loss of the Middle*, 1948) Sedlmayr interpreted true art as being "essentially situated in the middle, between the brain and the senses," and he accused the Moderns, beginning in the early twentieth century, of removing art from the healthy center core, from man, from anything human, and from balance. He alleged this process to have started with Picasso, who had painted jugglers, harlequins, circus people, and fugitives (in his Blue and Rose periods, 1901–6), and thereafter things where you could not differentiate between up and down (in his Cubist Period, 1907–10). This trend was carried on in the work of Le Corbusier and the Bauhaus, the Expressionists, and now the Surrealism of Salvador Dalí and his German acolytes such as Trökes. These modern, "mechanistic," painters showed "a preference for the unorganic," charged Sedlmayr, utilizing material that "replaces the organic with the unorganic." He employed arguments the Nazis had used against so-called degenerate art by comparing it to the doodlings of inmates of insane asylums when he wrote that modern (German) art was "in the antechamber of madness."[308]

Contemporaneous traditionalist thinkers were in agreement with Sedlmayr. One was Emil Preetorius, the chief stage designer in Bayreuth under Hitler and a former protégé of conductor Bruno Walter, an archconservative.[309] Like Sedlmayr, he too was out of a job at the end of the 1940s. A year before Sedlmayr he excoriated man's removal from an "organic existence" and urged his return to nature. Modern art was prone to decomposition, lamented Preetorius, deploring its "open, diffluent borders," where "the conduction of lines, coloring, the shaping of forms" had gone awry and "the design of space" had been dissolved. Preetorius's premise for art was that organic nature should motivate man to reproduce it – which was exactly what Baumeister's group rejected. Preetorius's pessimistic verdict was that "today's art, the modern art of the entire world is threatened by crisis, in that the formerly valid law of life governing the visual arts appears questionable."[310]

Sedlmayr was echoed by Karl Scheffler, once a champion of German Impressionism and a foe of humdrum Wilhelmian conceptions of art. But like Krannhals, he too became critical of abstract art at the beginning of the 1920s and, while he eschewed allying himself with the National Socialists, remained skeptical of the avant-garde. In 1950 he published *Kunst ohne Stoff* (*Art without Substance*), in which he cursed Picasso's works as "painted speculations," refuting his "doctrinaire Cubism." All abstract art was "marked by something inhuman, something satanic," held Scheffler, including the art of Klee, whose colors had the quality of noble rot. In sum, abstract art was the equivalent of atonal music – atonal music as defined by Furtwängler, who disdainfully had termed it "biologically inferior."[311]

In July 1950 Sedlmayr was challenged by Baumeister in a debate at Darmstadt that was highly publicized. Baumeister rehashed Sedlmayr's Nazi past and charged him with hiding behind the Catholic Church. "Sedlmayr is barely a democrat," reproached Baumeister, "nor does he genuinely serve the Church. His theory is as one-tracked as the racial theories of Alfred Rosenberg."[312] The fact that Sedlmayr received a chair in art history at the University of Munich in 1951 and Preetorius was appointed president of the Bavarian Academy of Fine Arts there two years later is a telling comment on the precariousness of modern art in Germany in the final years of the 1940s.[313]

Furtwängler's regressive opinion exemplifies that this reaction prevailed also in music. This was conspicuous at the Darmstadt summer courses, actively supported by the Americans even during insufficient quality-screening. For while some of the founding members were former Nazis, National Socialist content or related subjects were also featured. Choral compositions performed in the summer of 1946 had been created by syco-phants of Hitler and had served the Hitler Youth: the composers were Hugo Distler, Ernst Pepping, and Armin Knab.[314] Fellow sympathizers Fortner and Stürmer conducted these for ex-Hitler Youths, ex-Wehrmacht, and likely ex-Waffen-SS, impressionable adolescents still imbued with Nazi ideology and still closed to the sounds of Hindemith and especially Schoenberg. Undetected by the Americans, this was the wrong beginning of musical education toward democracy.[315]

Conservative tendencies in the West German music business after 1945 were supported by, among others, Fred Hamel, not coincidentally Hindemith's promoter in Darmstadt in 1947, a music critic and contributor to *Das Reich* who in the past had written that "the consequences of National Socialism naturally concern all areas of creativity, music not excluded."[316] Hamel became extraordinarily influential after he had joined the faculty of the Landeskirchliche Musikschule in Hanover and founded the journal *Musica*, soon a platform of restoration. He was aided by Walter Abendroth, a music critic from the Third Reich who eventually became the anti-Modernist head of culture for *Die Zeit*. From academe, scholars Joseph Maria Müller-Blattau, a former collaborator with the SS, Wolfgang Stumme, the Hitler Youth's one-time music chief, and Friedrich Blume, who had given a keynote speech at the "degenerate music" exhibition in 1938, joined Hamel's agenda.[317] Blume appeared at the 1946 Darmstadt event and declared, falsely, that youth had to be reintroduced to music after the war, in order to re-establish "continuity."[318]

Reactionary pressures were applied not just from within the musical establishment. Munich, as the seat of government for Bavaria, was dominated by the conservative Christian Socialists. Its minister of culture, Alois Hundhammer, in October 1948 prohibited Egk's new opera *Abraxas* after merely five stagings in May. The reason was not that Hundhammer thought Egk's music was avant-garde – it was shrill and off the beaten track, Egkian Modernist. Rather, to this dour Catholic and controlling minister certain scenes on stage appeared as fornication.[319] The affair proved that behind much of the political reaction in those years stood forces backed by the Christian Churches, not only through politics, but also in newspapers such as *Das Sonntagsblatt* and *Christ und Welt*, both published by the Protestant Synod. This was yet another example of an alliance between established religion in Germany and oppressive politics, joined by censorial media, which had found not just occasional expression during Hitler's regime.

Criticism of modern music as cacophony by retrograde culture elites then was common and taken to extremes in the case of jazz. For in the ears of the uninitiated, jazz sounded unintelligible and, by the social elites with knowledge of the classics, was falsely categorized as "atonal." This had been the practice since before the Nazis.[320] Moreover, jazz with its American origins was easily conflated with what was perceived as American culture by German conservatives, who honed a decades-long tradition of disparaging that culture, which, in their vernacular, was downgraded to mere "civilization." Venerated German composers and conductors such as Richard Strauss were in the vanguard of an anti-jazz campaign as early as the 1920s; Pfitzner fought jazz as the "musical expression of Americanism."[321] The Classical Modernists Orff and Egk, nationalists both, might utilize elements of the genre (as Egk did harmonically, Orff rhythmically), but never gave credit where credit was due.[322]

Both lines of attack against jazz were pursued with vigor after the situation gradually normalized and certain old cultural habits were again establishing themselves in post-war Germany. There were the literate polemics so typical of the educated classes of the past.[323] Moreover, in the more limited environment of concert recitals and clubs "jazz fans raised fears among cultural conservatives about a lack of respectability." One comment, tempered by racism, was that a jam session led by the Munich drummer Freddy Brocksieper in the Berlin club Badewanne satisfied "jungle instincts"; loosely dressed fans were criminalized by an association with the black market.[324] As new radio stations enriched their programs with – inevitably American – jazz, many infuriated German listeners employed invectives from the Nazi era in launching their complaints. In 1947 jazz was maligned as "the Negro's music" in letters to *Hör Zu*, the program guide belonging to conservative newspaper publisher Axel Springer: "This kind of singing should be left to American girls."[325]

The entire theme of German cultural superiority qua American-jazz disparagement presented itself in *Hallo Fräulein*, a 1949 film made by Rudolf Jugert and starring the German-American actor Peter van Eick as well as the Germans Hans Söhnker and Margot Hielscher. She plays Maria Neuhaus, a German singer who recently entertained Wehrmacht troops and now comes to lead a jazz band composed of DP musicians in an occupied German town. Van Eick impersonates an American officer, Tom Keller, in charge of the venture, including the organization of concerts, both for the U.S. Army and German civilians. Söhnker is Walter Reinhardt, a German architect, who helps with logistics. The main motif, of course, is the love triangle between the attractive young woman and the two men, where the older, more composed Reinhardt ultimately wins the girl in marriage. In the film, the jazz pianist Keller comes across as the more dynamic character, but also the more intemperate. Reinhardt, by contrast, is controlled and patriarchal. As Neuhaus croons jazzy numbers in the film, she is expertly accompanied by the flashy big band she or Keller leads. Reinhardt objects to the American-style music, and indeed the film includes scenes that show large parts of the German population in contempt of jazz. In choosing Reinhardt, Neuhaus submits to the superiority of German culture over American, but also as a German woman to a German man, which was the ultimate message of the German author of the script, Helmut Weiss.[326]

In literature, there was simply not enough produced by young authors until 1950 for conservative critics to make a stab. Their time would come during Adenauer's entrenched reign, which served as a damper on creativity, and their targets would be the writers Walter Jens, Martin Walser, Günter Grass, and, unsurprisingly, Heinrich Böll. Nonetheless, a few reactionary critics did rear their heads, after the establishment of Gruppe 47, according to Hans Werner Richter. Among them were Friedrich Sieburg, a former diplomat in Occupied France, Rudolf Krämer-Badoni, whom Richter had offended, and Hans Egon Holthusen, an ex-SS man.[327]

Nor did the new German film offer many areas for attack from outside, mostly because of Allied censorship and, after July 1949, the FSK, the German voluntary self-control mechanism. An obvious area was overt sexuality, which, as in the case of *Abraxas*, the Churches assailed whenever possible and on top of Allied controls. This was the case with Helmut Käutner's *Der Apfel ist ab* (*The Apple Has Fallen*) of 1948, which satirized Original Sin, showing Adam and Eve clad only in fig leaves, and offered for show the protagonist's wife *and* his mistress. There were also questionable portrayals of Heaven, Hell, and some angels. As Heide Fehrenbach has painstakingly chronicled, Minister Hundhammer received knowledge about all this before the film's release in Munich. He promptly decided that he "would not tolerate instances of moral poisoning," joining with Bavarian Catholic bishop Johann Neuhäusler who preached against the film in a sermon, then called a press conference. When someone there mentioned that the Nazis had disturbed showings of the film *All Quiet on the Western Front* in 1931, Neuhäusler replied that "even if the Church was silent on matters of decency during the Nazi period, it would be guilty of a violation of duties if it did not speak up now." Eventually accompanied by the Episcopal Information Office in Cologne and the Protestant bishop of Bavaria Hans Meiser, it was stated that the film appealed to erotic instincts and poisoned the minds of the young. National regeneration would be impossible, "unless moral libertinism is stopped, and the holiness of wedlock protected again."[328] Neuhäusler had been in a concentration camp for years during the Nazi regime, while Meiser had impugned marriages between "Aryans" and Jews even before 1933. But however different their individual pre-1945 histories, after the German capitulation both men worked vigorously to have all Nazi perpetrators acquitted.[329]

◆　◆　◆

Culture in western Germany after 1945 evolved as part of a triangular relationship: as a new society was forming aided by the politics of democracy, the arts, letters, and music unfolded anew, against the background and in constant recall of the Third Reich and its war. Mostly younger advocates of a constructive culture, as were the participants in Gruppe 47, were hampered in their efforts to inspire new representative democracy by older fellow artists such as Karl Hofer, who engaged in lachrymose exercises expressing sorrow for having been misled by Nazi criminals. Questions about their own guilt, however, were never considered and, even on the left, Jews and themes of the Holocaust remained taboo. Most extreme in that regard were former Nazis such as Ina Seidel or opportunists such as Hans Carossa, who had been able to survive, more or less comfortably, into the new era. On the political right, as the examples of Neuhäusler and Meiser show, ideologies of revanchism, restoration, and orthodoxy still were strong.

After the establishment of constitutive democracy in 1949 the task of progressive culture would have to be, in future, the defeat of such deleterious trends. Shifts in society contingent on the disastrous ending of the war – a demographic preponderance of women, an influx of refugees from the European East, returning POWs – would represent challenges for society *and* culture, as its Modernist advocates continued to ally themselves with left-liberal politicians. More questions would arise around the politics of memory, and in particular the past and future place of Jews.

CHAPTER TWO

◆ ◆ ◆

Defying Stasis (1950–1960)

THE 1950S IN West Germany were a period of political stability under the conservative leadership of Chancellor Adenauer, with social inequities gradually smoothed out until an equilibrium was reached in the early 1960s. The main theme was economic recovery, which reached a plateau at the end of the decade, after the storied "Economic Miracle" had started during its first half. The climate created by restorative tendencies in politics coupled with social and economic advances did not encourage new cultural initiatives, whose champions, nonetheless, persisted. That they were allowed to do so showed that democratic pluralism in society was working.

The FRG's growing stability was vouchsafed by the staunchly Catholic, authoritative, paternalistic Konrad Adenauer, who was supported in his efforts by long-standing pillars of society, leaders of industry, a conservative political clientele, the two Christian Churches, and reactionary intellectuals and culture elites. With their help, he won the general election of September 6, 1953, forming a coalition with right-of-center parties. In the elections of September 15, 1957, which were held on a pledge of "No Experiments," Adenauer's parties, the CDU and Bavaria-based CSU, won an absolute majority. His government was decidedly anti-Communist, not recognizing the GDR as legitimate and insisting that West Germany be bound closely to the Western Powers; he was personal friends with France's Charles de Gaulle and the U.S. foreign secretary, John Foster Dulles. Even after the

FRG received full sovereignty according to the terms of the Paris Accord of May 5, 1955, the West Germans, by an agreement of May 1952, allowed Allied troops to be further stationed on their soil. Also in May 1955, the FRG joined the NATO pact, and in July 1956 a law was enacted calling for rearmament and general conscription. Adenauer's position on German reunification was that it was desirable, but not to be achieved at the expense of the FRG's close alignment with the Western Powers, in particular NATO.[1]

From its beginnings, the Bonn government attained significant internal and diplomatic achievements that heralded stability for decades to come. Notwithstanding Adenauer's well-recognized tendency toward autocratic governance, the new rulers embraced democratic pluralism based on popularly elected political parties, heeded labor unions' concerns, and upheld the inalienable rights of man underwritten by the Basic Law of May 1949. This was wholly in keeping with Karl Jaspers's philosophy, which had recommended a German acceptance of responsibility for the malevolence of the Nazi past and attempts to make amends. The Karlsruhe supreme court disallowed the most dangerous neo-Nazi Party, the Sozialistische Reichspartei (Socialist Reich Party), in 1951, but also proscribed the Communist Party of Germany (KPD) in 1956, viewing both as dangers to the new democratic order. In theory, for a renewed flourishing of culture, this meant not only the protection of artistic freedom offered by the Basic Law, but also benefits arising from the FRG's joining UNESCO in July 1951. Its Article 1 pledged a commitment "to contribute to peace and security by promoting collaboration among the nations through education, science and culture." This was precisely the kind of multilateral agreement the Nazi regime had rejected.[2]

◆ ◆ ◆

The ever-increasing prosperity of the FRG became a hallmark only after the mid-1950s. Since its founding in 1949 there existed much social and economic hardship, some of which lasted well into the 1960s. It was an inescapable fact that in 1950 the FRG, whose social and economic fabric had been all but destroyed, was economically bankrupt; even with Marshall Plan aid, only hard physical work would change that. And work the post-1945 Germans did, inspired, not least, by the "rubble ladies" of Berlin, who had set stone upon stone to rebuild. But still by the fall of 1953 every third citizen of the FRG needed government handouts. Joblessness was widespread, and so were diseases, with antidotes scarcely available. Salk's anti-polio serum, for instance, came to Germany only after spring 1957. New fabrics to make clothes from were rare, hence Wehrmacht soft-cloth caps dyed an unsuspicious color and with Nazi insignia removed were a familiar sight.[3]

Almost everyone was affected by varying types of poverty. Near Stuttgart's main station, for example, in April 1950 a young woman was observed in a washed-out dress with a collecting tin, and before a judge she declared the money had been towards her own wedding.[4] Still, standing out were the refugees from the East and returning POWs. Of the first group, there were about 12 million by the mid-1950s, entire families who fled Poles and Russians, but also Sudeten Germans from the northwest of the Czech Republic and some from Slovakia, further southeast. Speaking unknown dialects, they were looked down on by their new hosts, who marginalized them socially until they were observed working hard.[5] POWs often found it difficult to reintegrate, especially if they had become war cripples. It was only in 1956 that the last of over 2 million POWs returned from the Soviet Gulag, after Adenauer had intervened in Moscow during 1955.[6]

A typical job open to war veterans was that of a traveling salesman who would set up a portable table on a city street and try to talk clusters of housewives into buying their wares, always with florid rhetoric. Actor Walter Giller personified such a hustler in the 1959 film *Rosen für den Staatsanwalt.*[7] I listened to several of those raggedy peddlers who had set themselves up on Königsstrasse in Krefeld, where my family had moved by 1950. They fascinated me with their powers of invention and imagination, like artists in variety shows. One, with a stump arm, threw kitchen utensils into the air, catching them like a circus artist, tools that allegedly could process produce in many different ways. These salesmen, some of whom also traveled from door to door, have been memorialized in novels, for instance by Martin Walser, who after the war was proprietor of an inn on Lake Constance. His main character Anselm Kristlein, of the now famous Kristlein trilogy, exhibited autobiographical traits.[8]

Already before the mid-1950s, however, these concerns were partially offset by the dynamics of recovery. As the main three reasons for the

Economic Miracle beginning in the early 1950s, Konrad Jarausch has listed an increase in industrial productivity, generous tax exemptions for businesses, and free-trade conditions for the FRG.[9] These developments were helped along by West Germany not only having been allowed to benefit from the Marshall Plan, but also from joining the France-centered Schuman Plan, in May 1950.[10]

Impressive benefits accrued as a result. Real wages increased between 1950 and 1960, with full employment setting in around 1955. Social benefits were extended, topped by dynamic pensions linked to gross wages. This enabled Germans to save more money than other European nationals. The manifestations were increased food and alcohol consumption per capita, the disappearance of old clothing, and furniture acquisitions: the newly designed kidney-shaped teak coffee table became a must-have for the upwardly mobile middle class. Vacation travel became the norm, especially to sunny Italy.[11] Elaborate radio and later television sets, refrigerators, motorcycles, and automobiles such as the Volkswagen were the new status symbols. In 1951 the first sports car, the Porsche 356, and the Mercedes-Benz 170 S cabriolet appeared in showrooms.[12] In the film *Das Mädchen Rosemarie* (*The Girl Rosemarie*, 1958), based on a Frankfurt woman who was murdered, the call girl Nitribitt drives a Mercedes-Benz roadster, and her clients from high politics and industry are seen in larger models.[13] Accoutrements of material progress were celebrated in popular song conjuring up exotic destinations, such as "Capri Fischer" or "Blue Hawaii."[14]

But there were drawbacks. The end of food-rationing in January 1950 made Germans overweight by 1952, and alcohol and tobacco indulgence became alarming.[15] Vacations to the south became the new token fetish. In the new-born federal "Wohlstandsgesellschaft," society of affluence, a materialistic value system tended to overshadow the spiritual, art, and culture. A hierarchy based on newly acquired wealth favored the nouveaux riches and accentuated old class differences, even if a belief in upward social mobility forestalled social unrest.

Constancy was assured, because West Germans in their search of consumption and status did not go overboard. They were in the shadow of Adenauer, who advocated progress through stability. Hence the nuclear family under patriarchal auspices returned. Slowly men were reasserting their authority over women, whose majority was attenuated and whose existence had to be rededicated to the roles of wives and mothers. This trend was supported by the gradual return of POWs, especially from the U.S.S.R., as "survivors of totalitarianism."[16] Well before the mid-1950s, therefore, a "divinely ordained natural order" was achieved, reinforced by the Christian Churches, where women had stopped working, as men resumed the bread-winning. To reinforce the idea of the family, Adenauer created a federal ministry for family affairs, appointing to it an observant Catholic and First World War veteran.[17]

Women's changed circumstances are illustrated in several films after the 1950s. In Rainer Werner Fassbinder's *Die Ehe der Maria Braun* (*The Marriage of Maria Braun*, 1978) the protagonist, whose husband is jailed, dominates her lover's business only during the immediate post-war years. She is fated to die in a house explosion as West Germany is set to resume a world-leadership role, here by winning the World Soccer Cup in Berne, in July 1954. Soccer is played by men, and they are well into reasserting their authority. In Fassbinder's film *Lola* (1981) the prostitute Lola, running a business with a male partner who is also her boyfriend, loses her independence as soon as she marries not him but a dour real-estate controller.[18] And in *Deutschland bleiche Mutter*, Helma Sanders-Brahms develops the role of Lene's war-returnee husband as one who asserts new superiority through increasing humiliations. There are flashbacks of the man shooting women in war who look exactly like his wife.[19]

In this social environment where familial mores harking back to Wilhelmine times were observed, a double sexual standard ruled. Men who preached sexual sobriety continued to prey on single or married young women for amorous adventures.[20] At the lower end of the social scale, literature identified the traveling salesman as one of several male-predatory prototypes. Martin Walser noted in his diary on November 10, 1951: "In this café there was no waitress with whom one would have wanted to sleep, therefore: nothing but out!"[21] Walser's hero, salesman Anselm Kristlein, through three volumes of extended novel describing the 1950s, constantly dallies with young women, his wife fully aware.[22]

Although stigmatized by the unwritten laws of polite society, the same double standard legally allowed prostitution. In this decade, every West German city with half a million inhabitants is said to have harbored approximately 20,000 sex workers.[23] And as the criminalization of abortion endured, homosexuality continued to be illegal according to laws the Nazis had introduced in 1935, and which were not repealed until 1969.[24]

◆ ◆ ◆

Despite Adenauer and Heuss having early on downplayed the issue, their government was impelled to recognize the Jews as Hitler's most suffering victims, to repudiate anti-Semitism, pay reparations to Israel, and welcome home Jewish expellees. However, while discriminating against Jews in Germany was illegal, the state had no control over anti-Semitic tendencies in society at large. This threatened the free development of culture.

Key administrations continued to rely on experts, many of those former politicians and bureaucrats with Nazi ties. After easy denazification, networks of cronies, already successful, smoothed their old friends' path to the inside of new power structures. Prestigious positions in the ministry of external affairs, for instance, were said to be attainable only for those having aided the legal defense for Nazi State Secretary Ernst Freiherr von Weizsäcker at the Nuremberg Trials.[25] Indeed, in the 1950s, one-third of all external-affairs officials in Bonn were former Nazi Party members. In October 1951 Adenauer had to admit that 130 officials of his foreign office had served under Ribbentrop. In addition, there were many former SS and Sicherheitsdienst (SD) officers.[26] In the economics ministry half of all functionaries were men with former Nazi ties, and in the justice ministry, among top bureaucrats, only 23 percent had not been in the Nazi Party.[27]

In the 1959 film *Rosen für den Staatsanwalt*, Wilhelm Schramm, played by Martin Held, personified jurists who as former Nazis had destroyed innocent lives: at war's end he had sentenced a soldier to death who allegedly stole some chocolate. During this time the Bundeskriminalamt, or federal crime fighters agency, employed Rudolf Thomsen, a former SS-Hauptsturmführer accused of having killed partisans, that is Jews, in Cracow.[28]

In 1952, Adenauer suggested that "we should now stop sniffing out Nazis."[29] He then proceeded to appoint two high-profile National Socialists to his cabinet in 1953, Theodor Oberländer as minister for refugees and Hans Globke as state secretary in the chancellor's office. Oberländer never answered to a post-war charge of having witnessed the lynching of Jews and leading anti-partisan routs as a Wehrmacht officer in Polish Lemberg in summer 1941. Globke had coauthored exegetical commentary of the anti-Semitic Nuremberg race legislation in 1936 and, during the war, was further involved "in the elaboration of laws that provided a juridical basis for the persecution of Jews and guidelines for the 'Germanization' of conquered peoples in the occupied territories."[30] Whereas Oberländer after public protests had to resign in 1960, Adenauer held on to Globke until he himself left office in 1963.[31]

The tendency of reactionary politicians under Adenauer to minimize the Nazi threat was paralleled by a public mood turning increasingly against the spirit of denazification. If during the Nuremberg Trials 70 percent of all Germans had endorsed Allied justice, by 1950 that same percentage judged the trials as unfair.[32] The fact that during the early 1950s hardly any war crimes were indicted met with German approval, and when in 1954 the 1951 Bundestag amnesty law was legally extended, people applauded.[33] Convicted war criminals were beginning to be released with almost total amnesty by 1958, fully approved by the Christian Churches.[34]

As for culture, upon arriving in Germany in the late 1950s the Jewish theater director Peter Zadek noticed that many artists "still were Nazis in their own secretive ways."[35] It has been calculated that of an unknown total, 190 film directors and scriptwriters who were active in the 1950s had worked in the Third Reich.[36] The list encompasses people who, while not Nazis, continued working in the Third Reich, such as Erich Kästner, and some incarcerated by the regime, such as the Communist Axel Eggebrecht. And it includes critics and journalists who were multitalented, such as Erich Ebermayer, a novelist, screenwriter, and playwright, so that a clear picture of a tightly delineated profession cannot be gained.[37]

Considering cultural professions, in journalism, for instance, Giselher Wirsing became editor of *Christ und Welt*, a religious weekly published by a conservative circle surrounding theologian Eugen Gerstenmaier. As an SS officer in 1938, he had followed Adolf Eichmann on his 1937 visit to Palestine, to explore the situation of the Jews. On April 20, 1940, the Führer's fifty-first birthday, Wirsing called Hitler "the great revolutionary and innovator in everything today" in the Nazi-owned *Münchener Neueste Nachrichten*.[38] The former *Jud Süss* film reviewer Carl Linfert, meanwhile, kept demonstrating expertise as a modern-art critic on radio and in the press, from his base in Cologne. [39]

The director of that 1940 film, Veit Harlan, attempted a West German comeback and, though not ultimately successful, caused enough adverse publicity to frighten many, who, in the cultural arena, were working for lasting change. In July 1948 a Hamburg court accused Harlan, who wished to resume work, of crimes against humanity. Former, newly rehabilitated colleagues such as Gustaf Gründgens vouched for him, and the charge that *Jud Süss* had been used by Harlan as an anti-Semitic weapon was refuted by his defense team. Harlan was acquitted by a sympathetic judge in April 1949. After appeal by the state attorney, he was again acquitted in May 1950.[40] He then commenced filmmaking; apart from obvious trash he produced a movie indicting homosexuality in 1957. This was also an attack on the cultural avant-garde, because one of the gay characters was an antique dealer with a penchant for electronic music.[41]

Next to newspapers, radio, and film, public opinion on the Third Reich could have been critically shaped by other media and institutions such as schools and universities. Instead, there were spaces in Germany where bragging about that regime was perfectly in order, within tight-knit veterans' groups at the beer table or anywhere among unreconstructed Nazis. War stories flourished in boulevard magazines such as *Der Stern*, *Revue*, and *Quick*, as the Wehrmacht was gradually cultivating an image of clean soldiery.[42] Within the larger public, not enlightenment but silence was the predominant attitude.[43] In both those realms the narrative of Germans as victims was upheld.

As a corrective, moral tales could have been published and memorials erected. As for those, Germans who thought of themselves as wronged scoffed at reminders about concentration camps. The only memorial set up on the site of a former camp was at Bergen-Belsen in November 1952, designed for official representational purposes only.[44] The few remaining synagogues too could have been utilized. But well-settled Germans were not interested; instead, those were often razed for other buildings.[45]

As for schools in this era, the essayist Hans Magnus Enzensberger (a brother of the younger Ulrich), who, according to filmmaker Alexander Kluge, was always "in rebellion," experienced them as "unbearable places."[46] Heinrich Böll was shocked to find out in April 1954 that in a Cologne school pupils had been taught about Frederick the Great's battle sites rather than learning about the extermination of the Jews.[47] As I recall from five

71

years in the 1950s Krefeld Gymnasium, schools were havens of muteness as far as the more immediate past was concerned. In history class, rather than learning about the Third Reich, we had to memorize the name of Alexander the Great's favorite horse; the years from 1900 to 1945 were simply blanked out. There were outright Nazis in the collegium who were known to have served in Nazi paramilitary formations. One was a dashing former leader of paratroopers. Most teachers applied physical punishment, and in textbooks fascistic contents remained unpurged. If, in other schools, National Socialism was touched upon, the 1944 military resistance to Hitler was highlighted, to demonstrate that Germans had been against the Third Reich and therefore could not be faulted. Other than that, in this Cold War era it was vicious Communism in East Germany that was the subject of social science.[48]

In universities, things were not much better; Enzensberger called them "centers of mediocrity ... a cultural wasteland."[49] When I attended the University of Munich in the fall of 1959, I searched in vain for professors of history who were researching the Third Reich. I should have gone to Bonn where the one exception was Karl Dietrich Bracher, born in 1922, who had spent three years as a prisoner-of-war in Kansas and also studied at Harvard (and became a jazz bassist on the side). Bracher was then working on the preconditions for the Third Reich, the willful destruction of parliamentary democracy in the late Weimar Republic.[50] A lucid article demonstrating Hitler's consolidation of power after 1933 was published by him in *Vierteljahrshefte für Zeitgeschichte,* a new journal brought out by the Institut für Zeitgeschichte, or Institute of Contemporary History, established in Munich in 1950.[51]

This institute became a beacon of enlightenment in matters of the Third Reich when elsewhere obscurantism reigned. But its founding too was fraught with problems, about its financial resources and who should lead it. After an uncompromised director had been found who later died in a traffic accident, at least two historians joined in the early 1950s who had been members of the Nazi Party. They were Helmut Krausnick, who had joined in 1932, and Martin Broszat, who joined in 1944 at the age of eighteen as a member of the Hitler Youth. Broszat later claimed never to have known he was a party member, as he was never notified to that effect, while serving in the Wehrmacht to the end. It is possible that in the throes of the final months of warfare a party notification never reached him, yet no one could ever become a party member who had not personally applied and signed for it.[52] "It is indeed very probable that he made a membership application or signed for it," judges political scientist Jürgen W. Falter, today's leading expert. Falter allows that Broszat could argue never to have become a party member, because his membership card could not be handed to him.[53] But apart from Broszat's own attitude, the mistake the institute founders made is embarrassing, by not having checked in the Nazi Party card file the Americans were holding in Berlin-Zehlendorf, because there the membership was recorded – as it was also in the case of Krausnick.

Well after the 1950s, both Krausnick and Broszat did superlative work through the institute with the aim of clearing the fog about Nazi rule. So did the two editors of the journal *Vierteljahrshefte*, published first in January 1953 by Theodor Eschenburg and Hans Rothfels.[54] However, although beyond reproach as a professor of political science at the University of Tübingen, Eschenburg had joined the SS early in the Nazi regime and lent his aid, at least once, in dispossession ("Aryanization") procedures against Jews.[55] Rothfels's case was more complicated. A baptized Jew born in 1891, he was a conservative, war-wounded veteran who condemned the Peace of Versailles and rejected the Weimar Republic. As a champion of German expansion in the East and fully in accord with Hitler's overall aims, he had been hopeful to remain as a professor of history at the University of Königsberg, accepted as an "honorary Aryan." But after his removal there in 1934 and having been manhandled by Nazis, he and his family moved to England in August 1939 and from there to America, where he eventually taught at the University of Chicago. It is certain that Rothfels qualified himself for the position with the institute as author of, significantly, a book on the German political and military opposition to Hitler, which he had issued in 1948 with H. Regnery, "America's most prominent conservative book publisher."[56] In an undifferentiated manner, it served as self-justification and legitimation for the German ultra-conservative establishment, leaving out marginal and also broader-based groups that resisted Hitler, such as the White Rose.[57]

There were few trials of suspected Nazi criminals after 1954. One was in Augsburg against former SS judge Otto Thorbeck and SS-Standartenführer Walter Huppenkothen, who had worked in Heydrich's office. Both were convicted as accessories to murder (having committed the murders themselves) and sentenced to penitentiary in 1955. In 1956, Thorbeck was acquitted by the Karlsruhe federal supreme court and Huppenkothen, sentenced to six years originally, was freed after merely three.[58] In 1957 followed the trial against Field Marshal Ferdinand Schörner, Hitler's last commander of the Wehrmacht, who was responsible for the mass-murder of civilians and thousands of Wehrmacht soldiers killed for desertion in the last weeks of the war. Schörner was sentenced to a mere four-and-a-half years in jail but released after three.[59] Next came the trial of Martin Sommer, an SS functionary responsible for torture and death at Buchenwald, in Bayreuth, during 1958. Sommer, too, received a milder sentence than he should have because he was ill during trial and had married his, much younger, nurse. This had made for sensational coverage in the yellow press as well as respectable journals of the kind that also featured stories about an untainted Wehrmacht.[60]

The most significant trial of the late 1950s was that of former SD-Einsatzgruppen members in Lithuania, held in Ulm during 1958. Some four thousand Jews had been killed in 1941. The case could only be dealt with because its main perpetrator, SS officer Bernhard Fischer-Schweder, living as a salesman in West Germany, had applied for reinstatement as a police official. He was condemned to ten years in prison, dying in 1960.[61]

During the Ulm trials, several publicists clamored for more judicial coordination at the federal level. Consequently, a central office was established in Ludwigsburg in December 1958, with federal powers to assemble evidence and delegate law courts to initiate prosecution. Not only did this shine a new light on the Third Reich and its criminality, but it also led to more tribunals, in particular the Auschwitz Trial in Frankfurt, 1963–5. Jews as victims now moved into the foreground. As the first director of this outpost, State Attorney Erwin Schüle was appointed, who had successfully conducted the Ulm proceedings.[62] Alas, it was long known by his superiors in Bonn that Schüle had been a member of the NSDAP and SA. In 1966 the USSR accused him of having shot to death Russian civilians in Chudovo during the fall of 1941, while serving as a lieutenant. Rather than repudiating these charges, Schüle decided to resign from his post, but the Ludwigsburg mission was not compromised.[63]

Some of those Jews following the Frankfurt proceedings were not certain whether Germans had fully come to grips with their responsibility for the Holocaust. In line with official policy towards Jews in general and Israel in particular, Adenauer by November 1949 had announced his readiness to compensate Jewish victims of Nazi terror materially as a "fundamental condition for establishing relations with Israel."[64] Yet while the FRG was thenceforth able to send millions of marks to Israel, formal recognition was not possible because of Arab protests. Arab nations had threatened to recognize the GDR if Bonn recognized Jerusalem. Nonetheless, because of good official relations between the two countries and with the Economic Miracle under way, Israeli Jews were moving to Germany, especially after the Luxembourg Agreement of September 1952, when reparations due to individuals would be taxed away by their government. This migration lasted until 1959, when waves of renewed anti-Semitism in West German lands were cresting.[65]

Hence there were approximately fifty new Jewish communities in West Germany, including around 25,000 people who had lived there before 1933.[66] Many had non-Jewish spouses. But also in these communities were other, often older, Holocaust survivors with East European backgrounds who found it harder to adapt.[67] These demographic peculiarities amounted to a socio-economic demarcation: while many of the German Jews found their way into conventional professions, with ninety-two Jews taken into the Bavarian bureaucracy as civil servants, for example,[68] formerly East European Jews tended toward more marginal occupations, such as proprietors or managers of entertainment establishments. In the Kaiserslautern area, for example, where U.S. soldiers were stationed, those Jews customarily ran the dance cafés, and they were equally conspicuous around Munich.[69] Others, however, were not doing so well, being pushed to the edge of existence despite reparation payments.[70]

For reasons not entirely clear, anti-Semitism was on the rise again from the early 1950s.[71] Much of it was simply a continuation of developments in the late 1940s – anti-Semitism had never gone away. Alt-Nazis were strong during the founding of the FRG; there were at least two parties with neo-Nazi tendencies, the Deutsche Partei and (until its dissolution) the Sozialistische Reichspartei, and Nazis successfully infiltrated the FDP. The fact that Bonn came to recognize Jerusalem as the capital of a new state caused resentment, and the Luxembourg reparations must have created envy among many Germans who in 1952 still had problems adjusting economically. Then there were those cases where Jews were officially favored in society, such as when they benefited from housing assignments or had better luck in landing jobs or being admitted to universities.

Several expressions of anti-Semitism suggest that the issue as a national phenomenon possessed systemic significance. Jewish pupils tended to be insulted in the very schools that refused to teach the Third Reich in history class. Old Nazi teachers were rarely fired; in the case of Offenbach high-school teacher Ludwig Zind, who had insulted a Jewish merchant in 1957, the prosecution collapsed because he escaped to Libya.[72] My own Gymnasium in Krefeld continued to be named, since 1938, after Ernst Moritz Arndt, one of the most ferocious nationalists and anti-Semites of the nineteenth century, who had labeled Jews "the impure flood from the East."[73] Illustrated weeklies such as *Quick* did not shrink from publishing anti-Semitic features and printing unflattering pictures, sometimes in the Nazi *Stürmer* manner; even dailies fell in.[74] Around Christmas 1959 a year-long wave of graffiti on Jewish sites culminated in the smearing of the synagogue in Cologne, which found countless regional imitations.[75]

At a cultural level, anti-Semitism surfaced as well, but more obliquely. The Polish-Jewish literature critic Marcel Reich-Ranicki, who had spent his youth in Berlin, insisted that he experienced it constantly after returning to Germany in 1958, even among well-meaning colleagues.[76] The Jewish poet Paul Celan, originally from Czernowitz but now living in Paris, thought he was a victim of it after repeated readings in Germany since 1952. And Fritz Kortner soldiered on as theater director in Munich under smoldering anti-Jewish sentiment for the remainder of his second career in Germany.[77]

◆ ◆ ◆

In the middle of March 1952, Generalmusikdirektor Günter Wand, the conductor of the Cologne Gürzenich orchestra who admired Schoenberg and liked, when possible, to perform compositions of the avant-garde, was at a dinner given by Hans Gerling, chief of a large multi-insurance firm. Wand had just conducted *Symphonia brevis*, opus 16, by Hanns Jelinek, a former Czech-Jewish student of Schoenberg and Alban Berg living in Vienna.[78] This was not a fiercely dodecaphonic work in the Schoenberg mode, but rather a piece showing "the particular blending of twelve-tone technique and traditional formal style."[79] During dinner Gerling, who was culture-minded but ultra-conservative, began making snide remarks about Jelinek, concluding with a hefty critique of Wand's Cologne music program and his predilection for the Moderns. What was meant as a eulogy for Wand turned into a rout. The conductor, a polite, quiet man, rather than erupting rose from the table discreetly, bathed in sweat, and left, never to interact with the Gerlings again.[80]

Gerling's attitude typified the conservatism blanketing culture in the FRG in the 1950s, indeed until 1963 when Adenauer finally left office. Enzensberger has characterized this deportment as one of "virulent anger toward modern art," and nowhere was this more obvious than on theater stages.[81] Theater had been pedestrian, newly emerging from a Nazi environment, and until the end of the 1950s there was not much change. Opera director Oscar Fritz Schuh went so far as to speak of an "artistic crisis."[82] More even than in the late 1940s, when a dramatist such as Borchert had been propelled to creative heights, the main problems were a dearth of fresh dramatic material and new authors, the overbearing presence of a worn-out actors' corps with its sense of entitlement – most as holdovers from the Third Reich – a multitude of mediocre directors, and, sometimes, insufficient government funding. This caused the left-liberal culture critic Joachim Kaiser of *Süddeutsche Zeitung* to lament the "defectiveness of today's theater business," and some years later his Stuttgart colleague Siegfried Melchinger to condemn "drought and a lack of direction in dramatic production."[83] Looking back on the past decade, critic Heinz Ritter complained at the beginning of the 1960s about the longevity of "the creators' pause."[84] The expatriate Austrian film director Berthold Viertel joined this chorus when he deplored in 1950s West German theater the embodiment of a Hitlerian "Reich Chancellery Style."[85]

Adenauer's dictum against experiments took hold at most stages, especially provincial ones such as Duisburg's where classical offerings were favored, because its audience "was not suited for experimental theater."[86] Instead, the classical German pieces continued to be featured, as well as foreign fare. Next to Schiller, Gerhart Hauptmann, and Shakespeare, Surrealist dramas by Ionesco and especially Beckett now became popular, but also French existentialists such as Sartre with his tragedy *The Flies* and the moralist T.S. Eliot.[87] A few new German authors were played whom Zadek would have classified as "harmless": Fritz Hochwälder, Manfred

Hausmann, Leopold Ahlsen, and Hermann Moers – all writing conventionally and forgotten today.[88] Few stages balanced that with works by the two path-breaking Swiss Modernists Friedrich Dürrenmatt and Max Frisch, who had no contemporary equals in Germany except Brecht, not least in recognition of the role the Zurich theater had played abroad as a proxy stage of quality throughout the Nazi years.[89]

But the landscape was uneven. In Ulm and Regensburg palaces had been erected to serve as new theaters, disproportionate to their mediocre productions.[90] Except for experimental highbrow niche creations of the smallest scale, West Berlin had merely three stages; it had lost its panache as the "artistic and spiritual" capital and was pioneer in the theater world no longer.[91] Brecht continued to be the star of the eastern German half, notwithstanding a few timid attempts by FRG stages to present his work.[92] Darmstadt's theatrical program, a carry-over of Modernism from the avant-garde music festivals, was considered excellent.[93] And the intimacy of the Munich Kammerspiele Kaiser judged to be in affinity with the admired Zurich stage.[94] On the other hand, Hamburg's Deutsches Schauspielhaus was merely solid, its *Peer Gynt* "frosty," and the actors not sufficiently inspired.[95] Heinz Hilpert's Deutsches Theater in Göttingen was hamstrung by insufficient public funding; Kaiser thought its performances "barren, verbose and boring."[96] The best stage was Düsseldorf's Schauspielhaus, under Gründgens until 1955, even though its prolific actors were susceptible to clichés and sterility, statues of themselves.[97]

Gründgens is said to have embodied the stasis of the Adenauer era, because on his stages he refused to experiment.[98] His old-guard attitude was one of observing *Werktreue*, interpretations intended to honor the playwrights, ignoring politics or customs of the day. Classical theater was Gründgens's forte; his signature performance was in Goethe's *Faust* as Mephistopheles, but he also directed or personified Schiller's Wallenstein or Philip II of *Don Carlos*. Modern pieces to fit the new times were usually flops, an example being, significantly, *Der Besuch der alten Dame* (*The Visit*) by Dürrenmatt.[99] Whereas in Hamburg after 1955 he was to lose magnetism because of age, Gründgens filled the theater to over 90 percent capacity in Düsseldorf, an extraordinary feat.[100]

A stage personality who eschewed *Werktreue* for the sake of opening the audiences' eyes to maladjustments in society and a need for change was Fritz

Kortner. As a former Jewish emigrant he had been instrumental in introducing Modernism into the Weimar Republic's culture. After largely retiring from acting he worked as a director – his work was known to be "unusual, exciting and new," whether it be Shakespeare or Beckett. He viewed his work as part of his own biography, condemning persecution, injustice, and suffering. How could such human theater not be political?[101] His artistry, influenced by Expressionism, all but vindicated his cantankerous manners – still, he treated his actors unsparingly. Once, when an actor begged for leniency because he had been in a concentration camp, Kortner shot back: Obviously not long enough! Yet in 1959, when Kaiser criticized Kortner's staging of Büchner's *Dantons Tod* (*Danton's Death*), he also conceded that this old master was still a "great director."[102]

While in America, Kortner had known Brecht, but they were not close. The left-wing, non-Jewish Erwin Piscator, yet another Weimar legend, also returned, managing only to work at smaller, provincial stages such as Marburg's, Tübingen's, and Giessen's, much as in Brecht's epic theater, and only in 1962 was he employed at the weightier Freie Volksbühne in West Berlin.[103] All the while, Jürgen Fehling, he too an old Weimar hand, was trying to revive his art in Berlin, Munich, and Frankfurt, yet, although revered by many, he was slowly losing his grip, until, mentally ill, he died in 1968 in a Hamburg sanatorium.[104]

The German theater scene was staid when Zadek returned from London to Germany in 1958, aged thirty-two. At the municipal stage in Cologne the institutionalized status of actors impressed him – in London, potentially always jobless, they had jumped from gig to gig.[105] But he also noticed that the Cologne actors would speak their lines statically, rhetorically, frozen, as if memorized and by rote, without inflection. For them, theater was either tragedy or comedy but nothing in between.[106] For himself, Zadek discovered psychology (at a time when Lee Strasberg was using that to train his students in America with "method acting"), particularly when he was offered a position in Ulm with a rare progressive Intendant of the younger generation, Kurt Hübner. Although Zadek disliked Kortner's rough ways, his tendency to overpower the spectator, he admired his "irresistible vitality," which he thought utterly modern.[107] With much of the ornery Kortner's approach on his mind, Zadek proceeded to develop his personal style, marked by "a combination of horror, wit, tragedy and psychology."[108] Zadek set about to transform the thespian's craft in West Germany substantially until in the 1970s he and some students of Brecht could take credit for having established a new theatrical performance mode.

Among established stage actors who also worked in film were Elisabeth Flickenschildt, Hilde Krahl, Mathias Wieman, and Gustav Fröhlich. All had been stars in the Third Reich. Beside them, a few younger ones were now emerging, such as Sonja Ziemann, Rudolf Prack, and Margot Hielscher, who had had minor roles. Hildegard Knef, Marianne Koch, and Joachim Hansen were neophytes. Dieter Borsche, although born in 1909, had only been in three Third Reich films; he and Hielscher had entertained the troops in the last years of the war, Borsche as member of a troupe playing for the SS in Auschwitz.[109] In the 1950s, specializing in physicians and priests, he became the darling of older audiences. Hardy Krüger, who graduated from a Nazi elite school, could not finish his role in the film *Junge Adler* (*Young Eagles*), because he was drafted into the army in 1944 at the age of sixteen. He then fought in the Waffen-SS, but survived to resume his acting career after the war.[110]

Such continuities also existed in the case of other film workers. In the early 1950s three major film-production companies arose, Bavaria Filmkunst AG, Universum-Film AG, and UFA-Theater AG, and alongside them many smaller outfits. But the large firms had the most money, much from the Bonn government, which therefore exerted content control. As the CDU politician Rudolf Vogel demanded, those subsidized firms were to make movies for popular entertainment to keep the masses quiet (an objective Goebbels would not have disagreed with) – uncomplicated content usually found in music or costume films. Vogel was not to be disappointed.[111]

The new German film industry flourished between 1951 and 1956, counting more than 554 million visitors in more than 4,000 cinemas in 1951 and more than 817 million in more than 6,000 theaters in 1956. But during this period, films had to compete increasingly with the new medium of television, and after 1956 the movie statistics worsened, so that by 1960 only about 605 million visited fewer than 7,000 theaters. In 1951, 56 films were made in West Germany, as opposed to 109 in 1956, and 85 in 1960.[112]

Willi Forst's *Die Sünderin* of 1951 was produced by a small company, as a continuation of the rubble-film genre of the late 1940s.[113] It featured a broken ex-Wehrmacht officer alongside a young prostitute (Hildegard Knef as Marina), alienated from her family and trying to make it on her own through the late war years and into the time of peace, sleeping around not only with Nazis but also American GIs. Then she meets Alexander (Gustav Fröhlich). Alexander's wife has divorced him as the loser he is, and Marina attempts to save him from alcoholism and, eventually, from the brain tumor that threatens blindness. The lovers struggle financially in the first post-war years, but there is an allusion to the beginning of prosperity as they take a vacation in Italy, where Germans soon will flock.[114]

Whereas this movie offended society's standards of decency, the series of Heimatfilme, or home films, which began where *The Sinner* ended, formed an opposite genre, emphasizing the importance of the nuclear family and traditional values. Because they were tailored to fit Adenauer's beliefs, 20 percent of all West German film production in the 1950s turned out to be Heimatfilme. One of them, *Grün ist die Heide* (*The Heath is Green*), was viewed by 20 million people in 1951, in a total population of over 50 million.[115]

The first such film was *Schwarzwaldmädel* (*Black Forest Girl*) of 1950. Its heroine is Bärbele Riederle, a country girl. That character's casting is programmatic: Bärbele demonstrates that women, after their gender-specific resurgence in the post-war period, must be cut down to size again. Riederle was christened Barbara, which is rendered as Bärbel, a diminutive form suggesting cuteness, and finally as Bärbele, infantilizing the name and the person. In the film, Bärbele is pretty but not bright, the ideal state for young girls hoping to be married. Her foil is Malwine Heinau, an independent, morally endangered showgirl from the city. Here a traditional, home-rooted value-set emphasizes the difference between the (clean) country and the (sullied) city, having originated with literary forerunners Ludwig Ganghofer and Peter Rosegger. Those were much in vogue during the "Blut und Boden" Third Reich. But now this theme is tied to social engineering in the new FRG.[116]

Sonja Ziemann and Rudolf Prack played leads in *Schwarzwaldmädel*, as they did in *Grün ist die Heide* a year later. This film contained multiple recipes for good behavior and taught loyalty to the Bonn Republic. Ziemann impersonates Helga Lüdersen who, with her father Lüder Lüdersen, has arrived on the North German heath after losing their homestead in Pomerania. Her depressed father is caught hunting game illegally by the young forester,

Prack's Walter Rainer. Lüdersen's daughter, as she falls for Rainer, urges her father to desist, and he redeems himself by catching a local criminal. Toward the end there is a luxuriant village feast, attended by both displaced East Germans and the native village folk. While the father will move to a city, the lovers remain in the country, to be married.[117]

The lessons are first that "Heimat" is a base synonymous with the FRG; it implies security in an unstable post-war world. Refugees from the East must integrate and become organic members of the new German community, for Bonn can compensate them. Moreover, as in the Black Forest film, country is superior to city. Opposite the city's corruption, justice in the country infallibly prevails, as proved by Lüdersen. Because he has contravened organic village laws, he must in the end be banished to the city. Next, as in Bärbele's case, women must be put in their place. Helga will marry an older, masculine forester, and Pomeranian friend Nora, rather than migrating to the uncivilized U.S., gets to be wed to a county judge.[118] The old-fashioned *ordo* suggested here is underlined by the presence of the county justice, and social divides are stressed further by the occasional appearance of a vagabond minstrel trio dependent on handouts. They intone folk tunes on harmonica, flute, and voice, some from the East that are also sung at the village festival, memorializing the post-war loss. The Germans-as-victims theme of the late 1940s resonates in those songs, but also in Lüdersen's lament that they are "the war's true victims." The Adenauer state's appeal to new-nation building predominates, as it shines through the verses.[119]

Other film genres represented the conservative establishment's response to specific social and political situations. After the mid-1950s youth unrest plagued large cities such as Berlin and Munich.[120] Many young men left for the French Foreign Legion, compounding a negative birth rate.[121] In part, these were reactions to society's ills over the previous ten years, in that teenagers resented the performance of their returned fathers. Many had been left to themselves during daytime when barely six years old, with keys to their flats around their necks (the so-called *Schlüsselkinder*), while their mothers were out working.[122] They had resented their fathers' late homecoming and resumption, often ruthlessly, of their patriarchal functions. Few juveniles, write the Mitscherlichs, wished to accept such role models.[123]

Also after 1955, American films were arriving in Germany that showed rebellious youths, chief among them *On the Waterfront* (1954), *Blackboard*

Jungle (1955), and *Rebel without a Cause* (1955).[124] They offered Marlon Brando and James Dean as new idols to admire, and eventually it was Elvis Presley whom especially the girls adored. Presley in particular posed a problem to authorities because he, already "the symbol of teenage rebellion" in the States, was seen as effeminate and the product of miscegenation, with African American blood in his veins.[125] All three American artists were viewed as dangerous by the establishment.

Alternatively, the West German film *Die Halbstarken* (*Teenage Wolfpack*) was made in 1956, featuring a Berlin youth gang that, after murdering an Italian merchant in his villa, gets taken out by police. Horst Buchholz, much resembling James Dean, plays the ringleader Freddy who is, significantly, outwitted by his girlfriend Sissy, portrayed by the sensuous Karin Baal. The actress was then a fifteen-year-old from the Berlin working class; she supersedes Freddy in evil, and so her appearance was modified in posters to give her face more of an Asian character, as that of some Red Army soldiers – this was at the height of the Cold War. Sissy's over-sexualization warns of the seductive powers of women, as evident, not least, in rock 'n' roll, and is yet another suggestion that women have no place other than in bedrooms and kitchens. Freddy, from a home with a despondent mother, apart from his unhealthy infatuation has been misled by circumstances, like so many of his peers, and therefore receives a chance at reconstruction.[126]

The zeitgeist demanded that other state-strengthening movies be made, hence a string of military films. West German rearmament required young men of a draftable age to step forward. Therefore teachings about the military opposition to Hitler were actually desired, for in such renderings the legend of the German army remained untarnished. As of 1955 the new Bundeswehr, led by ex-Wehrmacht generals with former contacts to the Resistance such as Hans Speidel, was interested in a national psychology acknowledging the FRG's right to defend itself within NATO, in case of a Warsaw Pact attack.

Already in 1954, the ground had been prepared for such a psychological shift with the film *Canaris*, in which the historic Wilhelm Canaris, chief of military Abwehr, is (falsely) shown to have been a foe of the Third Reich and (correctly) one of the key Wehrmacht resisters to Hitler, late in the war. A year hence followed *Des Teufels General*, a fictional screen account of General Harras's opposition authored, as already mentioned, originally as a theater play, by Carl Zuckmayer. Harras's character had been modeled on General Ernst Udet, a World War I Luftwaffe ace and former lover of Leni Riefenstahl, who committed suicide in November 1941.[127] Both characters, Canaris no less than Udet, were seen to be guided, in their respective film portrayals, "by an old-fashioned sense of duty and honour," which was in keeping with the Bundeswehr's self-conception.[128]

In this period the German film industry produced other movies with a conservative bent. They fell into the category either of escapism (from a dreadful past and often still grueling present) or authority endorsement. In this vein, a filmed version of Thomas Mann's novel *Königliche Hoheit* (*Royal Highness*, 1953) with Borsche and Wieman affirmed authority commingled with dreamy escapade.[129] In 1955 the *Sissi* film trilogy began, around Princess Elisabeth (Sissi) of Bavaria, who married Habsburg Emperor Franz Joseph, demonstrating obeisance as a private and public virtue.

At the close of the 1950s a few films were produced heralding the end of the Adenauer era and the beginning of more critical inquiries in the 1960s. They asked questions the conservatives in the cultural establishment would rather not countenance. In 1958 *Das Mädchen Rosemarie* questioned both newly acquired affluence and sexual bigotry in high society.[130] *Wir Wunderkinder* (*Aren't We Wonderful?*) traced the parallel careers of two men from the Empire through the Third Reich and into the post-war years – one a Nazi doomed to perish, the other an Everyman, with a clean vest who is rewarded with bourgeois bliss.[131] This was followed in 1959 by *Rosen für den Staatsanwalt* and, surprisingly, two anti-militaristic films.[132] In one, *Die Brücke* (*The Bridge*), seven sixteen-year-old boys defend a small-town bridge during the final days of the war against oncoming American tanks; all die, except for one who lives to tell the (true) story. The movie shows up the futility, even criminality, of sending unseasoned teenagers into a battle – teenagers who in the film appear gung-ho to defeat the enemy as if playing cops and robbers.[133] That aspect was justly criticized as unrealistic, for all German boys in such predicaments knew they were not in a game.[134] But many reviews found the director Bernhard Wicki's revelatory approach refreshing and his motives for it sincere. Another film of 1959, *Hunde, wollt ihr ewig leben?* (*Dogs, Do You Want To Live Forever?*), described the senselessness of the last stand by General Paulus's Sixth Army at Stalingrad and mourned the fate of the thousands who at film's end are marched off to

Siberia.[135] Yet all these movies, however well intentioned, expressed old themes of resentment. In essence, while German victims were offered commiseration and bad Nazis were condemned, sufferers other than those Germans were not mentioned, least of all the Jews.

◆ ◆ ◆

As a carrier of news and conveyer of culture, the West German radio network expanded in the 1950s. There was progress institutionally, in that a formula was found in 1952 that guaranteed German stations independence for creative programming with a minimum of governmental interference. A new broadcaster, Sender Freies Berlin (SFB, Radio Free Berlin), was established in June 1953; the original six stations covering all West Germany had expanded to nine in 1957. With the introduction of frequency modulation (FM) techniques, eventually there existed three channels for every station, with programming of ascending quality.[136]

Political pressure emanating from Bonn always threatened a high degree of alignment between political and news coverage on the one side, and conservative political direction on the other, until the early 1960s. Yet political right-wingers were always sufficiently resisted for compromises to be reached. That those restorative groups tried was typical of the Adenauer era, where establishment representatives defended assumed rights of entitlement, and that they could be successfully opposed – only a seeming contradiction – was a function of the working democracy Adenauer had, after all, helped to install.[137]

Conservatives held that a radio in the home should keep the family together. In the mornings there were programs for housewives, in the afternoons for children, and at 6 p.m. news or sports for the father. At night, all family members congregated to listen to the hit-parade, an operetta, or a variety show. More highbrow broadcasts featured Hörspiele, book reviews, or classical music. All offerings constituted "responsible journalism for a responsible democracy."[138]

The Hörspiel continued to excel. Hörspiel authors proliferated, not least because radio stations paid generously, among them early luminaries Siegfried Lenz, Heinrich Böll, Wolfgang Hildesheimer, and the champion in that group, Günter Eich. The dynamic Swiss duo, Dürrenmatt and Frisch, was also conspicuous.[139] Hörspiel production was encouraged by contests held at radio stations, such as Munich's (in 1950), and, since 1952, by a prestigious annual prize competition, endowed by the league of the war-blind, who were dependent on this novel cultural genre.[140]

The fifth winner of that prize, Leopold Ahlsen in 1955, had written a piece that engaged with issues from World War II. In his *Philemon und Baucis* he tells of an old Greek couple taking sides with German soldiers as well as Greek partisans, who hang them in the end.[141] This did not, as yet, constitute a principal discussion involving Jews as victims, but at least the victims were not Germans anymore. Closer to the core of the Holocaust was Eich's *Die Mädchen aus Viterbo* (*The Girls from Viterbo*). In this 1953 tragedy a Jewish girl is hiding, during 1943, with her grandfather from the SS in a Berlin attic until they are caught and deported. During this anxious wait, the girl fantasizes about a school class of Italian girls getting irretrievably lost in the Roman catacombs.[142] While here Eich grieved the fate of individual Jews, it was not yet a fundamental analysis of anti-Semitism as endemic to National Socialism. Playwright Rolf Hochhuth would be the first to deal with this more systematically in the 1960s.

In a Hörspiel for the Süddeutsche Rundfunk in Stuttgart during 1957, a piece that was edited there by Alfred Andersch and Hans Magnus Enzensberger, music by American jazz musicians was used.[143] This was symptomatic of the willingness of station managers to experiment with modern media, especially on the more demanding FM channels, and was a strong statement against anything the Nazis had done on the airwaves. Taking their cues from the AFN and later Willis Conover's shows on the Voice of America, jazz proceeded to be broadcast regularly, albeit in the late evening, first by the NWDR in Cologne, followed by Hamburg's NWDR/NDR, beginning in 1948. Cologne's disc jockey was Dietrich Schulz-Köhn, who had a legendary past as a convinced Nazi, who thought, incredibly, that he could integrate his personal hobby of jazz with Nazi ideology.[144] Jazz broadcasts in Cologne became a regular feature until his retirement many decades later. In 1950 the journalist Joachim Ernst Berendt, whose not wholly "Aryan" father had died in Dachau, initiated a similar program at the comparatively progressive radio station SWF in Baden-Baden.[145]

These broadcasts would acquire small but loyal followings, and so did those promoting modern music of the Darmstadt summer-course variety. Truly, this genre, from serial to electronic, could not have developed without a few avant-garde-minded radio stations, foremost again Cologne's and Baden-Baden's.[146] This was because they were able to acquire expensive instrumental, recording, and playback equipment, essential for the new electronic music. They also employed forward-looking experts, such as Heinrich Strobel in Baden-Baden and Herbert Eimert in Cologne. Moreover, they commissioned works, such as Henze's broadcast opera *Das Ende einer Welt* (*End of a World*) in the early 1950s, purchased by NWDR Hamburg. Its libretto had been written by the promising Wolfgang Hildesheimer, a habitué of Gruppe 47, and it was aired in December 1953. Kafkaesque, Surrealist, it dealt with a concert in a Venetian palace being flooded; the narrator leaves in a boat, with the audience holding hands above their chins and exclaiming, excitedly, "da capo."[147] Other stations, too, adopted New Music programs, such as Hanover's, Bremen's, and Munich's. But the SWF in Baden-Baden and the NWDR (later WDR) in Cologne remained unique because the SWF tied its work to music festivals organized in nearby Donaueschingen and the NWDR to experiments and concerts in Cologne's vivacious music scene.[148]

Alas, in the late 1950s the Hörspiel culture was endangered because of the ascendancy of television. Hörspiele tended to be replaced by television plays demanding all-round acting skills that not everyone could muster. In the beginning those plays were performed live because of the absence of visual recording techniques. But the acting remained wooden and lines were spoken as though read from scripts, with the image in constricted focus.[149] Although TV technology had been invented by the Nazis and was first used more widely during the 1936 Olympics, it had been imperfect and no match for Goebbels's radio.[150]

The first telecast occurred in Hamburg on December 25, 1952, with several hours of programming.[151] West Germany had fewer than 700,000 television sets in households in 1956, increasing to 4.6 million in 1960. Programming was set for the afternoons and evenings, with more on Sundays.[152] Throughout, as in radio, there was the Suchdienst, the Red Cross tracing service, searching for persons missing because of war and its turmoiled aftermath. Many of those questions remained unanswered.

Commercial-free at first, television legitimized itself through the regal spectacle of Queen Elizabeth's coronation on June 2, 1953, and a year later even more so during the telecasting of the European soccer match in Berne.

87

Because, like radio, it aimed to offer something to the entire household, television was politically considered as valuable for family cohesion. It soon became addictive. A good many films of yesteryear were shown, some of a questionable Nazi bent. It presented political magazines such as *Adenauer in Moscow* and made available parliamentary debates. It pioneered new forms of entertainment for West German habitués such as the detective series *Stahlnetz* (*Net of Steel*), initiated in 1958 (and patterned on U.S. archetypes). Today judged stilted, clichéd, and simplistic, it was hugely popular then. In the whodunits of the 1950s the main motives for misbehavior and crime were, rather than money plain and simple as in America, love or sexual distress, fear, loneliness, envy, and social marginalization – altogether more psychological sets of circumstances, more than tenuously related to consequences of post-war misery. Another popular series was *Unsere Nachbarn heute abend: Familie Schölermann* (*Our Neighbors Tonight: The Schölermann Family*, 1954–60), which presented the image of a harmonious family as a model for all citizens.[153]

A novelty in the German public-media world, and indicative of the new spirit of democracy, tolerance, and international cooperation, was *Der Internationale Frühschoppen* (*The International Morning Pint*) led by seasoned journalist Werner Höfer. It began on radio from Cologne, near Bonn, in January 1952 and was later also run on television, every Sunday before noon. The suave Höfer made it his habit to invite, for live broadcasts and telecasts, six journalists from different countries in order to discuss current affairs. The Höfer show was unique in content and format, including Rhine-wine tastings. Yet the moderator Höfer was vainglorious, tended to steer discussion toward his own perspective rather than preserving impartiality, and was often condescending to his guests. He reflected the new self-confidence of the Bonn government, based on economic achievements, populist certitudes, and ever-accruing diplomatic prestige. National Socialist topics or the Third Reich were omitted.[154]

Still, even with their deficiencies, topics such as Höfer's were rare on all nine or so West German television channels by the early 1960s. Whereas Nazi themes often served as background or action frames for fictional narratives, they were not problematized on TV. German guilt, or Jews as victims, did not figure. Only in 1958 were there three full features, one highlighting the fate of individual Jews and the Kristallnacht pogroms of

November 9–10, 1938; the other two were unconvincing. There was no contribution specifically written to deal with aspects of the Holocaust and to contextualize the phenomenon for the sake of public discussion.[155]

Newspapers and magazines increased in number after the founding of the FRG toward the middle of the 1950s, but then fell off because of consolidation. There were 137 dailies in 1949, for example, compared with the peak of 225 in 1954.[156] This favored press monopolies such as Axel Springer's. As in radio, the Adenauer cabinets saw printed news media as an ideal instrument for government control. Short of creating an information ministry as had Goebbels, the Bonn government attempted to take over *Die Welt* after the British had let it go in the early 1950s, but this failed.[157] Strongly believing that the press was subordinate to government and to be used as its tool, Adenauer's politicians exerted control over some papers, such as *Christ und Welt*, by subsidizing them.[158] Moreover, it created a substitute ministry, the Bundespresseamt, or Federal Press Office, which invited senior journalists to regular meetings in Bonn, obliging them to toe a party line. Lest they lose insider knowledge, these journalists were expected to "demonstrate insight into the wisdom of the government" in print.[159]

Like the government, 1950s journalists ostensibly believed in the Basic Law, parliamentary democracy, and the fraternity of the Western Allies. With anti-Communism a major touchstone and, consequently, the denial of GDR legitimacy, coming to terms with the Nazi past was secondary. This corresponded with the overriding mood in Bonn. As for the cultivation of a defensible legacy, the conservative opposition to Hitler, utilized as a spiritual foundation for the Bundeswehr and slowly reflected in academe, led commercial print media to blame the Nazi leadership and exculpate other Germans. Such a stance led to sympathies with Adenauer's inclination to tolerate compromised Nazis in his government, ignore German war crimes, and extend pity to convicted war criminals.[160]

The newspaper most obviously falling in line with Bonn's philosophy was the *FAZ*. Succinctly, Enzensberger said that it would "speak the language of the rulers."[161] Staffed with proven conservatives, many from before 1933, the paper was in favor of liberating former Nazi functional elites, desk perpetrators, and the military from criminal odium, since the main offenders had been punished.[162] In this manner and with a view to the new Bundeswehr, *FAZ* copublisher Paul Sethe attempted to relegitimize all former Wehrmacht soldiers.[163] He also called for Germany's reunification, decrying too close a connection with the Western Allies. This went too far for the chancellor, who now caused censorship mechanisms to set in: Sethe was impelled to leave the paper in 1955.[164] In his stead, at the end of the 1950s, Friedrich Sieburg, no less conservative, was put in charge of literature reviews; the newly arrived Jewish Marcel Reich-Ranicki believed Sieburg was hindering his integration into the *FAZ*'s staff.[165]

The *FAZ*'s liberal alternative was the Munich-based *SZ*. But, like the even more left-wing *Frankfurter Rundschau* (*FR*), it concentrated too much on local news, as highbrow readers tended to prefer the *FAZ*'s renowned cultural reviews.[166] Culture critic Joachim Kaiser, a former student of Theodor Adorno's, arrived in Munich only in 1959, to draw more discerning readers to the *SZ*.[167]

The *FAZ*'s corresponding organ in the north was Hamburg's *Die Welt*, always fraught with problems, not least financially. Axel Springer, born in 1912 to a mid-level newspaper owner, acquired it in 1953 from the British.[168] Springer's anti-Nazi stance had been motivated – typical for the Hamburg patriciate – by liberalism tempered by conservatism, on the British model and contrary to Nazi tastes. He had been something of a patron saint for the upper-class, anti-Nazi "Swings," with their love for American jazz and British fashions. He had befriended non-"Aryans" in his peer group, such as Erik Blumenfeld, a future shipyard magnate.[169] That relationship explains Springer's friendship with Jews and his support of Israel, which he shared with Adenauer. After the war Springer acquired *Hör Zu*, Germany's popular radio program guide, and later bought *Die Welt*.

Die Welt employed journalists who were tendentiously right wing such as, early on, Hans Zehrer.[170] Trying to control events in Germany by monopolistic media purchases conjured up the specter of totalitarianism, as this threatened to influence mass public opinion illicitly.[171] Charges by left-wingers such as Enzensberger that this was Springer's intention were not without foundation. The ramifications of Springer's monopoly possession of Bild-Zeitung, *Die Welt*, and *Hör Zu*, together with the daily *Hamburger Abendblatt* and the monthly journal *Kristall*, became dangerously obvious in the 1960s and 1970s.[172] Until 1960, with *Die Welt* for demanding readers, Springer forged *Bild*, a daily tabloid he had founded in June 1952, into a product of mass consumption, meeting the lowest common denominator in taste and education.[173]

To curry favor with the masses, until spring 1958 *Bild* mostly printed heart-rending human-interest stories, short and with many photos. Springer dictated that *Bild* should supply content to its readership in precut pieces, making independent thinking superfluous. Readers would then be able "to know without thinking."[174] More recently, *Bild*'s early texts have been characterized as "short and to the point, optimistic, libertarian, progressively minded, consumer-economics-oriented, but also thrilling, easily digestible and cut in rough anti-Communist patterns."[175] This meant publishing sports reportages, the weather, astrology, and, increasingly, sexualized copy.[176] Because it corresponded with the aesthetic mentality of many in a largely petit-bourgeois readership, Germany's majority population, *Bild* became so successful that by 1960 it was sold to nearly 3 million people per day.[177]

The illustrated weeklies were qualitatively above *Bild*, with Henri Nannen's *Stern* aiming for a higher standard. Episodes from the Third Reich for the sake of sales continued to be the aim mostly of magazines such as *Quick*, *Revue*, *Neue Illustrierte*, and *Constanze*, but sentiments of remorse were absent. Beauty tips for office secretaries and inside stories about film stars always took priority.[178]

Majority ownership of *Stern* was acquired in 1951 by Gerd Bucerius of *Die Zeit* (Zeit-Verlag publishing), assuring its higher standard.[179] As Bucerius's own weekly, *Die Zeit*, was struggling to uphold a liberal profile, alt-Nazis had to be removed. Richard Tüngel, the first chief editor and a major shareholder, had proceeded to hire more questionable journalists. When in the mid-1950s he counselled the retention of strong journalistic ties to Professor Carl Schmitt, who as a jurist had justified Hitler's overthrow of parliamentary democracy in the early 1930s, Dönhoff protested to publisher Bucerius. By 1957, Josef Müller-Marein, a former Luftwaffe officer who promised change, had replaced Tüngel.[180]

Right-wing influences, however, lingered at *Die Zeit*. Müller-Marein had published in the Nazi daily *Völkischer Beobachter*, and Countess Dönhoff herself, out of sympathy with fellow aristocrats, continued believing that Ribbentrop's state secretary Ernst Freiherr von Weizsäcker had been unjustly tried at Nuremberg.[181] Most noteworthy, the paper kept employing its music reviewer, Walter Abendroth. In the Third Reich his concerns had been "music and race" and the "decomposing effects of musical Jewry." It was a comment on the post-war period when Müller-Marein wrote in 1973, upon Abendroth's death, that the *Zeit* staff had hired him in the late 1940s because "we needed him, the highly educated man, who was so stimulating in all things cultural, if, time and again, a contrarian."[182]

Rudolf Augstein's obsession with the Third Reich resulted in more Nazi coverage in the pages of *Der Spiegel*; hence in 1952, 134,000 copies were sold, and, ten years later, 450,000 copies.[183] He also fancied himself a "replacement opposition in federal German politics" if and when the parliamentary opposition faltered.[184] Hence he wished to curb political corruption, reduce the power of Bonn ministries, and, like some colleagues on the right, work for a reunification of Germany without restrictive ties to the West.[185]

To continue coverage of the Third Reich, Augstein tended to call for help from Beelzebub in order to defeat the Devil. For example, he solicited insider information from Erich Fischer, a former SS major, who had worked for the Hitler Youth and Goebbels.[186] The result was more tell-all series about the Nazi regime and its immediate aftermath, some of which, like the one involving Diels, had morally dubious origins.[187] Augstein also acquired the collaboration of two former SS leaders as a more permanent part of *Der Spiegel*. Both men, Horst Mahnke and Georg Wolff, had been students at the University of Königsberg, that anti-East Slavic bulwark where Oberländer and Rothfels taught. They had been disciples of media professor Franz Alfred Six, a mentor of Adolf Eichmann, who oversaw the Inland SD for Reinhard Heydrich. When Six was head of an SD Einsatzgruppe on the march to Moscow in 1941, Mahnke was by his side. According to an original document published by Lutz Hachmeister, this unit liquidated 144 civilians, among them 38 "intellectual Jews," who had been found "dissatisfied and making trouble" in the newly erected ghetto of Smolensk. Wolff, meanwhile, had been posted to an SD commando in Occupied Norway, where he reported on the populace directly to Heydrich. At one time, Heydrich had accepted Wolff's assessment that Norwegians would not bend to Nazi rule with equanimity, implying the use of greater force.[188]

After the war, Six was condemned to twenty years of penitentiary by an Allied court for war crimes but was freed after four. He entered C.W. Leske publishers in Darmstadt, which then printed Augstein's first book, *Deutschland – ein Rheinbund*, a collection of his *Spiegel* columns. Mahnke was easily denazified after British internment. It had been in 1950 that both Mahnke and Wolff were able to begin their work for *Der Spiegel*.[189]

◆ ◆ ◆

The self-satisfied stability of the young FRG was reflected in a school of painting calling itself "junger westen," originating in the industrial Ruhr area shortly after its founding. Literalistic as well as abstract, it represented conditions created by industrialized society, showing off its technical, economic, and scientific progress cumulatively in the 1950s. Its protagonists advocated human acquiescence in industrial developments and technical processes as part of everyday life.[190] Concentrating on the moment shut out undue reflections on the past, the Nazi past in particular. Therefore, there was complacency underlying paintings by Heinrich Siepmann, Hans Werdehausen, and Thomas Grochowiak. Siepmann's work was characterized by the depiction of geometrical constructs, but also a certain lyric quality.[191] Werdehausen painted abstracts, sharply contoured static parts – one of his, a gouache on cardboard of black lines with red dots on a pale-blue and off-yellow background, is reminiscent of Klee, yet others recall Kandinsky.[192] Grochowiak's *Fördermaschinist* (*Miner's Machinist*) of 1950 shows a machine operator in a contraption surrounded by mechanical levers; later he designed a poster with a Bundeswehr Luftwaffe radio operator – earphones and three airplanes.[193] Other, unaffiliated, artists also from the Ruhr environs painted similar works suggesting compliance with routine not revolution, stasis not dynamics, and bespeaking domesticity and bourgeois contentment. Bruno Goller of Düsseldorf in 1955 created a "picture of pictures" (*Verschiedene Bilder*). It showed rectangles, some framed, inhabited, among other subjects, by a woman's upper torso, two roses, and a house cat stealthily navigating stairs.[194]

Meanwhile, the two major factions of the old guard led by Karl Hofer and Willi Baumeister were trudging on. To the extent that abstract art was now held to be superior to representational painting, Hofer himself was cumulatively discredited, against which he protested vainly.[195] Abstraction continued to be regarded as an antidote to once-established Nazi art, a path from which one must not stray. Such prescription was consonant with the inertia of the Adenauer era.[196] Hofer died, embittered, in April 1955, followed by his rival Baumeister four months later.[197]

Inertia in the West German visual-art scene was reinforced by generational cementation, because artists born after 1910 were hardly visible. Many of those had dwelt on Nazi themes and, unlike journalists or actors, found it difficult to change their genres and be newly admitted. Others who could have demonstrated against Nazi art had fallen at the fronts. "Junger westen," a much smaller group of younger, Wehrmacht-conscriptable men kept to quotidian themes endorsing the constituent values of the FRG, which rendered them legitimate even if they painted realistically.

A third group, in age resembling those of "junger westen," legitimized themselves through new abstractions; they were the Informel, or Tachists. Four of them formed the "Quadriga" group early in the 1950s and staged an exhibition at the Zimmergalerie Franck in Frankfurt in 1952. They were Bernhard Schultze, Karl Otto Götz, Otto Greis, and Heinz Kreutz. Of those, Greis, born in 1913, was the oldest, and Kreutz, born in 1923, the youngest.[198]

Their work occurred against the backdrop of artistic developments in the United States and France that, during the Cold War era, swept over the art scene in West Germany as well. In New York, which was to take the place of Paris as the art capital of the world, after European painters had influenced the Americans, Abstract Expressionists Robert Motherwell, Franz Kline, Willem de Kooning, and especially Jackson Pollock were changing the very way art was made and perceived, with Pollock famously throwing or dripping paint onto huge canvases laid out on the floor. He then worked on it with brushes and sticks, putting layer of paint upon layer, without necessarily heeding a sense of form or preset laws of color combination. Although Pollock himself never visited Paris, colleagues of his did, such as the French-Canadian Jean-Paul Riopelle, who arrived there in 1947, mingling with local artists such as Jean Dubuffet and Jean Fautrier. In 1948, Götz was in Paris, and the German painter Wols (Alfred Otto Wolfgang Schulze), who had been there since 1932, was most certainly in his company. Another German, Juro Kubicek, stayed in America during the late 1940s, returning to Germany in 1949 to start teaching art in Berlin.[199]

Apart from these individual interactions, the U.S. State Department and the CIA encouraged German–American cultural interchanges, to fortify the ideological bulwark against the Eastern Bloc. In the 1950s, many art exhibitions were organized in Europe, where the creations of de Kooning,

Mark Rothko, and Pollock were on display. In 1951 alone, Pollock paintings from Peggy Guggenheim's collection were shown in Amsterdam, Zurich, and Brussels, even though they did not yet possess the drip characteristics. A CIA-sponsored permanent Congress for Cultural Freedom was instituted during 1950 in West Berlin, with branches all over Western Europe, supporting such exhibitions, conferences, and newly created journals as *Der Monat* for Germany. To some extent, Amerikahäuser in large German cities struck the same note.[200]

Adherents of the Tachist school fulfilled unspoken requirements for art after the elimination of the Nazi system in a number of ways. They dared to experiment, they freely expressed their individuality rather than a state dogma, and they connected internationally. Influenced by the foreign paragons and ignoring pre-established color codes, they created a new method of painting for Germany by throwing paint out of a can or squeezing it out of a tube, onto canvas, which could then be worked on with a dry brush, stick, or spatula. The paint thus created highs and lows of material on the canvas surface, making the picture three- rather than two-dimensional. The content, the theme, was reaching out into space. Thus, the painting surface assumed a tactile quality. Motifs or forms were not prescribed, and usually form was dissolved – hence the moniker Informel, or Tachism, derived from the French word, *tache,* for "spot." Emphasis was on the material, such as the paint, and on the action of painting as such, rather than a final outcome. As was Pollock, Götz, for instance, was seen to be "painting" spontaneously, quickly and with broad strokes. Watching a Tachist painter paint was an aesthetic experience of equal importance to observing the finished work of art.[201]

In the specific artistic actions of the Tachists, a protest was implied against rationalization and established order, especially the order paraded and recommended by the structural fortitudes of the developing republic under Adenauer, with its well-defined bureaucracies, codes of moral law, and resulting good citizens' behavior, not to mention economic prolificacy. Some Tachist artists even related their defiant credo to the, often rationally laid-out, constrictions of the more recent past – a "reaction against National Socialism and the war."[202]

One who did was Gotthard (Joe) Müller, still a student at the Bavarian art academy when I met him in Munich during my Schwabing days in

1959–60. Like me in his early twenties, Joe had been born in Germany's easternmost provinces. He was a victim of the post-war dislocations described earlier. Toward the end of the war, he and his younger brother lost their father, a Wehrmacht colonel, and their mother, and were raised by a Polish family. Sometime in the late 1940s, Joe was located by the Red Cross tracing service and transferred to West Germany, but when he got there he spoke only Polish. By 1959 he was living a bohemian life in Schwabing, his hair long and his manners ever so casual. He complained to me about the staid school of painting at the academy and how he wanted to have his freedom. Müller liked squeezing equal amounts of paint from the tubes in an ever-repeating act, which produced similar shapes to those that would be made by a machine. The painting he gave to me he had called "Scottish Cross," something of a misnomer, but by introducing what he thought was a Celtic motif he meant to see it as outside the establishment and not to be confused with a Christian cross or Christian civilization, as it inspired the current political and social order. That he found smug. The regularity of his pattern, unlike the images produced by the earlier Tachists, shows that Müller created his work at the end of the classic Tachist wave, when more structure was returning to that art – delineated shapes and weighted color schemes. Similar to Müller's work is Günther Uecker's *Weisses Bild* (*White Picture*) of the same year, where, as in Müller's red background, a linen canvas had been tacked onto a wooden frame and then, unlike Müller's, been treated with regularly spaced nails, the whole thing being sprayed with white paint.[203]

In 1955 the series of documenta exhibitions was started in Kassel that would become a catalyst for new art in West Germany for decades. Kassel seemed like an ideal symbolic starting venue. Having lost 80 percent of its buildings, it was a reminder that Germany had suffered too. This appealed especially to unreconstructed nationalists. More forward-looking people saw the devastation as a sign of encouragement toward faster rebuilding, which corresponded to Bonn governmental thinking. The ruins of the classicist Fridericianum museum were chosen as a shell to be transformed, with new false walls and steles inside because, in founder Arnold Bode's interpretation, they allowed the integration of wide-open spaces outside. And finally, Kassel was very close to the border with the, still unrecognized, GDR, and this meant two things. One, it was economically challenged, as were all West German places near there, in the so-called *Zonenrandgebiet*, or border area. Large throngs of visitors were expected to fill up Kassel's treasury. Moreover, its modern art showing was meant to threaten East German Socialist Realism, which had been growing since the Eastern Bloc's anti-Formalism campaign had begun in the late 1940s.[204]

Arnold Bode, born in 1900, was a professor of painting at the Staatliche Werkakademie Kassel; he had been persecuted by the Nazis in 1933.[205] The idea for a redemptive exhibition that would reconnect the German art scene to an international standard that had, since 1933, overtaken the art of his countrymen, was Bode's own. But he chose as his advisors a group of four men, headed by the art historian Werner Haftmann. He was born in 1912 in West Prussia, and after acquiring his doctorate in art history in Göttingen in 1936 he worked as an assistant at the Institut für Kunstgeschichte in Florence (German-founded in 1887). He returned to the Reich to join the Wehrmacht in 1940 and thereafter was in a prisoner-of-war camp.[206] In Kassel he became the documenta's "chief theoretician" who would set all the "ideological guidelines."[207] Those revolved around what has come to be called Haftmann's "theory of continuity in the development of abstract art."[208]

During summer 1955 the exhibition showed the works of 148 artists – 640 paintings, illustrations, and sculptures in all – from fourteen countries, with most from Germany, France, and Italy. In keeping with Haftmann's view of art history, these were exhibits to testify to the consistency of Classical Modernism, with the German experience restored to what he viewed as a cohesive, unbroken trajectory. Hence Dubuffet's works represented France, Piet Mondrian's Holland, Marc Chagall's Russia, Carlo Carrà's Italy, and, naturally, Picasso's Spain. Henry Moore's *King and Queen* sculpture (1952/3) stood for Britain. For Germany, the main idea was to recognize Expressionist artists who had suffered from National Socialism and acknowledge them on a par with the international collegiate. Demonstrably, Haftmann had favored the œuvre of Expressionist artists active until 1933 and, even if encumbered, until 1945. Into this group fell the iconic Expressionists, such as Klee, Kandinsky, Ernst Ludwig Kirchner, and especially Emil Nolde. Haftmann, craftsmanlike, also placed much emphasis on profiling distinctive German artists' movements, such as "Die Brücke" (Dresden) and "Der Blaue Reiter" (Munich), putting them in the context of "the development of abstract art."

97

The exhibition, with its new structures amid the remaining derelict façades, attracted 130,000 visitors from July 16 to September 18.[209]

Everywhere, progressive critics were enthused. There was rapturous praise from local reviewers in daily papers such as Niels von Holst in *Badische Neueste Nachrichten* and Hans Curjel in *Schwäbische Donau-Zeitung*.[210] At the culture desk of *Die Zeit*, where the restorative Abendroth era was in recession, the renowned art critic Carl Georg Heise praised the exhibition as "the great panorama of modern creativity," which had been the result of a remarkable accuracy in selection. Haftmann was singled out as an expert completely in control of his field who even, in the preface to the catalog, had produced "a small masterwork."[211]

But there were also criticisms. In the *Bremer Tageszeitung*, Karl Bachler noted that despite the multitude of works, the very best of every artist's œuvre had not been shown, nor even something significant, for instance typifying the style of Picasso or Matisse. Artists appeared to have been picked at random, and several important ones, signifying historic developments, were missing.[212] Visitors looked in vain, for instance, for the Surrealists, with Salvador Dalí representing Spain. The new Abstract Expressionist school from the United States was non-existent – de Kooning, Motherwell, and Pollock – with expatriate Germans such as Max Beckmann and Josef Albers said to stand for America instead. From Germany, the Tachists were missing, and the Expressionists shown were mostly quite old, because those who had suffered under the Nazis were the ones to be favored. But the great majority of those were dead. The only artist featured who was born after 1920 was the Italian painter Roberto Crippa (b. 1921). From among the current Expressionists, such as Baumeister, only older works were displayed, and he himself was born in the past century. The German new beginnings after 1945 were, in fact, ignored. So were the Dadaists such as (the Jewish) John Heartfield, who had been a political left-winger, and the equally left-wing social critic George Grosz. The entire post-World War I Cologne Progressive School was left out, which had also comprised socially critical artists, among them the Jewish Jankel Adler. If sufferers from Nazism were to be highlighted, why were its ultimate victims such as the Jewish Otto Freundlich and Felix Nussbaum omitted, both of whom died in concentration camps?

The reason for the exhibition's skewedness was Werner Haftmann. He had an authoritarian streak that allowed only for the demonstration of the art genre he happened to believe in: German Expressionism as the core element of classic abstract art, in fact of any art. The group around Bode who had hired him in 1955 had known this about him. What escaped them and accounted for Haftmann's imperious demeanor was that he had been a Nazi active in the regime's administration of culture. During the early 1930s, just as Dietrich Schulz-Köhn thought that jazz should be incorporated into the Nazi system, Haftmann believed that German Expressionism was to be tolerated. He even went so far as to say that this style was quintessentially German and therefore a quintessential artistic expression of the Nazi creed.

What Haftmann kept from the denazification courts after 1945 and then from Bode was that as a student in Berlin (before he moved to Göttingen) he had joined the SA in November 1933. Furthermore, until February 1935, Haftmann was active in a circle of organized Nazi students who edited the journal *Kunst der Nation* (*Art of the Nation*), which aimed to encourage what they called "Nordic Expressionism," exemplified by Ernst Barlach and especially Nolde. Haftmann himself published in it during 1934 that artists of "Die Brücke" and "Blauer Reiter" stood for a new German departure because they had said no to Western civilization. This found unambiguous favor with Goebbels, who owned works by Barlach and Nolde. But the magazine was cashiered after Hitler decided that no form of Modernism was to be tolerated in art. Most probably to escape the wrath of Rosenberg, Goebbels's rival in the administration of culture, Haftmann moved to Florence a year later, after he had considered a position under the Nazi Party member Hans Sedlmayr, then in his art-history chair at Vienna. In 1937, Haftmann joined the party himself.[213] In 1944 he was stationed as a lieutenant with the XIVth Tank Corps in northern Italy, where he was responsible for hunting down partisans. In this capacity, he aided the SS during the torture of Italian civilians. In one documented case, he inserted his fingers into wounds that had been inflicted on a captive to make them worse. That victim was later shot, and Haftmann received the Iron Cross Second Class.[214]

It was therefore preposterous when Haftmann claimed, in the preface to the documenta catalog of 1955, that it was painful having to remember how "Germany isolated herself from united efforts in behalf of a modern European spirit," at a time when the National Socialist phenomenon amounted to a "workshop accident."[215] What he meant to suggest here was that the art of the Third Reich was a non-art and could be glossed over, that German Expressionism had in fact never been damaged and could now be continued as if nothing had happened. Even if this deviated from what he had believed in his student days, it was the official mantra he was now upholding: it legitimized him as an art expert in a pluralistic, democratic society and upheld his prerogative as the not-to-be-disputed custodian of a long-established German cultural tradition. In defining the canon, Haftmann's constant reminder of the *German* origins of Expressionism echoed the old nationalism rather than heralding integration with the international art scene.[216]

In the summer of 1959 the second documenta was staged in Kassel, again with Bode at the helm and Haftmann serving as *spiritus rector*. This time the accent was on art from 1945 to the present, hence late German Expressionists were featured, such as Ernst Wilhelm Nay, with his large-format *Freiburger Bild* of 1956. Altogether, over four hundred Artists were represented. Although Haftmann acted out his predilection for Abstract Expressionism, his concept was crisscrossed by the inclusion of works by Picasso, who had always denied being an abstract painter, and Henry Moore, who always broached the representational. They were part of an opening theme of historic Expressionists also including Klee and Kandinsky, with Klee, too, having painted figuratively at times. Haftmann now showcased contemporary American painters such as Joan Mitchell, de Kooning, and Pollock, whom he blithely situated within the German-European tradition. This time the Tachists were also included. And the political message was clearly, once again, against the Socialist Realism of the "East zone."[217]

Beyond that, Haftmann continued to infuse the exhibition with rhetoric that sought to assert his world monopoly as a visionary impresario on the one hand and, on the other, to fortify his persona as a man without a Nazi past. In cloudy oratory he spoke about artistic abstraction as a "universal language" now serving as an internationally binding vehicle of communication that henceforth would absolve the German people of their sense of historic guilt. Artists were, said Haftmann, the "seismographs of the historic moment." He bewailed past instances of wretchedness and human pain, summoning up camp inmates, political prisoners, and refugees, and tearfully commiserating with "the girl Anne Frank," who made the night "even darker."[218] People who knew him from the past must have been convinced he had done a credible job of reinventing himself.

◆ ◆ ◆

During the first half of the 1950s two luminaries of the West German classical-music scene exercised somewhat complicated rites of succession: in September 1953, Herbert von Karajan conducted his first post-war concert with the Berlin Philharmonic and, a year later, Wilhelm Furtwängler put in his last appearance, at the Berlin Titania-Palast. A mere ten weeks after that he was dead. A memorial concert in his name – Furtwängler's own unfinished Third Symphony – was not conducted by Karajan, but by his much lesser-known colleague Joseph Keilberth, in January 1956.[219] If Furtwängler had been a – sometimes difficult – favorite of Hitler, Karajan had been popular with Goebbels and Göring. As had Furtwängler, Karajan, as the most prominent music director in West Germany until the late 1980s, stood for a traditional canon in opera and orchestral music, not for Modernism.

Herbert von Karajan was the cultural incarnation of the FRG's Economic Miracle. Through his performances and, increasingly, recordings, often joined by his favorite soprano Elisabeth Schwarzkopf, Karajan became a media star par excellence, whose theatrical performances were enjoyed not only by the old educated *haute volée*, as used to be the case, but also by members of the new, upwardly mobile middle class, who would buy subscription tickets as a measure of their success. Karajan's natural gifts and personal eccentricities soon lent themselves to multimedia publicity – his aristocratic origins, his film-star good looks, his predilection for Porsche sports cars, his command of private airplanes and ocean yachts, multiple residences in Berlin, Vienna, and Salzburg. In Germany, he had no equals in what became polished show business of the highest order, with the similarly attractive Schwarzkopf keeping a lower profile. They were often joined by the up-and-coming young baritone Dietrich Fischer-Dieskau.

Often found in Karajan's programs were the works of Richard Strauss, whose music was also fetishized throughout, whereas his one-time embittered rival Hans Pfitzner's works were less often played.[220] The Strauss cult, like that around Karajan, was supported by a phalanx of pre-1945 established musicians, many of them active in the Third Reich, such as Schwarzkopf, the sopranos Tiana Lemnitz and Erna Berger, the pianists Elly Ney, Wilhelm Backhaus, Walter Gieseking, and Wilhelm Kempff, the flautist Gustav Scheck, and the cellist Ludwig Hoelscher. Among conductors, Karl Böhm was the most Strauss-centered musician.[221] The Strauss family attempted to extend the aura of the great Richard by passing the scepter, vicariously, to his grandson Richard junior, who had trained as an intendant under Heinz Tietjen in Berlin. In August 1952 he directed the premiere of *Die Liebe der Danae*, completed more than twelve years earlier, in Salzburg, under the baton of Strauss's old devotee Clemens Krauss, but it crashed.[222]

The conventional, culinary repertory concert and opera offerings in most German music halls, like Karajan in an extreme embodiment, signified the growing material comforts, the feelings of security and self-satisfaction, in Adenauer's republic.[223] Classical-music programs all over West Germany were exchangeable; the emphasis was on large-scale and showy productions, not intimate chamber music or song recitals.[224]

West Germany's traditional Modernists continued to flourish: Carl Orff, Werner Egk, Boris Blacher, and Gottfried von Einem. They had grown with the regional cultural establishments, affluently supported. Apart from performances, this guaranteed them posts at conservatories and opera houses. Their music remained safely tonal, with the most spectacular advances made, often disingenuously, in the area of rhythm, such as the variable meters in Blacher's work.[225] Newcomer Rolf Liebermann, scion of a wealthy Jewish family from Zurich, assumed the intendant's job at the Hamburg Opera in 1957. As a composer, he combined extended harmonies with elements of jazz – incorporating arranged big-band jazz passages, thereby giving up jazz's most important quality, individual improvisation.[226] There is proof that Orff much disliked jazz, on top of his disdain for the work of younger modern-music pioneers, such as Henze.[227] This sentiment was shared by Egk, and Henze's colleague Karlheinz Stockhausen smarted from Egk's having published a damning verdict regarding new experimental music: it belonged, stated Egk, "behind closed doors."[228]

Behind closed doors? That sounded like Herbert Eimert's electronic-music studio at the NWDR/WDR radio station in Cologne. The Rhenish metropole turned out to be a hotbed of modern-music experimentation. Not so Munich, where attempts at modern music under Karl Amadeus Hartmann were threatened, and not so in Hesse, where "modern music was disappearing from programs everywhere," except for Darmstadt's music festival. [229] Krefeld connected only sporadically to contemporary developments; the names of modern composers there were "missing."[230]

Radio stations such as Cologne's, which had public funds, could dissolve this dilemma, with modern-music festivals such as the revived Donaueschingen event tied to SWF Baden-Baden ("Tage für zeitgenössische Musik"), and Darmstadt's to Hessischer Rundfunk in Frankfurt. Hartmann's "Musica Viva" series survived because it was supported by Bayrischer Rundfunk in Munich, and Hamburg's NWDR/NDR had its own modern-music series, "das neue werk." This of course meant that station managers had to be in an avant-garde state of mind, as was the Social Democrat Hanns Hartmann (no relation to the composer), the intendant of the Cologne station, especially after its separation from Hamburg's in January 1956.[231]

The Cologne station was exemplary, even if Hanns Hartmann was, at various times, joined by like-minded culture brokers in the city – for instance, with reservations, Generalmusikdirektor Günter Wand of the Gürzenich Symphony and Heinz Schröter, after 1957 at the Musikhochschule. Others were the administrators of the gallery Der Spiegel, of the Kölner Gesellschaft für Neue Musik, and the painter Mary Bauermeister with her studio, where avant-garde artists of many colors congregated toward the end of the decade.[232]

With Hindemith being declared passé, the musicians of the Darmstadt event spent the early 1950s in a celebration of Schoenberg. In July 1951, eleven days before his death, his "Dance around the Golden Calf" from his opera *Moses und Aron* was premiered.[233] From 1953 to 1960 intimate interpreters of his music performed there – Schoenberg's brother-in-law Rudolf Kolisch on violin and his favorite pianist Eduard Steuermann.[234] All students now sought to emulate Schoenberg.[235] But by the peculiar dialectics of Darmstadt, his popularity was matched, in around 1953, by that of his student Anton von Webern (who had died in 1945), after a short-lasting fad for Béla Bartók. Bartók's "bent notes" and "wrong notes" alone, jests Alex Ross, qualified him as a Modernist, but he did in fact write a piano concerto with a twelve-note-row theme.[236]

As explained by Paul Griffiths, in Schoenberg's method of serialist composing, which he had made official in 1923, the constructed series was the result of an ordering of the twelve notes of the equal-tempered chromatic scale. The series could exist at twelve transpositional levels, all of which were considered as forms of the same series. Also included were the inversion, the retrograde, and the retrograde inversion at each transpositional stage in the complex, so that the series could be used in any of forty-eight forms.[237] In principally adhering to this method, Schoenberg's student Webern modified it and set accents of his own. In his early work he was fond of writing aphorisms of only a few bars, rendering his style pointillistic; he was always prone to use intervals of semitones; and he tended to divide musical lines among several dissimilar instruments and divergent registers, forming an angular sound and constantly shifting color. Without ever pronouncing rhythm and meter, he also had a propensity for canon and was fascinated by symmetry.[238]

In Darmstadt, Webern's compositions were performed after 1950, and fledgling composers incorporated his methodology into their work. Already in 1948 Peter Stadlen had played his Piano Variations, opus 27 – a first for Germany; his *Fünf Lieder*, opus 4 were featured a year later. In 1951, Webern's work, *Fünf Canons*, opus 16, was featured and Adorno spoke of him in a lecture.[239] In 1953 a musical retrospective was a highlight of Webern festivities; he would have been seventy. Thereafter an international group of young composers extended Webern's serialism, not without critical review; yet what intrigued them was his mathematical brilliance and his reductionist approach. They were Armin Schibler from Switzerland, Pierre Boulez from France, Bruno Maderna and Luigi Nono from Italy, and Karlheinz Stockhausen from Germany.[240]

From this group, Boulez, Nono and Stockhausen became instrumental in guiding the future Darmstadt programs. The 1925-born Boulez had studied harmony with Olivier Messiaen and regarded composing as a form of aesthetic research along scientific, logical lines. This led him to atonality. Later he was closely influenced by Schoenberg and the mature Webern. As a conductor, he encountered Darius Milhaud, Francis Poulenc, and Arthur Honegger. In around 1950, Boulez sought to develop a technique "whereby the principles of serialism could be made to govern the timbre, duration, and intensity of each sound, as well as its pitch." He wrote *Polyphonie X* for eighteen soloists, performed at Donaueschingen in 1951. A year later, Boulez's Second Sonata was played at Darmstadt. After famously having declared the death of Schoenberg, Boulez composed a more markedly serialist work, *Le marteau sans maître*, for a contralto soloist intoning three poems by former French Resistance fighter René Char, and for flute, strings, and percussion, recalling "the cellular style of late Webern." This signature piece was characterized as being cultivated by "a certain rhythmic monotony, emphasized by his use of the percussion in some of the movements. This is offset by certain tempo transitions, passages of broadly improvisatory melodic style, and – not least of all – the fascination of exotic instrumental coloring, underlining the work's basically static conception." Owing to its success and despite considerable notoriety because of his offensive prejudgements, Boulez began to teach at Darmstadt annually from 1954 to 1956, and then again between 1960 and 1965.[241]

Messiaen himself appeared in Darmstadt in 1949 and 1952, presenting his piano étude *Mode de valeurs et d'insités*, which demonstrated multidimensional serial techniques.[242] He impressed all the young composers there. Luigi Nono from Venice had his first work, *Variations* after Schoenberg, conducted by Hermann Scherchen in 1950 and then returned until 1960. He had been a student of Bruno Maderna, who arrived in 1954. Signally, Nono married Arnold Schoenberg's daughter Nuria in 1955. Taking cues from Messiaen and Webern, he enlarged upon serialism. For him, beyond merely a thematic function, it now had to become "the basis for the entire composition, determining not only pitch but also tempo, duration, register, dynamic and articulation."[243]

The leading light among those Young Turks was Karlheinz Stockhausen, born in 1928. A graduate of the Cologne Musikhochschule, he attended the summer course in August 1951. After meeting the Belgian Karel Goeyvaerts there he became intrigued with the older Messiaen when he listened to his recorded *Mode de valeurs et d'insités*. The next year, while studying with Messiaen in Paris, Boulez introduced him to the Parisian avant-garde. In March 1953, Stockhausen was with Herbert Eimert's electronic-music studio in Cologne, commencing Darmstadt instruction in 1956. He managed to invite the American composer John Cage in 1958, resulting in yet another paradigm shift.[244]

In 1954, Cage had already visited the Donaueschingen festival with pianist David Tudor, who could read all the new, complicated notations at great speed. Laughed at in Donaueschingen, their reception at the Cologne studio, where Stockhausen was waiting, had been marginally better. This pupil of Schoenberg had extended the master's dodecaphonic structure in unexpected ways. In the late 1930s he included live sounds not considered musical, such as from tin cans, and he was contemplating new sonic possibilities employing electronics. In 1938 the first piece with prepared piano was performed, with manipulated strings. In the last half of the 1940s, Cage was influenced by East Asian thought and picked up on silence as part of a musical soundscape. Impressed by Webern, in the early 1950s he reached a stage where "acoustic silence changed from being an absence of sound to being an absence of intended sound." As with his New York acquaintance Jackson Pollock who worked randomly, chance became a deliberate element of Cage's musical writing. He produced sounds that were marked by ambiguous notations, a state he called "indeterminacy." What has subsequently been termed "aleatoric" now described music created spontaneously and by chance. In Darmstadt in 1958 both Cage and Tudor gave concerts – using pianos, radios, and hammers – and directed seminars on experimental sound.[245]

Next to Darmstadt, the Donaueschingen festival to the south preferred more digestible types of modern music, such as Liebermann's showy big-band jazz concerto. Cologne's electronic studio to the north, on the other hand, became a serious catalyst for the musical avant-garde. It was founded by Herbert Eimert, originally a journalist who had had run-ins with the Nazis. As a Schoenberg disciple, he had written a book about the master, but finding him doctrinaire, had turned to Webern. In 1951 tape recorders for experimentation with tonal frequencies made electronic studios possible. Eimert had encouraged Stockhausen to visit Darmstadt. By 1953 both collaborated over tape recorders in Cologne. Here the Webernian serial model was modified by the addition of new sounds artificially generated through synthetic manipulation. New electronic sound makers facilitated the control of overtones, governing timbre and dynamics, and durations and intensities of new sinus tones. Whereas Eimert desired concentration merely on electronic music, Stockhausen wanted that together with conventional tone production. His *Gesang der Jünglinge* (*Song of the Youths*) of 1955–6 is one striking example. Here a twelve-year-old boy's voice, chanting a biblical text, was added to electronically produced signals after serialist-inspired manipulation.[246]

The charismatic Stockhausen and the more studious Henze, born 1926, along with Bernd Alois Zimmermann were the most significant figures of the West German Modern Music scene in the 1950s, even if Henze left for Italy in 1953, returning only sporadically. His artistic origins were in strong reaction to tendencies in the Third Reich. As so many village primary-school teachers, his father became a fanatical Nazi. Hitler Youth service for Hans Werner, who had started piano lessons and composing, was odious, and he was picked on by his peers. He witnessed with shame the desecration of Jewish synagogues around Bielefeld in 1938 and befriended French POWs during the war. In 1943 he was allowed to enter the Staatsmusikschule in Brunswick, studying piano and theory, and acquainting himself with the music of Stravinsky and, clandestinely, Hindemith. He listened at night to the BBC, as it broadcast forbidden music. There was whispering about concentration camps and mass executions on the Eastern Front. In early 1944, when Henze was serving as a radio operator with a tank squad, his father, now in the Wehrmacht, accused him of indulging in "Jewish Christmas symbolism." Eventually Henze landed in a British POW camp, returning to his war-widowed mother in August 1945.[247]

His early-discovered love of music fatefully determined the course of Henze's life, as did the conflict with his father, specific Nazi situations, and, finally, his homosexuality, a crime in the Hitler Youth and Wehrmacht. In music, Henze received composition instruction from Fortner in Heidelberg, from 1946 to 1948. Fortner not only introduced him to dodecaphony, but also took him to the first Darmstadt event in September 1946. There, also impressed with Stravinsky and Bartók, Henze conducted Hindemith and had his own chamber concerto performed, a neo-Baroque piece. After Hindemith, he fell under Schoenberg's spell until he tired of him too, in 1950. He was returning to a more conventional, tonal, approach. This led to ballets and theater scores and, later, his signature operas. Moving around much and having assimilated many musical styles, what he had arrived at musically by 1953 was a "lyrical, tonally oriented 12-note idiom." In the spring of 1953 Henze left Germany for Ischia, Italy.[248]

Part of the reason for this was Henze's view of much in the FRG as extensions of the Third Reich, which he identified with his father. He regarded especially the New Music institutions around Baden-Baden as pretentious, not-so-secret bulwarks of fascistic restoration. Donaueschingen director Heinrich Strobel, with a Nazi-sanctioned career in Occupied France behind him, he singled out. For Henze Strobel personified cultural power brokers who were chauvinists with patronizing attitudes, not really willing to remake a tainted Germany; instead, they were perceived as puppets of a sham-democratic Adenauer republic.[249] What dismayed Henze in particular about such people was their sexual and moral turpitude coupled with strong homophobic tendencies. Hatred of homosexuals in post-Nazi Germany was responsible for his own "fascism trauma" and was the main cause of his move to Italy.[250]

Two years younger, Stockhausen's hatred of the Nazi system was equally strong but more religiously fortified, for he was a pious Catholic. Demonologically, he once referred to the dictator as "obsessed by the Devil." His motivation, too, was personal: his mother Gertrud, mentally ill and housed in an asylum since 1932, was murdered there by the Nazis during "euthanasia" actions in 1941. The Nazis, with his party-member father's support, oppressed his religious freedom, causing life-long filial resentment. In 1944, Stockhausen, inducted into a field hospital just behind the Western Front, again and again after enemy raids saw "trees covered with pieces of human flesh."[251]

In 1951, Stockhausen, with a major in piano, graduated from the Musikhochschule in Cologne, the same year that he was introduced to serialism. Impressed, at Darmstadt, by Messiaen and Goeyvaerts beyond Schoenberg and Webern, Stockhausen composed, as his first work of significance, *Kreuzspiel* (*Cross Play*). This was a serial chamber piece, "an abstract musical process," according to the London *Times*, "played out by the unusual ensemble of piano, oboe, bass clarinet and three percussionists."[252] Here, instrumentation, pitch register and intensity, melodic form, and time duration were employed so that the individual musical segments assumed an almost geometric level of organization. The premiere of *Kreuzspiel* at Darmstadt in 1952 was so originally stunning that it caused a raising of eyebrows. Then, after having worked with Eimert in Cologne, Stockhausen composed *Elektronische Studien, I* and *II* (1953–4), deploying artificially produced sounds using sophisticated tape-recorder techniques. The next important piece was *Gesang der Jünglinge* in 1955–6. In these logically conceived electronic works Stockhausen saw embodied a divine order that for him was the very opposite of National Socialist-governed chaos and willful infractions of law.[253]

The Darmstadt international summer courses were born as an act of symbolic resistance against totalitarianism, in particular the Nazi dictatorship that had opposed individual artistic freedom, with its imperative to break new creative ground. It included in its ranks, of faculty as of students, childhood victims of the Nazi state such as Henze and Stockhausen and mature resistance fighters such as Helmut Roloff and Luigi Nono. Works of anti-Nazis were favored, examples being the œuvre of Messiaen, who had spent time in a Nazi POW camp, and the poetry, set to music, of René Char. Hindemith, who was then perceived as a victim of Nazism, was an early composer favorite; so were Schoenberg and Bartók, both of whom became refugees in the United States. The half-Jewish Theodor W. Adorno, a former exile, became predominant as a theoretician in Darmstadt. That Webern had been close to the Nazi movement was generally not known.

And it may not have mattered, because the festival organizers could not help compromising themselves in other ways. For one, early on they tolerated on their staff too many musicians who had flourished in the Third Reich – to mention only Bruno Stürmer – alongside those who had been opposed to it. Henze later said that there was a group of ex-Nazis whose names he could not remember. But he was hypocritical, for his own mentor Fortner was among those.[254]

Secondly, the cult about musical styles that were in themselves invariably fixed was only seemingly dynamic; it led to standstill. The constant, consecutive re-evaluations of modern composers, short of being enlightening in the long run, were confounding in the short run. What ought to have been a dialectic process turned out to be a course of musical-regime changes based on ever-mutating doctrinal interpretations of style, from Hindemith with his neo-Baroque whim to Schoenberg with his dodecaphony, from there to Webern and a different serialism, and then to the new generation of serialists and electronic composers such as Stockhausen. During any new composer's vogue, dogma reigned that one could not contravene. This made for an authoritarian aura of the kind one had initially wanted to defeat. One of the harshest expressions used by detractors during the 1950s against the Darmstadt courses, institutionalized as the Darmstadt School, was "dodecaphonic police."[255]

The worst offender in that respect was Adorno with his Schoenberg obsession, who lectured at Darmstadt consistently over the years after his return to Germany in 1949. In this era of the Cold War, during 1953 he was quick to chastise eastern European regimes for their adherence to anti-Formalist suppression of "modern art," an attitude he correctly likened to Goebbels's abusive cultural policy. Instead, Adorno saw Schoenberg at the end of an evolution from Bach's *Art of Fugue* to Beethoven's last quartets, whose achievement it had been "to overcome the inertia of formulaic polyphony through the artful fitting together of simultaneous voices." But at the same time Adorno exercised censure against anyone not keeping to the Schoenbergian master concept, and he singled out for special punishment the modern (and, significantly, not German) composers Nadia Boulanger, Dmitri Shostakovich, and Benjamin Britten, whose German premiere of *Peter Grimes* Henze, for one, had much enjoyed in Mannheim in 1946.[256]

Henze's flight to the Italian island of Ischia was as much brought about by disenchantment with German conditions in general as by what he called the "Darmstadt technocrats" in particular. To him they, always self-referential during Darmstadt's music routines, were little potentates who played themselves up in internecine warfare, hurting weaker ones in their way. Indeed, fierce battles of entitlement were waged. It was always a situation where, under the capable if unexciting festival director Wolfgang Steinecke, a Darmstadt municipal employee, Stockhausen went against Boulez, to whom he had ascribed a "satanic joy for destruction" even from their time in Paris, or Boulez affronted Henze. Stockhausen could not stand Henze, allegedly because of his relatively early return to a conventional tonal order, but in reality because he feared his rivalry: they were competing for ultimate recognition. Stockhausen also alienated the serialist Bernd Alois Zimmermann, who was less often in Darmstadt than in the Cologne studio, where Stockhausen could set upon him more easily. Not least because he felt marginalized as a composer, Zimmermann eventually committed suicide. At the end of the 1950s Henze was shunned even by his old friend Nono, and Nono himself left Darmstadt in disgust after Cage's last of three lectures in 1958, when a departure from European music traditions had been counseled.[257]

Therefore, for all the fructifying processes it instantiated to further modern music in Germany, the classic Darmstadt phenomenon lasted only through the 1950s, steadily losing influence, especially as an internationally inspirational venue of exchange. Similar to the Kassel documenta but for different reasons, it could not lay claim to having planted the seeds for new developments in Modernism, as the Bauhaus had in the 1920s. By the beginning of the 1960s, it appeared to have lost its creative nimbus, even though the number of participants, active and passive, had increased from 198 in 1950 to 343 in 1960. The resonance was scant: any Modernist music was banished to the few midnight programs that radio stations in the land thought they could take a chance on. With the ongoing rise of consumerism, the festival's agents were to become commercialized and its products commodified. By the 1980s it had turned into "a sleek establishment," with prestigious music publishers, automobile manufacturers, and radio and television stations acting as sponsors. If there was a gradual death of the avant-garde, Darmstadt could have personified it.[258]

◆ ◆ ◆

Meanwhile, since 1951, a different kind of innovation was under way in Bayreuth. It was nothing less than a remake of the Wagner festival.

Recently it has been said that since its inception in 1876, the Bayreuth festival had always acted as "a seismograph of German sensibilities," indicative of the period that produced it.[259] This was certainly true under Hitler. Considering Wagner's often-ominously portentous plots, with their artistically overwrought sets, artists acting and singing dramatically, and conductors of flamboyance and gravitas, the festival exemplified the Third Reich's claim to political and cultural world domination. In 1933 "what had been a Wagner festival became an outright Hitler festival," writes Frederic Spotts.[260] A few of Wagner's operas were used by the Nazis to teach the Germans political lessons. *Die Meistersinger von Nürnberg* was especially adaptable; in Berlin, for example, the third-act finale resembled a party rally. Moreover, after 1938, with all festival performances dedicated exclusively to the Wehrmacht, Bayreuth had sought to boost the moral support of aggressive warriors.[261]

Winifred Wagner's oldest son Wieland, born in 1917, assumed artistic responsibilities for reconstruction in 1951. A Hitler favorite during the Third Reich, showered with expensive gifts and exempted from war service, he had joined the party in 1938. He had aided his mother, Heinz Tietjen, and Emil Preetorius in running the festival from a design perspective. While his younger brother Wolfgang was wounded on the Eastern Front, Wieland assumed the deputy directorship of a concentration-camp satellite in Bayreuth in September 1944. From nearby Flossenbürg, thirty-eight inmates had been sent to the Bayreuth camp to help construct props for the stage. In day-to-day operations they were primarily supervised by Wieland's brother-in-law Bodo Lafferentz, a lieutenant-colonel in the SS. Here inmates were beaten, suffered from acute malnutrition, and were always on the verge of being shipped back to Flossenbürg, sometimes with fatal results.[262]

During the war, the opera house was largely undamaged. On April 14, 1945, American troops captured a bombed-out Bayreuth, entered the Festspielhaus, and, to Winifred Wagner's horror, played jazz on the grand piano. Black GIs were quartered in the residence. Wieland unsurprisingly decided to stay at the summer house in Nussdorf on Lake Constance, soon under French military rule with its lackadaisical permissiveness instead of the sterner denazification procedures under OMGUS in Bayreuth.[263]

The tasks ahead now were to denazify Bayreuth and plan for a new opening. Since Wolfgang Wagner had never joined the Nazis he was scot-free, but his mother was tried by German courts until December 1948 and ultimately classified as a minor offender, incurring a nominal fine. But she did have to agree to leave the festival business to her sons, and so she retired to a private life in Bayreuth and many more years of professing her admiration for Hitler. Deploring the new democratic establishment, she would enjoy the support of prominent ex-Nazis and have tea with Rudolf Hess's wife Ilse and Göring's widow Emmy. When Wieland Wagner was politically exonerated in late 1948, the path was cleared for a reorganization under the two brothers.[264]

The idea of a new beginning in Bayreuth was predicated on a determination to separate from, and repudiate, Nazism. Hence Wolfgang concentrated on management and Wieland on artistic direction. When Wolfgang, too, attempted opera production, he was not altogether successful. With his pre-1945 experience to guide him, Wieland was bent on demystifying the content and format of the festival: "He now wanted to emphasize human beings instead of Germanic heroes and gods," explains Hans Rudolf Vaget.[265] By keeping quiet on anything Nazi, he evidently thought that his reformation of the performances would usher in a new festival era and permanently undo that baleful history. But in so far as the Hitler style of Bayreuth had also been, in many facets, a copy or continuation of the traditional pre-1933 template, Wieland could have been under no illusion that he was abrogating deep-seated Wagner traditions, precious to many loyal devotees.

One of the first changes he implemented was to place the music ahead of the acting. But it was not the old Wagnerian style of musicianship that Wieland desired. His initial choice for conductor had been Clemens Krauss, who would guarantee a drier sound rather than the symphonic massiveness a Knappertsbusch churned out, but Krauss died unexpectedly. And so the tasteful Karajan conducted, along with the strident Knappertsbusch, during the first season of 1951. Making for a lean sound without "gluey pathos" and supported by excellent, disciplined choirs, Karajan came close to what Wieland had in mind. He was aided by younger singers who eschewed sentimental wobbling in singing. Wieland had taken a hand in their selection – the Hungarian-American Astrid Varnay and Austrian Leonie Rysanek, both dramatic sopranos, the German heldentenor Wolfgang Windgassen, and the American bass-baritone George London, among others, internationally. Many, such as Windgassen and Rysanek, returned to future seasons, in order to help cultivate the new, more cerebral, New Bayreuth musical style. The conservative Knappertsbusch found this and new pared-down stagings so unacceptable that he withdrew for 1953, after the second season. So did Karajan, but permanently, because of stylistic objections of his own.[266]

Wieland Wagner commenced the 1951 season with a production of *Parsifal, Der Ring des Nibelungen*, and *Meistersinger*. As music critic Werner Oehlmann observed, the "massive, awkward singer fortresses" of yesteryear had been replaced by "a slender and youthful Brünnhilde, a racy, passionate Isolde, a Wotan, whose godly highness and power were credible." Wieland produced the first two operas, whereas *Meistersinger* was fitted and staged by older associates. In *Parsifal*, instead of overstuffed stage props and constructions, he used a somewhat elevated, perfectly round disk as a stage, which was otherwise empty. Four giant, dark-golden pillars loomed in the background, representing the Grail Temple. There was much play with light and shadow, Rembrandt-style, which was to become a signature device of Wieland's in future. This was the beginning of his permutation from a denizen of the "temple" to one of the "workshop," as his daughter, the theater expert Nike Wagner, has described the events in retrospect.[267]

Signature stagings by Wieland Wagner to follow were *Tannhäuser* in 1954, with Expressionist tableaux visibly indebted to Klee. His own *Meistersinger* version arrived in 1956, full of abstractions and without cloying Nuremberg references – a *Meistersinger von Nürnberg* play without

Nuremberg. Outstanding was the dry oratorio treatment of the score, reminiscent of Orff s shapings, which Wieland Wagner always admired. Here the "Wach Auf" chorus was a tender morning song, as his grandfather might have wanted to compose for his old friend Mathilde Wesendonck. In his *Lohengrin* of 1958 there were no sets; this was a translucent affair with elegant decor – blue-in-silver, in daughter Nike's memory, allusions to Greek tragedy, and, much like *Parsifal,* stage as imaginary space. In *The Flying Dutchman* a year later, Wieland Wagner turned to a postmodernist Realism, using his grandfather's original, harsher Dresden score and flashy colors for costumes and sets.[268]

Yet still there were factors at play in Bayreuth that made the transformation, over time, not quite believable. For one, Wieland Wagner was strategically aided by personnel possessed of a Nazi past, such as the able lighting expert Paul Eberhardt and the experienced bookkeeper Heinrich Sesselmann.[269] More serious was the aesthetic predominance, if vicarious, of former Nazi-beholden artists such as the sculptor Arno Breker whose busts of Liszt and Richard and Cosima Wagner were installed and who was later commissioned to portray Winifred Wagner, customarily collecting large fees.[270] By recusing himself from the production of the first *Meistersinger* in 1951 Wieland Wagner relinquished control over potential Nazi influences, which predictably occurred; in his place, three artists who were not beyond suspicion took over.[271] One was the artistic director, Rudolf Otto Hartmann (no relation to Wolfgang Amadeus or Hanns), who had worked with Furtwängler in a 1943 staging of a Nazi-saturated *Meistersinger* opera. The other was Gertrud Wagner's, Wieland's wife's, uncle, the architect Hans Carl Reissinger, who was still beholden to voluptuous, excessive Nazi-type productions as a stage designer and whom critic Karl Heinz Ruppel now attested an "anodyne Naturalism bereft of imagination."[272] Quite up front were the three principal conductors of the first hour: Furtwängler with the introductory Ninth Symphony, Karajan, and Knappertsbusch – all of them once prominent in the Third Reich. After 1953, Knappertsbusch returned in the mid-1960s, to be touted by Wieland Wagner later as "the chief conductor of the Bayreuth festival since 1951." Ostensibly, the polished Karajan had left after 1952 over the new progressive style, rather than helping to institutionalize it; behind the scenes egos were clashing.[273] In 1951 as well, as a sign of fundamental change, the novelty of program booklets was introduced, with contents notoriously written by old Nazi Wagnerites and unrecon-structed anti-Semites.[274] Worst, when paying guests arrived in Bayreuth, they became aware of copies of Richard Wagner's nefarious screed *Judaism in Music* (1869) in a prominent bookstore and, walking up to the Festspielhaus, were offered neo-Nazi newspapers for purchase.[275]

Other circumstances left critics unconvinced. For all of Wieland Wagner's placing the music first, its quality was not consistent, owing mostly to changing conductors over time. Knappertsbusch's style just did not fit an avant-garde approach, and some conductors were judged as not to make the grade.[276] Moreover, the festival audience largely remained the same, showing off the wealth and power of the establishment, much of it still in synch with Nazism. To the extent that malicious tongues, for instance those in East Germany, were able to pronounce – vastly exaggerating – that much in Adenauer's society constituted a prolongation of the National Socialist era, its more sophisticated representatives could be said to be congregating here. Indeed, the forceful opposition of dyed-in-the-wool Wagnerites (and Nazis) to Wieland Wagner's experimental productions was long-lived and not easily digested by the brothers.[277]

Wieland had a problem with that, but also with his personal and profes-sional strategy of undoing the Nazism within himself by shrouding it in silence. He never talked about his experience under Hitler and never said, outright, that a certain move of his directorship was meant as an antidote to Nazi aesthetics.[278] Ideally, as became ever more obvious by the end of the 1950s, he wanted to get away from Bayreuth and altogether renounce anything that had to do not only with Nazism, but also with Richard Wagner himself.[279] This did not come to pass. By 1961 he had reversed his earlier priorities, actors and the stage now ruling over music again. His brother Wolfgang interfered increasingly with ho-hum productions of his own, and when the African American soprano Grace Bumbry was a Black Venus in that summer's *Tannhäuser* it created a scandal with the unendingly reactionary audience.[280] New Bayreuth had failed, and Wieland Wagner died from cancer in 1966. He was forty-nine.

◆ ◆ ◆

Jazz music became important in 1950s West Germany as yet another artistic articulation of anti-Nazism. The Nazis had opposed jazz in Germany, although it was expressly forbidden only on the airwaves, as of October 1935.[281] Between 1933 and 1945 adherence to a jazz culture for many Germans, especially in cosmopolitan Berlin and Hamburg, became an expression of protest against Hitler's totalitarian order. For it was remembered that originally jazz was the creation of two ethnic entities who, as racial minorities, were shunned and eventually persecuted in the Third Reich: Black people and Jews. Not all jazz musicians in Nazi Germany saw things that way, because many kept entertaining men and women and later the troops in clubs, and even joined Goebbels in a propaganda effort against the British. One who did so was the Munich drummer Fritz (Freddie) Brocksieper, who with a formation called Charlie and His Orchestra helped support the infamous anti-British radio personality "Lord Haw Haw" in a Berlin broadcast series during the 1940s.[282]

Brocksieper himself was of partly Jewish descent and, as far as he was concerned, happy to be allowed to continue playing the music he loved. Not indicted after May 1945, he went on entertaining fans mostly in the greater Munich area well into the 1980s, accompanying visiting American musicians such as the trumpeters Harry James and Dizzy Gillespie.[283] I very briefly played with his small group in a club, after I had arrived in Munich-Schwabing in the fall of 1959. After classical piano, I had picked up the vibraphone as an intriguing instrument in my late teens in Toronto, having arrived there from Krefeld with my family in March 1953. Considering jazz more interesting than the classics, I took lessons in harmony and vibraphone, lastly with Peter Appleyard, originally from Britain. Based in Toronto but increasingly in New York, Appleyard played with the likes of Zoot Sims and Benny Goodman. His style was advanced swing reminiscent of Lionel Hampton and only slightly touched by the developing bebop mode, which I then adopted, as I kept playing with groups in Canada and Europe on the side.[284]

In Schwabing, I did less university study than jazz work in various bohemian clubs at night, but also for the U.S. forces, in Munich itself and on bases close by. Having recently acquired Canadian citizenship, I called myself "Mike Carter," in order not to compromise my Bonn scholarship and Munich University student status, and, of course, one had to have a *nom de guerre*! I immersed myself in the Schwabing bohemian subculture, consorting with promising painters such as Joe Müller, students of the actors' academies, and various musicians, including some interested in the new electronic mode of composing. Few of the Schwabing scene's habitués were from Munich; its jazz impresario (and my "agent") was Youssuf, an Algerian Arab who resided illegally in the city, trying to escape from the North African colonial war. In February 1960 I played, along with other jazz musicians, in a benefit concert at the Deutsches Museum, not far from where Jewish DPs had set up vendor stalls ten years earlier. The next day, Monika Schlecht, Joachim Kaiser's colleague at *SZ*, emphasized the international makeup of the event in her review: "The two Blacks Bell and Harrison, who serve in the Munich detachment of the Armed Forces, performed on conga and bongo drums, the bearded Canadian Mike Carter swirled fire-red mallets on the vibraphone. The guitarist Ira Kriss is from the United States, the pianist Knut Haugsoen from Norway and the dark-haired Morris Gawronsky, who caused veritable fireworks on his drumset, is South African."[285]

The Munich clubs Brocksieper performed at were the Studio 15 and Klub Reitschule, Berlin had the Badewanne, Frankfurt the Domicile du Jazz, and Heidelberg, which was U.S. army headquarters, the Stardust Club for GIs, as well as Cave 54, West Germany's oldest jazz hangout. As a rule, American musicians played there, drafted professionals such as Bell and Harrison who were stationed in Germany and, increasingly, visiting artists such as Hampton and Goodman, the altoist Leo Wright, and the pianist Cedar Walton.[286] They were emulated by admiring young Germans who eventually formed their own groups. These were joined by older jazz veterans from the Third Reich such as Brocksieper, the trumpeter Charly Tabor, and the trombonist Walter Dobschinsky.[287] Frankfurt featured Emil Mangelsdorff on alto, born in 1925, who had returned from Russian captivity in 1949, and his younger brother Albert, who soon mastered the trombone. Together with reed players Hans Koller and Joki Freund, the Hungarian guitarist Attila Zoller, and pianist Jutta Hipp, who had escaped from Communist-ruled Leipzig, they formed a group heavily into bebop and the emerging U.S. West Coast cool jazz.[288] In Berlin, the conservatory graduate Michael Naura led a combo on piano, with Wolfgang Schlüter on vibes. They were fascinated by George Shearing's laid-back quintet sound, which that blind, originally British, pianist had made world famous.[289]

The Germans were awed by visiting American musicians and became quick studies, learning by listening and observing closely and copying them, a riff here and a lick there; the Americans gladly showed off their expertise.

These Germans had much to learn. When I later played in Heidelberg with the young American pianist Barney McClure, who back home in decades to follow would accompany vibraphonist Milt Jackson and other greats, he noticed, particularly of many drummers, "that they didn't 'swing.'"[290] (Later, when into the 1990s I occasionally played with the Emil Mangelsdorff Quartet and other groups, I was not aware of such deficiency.[291]) All the same, when the tenor saxophonist Stan Getz arrived from Denmark for a weekend at the Tarantel club on Schwabing's Feilitzschstrasse where I sometimes played, he used the rhythm section (piano, bass, drums) anchored there, including, it is true, an American drummer, and everybody took it for not just a party, but also a serious lesson in music.[292]

German-performed jazz in those clubs and some concert halls was complemented by what was featured on radio stations and an ever-growing number of jazz festivals. The American and British AFN and BFN networks had already broadcast jazz regularly since the late 1940s, and now their presentations became more entrenched. There was "Luncheon in Munich" and "Bouncing in Bavaria" on AFN, which also sponsored live shows with visiting American stars. U.S. radio administrators such as Johnny Vrotsos, the AFN program director, established close ties with Frankfurt's Hot Club. As they did for experimental modern music, German stations also made jazz their concern, especially at night. Joachim Ernst Berendt became a fixture at SWF Baden-Baden while Dietrich Schulz-Köhn made broadcast history as "Doctor Jazz" at Radio Cologne. Often their shows had a didactic streak, as did Dieter Zimmerle's at Radio Stuttgart, who with a "Masters of Jazz" series aimed to teach the distinction between mere dance music (as especially commercialized swing tended to lend itself to) and purebred jazz. The broadcasters also nurtured big bands such as Kurt Edelhagen's, first in Baden-Baden and then Cologne, and the Third Reich veteran Erwin Lehn's at Radio Stuttgart.[293] All of this was supported by the jazz programs of the Amerikahäuser (which were themselves assisted by the U.S. State Department and the CIA). Jazz festivals, which in turn spawned a growing recording industry, tended to be supported by local hot clubs, but Berendt and Schulz-Köhn were also early promoters of such events. The archetypal Deutsche Jazz-Festival in Frankfurt in 1951 was attended by 10,000 German fans, most of them adherents to the older, pre-swing, Dixieland style.[294]

But as a new art in the culture of West Germany, there was a lot that was not right with the music of jazz, and not just in the view of conservatives. Even enlightened critics and musicologists could not agree whether there was any value to it and doubted its capacity for enriching the post-1945 experimental artistic spectrum. Early on, there were negative reactions to jazz from men who, originally influenced by Nazi propaganda, disliked it as a token of Americanism and, worse, Black and Jewish influences. In 1948, during its reactionary era, Werner Höfer had published a critique of the emergent bebop in *Die Zeit*. Prejudiced, Höfer wrote that melody "mattered little," that, with the major and minor modes "liquidated," there were only "dissonances" and that "the simple, danceable rhythms" were "eliminated."[295] A year later a *Spiegel* reporter carped that bebop was bereft of music, contained only rhythm, and violated every rule of conventional harmony. Its improvisations were grotesque and beyond bounds; the most charitable thing one could say about it was that, like Schoenberg's serialism, it treated every one of the twelve notes as equal.[296]

The reference to Schoenberg was ironic, for neither his serialist compositions nor bebop improvisations were bereft of music or violated conventional harmony – they merely expanded the latter. Yet of all people who could have provided enlightenment, it was Adorno, the pioneer of Modernism currently propping up Schoenberg, who was putting down jazz. In so doing, he was building on preconceptions he had formed already since the end of the 1920s, when he had denied jazz recognition as an original art form and had contemptuously relegated it to the arts and crafts.[297] In 1953 he was writing that jazz, be it swing or bebop, was characterized by "the simplest melodic, harmonic, metric and formal structure," that it was monotonous and never-changing, that, instead of spontaneous improvisation, there was machine-like reproduction of memorized content, that musical patterns were ever repetitive. It needed a mass-audience base, and with or without it, it was resonant of impotence.[298]

The expert in Germany who was, in principle, in a position to contradict Adorno was Berendt in Baden-Baden, but his arguments were unconvincing. Steeped deeply in European traditions, like most critics and many musicians who approached jazz in Germany, he explained its genesis from the point of view of a Germanocentrist, even emphasizing the Prussian roots of Bix (Bismarck) Beiderbecke, a U.S. Dixieland cornetist from the

1920s. Overstating the case for jazz where Adorno understated it, Berendt held that European composers such as Stravinsky and Hindemith had influenced the Black man's music, quasi to make it legitimate, and he drew illicit parallels between the blues of boogie-woogie and the chaconne or passacaglia of the French and Spanish Baroque eras. He compared swing with "the mighty orchestral works of the Late Romantic period" and bebop passages with preludes by Debussy.[299] When he did mention autochthonous properties of jazz as currently played in America, he wrote of the inevitability of drugs as an essential aid of the jazzman's craft, thereby perpetuating legends that gave right-wing foes an opportunity to find fault with him.[300]

If articles by the likes of Höfer, Adorno, and Berendt had the potential to hurt rather than promote jazz in Germany, there were other detriments. One was jazz's real or imagined proximity to rock'n' roll, which was manna for the lower classes, as it was spread by the gyrations of Elvis Presley and films such as *Rock Around the Clock* (1956) with music by Bill Haley and His Comets. Highbrow critics associated rock'n' roll squarely with after-hours predilections of the working class and antisocial behavior in Munich and Berlin.[301] This was not helped by the practice especially of AFN radio hosts, but also of emcees at U.S. bases, who often mixed up jazz with rock'n' roll numbers, for the benefit of most GIs, but thereby confusing many educable young Germans. Then again, Chancellor Adenauer's good burghers did not care for a clear delineation – anything that was loud, bouncy, and incomprehensible could be branded as rock'n' roll, the harmonic similarities between rock's common musical structure and twelve-bar blues in jazz notwithstanding. Additional similarities in the dance styles, when jazz (Dixieland, swing, and even bebop) was danced as boogie-woogie, for example, aided the misconception.[302]

Whatever the situation in segregationist U.S.A., perceptions of jazz in Germany suffered from the fact that it had originally been generated by African Americans and that traditional musicians and innovative pioneers alike, such as Gillespie and Charlie Parker, were Black. Whether in this case the anti-Black prejudice among post-war Germans still stemmed from the racist Hitler era or was a consequence of U.S. occupation is difficult to ascertain; it was probably a combination of both.[303] There existed supercilious West German travelogues reporting on the United States, in which African Americans were treated patronizingly, at best. Their authors were linked to cultural revanchism in West Germany.[304] Whereas some of those writers argued that Blacks were doing socially and economically as well as could be expected under segregation, so that there were "even Black millionaires," others justified segregation outright. Their reasons hardly differed from the racial catechism of Nazi ideologues.[305]

Such skewed conceptions spawned specious analyses of the connection between African American culture and jazz, at the expense of the art form. Racist images of miscegenation were conjured up, such as that of a Black university professor from New Orleans, a friend of Duke Ellington's, embracing a white woman in dance: "the white hand on that black skin."[306] Like Adorno or those journalists, most of these writers wholly misjudged the true nature of American jazz, specifically its significance for African Americans: "The American is less interested in melody, as he is totally captivated by rhythm. His musical sensitivity is primarily a rhythmic one and as such it is original, naïve, even instinctual. He is, so to say, born with it. The purest manifestation of this predisposition, this instinctive feeling for rhythm, can be observed among the Negroes."[307]

Yet another anti-jazz polemic involved sexual corruption – the danger that a combination of African Americans and jazz would ravage German youth, in particular the pretty German girls in relationships with GIs. The erotic quality of jazz had been one of its trademarks since its inception, but it could be used by enemies of the genre by construing connections to milieu factors commonly associated with sexual promiscuity. This had been at the core of many Nazi arguments. And in post-war western Germany, the natural association of jazz with sex was undeniable.

Despite all the encumbrances, how viable was jazz in the context of other new cultural developments in post-war Germany? If Bayreuth's resurgence was questionable, Kassel's documenta a limited success, and Darmstadt suffering from authenticity quarrels, was jazz a convincingly novel art form? One measure might have been international comparability and pioneering reputation, something that distinguished culture in the Weimar Republic. On that count, new German films were only watched in Austria and parts of Switzerland; Bayreuth, Kassel, and Darmstadt were already doing reasonably well by around 1960 but left room for improvement. In the case of jazz, the Germans were hardly pace-setting, but then again, this was not their original art. However illustrative of this situation, the story of one of West

Germany's most gifted new jazz talents, pianist Jutta Hipp, who tried to succeed internationally, is revealing.

Hipp became a close friend of Frankfurt's saxophonist Emil Mangelsdorff, after she had fled from Leipzig to the Western Zone, where a hard life awaited her. An attractive brunette, she suffered from abject poverty, depression, and alcoholism, and had trouble maintaining romantic relationships. She had given up a son for adoption whom she called Lionel, after Hampton, from a Black GI. As a pianist, she played in various musical combinations all over Germany, preferring small-group settings. In 1954 the British impresario Leonard Feather heard her in Duisburg, as he chaperoned a tour by American jazz stars, the singer Billie Holiday among them. Struck by her piano solos, he persuaded her to move to New York. This she did in 1955, and then Feather launched her with a trio at the storied Hickory House. She recorded albums with stars such as Zoot Sims and played at the Newport Jazz Festival. But then things became difficult. Afraid that she could not keep up with American bandsmen, she lost confidence in her own playing. Depressed, alcoholic, and probably on drugs, in 1958 she stopped performing altogether; instead, she joined a New York garment factory as a textile worker. She retained this job for the rest of her life, never touching piano keys again. Before she died of pancreatic cancer in April 2003, wrote *The New York Times*, she was living alone in Jackson Heights, without a piano. She had earned $40,000 in royalties since 1956, which Blue Note Records could not pay her because they did not know her address. All told, she had made three albums that were sold in North America, Europe, and Japan over five decades, but never knew about it. Hipp was seventy-eight at her death.[308] Hers was not a success story for German jazz abroad.

◆ ◆ ◆

In 1983 a German literature scholar remarked, correctly, that the post-war *belles lettres* in the FRG included self-reflective and self-pitying examples belonging to the rubble genre, as in rubble films, but were hardly dominated by pronouncements against National Socialism and the Third Reich.[309] By 1961, said another, Walter Jens, professor at the University of Tübingen, there had been a change, but he mentioned only stylistic features, not the noticeable shift to scrupulous examinations of German history between 1933 and 1945 that had occurred increasingly in the late 1950s.[310] The writers of that period were concerned, already since the early half of the decade, about what they saw as manifestations of Nazi phenomena extending into the FRG. Their literary work was inspired by questionable developments under Adenauer's regime; they reflected on them, as well as on their ultimate cause – the Third Reich.[311]

Approaches to this complex set of problems were not uniform. An early 1950s author, Wolfgang Koeppen, was interested less in the Third Reich than in the calamitous changes it had wrought. Nothing predestined him to write three novels between 1950 and 1955, in which he voiced his unease. Born in 1906, he had a checkered career in theater, cabaret, and as a writer, and for unknown reasons got into trouble with Goebbels's writer's chamber. In 1951 he found his stride as a novelist. His novel *Tauben im Gras* (*Pigeons in the Grass*) made it clear that he disliked how Germans were behaving under Allied occupation, but he also criticized the Allies.[312] He described one day in Munich, under American military rule, after the 1948 currency reform, which saw various people suffering from different forms of discontent. There is the unreconstructed Nazi Frau Behrendt, the mother of Carla, a young war widow who dates a Black GI, and a Nazi countess posing as a victim of totalitarian rule.[313] A German male servant is killed by a Black soldier. The novel has no hero, and its only message is outrage over dismal conditions in post-war Munich, but when exactly the plot was intended to have taken place Koeppen does not make clear, so that later reviewers of his book guessed around four different years, from 1948 to 1951, as a historical narrative framework.[314]

In 1953, Koeppen published *Treibhaus* (*Hothouse*), a novel about Keetenheuve, a German returnee from exile, who chose to be elected as an SPD member to the new Bundestag. This faceless hero is disappointed with the political landscape, for he discerns a lack of real change; there are Bundeswehr generals, for example, reared by Hitler. The Third Reich lingers as a gloomy silhouette in the background.[315] Keetenheuve is obsessed with his personal failures as a politician and a man – obsessed with his ex-wife, the daughter of a Nazi Gauleiter, his sexual impotence and alcoholism. Finally, he decides to seduce a Salvation Army member who is in a lesbian relationship. But failing this he resigns life and throws himself into the Rhine.[316]

Significantly, the novel appeared shortly after the general elections of September 6, 1953, in which Adenauer's supporters were hugely successful and which ushered in measures toward rearmament that Koeppen (and his foil Keetenheuve) opposed, but which roused affirmative energies even on the political left.[317] The general mood of the educated reading public was in accordance with this. If this was one probable reason for the novel's lack of success, Koeppen's treatment of the main character not only as a failed male without any endearing qualities, but also his depiction of women either as easy sexual booty or lesbian stereotypes was fundamentally misogynist and unacceptable to female readers.[318]

Koeppen's third novel of his trilogy, vaguely inspired by his exemplar Thomas Mann, was *Tod in Rom* (*Death in Rome*), published in 1954. It contained the most obvious references to the Third Reich by highlighting the after-1945 career of Judejahn, a former SS general condemned to death in absentia now serving an unnamed Arab state. Judejahn is in Rome to meet family members; his brother-in-law, also a former Nazi functionary, is now a lord mayor, a slick servant of the new democracy. His nephew Siegfried is a queer serialist composer, sexually conditioned in a Nazi elite school. Judejahn's own offspring, Adolf, has become a priest (a reference to Martin Bormann's repentant son Martin Adolf). The composer's friend is Kürenberg, a conductor bearing a resemblance to Karajan who is married to the beautiful Jewish Ilse, whom Judejahn will shoot dead at the end of the novel, in fulfillment of a last promise to the Führer, to kill Jews.

Judejahn is sketched as a repulsive character. It is suggested that there are more like him and that German democracy, therefore, is not safe. Yet despite Koeppen's well-intentioned warnings, this novel too met with little success. His entire trilogy, with its stark moralism, had failed.[319] Apart from the – then hard to bear – sexual emphases, two factors were responsible for this. One, in all three books every character was so negatively described that no West German citizen could identify with any of them. Even the least offensive ones hardly had redeeming qualities. Even if it was realized that Bonn's nascent democracy had embarked on a shaky experiment, they needed confidence that none of Koeppen's characters inspired.[320] Second, even if Koeppen's social and political analyses were apt, even prescient, his novels arrived too early, because the public could not yet comprehend the phenomena he described, which did not match their experience.[321]

A first attempt to characterize conditions in the Third Reich without naming it was made in 1950 by the twenty-seven-year-old Walter Jens in his novel *Nein – Die Welt der Angeklagten* (*No: The World of the Accused*). He drew the outlines of a dystopian setting that was reminiscent of Franz Kafka or Aldous Huxley, but also evoked later works of international literature such as Arthur Koestler's *Darkness at Noon* and George Orwell's *Nineteen Eighty-Four*. Although those books were published in 1940 and 1949 respectively, Jens apparently did not know them. Yet it is likely that he read Kafka's *The Trial* and possibly took Dostoyevsky's grand inquisitor in *The Brothers Karamazov* as a model for his supreme judge in *Nein*.[322]

The plot of *Nein* is frightening. In the fictional town of Braunsberg the writer Walter Sturm is summoned to an interrogation. In the state building he is shown unknown burghers being kept and tortured. In a narrow cell stands a man with water over his knees. "'See this,' said the officer as he pointed downward, 'as soon as the man stumbles, it's over for him. On the slanted walls, above the water surface, there are small shards. And here is the ring of nails!'" The officer explains that mathematicians have worked long to devise this fiendish scheme, a statement that Jens could have intended as a reminder of the intricate entrapments of Auschwitz crematoria designed by German engineers. "I would not advise the man to fall down. He has no choice but to stand in the icy water or tear his belly on the nails."[323] Sturm realizes he is living in a police state with only defendants, witnesses, and judges. Everybody can be called upon to fill any of those three functions. So nobody is free and everyone can spy, must spy, on everybody else. Back in town, Sturm discovers that his lover, a physician, has betrayed him, but also lost her job in a clinic.[324] Finally he sits opposite the supreme judge, who wants him to assume his post. Sturm will now have to rule over all the subjects, mercilessly. But he declines and is shot.

With the judge's words, Jens pinpointed much of the philosophy that fortified the governmental mechanism of the Nazi regime. In addition and coincidentally, he presciently articulated the principles by which Axel Springer's demagogic *Bild-Zeitung* would be run only two years hence. But Jens failed to make a deep impact at the time because he did not actually name the Nazi state and because the book possessed the stylistic weaknesses of a new author that critics found not easily forgivable. In fact, they preferred to dwell on those weaknesses rather than take Jens's serious lesson to heart. Further novels by Jens, who came to make his living primarily as an academic, dealt with different topics, and *Nein* would be forgotten.

During 1957 Alfred Andersch, who had assisted Hans Werner Richter with *Der Ruf* and the founding of Gruppe 47, treated would-be fugitives from the Nazi regime in *Sansibar oder der letzte Grund* (*Zanzibar or the Final Reason*). This is the first West German novel dealing squarely with the Third Reich, but again not yet naming it. It tells of four people wanting to flee on a fisherman's boat from the Baltic coast to Sweden, on a summer day in 1937. Wishing to stay on shore is the pastor Helander, but he wants a wooden Barlach figure of a young monk reading Scriptures to be taken from his church to safety. Fisherman Knudsen must escape his niggling wife, who is mentally disturbed. A beautiful young Jewish woman, Judith Levin, arrives from Hamburg to find refuge; after the suicide of her mother, she is threatened with arrest. Gregor, a young Communist, must leave Germany for fear of persecution. Finally, a local teenager inspired by Huckleberry Finn wishes to escape drab quotidian realities. Nazis arrive to fetch the statue and Helander gets shot. Knudsen, the girl, and the boy finally arrive in Sweden, but only the girl disembarks. For Knudsen knows his wife will perish unless he returns, and the boy, not to endanger Knudsen's life, must accompany him. Gregor too resigns himself to staying in Germany.

Apart from his good intentions, there were too many things Andersch got wrong. First, the Barlach statue. While in July 1937 the end of Modernist art had been declared through the exhibition of "degenerate art," which also censured sculptor Ernst Barlach, it is unlikely that in that same year examples of his art would be hunted down, especially in Lutheran churches that were in general conformity with the regime.[325] Going after a pastor known as an opponent to the state was likely but tying his fate to a Barlach statue absurd. Most Protestant clergymen who resisted did so not because of the Nazis' treatment of the Jews, as the novel implies but because the government would dispute the Church's institutional independence.[326]

Second, neither individual Nazis nor Nazi formations are mentioned by name in the novel; they are abstracted as "The Others", suggesting, as had been done before, a division between blameless Germans on the one side and demonic forces, such as those hunting for Helander, on the other. Andersch stayed deliberately vague about the appearance of the men who eventually catch up with Helander; they are supposed to be dressed in black but with hats, which would suggest the SS in the first instance and the Gestapo in the second.[327] Demonization of "The Others" was what many

Germans engaged in after 1945 to exonerate themselves, something that was supported by right-wing intellectuals.

Third, the ambiguity regarding Knudsen's wife. If she was mentally unwell, readers have concluded that she was threatened either by a concentration camp or by "euthanasia" actions.[328] Neither of these made sense in 1937. No one who was simply ill would have been sent to a concentration camp, unless this person could be classified as "asocial." Instead, she would have been committed to an asylum and possibly have fallen victim to "euthanasia" action when it began in late 1939, but Knudsen could not have known that two years earlier.

Finally, Andersch's treatment of the Jewish Judith Levin. She is portrayed as someone in immediate danger for her life.[329] But in 1937 no German Jew of any age or gender was yet threatened by incarceration or, worse, genocide. Although the Nuremberg Laws of 1935 had decreased the Jews' legal status, Kristallnacht was still to occur in November 1938, which only then prompted many Jews to seek emigration. However, as the former Auschwitz inmate and Germanist Ruth Klüger has argued, the equating of a Barlach figure with a Jewish person as an object of persecution devalued the cause of the Jew in her quest for safety.[330] And, as Reich-Ranicki mentions, the portraiture of Judith as an attractive woman, "a stranger with a beautiful, tender, outlandish, racy face," insultingly used the language of the enemy, for a Jew from Hamburg was neither a stranger nor should her face have been characterizable as "outlandish" or "racy."[331]

The moralist Heinrich Böll, who into the 1950s simultaneously had condemned war and lamented the suffering of Wehrmacht soldiers and their enemy victims, continued those themes into the 1950s, but now added criticism of Nazis to his concerns. In *Wo warst du, Adam?* (*Where Were You, Adam?*), of 1951, he described the fate of soldier Feinhals who suffers with his comrades on the Hungarian front in early 1945, as he falls in love with a Jewish girl just before she is scheduled to be killed by a sadistic concentration-camp commandant. With his love of choral music, asceticism, and merciless, meticulous camp management, this man, Filskeit, is eerily identifiable as a composite of the fastidious Himmler and Heydrich, an accomplished violinist. Next to this girl Ilona, Feinhals appears as a victim of Nazism and its war; he is cheated out of love by the SS and finally loses his life on a crawl to reach his parents' house back home, shot from a tank. The ending leaves open whose tank this actually was – from the Waffen-SS or the advancing U.S. army, hinting that guilt for German deaths lay not only with criminal Nazis.[332]

At the time, Reich-Ranicki, whose unshakable paragon was Thomas Mann, charged Böll with too much black-and-white description, leaving little room for nuances.[333] Böll was also guilty of that in his next two novellas, in which his empathy was extended to the suffering of post-war German civilians. The agonies of war-damaged ex-soldiers, the plight of their wives and war widows, and that of their partly orphaned children were in his sights in *Und sagte kein einziges Wort* (*And Never Said a Word*, 1953) and *Haus ohne Hüter* (*The Unguarded House*, 1954). In the former, already discussed (see Chapter 1), the war veteran Fred Bogner, in addition to his alcoholism, is portrayed as someone "who sold door to door and whom my mother never refused."[334] *Haus ohne Hüter* deals with two war widows, and their children and new suitors, unmistakably indicting the war, during which one of the characters, a former lieutenant, was responsible for one of the husbands going missing. Jews, too, are described as victims, and SA and SS atrocities are outlined in detail.[335] The book is a first indication that Böll was becoming politically committed.[336] Like Koeppen, he was deeply concerned about impending rearmament, and he continued his criticism of the Catholic hierarchy.[337] Ever a staunch Catholic, Böll became increasingly scornful of the Papal Church, which after 1945 he saw in a conspiracy with political rulers, especially from the CDU and CSU.[338]

In 1959, Böll published his first major novel, which put him on the path to international fame – here the theme of German self-pity had been largely removed. It was *Billard um halb zehn* (*Billiards at half past Nine*), about three generations of architects, in what is surely Cologne, who construct a Catholic abbey under Kaiser Wilhelm (Heinrich Fähmel), raze it during the Second World War (Robert Fähmel), and are in the process of rebuilding it during the late 1950s (Joseph Fähmel).[339] The Fähmels are a split family, divided into "beasts" and "lambs," with the beasts having sided with the Nazis and now the powers that be, and the lambs bent on peace, reconciliation, and reconstruction. Other beasts and lambs are surrounding this family on September 6, 1958, as Heinrich Fähmel gets set to celebrate his eightieth birthday, and multiple events unfold. The novel received much flak for its overly compounded, confusing structure, for what seemed to be irrational flashbacks and logical incoherence, for too much cloudy symbolism, and, again, for too few character nuances. But it drove home that Böll was beginning to see too many Nazi influences in society and government everywhere. There is Nettlinger, with heinous crimes during the Third Reich behind him and now back as a police president (the arch-beast), and Schrella, a former resister now returned from many years of exile abroad (the arch-lamb). There are Catholic monks who participated in Nazi festivities (lambs converted to beasts). At the end, Johanna, who is a lamb, and the wife of Heinrich, who is a beast, tries to shoot Nettlinger, but wounds another government official, another beast, instead. She is supposed to be clinically insane, but Böll leaves no doubt about her mental lucidity and moral integrity. The novel, while granting revealing insights into the Third Reich as did its forerunners, now establishes negative continuities from 1933 to 1959 in West German politics, society, and culture as chief elements for Böll's narrative trajectory from here on.[340] Based on the novel, Kaiser called Böll "the poet of our dark years."[341]

Martin Walser was, like Walter Jens, a younger representative of the new German literary scene. Born in 1927 in Wasserburg, a borough on Lake Constance, his parents, proprietors of a modest inn, were members of the petite bourgeoisie, as was Böll. Walser, who in 1951 obtained a doctorate on Kafka, always considered himself an upwardly mobile petit bourgeois. Hence a leading theme of his early novels was the upward mobility his main characters found themselves in, Hans Beumann of *Ehen in Philippsburg* (*Marriages in Philippsburg*, published in English as *The Gadarene Club*) or Anselm Kristlein, an extension of Beumann and ultimately of Walser himself, in *Halbzeit* (*Half-Time*) and later. They viewed "the big wide world from the perspective of the little man."[342] After Hitler Youth service and a non-dramatic stand in the German Alps as a Wehrmacht skier, Walser turned to the modest parental business, then to studies in Tübingen, where he met Jens. Journalistic work followed on print media and in Stuttgart radio. Marxist-influenced, he published his first novel, *Ein Flugzeug über dem Haus und andere Geschichten* (*A Plane Above the House and Other Stories*), in 1955, an anarchist reaction to resurging affluence and its attendant social excrescences. It was Kafkaesque, an assortment of unconnected short stories about weird people doing and experiencing weird things. In one story, a young unnamed man who only lies around in bed receives blocks of ice from mute workers, every day at the same hour, on a table. "The ice lay on the table and melted. Water flowed in small rivulets through the dust that covered the floor."[343] Uncannily, the surreal quality of this prose coincided with what some German artists, such as Heinz Trökes, were attempting to achieve in painting at this time.

Walser's criticism of West German society was continued, far more strongly in his 1957 novel *Ehen in Philippsburg*. Its four chapters describe moral decay and the decomposition of marital ties against the background of economic recovery.[344] Walser began it in October 1954, completing it in August 1956. Next to young Beumann's own development as a young careerist, the lives of two couples are chronicled, admittedly in Stuttgart, habitually the main venue of Walser's mature novels. A gynecologist and a lawyer have extra-marital affairs, a wife commits suicide, and a motor-cyclist is killed as a consequence of drunk driving. Beumann, illegitimate son of a country waitress, manages university and enters the city's media network, supported by manufacturers of home electronics, whose daughter he impregnates and then gets engaged to. But he favors the sexually alluring Marga, who had earlier rejected him. After he finds her at a fancy strip club, he takes her as his mistress. In this affluent scenario typical of society during the Economic Miracle, the couple listen to jazz, code for new, careless, swinging times.[345]

If it was to be Böll's mandate only two years later to expose excesses of West German society as well as to show the impact of malignant Nazi residues, where then was Walser's thrust in that respect? His diaries of the 1950s offer no clue; libido-obsessed, Walser sketched scenes of male–female seduction obviously to be used in later writings, all of them quite misogynistic.[346] But there are no references to Hitler or the Nazi period, and barely to World War II.[347] Yet a closer look at *Ehen in Philippsburg* reveals that what Walser did was reflect the attitude of the times: his characters do not contemplate the Nazi era because citizens of the FRG did not either. "That which remains unsaid always belongs to what was actually said," Walser remarked many years later.[348] In the mid-1950s, covering the past up in silence was what was helping Germans to concentrate on the economic and social reconstruction of the country and forget their guilt, even though, as Jaspers and the Mitscherlich couple had been warning, this was morally questionable and futile in the long run.

Both Jaspers and the Mitscherlichs had insisted that the Third Reich had not been an accident, but the consequence of human will, and Günter Grass, Walser's exact contemporary as a writer, proceeded to show this symbolically by having Oskar Matzerath, his lead character in the novel *Die Blechtrommel* (*The Tin Drum*), make a decision. On his third birthday, September 12, 1927, Oskar's decision is to allow himself to fall down a flight of stairs, so that he will stunt his growth.[349] Germany elected to stunt her growth within the family of nations by inviting Hitler to seize absolute power: Oskar committed his act at the age of three; Germany's was in the year of 1933.

Günter Grass was born on October 16, 1927, in a lower-class suburb of Danzig, then a Free City under the League of Nations. His father, a grocer, was a Lutheran Rheinlander and his mother a Catholic Cassubian, member of a Slavic minority related to the Poles. Grass always identified as a Cassubian, taking Catholicism half-seriously. After Hitler Youth, Grass became a tank gunner, fighting the Red Army. Having endured a U.S. POW camp, he worked as a miner and stonemason. In Düsseldorf and, after 1953, in Berlin, he studied sculpture and graphics. He took up writing in the early 1950s, his first work being a collection of poetry that he himself had illustrated, and smaller stage plays.[350]

Grass's first novel, *Die Blechtrommel*, was published in 1959 and became an almost instant success. In allegorical fashion, it pictured pre-Nazi life in League of Nations Danzig, the advent of the Nazis in 1933, the takeover of the city by the Wehrmacht and SS in 1939, and life in immediate post-war Germany, now in Düsseldorf. This is the framework for the autofictional life history of Oskar Matzerath, the dwarf who tells it from his bed in a Düsseldorf insane asylum in the late 1950s. Insecurely, grotesquely, and in ill-focused shots, sequences emerge of a poor grocer's life, Alfred Matzerath's in Danzig, as he suffers the adultery his wife Agnes commits with her cousin, the Polish Jan Bronski, so that it is questionable whether Oskar is his own son. Agnes dies sitting on a toilet after overeating fish, and Bronski is killed during the Nazi advance on the Polish post office where he worked, in September 1939. Matzerath takes in the fifteen-year-old Hitler Youth girl Maria, who awakens Oskar to sexuality but simultaneously becomes the father's mistress. She bears a son, Kurtchen, who could be either's child. During the war, Oskar meets up with a miniature circus unit and joins them in troop entertainment, a Goebbels mandate, on the Western Front in the Rhineland. Before he is shipped off to the Düsseldorf institution after war's end, Oskar witnesses the death of his father: after trying to swallow his Nazi Party badge he is shot by an invading Red Army soldier.

This, Hans Magnus Enzensberger wrote shortly after the novel's appearance, is symbolic, for swallowing a party badge could not end the Third Reich.[351] Grass himself was less convinced; in 1974 he declared that the process of coming to terms with the Nazi past consciously had not been within his remit.[352] Perhaps not consciously, but it is obvious to the reader that Oskar's story is told entirely from a perspective relative to Nazism, before, during, and after Hitler's regime. Grass's own uncertainty comes through repeatedly in the novel.[353] As if Grass himself had had doubts about his own dual ethnic heritage, these are expressed in the dubious paternity of Oskar – his father could have been either a German or a Pole. Oskar is stymied at three, at once looking like a child who cannot comprehend developments in the Third Reich, and yet with an obviously developing brain that sees, hears, and understands all and hence cannot claim innocence. Oskar's entire telling of his biography is unreliable – mostly in opposition to the Nazi regime and in sympathy with Sigismund Markus, the local Jew who sells him his drums, but sometimes in stark compliance, as he joins the uniformed gnomes on the Western Front.[354] Apart from reflecting Grass's personal insecurities, the farcical nature of events is designed to capture the reader's attention to pay close heed to the images conjured as significant manifestations of a fascist, totalitarian state. The macabre qualities of the encountered events no less than the "somewhat fuzzy and shadow-like" figures who appear de-demonize, de-sanctify that state.[355] For example, in one of the best scenes of the novel, as Oskar hides with his tin drum underneath stadium bleachers, he drums a Hitler Youth march off tune and forces the uniformed boys into playing a Charleston, once he has loudly established the syncopated rhythm.[356] Oskar loved jazz.

In 1959 most reviews were enthusiastic. At a time when synagogues were newly defiled throughout Germany, progressive critics welcomed this bizarrely original attempt to reproach the Nazi past. Kaiser, who in 1958 heard Grass recite two manuscript chapters at Gruppe 47, acknowledged "a wild energy of expression" and called what he heard "wrathful, beast-like, full of evil phantasies."[357]

Yet early in 1960, Reich-Ranicki found fault with Grass's depictions, which, he wrote, had not been clearly delineated. In particular, he dismissed as ludicrous a nightclub scene where patrons cut away at onions in order to facilitate weeping, now that totalitarian constraints on behavior had been removed. Reich-Ranicki's scorn extended to Grass's overall style, his garrulousness, his overloaded prose with undigested bits and pieces, his forced humor, and his overall lack of taste. Yet the deeper meaning behind Grass's fantastic turns of phrase escaped the critic, and he completely ignored the author's ultimate achievement, having caricaturized, having rendered questionable *and* laughable the achievements of the Hitler period.[358]

Why would he, a Polish Jew who had escaped from the Warsaw Ghetto, react in such a hostile manner? The answer lies in the peculiar sensibilities of the critic, if not also of Grass himself. Early in 1958, not yet famous, Grass had visited Warsaw as a representative of the new West German literary scene. He received Reich-Ranicki, then still a resident of Warsaw and representing Communist Poland's literary establishment, in the Bristol Hotel's lobby, unshaven, unkempt, slumped into an armchair, and unwilling to engage with him on personal or professional terms as they went for a walk. Eventually, Grass told of his epic work in progress, but his visitor "did not want to hear about the planned novel." They parted unceremoniously.[359] Later it came to light that Grass had consumed a whole bottle of vodka at lunchtime because he, the experienced cook, found himself dining alone and disliked the food. Grass himself may have been uneasy, as a half-Slav, meeting a survivor of the Warsaw Ghetto. There was going to be a postlude when later in the year, Reich-Ranicki, who, after all, was Polish-born but grew up in Berlin until deported back to Poland in 1938 and then ghettoized, met Grass again, at the Gruppe 47 gathering in Grossholzleute in October 1958. According to the critic, who had permanently moved to Germany only three months earlier, Grass approached him between readings for conversation: "What are you now – a Pole, a German or what?" "Half of me is Polish," Reich-Ranicki replied archly, "half of me is German, and all of me is Jewish." The next day, Grass won that year's literature prize for his readings from *Die Blechtrommel*.[360]

That prize was the seventh Gruppe 47 had awarded since its creation, with Günter Eich as the first winner in 1950. There was a prize, in 1951, for Böll in Bad Dürkheim and in 1952, in Niendorf, for Ilse Aichinger.[361]

Walser received his prize in 1955 in Berlin, for his first short stories.[362] In 1948, Aichinger, whose mother was a Viennese Jew, had published a largely autobiographical novel about a non-"Aryan" girl in a large city in fear of Nazi dragnets. Her 1952 contribution was a short story about a woman told backwards, beginning and ending with her death.[363] In 1953, Ingeborg Bachmann, an Austrian like Aichinger, was honored, for a selection of poetry.[364] When first she had appeared, in 1952, she seemed fragile, vulnerable, and, to the overwhelmingly male participants of the meeting, eminently protectable. Grass, that strapping fellow with the walrus moustache, thought that she was "mousy."[365] Born in Klagenfurt in 1926, Bachmann, like Aichinger, was not really part of the new West German literature scene, although, after the 1938 Anschluss of Austria, the Nazi background of her childhood was similar to that of Walser's or Grass's. In her case, there was a Nazi father whom she came to detest even during the Third Reich, as she proceeded to transfer her hatred of him to all men, whom she generically regarded as fascistic. As she made clear in writings later in life, she believed that men were out to exploit women and thrive through the abuse of their bodies and their talents, as she later thought her lover Max Frisch had done. She died, a drug and alcohol addict, in October 1973, after having set her bed on fire through careless smoking. Some thought it was suicide.[366]

From the beginning, the left-leaning Richter had charged Gruppe 47 with the mandate not of politics but of democracy, in a quest to help reform society and politics, ridding them of the Nazi scourge. But although political debates during meetings were off limits, this is what it now became, an avatar of the ideological left, favoring Social Democracy. Social Democrats such as Günter Grass encouraged this development. It received additional impetus after the failed Hungarian insurrection in 1956 and Adenauer's move toward nuclear armament in 1958, which frightened these left-leaning literati.[367]

Not unlike Darmstadt, over time there were always those who accused Gruppe 47 of being a self-appointed, exclusive clique, a censorship bureau that dictatorially decided what was literature in Germany and what was not. Richter himself stood at the center of such accusations. The charges intensified after many viewed what were manifestations of a growing institutionalization and attendant gentrification with alarm. These came about as a consequence of increased funds for prizes, rising interest by publishers, and expanded media coverage.[368]

By the mid-1950s the meetings had mutated to "super parties," to which well-dressed men and women, approaching middle age, arrived in expensive cars, intending to have a good time. This certainly held true for Walser, who disliked the daily proceedings, preferring instead the evenings with much wine, schmoozing, and natter.[369] Indeed, the original 1947 meeting at Bannwaldsee, when participants had been in shabby clothes and subsisted on self-caught fish, was a distant memory.[370] In 1956 a critic anticipated that the anniversary gathering one year later would be conducted "with much momentum," and so it was.[371] There congregated, in Niederpöcking on picturesque Lake Starnberg, a select group of people, "correctly attired men of medium age mostly, here and there a fluff of gray hair," next to "elegant women in the tapered, casual dresses en vogue this fall."[372] When Gruppe 47 met again in 1959 at the Elmau Castle resort near Garmisch-Partenkirchen, it was placed on a level with the Frankfurt book fair and labeled a "big event."[373]

Over time, Gruppe 47 also had to ward off accusations of anti-Semitism. Those arose after a guest visit by the poet Paul Celan to the Niendorf meeting in 1952. Bachmann, who then was just at the end of a love affair with him, had brought him along. Richter invited Celan to read from his poems, those somber, lyrical, elegiac pieces decrying the might of blond-haired Germans and the death of dark-haired Jews in concentration camps. Celan knew of what he spoke. Born Paul Antschel in 1920 in polyglot Czernowitz (Bukovina) to Jewish parents, he had grown up speaking his mother tongue German as well as Romanian and studied literature at the University of Bucharest, then medicine in Paris. In 1942, after his return to Czernowitz, he was indentured to a Nazi work detail. He survived the war but his parents had been killed. He fled to Vienna, where he became Bachmann's lover, and then again moved to Paris, whence she fetched him in 1952.[374]

Well into the late 1960s before he jumped into the Seine, depressed and paranoid, to end his life on Hitler's birthday in 1970, Celan attacked West German authors for anti-Semitism, in particular Böll. Celan, to whom his friend Günter Grass always ascribed "exaggerated fears," communicated about Böll with Max Frisch, whose sympathy he craved as a mutual friend of

Bachmann. While it is true that certain German men of letters disparaged
Celan, his blaming of Böll was misplaced (and Frisch told him so). As far as
Gruppe 47 was concerned, he did receive a less than enthusiastic reception
after his reading, but this was not inspired by anti-Semitism. Rather, his
listeners were stunned, because they were not used to his kind of emphatic
recitation. In Richter's recollection, Celan expressed too much pathos;
someone else said that he read "like Goebbels" – without a doubt an unfortunate turn of phrase.[375] But Gruppe 47 was not anti-Semitic, the best proof
of which was that in Niendorf Celan himself received a Third Prize (after
Aichinger's First and Walter Jens's Second). Gruppe 47 had always invited
Jews, Wolfgang Hildesheimer and Walter Maria Guggenheimer being
among the founding members, and the original hostess, Ilse Schneider-
Lengyel, was married to a Hungarian Jew. Aichinger herself was half-Jewish.
The enemies of Celan were in fact enemies of Gruppe 47, and they included
a former SS man and a circle of ultra-conservative literati.[376]

◆ ◆ ◆

Whatever the advances in West German culture after 1945, in literature
serious new reactionary impulses came from the former Luftwaffe fighter
Gerd Gaiser, who wrote in the Cultural Pessimist mold.[377] He had published
a collection of poetry in 1941 hailing the regime's early victories. And in a
poem *Riders in the Sky* he had celebrated the exhilarating effect the Führer's
voice had in 1940 on a battery of tired airmen resting on the ground, as it
reached them through a radio in an open window.[378]

Gaiser's first post-1945 novel was autobiographical, *Eine Stimme hebt
an* (*There Was a Voice*, 1951), about the experiences of Oberstelehn, a World
War II veteran officer, in the countryside during the late 1940s. The
conservative Oberstelehn is rooted in the soil, distrustful of the people
around him, but condescendingly sympathetic to the local women, some of
them war widows. He himself is separated from his wife. The tragic war was
not his or any German's fault, and nature is still his to enjoy; he is content
to be a forest worker.[379] Clichés from Nazi-type literature prevail. The foregrounded "Blood-and-Soil" theme, as a pre-industrial trajectory, spells
out the difference between country and city: the woods and an honest
forester are contrasted against "industrial landscape, dull-green and iron-
red," "long-bodied, ugly rats," and girls who need "champagne for their

profession and who rise to attention when the fifty-marks bill crackles in their stockings."[380]

Those motifs recurred in the second novel of note, playing in the 1950s, with an even stronger accentuation of light and shadow. In *Schlussball* (*Final Dance*, 1958) the fair-skinned, beatific Herse Andernoth is purity incarnate and the darkish Rakitschs, mother and son, are the fount of evil. Frau Andernoth, a war widow, has a teenage daughter, Diemut (again this anti-quated, pseudo-Germanic name, suggesting modesty), who – symbolically – refuses to cut her golden braids. The plot is simple: the one-time officer Soldner, again displaced and dispossessed, finds a provisional job as a teacher in a mid-sized town, from which he is eventually fired. Having lost his wife, he woos Andernoth, who remains virtuously true, however, to her missing husband. Soldner is suspicious of Frau Rakitsch, who talks loud, smokes cigarettes, and deals in revealing lingerie, and her son, a rakish good-for-nothing who pursues Diemut and at the end is subdued. Without Gaiser ever coming out and saying so, Reich-Ranicki correctly identified them both as Jewish, for they "communicated like a tribe which twisted and turned until emerging on top."[381] Gaiser reproached the growing materialistic excesses of the Economic Miracle and mourned the good old days.[382] Both Reich-Ranicki and Jens have pointed to Gaiser's preference for the country-side over the city, which he, in typical conservative fashion, associated with unhealthy intellectualism.[383]

Within the old-school camp of literati that greeted Gaiser's work, Friedrich Sieburg stood out, the literature critic of *FAZ*, joined by the former SS man Hans Egon Holthusen, a future director of the New York Goethe House, as well as journalist Günter Blöcker.[384] Holthusen and Blöcker made explicit a particular dislike of Paul Celan so that he claimed to be pursued by an anti-Jewish cabal in West Germany's literary establishment. At the same time, Holthusen and Blöcker left no doubt about their dislike of Gruppe 47.[385]

Sieburg polemicized against Richter's Gruppe 47 and progressive, social-critical films in equal measure. *Die Sünderin* (1951), in which Hildegard Knef showed some nakedness and lived in sexual sin met with his particular disapproval. In 1954 he contrasted "the absolute emptiness that the face of the actress conveys" with the "naturalness" of Greta Garbo's beautiful features, calling Knef's acting strained and the entire movie an expression of "the yawning boredom characterizing contemporary erotics." His overall judgment was that with this film inferior art was being thrown to "defenseless people" for the purpose of mass consumption.[386]

Die Sünderin was the one aesthetically daring piece of art conservatives in all camps used to demonstrate their fundamental discontentment with post-war modern trends. Those trends were suspected of other movies also, since, as Karl Korn averred, "there exist direct links, from this or that film, to heavy crime."[387] Such fears proliferated after Helmut Käutner's film *Der Apfel ist ab* (*The Apple Fell*) of 1948 had already been indicted. Now the FSK mechanism, the voluntary self-control instituted in 1949, was expected to set in: nakedness, adulterous relationships, and any forms of prostitution were declared taboo.[388] *Die Sünderin* was further accused by the Catholic Church because of Marina's and Alexander's suicide, by its laws a mortal sin. Priests, joined by Lutheran pastors, agitated from their pulpits, and both Churches organized protests. They were aided by conservative politicians such as the CDU's Josef Gockeln and other conservative publicists writing for Christian papers and right-wing dailies.[389]

In music, educators formerly associated with the Hitler Youth attempted to revive communal singing, folk-dancing, and folk music as a thrust against the new Modernism and to gain influence in the popular-music field.[390] This group was led by Fritz Jöde, born in 1887 and with a checkered career as a youth-music leader until 1945. In the Weimar Republic he had been a pioneer of the German youth movement, in particular its back-to-the-Volk music ambitions with its emphasis on communal singing to the accompaniment of the simple recorder, harmonica, and guitar. As such, the Nazis had accommodated him after 1933, to use his talents for the Hitler Youth. Indeed, one of his assistants, Wolfgang Stumme, became the chief of music under Baldur von Schirach. But the Nazis convicted Jöde as a predator who had seduced underage girls, and he was dismissed in 1936. West Germans, not probing those circumstances, employed him at the Hohner Academy for folk music in Trossingen in 1952, where the mouth organs were made.[391]

Already in 1950 Jöde started a new music journal, *Junge Music*, to aid in the resurrection of the old communal culture for music education. He was joined by former Nazi Party member Wilhelm Twittenhoff, once a student of his and an assistant to Orff, before he became a staff member at the

Hitler Youth music academy in Weimar. In 1953, he was director of a youth-music school in Hamburg.[392]

Four other collaborators were Felix Oberborbeck, Walter Wiora, Gottfried Wolters, and ex-Hitler Youth music chief Wolfgang Stumme himself. Oberborbeck, a Goebbels minor functionary, taught for the Hitler Youth at Weimar and after the Anschluss helped shape the traditional Graz music school into a political academy. Already by 1949, he had managed to secure for himself a teaching position at a school in Vechta.[393] Wiora had a multiple Nazi background and Wolters bore the official title "Composer of the Hitler Youth" – but they both found new jobs.[394] Stumme returned in 1949 from Soviet captivity, eventually to become a faculty member of the renowned Folkwang Academy in Essen.[395]

In an early issue of *Junge Musik*, Jöde spoke of Weimar youth-movement music as having been hijacked by Nazi forces, intentionally omitting that the hijackers had been his own young crew, the youth-music advocates turned Hitler Youth leaders, and that this trend had begun long before 1933.[396] In 1951 he capitalized on high youth unemployment, as he planned to attract the young to right-wing causes through the utilization of traditional youth-movement song. Advocating the "inner convalescence of our people," he insisted that a youth that was singing and making music would be essential "in our restoration." It was clear that an infiltration of the overall youth culture was much more important than mere technical questions of musicianship teachable in workshops. Hence against a larger ideological background, outposts should be established all over Germany to direct musical life for the young, beyond what home and school would offer. As a first step, Jöde invited pedagogues, regional politicians and administrators, private music teachers, and parents to a meeting in Göhrde at the end of May, for discussion and devising a strategy.[397]

The meeting in Göhrde mobilized older youth-music functionaries whom Jöde knew well, but also younger ones who were searching for an organizational framework in those uncertain times, including young men and women from the refugee organizations lamenting the loss of the eastern territories.[398] This was followed up with an invitation to "Festive Days – Young Music" in Wanne-Eickel, in the industrialized Ruhr, where there were thousands of young unemployed, at the end of April 1952. Several certified lay-music organizations participated, and the federal ministry of the interior in Bonn lent institutional support along with coal-mining industrialists, as the Jöde group's excoriation of Communism and the GDR resonated with Cold Warriors. They all had reasons to worry, for the GDR had organized a Deutschlandtreffen (All-German Meeting) in 1950 and had staged a World Festival in East Berlin in 1951, including singing groups, which were attractive to large crowds of young people from the FRG.[399]

The Wanne-Eickel gathering assembled around one hundred participants and, as foreseen, became much more important from an ideological than a musicianship perspective. Every organization, choir, and harmonica group present was reminded, "above all, to fulfill a social duty" – to build a new Volksgemeinschaft "from all strata of the industrial population." Wolters performed twice with his Norddeutscher Singkreis to set a community example for all as far as music went. He offered compositions that would have been welcomed on every concert stage of the Third Reich: Orff's *Carmina Burana* (1937), Hugo Distler's *Choral-Passion* (1933), and Stravinsky's neoclassical *Mass* (1948). Other choral composers featured were the Nazi bards Armin Knab and Heinrich Spitta. All this output was suited to defeat charges of musical obscurantism – contemporary and demonstrably tonal at the same time. In the end, to serve a higher purpose than those strictly musical, several possibilities of organizational amalgamation were discussed, with the ulterior objective of securing a leadership advantage for Jöde and his men.[400]

The ultimate success of this meeting was questionable, for it took two more years for the Jöde faction to stage its next large event, at a time when Twittenhoff had already been designated as his, much less charismatic, successor. The group convened in Passau, after a disastrous flooding of the Danube there – not a good omen. Supported by the resources of the profoundly conservative Passau administration – a wealthy town in deeply Catholic Bavaria – it was possible to invite folk and music groups not only from North Germany, but also from outlying countries such as France, Great Britain, even Yugoslavia and Turkey, most certainly groupings with their own right-wing agendas. Over 4,000 came in July and 3,000 of them boarded ships to float to Engelhartszell, some 20 miles down the river in the Austrian borderland of Schärding, evoking Hitler's 1938 Anschluss. The international flavor of the meeting was reminiscent of visions the National Socialists had had for a united Europe under German suzerainty, in cultural, economic, and political respects. It was something those former

Hitler Youth leaders had dreamed about as a glorious future for themselves in the early 1940s, and here it was, a fond memory realized for a couple of days or so – and hopefully again, more permanently. These imperialist, irredentist chimeras were reflected in the songs intoned and the music played, for it was imperative to again "build bridges." The performance venues for this were a Nibelungen hall and a – lately underused – Nazi Thing site (a multiuse outdoor stage). And the music offered was appropriate for the occasion: after denunciations of the avant-garde in several of the speeches, as in 1952, neoclassical compositions by Stravinsky and Hindemith were played for a neoconservative audience, and also, as in Hitlerian times, madrigals and oratoria by Monteverdi, Schütz, and Gabrieli.[401]

It is a measure of the failure of Passau as a community-forming catalyst that the next meeting took a full three years to organize. For either in musical or political terms nothing came to pass. Yet come 1957 there were fewer incentives for Twittenhoff and his men than before, for within a growing prosperity for ever larger sections of adolescents any longings for pre-1950 good old days diminished. Within the new West German materialism, American Pop art set new standards and films such as *Rock Around the Clock* were stronger than any old or neo-Nazi symbolisms. Rock 'n' roll was en vogue for boys and girls who twenty years before, like Twittenhoff and Wolters, would have practiced the recorder and danced a Rheinländer, and jazz and swing-dance were making inroads. At the same time the former Hitler Youth leaders were faced with occurrences of juvenile delinquency, certainly in larger cities, of the kind they could not easily comprehend and did not know how to deal with. When they had had their say decades ago, such outbursts would have been instantly quashed with policing mechanisms available to a totalitarian regime. But that youth rebellion could be a facet of democracy to be tolerated in pluralist societies was something their authoritarian mentality could not fathom.[402]

Before the gathering in Münster, Twittenhoff ruminated about the prevalence of Cossack and cowboy songs among West German youth groups and remarked on the need for a genuine youth song that was now sorely lacking. While his first statement was without foundation, the dearth of home-grown popular music of some quality against the flood of American influences was palpable.[403] To counteract those, a pseudo-jazz musical was offered in Münster, *Halleluja Billy*, of unknown origin and staged by a lay-musical group, tame in dynamics and with Christian themes. As an alternative to rock 'n' roll and swing dance, "open dancing" was introduced, chaste ascetic exercises, the hallmarks of which were group formations, simplicity of movement and discipline.[404]

Although five thousand participants were seen in Münster during summer 1957, the youth leaders themselves declared the events there to have been a letdown. Twittenhoff's own assessment was that the citizens of Münster itself had not been interested in the many events planned for variously talented youth groups – singers, musicians, dancers, sports enthusiasts, and lay actors – and that the press had offended them with total disregard. But worse, as he saw it, the homogeneity aimed at for all the groupings (in analogy to a cultural and ethnic Volksgemeinschaft) had not come about, as every young faction remained interested only in its own pursuits.[405] Consequently, no single leader, musical, social, or political, was able to emerge, anointed to lead the way to a future fit for Germans. "Junge Musik," the movement, as a fresh incentive to classless unity, was at an end before it had really had a chance to prove itself. And so was, for the time being, a National Socialist resurgence.[406]

Still, the nefarious judgments former members of the Nazi music establishment exercised against post-1945 progressive music must not be underestimated. When they had the power, they used it ruthlessly in the interest of what they chose to view as tradition. Hence at the end of 1959, Cologne Generalmusikdirektor Wolfgang Sawallisch rejected the score of Bernd Alois Zimmermann's new work, *Die Soldaten*, which called for several acting levels and projection screens, at the time of its premiere as "unplayable"; Sawallisch, at the age of eighteen, had been in charge of a Hitler Youth choir at Radio Munich.[407] Another traditionalist musician was Alois Melichar, a film composer who had written the musical score for . . . *reitet für Deutschland* (1940/1), an irredentist movie with anti-Semitic overtones, and *Baku*, a 1941 anti-British propaganda film.[408] After 1945, Melichar found himself neglected and began to rage against the Modernists who, in his opinion, were taking over everywhere. He reserved his fiercest offensive for Schoenberg, in a book of 1960, where he castigated the composer and his "twelve-tone fascism," trying to justify his particular brand of anti-Semitism.[409] In 1954 he deplored that composers such as himself, Robert Heger, Armin Knab, and Walter Abendroth had been eclipsed by "the atonal clique."[410] He regarded Henze's 1952 ballet *Pas d'action* as "pitiful rubbish" and the composer himself as surrounded by "faggot laddies."[411]

More dangerous were Friedrich Blume, the musicologist who had managed to make an appearance at the 1946 Darmstadt festival, and music critic Abendroth, because they reached a larger audience. Blume, born in 1893, like Jöde became involved in the Weimar-republican youth-music movement. He too had strong Nazi connections having been, from 1939 on, at Kiel University as a full professor. In his book *Das Rasseproblem in der Musik* (*The Problem of Race in Music*) of that year he contributed a musicological essay to a festschrift in honor of Hitler's fiftieth birthday, in which he cast doubts upon the Jews.[412] Still, he was allowed to reoccupy his chair in 1947. In 1949, the psychologist Albert Wellek, with old Nazi connections, published an article in one of Blume's anthologies attacking atonality based on Alfred Rosenberg's reasoning.[413] Blume himself issued forth diatribes against electronic music, of the Eimert and Stockhausen school. The "tonal system" was being exploded, charged Blume, with tonality a thing of the past. Ultimately, it would be wrong to call the new end-product "music."[414] Thus slandered, the young garde attempted a concerted rebuttal, with Boulez, Eimert, Zimmermann, and Stockhausen participating.[415] But they were themselves divided, and Blume, in concert with Melichar and Abendroth, continued his offensives unabated, not least in his lecture halls at Kiel.

Using as his platform monographic publications and, beyond his retirement in 1955 from it, Hamburg's *Die Zeit*, Abendroth was doing his best to undermine the new cultural developments he so detested. A fierce opponent of jazz or anything American, Abendroth was predictably a loyal follower of the traditional Bayreuth festival.[416] In 1933 he had written hymnically that the Führer had come forth with a complete understanding of the Wagnerian concept that, so he wrote a year later, was beautifully manifest in the 1934 *Meistersinger* performance.[417] But ten years after that, Abendroth disagreed with Wieland Wagner's work in Bayreuth under Wilhelm Tietjen, even though he retained faith in Tietjen's overall direction. Come 1951, Abendroth was vexed that Wieland, together with his younger brother Wolfgang, should be granted license to stage the master's operas in a new Bayreuth.[418] He waited until Wieland Wagner's own production of *Die Meistersinger* in 1956 finally to deliver a deadly blow.[419]

Abendroth came to have a differentiated view of Modernism in music. The more restrained in form and the more tonal twentieth-century compositions were, the more he could countenance them. Hence, he appreciated the works of Orff and Egk. Hindemith and Stravinsky's later œuvre also agreed with him, because their neoclassical forms, melody and harmony, guaranteed order. But he found Benjamin Britten problematic, whose style he deemed too "eclectic" and whose opera *Billy Budd* touched him negatively. Abendroth suspected abstraction, and he chastised deliberate construction in musical composition, as he found it in Virgil Thomson's work: "a typical product of the intellectual café, nihilistic in essence, artistic in conception and a textbook example for that dangerous point of departure where spiritual freedom, misunderstood, will turn into anarchy."[420]

This led him to Schoenberg's progressivism, which he regarded as the apotheosis of contrivance in music. During the very early 1950s, when Hindemith's backward-looking modern music dominated the avant-garde, Abendroth appeared reassured that Schoenberg's work moved only a small fraction of German musicians and connoisseurs.[421] But this had changed by the middle of the decade, as Abendroth was beginning to denounce the "dogmatic dictatorship" that was bent on defining contemporary creative norms only in one way, amounting to a music-theory "power grab." Just as the Nazis had deprecated Sigmund Freud, so Abendroth, too, construed arguments associating Schoenberg's methodology negatively with psychoanalysis.[422] Then, in an article of 1958, in which he endorsed a recent book by his friend Melichar, he condemned the work of Schoenberg, Webern, and all the Donaueschingen and Darmstadt composers who had followed them.[423] And a year later he added, wrongly, that over more than three decades twelve-tone music had remained "without any true resonance."[424] By this time, however, he was not sufficiently powerful any more to cause lasting damage.

◆　◆　◆

The 1950s were characterized by, politically, unshakable stability and, economically, the return of prosperity, predicated on the division between East and West Germany as sanctioned by the Cold War. The early trials of the worst of Nazi war criminals were accompanied, culturally, by retrospectives in literature authored by – at the time – youthful participants in war and, related, experimental musicians at the Darmstadt music courses. Experimentation became a hallmark of the emerging arts, as it showed in jazz, radio Hörspiele, or the Informel painting school, sometimes with nods of indebtedness to the United States or France. In the interest of a vibrant democracy, those artists' critiques extended, in part, to the new materialism that was an outgrowth of the Economic Miracle.

German themes of martyrology were, however, continued in such cultural products as Heimatfilme, the novels of a Gerd Gaiser, or articles by Walter Abendroth, as well as ex-Hitler Youth attempts to revive folk music. Would such phenomena finally disappear in the 1960s, as all protagonists were getting older and inveterate Nazis were dying out? Would it not, finally, be time, if not for reconciliation, then for introspection, an examination of one's own relationship to the Third Reich and how to cope with the nation's gravest of offences in the last century, nay all of history? As the 1950s saw recurrent anti-Semitism, in the decade following the Germans were in for a fundamental reckoning concerning mass murder and Auschwitz. Culture mavens had to deal with this as well as define their own status, vis-à-vis their mentors and an emergent, restless generation, bent on faulting their parents.

CHAPTER THREE

◆ ◆ ◆

The Clash of Generations (1960–1970)

O NE OF THE problems of early 1960s West Germany, which became
a key contributor to student unrest later in the decade and inevitably had ramifications for culture, was the permeation of university
and research institutions by old Nazi elements, by academics who had once
again fully established themselves, and residual fascist dogma. I experienced
this at a lower level at the University of Munich in 1959–60, and in Heidelberg
and Koblenz at a higher and acutely personal level some two years later. In the
autumn of 1959 in Munich, I was in a postgraduate seminar taught by Fritz
Valjavec, a full professor of southeast European history. He was a German
from the Banat, touted as an expert on the Balkans. I found him very knowl-
edgeable, overseeing the complex post-World War I history of the Balkans, in
particular minorities issues. Early in 1960, with a major thesis in mind, I was
informed by a sign on his office door that Professor Valjavec had just died.
Years later archival evidence was published to the effect that Valjavec had been
investigated as a member of Otto Ohlendorf's SD-Einsatzgruppe D. It had
massacred one hundred Jews in Czernowitz in July 1941, including, possibly,
Paul Celan's parents. It emerged that Valjavec had been under investigation for
war crimes. After the war he had concealed his past and obtained that chair at
Munich, as his expertise was in great demand.[1]

Those fleeting get-togethers with the affable Valjavec had no personal
consequences for me. This changed two years later when I had put full-time

professional jazz-musician ambitions aside, apart from occasional gigs in Heidelberg's Cave 54. Instead, I had decided to work toward a doctorate in modern German history at the University of Heidelberg. Armed with a 1961 MA certificate from the University of Toronto, I became a doctoral student of Professor Werner Conze, wishing to investigate the Ahnenerbe. This was Himmler's research organization in the SS, through which he had attempted to control German culture and, in the universities, research in the humanities, natural science, and medicine. Hence in summer 1962 I entered, on Conze's recommendation, the Bundesarchiv (Federal Archives) in Koblenz for primary research. The voluminous files of the Ahnenerbe, which had been used by the Americans during the Nuremberg Doctors' Trials, were deposited there in the original. After two weeks of work I was summoned to the office of a deputy director, Dr. Wolfgang A. Mommsen, a grandson of Nobel laureate Theodor Mommsen. In the shrillest of voices, Mommsen accused me of having misplaced documents and berated me as a person unfit for research. I was told to pack my things and never to return. Stunned, and knowing I was innocent, I consulted with Conze back in Heidelberg, who appeared surprised. But he did not get on the phone to Koblenz to insist on my reinstatement. It became obvious to me that someone wanted to prevent me doing research on the SS. But because I knew that microfilm copies of the Ahnenerbe correspondence were in the National Archives in Washington, I embarked for New York, on borrowed money. Boarding in the YMCA near the White House, I spent strenuous months in Washington copying from microfilms, unearthing the history of the Ahnenerbe, which in 1966 became the subject of my Heidelberg dissertation and, in 1974, the basis for my first book.

As I had suspected, I had been thrown out of the Bundesarchiv on a pretext, for I found Mommsen's name in the Ahnenerbe files repeatedly. A Nazi Party member since 1937, he had assisted it in the looting of archives in occupied eastern territories.[2] In March 1942 he witnessed but, according to his diary, did not participate in, the shooting of the Jews in Riga: "There should be nothing left," he noted, "now it's the turn of the Jews from the Reich, who are allowed to shovel snow here for a few days on their way to death."[3] According to archival research by Ernst Klee, the USSR wanted Mommsen after 1945 for war crimes. But as he had managed to ingratiate himself with the Western Allies, he was allowed to process documentary materials for upcoming Nuremberg Trials. Thereafter, he re-entered the archivist's profession in 1952, becoming president of the Federal Archives in 1967. In 1972 he received the Federal Cross of Merit from Bonn.[4]

◆ ◆ ◆

In the early 1960s, the Bundesarchiv was involved in preparations for the Auschwitz Trial, under the Hessian Chief State Attorney Dr. Fritz Bauer in Frankfurt. The trial and two subtrials were to have an important impact on the collective self-reflection of Germans, often discursively: they exposed Nazi criminals to wide-open scrutiny; for the first time they centered on Jews as victims of Nazi wrongdoing; and ultimately, they influenced literary and artistic output. Despite Bauer's central initiative, the main trial in 1963 did not come about so much as the result of single-minded strategic planning than being born of several impulses, some of them determined by happenstance.

Significantly, Bauer was not a typical representative of the Bonn juridical system. Born in 1903 in Stuttgart, he had had good reasons to leave Germany, after incarceration by the Nazis, for Sweden – as a Jew, a practicing Social Democrat, and a homosexual. When he returned to Germany in 1949, he was appointed to a high justice position in Brunswick. After 1952 in Frankfurt, he became interested in a full restitution of the rule of law, advocating for the prosecution of Nazi criminals. His longer-reaching aim was to enable comprehension of the most recent past for the purpose of avoiding mistakes in the future, hence his attentiveness to history. "Coming to grips with our past means to sit in judgment over ourselves," he said in July 1962, "in judgment over the dangerous aspects of our history."[5] In all of this, he felt he was inadequately supported in the restorative climate that was the hallmark of the early FRG.[6]

Adolf Eichmann was an important factor in the process leading to the Frankfurt trial. Since becoming the chief attorney for Hesse in Frankfurt, Bauer knew Eichmann was hiding from justice as early as 1956; he wanted to bring him to trial in Germany. But efforts to enlist West German help repeatedly came to naught. Because he thought it would be safe, Eichmann was looking forward to returning to Germany from Argentina sometime in 1960. However, the Israelis, tipped off by Bauer, kidnapped Eichmann in Buenos Aires on May 11, 1960, put him on trial in the spring of 1961, and condemned him to hang for organizing the mass killing of Europe's Jews in December of that year.[7]

The Eichmann Trial created a precedent for justice to be meted out for the genocide of Jews internationally that even reluctant Bonn bureaucrats found difficult to ignore. After the 1958 Einsatzgruppen trial in Ulm and the formation of the Ludwigsburg prosecution agency, it added further impetus to progressive German jurists to bring Nazi murderers to heel. Bauer especially was looking out for killers other than Eichmann, and already in 1959 he had secured permission from the supreme court to go ahead with a trial, at Frankfurt, of former Auschwitz personnel. Regional courts all over West Germany opposed him, because they wanted to go ahead on their own, not least in order to attenuate and render powerless judicial proceedings. Since 1959, however, Bauer had managed to interview 1,300 witnesses, most from Auschwitz, as testimony for *his* trial, beginning in December 1963.[8]

He was aided by a personal intercession and a stroke of good luck. In March 1958 a letter from an Auschwitz victim alerted him to main perpetrator Wilhelm Boger, now living near Stuttgart. In 1962 the press coverage of Rolf Mulka, a medal-winning sailor from the German Olympic team of 1960, led to the discovery of his father Robert Mulka, the former deputy commandant of Auschwitz, now a merchant in Hamburg.[9]

As the trial initially of twenty-two defendants unfolded in Frankfurt, German and international visitors paid close attention. To observers such as Martin Walser, who assiduously attended for weeks in early 1964, the ordinariness of the culprits was remarkable. They could have easily been confused with regular German citizens, in the manner that Hannah Arendt had cited psychiatric assessments describing Eichmann at his Jerusalem trial as "normal" a few years before.[10] Walser was shocked by the singular atrocities that came to light: "Oswald Kaduk, 57, butcher and orderly, SS-Unterscharführer. Placed a walking stick over inmates' necks and then stepped on it. Pulled the stool from under inmates to hang them, shots in the back of the neck at the Black Board with Pistol 08 with inserter, drove over inmates with a motorcycle, selected inmates and led them to be gassed."[11] When I visited the courtroom on a day-trip from Heidelberg in April, like Walser I was struck by the everyday appearance and manner of speech of the defendants, which matched the quotidian course of trial dealings.

Robert Mulka maintained that he never set foot in the camp and had only heard about gassings, never asking further.[12] Wilhelm Boger, a brutal police investigator even before Auschwitz, was a member of the SS political division. He built a torture chamber and installed the "Boger Swing," a contraption twisting inmates before beatings and false confessions. "The purpose of such stepped-up interrogation was fulfilled when blood came out of the pants. I never beat anyone to death, I followed orders," stated Boger in Frankfurt.[13] Franz Lucas was a physician who finally admitted that he had assisted his colleague Josef Mengele during selections on the ramp.[14] And I observed Pery Broad, who had come to Germany from Brazil as a child and, as a volunteer for the Waffen-SS, in 1942 was in Auschwitz. This unassuming man of middle age, too, was charged with selections on the ramp, and, especially, the murder of Romani. Henryk Eisenman, a Polish survivor of Auschwitz whom I interviewed later, called him a "sadist," but Broad was also known to enjoy jazz. Auschwitz did have its swing band, "The Merry Five," for the amusement of SS men, so when in the mood, Broad would join in on accordion. Does music temper human cruelty? Does music temper fascism? In reality, Broad had a perverted sense of aesthetics. In Auschwitz, he had a reputation for killing the most beautiful girls first.[15]

In August 1965 judgment was pronounced on the twenty remaining defendants. Three were acquitted for lack of sufficient evidence, six received a life sentence, and eleven got off with lighter punishment. They had meted out terror and death to 1.3 million men, women, and children, the great majority of them Jews, between 1941 and 1945. Although all the offenders acknowledged participation in torture and killings, none accepted personal guilt.[16]

The public reaction to the trial in West Germany was ambivalent. Overall, it was a sign of the progress of formal democracy that most citizens approved of the proceedings – and they might even be taken as a sign of contrition. The trial was interpreted as "a cultural watershed. It was both a focal point and a wellspring for the politics of memory in the Federal Republic."[17] It spawned enlightening newspaper coverage, such as in the *FAZ*, and a television documentary, *Das Dritte Reich*. It specified the image of the Third Reich and its helpers as one not just ruled by Hitler's immediate clique.[18] At a more elevated level, the expert assessments authored by historians of the Institut für Zeitgeschichte, such as Martin Broszat's, not only aided the trial jurists, but, when published, also further research on the Third Reich.[19]

But on the other hand, letters to the editor and such showed that many Germans were opposed to it.[20] Progressive jurists around Bauer deplored that the Auschwitz crimes were treated as individual transgressions and not singled out as systematic genocide organized by the state.[21] Others again rued that the Jewish element had been downplayed.[22] The most serious criticism was that many known culprits had escaped justice and that in Frankfurt too lenient sentences had been pronounced.[23]

Perceived deficits were partly due to the fact that as a basis for sentencing, the laws as they obtained before 1945 had to apply, and this favored the defendants.[24] Moreover, Bauer's mandate did not enjoy majority support among Hessian jurists, and the presiding justice was found to be Nazi-compromised: Hans Hofmeyer was later accused of having participated in forced sterilization cases at a hereditary-health court in Giessen and of having been part of a department which, at the end of the war, oversaw the establishment of the itinerant drumhead courts-martial that strung up Germans loath to engage in last-ditch combat, on trees and lampposts.[25]

Bonn's dislike of Bauer's doings in Frankfurt was based on the fear that the exposition of Auschwitz crimes of such magnitude was hurting West Germany's international image, notwithstanding its official policy of good-will with Israel. As one of several politicians, Franz Josef Strauss, the chairman of the CSU and a former minister of defense, had raised objections. In August 1965, journalist Dietrich Strothmann accused him of obstinacy, in that he repudiated "acknowledgment of the ineradicable guilt of many Germans for the mass murder and the necessity of *all* Germans to gain clarity about the causes and consequences of those deeds."[26] Undeterred, Strauss again became minister of economics under Chancellor Kurt Georg Kiesinger in 1966. His uninterrupted presence in Bonn symbolized the permanent power conservatives exercised in federal politics from 1949 well into the 1970s.

The 1960s lacked the political stability of the 1950s, not least because of greater dynamics in the economy, in society at large and the arts and letters in particular. There were no fewer than four chancellors, one of them a Social Democrat. After the general elections of September 17, 1961, the CDU lost its absolute majority, with the SPD and FDP gaining; hence the centrist FDP entered a coalition government with CDU and CSU. After pressure from the FDP, the aging Adenauer in October 1963 ceded his office to Ludwig Erhard, the widely admired former economics minister. His economic governance had turned the storied "miracle" into normality. In 1965 the CDU won again, as did the SPD, with the FDP losing pointedly. The result was a Grand Coalition between CDU and SPD of December 1966, with Kiesinger as chancellor and Willy Brandt, the SPD's leader since 1964, as foreign minister. There was now practically no party opposition in the Bonn parliament. More middle-class voters had voted for the SPD since its renunciation of radical Marxism in 1959; it had become more of a people's party. Brandt became chancellor in 1969, after a mild recession in 1966–7 had led to elections. Along with a strengthened SPD, a weakened CDU and a battered FDP returned. For the first time in the FRG's history, the CDU/CSU was forced into parliamentary opposition.[27]

Despite continued economic progress that practically abolished unemployment, making many more citizens of the republic wealthy, and which helped subduing political extremism both on the right and left, there were several critical developments in the 1960s with important repercussions, real or potential, in the arts and culture scene.[28] These were the *Spiegel* affair of 1962, the passing of emergency legislation in 1968, and protracted deliberations in society and parliament regarding a statute of limitations for Nazi crimes.

In the case of *Der Spiegel*, its journalists had placed into doubt the state of military security of the FRG in October 1962, by questioning the prioritizing of atomic over conventional weapons. Thereupon Defense Minister Strauss recognized a chance to ruin it. He searched *Spiegel* offices, clapping Augstein into jail. But on the left, this was seen as an attack on press freedom with Nazi methods and, subsequently, Strauss was forced to resign his portfolio and Adenauer, who had charged the magazine with "treason in our land," lost credibility. This contributed to his own retirement months later.[29]

Since late 1962, therefore, conservative politicians in Bonn were bent on strengthening their position against the left. They threatened using expanded emergency powers imbedded in the Basic Law. Fearing this, students and left-liberal faculty, including historian Karl Dietrich Bracher, protested on the Bonn University campus during May 1965. They were afraid of a repeat of Nazi tactics that had abolished essential freedoms in

1933. In July, after Rolf Hochhuth had issued his play *Der Stellvertreter*, which was critical of papal as well as Third Reich authority, Chancellor Erhard publicly denigrated him and his consorts as "pipsqueaks."[30] After the formation of the Grand Coalition in December 1966, extended laws were more intensely discussed in Bonn. As part of the government, the SPD promised conditional support given parliamentary guarantees. At this point, Brandt and his party cohort did not appear overly concerned by Karl Jaspers's warnings of militarism à la General Franco in Spain, or of totalitarianism à la Hitler.[31]

The new emergency powers became law on May 30, 1968, having been passed by the required two-thirds majority in parliament with the SPD's support.[32] The polarization was complete: while the Springer press of *Welt* and *Bild* and reactionaries everywhere triumphed, the leftist camp, students, intellectuals, and artists, was outraged, yet impotent. In vain, one left-oriented young journalist, Ulrike Meinhof, had warned weeks before that it was of vital necessity to defeat the emergency laws in order to "disempower the dictators in state and society."[33] Like Jaspers, she cast a wary eye on major politicians of the right in Bonn: Interior Minister Gerhard Schröder who, however committed, had been in the NSDAP, Federal President Heinrich Lübke who could not extricate himself from suspicion that he had constructed concentration camps, and Chancellor Kiesinger himself, a former broadcast specialist in Ribbentrop's and Goebbels's ministries. In November 1968, during a CDU convention in Berlin, Beate Klarsfeld, a twenty-nine-year-old German whose Romanian-French husband Serge had lost his father in the Holocaust, advanced to the podium and slapped the sixty-four-year-old Kiesinger in the face with the cry: "Nazi, Nazi!" It was as if the young woman was hitting her own father. Klarsfeld was sentenced to a year in jail, which progressives considered preposterous in light of the recent, relatively lenient, Auschwitz Trial judgments.[34]

Given its philosophy of permissiveness, from the beginning of the republic the right-wing-majority government was always bent on reducing the effectiveness of Nazi-crime prosecution by instituting a statute of limitations. Conservatives wished to set 1940 as the start of a twenty-year period leading to amnesty in 1960, meaning no wartime murder trials after that year. Parliamentary opposition at the time, by the Social Democrats, was deemed defeatable.

But except for the elimination of manslaughter as an object of prosecution, a statute of limitations did not come to pass in 1960, not only because of SPD objections, but also because of continued accusations by the GDR. Israel, the international community, and especially the International Auschwitz Committee also exerted pressure. In addition, thousands of returning POWs from the Soviet Gulag had to be considered for questioning, and cases from Ludwigsburg central had yet to be processed.[35]

Moreover, when the debates continued in the first half of the 1960s, they stood under the shadow of the unfolding Auschwitz Trial; hence no statute was passed in the 1964–5 legislative period either. After Lübke had been re-elected as federal president in 1964, there was further pressure from around the world as well as from the formerly persecuted. After the SPD had proposed the total abolition of limitation for murder and genocide in parliament, a compromise was reached, retroactively moving the beginning of the twenty-year limitation period to 1949, making a new debate obligatory in 1969.[36] During that year, Ludwigsburg central announced there were many more cases to be tried. This time, on Chancellor Brandt's initiative, it was decided to delay a decision for another ten years, thus safeguarding the status quo.[37]

◆   ◆   ◆

The students' rebellion of the late 1960s was initially caused by inadequacies in the universities. They found the subject matter being taught infected with Nazi ideas, prescribed comportment in classrooms as outmoded as academic rituals, and many of the professors themselves to have been Nazis and to have uttered Nazi ideas. When I entered Heidelberg University in the fall of 1961 to study with Werner Conze, I did not know of Conze's own Nazi background; instead, I was drawn to him because by that time he, next to Bracher in Bonn, was reputed to be interested in the teaching of Third Reich history. Indeed, in 1959–60, he had made a reputation in that field – but not as a writer.[38]

I had become acutely interested in the study of Nazism and the Third Reich after a trip I had taken from Munich to Jerusalem and back with a fellow scholarship student from Winnipeg, throughout March and April 1960. We went by bicycles, hitchhiking, and train to Israel, and back again through Syria, Turkey, Greece, and Italy. The trip alerted me to the situation of the Jews, both in terms of the Arab majority they were now surrounded by and their recent past in a National Socialist-dominated Europe, in ways I had never imagined before, as I had studied modern European history back in Toronto.

Two or three events in particular made me more aware of that history. Outside Beirut we were picked up by a younger man, tall and elegant, in an American car with a chauffeur who took us through Syria and Jordan for two days. Obviously rich, he called himself Hussein Amin and claimed to be the son of Amin al-Husseini, the grand mufti of Jerusalem who had met with Hitler in Berlin in November 1941 to discuss policy against the Jews in Palestine. In the car, he launched into a tirade against Jews, declaring that through Himmler's relatives he had been given fifty thousand photographs of Jewish concentration camp inmates. How despicable they were! Later, during a longer stay at Givat Brenner Kibbutz in central Israel, Ernest Redekop and I noticed several people with tattoos on their lower arms – survivors of Auschwitz. Involving them in conversations about their Third Reich experiences proved near impossible. A few weeks later Arabs we met while hitchhiking from Haifa to Tiberias told us about having been expropriated by the Israelis. In the end it was difficult to receive a clear picture of people's privileges and their suffering, and where responsibilities lay. I wanted to know more.[39]

As a doctoral student of Conze's in autumn 1961, I found that he was mostly teaching non-Nazi topics. Only later did I learn about his complex personality. With a highly educated, upper-bourgeois family background, the 1910-born Conze had been significantly shaped by the right wing of the German youth movement. With its restorational aims, it lamented the Treaty of Versailles of 1919 and clamored for the return of German territory lost to its eastern neighbors. He entered the University of Königsberg and came under the influence of Hans Rothfels, the *völkisch* sociologist Gunter Ipsen and the economic "Blood-and-Soil" chimera of Theodor Oberländer, whose staff he joined.[40] Besides teaching there, Oberländer was the local leader of Conze's fraternity, Deutsche Akademische Gildenschaft, with racist, irredentist origins. Some of its members had been involved in the Munich Hitler Putsch of November 1923 and now promoted new colonial forays into Poland. Conze acquired his doctorate with Rothfels in 1934 and, later in the Wehrmacht, became a captain at the Eastern Front. A member of the SA since 1933 and the Nazi Party since 1937, in 1943 he was also a faculty member at the new Nazi University of Posen (Poznan). The year 1946 found him, released from a Soviet POW camp, at the University of Göttingen, war-wounded and lowly placed in the faculty. In 1955 he became an associate professor of history in Münster, changing to Heidelberg for a full chair in 1957.[41]

It appears that the nationalist firebrand of Königsberg was, in important ways, a different man from the historiographical innovator of Heidelberg. Rothfels's scheme of an *Ostpolitik* that plotted a resurrection of thick German settlement in the European East, à la the medieval Teutonic Order and later also underwritten by Oberländer, intrigued Conze. Already before the war he imagined the return of Polish-occupied German territory to the Reich and other pro-German demographic changes in the East. There, he singled out Jews as the cause of population imbalances in that, allegedly, they crowded the urban spaces, and hence he advocated for a "dejewification of towns and marketplaces." After September 1939 this would facilitate a move of Poles into those towns and of Germans from the Reich to be settled in the formerly Polish countryside. Where those urban Jews should go he never elaborated – Madagascar, further east in Europe, or Central Asia? Mass killings? Whatever he envisioned, there is no question that as a confirmed anti-Semite and imperialist-minded hypernationalist Conze agreed with many of the Nazis' policies.[42]

Conze came to Göttingen in large part through its medievalist Reinhard Wittram, a veteran National Socialist from the Baltic who knew him from Posen. In 1956, Conze became involved in a large-scale project to document the expulsion of Germans from the European East starting in 1945 – it was an ironic reversal of his earlier theme. This was headed by his old friend Theodor Schieder, a historian with similar research interests from Königsberg, where Schieder, under Rothfels, had become a professor. Schieder now had a chair in Cologne. Rothfels, after his return to Germany in 1951, also joined the project. Officially it was overseen by Peter Paul Nahm, state secretary in the Bonn ministry for refugees, headed, after 1953, by Oberländer.[43]

Beginning in the mid-1950s, Schieder and Conze became the most important historians of modern Germany in the FRG, not least because of the latter's groundbreaking visions of what a new social history should be and the development of novel methodologies derived, in part, from the French *Annales* school, in particular Fernand Braudel. In the 1970s, Conze alone was recognized as the "founding father of West German social history."[44] Initially Conze had been inspired by the history and sociology of ethnicities, at that time with the *völkisch* bias toward everything German, which he had learned from Rothfels, Oberländer, and the race-conscious sociologist Ipsen. But now Conze developed a version of *Sozialgeschichte* that was value-free, encompassing the teachings of Max Weber and, critically, Marx. Having left Nazism behind, he published a first milestone in the development of his new discipline, his 1955 article on the German underclass of the nineteenth century. It appeared in the conservative *Vierteljahrschrift für Sozial- und Wirtschaftsgeschichte*, in which he showed himself fully conversant with Marxist theory and the developmental outlines of various social strata.[45]

After 1957 in Heidelberg, Conze came across as a conservative personally and a liberal academically. In accordance with his, plausible, Saul/Paul conversion he developed an affinity for progressive subjects his students might pursue, encouraging them to experiment, often beyond actual *Sozialgeschichte*.[46] This explains why he permitted me to conduct research on the SS Ahnenerbe, without assigning me the topic; I had to consult with Hans Buchheim, one of the Institut für Zeitgeschichte experts for the Auschwitz Trial. Mine was only the second dissertation on the Third Reich Conze allowed.[47] In his teachings he still tended to cling to old-fashioned and even reactionary content: in seminars he tried to justify Chancellor Heinrich Brüning's authoritarian stance after 1930 and cast doubt on William L. Shirer's epochal *The Rise and Fall of the Third Reich*, just published.[48] In 1962 did he want to sabotage my research in the Bundesarchiv? He was a man of networks, and the Königsberg network, now active again, provided lifelines.[49] It is likely that he knew archivist Wolfgang A. Mommsen from both their war work in the Baltics and Poland. Hence, he may have been honor-bound not to interfere with any actions that Mommsen's own network, which coincided in part with Conze's, felt necessary to decide upon. It is unlikely, however, that he was in direct cahoots with Mommsen, or he would not have allowed my initial presence in Koblenz. In 1966 he passed my dissertation, and later others in that field.[50] Later Conze came around to admitting mistakes that had been made before and after 1945, as he spoke to a congregation of his party, the CDU/CSU, in March 1968, amid the student rebellion: "Crimes remained long unpunished, there was not enough free and open discussion of the problems of individual as well as public entanglements. If it was still alive, the generation of fathers became questionable to its offspring. Many conflictions of the political mentality in West Germany are traceable to the failure in resolving the pressing problems during the first years after 1945."[51] Here Conze recognized the roots of student unrest in the wrongdoings of Nazism, with generational conflict as their consequence.[52]

In the early 1960s Heidelberg was home to several more professors who had been Nazis, any post-1945 ideological epiphany notwithstanding. Wilhelm Emil Mühlmann was the head of sociology. A member of the SA and NSDAP, he had written books on race and the breeding benefits of "well ordered and organized warfare."[53] Heinrich Bornkamm held his chair of church history in the theological faculty. Once in the SA and Nazi Teachers' League, he defined what was to be expected from the Lutheran Church of the 1930s – to protect "the *völkisch* substance" from Bolshevism and Jewry.[54] Bornkamm's colleague Karl Georg Kuhn had gone further. In April 1933 this young theologian, long a member of Nazi organizations, had supported the anti-Jewish boycott in Tübingen with a public speech, in which he maintained that "international world Jewry had declared war on the new Germany, not with weapons but with words," and hence a Nazi boycott of Jewish businesses would help stem the "unhindered Jewish drive to power" and finally contribute to the "solution of the Jewish question."[55] Ernst Forsthoff, who in 1952 reoccupied the Heidelberg chair in law that he had lost in 1945, during the Third Reich had justified both the totalitarian state that had "neutralized the private character of individual existence," and also demanded that "the Jew," as enemy, "be disposed of."[56] In the 1960s, these writings were hard to locate. Heidelberg's university library had a so-called poison cabinet, which was said to contain Hitler's *Mein Kampf*, but, likely, also the publications of scholars who could be embarrassed – so students had difficulty accessing them.

It would fill volumes to list faculty with similar backgrounds and post-1945 histories for all West German universities. Significantly their students, alerted in no small measure by the Eichmann and Auschwitz trials, were beginning to question how and what they were being taught, and by whom. Criticism of the universities and their mandarins was not fixed on Nazi reputation alone, but also on a perceived sense of entitlement students identified as an insalubrious heritage of the pre-1945 era. And this was combined with disapproval of the political setup at universities, where a hierarchical structure favored full professors at the top and left no room for participation in university administration by untenured lecturers, professorial assistants, and the student body. University reform, therefore, as it was now beginning to be demanded, meant the purging of the faculty, combined with a sharing of power by the young. This call for a "democratic university," as Berlin's student representative Peter Müller pleaded for in the first half of the 1960s, was resisted by the elders, making for a generational struggle and engendering a "culture of suspicion" Conze could never have imagined.[57]

Protest against the universities, by midlevel instructors and students subordinate to full professors, took various shapes and forms from 1960 to 1969, and was acted out at several stages. Ultimately the anti-Nazi accusations were conflated with recriminations against the, purportedly imperialist, United States. In Heidelberg in 1960, Michael Buselmeier began to study art history and German literature; he found the professors "theatrical" and possessed of "authoritarian gestures." They aped the oratory of great poets, Goethe or Stefan George, and were sure to impress everybody around. When Peter Wapnewski, a Germanist who had accepted a call to Berlin in summer 1966, held his closing lecture, he artfully conjugated sentences in Walther von der Vogelweide's middle-high German and sanctimoniously shed tears before his class. By that time Buselmeier had already joined mass demonstrations, led by the Socialist German Student League (SDS), whose national chief was Rudi Dutschke, demanding fundamental reforms of the university system.[58]

In 1960 also, disturbed by the synagogue smearings, students at the Free University of Berlin (FU), with the SDS in the lead, took the initiative in organizing a seminar themed "Overcoming Anti-Semitism," which carried on into 1965. Berlin was the first hotspot of student unrest because of the principles of liberty the new university had been based on since 1948; and also because left-wing students who resented being drafted into the Bundeswehr went there, as its special status accorded by the four Allies made them exempt from conscription. In 1965, Ekkehart Krippendorf, an assistant in the political-science department, spoke out against the rector, accusing him of having prevented Karl Jaspers from speaking on campus.

When he also objected to a year-long university ban on the left-leaning journalist Erich Kuby, his employment was terminated. This sparked the first large-scale demonstrations on the Berlin campus, rhetorically against the American involvement in Vietnam (therewith connecting to the more original protests at Berkeley), but at the core always with the specifically German cause in mind: "We wish to demolish authoritarian forms of governance in the university and in society, and practice, here as there, democracy," as student leader Knut Nevermann formulated in 1967.[59]

Soon, the action was everywhere. In the University of Tübingen, the academic leadership attempted to counter criticism of past practices that had been leveled nationwide in the student press in 1963–4, by organizing a lecture series in which faculty members of various disciplines participated. But the lectures were considered exculpatory and self-serving.[60] In Bonn during 1964 there was objection to the appointment of Hugo Moser, a Germanist said to have a Nazi past, as rector of the university, but its administration persisted, nonetheless. The dissent had been initiated by Walter Boehlich, a former university assistant with a Jewish mother.[61] In Hamburg, the SDS organized go-ins to disrupt lectures, calling for the early retirement of tainted professors.[62] And in Frankfurt the local SDS displayed large placards with images of Beate Klarsfeld hitting Kiesinger, carried through the streets by throngs of students. This was in 1969, when the student revolution had all but failed.[63] Although there was some university reform in the 1970s, it hardly met the aims of the original student protesters.[64]

In the rejection of their elders, the students' rebellion of the 1960s has been compared to the German youth movement after World War I that Conze belonged to.[65] Whatever the similarities, there was one decisive difference. Whereas the youth even before World War I objected, first, to the bourgeois complacency of their parents and, thereafter, to their failure in having lost in battle, post-1945 adolescents of the upper-middle classes, those in universities, reacted to perceived crimes of their fathers as Nazis. Konrad Jarausch has correctly observed that "rebellious youths began their crusade at home by pointedly asking their fathers or uncles about their roles in the Third Reich."[66] As Helmut König has put it, for these young people National Socialism was not yet a closed chapter and part of history, but an imminent danger to current society in the FRG, as formal democracy appeared merely as one variant of several possible gubernatorial expressions of fascism.[67] The contours of this generational conflict were shaping up to make visible those who were born between 1935 and 1945 and came to have a reason to ask their progenitors how they personally related to the Nazi past, on the one side, and those born between 1900 and 1925, who would have to answer, on the other.

Student unrest in the streets of university towns persisted until March 1970, when the SDS dissolved itself in Frankfurt. Its two blackest days occurred when on June 2, 1967, during a state visit by the hated Shah of Iran, Reza Pahlavi, thought to be a servant of the United States, the student Benno Ohnesorg was shot dead by police in Berlin. And on April 11 of the following year student leader Dutschke himself was shot at by a fanaticized young right-winger, also in Berlin; put out of commission, he succumbed to his injuries eleven years later.[68]

Although it left traces later, the intellectual and artistic legacy of Dutschke's movement in immediate terms was not impressive. The New Left critical theorists Adorno and his erstwhile assistant Jürgen Habermas, who had been sympathizers of the movement in the beginning, were themselves criticized and distanced themselves at its end – the venal Adorno shocked that he was so unloved.[69] Two novels ensued, characterizing members of the movement, one a failed student who leaves for Italy disappointed, only to be arrested on his return to Germany, the other, who never manages to find an academic profession and becomes, in resignation, a primary-school teacher. Both novels aptly describe the follies and failures of a movement that was historically justified yet was not allowed to come to fruition because of obstinate forbears.[70]

◆ ◆ ◆

There was a generational issue raising questions of responsibility and guilt within the ascending West German writing class as well. Some of the leading authors of a certain generation who were now moralizing, reminding their readers of the wrong turns taken before 1945, were themselves tied to the Third Reich, without, however, fully divulging it. Their generation was the one born between 1920 and 1930, which would have made them too young to have played a decisive role in the Hitler state, but too young also to become parents who would be questioned during a student revolt.

Heinrich Böll, born in 1917, did not belong to that age cohort, and neither did he have any formal ties to the Third Reich that he might have wanted to suppress after 1945. Eventually it could have been incumbent on his three sons to ask him questions as a father. Did they query him about what he did in the Wehrmacht during the war?

Perhaps they asked him what he thought. Böll's contemplations as a soldier were neither disinterested nor neutral. His deeply Catholic family, especially his mother, detested Nazism, although one of his brothers later joined the SA, possibly as an alibi.[71] In school, he dissected *Mein Kampf*, abhorred by its grammar and syntax. Then, at Cologne University, he studied German literature under Ernst Bertram, sympathetic to the Third Reich, whom Böll found learned and sensitive.[72] In the Wehrmacht, being stationed behind the front in 1939, he longed for action.[73] Then sent to Bromberg (Bydgoszcz) in western Poland, he was struck by the dirt and disorder reportedly caused by the Poles ("bedbugs," "whores") and was touched sympathetically by Volksdeutsche living there, in sync with Nazi propaganda.[74]

Böll's view of war, then, was romantic; he wanted victory for the Germans, not seeing that they were often the same as the hated Nazis. At the dawn of Hitler's invasion of the USSR in spring 1941, being at the front would be a wish fulfilled – "surely it must be wonderful to move into the infinite spaces of Russia."[75] German culture was "certainly the best in the world" and needed defending.[76] Including Catholic Christendom, Germany's heritage had to be shielded, especially from the noxious effects of the French Revolution, so difficult "it can hardly be imagined" – in a letter from Calais, 1942.[77] Before and after the 1943 battle of Stalingrad, Böll insisted that Germany be victorious, imagining for himself "a colonial existence perhaps here in the East after the war."[78] In his diary from 1943 to 1945, Böll recounted the horrors of war, but was silent on its ultimate purpose and the German dictatorship.[79]

Martin Walser, born in 1927, belonged on the 1920–30 cohort; he experienced the Third Reich as a boy in lakeside Wasserburg. Over time, much of his writing divulged details about service in the Hitler Youth and soldiering in a ski patrol in the Alps. In 2017 he told his biological son Jakob Augstein that not his father, but his mother had joined the Nazi Party in 1932, for the sake of the family business. He admitted to having been an enthusiastic member of the Kriegsmarine division of the Hitler Youth when ten years old, in 1937, eventually winning the Reich championship in marine signaling. Late in the war he had wished to join a tank division, but was rejected because of his eyes; hence the infantry and hoping for a commission.[80] As for his Nazi Party membership from April 1944, at age seventeen, details of which had recently been discovered in the Bundesarchiv, he said that a local Nazi official had put his name forward without him being asked.[81]

This reportage needs examining. A Nazi Party entry by Walser's mother merely for the sake of business makes little sense in a Catholic hamlet with very few Nazis in 1932. Hence his mother, whom he characterizes as a "naïve anti-Semite," must have been a convinced rather than opportunistic National Socialist.[82] She could have had an influence on his eagerly joining the Hitler Youth. Contrary to Walser's assertion that Hitler Youth member-ship was compulsory in 1937, such service was obligatory only in March 1939;[83] and even then refusal was possible, as practiced by Walser's contem-poraries Joachim Fest and Joachim Kaiser. After caricaturizing the Führer in school, the one-year-older Fest, facing expulsion, moved with his family from Berlin to Freiburg in 1941.[84] Kaiser, born in 1928, protested to his father, a country doctor in East Prussia, so another doctor then signed medical-release papers for Joachim to avoid the Hitler Youth.[85]

As for Walser's automatic party membership, he claims to have been surprised that what applied to Martin Broszat also applied to him. Nazi Party membership was not designed to occur without a candidate's original signature on an application form.[86] That a Nazi official should have nomi-nated Walser clandestinely appears highly unlikely.[87] The question therefore becomes: Was Walser really truthful regarding the Nazi circumstances of his early youth?

As for Günter Grass, half a year Walser's junior: as he divulged publicly and also in mildly encrypted form in novels, he joined the Hitler Youth, was in an anti-aircraft flak emplacement, and was then drawn into the compul-sory Reich Labor Service, preliminary to the military. Being declined for the U-boat fleet in 1944, he was drafted into a Panzer division, where he served to the end at the Eastern Front.[88]

But there was more to it. In 2006, in a mixture of self-accusation and carnival, Grass divulged that his tank formation was the "Frundsberg"

Waffen-SS unit and that he had not only not resisted being moved there, but had welcomed it, for adventure's sake. He went further, admitting that as a pupil he had witnessed the execution of his Cassubian uncle, the persecution of a fellow student – a Jehovah's Witness who would not touch a gun – and an oppositional teacher, who vanished into Stutthof concentration camp near Danzig. He had also encountered a sensitive female teacher who showed him German Expressionists such as Dix and Klee. But he did not encounter any Jews, or so he said, nor did he mention the anti-Semitism that surely must have been prevalent in the SS unit he served with.[89]

Why did Grass wait until 2006 to reveal such key details, when from 1959 until then he had been acting as an enlightened preceptor for current generations? He never explained, other than citing authorial privilege as to when to tell all. Seemingly in contradiction to the revelatory nature of his novels, he publicly stated in January 1974 that he was not interested in "coming to grips with the German past."[90] What would facilitate this reluctance was that in the final turmoil of the war no SS runes had been tattooed onto his upper arm, as was the norm. He also insisted that he became aware of Nazi crimes only when Baldur von Schirach assumed all blame for misdeeds possibly committed by the young at Nuremberg, which, Grass said, woke him up. Instead, he had remained confident that he was on the right and winning side. Really? Schirach's Nuremberg statement occurred in May 1946: did Grass have to wait that long to grasp the enormity of Hitler's crimes and the likely coresponsibility of German youth?[91] Kaiser, who had listened to radio news at home, openly disagreed with Grass's confessor version because he had known that the war was over for Germany after Stalingrad.[92] Was Grass really innocent at the end of Nazi rule, before he entered a U.S. POW camp? This may well be doubted. Significantly, he asked Volker Schlöndorff, the director of the *Blechtrommel* movie in 1979, to cast his alter ego, Oskar Matzerath, in a black SS-like uniform while with the propaganda unit at the front; only the SS insignia were missing. Signs of an uneasy conscience rather than a private joke? According to the available evidence, the question to Grass today would have to be, not why he joined the Waffen-SS when scores of Hitler Youths tried to avoid this, but why he waited until 2006 to inform his legions of followers.[93] One explanation could have been the Nobel Prize Grass had justly been expecting ever since the international success of *Die Blechtrommel*. After receiving it in 1999 it was prudent, for decorum's sake, to stay quiet about his past for a while.

Grass was comparatively fortunate to have been assigned to a Waffen-SS unit at the front rather than in a concentration camp. As a guard there, he might have been tried as an accessory to murder decades later by a German court. This happened to Grass's exact contemporary Bruno Dey, drafted into the SS aged seventeen in August 1944 and serving as a guard in Danzig-Stutthof for a year. In 2019, accused by a Hamburg court, Dey acknowledged "hearing screams from the camp's gas chambers and watching as corpses were taken to be burned," but, incredibly, at the time did not recognize that guarding a camp was a criminal action. In December 2019 he received a suspended prison sentence.[94]

Having co-founded, in 1959, Germania Judaica, a Cologne archive that housed documents on the history of the Jews in Germany, Böll closely followed the SS trials and particularly the Frankfurt Auschwitz proceedings. He endorsed Adorno's dictum that after Auschwitz it was impossible to write poetry; feeling so strongly about the subject, he hyperbolically amplified it in one of his public lectures: "After Auschwitz, one can no longer breathe, eat, love, read."[95]

An admirer of Rudi Dutschke early on, like many active in the left-leaning intelligentsia, Böll looked on the initial student demonstrations sympathetically. He spoke at student meetings, for instance in protest against the pending emergency legislation, comparing it with the FRG's earlier plan to rearm. Yet as the 1960s wore on, like Habermas and Adorno he became wary of the students' progressive violence and counseled moderation, only to be jeered by his younger friends. Increasingly, they tended to see in him a father whose onetime war service was suspect.[96]

As in the 1950s, Böll went against the social and political order, within which he identified the Catholic Church as a major supporter of the Third Reich. The regnant, Catholic-majority CDU for him, especially under Adenauer, was always dangerously close to a monopoly party with authoritarian traits.[97] Hence he opposed the chancellor's intention to establish a government-controlled television channel in November 1960, when Grass, Enzensberger, and Walser supported him. He was dead set against the SPD joining the CDU in a Great Coalition in 1966, claiming publicly that "the CDU has destroyed Christianity in this country, the SPD Socialism."

After Klarsfeld's slight against Kiesinger, Böll sent her flowers. Kiesinger to him represented "well-groomed, middle-class Nazis, who dirtied neither their fingers nor their slates and who now continue after 1945 to parade shamelessly across the countryside."[98]

Always the pious Christian, Böll condemned the Catholic hierarchy as hypocritical, failing its flock in essential services.[99] Böll accused it of ethical compromise, in collusion with the CDU. He charged it for having prayed for a Nazi victory, with the bishops siding with the Nazi brass when the lower orders were being tortured in concentration camps.[100] He had already touched on this in *Billard um halb zehn* in 1959, but in the late 1960s it exploded for him when he learned that a Munich bishop, Matthias Defregger, had been involved in an Italian hostage shooting in June 1944 as a Wehrmacht captain (although never convicted in a court of law). When the Bavarian Catholic leadership tried to hush this up, Böll accused it of acting "almost like a mafia."[101]

On the whole, Böll retained his respect for the lower clergy. In his novella *Ende einer Dienstfahrt* (*The End of a Business Trip*, 1966) he portrayed with friendly brush strokes a priest who is worldly-wise and tolerant, including in matters of sexuality. But in this work, Böll's fierce displeasure at West Germany's renewed militarization found expression in a Bundeswehr jeep that is torched. He also made fun of the FRG's long-winded legal system, possibly an allusion to the Auschwitz Trial with its askew sentences, by describing a court case with a suspect in jail, who is allowed to make his girlfriend pregnant behind bars.[102]

Böll reserved ultimate wrath against lingering Nazi influences and a corrupted higher clergy for his novel about Hans Schnier, the son of former Nazi industrialists who at the end of the narrative ends up as a carnival clown in Bonn. In *Ansichten eines Clowns* (*The Clown*, 1963), Schnier, as a Protestant standing out in the Rhenish Catholic milieu, cannot marry his girlfriend because she insists on Catholicism being practiced at home. The unhappy Schnier's other great lament is that he remembers the death of his sister Henriette, a victim of late-war activities because of her fanatical mother. He himself is forced into an uncomfortable dinner with his former tormenter from the Hitler Youth.[103] The story evoked months-long controversy after having been serialized, before book publication, in *SZ*.[104]

As both Walser and Grass were born between 1920 and 1930, neither they nor their parents held agency in the Third Reich, and therefore they could start afresh after 1945, shaping a new era. Their age cohort, however, possessed its pitfalls. Sometimes called the 45ers, this generation was not free from collusion with older Nazis, and at its younger end could be identified with rebellious students.[105] Walser and Grass's birth year of 1927 may explain their intermittent silence about formal Nazi associations.

Whereas Böll was disabused of political parties, Walser, sympathizing with the radical left, at first supported the SPD. In 1961 he published essays by progressive colleagues, Enzensberger, Grass, and Eggebrecht among them, endorsing Willy Brandt in his electoral bid against Adenauer, with some reservations. He accepted the division of Germany, and later the Berlin Wall, as punishment for Nazi sins. After a futile argument with Richter about more democracy in Gruppe 47, during 1964, his criticism of the SPD intensified because of Brandt's accepting attitude toward the Western Powers' role in Vietnam. Chancellor Erhard's anti-intellectual "pipsqueak" quote of July 1965 incensed him. Although he sympathized with the university students, he condemned their rough-and-ready street behavior. Like his colleagues he lectured, with a left-wing agenda, on emergency laws or Vietnam.[106] By 1969, he had found the SPD, in coalition with the CDU, too right-wing. Hence, he approached but never joined the new German Communist Party, Deutsche Kommunistische Partei (DKP), a legalistic refounding of the forbidden KPD and, Walser may have known, a creature of the GDR. He was now one of those critical intellectuals who, in Ralf Dahrendorf's estimation, "exist on the edge of their society, but remain within it."[107]

From its beginnings, Walser viewed the Auschwitz Trial as a necessary function of democracy at work. The German state had instantiated the phenomenon of Auschwitz, and, under a changed government, the same state had to accept responsibility and deal with it by an accepted code of law. From his courthouse notes and "Our Auschwitz," an article he published in 1965, it is clear that he refused demonization of the culprits, whom he conceived, much as Arendt did, as ordinary human beings. He proposed that every German could have had the unfortunate fate of ending up in Auschwitz as a guard, and that apart from the SS who were in Auschwitz, nobody knew about the camp. This conclusion was problematic, as Walser should have known. He was taken to task by his old friend Ruth Klüger, the survivor of Auschwitz with whom he had studied at university. Walser's final view of Auschwitz was incomplete because he failed to appreciate its intrinsic significance for the history of the Shoah. Auschwitz was not unique because it exterminated "innocent Jews, Communists and so on," as he wrote in his essay, or "Jews and Slavs," but because it was the apotheosis of a centuries-long death wish by the Germans for the Jews.[108]

In his literary production, Walser continued the autofictional saga of his hero Hans Beumann. Now Beumann, during the 1950s, becomes Anselm Kristlein – a little Christ with a fragile halo, more of zinc alloy than gold, who suffers but has staying power. Like Böll, Walser cared about Nazi continuities and conservative establishment controls, but, not an uncritical Catholic himself, he exchanged the former's concern about the Church for a preoccupation with sex. His first of three new novels, *Halbzeit* (*Halftime*, 1960), was overly long, containing nonsense words, sentences, and paragraphs. But marked by writerly enthusiasm, it attracted the reader's attention for the psychologically sensitive portrayal of characters and plot. That was of the nearly perfect ascent of traveling salesman Kristlein to middle management within nouveau-riche society. Walser followed up with *Das Einhorn* (*The Unicorn*) in 1966, in which Unicorn Kristlein, now an author, has become even more phallus-conscious as he is researching "love." Whereas the Grimms-Märchen-like *Einhorn* lacked the panache of *Halbzeit*, it served as a convenient trajectory for the middle-age biography of Kristlein, now gradually descending from a climax, a jinxed journey that would end tragically in the 1973 book *Der Sturz* (*The Fall*). Overwrought with grotesque sexual escapades in between several outlandish scenarios, stretching belief, this completed Kristlein's trilogy.

Kristlein's livelihood and upward social mobility depend on affluent consumer society. He is always an insider, unlike Oskar Matzerath, who remains an outsider in his *Blechtrommel* narrative to the end, in his Düsseldorf asylum bed. And yet Kristlein always regards his environs suspiciously. He knows they are the outgrowths of success overwhelmed by complacency. But he partakes in everything as the parvenu that he is, a waitress's illegitimate son and failed university student, married to a professor's daughter. He attends huge parties of the rich, who enjoy Mercedes and rock lobster imported from South Africa. He shares their conceits, as they flaunt the accoutrements of education, such as rare-book libraries and Steinway grands. On those, "three piano-playing physicians" can nicely show off. Kristlein and his coprotagonists are conversant with Orff, van Gogh, Heidegger, Böll, and Adorno, subjects of pseudo-intellectual small-talk, and he himself can perform Beethoven piano sonatas, fourhanded, with his wife. His boss, the industrialist Frantzke, whose business is advertisements for toothpaste, receives an honorary doctorate and establishes a "Frantzke Prize" for New Music composers, and society ladies pose as novelists. A true dilemma for the well-off is described in *Das Einhorn*: "The poor rich man, he still feels full from eating lunch and has not lost many pounds during the afternoon and yet, he is supposed to eat again at night . . . It's not that the rich want to eat better, they have to."[109]

German society, including the CDU, is dominated by an insidious confluence of old Nazi impulses and modern pioneering initiatives, which characterize its progress. Emblematic of this is Dr. Fuchs, a marketing expert responsible for staggering ad sales, known to have been in the SS and acquainted with Goebbels's propaganda techniques. Eventually, he is arrested for Jewish mass murder. Both novels feature accomplished Wehrmacht, SA, and SS veterans, now shining in social circles. But reminiscing can be risky: tales from the Russian front, where Kristlein saw children killed as targets during pistol practice, frighten two young women in a bar.[110]

Despite having authored "Unser Auschwitz," Walser appears to neglect the Jewish problematic. Jews as victims of genocide remain a dark cipher, some problem way back in history but not associable with good Germans. Much of Kristlein's sexual interest is bound up with the alleged reputation of young Jewish women as passionate *and* promiscuous. In *Halbzeit*, there is Susanne, a survivor of the Holocaust, trying to re-establish her bearings. In *Das Einhorn*, Kristlein meets Orli, whose Jewish mother fled Vienna and who easily ditches her boyfriend for him. Like other women, Susanne and Orli are portrayed as sexual objects, solely to lift his ego.[111]

Critics were divided over *Halbzeit*, given its length and convoluted style, and some rejected *Das Einhorn* for an even more outrageous plot.[112] Sieburg of the *FAZ* was in the forefront, condemning *Halbzeit* for its "nine-hundred frozen pages," but acknowledging Walser's "genius of German language."[113] Marcel Reich-Ranicki stated that never had such a bad book pointed to so much giftedness.[114] Walser's response was that "M R-R holds my books in ill regard, because he does not know what it's all about . . . I hold my books in ill regard, because I know what it's all about."[115] At this time Walser was fiercely competing with Böll and Grass for placement on bestseller lists. In particular he envied Grass, whom he accused of hiding behind "the irremovable immunity of his success," and looking down on colleagues less well received.[116]

With Böll and Walser avoiding party-political affiliation, Grass never wavered in his support of the SPD, especially under Willy Brandt, although he joined the party only in 1982. In 1961 it was Brandt, then lord mayor of Berlin, who sought out Grass after asking Richter for an introduction. Grass had just linked up with other left-leaning intellectuals, such as Habermas, in a condemnation of Adenauer for having impugned *Der Spiegel*. In accordance with the SPD's 1959 abandonment of orthodoxy, henceforth favoring reform not revolution, he aided Brandt in electioneering. In campaigns from 1965 to 1969, he delivered fifty-two speeches in forty-five municipalities during 1965 alone. However, he was shocked that Brandt should agree to a Grand Coalition, "a really awful marriage," with Kiesinger in late 1966, and so he wrote a letter, asking Goebbels's former expert to desist.[117]

As for the students, Grass just like his colleagues welcomed their initial moves. But the constantly radicalized students disliked Grass's more evolutionary vision, opening a dangerous rift. While he was in sympathy with the students' questioning of their parents' role during Nazi times, Grass saw this original quest as taking the wrong turn. He was skeptical of their attacks on Iranian authoritarianism and on the United States for its Vietnam policy. And so he distanced himself from student rallies as soon as 1968, advising Adorno and his circle to do the same.[118]

However convincingly, Grass grappled with the student dilemma in the novel *Örtlich betäubt* (*Local Anesthetic*), in 1969. At the height of campus unrest in Berlin two Gymnasium teachers mentor two seventeen-year-olds, in sympathy with the students. Based on the students' battle cry "Burn, Warehouse, Burn!" Phillipp and his girlfriend want to immolate the dachshund Max in front of historic Café Kranzler.[119] This was Grass's reminder of the use of napalm in Vietnam by the Americans, seemingly endorsed by Bonn; but it also pointed to the burning of Auschwitz prisoners in crematoria.[120] The woman teacher, within a framework of generational conflict, hates herself for her Hitler Youth past, and both mentors want Phillipp to let go.[121] Her colleague, born like Grass in 1927, is sketched as a reluctant educator who finds it difficult to adjust to the emergent Economic Miracle as he attempts to follow an altruistic path.[122]

Student unrest is only one of several motifs in *Örtlich betäubt*; driven by his own SS history, the Nazi past and its post-war ramifications were always more important to Grass. This is shown by *Katz und Maus* (*Cat and Mouse*, 1961) and *Hundejahre* (*Dog Years*, 1963). These were sequels in the Danzig trilogy that began with *Die Blechtrommel*. In *Katz und Maus*, Grass portrays Mahlke, a half-Polish Gymnasium pupil with a large Adam's apple, who steals a Knight's Cross from a visiting officer in order to cover it up. He then decides to earn his own medal by joining a tank commando, but on furlough opts to desert to a Swedish steamer anchored near the Danzig coast. Thwarted, Mahlke then disappears in a Polish shipwreck.[123] In choosing a tank command, Mahlke emulated Grass's own enthusiasm after having climbed into his SS Panzer; Mahlke vanishes, as did Grass's SS persona when he reappeared in Germany.

Grass wrestled with the interplay of continuities and disruptions again in *Hundejahre*, where his main conduit is the dog Prinz, a German shepherd given to the Führer by Danzig's Gauleiter Albert Forster. After the attempt on Hitler, Prinz swims toward western shores through the Elbe in 1944. As Pluto, he subsequently accompanies former SA man Walter Matern as he takes revenge for his Nazi past by devastating other ex-Nazis all over Western Germany, especially with sexual attacks. Grass may be recognizable in the dog, or possibly Matern, and allusions to Nazi continuities are frequent, but this is overall the weakest in the trilogy, "at narrative perspective levels three times broken," because of crude allegories and unconvincing satire bordering on the burlesque.[124]

Becoming increasingly famous in the 1960s, Günter Grass was, by all accounts, the most stalwart supporter of Richter and his Gruppe 47. Kaiser called Richter the "father" of the group and Grass the expert "technician," a "mighty uncle," who could grant or withhold blessings.[125] Grass helped Richter to face opposition by conservatives and even insiders; among the former were, undeterred, Holthusen, Sieburg, and Blöcker.

In the *FAZ*, Sieburg continued to question the accomplishments of Walser, Böll, and Grass, and with them the entire Gruppe 47, which had to own up to several shortcomings close to its dissolution in 1967.[126] Günter

Blöcker claimed in October 1962 that it had become a "totalist clique seeking to suspend democratic fair play through Group resolutions."[127] During the following year, CDU politician Josef-Hermann Dufhues reinforced the charge of literary monopoly control by calling it a "secret Reichsschrifttumskammer," evoking Joseph Goebbels.[128] And in 1964, the deeply conservative Hans Habe, formerly of the *Neue Zeitung* in Berlin, thought Gruppe 47 "a sort of Hitler Youth" exercising "opinion terror " and "dictatorship."[129] He may have been put off by its notorious absence of remigrants, but Habe was known to be a far-right stalwart.

Gruppe 47 met annually from 1960 to 1967, in Germany and abroad, concerning itself with important issues such as the *Spiegel* affair, the Auschwitz Trial, and the Grand Coalition.[130] Its 1960 meeting in Aschaffenburg was, as before, characterized by mass attendance, glitz and glamor, publishers' clout, and glaring publicity. The gathering in Göhrde one year later suffered from internecine warfare between Walser and Reich-Ranicki.[131] In 1962, the influential journalist Rudolf Walter Leonhardt sought to rescue it by arguing in favor of literary pluralism, for it represented only one of several trends.[132]

Because of its growing size and "mass publicity," Böll, for one, thought less of Gruppe 47 in 1965. When Richter called a meeting at Princeton for April 1966, Böll decided not to attend. At the Ivy League university, Böll would have found himself justified. Several readings were by younger unknowns, below acceptable levels of quality. Politicizing events, the FDP parliamentarians Hildegard Hamm-Brücher and Ralf Dahrendorf were in the audience, and there were exchanges with American university students and literati such as Allen Ginsberg and Susan Sontag. Anti-Vietnam demonstrations and television crews distracted from readings. At one point, a young Austrian with shoulder-length hair read from his work in progress, an unexceptional detective story, and later he rose in fury. He characterized Gruppe 47 as behind the times, lambasting its "descriptive literature." Taken aback, Richter asked who the young man was. His name was Peter Handke.[133]

In the early summer of 1967, Handke told Richter that he had no intention of looking at Reich-Ranicki's back while he waffled on endlessly; therefore, he could not be at Gruppe 47's next meeting.[134] At the Pulvermühle inn near Bayreuth some weeks later, Gruppe 47 was dismantled by rebellious students in the shape of an SDS detachment from nearby Erlangen, who saw in the literati parents who had failed them. They clowned around the premises with a Viet Cong flag, broke into readings without invitations, and intoned: "The Group is a paper tiger!" While some of the participants, cheered on by an enthusiastic Walser, sided with the students, others, led by Grass, protested.[135] But this was the death knell for Gruppe 47; after 1967, it never met again.

However, Gruppe 47 had long been threatened by structural fissures resulting from personality difficulties and unbridgeable differences. Not the least of those originated with Walser on the one side and Reich-Ranicki on the other, with both colliding often. Beyond that, Walser objected to Gruppe 47's prize-awarding practices, disliking "how it exercised criticism and forwarded its valuations."[136] From the early 1960s on, Walser regularly challenged Richter on many policy issues.[137] In April 1962 he published a satire about Gruppe 47's five major critics – Kaiser, Reich-Ranicki, Jens, Walter Höllerer, and Hans Mayer – sternly questioning its growing calcification.[138] Later he demanded a left-wing change, which Richter, defying party politics, rejected. This was topped in 1964 by a Walser essay urging more socialization. He rebuffed the notion of Gruppe 47 as a "brand" that did business at some "literary country fair," calling it a "patchwork quilt" and asking for fundamental reforms: "Let's try it democratically. That would be something new."[139]

In his critics' satire, Walser had not singled out Reich-Ranicki for special punishment. He by this time was unpopular to the same extent that Kaiser, who, even in offending would be gracious, was much loved. With his ornery personality, his fear of anti-Semitism, and his tendency to condemn authors outright, Reich-Ranicki, whom some compared to Rumpelstiltskin, was becoming a liability for Richter, because, even though he was disliked within Gruppe 47, he was identified by the public with it.[140] He impressed everyone as a showman except those authors who were liable to be criticized.[141] The matter of his Jewishness was important and necessary to defend, because enemies such as Sieburg, who called him a "former trained Communist" and "most turbid figure," held old Nazi resentments against him.[142] Yet already in the fall of 1961, Richter was confronted with the threat of writers staying away if Reich-Ranicki's visitations were to continue, and he asked the author Siegfried Lenz what to do: "Criticism is becoming much too academic, officious, and is assuming a life of its own within the group. It does not serve the author but is harmful to him."[143] In the end, however, it was Richter who capitulated, with Reich-Ranicki famously surviving him.

◆ ◆ ◆

In the 1960s conventional repertory theater much resembling that of the 1950s was overshadowed by new theater staged by young progressives and inspired by the two main developments of the decade – the Eichmann and Auschwitz trials on the one hand, and the university student uprisings on the other. Those young stage directors were not quite young enough to be the sons of a Gustaf Gründgens or Heinz Hilpert, but they certainly viewed themselves apart from them, and if they had been asked to adopt an artistic father, they would have chosen Erwin Piscator with his political theater, Bertolt Brecht with his epic theater, or Fritz Kortner with his critical-realistic theater.[144]

In that progressive group, the two most important directors were Peter Palitzsch and Peter Zadek, with Palitzsch being a direct spiritual descendant of Brecht. Born in Silesia in 1918, he served in the Wehrmacht, followed by a POW camp. Trained as a graphic designer before the war, he first worked at the Dresden Volksbühne under Soviet occupation and then moved to East Berlin, as Brecht's assistant at the newly founded Berliner Ensemble in 1949. He worked in Stuttgart in 1958, after Brecht's death two years earlier, presenting the world premiere of his *Der aufhaltsame Aufstieg des Arturo Ui* (*The Resistible Rise of Arturo Ui*), a biting persiflage targeting Hitler, and thereafter directed plays in both East and West Germany. He was in Ulm producing Brecht's *Der Prozess der Jeanne D'Arc* (*The Trial of Joan of Arc*) before the construction of the Berlin Wall on August 13, 1961. In it a visionary criticizes the authorities – taboo in the GDR at that time. Although regarded suspiciously, Palitzsch decided to remain in West Germany once the Wall was up.[145]

Palitzsch guest-directed until he was hired by Stuttgart, with its reputation as a modern theater, in 1966. There followed more Brecht readings, but also enlightened interpretations of the classics, such as Shakespeare's, whose histories of the English kings he adapted into "a topical and relevant trilogy," *The War of the Roses*, with which he toured. He strove to make classical pieces ideologically and socially relevant. But he also produced newer foreign authors such as Beckett, O'Casey, and Pinter, and Germans such as Walser and

Tankred Dorst, who were implicitly critical of society. In 1967, Palitzsch staged Barbara Garson's *McBird*, satirizing the American president Lyndon B. Johnson, which earned him the unremitting hostility of the CDU.[146]

If Palitzsch's style was very Brechtian, dry, ascetic, and rational, director Zadek's was, as in the past, sensuous, slapstick, and entertaining, much geared to light-hearted English musicals, but often not so light-hearted.[147] Yet whatever their differences, Zadek had immense respect for his colleague. When he left Ulm with Intendant Kurt Hübner's team for Bremen in 1962, where he stayed for five years, he began to do theater in a style that he called "show-off experimental," the Bremen Style, comparable only with what Palitzsch was doing in Stuttgart.[148] Zadek turned into a super realist, surpassing the Expressionism of the admired Kortner. Like Palitzsch, he took on old and newer classics and turned them into shocking contemporary theater. Before his time, of course, Bremen's theater tradition had been as dull and provincial as Ulm's. Zadek delighted in grotesque spectacles such as decapitations on stage and large baby dolls being sexually molested and torn apart. His actors were instructed to use body language, explicit to the point of obscenity.[149] Thus he brought to the attention of the complacent Bremeners works not only by Shakespeare and Schiller (*Die Räuber*, *The Robbers*, against a background of giant comic strips by Roy Lichtenstein), but also Brendan Behan's *The Hostage*, Meredith Willson's Broadway hit *Music Man*, and John Osborne's *Luther*.[150]

Zadek was conscious of being a Jew who had been forced out of Germany as a child. He felt uneasy in the Adenauer era and during the Great Coalition beginning in 1966, under the ex-Nazi Kiesinger. Already in the early 1960s, having been offered a West German passport, he refused to accept it.[151] When he chose to interpret Shylock as a Jew the way he saw him, Hellmuth Karasek, an enraged left-wing critic, asked him how he, as a Jew, could project anti-Semitism onto the stage. Zadek's answer was that, as a Jew, that was his privilege. His Shylock was a figure "turning into Devil, because he was always treated as a devil by the others."[152] He was unsparing in his treatment of ex-Nazis. When one of his actress-girlfriends sought a *nom de plume*, he chose to call her Judy Winter, a Jewish-sounding name she henceforth kept, to permanently spite Nazi relatives.[153]

The student revolt beginning in the mid-1960s turned Zadek's cranks of invention in unforeseen ways. Hübner had asked him to read a novel by

Thomas Valentin, a Gymnasium teacher, *Die Unberatenen* (*Those Not Advised*); this work of mediocre merit with an unappealing title was published unspectacularly in 1963. It was about Rull, a pupil who challenges the collegium because of its authoritarian tendencies and empathizes with the fledgling student protests, only to be irritated by them and remain isolated, expelled from school in the end. Zadek, who identified with Rull as he shunned mass demonstrations, fashioned a play from this book and performed it in 1965 on the Bremen stage, turning it into a movie in 1969.[154] In 1967, he took note of Rudi Dutschke but became as suspicious as Rull: "The political comportment of the Berlin students already implied violence."[155]

Moved, since 1959, by his thoughts about possible consequences of the Third Reich, Walser was the first of the 45ers to compose what has been called documentation dramas, plays that reflected on the Nazis amid their crimes. He was motivated by Nazi medical misdeeds, as divulged in 1960 by Mitscherlich, and by what he learned about the Eichmann and Auschwitz trials. Next to his novels *Halbzeit* and *Das Einhorn*, his reactions were mirrored in two plays, *Eiche und Angora* (*The Rabbit Race*) of 1962, and *Der Schwarze Schwan* (*The Black Swan*), written in 1964.

In *Eiche und Angora*, Walser allowed himself to be influenced by Arendt's impression after the Eichmann Trial that ordinary Germans, not deranged ones, were responsible for Nazi crimes. These thoughts later entered his ruminations about Auschwitz, when he published his "Our Auschwitz" essay in 1965. From Mitscherlich's book, *Medizin ohne Menschlichkeit*, which sold about 75,000 copies in 1962, he learned details about SS medical experiments in concentration camps.[156] Those also influenced his plot in *Der Schwarze Schwan*.

In his first play of 1962, just as he would not single out the Jews as chief victims in his essay "Our Auschwitz" or in the first two Kristlein novels, Walser created not much of a place for them. His main victims are Communists, a Pole accused of race defilement having slept with a German girl, the girl herself who has her head shorn, and Germans subjected to medical experimentation. A Jew is mentioned who wanders in the woods looking for his vanished sons, and another one, cast shadowy, post-1945, as a negative stereotype in the role of a wealthy (and possibly usurious) entrepreneur. Apart from the medical experiments, which leave a former Communist castrated, Walser pays attention to the seamless integration of former Nazis into post-war, small-town German society – a former SS physician, a Kreisleiter turned wealthy restaurateur and a town mayor, and two upper-school teachers, one of whom is an ex-member of the SA.[157] The play was premiered by Helmut Käutner at the Schillertheater in Berlin on September 23, 1962. Perhaps because of Käutner's lackluster engagement with the explosive motifs, but also because many in the audience recognized themselves before and after 1945, it was not a success, so that already at its third performance the auditorium was half-empty.[158]

Jews were also not central to Walser's second drama of 1964, introducing two former Nazi physicians. In "Der Schwarze Schwan," Walser meant the double use of the letter S to stand for SS insignia, which would tally with the color "schwarz," the color of SS uniforms.

The two SS physicians, Goothein and Liberé, are trying to cope with their pasts, Goothein presumably with an Auschwitz record and Liberé active in "euthanasia."[159] Goothein has served jail time and Liberé seeks to evade capture under a false name. Well adjusted to West German society, they wish to calm their bad conscience – an old Walser theme. Here, next to Germans, Jews figure as victims only secondarily. The main theme is generational conflict, as Goothein's son Rudi questions his father's involvement in Nazi crimes and wants him and his colleague to repent. Failing in this, the starry-eyed idealist Rudi, vaguely Hamletesque, is declared mad and consigned to an insane asylum under Liberé's care as punishment for seeking the truth. He assumes his father's guilt and kills himself at the end.[160]

The premiere occurred in October 1964 in Stuttgart under Palitzsch, and again the reviews were mixed. Critics, including Reich-Ranicki, noted that this dramatist was in the end not convincing because he lacked a talent for theatrical verisimilitude: "Walser cannot translate emotions, events, developments of fate into verbal expressions – only attitudes, outlets, false repentance." Walser himself decried that there were merely eighteen stagings in the next four years, including stagings at theaters in the GDR.[161]

At the play's appearance, it had already been eclipsed by Rolf Hochhuth's Der Stellvertreter as far as the critical themes of the decade were concerned. It was the first literary work to treat the genocide of the Jews by stressing the ordinariness of German perpetrators and the complicity of the Catholic hierarchy and German industry, backgrounded by generational conflict. At its premiere on February 20, 1963, Hochhuth wished to demonstrate West

Germans' willingness to suffer former Nazi criminals with impunity. Born in 1931, he had become a bookseller. Then, as an editor with the Bertelsmann publishing house, he married Marianne Heinemann in 1957. Her mother, the kindergarten teacher and Social Democrat Rose Schlösinger, had been decapitated by the Nazis as a member of the Red Orchestra in 1943.[162]

The action is set in August 1942 to November 1943, with the two main protagonists being Pope Pius XII and a young Jesuit padre Riccardo Fontana, who accuses God's deputy of keeping quiet about the ongoing murder of the Jews. This establishes the first set of two intergenerational-conflict scenarios, with the pope, as father, not acceding to Riccardo's plea to protest against Hitler's schemes.[163] Fontana's quest is aided by Kurt Gerstein, a Lutheran spy posing as an SS officer, bent on sabotaging SS crimes. On the SS side a doctor resembling Auschwitz physician Mengele and SS Professor August Hirt, a human-skull collector, join Adolf Eichmann. High military charges and a Ruhr industrialist appear, with business interests in Auschwitz. Italian Jews are being caught by the SS in Rome, deported to Auschwitz, and – the girl Carlotta – killed there. Her foil is Helga, a callow nineteen-year-old German blonde, who serves as the doctor's sex interest. Hochhuth had read Nuremberg Trial transcripts, some excerpts from Goebbels's diaries, and the pope's own speeches. Eichmann Trial records and Arendt's Eichmann book were also available to him.[164]

The mediocre, everyday character of the SS thugs – in keeping with Arendt's characterization – becomes apparent during the first scene, which takes place in an SS pub at Auschwitz, with beer, liverwurst sandwiches, communal bowling, and bawdy jokes creating an atmosphere of small-town familiarity and – in the doctor and the waitress Helga – the sexual intimacy then typical of the German petite bourgeoisie. Eichmann plays the mouth organ, that quintessential folksy instrument in German lands. Obviously, these goons are not monsters but ordinary Germans. "Normal people," Hochhuth elaborated, "who today would earn their living as letter carriers, judges, social workers, traveling salesmen, pensioners, state secretaries, or gynecologists."[165] Later, during scenes in Rome, the pope and his entourage appear as autocrats merely concerned about safety for their Catholic flock – hence the compromising Concordat with Berlin of September 1933 and the exclusion of *Mein Kampf* from the Index.[166] Fontana, deeply disappointed by the pope's lack of action, assumes the identity of a deputy of God himself by infiltrating Auschwitz and getting shot, as a sacrificial lamb.

Hochhuth meant the relationship between the Germans and Hitler, as an Übervater, to serve as a parallel to that of pope and priest, in a constellation of generationally determined tension. He had included himself in this equation, as he reminisced how, as a Hitler Youth, he had been compelled to acknowledge the authority of a loathsome Führer: "My father's name is Hitler."[167] Significantly, as his play was being performed in Germany, university students welcomed this cue for collective protest; therefore, it acted as a trigger.

The drama was produced only when Rowohlt had finally agreed to print it.[168] It was made for remigrant Piscator, then at the West Berlin Freie Volksbühne, because it accorded with his principles – documentary realism, social criticism, and morally didactic input. The play, with Dieter Borsche in the role of Pius XII (he who had formerly performed in Auschwitz), became highly controversial with audience and reviewers.[169] Germans' lingering reluctance to submit to criticism expressed itself by the refusal of theaters especially in Germany's western half to stage it, and by outrage not just from Catholics. Unlike in Paris or New York, West Germans only timidly scheduled performances until 1964. In Düsseldorf, for instance, the anti-papal dialogue was much toned down. In heavy-industrial Essen and Bochum, the tycoon Baron Rutta's character was omitted.[170] In the Bundestag, Chancellor Adenauer and Foreign Minister Schröder deplored the adoption of the play, and later, when Chancellor Erhard made his comments about "pipsqueaks" in July 1965, he was aiming them at Hochhuth.[171]

By contrast, foreign scholars of the subject matter ceded much praise to Hochhuth for having brought Vatican–Nazi relations into the forum of public discussion, and intimated that his play served in the interest of serious fact-finding. The French political scientist Alfred Grosser, himself Jewish, said that it became clear, after more research, that the Vatican had been even less reluctant to stand up for potential Jewish victims than Hochhuth had indicated, and the Israeli historian Saul Friedländer, apart from elucidating the Hitler–Pius relationship, drew in sharp outlines the figure of Gerstein, who after the war was found dead in a French prison.[172]

Auschwitz, Eichmann, and Jewish genocide victims were the subject of two further plays, by Peter Weiss and Heinar Kipphardt. Weiss, born in 1916 near Berlin, had moved with his Christian Swiss mother and Hungarian-Jewish father via England from Prague to Sweden by 1939. Remembering his southeast European grandfather in the kaftan, he spent a tortured time in Sweden, eventually laden with guilt that he had escaped extermination. He became a painter and documentary-filmmaker; early writings of his are filled with self-doubt and self-recrimination, worries over sexual ineptitude, incest, and sadism, thoughts of loneliness, and objections to his father, who had converted to Christianity.[173] He was only nominally a German writer, publishing simultaneously in Swedish and travelling to Germany merely sporadically, sometimes to attend Gruppe 47 meetings. He joined Gruppe 47 in Princeton in 1966 and as a convinced Marxist kept company with those denouncing the Vietnam War.

Weiss was already famous on account of a 1964 play about the murder of Jean Paul Marat. His new drama *Die Ermittlung* (*The Investigation*) was premiered in October 1965, simultaneously by thirty theaters in West and East Germany, the principal ones being Piscator's Volksbühne, for the same reason as Hochhuth's drama, and Palitzsch's in Stuttgart. In vain this Brecht disciple wanted to install a giant mirror over the stage, so that all members of the audience could recognize themselves in it as part of the accused at the Frankfurt trial, who were represented on stage. The play consisted of some dialogues from that trial, used verbatim by Weiss, after many visits there. He had chosen lines he thought to be most representative of those spoken by accusers, witnesses – often nameless, depersonalized victims – and the accused; altogether eighteen defendants, in a sequence of eleven cantos, for example, archly Brechtian, "Canto of Cyclone B."[174]

Structurally, this oratorio was vaguely modelled on Dante's Inferno in *Divina Commedia* and offered strong language that projected the horrors of Auschwitz, but at the same time, in already proved fashion, made clear the banality of evil there, committable by Everyman German. The first lines defined the play's Auschwitz setting: "Judge: Witness, you were the head of the train station where transports came in. How far was the station from the camp? Witness 1: 2 kilometers from the old barracks and maybe 5 kilometers from the main camp."[175] Guard Pery Broad divulges: "There were two tables. On one table were the boxes with the numbers of the living. On the other table the boxes with the numbers of the dead. There we could see how many from a transport were still alive. After one week, from 100 still a few dozens were alive."[176] Weiss chronicles the vanities of Auschwitz's pharmacist Dr. Capesius, who stole valuables for use in a post-war beauty business.[177] Weiss also singles out heavy industry's involvement with Auschwitz. Processing human remains such as bones and hair, well-known German businesses made billions, investing these in post-war enterprises, currently "in a new phase of expansion."[178]

Weiss's Auschwitz verities engendered criticism mostly for his Marxist interpretation of the Holocaust. His detractors charged that he had, in too facile a manner, adopted the East German thesis that not Hitler but German monopoly capitalists were responsible for the Holocaust.[179] They would, of course, include broad segments of German society, hence Palitzsch's mirror idea. Yet another grouse was that Palitzsch thought inmates and guards were interchangeable, therefore leveling all guilt.[180] In any event, Piscator's Freie Volksbühne, which had employed Marxist composer Luigi Nono's music, received threats and about two thousand cancellations from its subscription membership.[181]

Heinar Kipphardt's documentary piece of 1965 dealt with Eichmann's historic attempt to barter for 10,000 trucks in return for 1 million Hungarian Jews to be allowed to emigrate in spring of 1944, "to sell one million Jews," as Eichmann put it on stage.[182] Joel Brand was the Jewish negotiator opposite Eichmann, finding himself increasingly deserted by Jewish organizations and the British. They feared a flood of newcomers in Palestine and did not wish to interfere with the planned invasion of Occupied France.[183] Kipphardt's drama documented how the dialogues between all sides led to nothing and, consequently, the Hungarian Jews were doomed.[184]

Kipphardt, like Hochhuth and Weiss, had grown up in opposition to the Nazi regime. His estranged father, as a Social Democrat, had been in a concentration camp and then, punitively, at the Eastern Front. Young Heinar, too, a medical student, by 1942 found himself in Russia. In early 1945 he deserted, became a psychiatrist, and, in East Berlin, began a literary career. A sworn Communist, he left the GDR, initially prompted by the Hungarian uprising, in 1959. His drama about Joel Brand premiered at the Munich Kammerspiele in 1960.[185]

Kipphardt wrote his play aged forty-five, under the impression that West German historians had not researched the Third Reich sufficiently.[186] He chiefly wanted to point out the suave comportment of Eichmann, who easily slipped into SS middle-management as any German could have. As Kipphardt formulated it: "Had I grown up like Eichmann in similar circumstances, would I have become Eichmann? If so, why? If not, why not?"[187]

Kipphardt continued his writer's career, and in 1969 became dramaturge at Münchner Kammerspiele, where his work had first appeared. In 1971, before staging a play by the East German songwriter Wolf Biermann critical of Bonn elites, Kipphardt planned to publish in the program notes slights about pillars of the republic. Although such copy never appeared in print, the Social Democratic government of Munich fired Kipphardt. In Bonn, the SPD was then the leading party. Among others, SPD supporter Günter Grass, whose friend Willy Brandt was now the chancellor (whose own sons Lars and Peter Brandt had recently starred in a film version of Grass's *Katz und Maus*), had learned of the plan, and denounced Kipphardt as "stupid and dangerous to public safety," a man who as dramaturge would falsify theater.[188] But in a backlash many writers now protested, seeing in this action "a singular intervention in the necessary political and artistic autonomy of a theater."[189] The incident demonstrated how free-floating intellectuals of old had meanwhile become part of the establishment, comfortably aligned with power and afraid of criticism. It was also premonitory of the conflicts that were to come, for the arts and letters, in the decade just ahead.

◆ ◆ ◆

Whereas theaters in most West German towns continued to be heavily subsidized by municipal governments, this was not so with movie houses, invariably privately owned. Because cinema audiences continued their decrease from the 1950s, the movie houses vanished; accordingly, many were converted into supermarkets, symbols of the Economic Miracle. If in 1960, 605 million viewers had visited 6,950 movie halls in 1960, only 160 million did so in 3,446 movie halls during 1970. Large movie-production companies went bankrupt, as did Ufa-Film-Hansa in 1962 – marking an early crisis point for the industry – and Universum Film AG, after losing money hand over fist, was absorbed by the mass-market company of Bertelsmann, serving a less intellectual clientele. Smaller companies, such as the one that had produced the artistically interesting *Die Sünderin*, fared similarly. The problem was twofold: film quality had been decreasing steadily since the mid-1950s even for keepers of minimum standards, and television's rise was unstoppable.[190]

For projected yet ultimately futile mass consumption, the film companies extended successful motifs of the 1950s, by emphasizing the veiled sexuality of the Heimat films to make outright sex flicks and inventing foreign settings, such as Austria had been for the Sissi films, to titillate the romantic imagination. As West Germans were becoming more accustomed to vacationing in the European South and their geographical horizons widened, film scenes beyond the republic's borders became a new movie norm. In new pulp-movie confections, detectives had to operate in London, often enacting Edgar Wallace crime themes, and adventure novelist Karl May's characters roamed the American Wild West. Other German adventure films developed plots in Hong Kong, Venice, and Mexico. The new sex films, soft pornography barely tolerated by FSK, were set in Germany, however, to suggest hometown familiarity, usually in the provinces (e.g. in the farmer's hay), which was the geographic link to the classic Heimat films.[191]

In February 1962 twenty-six film artists seized the occasion and issued a statement calling for a new beginning in film creation at a short-film conference in Oberhausen. It was, not coincidentally, also the time of a chipped political establishment, in a changeable atmosphere where the *Spiegel* affair was about to break and a compromised Chancellor Adenauer was on the verge of retreat. Inspired by what they conceived of as the avant-garde team spirit of Gruppe 47, these Young Turks, most of them aged around thirty and from Munich, distanced themselves from "conventional German film," which they declared broken in their published Oberhausen Manifesto. They had long been frustrated by the established filmmakers who had spurned them, not allowing them the use of their studios, for instance in Munich-Gaselgasteig, and other affronts. Now they were clamoring for new freedoms. "Freedom from the industry's conventions. Freedom from the influence of commercial partners. Freedom from the patronage of interest groups." They grandly proclaimed the death of "Papas Kino" – Daddy's cinema.[192]

Rather than churning out routine footage, these were auteurs who wanted to make precious authorial films. Some of them had been influenced by the new French school, the *Nouvelle Vague*, or by German Expressionists from the past. Volker Schlöndorff had been Louis Malle's assistant in Paris, and he and Alexander Kluge admired Fritz Lang. Their operating premise was to question anything from the more recent German past and its ramifications after 1945, in society as well as in the arts. Hence they were positioning themselves squarely against the older generation; "Papas Kino," they said, was an instrument in the attempt of the fathers to continue silencing the sons.[193]

Kluge and his friend Edgar Reitz were activists who charged ahead with attempts in Bonn to secure more funding for artistically experimental rather than ordinary commercial films. In 1965, after Adenauer and some of his more intractable CDU politicians had left the government, more pliant lawmakers were willing to hear out the young filmmakers. They secured from Bonn, for future film projects starting in 1966, loan financing that enabled some, if not all, to realize long-held plans, so that altogether twenty-five new film productions were aided.[194] Hence Kluge made *Abschied von gestern* (*Yesterday Girl*), the story of a Jewish girl from the GDR attempting to find her way in West Germany, and Schlöndorff produced a film about pre-fascist conditions in a Habsburg prep school, both in 1966. In 1968, Werner Herzog made *Lebenszeichen* (*Signs of Life*), a critique of Nazi Germany waging senseless war in foreign lands.[195] For these films the costs were kept low by filming in friends' apartments, often in Schwabing, and employing, for pocket money, those friends in minor roles. This imparted a certain hand-held-camera, improvisational, authorial quality to those films, as did the type of female portrayed. These were not the sex-bombs of older commercial films, but young women acting intelligently and confidently – as did, brilliantly, Alexandra Kluge – a physician in real life – in *Abschied von gestern*. It was not just Alexandra, Alexander's younger sister, who had an atypical background: Anita Pallenberg had studied graphic arts in Munich and then lived in New York and London; and Heidi Stroh had been a nightclub dancer in Rome. She had "crooked legs" and "a fat bosom," confessed Stroh, but invariably she and her companions assumed intriguing leads in new movies that subscribed, not least, to modern notions of women's emancipation taking root.[196]

Alexander Kluge and Edgar Reitz, true idealists, went further than just planning nouveaux movies; they also cared about recruitment. Realizing that the conventional film companies had no interest in creating conditions for quality and permanence in the film arts, they organized a department for film studies at the privately-run Ulm academy for design, the Scholl Siblings memorial, in 1962. Here they themselves taught for many a semester, while regular film schools were finally founded on a state-supported basis – one in Berlin in September 1966 and one in Munich a year later. One of the first graduates from the Munich academy was a young man from Düsseldorf, Wim Wenders, the son of a surgeon. In Berlin, a would-be student named Rainer Werner Fassbinder from a broken home in Munich failed the entrance examination twice and was rejected, but another, Wolfgang Petersen, was in the first graduating class. In 1981 he rose to fame with his film *Das Boot*, demonstrating the futility of the Nazis' U-boat campaign. Another graduate in Berlin was Holger Meins from Hamburg. He made a short film about Molotov cocktails in 1967.[197]

Intergenerational tension, which motivated much of the protest generated by the incipient Neuer Deutscher Film (New German Film, NGF) group in Oberhausen, was the lead theme in one of its members' early work in 1966, Peter Schamoni's *Schonzeit für Füchse* (*No Shooting Time for Foxes*). Here two young men from well-situated Düsseldorf families catch themselves in dissoluteness, after having been socialized by their elders – amnesia about the past coupled with dedication to the good life of West Germany's post-war revival. They reflect and decide to reject the ideology of materialism, applying themselves to nobler causes. But they fail – victims of an irreversible upbringing? – as one of them emigrates to Australia to run a crocodile farm and the other pursues journalism, seeking more meaningful topics.[198] Like many of its genre, the film was not commercially successful, but it won the Silver Bear at the Berlin film festival of 1966.

Peter Schamoni, from a prolific family of artists, was thirty-four when he made his film; Volker Schlöndorff was twenty-seven. *Der junge Törless* (*The Young Törless*) of 1966 was based on a novel by Robert Musil, the Austrian author married to a Jew who had been at odds with the National Socialist regime.[199] For this film, Schlöndorff sharpened some of the points Musil had made in his template of the novel. The plot, if historically transposed to the 1920s, would have constituted a warning against pre-fascist practices inherent in male-centered military institutions and thus served as an oracle anticipating the Third Reich. In Schlöndorff's narrative of a Habsburg cadet school in around 1900, inmate Basini is incrementally molested by two comrades, Reiting and Beineberg, while a friend of theirs,

Törless, looks on bemused, sometimes taking the torturers' side, sometimes the victim's. Whereas the roles of Beineberg and Reiting are clear-cut as those of fascists (i.e. Nazis), and Basini's as a Jew who committed minor misdemeanors serving as an excuse for the martyrdom to follow, Törless's position is more ambiguous. In the end he comes across as the ordinary German who watched the ascendancy of evil forces, accommodating himself to them in order to survive in comfort. Hence Schlöndorff had addressed the problem of fellow travelers of Nazism until 1945, who feigned innocence after World War II.[200]

The most vocal advocate at the Oberhausen meeting in 1962 had been Alexander Kluge; over time he also proved to be the most versatile and authoritative of the NGF group. He was born in 1932 in Halberstadt, old enough to be impressed by the Third Reich as a child. The son of a physician, he remembered it most vividly when his upper-bourgeois house was destroyed in 1945 – including opulent chandeliers later figuring in some films. The war memories of his main character Anita G. in *Abschied von gestern* – SA troopers, menacing German shepherds, polite family gatherings around a decorous living-room table, music of the classics and by popular star Zarah Leander – were also his own. Close to Adorno, Kluge received a doctorate in law and then entered the legal profession working in Frankfurt, where in around 1960 he met up with Fritz Bauer whom he venerated and would include in a film. He was interested in the human and literary perspectives of legal cases and published *Lebensläufe* (*Curricula Vitae*), aphoristic short stories with often Kafkaesque themes, from the Third Reich during the war. One deals with the skull collection of SS Professor August Hirt in Strassburg, another with a Jewish man and woman whom the SS had placed in sexually compromising situations, anticipating intercourse.[201] Next, Kluge published a volume, *Schlachtbeschreibung* (*Battle Description*), that documented the last days of Stalingrad – a mixture of fact and fiction.[202] Kluge, no professional historian, sought to create a tapestry of events he placed within the larger "question of tradition" in German society and culture, shocking readers, prompting them to think, and leaving all answers open.[203]

Kluge's 1966 film *Abschied von gestern* was based on a short story in his *Lebensläufe* volume, about a young Jewish woman Anita G. (Anita Grün) who, after release from a concentration camp, fails to make a life for herself in the GDR and moves to West Germany in around 1960. But here, attempts to assimilate also fail. She becomes a habitual petty criminal, is arrested, and is tried in a court of law by an ex-Nazi. After she gets out of jail, she fails again, and has casual sexual encounters until she falls in love with a married bureaucrat in Frankfurt, who impregnates her. At the end she travels alone like a vagabond, landing again in prison, to give birth and then to serve another, indeterminate, sentence. The long-term outlook for her is calamitous.[204]

Kluge's engagement with the narrative of Jewish persecution under the Nazis both in literature and film was novel for its time, not least because of a convincing depiction of suffering on the part of the helpless character Anita G. By 1963 he had of course read Mitscherlich and followed Eichmann and Auschwitz trial proceedings. Never had the theme of Jewish remigration been treated so convincingly in prose, much less dramatized. From this film with its Freudian inflections, it is obvious that the men who pursue Anita represent the patriarchy Kluge suspected behind the Nazi state; Anita runs away from every uniform in the republic, be it a streetcar conductor's or a policeman's. The complex ending symbolized for Kluge the monstrosity of the Third Reich in all its far-reaching consequences and, more importantly, problems of historiography with special reference to the genocide of Jews.[205]

Kluge's film, easily the most impressive generated by the NGF movement, won many prizes but commercially, like the others, it was a write-off. His originality in thought and technical creativity did not escape scrutiny. First, both his books of prose were criticized for their mixture of truth and fiction, for the artificial collage of scenes originally incoherent. There were charges of "invented true stories" for *Lebensläufe* and cavalier deployment of evidence in *Schlachtbeschreibung*.[206] Thereafter, Kluge made several more, less successful, films, trying to force onlookers to assemble perceived sequences in their heads according to an individual law of selection that critics thought questionable: there was no thread.[207] More recently, Eric Rentschler has found this technique to have been a hallmark not just of Kluge's, but also of other New German Films, resulting in "an elliptical and often jerky quality in which staged fiction and found reality frequently came together."[208] But even if the film techniques were acknowledged as novel, most themes were said to be quotidian, banal, and narcissistic, dealing with heterosexual relationships, marriage, separation, social outcasts, normal family life.[209] None of the innovators, observed the progressive Wolfram Schütte in 1967, had, unlike Hochhuth, been rewarded with the resonance appropriate to their efforts. "This shows," he said, "how far our young film is removed from the true criticism of our society."[210]

◆ ◆ ◆

In the 1960s the dailies *Frankfurter Allgemeine Zeitung* and *Süddeutsche Zeitung* continued to hone their marques as the conservative and liberal medium to go to, respectively, as did *Frankfurter Rundschau*, with its Social Democratic pedigree.[211] The weekly *Die Zeit*, under Bucerius and Dönhoff, became a bedrock of enlightened liberalism in the country.[212] Illustrated weeklies such as *Der Stern*, *Quick*, and *Revue* served the masses with stories and pictures, in varying degrees of quality, but playing by democratic rules. *Der Stern* remained on top. Defying Bonn's tendency to chaperone journalism, politics was emphasized more, supplanting human-interest stories.[213] *Die Welt* as the brainchild of the combative Axel Springer continued conservatively, and so did his mass organ *Bild-Zeitung*, but with an undereducated target group.

Rudolf Augstein, with his democratic disposition, further built *Der Spiegel* into a conveyor of news, keeping it left of center politically. Without party ties, *Der Spiegel* confronted government or society more easily, siding with none. It saw fit to move against "the monopolies of power in mass society, the state as well as the Churches, the cultural establishment, business associations, employer as well as workers' organizations, political parties, and all manner of interest groups." It placed its approximately 2 million, higher-educated, readers in a position of being singled out, by offering them special insights rather than profound analysis or arguing for change. It remained interested in political corruption and malfeasance as under Franz Josef Strauss, industrial exploitation, and compromised celebrities. Because of its suspicion of monopolies of power, it assumed the role of an extra-parliamentary watchdog long before rebelling students claimed that function. As far as they were concerned, Augstein kept them at a critical distance; he approved of their concerns in principle while disdaining manifestations of violence.[214]

Cynically, the Marxist Enzensberger classified *Der Spiegel* as "a *Bild-Zeitung* for sophisticated users."[215] Unlike Springer, however, Augstein avoided influencing his readers ideologically. It is true that Springer wanted to impute a conservative, non-critical worldview to an intellectually cumbrous readership, and this was demagogic. For this he concentrated on two overlapping enemy fixtures: traduced from the late 1950s was the GDR and, after 1966, there were student protests. *Der Spiegel*, on the other hand, with a pro-democracy animus, wished to encourage independent thinking. Whatever their difference in business models, *Bild* always sold twice the number of copies to its more underprivileged readers, even if students successfully blocked paper delivery at the end of the decade.[216]

Significantly, media tycoon Springer repeatedly attempted to acquire a private television station during the 1960s.[217] Adenauer, too, finally desired a proprietary TV station for use by the central government. But the German state premiers demurred. After a final supreme-court decision in their favor, the plan was dead in December 1960. Now a second television network was established under decentralized Länder auspices, by April 1, 1963, head-quartered in Mainz, and eighteen months later a third channel.[218] By 1969 all the Länder had more television input.[219]

At the expense of cinemas, the number of TV viewers rose from 2.13 million to 16.4 million between 1958 and 1970.[220] Television continued programming beyond the capacity of radio, and color transmission was introduced in August 1967.[221] Pure entertainment telecasts increased in number, several with a didactic bent, such as "film clubs," but also films from the (older) movie world. The international scope was widened, for large sportscasts such as the 1960 Rome Olympics or prefabricated detective series, imported from the U.S. and Britain. Germany soon had its own TV-commissar format, improvements on *Stahlnetz* from the 1950s, such as *Derrick*, with the hugely popular Horst Tappert, an SS Death Head's Division veteran.[222]

More pedagogical and serving democracy were political series. Werner Höfer's high-flying interviews on *Der internationale Frühschoppen* fell short here, because they avoided questioning Bonn. In contradistinction, *Panorama* became so irreverent that Bonn tried to censure it in 1962.[223] Some of its protagonists were part of the 45er generation, convinced democrats and energetic supporters of a pluralistic society; others were only a little older: Rüdiger Proske, Gert von Paczenzki, and Joachim Fest, Helmut Karasek, Carola Stern, and Bernt Engelmann.[224]

As anchor of *Panorama*, von Paczenski questioned the past of Theodor Oberländer, while Claus Hinrich Casdorff, leading a new TV magazine called *Monitor* he founded in 1965, drew Franz Josef Strauss into "crossfires."[225] The magazine also reported from the Eichmann and Auschwitz trials and probed other Nazi careers. Eichmann aides Wilhelm Harster and Erich Rajakovic, who had been hunting Jews in Europe, were shown as they were being tried in West German courts.[226] In 1962, *Panorama* went after Wolfgang Fraenkel, the Lübke-appointed federal attorney at the supreme court, who was suspected of having meted out death sentences for petty crimes in Nazi Germany. Faced with the journalists' evidence, he resigned.[227] As with film, television briefly overtook radio in the early 1960s, but over time there were new uses for audiotechnology. One was in automobiles, as more became affordable and people traveled more. New transistor radios appealed especially to younger persons, and radio, unlike television, was able to entertain night workers. After the introduction of stereophonic systems, music lovers benefited. By the end of the 1960s radio broadcasting had evolved as a sensible complement to TV, and since the cost of receivers steadily declined, Germans often owned more than one.[228]

Radio content changed in terms of music, what with its many formats – traditional pop and classical, hit-parade songs, and operatic airs, rock 'n' roll, electronic music, and modern jazz. There was a greater diversity of stations, rounded off with AFN and BFN, and neighboring Radio Luxembourg. AFN and BFN continued to be extremely popular in the pop and jazz fields, and picking up English jargon was a welcome extra in German youth culture.[229]

Toward the end of the 1960s the Hörspiel, long a mainstay of democratic Germany, underwent some characteristic changes. It proceeded to make use of novel stereophonic techniques and attained autonomy as an independent art form not obviously derived from, and instead of, literature readings. Nor did it want to mimic stage plays. With the capabilities of tape recorders, words and soundbites could be spliced, reversed, and otherwise manipulated, as in music composition, so that a collage of sound sequences could be created, mixed behind or into actors' locutions. As in the art of John Cage, moments of silence were often part of these constructions. The electronic-music composer Mauricio Kagel who in the 1960s was prominent in the German New Music scene and who excelled with new offerings for radio, practiced what connoisseurs called 'Ars Acustica'. Said Kagel: "Hörspiel is neither a literary nor a musical genus, but simply an acoustic one with uncertain subject matter."[230]

Even as Hörspiele adapted themselves to accommodate such inventive methods, in their experimentation they strove to be more relevant in terms of content. This included more attempts than in the 1950s to come to grips with the Third Reich. One such piece, by Franz Mon, operated with repetitive phrases containing the word "Eichmann" as a leitmotiv, in order to deeply impress itself on the consciousness of the listener.[231] Another piece, *Ein Blumenstück* (*A Flower Piece*), by Ludwig Harig, was based on the homely entries into a diary by Auschwitz commandant Rudolf Höss, recently edited and published. Maudlin impressions of a German family idyll were transmitted, of flowers in the garden of Höss's family, who lived with him outside the camp, validating Arendt's judgment of the ordinariness of German Nazi murderers. But Harig spun subtle symbolisms. Some flowers were said to contain yellow stars in their blossoms, some butterflies bore brown crosses, and everywhere a black bogeyman.[232] This radio play played with color, signifying subjugation and victimhood.

◆ ◆ ◆

Günther Uecker, whose artwork of white canvas with nails was introduced in Chapter 2, was not a member of the Tachists (Informel) of the outgoing 1950s, although some of his earlier pieces, overlapping with creations of that group, certainly bore a resemblance.[233] He was a constituent member of "Group Zero," which opposed Informel's monotony, emptiness, and abstractions. A painter who made the transition from Informel to "Group Zero" was Otmar Alt. In the late 1960s he specialized in two-dimensional color fields and three-dimensional colored objects, for example animals, molding them into puzzles.[234]

Concurrently, Horst Antes and Konrad Klapheck worked to defeat the abstractionism of Informel by re-establishing representational art ("Neue Gegenständlichkeit"). They wished to be in the world, not away from it. Klapheck, born in 1935, painted tangible subjects such as typewriters, and after 1963 they became somewhat more abstract and received an ironic twist in the manner of Surrealism. Antes, earlier touched by Informel as well as Willem de Kooning's Abstract Expressionism, became known by his signature stock character, head and limbs without torso and with firm contours. His pictures represented "a condition or state of being as metaphors of human existence, defined in part by the associations of the accessories accompanying the figure – everyday objects such as furniture; animals and creatures resembling snakes or sperm; and geometric forms or archaic cult objects."[235]

"Group Zero," with ties to the *Nouveau Réalisme* of Paris artist Yves Klein, was an international group of artists founded in Düsseldorf in 1958, led by Uecker, Heinz Mack, and Otto Piene. They moved from monochromatic painting to new representational, and to object art via kinetic art and light art.[236] Uecker, five years older than Klapheck, attempted a light-and-shadow play highlighted by kinetics with his painted-over nails and canvas and rotating spheres on specially cut wooden boards. After the horrors of World War II, his overriding concern was an existential threat to mankind, including threats from Modernism, and a preservation of humanity.[237] Heinz Mack (born in 1931) worked with aluminum foil and corrugated glass to produce light reliefs. He made steles from aluminum, as in *Silver Stele*, where aluminum was stamped onto wood in 1966, with the aim of "structuring and extending both nature and the human environment." In 1963 he stopped painting oil on canvas.[238] The connection between art, nature, and technology (as in light and movement) was the objective of Otto Piene, born in 1928. In 1959 he produced *Light Ballet*, where light from moving torches was projected through grids; this stimulated the viewer's perception of space. Combining these grids with sources of fire such as from candles resulted in smoke traces and fire paintings, in which the paint was burned.[239]

However much these artists may have been concerned about the present and future of mankind, they showed little regard for Germany's more recent, compromised, past. The name "Zero" implied a complete break with bygone cultural traditions such as early 1920s German Expressionism *and* their political contexts. These artists were members of the 45er cohort who wanted to forge new paths for themselves without much retrospect.[240]

Such was not the case with Georg Baselitz, who was born in 1938 in Saxony and trained in the GDR's authoritarian environment. He was expelled from the Hochschule für Bildende Künste in East Berlin in 1956 because of "sociopolitical immaturity." Subsequently, in West Berlin, his works became marked by a new brutal realism.[241] He wished to bring back artistic traditions the Nazis had scorned, he said, such as Expressionism, but in doing so he subjected that genre to a process of alienation, painting his human figures as conspicuously ugly, as in his oil canvas *Der geteilte Held* (*The Divided Hero*) of 1966, and placing disproportionately small heads on their torsos, as in *Die grossen Freunde* (*The Great Friends*) of 1965.[242] This was to emphasize his idiosyncratic avant-gardism, which remained critical of both Germanys as avatars of Nazi attitudes. To alarm the public, he turned to provocation. At a West Berlin exhibition in 1963, for example, he showed a painting called *Der Nackte Mann* (*The Naked Man*), and another entitled *Die Grosse Nacht im Eimer* (*The Great Night in the Bucket*), both confiscated for indecency.[243] That was his protest against the elders. He was cynical about the most recent past and its perceived protrusions into the present, and the traditions undergirding them.[244] Cynically, he drew a line from Dürer to Nolde: "The tradition of German art is the tradition of ugly paintings."[245] In 1969, in defiance of his past aesthetics, he began presenting his pictures upside down.[246]

Baselitz stretched the hitherto accepted rules of art in order to articulate his discomfort with the establishment. The protagonists of the Fluxus movement, on the other hand, abandoned those rules altogether. Fluxus was, technically, the American and German extension of a new art form called Happening; Fluxus events were said to be more suitable for the stage. During acts of Fluxus there were also clearer manifestations of interdisciplinarity, as musical performances were joined by (were confluent with) visual artistry and mock theatrics. Happenings had what appeared to be simultaneous roots in North America *and* Europe. In 1958 the thirty-one-year-old Abstract Expressionist painter Allan Kaprow, influenced by Pollock, staged Happenings in New York. Taking his cue from Pollock, Kaprow himself engaged in "action painting," which was an aesthetic "in multimedia directions, at first by bulking up his canvas surfaces with hunks of straw and wadded newspapers and adding movable parts that viewers were invited to manipulate." Influenced, furthermore, by Cage, he began using a combination of choice and accident to create "non-verbal, quasi-theatrical situations in which performers functioned as kinetic objects," and in which the role of the single artist-genius was de-emphasized and audience members became active participants in action events. In October 1959, Kaprow scripted an event – they later became more spontaneous – assemblages of movement, sound, scent, and light, with instructions given to performers and viewers. Spectators were asked to move on cue to experience a woman squeezing oranges, artists painting, and a recital performed on toy instruments.[247]

Seemingly in isolation from Kaprow, the German lithographer Wolf Vostell, born in 1932, participated in Happenings in Paris during 1958, at that time incorporating auto parts and a TV set. He based his new art on the idea of "Dé-collage," an image he had formed after a 1954 plane crash, which for him was "a visual force that breaks down outworn values and replaces them with thinking as a function distanced from media."[248] Happenings could include representations of Nazi times and, deeper, the genocide of Jews: Vostell had had to flee Hitler with his Jewish mother. Hence his event of November 1964 was signally meant to shock the public into memorializing Auschwitz, as he led buses filled with some 250 onlookers from one strange scenario to another, in Ulm, where the martyred Scholl siblings had been raised – from a military airfield with howling airplane engines to a car wash, where Vostell had his car cleaned, then sprayed with yellow paint (the color notoriously stigmatizing Jews) and again washed, and again sprayed, with the paint-covered car eventually being driven against huge chunks of raw meat, so that red blood and yellow paint comingled. In an underground parking garage, gas masks were distributed to the many members of the audience, bicycles and perambulators were pushed, and persons posing as corpses were dragged around on blankets. The municipal slaughterhouse was the penultimate station before a sauna was visited, to conjure up the past reality of gas chambers.[249]

By this time those German Happenings were also being organized under the label of Fluxus (as they came to be in the U.S.). The standard-bearer here was George Maciunas, an American architect and art historian who worked for the U.S. Army in Wiesbaden. In September 1962 he mounted the first Fluxus concerts there, joined by other Americans and the Korean composer Nam June Paik. The piece *Piano Activities* was performed, during which Paik sawed up a piano.[250] A year later Maciunas issued a "Fluxus Manifesto," which made clear that Fluxus had aesthetic roots in Dada and paid artistic tribute to Marcel Duchamp, with his presentation of a urinal as art in 1917. The manifesto stated, among other exhortations: "Purge the world of bourgeois sickness, 'intellectual,' professional & commercialized culture, PURGE the world of dead art, imitation, artificial art, abstract art, illusionist art, mathematical art." And: "PROMOTE A REVOLUTIONARY FLOOD AND TIDE IN ART, promote living art, anti-art, promote NON ART REALITY to be grasped by all peoples, not only critics, dilettantes and professionals."[251]

And so from the early 1960s on, until about the end of the decade, there existed a sworn confraternity of Happening and Fluxus practitioners, at the core of which were Germans and, warmly embraced, foreigners who came and went: Vostell, Maciunas, Paik, Kagel, Cage, Stockhausen, the American cellist Charlotte Moorman, who (after her return to New York later in the decade) preferred performing topless, and Bazon Brock, who always intro-duced himself with a headstand. By 1963, Paik was staging actions at the Galerie Parnass in Wuppertal and at Technical University Aachen.[252] In 1965, at the Galerie Parnass, Vostell, who liked working with automobiles, had a car crushed between two locomotives. The event was witnessed by fellow Fluxus artists Brock, Moorman, Paik, and the Düsseldorf art professor Joseph Beuys.[253] In their opposition to social, political, and artistic currents these artists toward the end of the decade indulged in outgrowths of their movement that contributed to its ultimate demise: in December 1969, Otto Mühl mounted an action at which, after a poetry recital, a pig was slaugh-tered on stage, the guts of which, mixed with flour and milk, were then spread on a naked young woman, on whom the artist defecated.[254] By any standards this was misogynous and aesthetically revolting.

The painter and sculptor Joseph Beuys's first Fluxus event occurred in early February 1963 when he joined Maciunas, Paik, Cage, and Vostell, and a young Japanese filmmaker named Yoko Ono, at the Düsseldorf art academy for a "Festum Fluxorum-Fluxus." Beuys, who played cello and piano, performed his *Siberian Symphony, First Movement*, in which he used a dead rabbit. He later recalled: "The Siberian Symphony was a composition for piano. It began with a free movement that I composed myself and then I blended in a piece from Erik Satie; the piano would then be prepared with small clay hills, but first the hare would be hung on the slanting blackboard. In each of these small clay hills a bough would be placed, then, like an elec-trical overhead wire, a cable would be laid from the piano to the hare, and the heart would be taken out of the hare. That was all; the hare was actually dead. That was the composition, and it had for the most part sound."[255]

Beuys would become West Germany's most famous visual artist in the 1960s. Brought up, since 1921, in Lower-Rhenish Cleves, the Catholic Beuys ended up as a Luftwaffe soldier on the Eastern Front in 1940. He was enthusiastic about his jobs as airplane radio operator, gunner, and pilot.[256] Later, in March 1944, according to his own narrative, he was thrown from a dive bomber and found unconscious in the snow by Crimean Tartars. They looked after him for several days, covering him with felt to keep him warm and applying to his head layers of fat for healing.[257] Found by the Wehrmacht, Beuys recuperated sufficiently to be redeployed until the British took him prisoner in 1945.[258]

Thereafter, Beuys studied with the sculptor Ewald Mataré at the Düsseldorf art academy. Mataré recognized his master student's talents, but friction interfered because Beuys was beginning to entertain unconventional ideas and his teacher became envious. Beuys worked as expected of him until about 1949, when he created a "Christ in the Can" sculpture, which was a figurine placed in a wooden cigar box.[259] In the mid-1950s, Beuys, ill with depression, was watched over by Hans and Franz Joseph van der Grinten, farmer brothers near Cleves, who helped him to recuperate and thereafter curated his œuvre.[260]

Beuys then developed what he termed Soziale Plastik (Social Plastic), placing communally valuable work by an artist over individual self-interest. Man had to be artistically educated – "it was only when art was integrated into all areas of living and learning that a spiritually and democratically productive society could exist."[261] To make Soziale Plastik, Beuys needed the felt and fat he remembered from his Crimean ordeal, during which, in retrospect, the Tartars appeared as moral exemplars. The Tartars were the denizens of the steppe, and the feral animals surrounding them were creatures of the steppe – rabbits and stags, moose, sheep, and bees. The steppe was Russia, Crimea, Siberia, the wild, beyond the horizons, not like anything in the civilization-spoiled West. Beuys took to the archetypal representation of animals that were for him "an equivalent for nature, for the primitive and for elements untouched by civilization and technology."[262]

Joining the Happening and Fluxus scene during the early 1960s in the Rhineland, Beuys preferred working with margarine or lard blocks on chairs, wrapping objects such as pianos in felt and holding up rabbits as symbols of community and peace. For himself, he adopted the role of a shaman, with a felt hat as the visible symbol of specialness. According to Mircea Eliade, shamans, often strangely attired, possess the power to heal, but are themselves stricken with illness.[263]

That Beuys's personally arranged Fluxus events claimed significance as redemptive ceremonials only a shaman could minister to was shown in 1964, when on July 20 in Aachen, before an invited audience, he threw detergent into a piano, tried it out for sound, and, rejecting it, emptied a wastepaper basket into it, then drilled a hole. Beuys drilled according to brown notations on a music sheet. Then, while Bazon Brock played from tape a portion of Goebbels's Berlin Sportpalast speech of February 1943 ("Do you want total war?"), he melted layers of fat on a hot plate. But an acid bottle exploded on a student who then hit Beuys on the nose. Heinrich Riebesehl's on-the-spot photograph of a nose-bleeding Beuys holding up a crucifix is still iconized today. It, like no other reliquium, underscores the reputation Beuys then wished to be known by, that of artist as all-healing, of victim as savior, of student as preceptor.[264]

Although to onlookers Beuys the entertainer often seemed to overshadow Beuys the artist and educator, he is important in his paradoxicity, because he created many of his works under the influence of the Third Reich and Auschwitz. On the one hand, when young he had accepted life under Hitler as normal, enjoyed the romps of the Hitler Youth, in whose midst he traveled to Nazi shrines in Nuremberg, and entered the Luftwaffe excitedly.[265] He was reading books by Ernst Bertram and Heinrich Lersch, both known as National Socialists.[266] To his parents he wrote on December 20, 1942, from Königsgrätz (Sadová) that 1943 would be without pain and problems "if we all, as a matter of course, do our duty without fear and look fate into the eye with full strength."[267]

On the other hand, such stoic acquiescence with Nazi life covered up disruptions that affected him accretively, until his anguish lent him the power of expression in his art. In 1938, when he was seventeen, he attended a book-burning in Cleves during which he was able to salvage from the pyre novels by Thomas Mann as well as sheets with imprints of the sculptor Wilhelm Lehmbruck's works and drawings by George Grosz. Lehmbruck, as he may have known, although dead since 1919, had had his works defamed during the exhibition of "degenerate art" in July 1937.[268] In 1943, Beuys's childhood friend Fritz Rolf Rothenburg, a follower of the philosopher

Rudolf Steiner, died in Sachsenhausen concentration camp – Beuys later dedicated an exhibition to him.[269] As a student of Mataré, he became aware of the master's suffering under the Third Reich; Mataré had been dismissed from his Düsseldorf chair in 1933.[270]

Among several interpretations of why Beuys manipulated felt and fat for purposes of his art and liked to perform with dead rabbits, the most convincing one relates to the genocide of Jews. The Geneva art and design scholar Gene Ray has offered an explanation. In Beuys's recurring paradigms, felt represented the mountains of hair shorn from Jewish victims' heads in Auschwitz before they were gassed and stored in the Kanada depository. Body fat was what remained after incineration in the Auschwitz ovens. From hair the Nazis manufactured mattresses for civilians and gaskets for U-boats. From residual fat they made industrial products (some later said soap). The totem of the dead rabbit represented victimhood, as it did in Walser's 1962 play *Eiche und Angora*, yet his hair coat also could be processed for felt. Beuys himself was a victim, in a bomber accident, but he was also a perpetrator, a Nazi Luftwaffe pilot who enabled the behemoth that was Auschwitz.[271]

From the 1950s onward, Beuys's artistic work, including Fluxus, was interspersed with demonstrations on behalf of Jewish Holocaust victims. In 1957–8 he participated in the first round of an international competition for a memorial at the Auschwitz site. In one submission, Beuys drew over a fold-out panoramic photograph of the camp complex that was later added to the contents of his vitrine *Auschwitz Demonstration 1956–1964*, where he had deposited thirteen other separately titled and dated objects, including the 1964 Aachen Fluxus hot plate. The Auschwitz memorial competition jury, chaired by Henry Moore, adjudged this and Beuys's other submissions, a design of three elevated geometric forms, tracing the path of the Jewish victims from the main entrance gate to the gas chambers and crematoria. With the oblique referent Auschwitz, among the objects in the vitrine there were eventually a corroded and discolored metal disk with a blood sausage and other sausage fragments tied with strings, two straw-filled wooden tubs with one containing a mummified rodent and the other a folding carpenter's ruler, a crucifix modeled from clay and an old biscuit in a shallow soup bowl, a pencil drawing of a traumatized girl, and an object group enclosing two medicine phials and a pair of sun-lamp goggles.[272] In 1958, Beuys designed a wooden gate for a Büderich memorial, near Cleves. His pencil and watercolor sketch, when completed, uncannily resembled the opening of a crematory at Auschwitz-Birkenau.[273] And a few years later, as *The New York Times* observed, Beuys produced a sculpture of a small toboggan on which were tied the bare necessities of life on the run.[274]

In 1961, after the envious Mataré had forestalled a much earlier possible appointment, Beuys became an untenured member of the Düsseldorf academy.[275] Thus he joined the West German establishment, which he always saw in need of education. Predictably, he sided with the students in their unrest. A first collision with the academy occurred on July 20, 1964, the twenty-year anniversary of Count Stauffenberg's failed coup against Hitler. During his Aachen Fluxus event, Beuys declared that the Berlin Wall should be increased in height by 5 centimeters. This provocation, after legal complaints by former Hitler resisters, almost cost him his Düsseldorf contract.[276] On June 22, 1967, some twenty days after the shooting of Benno Ohnesorg in Berlin and as a demonstration against the academy, Beuys founded the Deutsche Studentenpartei (German Student Party), which he viewed as a Soziale Plastik, later naming it Fluxus-Partei. It was to support complaints by progressive students in Düsseldorf about deficient academy representation. Beuys's action showed itself in numbers. From eighteen students in his classes before 1967, their presence jumped to forty-nine in the winter semester 1968–9.[277] But he went further. In 1967, as professor of sculpture, he opened a special program: "For ten minutes he stood before his audience, barking, hissing and whistling."[278] Many of his left-leaning colleagues tolerated these escapades, until nine of them signed a declaration of non-confidence against him on November 24, 1968.[279] At the time, the rector, Eduard Trier, expressed concern: "The limitless 'expansion of the art concept' (Beuys)," he stated, "not only would endanger reforms begun already in 1965, but would take to the point of absurdity the self-understanding of an academy for the visual arts."[280] Beuys's days in higher education were numbered.

At the Kassel documenta 3 in summer 1964, Beuys was not represented, because contemporary art was on the whole ignored, but at the documenta 4 in 1968 a special room, "experimental space," was organized for him. Under Arnold Bode's and, again, Werner Haftmann's direction documenta 3 got underway a year too late, because of intra-party wrangling over policy.[281]

But that was the least of the problems. Documenta 2 had finished with a 300,000 DM minimum deficit, and although Bode officially had to assume the blame, he tried to hold others responsible.[282] Under the continuing influence of Haftmann, traditional Modernism was to be featured in 1964, to the exclusion of anything most recent, and he himself issued a glib declaration that "art is what famous artists do."[283] Realizing this oxymoron for what it was, the embarrassed Bode attempted to counteract set policy by establishing a secret attic "for everyone's surprise and good humor." Here the œuvre of "Zero" artists such as Uecker and Piene was on display. Uecker showed his signature nail pictures, producing light and shadow, and Piene featured a "light ballet," sending light from spotlights through rotating spheres.[284] Haftmann, meanwhile, tried to gather praise with a vitrine of 500 drawings since Cézanne and Van Gogh – the end of the nineteenth century – which connoisseurs found humdrum.[285] But some exceptions notwithstanding, Haftmann made no secret of the fact that, to him, the traditional Modernist, "Zero" was anathema. Moore's sculptures in the center, perhaps, saved the exhibition in the end.[286]

While Robert Rauschenberg's was one important example of American art in 1964, the Americans dominated documenta 4 in 1968.[287] With Haftmann gone, there were fifty-seven U.S. artists at this "documenta americana," out of one hundred and fifty altogether. The Americans mostly showed the Pop art that Rauschenberg and Andy Warhol were famous for. But the winds were changing ever more strongly in the students' direction, and so even the reasonably accommodating if always autocratic Bode had to subject himself to democratic procedures when establishing committees and choosing works of art. This process was so alien to some veteran fellow organizers, to say nothing of Haftmann, that they resigned in protest. Even so, this and the thematic paradigm change under the American banner was not enough for the representatives of student interests, such as Beuys's devotees Brock and Vostell. They deplored the absence of large-scale social criticism. Hence Brock set up a "visitors' school," to teach attendees correct perception, and Vostell organized a protest named "Honey Action." This called for the disturbance of a press conference by younger artists with a placard: "Prof. Bode! We blind people thank you for this beautiful exhibition."[288] Art critic Gottfried Sello found such action redundant, for was not the FRG pursuing an enlightened culture policy? Those protesters were the very same people for whom the exhibition had been made and "who should identify themselves with it, those so-called progressive forces, artists and students."[289]

◆ ◆ ◆

Haftmann's resignation in 1964 was not just because of his new appointment as director of the Nationalgalerie in West Berlin. His doctrinaire opinions of what modern art should be irked a majority of contemporary experts. He envisioned expressions of Modernism as a historic stream, up to a certain point defined by him alone (such as Cézanne's work), dismissing anything beyond that. Moreover, he viewed art as absolutist, in isolation of social causes and consequences; and, beyond the idolatry of individual hero artists, he rejected the reality of artist collectives and artists' trends.[290]

This explains Haftmann's obdurate crusade on behalf of Expressionist Emil Nolde. He knew that Nolde had a Nazi past marked by an admixture of nationalism, Jew-hatred, and opportunism. Haftmann became part of a cabal to further Nolde's fortunes when he resurfaced after relative isolation in the Third Reich, and who then lived and worked till his death in 1956, aged eighty-nine. In his heyday in the early 1900s he had sparred with Max Liebermann, the head of the Berlin Secession, and Paul Cassirer, the art dealer. This had resulted in Nolde's principal hatred of Impressionism, of the French and Jews, and led straight to his admiration of the Nazi movement as early as 1920. Residing after 1925 in the North Frisian hamlet of Seebüll, he became a great follower of Hitler during the Third Reich but was unsuccessful as a champion of "Nordic Expressionism," which Goebbels failed to establish, against the Führer's orders. He plotted against fellow artists, such as Max Pechstein, whom he falsely denounced as Jewish, and hobnobbed with Röhm and the Himmlers. However, by the time of the "degenerate art" exhibition in July 1937 he had not been able to prevent 1,052 of his works from being confiscated from public displays and 48 exposed as depraved.[291]

Nolde's fate deteriorated after that. In August 1941 he was expelled from Goebbels's Reich culture chamber and then allowed to paint only in private, which he did, isolated, in Seebüll.[292] After the war he stylized himself as a victim of the Nazis. Although under suspicion and a "controversial figure," in Jonathan Petropoulos's words, he collected federal-republican honors. He became an art professor and received the Order Pour le Mérite, Bonn's highest award. In 1952 he was given the Culture Prize of the City of Kiel, and in 1955 his work was represented in documenta 1.[293] A year later he reissued his 1934 memoirs, purging them of anti-Semitism.[294] He kept his past shrouded, avoiding the Third Reich, but, relates Petropoulos, "allegations and rumours persisted." In 1948 he married for a second time: Jolanthe Erdmann was a much younger woman who would assist him in his secretiveness. After his death in 1956 she limited access to his papers, now with a private foundation in Seebüll. Questions from outside were warded off.[295] In 1963, Haftmann published a Nolde biography, characterizing the painter as "a totally inexperienced and wholly naïve person" who, never an anti-Semite, had, at the beginning of the 1920s, merely suffered from "political misunderstanding" by having been lured to National Socialism.[296]

In 1964 an art exhibition in Aachen featured Nolde's 1927 oil on plywood *Schwüle treibende Wolken* (*Humid Clouds Drifting*), as well as his 1930 watercolor *Junge Frau mit Pagenfrisur* (*Young Woman with a Pageboy Hairstyle*). It was an event typical of several at the time, some of them showing Nolde exclusively.[297] The painter was described as a former member of the Dresden "Brücke" movement as well as the Berlin Secession, and as having resided, since World War I, in Berlin and Seebüll. The last sentences of the short biography read: "1933 defamed as 'degenerate.' 1941 forbidden to paint. Also, graphic artist and sculptor."[298]

This victim-resistance legend was to be written in stone four years later in *Deutschstunde* (*The German Lesson*), a novel by Siegfried Lenz, a contemporary of Grass and frequent visitor to Gruppe 47. Lenz's hero is Expressionist painter Max Ludwig Nansen, in isolation at some fictitious place in Schleswig north of Hamburg, an expellee from the Nazi culture chamber and forbidden to paint. The likeable, pitiable Nansen was immediately recognized as Emil Nolde. Lenz had written a "masterpiece," wrote *Die Zeit*, "whose earnestness is full of grief."[299] The book was an instant bestseller, translated into nineteen languages, and Lenz became the highest-earning West German author after Grass. A popular television film followed in 1971.[300]

The novel (and Nolde) attained even more credence once Lenz's close friend, Federal Chancellor Helmut Schmidt, had taken up the cause. Schmidt had exposed himself as a foe of Modernism when he approached the editors of the Rowohlt publishing house, urging them to discard the avant-garde by stopping the republication of works by Brecht and Kafka.[301] But in early February 1982 he opened a Nolde exhibition in the Bonn chancellery, speaking about the "political injustice meted out to art and artists during the Nazi dictatorship." He mentioned his predilection for German Expressionism, in particular his closeness to Nolde, whose work he had first encountered as a student, when it was banned. He had read – evidently in Nolde's first, later purged, autobiography – about the painter's attitude to Expressionism, Futurism, and Cubism, and "the questionable aspects of a so-called free art establishment." He explained that he and his friend Lenz had been spending time on the Danish island of Alsen, where Nolde had stayed early in the century, in dire material circumstances. Over the years he had also spent many contemplative hours in Seebüll, Nolde's place of enforced isolation. At the end of his speech, Schmidt emphasized the didactic importance of Nolde and his œuvre, stating that beyond the German frontiers there would be many who would have to discover the artist for themselves in future.[302]

The background to Siegfried Lenz's preoccupation with Nolde's past is as murky as that of his friend Helmut Schmidt's. There is consensus that Lenz knew fully about the painter's compromised history; until his death in 2014, no one bothered to ask him point-blank.[303] But if Lenz knew, so must have Schmidt. Lenz, the young East Prussian, like so many spent time in the Hitler Youth and later was drafted into the Kriegsmarine.[304] Not known as an enthusiastic National Socialist, he still joined the party as a young man, denying this later, as did Walser.[305] Immediately after the war, as a journalist for *Die Welt* in Hamburg, he became a fervent democrat who was wedded to the SPD. On the side, he wrote prose against dictatorships.

Whether, for a white-washed portrait of Nolde, he was in touch with Haftmann in Berlin, who was ever losing credibility in West German art circles, is possible, but not proved. On the other hand, he probably read Haftmann's 1963 hagiography of Nolde, while never bothering to check out the painter's papers in Seebüll.[306] Expert Bernhard Fulda speaks of Lenz's affinity for Nolde via the common ground of Schleswig they trod, and Lenz's close interest in Nolde's retreat of Alsen, where Lenz had owned a house since 1957.[307] After the exciting, and profitable, depiction of Nazis and their victims in novels especially by Böll and Grass, it is reasonable to assume that Lenz, after a non-exceptional career thus far, was looking for bombshell success of his own. Hence Nolde as a sufferer from Nazi arbitrariness was a clever choice; inaccuracies could be excused on the grounds of poetic license.

As for Helmut Schmidt, he knew Lenz since his play *Zeit der Schuldlosen* had been staged in Hamburg in 1962, while the politician was a senator for the interior there. Nolde paintings on loan from Seebüll had decorated his office since the beginning of his term as chancellor in 1974.[308] It is clear that Professor Martin Urban, director of the Seebüll Foundation since 1963 and singled out in Schmidt's speech of February 1982, was either keeping the chancellor in the dark or was in cahoots with him about Nolde's explosive correspondence and the need to keep it under cover.[309] The best one may assume of Schmidt, one of whose grandfathers had been Jewish, was that he did not ask any questions; the worst is that he knew.

In 2013, after the death of Jolanthe Nolde, there was a regime change in Seebüll. Christian Ring, the new curator of the Seebüll Foundation, finally opened the doors to Nolde researchers such as Fulda and, as 25,000 documents were revealed, they began to unravel the legend. In April 2019 an exhibition was organized in Berlin to make explicit Nolde's sympathies for the Nazi rulers and the real circumstances of his "inner emigration" retreat. For this purpose, Chancellor Angela Merkel let go from the chancellor's office two of the Nolde paintings it had inherited from the Schmidt collection. On that occasion it was reported that additional examples of Nolde's "glowing adoration of Hitler" had been found to be shown in public, and of Nolde's "hatred for the alleged machinations of Jewish gallerists." Yet there were also letters deploring the fact that during Hitler's regime his, Nolde's, art form, Expressionism, had met with rejection among culture lovers.[310]

◆ ◆ ◆

As had begun in the 1950s, in the 1960s West German audiences preferred listening to classical music that was easy on the ears. Furthermore, they wanted to use their listening experience as part of a cultural consumption process that confirmed the material benefits they were increasingly enjoying. At the peak of the Economic Miracle, everything had to serve their sense of entitlement. To be seen going to the opera was important, with expensive cutaways and décolletés to be noted; driving in a Mercedes to hear music in a concert hall made the journey more important than the goal; checking out the high frequencies of *Ein Heldenleben* on the car's new Blaupunkt radio became a ritual. For all this, Richard Strauss was as good as Verdi or Mozart. Compositions by the established masters thrived in German concert halls, without ever topping operettas. The recording industry, especially Deutsche Grammophon with Herbert von Karajan supreme, became a golden goose, because its recordings were status symbols. Under those conditions, the limits of musical performance were predictable. In Nuremberg, when Alban Berg's opera *Lulu* had been staged, the local critics were dismayed. "*Lulu* does not mean very much to us," scorned Fritz Schleicher, "an antiquated text [by Frank Wedekind], combined with super-modern twelve-tone music, does not amount to a whole."[311]

The limit were new presentations of Baroque music through the contrived use of original instruments and compositions by traditional Modernists such as Orff, Egk, von Einem, and Blacher.[312] But even with those non-radical composers on the programs, music establishments continued to be threatened with a loss of subscribers, as in Kiel, and musicians refused to play scores, as in Nuremberg and Cologne.[313] Here, Gürzenich maestro Günter Wand became less interested in Modernism. He got into a disagreement with Bernd Alois Zimmermann, who had written music and libretto for his opera *Die Soldaten* (*The Soldiers*). Zimmermann's avant-garde score contained twelve-tone passages and unusually thick orchestral instrumentation. About this, Wand became increasingly apprehensive, scared of the "stylistic over-complications" that Wand had warned Zimmermann about as early as 1957. As time wore on, Wand found other complications, such as metric inconsistencies, so that on the whole the conductor eventually declared the opera unplayable and never conducted the score. Undaunted, Zimmermann kept insisting on post-serial, aleatoric methods of composition, on tape assemblages and electronic voicings. He employed non-musical sounds à la Cage and artificially manipulated soundings from conventional musical instruments. After conductor Wolfgang Sawallisch's rejection in 1959, Michael Gielen performed the full opera on stage in February 1965. Sagely, Gielen later said: "From Beethoven onward, so-called unplayable pieces become playable with time."[314]

Meanwhile, Modernism also suffered at Bayreuth because of Wieland Wagner's overextended if well-intentioned theatrical innovations and, subsequently, his younger brother Wolfgang's disdain of them. By reversing his earlier stand and again placing acting over music, Wieland Wagner resorted to neo-Shakespearean stagings. His motivation being, in Nike Wagner's view, a permanent purgation of earlier complicity with Nazi wrongdoing, the older Wagner adopted a defiant stance for himself, using alienation to defeat Wagnerism. Reminiscent of Brecht in his quest to provoke and offend, Wieland Wagner in his 1961 offering of *Lohengrin* presented what some perceived as a sex orgy by the dance troupe in the Bacchanal. They charged that he cynically employed the young American soprano Grace Bumbry on stage as Elsa – a Black sex symbol for white German male consumers. (His justification might have been to shame the racist Nazis.) His 1963 production of *Die Meistersinger* featured an Elizabethan theater with wooden floors and gallery. Rather than a patrician tradesman, Hans Sachs appeared as a "shabby cobbler." Everywhere Wieland planted stark scenery, conjured unexpected scenarios, and sounded loud language. Connections between actors now were sexualized where formerly they had been erotic, the people were dancing the samba, demonstratively there was no Nuremberg, just an anonymous stage. Wieland Wagner was breaking every rule of good taste.

For his 1965 production of *Der Ring des Nibelungen*, Wieland allowed his imagination to run even wilder. After Henry Moore had declined, he himself designed abstractions and symbolisms as props; the Giants had no clubs, Donner had no hammer; there were science-fiction type sets for *Götterdämmerung*; and Siegfried, Wotan and Fricka slept standing up. Emendations offended the traditionalists such as when Siegfried was given no funeral procession. Moreover, thinking less of it, Wieland was accused of messing with his grandfather's music, deleting, cutting, and pasting bits into *Holländer*, *Tannhäuser*, *Lohengrin*, and the *Ring*, causing more friction – especially with conductor Knappertsbusch. Friction must have been exacerbated by the fact that Bayreuth was now going out of its way to welcome Jewish artists and visitors, whereas Knappertsbusch was an anti-Semite of long standing. Thus was the pro-Jewish Wieland denazifying himself, by de-Wagnerizing Wagner, by denaturizing Bayreuth.[315] Kaiser spoke for many critics of the progressive left when in 1964 he uttered doubts about Wieland Wagner's idiosyncratic concepts. Correcting Richard Wagner could be effective only once one operated on the basis of the given, "with the word, the tone, the letter and the sound."[316]

1. Hildegard Knef and Ernst Wilhelm Borchert in the first post-war German film, *Die Mörder sind unter uns* (1946). Although Knef's face is mask-like in this still, her overall radiance belied her role as a recent concentration-camp inmate.

2. Heinrich Böll, typically, with a cigarette, in 1961. He and his family suffered from hunger after 1945. The family acquired the habit of smoking and drinking at the fronts during World War II.

3. Actor Fritz Kortner with his wife, actress Johanna Hofer, in 1962. Kortner found it difficult to be re-integrated into West German society as a Jewish emigrant.

4. Hanna Schygulla in Rainer Werner Fassbinder's film, *Die Ehe der Maria Braun* (1978), showing how a single woman could overcome post-war misery and partake in the material blessings of West Germany's early Economic Miracle.

5. Sonja Ziemann and Rudolf Prack, role models as lovers in the emergent Federal Republic, in the Heimat film *Grün ist die Heide* (1951). Her wholesomeness reinforced his paternalism; his uniform evoked respect.

6. Starting in 1951, the Bayreuth festival featured Richard Wagner's operas. Here Wolfgang and Wieland Wagner are planning to take charge.

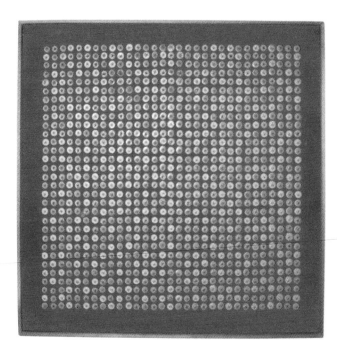

7. This painting by Gotthard (Joe) Müller of Munich, entitled *Scottish Cross* (*c.* 1959), was influenced by the new Tachist School, in clear repudiation of earlier, conventional, forms.

8. The writer Hans Grimm was a leader of cultural reactionaries well into the 1960s. This photograph taken in 1930 shows him aged fifty-five.

9. The German-Jewish judge and prosecutor Fritz Bauer initiated the Frankfurt Auschwitz Trial (1963–65). He became disillusioned toward his death in the late 1960s.

10. Marcel Reich-Ranicki, the brilliant Polish-Jewish critic who came to reign over the West German book market, in the early 1960s.

11. David Bennent in his role of Oskar Mazerath, in Volker Schlöndorff's film *Die Blechtrommel* (1979).

12. Martin Walser and Günter Grass, the two titans of literature after Heinrich Böll, best friends and always arguing, in 2007.

13. The composer Hans Werner Henze in 1957, aged thirty.

14. Leading West German Modernist composer Karlheinz Stockhausen in 1994 at one of his electronic instruments.

15. Alexander Kluge, one of the first and, arguably, the most original among the founders of the New German Film, in 1983.

16. During the founding of the Filmverlag der Autoren in Munich, in April 1971. From left to right: Hark Bohm, Rainer Werner Fassbinder, Bernhard Wicki, Rudolf Augstein.

17. *The Pack*, an installation by Joseph Beuys of 1969, on display in Düsseldorf.

18. Television host Werner Höfer at the Frankfurt Book Fair in 1978.

19. Socialist Students Union (SDS) leader Rudi Dutschke leading students in protests through the streets of West Berlin, February 1968.

20. Theatre director Peter Zadek, *c.* 1977.

21. Rolf Hochhuth, on the left, during a discussion of his play *Der Stellvertreter* among students in West Berlin, March 1973. Erwin Piscator is on the right.

22. Defendants Thorwald Proll, Horst Söhnlein, Andreas Baader, and Gudrun Ensslin, on trial in a West Berlin court after having committed arson in Frankfurt, in October 1968.

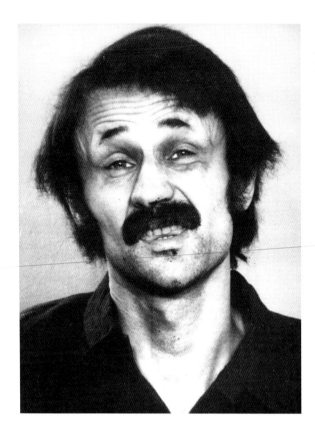

23. Holger Meins, before his death after a hunger strike, in November 1974.

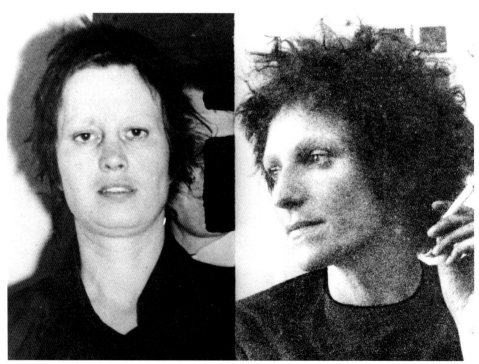

24. Ulrike Meinhof and Gudrun Ensslin in prison, May 1975.

25. Hanns Martin Schleyer in March 1976, eighteen months before his execution by the RAF.

26. Gerhard Richter's artistic commemoration of Ulrike Meinhof, 1988.

27. Günter Wallraff as Turkish guest worker Ali on the cover of his book with Kiepenheuer & Witsch, Cologne 1988.

28. Historian Professor Ernst Nolte in his West Berlin study, in June 2006.

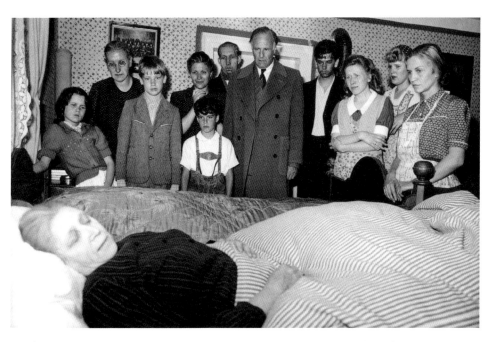

29. A scene from *Heimat: Eine deutsche Chronik*, a television series by Edgar Reitz, 1984: Katharina Simon, the matriarch, has just died.

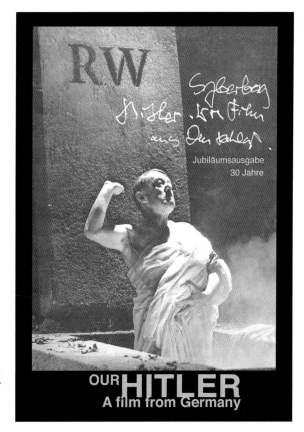

30. A scene from Hans-Jürgen Syberberg's 1977 film *Hitler: Ein Film aus Deutschland*.

31. Film director Volker Schlöndorff lighting a cigarette for film director Margarethe von Trotta.

32. Artist Anselm Kiefer in front of his painting *Der fruchtbare Halbmond* (2009), in October 2011.

After Wieland's death in 1966, Wolfgang Wagner found a way back to naturalist patterns in his quest to undo New Bayreuth. The Greek deities Wieland had created once again became Germanic gods. Other symbolisms were replaced with realistic constructs. Thus, in the 1967 production of *Lohengrin*, not a neo-Greek mystery in oratorio style but a down-to-earth medieval fairy-tale romance, the image of a real swan appeared, with a vastly magnified plumage (which Wieland would have rejected). Colorful, luxuriant costumes were designed of "a certain architectonic solidity." The 1968 *Meistersinger* were warm, realistic, and played in Nuremberg. The romantic realism was conservative, featuring a large, wooden-framed hall one could feel welcome in. This was the expression not of frustration and rage, but of affinity and compliance with the profuse, ingenuous West German self-satisfaction over affluence well-deserved. Contemptuously, satirists termed this "Broadway-medieval." The style was assuredly conventional with not a trace of Modernism, especially under the staunch traditionalist directors Wolfgang Wagner hired, such as Munich's August Everding, who produced a solid *Flying Dutchman* in the 1969 season.[317] *Die Zeit* found it reliably mediocre.[318]

◆ ◆ ◆

Officially defying old-school traditionalism, the Darmstadt festival in the 1960s was nonetheless on its way to becoming the "sleek establishment" of twenty years later, losing much of its original spontaneity and charm.[319] Certainly, many accomplished international musicians were performing and teaching there, the brothers Alfons and Aloys Kontarsky on piano or the percussionist Christoph Caskel. Cage's pianist David Tudor was still there, as was the Swiss oboist Heinz Holliger.[320] Headteachers were still Stockhausen, Boulez, and Kagel, all now residing in the FRG.[321] Tona Scherchen, Hermann Scherchen's daughter, presented interesting compositional turns in a new piece for flute, and the Munich Siemens Studio convincingly demonstrated the result of its collaboration with Darmstadt's electronic experimentation.[322] Young musicians composed collectively when in 1967 Stockhausen's *Ensemble* was created, and in 1968 when his *Musik für ein Haus* originated.[323] Michael von Biel, a young musician of great promise, later established cross-connections to Beuys and Fluxus.[324]

But criticism mounted. The instructors' internecine warfare had not let up, with Stockhausen at his worst. "True, there were no people being liquidated," said one participant later, "but there was certainly character assassination."[325] The quality of instruction suffered, as Stockhausen and others intimidated students with self-referential lectures rather than teaching composition. A pompous Adorno held forth on university topics, not music theory, and often inarticulately. In 1961 he explained in squiggly language that "the discomfort of emancipated music with the circumstance that everything is allowed to be allowed, multiplies just like the violent world order." And in 1965 he imparted his insight that "since form does not exist anymore, everything must of necessity become form."[326] During 1962, in another such hours-long lecture, Stockhausen ruminated about "pluralist society," "modern life-style feeling," and "Occidental Man," on a *Reader's Digest* level, as malicious tongues wagged.[327] By the mid-1960s illustrious docents took to leaving Darmstadt forsaking discussions, investing their (liberally subsidized) fees in the Schneckenschröder restaurant, a culinary Odenwald hotspot serving snails.[328] As an in-group these docents were meeting periodically in select places throughout Europe, such as Stockholm or in Donaueschingen, to talk shop. "They always see each other again, they are always among themselves," was one snide comment.[329]

Many novitiates now came to Darmstadt ill prepared, lacking fundamentals. They did not learn much more in badly designed new courses; nothing truly new was taught to them. Indulging too much in Happening or Fluxus-like events, they were in thrall to percussion, with several instruments far beyond the musical realm. There was altogether too much noise. Their compositions were, with rare exceptions, superficial – "lethally boring," thought one critic. Economic Miracle contentedness threatened to envelop teachers and students alike, turning Darmstadt into a status symbol.[330] All around, things were so comfortable that generational conflict did not well up. Rather than antagonizing their masters, the students copied them, careful not to upset the institutional equilibrium.

Happening and Fluxus, of course, proved that time did not stand still at Darmstadt; Stockhausen's mistress, the painter Mary Bauermeister, attended at least one such event. At her studio in Cologne's Lintgasse she arranged meetings for the likes of Kagel, Vostell, and Paik.[331] Bauermeister and Paik's Happenings were a marriage between painting and music – as in Düsseldorf in 1963, when Joseph Beuys performed his *Siberian Symphony* with a dead rabbit.

Cologne was West Germany's center of Modernism, a legacy of the Dada avant-garde there in the 1920s. Apart from Bauermeister's loft, it was home to the electronic studio of the WDR and several public and private academies and galleries. The Korean Paik was in Cologne from the end of the 1950s. With snippets of discarded WDR audiotape he produced *Hommâge à la John Cage*, connecting music, speech, and action, which Darmstadt rejected. He then performed it in Cologne's Galerie 22. With reference to Duchamp and Dada, he claimed to "complement Dadaism with music," wishing to shock even advanced Modernists.[332] At her atelier, Bauermeister organized a festival in mid-June with the Americans Tudor, Morton Feldman (an experimental-composer friend of Cage's), and La Monte Young, a veteran of modern jazz interested in microtones. Also in attendance were Stockhausen, Boulez, and the light-manipulating painter Günther Uecker.[333] Of Paik's *Hommâge* presentation there, the local critic Heinz-Klaus Metzger wrote: "It is the most extreme in shock that music currently is capable of, Dadaism multiplied with Expressionism to reach into the unknown."[334]

In early October 1960, Paik joined Cage, Tudor, and others in Bauermeister's studio in the performance of Cage's *Cartridge Music with Solo for Voice 2* and his *Music for Amplified Toy Pianos*. They also presented La Monte Young's *Poem for Chairs, Tables, Benches, etc. (or Other Sound Sources)*, followed by Paik's own *Etude for Piano*, during which Cage's tie was cut off and his and Tudor's scalps shampooed. Paik later elaborated, in a Dada style: "I play the ensuing part of Chopin's Ballad and I go to John Cage and cut his under shirt . . . But I find his short tie therefore I cut it, too and shampooed Cage (and Tudor). I come back to Piano and play Chopin's nocturne Fis DUR then play tape recorder."[335] A year later, in another such piece, Paik threw beans against the ceiling and at the audience. At the end, there were the sounds of women screaming, radio news, children's noise, classical music, electronic jingles, and Haydn's string-quartet template for the *Deutschlandlied*. The piano was attacked and almost turned over. All the while Bauermeister mimicked a painter and Stockhausen a conductor, while the conductor's child with wife Doris was playing on the ground with building blocks. Caskel was feeding goldfish.[336]

This was neo-Dadaist art, and Duchamp's art, because elements of deconstruction figured prominently. It was "destruction art."[337] The Modernist composer Dieter Schnebel sanctioned it wherever "instruments are taken apart," because then the play verily became "theater."[338] Boulez attained the pinnacle of such art, for as an actionist in his own right he wallowed in allegorical destruction. He, who had denounced Stravinsky's *Rake's Progress* and declared Schoenberg dead some years earlier, maliciously reminded Stockhausen that composing with the aid of sound tapes was futile, for those tapes would die.[339] He also denied the existence of good operas ever since Berg's *Lulu* (1935), and in June 1967 declared that every opera house should be destroyed. He appeared to have synchronized this plea with the exploits of the more radical of the restive students who were protesting against a performance of *The Magic Flute* that the Shah of Iran had come to enjoy at the Berlin Opera. As if rustled up by Boulez, a bomb was nearly placed there, and Benno Ohnesorg was killed by police.[340] "Boulez was, in the end, more a repressive force than a progressive one," judges the American composer Matthew Aucoin.[341]

Still, the aesthetics of destruction were hardly exclusive to these esoteric classicists, for they existed also in contemporaneous Pop art, so their origins are uncertain. Already in 1960, in Hamburg Reeperbahn clubs, John Lennon of the early Beatles appeared on stage, clad in underpants with a toilet seat around his neck, to shock his audience.[342] On his German tours during the decade, Peter Townshend with his rock band The Who regularly demolished his guitar. And the Rolling Stones invited destruction after their concert at the Berlin Waldbühne on September 15, 1965, when a fanatical crowd joined the band on the boards, swaying with its rhythm, only to wreck the inventory of the site thereafter.[343]

If the music of these habitués of Modernism was hardly distinguishable to the common ear, for the in-group culturati characteristic marks were salient. Here Stockhausen remained the leader, with his iconic valence rising. His compositions developed against criticism by experts such as Eimert, who expressed discomfort with serialism when he stated that the tone row had still not been fully thought through and therefore was incomplete. Nor had anyone yet fully mastered the uses of "space and time." Schoenberg's original concept of an "emancipation of dissonance" had become stuck in development, he charged, for a "twelve-tone tonality" was not as easily discernible as a conventional, Pythagorean triad.[344] When musicologist Carl Dahlhaus spoke of the 1960s as "the post-serial decade," he appeared to agree with Eimert, meaning that one could now move ahead with newer ideas and constructs.[345]

Stockhausen set out to do just that. An orthodox serialist in the 1950s, influenced by Schoenberg and even more so by Webern, in judging that the original tone-row principle was broken, he thought about extensions, aiming for "a chosen sequence of proportions for pitch, duration and volume." He came up with a musical unit he called timbre – "different experienced components such as color, harmony and melody, meter and rhythm, dynamics and form." By the beginning of the 1960s this had resulted in a change, certainly for Stockhausen's own music, but also for that of others. In all, it represented "a significant departure from the original formulation of serialism," as musicologists have found.[346] A case in point was Stockhausen's own *Momente*, beginning in 1962, which was based more on subjective criteria of perceptible musical characteristics shaping scores than allowed by the stricter rules of serialism. This was a celebratory cantata for soprano, choir, brass, percussion, and electronic organ, with an open concept, where interpreters were no longer guided by fixed score notations, but merely short text-sets inspiring free music-making – which Stockhausen termed "intuitive music."[347] Next came *Mikrophonie I* (1964) and *Mikrophonie II* (1965), in the latter of which he attempted a synthesis of human voice and electronic music, reminiscent of *Gesang der Jünglinge* of 1956. The voices of six sopranos and six basses, supplemented by an electronic Hammond organ, all on stage, were modulated electronically by the conductor using a mixer, mutating the sound, suppressing frequencies, and controlling volumes. The result was music from four loudspeaker groups.[348]

In Stockhausen's *Musik für ein Haus* or *Music for a House* fourteen composers and twelve instrumentalists were planted in four self-enclosed rooms to perform compositions, for instance *Auflösung* (*Dissolution*) by the American John McGuire in one room (for horn, trumpet, and piano), and *Transzendenz* (*Transcendence*) by the Czech Jaroslav J. Wolf in another (for trombone and double bass), lasting altogether four hours. Mixers available to musicians in each room permitted modulation. Although agency thus lay with the players, centrally a modulator-conductor had ultimate control. With difficulty, the piece was premiered at Darmstadt in 1968, when

Holliger and Aloys Kontarsky excelled.[349] The year before Stockhausen's somewhat similar piece *Hymnen* (*Hymns*) had resulted in a scandal, after it was discovered that he had utilized "Die Fahne hoch," the first strophe of the Nazis' blood-curdling *Horst Wessel-Lied* calling for the death of all Jews. He had been warned there would be bad blood. "Bad blood," said Stockhausen, "but I did not mean it like that. It is only a memory." Stockhausen's notoriety was already well cemented; his portrait had appeared on the Beatles' *Sgt. Pepper's Lonely Hearts Club Band* album cover.[350]

Although Bernd Alois Zimmermann shared Stockhausen's collage and montage techniques, as he was composing *Die Soldaten* up to 1965, he eschewed electronic-sound manipulation. He, too, had been influenced by Schoenberg and serialism at Darmstadt, but also Milhaud, Hindemith, and Bartók.[351] At Darmstadt as a student of serialism in 1949, Zimmermann experimented with a multilayered method of writing opera, which he perfected during work on *Soldaten* in the years after.

Influenced by Berg's *Wozzeck* and *Lulu*, this musical drama, in its pluralist complexity, combined different levels of time, plot, and space, which in a performance was expressed in various, often synchronous, scenarios that in reality were spatially and time-removed.[352] Although largely serialist, if not slavishly dependent on the Second Viennese School, the opera incorporated music from the Renaissance to Strauss's *Rosenkavalier* and even jazz passages; Eimert called it "total music theater, a grandiose Gesamtkunstwerk." For this, the required orchestra was huge, altogether 120. The percussionists alone stood out: they featured mounted and hand-held cowbells, suspended iron bars, whip as well as marimba, vibraphone, and all sorts of drum hardware. Zimmermann's debt to Alban Berg was forcefully expressed, for his heroine in *Soldaten* was called Marie, as in Berg's *Wozzeck*; there were randy soldiers as there were in Berg's opera; and Marie was rendered a prostitute like Lulu. The opera came in fifteen scenes, as did *Wozzeck*, and there was also a countess, as in *Lulu*. In addition, Zimmermann shared in the social criticism Berg had wanted to convey: the plot was around a girl from the solid middle class who falls prey to repeated soldiers' seduction attempts and is not saved either by the aristocracy, whose members are complicit in the tragedy, or by her own class, including her status-conscious father.[353]

In the opera, the sexual licentiousness of the military was easily identifiable with the abuses of fascism, even, specifically, National Socialism, but such parallels became intentionally more obvious when Zimmermann composed one of his last works in 1969, *Requiem für einen jungen Dichter* (*Requiem for a Young Poet*). It was an oratorio for narrator and widely differing instruments. Here Zimmermann gave sound not only to the voice of Stalin, but also that of Goebbels and of Hitler ("I lead you back into that homeland, which you have not forgotten, and which has not forgotten you!"). In this work, another sentence is spoken: "There is nothing to be expected but Death."[354] Zimmermann killed himself on August 10, 1970; he was nearly blind from disease, but had also suffered severely from depression and what he thought were "cliquish" attacks on him.[355]

That loose Cologne group was augmented toward the end of the 1950s with the arrival of two Jewish musicians, Mauricio Kagel from Argentina and György Ligeti from Hungary. Both men had lost relatives in the Holocaust, and the fact that they were accepted by their West German colleagues is testimony to the aura of freedom and tolerance in which extreme artistic experimentation such as in Cologne was possible, notwithstanding disagreements in substance and personal bickering. Henceforth, their permanent residency demonstrated, as did the difficult Auschwitz Trial, how far West Germany with its new democracy had already come in the early 1960s when compared with a decade earlier, in attempts, however strained, to defeat the Nazi past.

Mauricio Kagel, born in 1931 in Buenos Aires, took Zimmermann's choreographic montages to new extremes. He had arrived in Cologne in 1957 on a Bonn scholarship, attending Darmstadt summer courses in 1958. In Argentina he was a largely self-taught polymath, accomplished in piano, cello, singing, and conducting.[356] His earlier-described involvement with Hörspiele shows that he mastered ballet, theater, and film equally well, either discretely or in varying combinations. He favored the application of "subversive rhetorical gestures such as paradox, disjunction and irony."[357] Aesthetically deconstructive as in Dada was his tendency toward alienation, falsification, and replacement of conventional cultural output and commercially available instruments. His piece *Sur scène*, for example (1958–60), was sonically and logically distorted, a lecture on the goals of contemporary music accompanied by disconnected fragments of instrumental sound, vocalization, and mime. And in *Der Schall* (1968), Kagel used old or invented instruments, fashioned from household appliances, cash registers, and sirens. Ultimately, Kagel's jarring sounds were a consequence of his personal politics: in Buenos Aires, he had opposed the neoclassical style of a Hindemith or Stravinsky dictated by Juan Perón's authoritarian regime, and his despairing sense of anarchism had been further strengthened after reflections on the disastrous role of socialist fighters in the Spanish Civil War.[358]

His compositional approach in Argentinian days had been a quasi-serial technique "internally subverted by perversely uncontrollable elements and exaggerated demands for precision, implying a subtle critique of formal control." Here orthodox serialism was already tempered by aleatorics.[359] Then he integrated visual elements into his multidimensional works, calling this "instrumental theater." Those scores contained not only the musical material, but also specified the gestures of performers and their movements, as well as lighting and sets.[360] He created two films, *Hallelujah* (1967–8) and *Ludwig van* (1969–70), attacking Beethoven cultists (in the second feature he caricatured Nazi pianist Elly Ney, who disturbingly always made herself look like the master and died only in 1968), where music functioned as only one of several symbolic elements, the others being textual and visual. Scoring used graphic symbols instead of conventional notation. Such "forceful, aggressive-virile elan" impressed other artists, reminding Henze, for one, of the Spanish filmmakers Luis Buñuel, Fernando Arrabal, and, later, Pedro Almodóvar, a strange combination, thought Henze, of Catholicism, Inquisition, and Dada.[361]

Kagel's first opera, *Staatstheater* (*State Theater*, 1967–70), was also starkly anti-institutional and reminiscent of Boulez. He described it as "not just the negation of opera, but of the whole tradition of music theater." It had nine sections, each with soloists, chorus members, dancers, and players undermining the accepted performance standards, with chorus members singing overlapping solos, soloists concertizing in ensemble, and non-dancers performing in a ballet. It featured twenty minutes of anti-musical sound that disturbed the audience. At the end of the work sensual, overwhelming mass scenes reversed the anarchistic chaos of earlier sections, with a finale suggesting institutional conformity.[362] After several such unorthodox performances, musicians protested, threatening a strike. Kagel understood this, but he thought ill of the often still acerbic reactions of his German critics. As he told Stockhausen, "what I dislike is the tone, for it sounds like eight o'clock in the morning in the concentration camp, and that I know fairly well from what I have been told."[363]

Then again, after Ligeti had arrived from Vienna, he found that in the Cologne infighting Kagel, no less than Stockhausen, wanted to be number one. "And I, personally, have no ambition to be first or to be important."[364] Arguably, Ligeti later became more important than Kagel and even Stockhausen, after musical scores of his were used in films by Stanley Kubrick: *2001: A Space Odyssey*, *The Shining*, and *Eyes Wide Shut*.

Ligeti, born in 1922 and originally from Romania, in 1944 was put into a forced-labor gang under fascist Hungarians and then forced to carry explosives on the Eastern Front. Under the Nazis later that year, he managed to escape death camps. Post-war, although he had lost relatives, he was able to move to Communist-governed Budapest and begin conservatory studies. Ostensibly working on Bartók, considered safe under new totalitarian strictures, Ligeti secretly (and incredulously) familiarized himself with dodecaphony by studying Thomas Mann's new novel *Doctor Faustus*, which highlighted the fictitious Modernist composer Adrian Leverkühn. He was in Hungary by 1949, where Soviet-decreed anti-Formalism was being enforced; "musical innovation was as impossible as political dissent." Ligeti escaped this by fleeing to Vienna during the 1956 uprising, thereafter managing to reach Cologne, aware of the avant-garde experiments taking place there.[365]

What could Ligeti do differently from what had already been done? He has been credited with radically new approaches to composition. In his works "specific musical intervals, rhythms, and harmonies are often not distinguishable but act together in a multiplicity of sound events to create music that communicates both serenity and dynamic anguished motion."[366] Early, Ligeti went beyond Webernian constructs by becoming interested in unmeasured rhythm and orchestral clusters, as shown in his first significant composition, *Apparitions* of 1958–9. More homogeneous and static handling of orchestral clusters is apparent in *Atmosphères*, of 1961, "almost a single cloud, drifting through different regions of color, harmony and texture," whether in the form of sustained tones, or what Ligeti named "micropolyphony." There were dense weaves at the unison, where the lines moved at different speeds and were not separately identifiable. *Atmosphères* was for large orchestra with no percussion, as Ligeti wanted to banish rhythmic articulation from a music of constant timbre and textural flux; a music, as he

215

said, "without beginning or end."[367] This soon became successful around the world. Ligeti then created another cluster composition, *Volumina* (1961–2), a piece for a solo player, an organist, and graphically notated. In 1963–5, his *Requiem* was characterized by "extravagant vocal behavior" and choral and orchestral micropolyphony. Again Ligeti attempted to obliterate the differences between instrumental and vocal sounds, and the contrast between soloist and orchestra was minimized, as in his *Cello Concerto* (1966). Ligeti became increasingly fond of chords with no clear diatonic sense, but, positing the principle of canon, this allowed him, in this emergent post-serialist age, to access the continuity of conventional tonal music. His composition *Lontano* (1967) for full orchestra, and again with closely woven textures, sounded harmonic, in large part out of respect for the late nineteenth-century Romantic symphony. Obviously, Ligeti, ignoring electronics, was returning to traditional instruments, but he continued to prefer experimentation with pitch: in *Ramifications* (1968–9), two string units were called upon to play similar music in different tuning systems, a quartertone apart from one another.[368]

◆ ◆ ◆

As ever, Hans Werner Henze also eschewed manipulating sounds with gimmicky machines and, in self-imposed exile, as he always emphasized, he tried to stay away from Cologne and its spiteful confrères. To the extent that he rejected electronic music, he was finding himself in sympathy with the neoclassicism of Stravinsky's middle period, and yet always reverted to twelve-tone structures as a working matrix.[369] But because he was in West Germany frequently, not only to have his works performed there, but also to garner recognition and even to teach in Cologne, he was thought unprincipled by his German colleagues.[370] The fact was that he needed money and was getting lonely by himself in Italy, having to suffer tension with his on-and-off friend Luigi Nono, both over composition and ideology, and missing the company of Ingeborg Bachmann. When in October 1973 she died, Henze was devastated.

In interpersonal, collegial relations Henze suffered setbacks; he often felt slighted. He agonized over what he saw as attempts by his publisher, Ludwig Strecker of Schott's Söhne in Mainz, to sabotage his opera *Elegie für junge Liebende*, commissioned by SF Stuttgart.[371] Later, in Munich, stage props had been designed for its performance without prior consultation, forcing the singers backstage.[372] After the production of Henze's opera *Prinz von Homburg* in Frankfurt, Adorno told him that it was not chaotic enough: "New Music must be chaotic." Henze had resented Adorno ever since he had been at his home, decorated with crocheted doilies, where he had accompanied himself on piano, warbling his own songs.[373] *Prinz von Homburg* was also targeted by Boulez when he claimed in a *Spiegel* interview that it was an unfortunate rehash of Verdi's *Don Carlos*, and that Henze was a lacquered barber who was paying homage to a very superficial Modernism.[374]

Bachmann had been the librettist for *Prinz von Homburg* after Heinrich von Kleist, which, having been completed already in 1958, premiered in Hamburg only in May 1960 under Intendant Rolf Liebermann, in not altogether happy circumstances. The opera's director, movie maven Helmut Käutner, did not find himself comfortable in this new idiom. Henze had intended the new young lyric baritone Hermann Prey in the title role, but he took sick and was replaced by Vladimir Ruzdak, a much older singer of swarthy complexion not suited to the part, whose voice critics deemed adequate but whose comportment Henze himself found "heavy-blooded." Conductor Leopold Reichwein was incapable of resolving a technical glitch in the amplification system that resulted in aural imbalances during trombone glissandi.[375] Consistent booing music critic Josef Müller-Marein attributed to stupidity and ignorance, the usual execration against Modernism, for he found the opera itself "beautiful, a magnificent work."[376]

Henze's next opera, *Elegie für junge Liebende* (*Elegy for Young Lovers*), about a poet who abuses a young couple to enhance his creative output, was premiered in Schwetzingen in 1961. It showcased a composer still unsure about his choices in musical technique, for he was said to deploy several at once, dodecaphony and polytonality, or harmonics that somehow utilized dissonance. They "relieve each other, penetrate one another, and meld to form a third, perhaps a wholly original Henze style in gestation," remarked Abendroth, in an unusually balanced critique. Henze was said to be too fond of "dramatic sound effects" and in danger of sounding like a film composer.[377] After Christoph von Dohnányi had premiered Henze's *Die Bassariden* (*The Bassarids*) in Salzburg in August 1966, with a libretto by Auden about the cult of Dionysus, the text was deemed overloaded and too full of Greek mythology. The music suffered, once again, from an assortment of styles, using, among other devices, twelve-tone rows with an ultimately conventionally tonal sound output.[378] Thereafter Henze reworked his piece, and after Dohnányi had performed it a second time, in Frankfurt, he was not certain whether any of the alterations had solved "the problems."[379]

Around this time Henze was beginning to be interested more in left-wing causes. Long a friend of the prolific Communist composer Paul Dessau, a former collaborator of Brecht's, who was residing in the GDR, Henze liked to visit him, crossing from West to East Berlin.[380] He was also influenced by the left-radical views of Nono and the – sometimes expatriate – Marxist Enzensberger. In addition, he was friends with the extreme-radical millionaire Milan publisher Giangiacomo Feltrinelli, who in March 1972 would blow himself up in a terrorist explosion gone wrong, and other Communists.[381] No doubt his resentment of West Germany, his contempt for accredited establishment, whether it be the Bonn government – for him an outgrowth of the Third Reich – Donaueschingen or Darmstadt, contributed to shaping the composer, over time, into a *homo politicus* on the ideological far-left.[382]

After having spoken critically in public as early as 1963, Henze first exposed himself as a left-winger in 1965 when, urged on by the sympathetic Bachmann, he joined Grass in a vigorous campaign for the Social Democrats and Willy Brandt.[383] On September 4 he gave a supportive speech in Bayreuth, carefully edited by Bachmann, whose audience included the Grass and Brandt couples, Kortner, and the minister of economics-to-be Karl Schiller. Henze railed against the government, then under Erhard (to be re-elected in October), castigating his earlier remarks about artists as "pipsqueaks" and extolling the virtues of Heine, Tucholsky, and the Mann brothers. They were chased out of Germany, Henze complained, implying, falsely, that a similar fate had befallen him. Excoriating "the murky instincts" of the Germans, he stressed what purchase musicians possessed within society, for they were able to speak up and define abuses, despite or perhaps because they worked with counterpoint and song. They, like their fellow upright citizens, abhorred the thought of Germany adopting nuclear weapons, "bludgeons for future crusades." Henze emphasized again, disingenuously, that he loved his "German fatherland," despite being "rejected"; for his part, he was assuming the burden of the recent past, characterized by militarism and Auschwitz, and he denounced a new, revengeful, racist Germany intent on recovering territory it had lost "through historic guilt."[384]

Hyperbolic as such utterances were, they established the composer firmly on the republic's left-political spectrum, notwithstanding his continuing Italian residency. In autumn 1967, through Enzensberger, he got to know Rudi and Gretchen Dutschke and members of their SDS entourage, among them the Chilean expatriate Gastón Salvatore who now wrote German poetry, some of which Henze later set to music. He was much taken with Dutschke's charisma, his obvious intelligence, and interest in questions of art and culture, even though Henze was critical of his pseudo-sociological party-lingo. During his extended stay in Berlin, early in 1968, he was in touch with left-leaning members of the Gruppe 47, which he himself had once attended, like Peter Weiss and Reinhard Lettau, and participated in pro-Viet Cong demonstrations at the Technical University, where he had spoken years before. He attended a performance of Berg's *Lulu*, conducted by Karl Böhm. But now he had become alienated even from this progressive Berg opera, finding the libretto philistine and the music bawling. A few months later, when Henze was in Beirut, Dutschke was shot in the head and Henze immediately flew back to Berlin. His attempts, together with Enzensberger, to persuade the Intendant of Berlin's radio station SFB to broadcast pro-student-revolutionary content led nowhere, but he rendered a more important service to the SDS's cause by receiving the injured Dutschke for months at his villa in Marino for badly needed recuperation.[385]

What did Henze's new leftist philosophy consist of? He went much further than his original allies Grass and Brandt in stating that Western European societies, including Germany's, needed to be totally cleansed by social and political revolution, and to this extent he concurred in much of what his SDS friends were proclaiming. It would be a drawn-out struggle, a long march that, as Dutschke was wont to say, would have to penetrate all bourgeois institutions, foremost those of learning and art. On this march the artist, in particular the musician, would have to play his part. In order to "help Socialism," apart from going into the fields and engaging in manual labor – a Maoist imperative – a musician would have to compose music for schools, for students, for children, rather than for consumers who craved culinary feasting, as Richard Strauss's music was notoriously for. In present circumstances, music had to become subversive, as some of Beethoven's music was, as some of Mozart's music was, intoning "utopian concepts of freedom." Altogether, such a novel, radical approach would eventually separate all of art from its consumerist ingredients and help bring about the political revolution. "When we say music instead of weapon," summed up Henze, "then we have pretty well indicated what music could be in the revolution."[386]

Henze's delusions about music as "an explicitly political phenomenon" put him into a quandary towards the end of 1968, when his new Communist-inspired oratorio *Das Floss der Medusa* (*The Raft of the Medusa*) was scheduled to premiere in the Ernst-Merck-Halle of the urban park Planten un Blomen in Hamburg, sponsored by the NDR radio station, to be simultaneously broadcast, under Intendant Ernst Schnabel.[387] Its theme was the fate of (originally) hundreds of Senegal-bound French soldiers on a raft in the Atlantic drifting toward the West African coast, after its frigate *Méduse* had hit a reef after the Napoleonic War. It was sighted on July 17, 1816 by the brig *Argus*, with only fifteen survivors on board. This oratorio, with a questionable revolutionary timbre, Henze dedicated to Ernesto Che Guevara, the harbinger of revolution and friend of Fidel Castro, who had been killed in the Bolivian jungle in October. The text was by Schnabel, using citations from Dante's *Divina Commedia*; this former Kriegsmarine commander had long been enlightened, and the work was commissioned by NDR Hamburg with 80,000 DM to be paid to Henze.[388]

According to witnesses, this is what happened on Monday, December 9, 1968: before the broadcast-performance, university students from Hamburg and Berlin affixed posters to the stage with slogans such as "Expropriate the Culture Industry!" But no sooner had technicians of the station removed these, than a placard with Che Guevara's portrait was planted near the conductor's podium. Simultaneously, members of the SDS project group "Culture and Revolution" distributed flyers entitled "In Matters of Henze," which contained a radical message: "The concert was supposed to be for workers, but now the bourgeoisie is being entertained. The advocates of class culture have schemed to prevent art from reaching its designated goal. Thus the concert will, once again, make sure the ruling system is further prolonged." As the station's program director tore up the Che Guevara poster, the students placed a black and a red flag near the conductor's podium. At this point members of the chorus, the singers of the radio station, protested with the chant "We are artists not politicians." Henze now took the microphone to plead with everyone to commence the performance. "Without the red flag," demanded the choir. But Henze, through his microphone, insisted on keeping the flag. Soon the choir members were filing out of the concert hall, while the tumult in the hall increased. Amid the bedlam, the program director called the police. As Schnabel and Henze shielded the students, who were now being targeted by the police, Henze joined them in clapping to the Ho Chi Minh rhythm. However, he then declined the demand of the youthful audience to enter a discussion, instead fleeing through a back door. That same night, six students and Schnabel, who had attempted to mediate, were arrested. Rather than broadcasting the original premiere, which had thus been filibustered, the radio station aired a tape of the dress rehearsal.[389]

Henze's dilemma was that at one and the same time he had tried to be the piper at two weddings. In one instance, he had committed himself ideologically to the students' leftist cause by honoring Ho Chi Minh and Che Guevara, in the treatment of a requiem that topically had no revolutionary content except for paying tribute to an amorphous nineteenth-century underclass. In another he had remained an ally of cultural commercialism, having contracted with a highbrow cultural establishment that was to pay him generously: he who had denounced the commodification of music was now selling it himself. Critics on both sides of the ideological divide deplored that he had first made a show of helping students, only to desert them in the end, while a co-creator, Schnabel, was allowed to be detained by police. Critics labeled Henze neither a "revolutionary type" nor a "revolutionary musician," but an armchair Communist, who, for all to see, hosted the revolutionary Rudi Dutschke, but did so in a sumptuous Italian villa no other member of the rebellious student crowd had access to.[390]

It did not help that another affair involving Henze was concurrently reaching its peak. The baking-powder Dr. Oetker concern in Bielefeld, now owners of capitalist assets such as ships, banks, and insurance companies, had commissioned Henze to help in the inauguration of a new museum, named after Bielefeld's deceased burgher Richard Kaselowsky, who, as it now turned out, had been a member of Himmler's financial-support circle, Freundeskreis Himmler.[391] Henze's especially composed piano concerto was supposed to be a highlight of the planned celebrations. When, at about the time of the Hamburg fiasco, Henze was confronted with the facts of his involvement, rather than distancing himself completely from the project and returning his 50,000-mark commission or gifting it to charitable causes, he announced that his performance would still be taking place, now merely as a "musical manifestation." But even well-meaning critics found that sidling up to would-be revolutionaries while taking money from the very institutions they were trying to destroy damaged Henze's personal and aesthetic integrity.[392] Henze had failed to make music into a handmaiden of revolution in West Germany.

◆ ◆ ◆

In the 1960s several climaxes congealed to form a cultural apotheosis: the Auschwitz Trial sought to come to grips with Germany's greatest failure as a nation, which resulted in the mounting of inquisitive stage plays; innovator Beuys set new accents in the visual arts, as did Stockhausen and Kagel in music and broadcasting. But there were also setbacks hampering progress. With growing pains for new forms of culture over, hotbeds of invention such as Gruppe 47 and the Darmstadt summer courses began to institutionalize themselves, fell victim to ossification, and – in the case of the Gruppe – died. Art exhibitors in Kassel were being questioned. The student rebellion at the end of the decade raised, anew, existential questions regarding the Germans' culpability for dictatorship and war, which prompted some of the literati to divulge more, but still by no means all, fragments of their past.

Unanswered questions in the 1960s were programmed to lead to the violence of rebellion in the 1970s. A terror regime by young, unsatisfied, middle-class would-be intellectuals and artists unfolded, fiercely suppressed by the state. It would have to be seen in what ways, if at all, the arts and letters were subject to this.

CHAPTER FOUR

◆ ◆ ◆

New Uncertainties (1970–1980)

U LRIKE MEINHOF WAS the spiritual head of the Red Army Faction (RAF), which terrorized the Federal Republic in the 1970s. She herself acknowledged the intellectual debt of the student and, by extension, her own movement to "the intellectual left," in June 1970.[1] She was by far the most perceptive and energetic leader the RAF produced. Intellectually curious, she wished to research issues from the roots, and brilliantly argued analytically, although less lucidly in her final prison years.[2] She was also compassionate, within her tightly defined charitable orbit. With tears in her eyes, she followed the proceedings against SS-Obergruppenführer Karl Wolff, Himmler's right-hand man, in August 1964, who was accused of the death of more than 300,000 Jews in Treblinka. "Her questions were exact and intelligent," remembered Reich-Ranicki, who was also in court; "they revolved around a central problem: How could this happen?"[3] During the Berlin visit of the shah in June 1967, Meinhof published an open letter in which she denounced the notorious abuses in his empire.[4] She had been emphatically against what the left viewed as offenses by the Bonn government – the employment of old Nazis, remilitarization, planned atomization, and the emergency legislation.[5]

Born in 1934, she grew up in Jena, where her father, a museum official, was a Nazi Party member. Her mother's father, a Socialist, had been deposed as a teacher in 1933. The father died in 1940, so that Ulrike was raised by her mother; the family was piously Lutheran. By early 1945, Renate Riemeck had moved in, a sophisticated former Hitler Youth leader, who rebuked the regime, easily convincing Frau Meinhof. Still in 1945, the family and Riemeck moved to Oldenburg, and after Frau Meinhof's death, Riemeck became Ulrike's foster mother, if not more. Ulrike then studied pedagogy and psychology, yet never formally graduated. In 1958, in Münster, she became a member of the SDS. Meanwhile, Riemeck had converted to Communism, which resulted in her dismissal from the pedagogical academy where she had been teaching. This profoundly impacted Ulrike.[6]

In 1958 she also met Klaus Rainer Röhl, who had cofounded a left-leaning student magazine, *konkret*. This was to be patterned on the literary journalism of the Weimar-republican *Weltbühne*. Only years later were suspicions confirmed that *konkret* was financed by the GDR. A year younger than Grass, Röhl had been a Danzig schoolmate; the two shared Hitler Youth experiences, but were not close. In January 1960, Meinhof became chief editor of *konkret*, and one year later she was married to Röhl; the couple had twins in 1964.[7]

In that year the East Germans cut financing for *konkret*, and the popular magazine was turned into a commercial medium in the manner of *Quick*, offering sex and scandal stories. Meinhof, notwithstanding her Marxist beliefs, became a star journalist, freelancing on the side, visible on television and in public debates. Among the glitterati, it was chic to invite her socially and thus to demonstrate a token interest in the left. But under the impact of the SDS, she gradually resented her luxurious life with Röhl. Disabused of the consumerism of affluence, her large Hamburg villa and expensive vacations in Sylt, Meinhof divorced him in 1968.[8] Residues of Nazism in German society and politics now concerned her more.

The second-most important woman in the RAF, Gudrun Ensslin, had a different background. Born in 1940 as the daughter of a Lutheran minister in Stuttgart's suburb Cannstadt, she had studied literature under Walter Jens in Tübingen and by 1962 had become the girlfriend of a fellow student there, Bernward Vesper. He was the son of Will Vesper, one of the Third Reich's prominent poets. The young Vesper had coopted Gudrun in the reissue of some of his father's writings, which, surprisingly, she had agreed to. Will Vesper had remained a Nazi after 1945. He notoriously kept books around the house that supported Nazi lore, such as a volume by Hanna

Reitsch, who had attempted to fly the Führer out of Berlin at the last minute, and literature about Hess. He still socialized with the like-minded: Hermann Schäfer, Winifred Wagner, and Agnes Miegel. He compared cats, as a race from the Orient, with Jews, insisting that true Germans, like Hitler, prefer dogs. Hence the Vespers' cat, Kater Murr, was shot in an act the father knew would hurt his son. For Nazi ideology demanded that fathers be hard on sons. Will Vesper had often meted out punishment with his belt or lecturing, belittling and shouting at Bernward. Yet although the boy had hated his father, he had promised to carry out his last will, the republication, before Will Vesper's death in March 1962.[9]

At first, Bernward Vesper and Gudrun Ensslin envisioned a new edition of all of Will Vesper's works, including left correspondence and reviews, in a seven-volume set, ideally before the Frankfurt book fair in September 1963. They founded a small publishing firm, "studio neue literatur," named after Will Vesper's Third Reich book series "Neue Literatur" and housed partly at Bernward's paternal estate in the Lüneburg Heath and partly at Gudrun's Cannstadt home. Ideologically they moved to the left with a planned anthology of works not only by Vesper père and the Hitler Youth bard Hans Baumann, but also the Marxists Anna Seghers and Brecht. This appeared in 1964.[10] The thread was opposition to the Bonn establishment, as Will Vesper had upheld it, strengthened by the *Spiegel* affair in autumn 1962, in which they took the magazine's side against Bonn. In curating Will Vesper's work, they held that although he had been a Nazi, he had not followed a party line, always preserving his freedom of opinion. They conveniently chose to overlook his anti-Semitism and extreme veneration of Adolf Hitler.[11]

At the beginning of 1964 the couple moved to West Berlin to continue their studies of German literature at the Free University. On Jens's suggestion, Ensslin looked up his colleague Eberhard Lämmert, with a view to beginning a doctoral dissertation. Thus, she discovered that Lämmert was urging structural and thematic reform for German literature studies, to break with Nazi traditions.[12] This impressed Ensslin, who by 1965 was losing interest in the Vesper editing chores, and so both she and Bernward drew close to Social Democratic opponents of the Bonn government. They joined Günter Grass's electoral campaign for Willy Brandt. However, when Brandt linked up with the CDU in the Grand Coalition of December 1966, both of them, anti-Bonn, turned away from the SPD. In March 1967, their son Felix was born. This was during nascent student unrest in Berlin, when they were already well assimilated in the restive student subculture, which attracted many would-be-bohemians, beatniks, and hangers-on. Among them was Andreas Baader, a charismatic, handsome dropout originally from Munich, whom Ensslin fell for in June. The student Benno Ohnesorg had just been killed. Dissatisfied with publishing chores and academic work, Gudrun separated from Vesper and their infant son and teamed up with Baader, who himself left his own small child and an artist couple he had lived with in a ménage à trois. On April 2, 1968, Ensslin and Baader led two friends in setting on fire two department stores in Frankfurt, causing damage but no injuries.[13] In a fall trial, Baader, Ensslin, and the two collaborators were each sentenced to three years. During it, Meinhof, in sympathy, interviewed the defendants at length.[14] Later, she published an article saying that department stores protected the interests of capitalists who exploited human beings who were slaving for their benefit. Therefore, so she then wrote in *konkret*, it would "always be better to ignite a department store than to operate a department store."[15]

Pending a final judgment by the supreme court, all culprits were temporarily freed in June 1969. But after confirmation of sentences in November, Baader and Ensslin absconded to Paris, then, via Rome, returned to West Berlin in the following February. Here they hid in Meinhof's apartment. In April 1970, however, Baader was rearrested, having been caught speeding. He was freed from his Berlin prison in a spectacular action led by Ensslin and Meinhof on May 14, 1970, during which a librarian was gravely injured. Joined by accomplices, the three then went underground, signifying the beginning of the Baader-Meinhof gang and their war against the establishment.[16]

◆ ◆ ◆

In the ensuing waves of terrorism, thirty-seven people would die on the victims' side and twenty-seven on the assassins', during actions that culminated in October 1977 and continued, attenuated, until the early 1990s.[17] While the trio led by Meinhof was in hiding, in Germany or with Palestinian insurgents in Beirut, she declared on a recorded tape for *Der Spiegel* that a "Red Army Faction" would be formed and that, "naturally, shooting is permitted."[18] One year later, in July 1971 in Hamburg, the first terrorist killed by police was Petra Schelm, a twenty-year-old make-up artist in training. The first policeman slain was also from Hamburg. While the RAF was growing, banks were robbed, and people suffered, Meinhof, Baader, and Ensslin remained at large until June 1972, when they were arrested along with Jan-Carl Raspe and Holger Meins, who had made that film about Molotov cocktails. All five now formed the unofficial core of the terrorist movement, issuing new commands even when behind bars.[19]

In November 1974, with more than fifty terrorists in jail, Meins died from self-induced starvation in Wittlich prison, thus laying the grounds for a legacy of martyrdom the outlaws were about to construct, insinuating torture and murder on the part of the prosecuting authorities.[20] The so-called Holger Meins Command stormed the FRG's Stockholm embassy in April 1975, demanding the release of twenty-six RAF prisoners. Two diplomats and two terrorists were killed. A month later the four remaining core members were arraigned in Stuttgart-Stammheim, awaiting trial, but Meinhof hanged herself on May 9, 1976. The next day there was a demonstration in honor of her death in Frankfurt, which led to severe altercations with the police. In April 1977, Baader, Ensslin, and Raspe were sentenced to life imprisonment; forthwith they would be housed in a specially built maximum-security prison in Stammheim.[21]

Meanwhile, the original RAF had regrouped, collecting former sympathizers and now calling itself the June 2nd Movement after the historic death of Ohnesorg on June 2, 1967. Their *raison d être* was total solidarity with captured RAF members of the first hour.[22] Hence on September 5, 1977, the "German Autumn" began, when industrialist Hanns Martin Schleyer was kidnapped in Cologne. The specific goal was to hold him, pending the unconditional release of the RAF Stammheim prisoners and others. As German authorities refused to give in, a Palestinian commando hijacked the Lufthansa passenger jet *Landshut* on a flight from Majorca to Frankfurt, eventually forcing it to land in Mogadishu, Somalia. After the Palestinians had killed the pilot, eighty-six passengers and the remaining crew were freed by GSG-9, a newly formed German federal police commando unit clandestinely flown in. The same day, October 18, Ensslin, Baader, and Raspe were found dead in their cells, the woman by hanging and the men by gunshot. Schleyer was found murdered the next day, in

Mulhouse, France. This shocked most of the republic's citizens.[23] Martin Walser, who had, after a meeting years earlier, found Schleyer to be quite agreeable but resembling a Borgia family member of the Italian Renaissance, wrote in his diary: "This is the worst." His wife Käthe was in fear of her husband's life.[24]

Shortly after Schleyer's abduction in September 1977, social theorist Jürgen Habermas wrote to the left-liberal political scientist Kurt Sontheimer in Munich that he, Sontheimer, had been wrong when he had assumed "a causal relationship between leftist theories and the acts of terror, which today are committed in the Federal Republic."[25] Habermas was embarrassed by the far-reaching consequences of his and Adorno's 1960s preachments that had done their part to spawn student unrest. As Sontheimer had seen clearly and as he had emphasized in a recent television broadcast, the current terror was an outgrowth of such unrest, albeit one that SDS leader Rudi Dutschke had not envisioned, far less desired.[26] For Dutschke's long march through the institutions of power was meant to result in transformations within government and society over time, including the universities; he never planned on waging actual war against the established democratic order. In fact, the SDS unequivocally dissociated itself from the first of the terror actions, the Frankfurt department store arson, in the spring of 1968.[27]

If judged by their writings, Dutschke was much inferior to Meinhof. Although he had a good background in Marx and Engels, he had contaminated it with Mao and Ho Chi Minh and succumbed to the SDS's pseudosociological vernacular. With her impressive theoretical background, Meinhof also put Ensslin in the shade, who mostly wrote gobbledygook, to say nothing of Baader, who in what he thought were political pamphlets exulted in expletives, habitually demeaning women.[28]

Ensslin was merely a bad copy of an intellectual, made worse by her insistence on originality. From the University of Tübingen she failed to graduate; instead, she attained a primary-teacher's certificate in the provinces with average grades. She was set to start school teaching when Jens's recommendation sent her to the Free University. She took punctilious notes in lectures and slavishly followed trends. First beholden to the deeply serious Christendom of her Lutheran father, the minister, she was then drawn to whatever enlightenment came out of Jens's casual but fashionable Friday colloquiums, where she met Bernward Vesper. Through him, she became persuaded of the value of old Nazi lyricism as generated by Will Vesper, and then came more enlightenment through the FU's Professor Lämmert. From there she easily navigated to Social Democratic gospel à la Günter Grass and then, seemingly abruptly through the magnetic influence of Baader, to extreme activism. Throughout all, the slender, long-haired blonde maintained perfect composure and followed the calls of fashion as much as her funds allowed – always strikingly made up and showing off a red leather jacket at the time of her Berlin trial in 1968.[29]

Andreas Baader, also a fan of leather, shared her sense of style, impressiveness, and grandeur. Three years younger than Ensslin, he was the son of a Munich municipal archivist who held a doctorate, as had Meinhof's father, who had gone missing in a Soviet POW camp. The attractive child was pampered by his mother and aunt, and as an adolescent he drifted into the Schwabing artists' scene, spending time with the experimental Action-Theater, where another denizen, Rainer Werner Fassbinder, called the shots. There he met Horst Söhnlein, who later assisted him, Ensslin, and another terrorist, Thorwald Proll, in the Frankfurt immolations. Baader was a failure at school, work-shy and with a proclivity for brawls and petty criminal activities, a specialty being joyrides in stolen cars. He was even more ostentatious in dress than Ensslin and his mannerisms were outré. Unlike Meinhof's, and perhaps Ensslin's, Baader's life was driven by no altruistic motives; he merely exhibited narcissism. He was a sentimentalist, a facile seducer of women, and, some say, also of men. After he had moved from Munich to Berlin, he merged with university students who were more interested in a bohemian lifestyle than serious study, like those in the communes. By them he was introduced to SDS circles, where eventually he met Ensslin.[30]

At the time of the White Rose student insurrection in Munich during 1942–3, Baader's father had become interested in the anti-Hitler resistance, but never followed suit. Ensslin's parents had been influenced during the Weimar Republic by *völkisch* thought as members of the German youth movement; this explains their tolerance of Will Vesper, with his maudlin love of "Blood and Soil." During the Third Reich, Helmut Ensslin supported the Confessing Church of Martin Niemöller, then joined the Wehrmacht voluntarily before being drafted. Only Meinhof, who looked up to Sophie

Scholl, was old enough to have grown up with a consciousness of anti-Hitlerism toward the end of the war, and her subsequent disgust of anything Nazi thereafter was patent.[31]

Judging by Meinhof's paramount influence alone, abhorrence of Nazism and the Third Reich was a major trigger for action in the RAF, as it had been, more distinctly articulated as intergenerational conflict, in prior student unrest. As has been well qualified, the RAF was "content with a stylized understanding of the Nazi dictatorship, they saw analogues everywhere, even in the democratic United States, and used their imaginative rhetoric to justify 'resistance' against what they considered neofascist dangers."[32] Anti-authority rhetoric was introduced early into the discourse when Ensslin, who along with her siblings had questioned her parents' behavior during the dictatorship, declared shortly after Ohnesorg's death on June 2, 1967 that "this is the generation of Auschwitz – you cannot enter into discussion with them!"[33] In more serious argumentation by RAF ideologues, led by Meinhof, the decades-old (and GDR-sponsored) formula was repeated, by which Nazism was an outgrowth of capitalism and Auschwitz the apotheosis of that logic. Hence RAF activity was the nemesis of such linear development.[34]

To be sure, personal experiences had an important bearing on such thinking, because, apart from Meinhof, several of the terrorists' parents had either suffered or profited significantly from Nazism. Into the first category fell Hans-Joachim Klein, Thomas Weisbecker, and Stefan Wisniewski. Klein was born in 1947 as the son of a woman who had been imprisoned in Ravensbrück concentration camp after committing what the Nazis regarded as "race defilement" with a Jew. His mother killed herself shortly after his birth and he was brought up by a policeman father who regularly beat him.[35] The father of Weisbecker, born in 1949, as a half-Jew had been in Buchenwald, his grandfather in Mauthausen and Auschwitz, and his uncle murdered.[36] Wisniewski was born in 1953 as the son of a German woman and a former Polish forced laborer who died eight years after liberation from Nazi rule. In the Black Forest village where he grew up regional notables, onetime SA and SS men, had to be kept from learning about the boy's origins lest he suffer reprisals.[37] The second category included Birgit Hogefeld, born in 1956. Her father was said to be a Nazi who spent eight years in the Wehrmacht and then returned from the Soviet Union as a broken man, embittered after years of deprivation. When her name appeared on the most-wanted list all over West Germany, he experienced revenge.[38]

Concentration-camp symbolism was effectively employed in the RAF and its successor organization's self-representation, often picked up and uncritically dispersed by the public media, chief among them *Bild*. Direct comparisons with the victims of Nazism were facile, as Ensslin ruminated in her letters from Stammheim about lampshades made from human skin in Buchenwald or "das System Auschwitz."[39] In her Cologne cell before Stammheim, Meinhof told of Zyklon B gas and "Auschwitz fantasies," and warned of "Treblinka, Maidanek, Sobibor" punishment schemes by the authorities to keep the proletariat in line.[40] A favorite ploy was to compare the appearance of Holger Meins after his hunger-strike suicide in 1974 to that of a "Muselmann," typical concentration-camp corpse, with his hollow eyes and sunken cheeks.[41]

There is no question that all members of the terrorist units were incensed by the presence of former National Socialists in the Federal Republic's political and industrial, social and educational structures. RAF member Inge Viett experienced this at the most primitive level, as she was growing up, in the 1950s, in a household in North Germany where visitors uttered "Heil Hitler" when they entered and "Heil Hitler" when they left.[42] Subsequently she claimed to have found out that "onetime mass murderers were decorated as heroes of democracy."[43] Viett and others deplored the continued influence of former Nazis in higher and highest places in federal-republican government.[44] Meinhof, best informed as usual, early on deplored the insouciance of Adenauer-protected men such as Lübke and Kiesinger, Oberländer and Globke, and denounced Bundeswehr generals such as Friedrich Foertsch, whom she accused of having served under Hitler.[45] After chief federal attorney Siegfried Buback was murdered in April 1977, the terrorists charged that he had been in the Nazi Party and publicized his membership number.[46]

Former Nazi Party and SS membership was a key reason why Hanns Martin Schleyer was selected as an archetypal victim to be held for ransom toward liberation of the Stammheim captives in September 1977. For Inge Viett (who was sentenced to five years in prison) he was the "fattest magnate of capitalism, with the fascist past, whose war and post-war careers reflected both character and morals of post-war West Germany."[47] Her cofighter

Peter-Jürgen Boock (who served seventeen years) stated that as employers' union head and former SS officer Schleyer was, for the RAF, "the most important link between the Nazi period and federal-republican present."[48]

Schleyer's Nazi credentials were, in fact, striking. He was guilty of having uttered sentences such as "The German concept of fealty should never be used in connection with Jews" and "Selection always means eradication."[49] Haughtily, he never renounced his Nazi past.[50] Born in 1912, he was the son of a Nazi justice and son-in-law of the chief physician of the SA. His was a stellar Nazi record: Hitler Youth, Nazi student administration, and SS. During the war he served in Prague under the governance of Heydrich, with partial responsibility for the integration of Czech industry into German armaments. Post-1945, in French custody, he downplayed his Nazi functions and then distinguished himself in West German industry, especially at Mercedes-Benz Incorporated.[51] Schleyer's demise at the climax of the RAF campaign exemplified his goodness of fit as a proxy father for the entire disillusioned RAF generation.[52]

By wielding their weapons, the terrorists caused changes to German society and politics. Those compounded existing crises in the making since the late 1960s, whose root causes lay elsewhere. Apart from a birth decline, the economic boom since the 1950s was slowing toward the end of the 1970s, aggravated by an energy crisis in 1973. Stagnating wages during inflation and unemployment were becoming precarious.[53] The appointment of Helmut Schmidt as chancellor in May 1974 was therefore welcomed, because his previous portfolios seemed right. He had experience as a Hamburg senator, managing a terrible flood, and had acquitted himself well in Bonn as minister of finance and economics.[54] On September 5, 1977, the day Schleyer was kidnapped, *Der Spiegel* accused the coalition government of SPD and FDP of blatant shortfalls as a result of political misjudgment – "faint economy, growing joblessness and imminent pension failure."[55] But the magazine also noted that, fortunately, prospects had been held out of more employment for new personnel in the interest of "inner security," "flight protection," and "reactor safety" – unmistakable references to the terrorist threats and their putative controls.[56]

Initially, the right-wing Social Democrat Schmidt was trusted with the economy and with providing more security to an increasingly endangered commonweal. Many saw him as an antidote to Brandt, with his fateful decision-making and lax private morals. Brandt had to admit responsibility for having employed Günter Guillaume, a GDR spy planted in Bonn years before.[57] Moreover, Brandt was close to the arts and letters; they were suspected of sympathizing with the terror scene.[58]

The CDU/CSU meanwhile, while having lost the majority in the federal elections of 1972 and 1976, during the 1970s underwent a remake that removed it from Adenauer's ultra-conservatism and, with some exceptions, from former Nazis. In their stead, new energetic men with untarnished reputations came to the fore. Some were minister-presidents, others state secretaries or lord mayors. Among the former, Bavaria's Strauss remained the most problematic, despite his charisma and intelligence. After the *Spiegel* affair, he was making a comeback. But even the Bundesrat, with a veto on many Bundestag decisions, after being staffed with many more enlightened Christian conservatives, as a group moved to the left. The most significant change for the CDU came with the arrival of Helmut Kohl, who for most of the 1970s was minister-president of Rhineland-Palatinate as well as leader of his party. Kohl, a liberal by old-fashioned CDU standards, was interested in pluralism and social change and much in favor of an entente with the GDR, which the FRG formally recognized in December 1972, without entirely forgoing claims for unification.[59] Kohl now proceeded to normalize relations between the two states further by pursuing *Ostpolitik*, a theme prodigiously begun by Willy Brandt.

To defeat terrorism, Bonn passed three consecutive pieces of legislation, beginning in 1974. Already before then anyone vaguely suspected of taking the terrorists' side was set upon by the authorities. In Frankfurt during 1971, the police searched the flat of the writer Jürgen Roth, author of a short polemic, "Is the Federal Republic a Police State?" The sociologist Brigitte Heinrich was apprehended on suspicion of having aided terrorists. After fruitless weeks-long searches, she had to be released. Another left-wing intellectual, Eva-Maria Michel, was jailed after aiding "Rote Hilfe," which assisted terrorists in flight. Her husband Karl Markus Michel, who like her was close to Enzensberger, was also suspect.[60] Journalists in particular were in danger of becoming the prey of investigators.[61]

In December 1974 the Bundestag allowed the prosecution of attorneys mistrusted as clandestine collaborators of RAF members. Anyone close to those lawyers was imperiled. In August 1976 an additional law attempted to forestall the formation of terrorist cells, making eventual expressions of sympathy with terrorists a felony. Then, in 1978, the authorities were given leave to expand searches of private buildings and intensify personal controls.[62]

As a consequence, the nation was split into three parts in the cataclysmic autumn of 1977. There were those who notoriously felt insecure even under a strong-armed Chancellor Schmidt. Their outrage was fanned by right-wing CDU politicians such as Hessian delegate Alfred Dregger and intellectuals such as Professor Golo Mann, a close friend of Strauss's, who demanded the reintroduction of the death penalty and summary executions for RAF members.[63] Others, such as Habermas, placed confidence in Schmidt's cabinet, trusting the mechanisms of parliamentary democracy and its executive in action.[64] Others again, intellectuals and artists on the left, were fearful of governmental agencies overreaching themselves as in a witch-hunt, threatening the inalienable rights of man.[65] "Elephants are facilitating the disassembly of the constitutional state," cautioned Rudolf Augstein in September 1977.[66] He and Böll were now more afraid than ever that the FRG was on the way to becoming a police state. Policemen were working seven days a week on terrorism, also catching in their dragnets many ordinary criminals. People's rights were being violated to the point of ridicule: in Berlin, a young woman who vaguely looked like wanted terrorist Angelika Speitel drastically changed her hairstyle, after having been caught three times by police.[67]

Moreover, anti-terrorist measures implemented since January 1972 in the public service were now causing great concern, particularly among the young. For Brandt had met with officials of the states to initiate an automatic background check on any applicant for state employment. The new Radikalenerlass or Radical Decree, anchored in the Basic Law of 1949, was in the spirit of combating extremism, on the left or right. Yet the blanket manner in which the policing of individuals occurred damaged not only innocents, but also Brandt, the SPD, and the FRG as a whole. Over a thousand cases were processed until 1979, when the Schmidt cabinet moderated the practice, having realized that almost all the young people were good citizens.[68]

As it turned out, the measure affected mostly schoolteachers and some junior university faculty. An early victim was Ekkehart Krippendorff, the student of politics and admirer of Jaspers, born, like Meinhof, in 1934. In

1959 he received his doctorate under Eschenburg in Tübingen. Having spent 1960–1 at Harvard, Yale, and Columbia, he was assistant to a professor at the Free University in Berlin from 1963 to 1968. Here he represented students' interests, so that already in 1970 his path as a tenure-track academic was blocked. Even after having obtained full qualifications, a promised chair at Konstanz was withheld from him in 1973. Only in 1978 did the FU rehire him as a full professor, after stays in Britain and Italy.[69]

Many West Germans were convinced the Stammheim prisoners had been murdered and the government wanted to turn the nation into a police state. From the beginning of RAF arrests beyond the German Autumn of September–October 1977 the terrorist captives were idealized as martyrs and "political prisoners" in left-wing circles.[70] They were said to be ill-treated and subject to what all outside supporters, especially the second-generation "June 2nd" terrorists, soon identified as "isolation torture."[71] The frequent use of Nazi paradigms, actively encouraged by the prisoners themselves, was key in this. Another such term was "Vernichtungshaft," or "eliminatory incarceration," also facilely borrowed from the Nazis' vocabulary, as they had used this against the Jews.[72] There were liaisons, mostly through complicit lawyers, to human-rights organizations such as those associated with the United Nations and Amnesty International, and the "Rote Hilfe" network to help financially with the defense. Nationally and internationally, left-wing intellectuals and journalists were coopted to beat the drums for the captives, Enzensberger and Engelmann among them.[73] Terrorist Hans-Joachim Klein chauffeured Jean-Paul Sartre from Paris to Stammheim prison on December 4, 1974, to interview Baader; Sartre then spread the word, well intentioned and ill informed, and soon other intellectuals in France, including Michel Foucault, were on the side of what they thought were persecuted champions of democracy.[74]

Holger Meins, after transport to Stammheim on April 28, 1974, was especially useful in this cause. With the RAF's characteristic affinity for publicity, his hunger strike was instrumentalized by the comrades outside, as his preventable death on November 9 was conveniently presented as "execution" to the outside world.[75] In reality there was no murder and charges of torture and isolation were unsubstantiated. At the beginning of her prison ordeal in Cologne, Meinhof was in an isolation cell under worse than normal conditions, similar to the four others elsewhere. But after Meinhof's death when the remaining three were in Stammheim, they became preferential prisoners, entitled to books, typewriters, radios, and television sets. They also communicated with one another and visited each other's cells, until the fall of 1977. Attorneys smuggled in contraband. Significantly, when Meinhof had hanged herself in 1976, she had done so with rope easily at her disposal.[76] When Baader, Raspe, and Ensslin were found dead in their cells on October 18, 1977, they had coordinated their suicides beforehand, to occur simultaneously.

◆ ◆ ◆

Left-of-center intellectuals and artists were touched by the RAF because of class affinities and ideological sympathies. Meinhof was a journalist, Ensslin had been in publishing, and Meins attended a film academy. However unsuccessful, in his knockabout youth Baader had mingled with the bohemians, and Raspe had ambitions as a writer. Most of them came from upper-middle-class homes.

Meinhof's situation especially from 1970 caused Heinrich Böll to switch his authorial attention from residual problems of the Nazi era to the new problematic posed by the RAF. In 1971 he published *Gruppenbild mit Dame* (*Group Portrait with a Lady*), describing the life of a young Cologne woman, daughter of a well-to-do builder, as she clandestinely loves a Soviet prisoner-of-war, a forced laborer among German civilians. Again, Böll fumed against Hitler's Wehrmacht, conjured up images of gold teeth yanked from Jews, and denounced the Catholic establishment.[77] In January 1972 he defended Meinhof in a *Spiegel* article, extending his criticism to Adenauer and his FRG for their protection of old Nazis and premature release of war criminals. He favorably compared the fugitive Meinhof with those criminals, insinuating that she was less deserving of long-term imprisonment than Göring or von Schirach. Meinhof was entitled to clemency; her "group's" fairness to policemen should be reciprocated; they were merely "desperate theoreticians" and should not be prejudged; poor Meinhof was liable to be lynched once caught.[78]

The unreasonableness of such argumentation was countered by the SPD justice minister of North-Rhine-Westphalia, Diether Posser, who claimed that Böll belittled the RAF's danger; that they, not the police, had resorted to guns first; that in West Germany, not a country of lynch justice, clemency could not legally be offered to those not yet tried or convicted.[79] The *FAZ*'s conservative Dolf Sternberger seconded this, for the gang's ideal of a lawlessness was anathema to the FRG with its Basic Law.[80] State organs took action. Backed by emergent anti-terror legislation, policemen visited Böll in his Eifel mountain country house in early June.[81]

All of a sudden, Böll found himself in the center of controversy. His position was unambiguously clear, with Joachim Kaiser conceding that amid much public animosity against Meinhof and her accomplices he was becoming the FRG's moral alibi – "festive jackass, statue, decorated conscience of the nation"; and Böll proceeded to make a Meinhof-like figure the subject of his next novel.[82] Katharina Blum, in *Die verlorene Ehre der Katharina Blum* (*The Lost Honor of Katharina Blum*) is a young, un-attached, woman who allows a deserter from the Bundeswehr to stay over one night and in her bed; hence she resembles the citizens who were warned about collusion with the RAF, and he is like an RAF member, because police suspect him of being one. Infatuated with him, she subsequently tries to shield him during police interrogations, getting herself deeper and deeper in trouble. Counting against her is that she sent him to a hideout owned by a city luminary, a married man who desired her as his mistress. In the end she shoots a tabloid reporter after he tries to force her into sex, the fugitive is caught, and they both go to prison. Devoid of all other Third Reich symbolisms, there is only one "old Nazi" in this novel, who previously handed her the murder weapon.[83] Although Böll was applauded by left-liberals, he was chastised by conservatives for what looked like a defense of the Baader-Meinhof gang and, even if he had meant the *Bild-Zeitung*, for not respecting press freedom.[84]

Henceforth, Böll strove to justify the role Kaiser had assigned to him in 1972. He polemicized against *Bild*, characterizing it as an undemocratic element in society. He invented personalities for satire who had everything or nothing to do with Ulrike Meinhof or Gudrun Ensslin, whom in particular he credited with "spirituality."[85] He suggested, hardly in jest, that the broken student Dutschke should be appointed to a university professorship. Conceding that the terrorists' activities were "cruel," he nevertheless insisted on a connection between the student uprising and the National Socialist past.[86] For all their crimes, the RAF and its successor organization deserved their day in court, rather than falling victim to police arbitrariness.[87]

In 1979, two years after the apotheosis of German Autumn, Böll published *Fürsorgliche Belagerung* (*The Safety Net*). This novel's literary value disappointed. Although a creation of "that great poet of compassion," Reich-Ranicki called it "a weak and questionable, and partially a downright fatal book."[88] Its hero, a newspaper magnate with a Nazi past, resembles Schleyer. The likeable Fritz Tolm's estate is heavily guarded by federal security; his and his wife's movements are restricted. But in the end it is burned down by his grandson, whose name is Holger, after Holger Meins (in all, and quite clumsily, no fewer than three Holgers populate the narrative), and whose parents were terrorists. Holger's mother, Tolm's former daughter-in-law, resembling Ensslin, in this story gives herself up; sympathetic young men and women, jobless, suffer from the Radikalenerlass.[89]

Late in 1972, Böll received the Nobel Prize in literature, ostensibly for his novel *Gruppenbild*, but in large measure for what was seen as his fight for human rights.[90] It was for altruistic reasons Martin Walser could not claim that explain his ridicule of Böll as a man of "public goodness."[91] Walser suspected that Böll's reception of the prize was due to cronyism involving the critic Hans Mayer, head of the West German Nobel delegation. Whatever truth there was in that, now, as in later years, Walser was to be disappointed.[92]

In politics, Walser continued steering to the left, but he forsook the orthodox DKP, as he became increasingly suspicious of the GDR, its financier. He visited the Soviet Union and, as Reich-Ranicki would later carp, had much good to say about it publicly. He supported the SPD and, as all leftist liberals, deplored Bonn's support of American policy in Vietnam. Although he appreciated that the students' rebellion and RAF activities were, in part, a consequence of that, his empathy for the terrorists was limited.[93]

On the Third Reich and the Holocaust, Walser qualified his approach of the mid-1960s that any German could have worked at Auschwitz (the converse of which had been that no one could be singled out as *especially* evil). In 1979 he articulated that the German people were collectively as guilty as those criminals, no single individual could be held responsible, and their crimes should fall under a statute of limitations. The crime of Auschwitz was so great as never to be atoned for.[94] This explains why already in his novel *Der Sturz* in 1973 he made light of known Nazi criminals by ostentatiously using their names, such as that of Oskar Dirlewanger, a particularly vicious SS commander.[95] He also treated Nazis, SS, and race scientists as people like you and me.[96]

In 1976, Walser published the novel *Jenseits der Liebe* (*Beyond All Love*), which some readers thought worse than *Der Sturz*, with its chaotic plot and implausibly grotesque sexual configurations. It introduced Franz Horn, of average intelligence, weak-willed, lethargic, and ultimately heading for failure professionally. Walser identified on several counts with Horn, and in Horn's boss Arthur Thiele he sought to characterize his publisher Siegfried Unseld of Suhrkamp, with whom he was beginning to disagree, and in Horn's senior colleague, Dr. Horst Liszt, the fellow writer Uwe Johnson, with whom he had a tempestuous relationship.[97] The book was immediately savaged by Reich-Ranicki, who wrote: "An irrelevant, a bad, a miserable novel. It is not worth the trouble to read even one chapter."[98] Less damning was Kaiser, who thought it a "weak Walser text" recycling well-worn themes.[99] However, just those themes fascinated others, for Walser had again demonstrated the fragility of today's existence amid a phony affluence, with its tokens of materialism and outward success.[100]

Two years later, Walser presented *Ein fliehendes Pferd* (*Runaway Horse*), a novel about two middle-aged men, alter egos to each other, resembling both Anselm Kristlein and of course Walser. It is the story of two former high-school comrades who meet accidentally on vacation near Lake Constance. One is reticent and culturally pessimistic, the other self-confident, gregarious, open to life's enjoyments. But during their competitive meetings their personalities unravel, one revealing himself a failure in life who has lived through lies, the other fully succumbing to futility and forlornness.[101]

This time, Reich-Ranicki was pleased. Walser had shown insight and maturity; he had managed to defeat an often-exorcised crisis, in a "most modest and most convincing epic work." The critic noted "that this prose is alive, that the two central figures are neither phantoms nor marionettes and that Walser has finally freed himself from abstraction."[102] The author, however, was humiliated to have been treated so condescendingly.[103] Reich-Ranicki's review was a mirror image of the one he had published two years earlier about the travails of Franz Horn. At that time the critic's judgment had driven Walser to an existential crisis, because he had suggested that the author was not merely a bad writer, but one who operated beyond commonly accepted literary rules. In spring 1976, Walser's loathing had been so great that he considered slapping Reich-Ranicki's face, for in twenty-five years he had never come across "a harsher, more malicious hatchet job."[104] He also suspected Reich-Ranicki to have conspired with his publisher Unseld – whatever that case may have been, the relationship between author and critic from 1978 on was only to get worse.[105]

Walser appears to have been much more concerned about his standing in the West German literary world than any of his colleagues in the 1970s, for he continued obsessing about the bestseller lists.[106] Hence he took umbrage at his closest rival, Grass, who in November 1974 for his own publicity had blamed him for not rooting for Soviet dissident Aleksandr Solzhenitsyn, as was then in vogue in left-wing circles.[107] Grass issued his allegation three months before his own political star fell along with his mentor Willy Brandt's, in May 1974; he and Brandt had been on a famous penitence journey to Warsaw four years earlier. Although Grass was on good terms with Helmut Schmidt, he never again worked for the SPD as he had done in the 1960s.[108] To Brandt he wrote that with his resignation as chancellor Social Democratic politics would lose an "essential dimension" – hence he too would have to step back.[109] In 1972 he pronounced judgment on the RAF, denying the Baader-Meinhof gang "revolutionary theory" and instead attesting it a "Bonnie-and-Clyde" character.[110] Thereafter he, who had known Ensslin and Meinhof well in the late 1960s, abstained from comment. His abstinence reflected itself in contemporary writings, with the RAF "an unacknowledged presence." In his novel of 1972, *Tagebuch einer Schnecke* (*Diary of a Snail*), Grass referred to the 1969 federal elections but did not mention the incipient RAF. This he would do in *Der Butt* (*The Flounder*) of 1977, where he described law-court proceedings much like those in Stammheim. But he deflected from the youthful terrorists when he suggested that "it is the generations responsible for Auschwitz who are really on trial."[111]

Like Walser, Grass had his share of problems with critics, especially Reich-Ranicki, who first had tried to smother him with his disapproval of *Die Blechtrommel* in 1960. Reich-Ranicki's censorship of *Örtlich betäubt* of 1969 was only a little more benign. And in 1977 for this reviewer *Der Butt* became "an artistic failure."[112] The reviewer's position in West German literature by the 1970s was unique in three ways. First, he was a Jew once persecuted by the Nazis, who had made a successful post-war career among Germans. As such, secondly, he was the shrewdest critic capable of incisive judgments no author in the country could escape. And thirdly, he issued those judgments from a position of seeming political neutrality, although this former Stalinist now tended to the liberal left. His considerable energies could therefore not be harnessed in the service of others, and he could not be bought by others, in politics or elsewhere. Instead, he possessed the air of someone with ideological unapproachableness. What drove such an iridescent personality to exercise the influence that he did?

As he made clear in his memoirs, Reich-Ranicki continued in the 1970s to suffer from what he perceived as anti-Semitism, however politely it was couched.[113] Physically, he resembled the cliched caricature of the Jew that the Nazi *Stürmer* had constructed, and evoked negative feelings certainly in Walser. In spring 1976, at the height of his fury, the author of "Our Auschwitz" remarked that Reich-Ranicki should not have the "tastelessness" to regard his criticisms of him as expressions of anti-Semitism.[114] And when in November 1978 the writer heard that the book critic was compulsively using a razor every evening, he reasoned this had to be "a habit from the ghetto." For in the ghetto, whoever did not always look his healthiest was speedily selected for death.[115] Some thought even then that Walser was operating "at the border of anti-Semitism."[116] Decades later, Walser condemned Reich-Ranicki to a literary death in his novel *Tod eines Kritikers* (*Death of a Critic*), describing the Jewish protagonist André Ehrl-König, who talks with his hands and bounces his "bald and massive head" up and down, as so "small and ugly" as a child that his mother had had to reject him.[117] Walser's sentiments revealed that even enlightened Germans could not resist the racist stereotyping that had been implanted in their minds by a manipulative fascist state when young.

In truth, the peer of literary criticism overstepped his competency in a number of ways. Reich-Ranicki pushed writers in the direction that *he* wanted, disregarding their own initiatives, as he openly admitted in January 1989.[118] He misrepresented the writers' work, by, for example, imputing "frigidity" to Böll's Katharina Blum character when the author had not implied that.[119] He accused Walser of abstractionism when none had been engaged in.[120] And both in 1977 and 1979 he claimed there were no literary new talents when those that he had detected did not meet his excellence criteria.[121] Most fatally, he was liable to ascribe both brilliance and incompetence to an author's work, as in the case of Walser's *Halbzeit*."[122] Later, in Walser's *Jenseits der Liebe*, he found a "mixture of vitality and sterility" and in the next sentence called Walser temperamental.[123] On the occasion of Böll's *Fürsorgliche Belagerung* he pronounced: "Who other than Böll in these lands can afford to write so badly."[124]

Was Joachim Kaiser of the *SZ* Reich-Ranicki's foil? More on the left, he did not exude his Frankfurt colleague's exotic fascination. Unlike him, Kaiser always remained within good taste and a self-understood code of ethics. This is why Walser feared his disapproving comments more than Reich-Ranicki's. On the occasion of *Jenseits der Liebe*, he claims to have been hurt by such comments, "rationally" formulated as could have been expected.[125] Two years later, Kaiser was less than thrilled with *Ein fliehendes Pferd*.[126] Still, during a social visit by the Kaiser couple to the Walsers in Wasserburg in September 1979, all was well if not perfect. "Posing only, but it was pleasant," noted Walser, "we didn't hurt each other. So I hope."[127]

◆ ◆ ◆

Theater continued to be highly political in the 1970s, and dramatic plays and docudramas appeared whose subject matters oscillated between depictions of Nazism and West German defects, RAF terrorism, and Marxist-inspired nation states. The extreme left-of-center essayist Hans Magnus Enzensberger wrote a play about Fidel Castro's Cuba, *Das Verhör von Habana* (*The Havana Inquiry*), which was premiered at the Ruhr-Festspiele in Recklinghausen and East Berlin simultaneously, during June 1970. Enzensberger, born in 1929, was brought up in Nuremberg in a dwelling next to that of *Der Stürmer* publisher Julius Streicher, whose evil vulgarity he later remembered with revulsion. His was a background similar to that of his peers – the father a Nazi Party member, he himself a reluctant Hitler Youth listening to the BBC "with bedsheets over our heads so the neighbours couldn't hear," and fighting American tanks in the end.[128]

At the University of Erlangen, the German literature department dissuaded Enzensberger from writing a doctoral dissertation analyzing Hitler's compositional style. There were at least two former Nazis there: Hans Schwerte, who was hiding his true identity as a former SS functionary, and Heinz Otto Burger, an SS veteran and former specialist in Nazi race typology.[129] Enzensberger graduated, in 1956, with a thesis on the Romantic poet Clemens Brentano.[130]

Because of the country's "inability to deal with the Nazi past," Enzensberger drifted ineluctably into the Marxist camp. Disabused of half-hearted attempts at democracy, he moved abroad, but returned regularly to Germany, where he befriended Hans Werner Richter and soon was a habitué of Gruppe 47. Richter especially liked his poetry, which he compared to Heinrich Heine's. In Frankfurt in June 1961, in a speech, Enzensberger constructed a historical parallel between Auschwitz and the Algerian war of independence.[131] Then he accused the *FAZ* of having neglected the Algerians' side as well as the Auschwitz Trial, but, as was his wont, overextended his arguments.[132]

Ever since its revisionist program of 1959, Enzensberger, more than Walser or Grass, had been suspicious of the SPD's more bourgeois flavor. Yet in 1961 he assisted both in an anthology of essays to aid Brandt's campaign; there was little enthusiasm for the SPD, yet it was still acknowledged as the only alternative. In July 1965, Chancellor Erhard's "pipsqueak" remarks irked him much. As the SPD was even closer to governing, Enzensberger founded *Kursbuch*, an annual series of anthologies he edited – essays, reviews, reprints and commentaries, by authors of a left-wing persuasion. It became required reading for the incipient student movement, which he much applauded. Walser's piece, "Our Auschwitz," was originally published there. After a visit to Moscow in 1967, Enzensberger fell in with the crowd surrounding Dutschke back in Berlin, including Gudrun Ensslin. In 1966 he was in Princeton with Gruppe 47, joining those who were protesting; near the end of the decade he was convinced that the FRG constituted "a masked, yet institutionally secure, everyday fascism."[133]

In late 1967 this visible public intellectual was invited on an eight-month fellowship to Wesleyan University in Middletown, Connecticut.[134] But early in 1968, after Fidel Castro had contributed to his *Kursbuch*, Enzensberger visited Cuba, resigning his Wesleyan position, "after three peaceful months." In a letter to *The New York Review of Books*, he claimed "the class which rules the United States of America, and the government which implements its politics, to be the most dangerous body of men on earth," for its aim was "to establish its political, economic, and military predominance over every other power in the world." He mentioned states such as Guatemala as U.S.-manipulated. They were all governed, "with American support, by oppression, corruption, and starvation." The current situation in the United States reminded him of Germany in the 1930s – "there was a lot of racial discrimination and persecution going on." To protest this, he wanted to visit Cuba.[135] Later *The New York Times* informed its readers that Enzensberger regarded American foreign policy as "an attempt to impose the will of the United States on smaller countries throughout the world."[136]

Back in Cuba again during fall 1968 for longer, Enzensberger and his Russian wife resided in a luxury hotel. If this was not arrogance he, contemporaneously, published an article in *Kursbuch* proclaiming the death of all literature – a bombast reminiscent of Boulez, who had pronounced the death of Schoenberg some time earlier.[137] Having returned to Germany after several months, he composed his docudrama *Das Verhör*, which was based on interrogation transcripts of exiled Cubans who, part of a larger band, had failed in their coup from Florida, in the Bay of Pigs, in April 1961. As Enzensberger alleged, those prisoners had not been punished by Castro's forces, merely questioned, and with his recapitulation of the inquests he wished to demonstrate Castro's magnanimity.[138] In summer 1970 he had his play performed in industrial Ruhr Valley Recklinghausen (ideally for a workers' audience) and East Berlin's Deutsches Theater, with actors mimicking several interrogators as well as exiled Cuban captives. Fascist verisimilitudes were conjured up, interrogator Franqui reminding defendants of "Franco, Nazism and Hitlerism" and "torture and the murders" under Castro's predecessor, Fulgencio Batista. Enzensberger pictured Castro's interrogators as judicious and the interrogated as flawed.[139]

The reviews were mixed and, in West Germany, mostly negative, whereas in East Berlin there were some laughs.[140] It was next to impossible to fascinate industrial workers in Recklinghausen with stories from a Communist dictatorship, because they, who in the 1970s were driving Volkswagen and enjoying vacations in Rimini, could not identify with an impoverished Latin American proletariat.[141] Such identification was even less likely during a WDR telecasting, which reached all social strata. Moreover, Enzensberger's suggestion (in the preface of the play) that the Cuban prisoners in his drama were exchangeable, in that they could just as well be Swedes or West Germans, stretched the limits of credulity. "Drawing the parallel from the exploited sugar-cane island to the industrialized nations of central Europe is impossible," wrote the *FAZ*.[142] And when Heberto Padilla, the Cuban poet to whom the work had originally been dedicated, a year later in a (probably forced) act of self-criticism accused himself of having betrayed the Cuban Revolution and charged Enzensberger (and Sartre, Simone de Beauvoir, and Susan Sontag) with being agents for the CIA, the playwright found himself downright embarrassed.[143] Enzensberger lost more credibility when years later he was impelled to declare Cuba a failure as a Marxist polity, for "they had botched it completely. Cuba was a one-man show: For me, this experiment was over."[144]

Enzensberger's play was not performed by the leading progressive stage directors of the time, Peter Stein, Peter Palitzsch, Claus Peymann, and Peter Zadek, not even at Stuttgart, whose theater was among the most advanced.[145] Although the more Marxist-oriented among them, such as Stein and Palitzsch, may have shared his eschatological visions, his drama was ignored, either because of its low adaptability or poor popularity ratings.

The Kortner disciple Stein, born in 1937, came to the fore in 1969 in Bremen, with a new staging of Goethe's *Torquato Tasso*. In his bid to politicize theater, he set it in contemporary surroundings and spiked it with salient messages for the citizens. Tasso was played by the brilliant young Swiss actor Bruno Ganz, later a favorite of Zadek's. Already in Munich in 1967–8, Stein, at the Kammerspiele, had presented a *Vietnam Discourse* by Peter Weiss, replete with a money collection for North-Vietnamese fighters, whereupon the conservative Intendant August Everding, the one who would produce a staid festival at Bayreuth during 1969, had fired him. In 1970, after the guest appearance in Bremen, Stein worked at the West Berlin Schaubühne, which, rebuilt and reopened, became pure-bred post-Brechtian. Here Stein staged Brecht's *Mutter* (1970), the *Optimistic Tragedy* of the Stalinist Soviet author Vsevolod Vishnevsky, about the anarchist sailors' regiment of 1918, and Maxim Gorky's *Dachniki* (*Summerfolk*, 1974), the theme of which was women's emancipation. In December 1977, two months after Schleyer's assassination, Stein, behind the fascist façade of the Berlin Olympia stadium, presented strophes of lamentation and mourning adapted from Hölderlin's *Hyperion*.[146]

In 1972, Peter Palitzsch moved from Stuttgart to Frankfurt to initiate an experimental model of inclusive participation ("Mitbestimmung") for all workers in the theatrical production. Briefly, this became as pacesetting as Palitzsch's new interpretations: after Stuttgart's Shakespeare, he now staged Beckett, O'Casey, and Pinter. Under student-movement influence, committees representing all stage workers shared planning and repertoire decisions but failed in determining an actor's salary and casting. This remained contentious, "because actors cannot themselves decide who would play what part." Disappointed, Palitzsch quit in 1980 and moved to other postings, among them the Berliner Ensemble. Yet while "Mitbestimmung" lasted, some phenomenal successes transpired, such as Lessing's *Emilia Galotti* and Wedekind's *Frühlings Erwachen* (*Spring Awakening*). During the German Autumn of 1977, Palitzsch performed Brecht's *Die Tage der Commune* (*Days of the Commune*), which suggested ideological proximity to terrorist goals and therefore became highly controversial, but he persisted, owning up to his Brechtian pedigree.[147]

From 1972 to 1977, Peter Zadek continued his meteoric career in Bochum, obsessed as he was with Shakespeare. He worked with promising, unconventional young artists such as actors Ganz and Ulrich Wildgruber. His protean directors were Werner Schroeter and the ever-moody Fassbinder, with whom Zadek often clashed. An exceptional talent was Peer Raben, who was versed in the composing of stage music as well as chansons, several of which were based on Enzensberger's poems. Zadek loved this young troupe and they loved him, even to the point where personal relations, love triangles, became rather complicated.[148] He managed four Shakespeare productions in that five-year span, of *The Merchant of Venice*, *King Lear*, *Othello*, and *Hamlet*, which he later called "punk Shakespeare."[149] As an "anarchic Romantic," he wanted to take Shakespeare out of fancy bourgeois settings and return him to his popular roots, but also to scandalize the theater subscribers.[150] As Hugh Rorrison recorded, "For *King Lear* the cast selected their own costumes from a heap on the rehearsal room floor. Lear dandled Cordelia on his knee in a pink tutu. Ulrich Wildgruber, a lumbering, inarticulate Othello, mauled a sunbathing Desdemona, smearing her body and bikini in black greasepaint."[151]

Unlike Stein or Palitzsch, who were concerned with the realization of Marxism in society and at the same time worried about the outgrowths of terrorism, Zadek had no ideological axes to grind. Rather than the RAF, whose political anarchism corresponded somewhat with his own artistic temperament, he continued to be worried about Nazis. As a remigrant Jew, he was concerned about the Jews' place in post-war Germany and his own situation there. Again, he experimented with Shylock, now casting him as a wicked, obnoxious Jew of the *Stürmer* variety, meaning to tell his audience that Jews were, like everybody, good *and* bad. One had to live with good and bad people and make do, casting no praise or blame.[152] At the same time, Zadek was concerned for everybody's safety when threats came his way. After the murder of Jewish Olympic athletes in Munich in September 1972, he received a written threat: "If you don't bugger off, you will come to a bad end!"[153] It was a time, recalls Zadek, when people here and there received small letter bombs that exploded on opening. He himself got more threatening letters. His superiors were unmoved, and Bochum police laughed at him, saying: "Your worries are unfounded, especially since it is your secretary who is opening the letters."[154] Eventually, two off-duty policemen impersonating drunks threatened the premises; when actress Hannelore Hoger was mugged by neo-Nazis, still the police played things down: "Naturally there is nothing one can do."[155] Zadek writes that thereafter he became more conscious of his Jewishness, as he sensed "the increasing anti-Semitism" around himself.[156]

Zadek was replaced in Bochum by Claus Peymann, who arrived for the 1979-80 season with his entire theater corps from Stuttgart, protesting how he had been treated there. Like Stein, Peymann was born in 1937, son of a Nazi father and anti-Hitler mother. He heard about concentration camps when a boy; wooden crates were distributed in his hometown of Bremen containing the, often bloodied, personal belongings of Jews. However, GIs coming to occupy Bremen after 1945 brought a culture of tolerance with them that influenced his lifestyle as he was growing up. He joined left-leaning circles, becoming a denizen of bohemian locales, dressed in black, cherished jazz, and traveled to Paris. In the 1960s he was a director of university student theaters, for example in Heidelberg, where he performed Walser's anti-Nazi piece *Der Schwarze Schwan*.[157]

From 1974, Peymann was in Stuttgart when important RAF events unfolded. Sympathetic to their cause but by no means a collaborator, in April 1976 he put on stage the Camus play *Die Gerechten* (*The Just Assassins*), about two nineteenth-century Russian anarchist assassins, one of whom suggested Meinhof, just then in Stammheim. Peymann exhausted his potential when he showed a film about entering a Stuttgart streetcar, with Stammheim as the destination, the audience finding this hard to take. A year later he attempted to produce Meinhof's early play *Bambule*, which dealt with hard-to-educate girls, but this was prohibited by his superiors. As terror was increasing everywhere, things were coming to a head for Peymann.[158] In June 1977, Gudrun Ensslin's mother, Ilse Ensslin, approached him with a letter to be posted on the theater's bulletin board. It asked for financial aid toward the dental treatment of Stammheim inmates, because 7,000 DM was needed for urgent tooth repair. Frau Ensslin made a plea for "a onetime sum of support."[159]

At this point, Peymann had several counts against him. On August 29, *Bild*, under the heading "New Teeth for Terrorists – from Donations," wrote that Gudrun Ensslin had received 3,000 DM for new teeth because she had rejected prison treatments. *Bild* added that after Frau Ensslin's plea, director Peymann had delivered "a higher amount."[160] Even though it was later said that most of the money was for Raspe, Peymann had given the impression that he supported core terrorists. His name had appeared in the uncharitable *Bild-Zeitung*, Stuttgart theater's opera choir had stood up against him, and so had Stuttgart's police union. Consequently, the ruling CDU of Baden-Württemberg demanded his dismissal, although the sympathetic CDU lord mayor, Manfred Rommel, stood behind him. Still in August Peymann himself announced his departure, even though Böll had stated in the *FAZ* that he had done nothing wrong.[161]

By that time, Schleyer had been abducted, then came his murder, the disaster at Mogadishu, and the Stammheim suicides. Peymann was one of those who had reason to doubt they were suicides. He expressed his continued suspicions of the connection between Nazi interests and government on stage when in July 1979, just before his leave-taking, he produced *Vor dem Ruhestand* (*Before Retirement*). It was a brand-new drama by Austrian playwright Thomas Bernhard about a family of three adult siblings, in which German federal justice Rudolf Höller is a former high-placed SS officer. He lives with two sisters in an apartment where he dons his old SS uniform each year on October 7, in honor of Himmler's birthday. On that day, also, he sleeps with his sister Vera, an equally fanatical Nazi who admires him, while the paralyzed Clara, helpless in a wheelchair and an anti-Nazi, withers away in frustration.[162] Obviously, Bernhard and Peymann were lashing out against leading CDU politicians, such as lawyer Karl Carstens who, a former member of the SA and NSDAP, in July 1979 was poised to take office as new federal president.[163] A blanket reference was to former Minister-President Hans Filbinger in Stuttgart, who had backed the cabal against Peymann: the main lead Höller is a high-placed judge. Filbinger was currently being unmasked as a formerly Nazi jurist; Rolf Hochhuth was completing another play, *Juristen* (*The Jurists*), about him to be assigned to Peymann, but it was incomplete for Stuttgart. It was premiered later during 1979 in Hamburg.

By that time, Filbinger had already been forced to abdicate the Baden-Württemberg premiership. Hochhuth's play had dealt with the Radikalenerlass, which Filbinger had pushed in his state. The character of the young man Klaus is a victim of it, about to graduate as a physician, he is unable to find hospital work when he visits Heilmayer, a high-placed politician, easily identifiable as Filbinger, who in the end offers no assistance.[164] But this was an anticlimax. Hochhuth had already caused Filbinger distress with an earlier publication, for which he had collaborated with *Die Zeit*. On February 17, 1978, the prepublication of a novella, *Eine Liebe in Deutschland* (*A Love in Germany*), had begun. It dealt with the fate of Pauline Kröpf, a small businesswoman, consigned to Ravensbrück concentration camp, and Stasiek Zasada, a Polish forced laborer, executed by Nazi law enforcers after their love affair was found out.[165] In an adjoining, explanatory article in *Die Zeit*, Hochhuth had spoken of "a terrible jurist" and such jurists' continuing presence in the Federal Republic, expressly mentioning Filbinger in Württemberg as an outstanding example.[166] Why single out Filbinger? It had just been revealed that, as a Kriegsmarine judge – and unrelated to any "race defilement" case – he had caused the execution of young sailor Walter Gröger merely days before the Third Reich's end. Gröger had been absent without leave but had returned to face proceedings. After research more such cases came to light, yet Filbinger liked to pass himself off as a resistance fighter. After that *Zeit* publication, Filbinger, earlier an opponent of Böll in the pro-Meinhof case, filed a civil suit in Stuttgart against both Hochhuth and *Zeit* publisher Bucerius, which was disallowed in May. Then Filbinger crowed that "whatever had then been right cannot be wrong today," and conspired in getting Peymann to resign. However, as it was henceforth legal to call Filbinger a "terrible jurist," he himself was impelled to resign in August.[167]

Hochhuth was aware of the continued presence of former Nazi attorneys and judges who had pronounced death sentences against unruly soldiers in the disintegrating Wehrmacht. He knew this to be one of the few remaining weak spots in post-Nazi West Germany. In the early 1970s, Hans-Joachim Rehse, a high Schleswig-Holstein administrator, had made headlines. This former judge of the notorious People's Court was put on trial in 1967, having been responsible for at least 231 death sentences against German civilians. After German courts found him guilty of abetting murder, he was ultimately acquitted on appeal and the legitimacy of those wartime sentences was upheld. A presiding higher judge later said, much like Filbinger, that Rehse had followed the laws of the time.[168] National outrage overflowed, an impressive sign of democratic awareness. One vocal protest was by Meinhof, who lamented that Nazi criminals were still at large as concentration-camp guards or justices.[169]

It is a fact that throughout the 1970s many such tainted jurists were living in the Federal Republic unmolested, practicing law or enjoying generous state pensions.[170] But so were other legal professionals, who were trying to use what influence they had to hinder democracy by obfuscating the truth about themselves and that of Nazi crimes. One of them was Dr. Alfred Seidl, who as lawyer for Professor Walther Wüst first went after my 1966 Heidelberg dissertation on the SS Ahnenerbe and subsequently the book I published on it in 1974, in order to have them both annulled or trashed.[171]

Seidl, born in 1911, had a stark Nazi past. In 1938 – when Wüst was dean of the philosophical faculty there – he obtained his doctorate in law at the University of Munich with a dissertation justifying harsher interpretations of criminal law. His supervisor was the criminologist Professor Edmund Mezger, who later published writings by jurist Hans Frank, the future butcher of Occupied Poland. Seidl defended Frank, before his execution, at the Nuremberg Trials. He also represented Hess and several SS generals, justifying the Third Reich exhaustively – for example, the attainment of Lebensraum through war in the East had been necessary because the German people needed it; conditions in the concentration camps had become unbearable only after Allied bombardments.[172]

His duties at Nuremberg completed in 1946, Seidl followed a far-right policy, determined to rehabilitate the Third Reich. He called for the immediate release of Hess from Spandau Prison, drawing closer to neo-Nazi publisher Gerhard Frey, who distributed the *Deutsche National Zeitung*, always on the edge of legality. Admired by Strauss, Seidl was appointed Bavarian minister of the interior in 1977. Now he rooted for the reintroduction of the death penalty and actively supported the Radikalenerlass. He had a hand in at least one case, of a Social Democrat rejected for a career in the civil service because she was deemed unfit.[173]

Walther Wüst and his attorney Seidl went after me after I had issued my Heidelberg dissertation on the SS Ahnenerbe in late 1966, because here I had accused Wüst of murder. As could be proved, he had delivered the Scholl siblings of the White Rose resistance group to the Gestapo as rector of the University of Munich in February 1943. And although SS Colonel Wolfram Sievers had already been hanged at Nuremberg as the Ahnenerbe's secretary-general, Wüst, also an SS colonel, had headed it when it caused human beings to be tortured and killed. It selected Soviet citizens for skull and skeleton collections and conducted terminal medical experiments on Jews and Soviet POWs. In the course of these activities innocent men, deemed, through Ahnenerbe research, to exist below the German master-race, died.[174] In 1974, after a total rewrite for publication, I had deleted the murder charges, but, all the same, Wüst did not want to see my book on the market.

During research, I had interviewed twenty or so former members of the Ahnenerbe, some of them still active in universities. I had started with Wüst, who was living in Munich waiting to be reinstated as professor of Indology, which he had taught there until 1945.[175] Although these former SS officers were wary of me, they wanted to talk, in order to find out how much I really knew. To escape blame they always sent me on to the next comrade, insinuating that he was responsible for whatever questionable activity I wanted to probe. I missed several important collaborators of Wüst, not only because some were now dead, but also because a few had changed their identity. One such person, whom I could have interviewed at the University of Erlangen, was Enzensberger's likely teacher, the German literature scholar Dr. Hans Schneider, now calling himself Hans Schwerte. Schneider had been part of Himmler's effort to utilize pro-Nazi Dutch cultural groups in the Occupied Netherlands in a campaign for a Greater Germany (within which the "Aryan" Dutch were to be coerced). If, after 1945, this was bad enough, the real reason Schneider was hiding was that he had played a part in the procurement of contraptions to separate human flesh from bones to be used for skeleton collections in Strassburg under August Hirt. He had also been asked to procure medical instruments to assist terminal experiments by Ahnenerbe physician Siegmund Rascher in Dachau. Although Schneider never did find Dutch machinery for Strassburg, the requested implements for Dachau were delivered – with or without his help. Therefore, Schneider had reason to fear questioning once the Allies got to him. And so he remained in Erlangen under the fictitious name of Schwerte, having remarried his wife for the records and faking a new relationship with his small daughter, and then moved to the Technical University of Aachen, where eventually he became its rector. He was found out in 1993 by Dutch journalists who checked his current vita against Ahnenerbe facts (and called me on the phone), whereupon he lost his pension and all civic honors he had collected since 1945.[176]

Seidl's quest to have all suspicion against Wüst quashed by suppressing my writings was beginning to falter in the late 1960s when State Attorney Fritz Bauer informed me that an investigation of the professor's role as curator of the Ahnenerbe was underway.[177] Evidently his team had come to the conclusion that Wüst had been more than just a titular head of Himmler's research organization, as he had always claimed, not least to me in our Munich conversations. When Wüst died in March 1993, legal proceedings had been initiated against him on charges of murder.

◆ ◆ ◆

In the 1970s increasing unemployment became a major problem in the Federal Republic for the first time. Non-German workers who had been hired when they had been needed for reconstruction since the 1950s were to become its first victims. Politicians on the political right appeared to be playing heartless roles in this. Dead set against the integration of foreigners already living in Germany, they devised methods of moving them out of the country, using unemployment as a pretext.[178] Filbinger of Baden-Württemberg thought up a complicated rotation scheme that would entice foreign workers financially to return to their homelands.[179] It was seriously considered in Bonn but ultimately rejected, thought to be too expensive and incapable of warding returnees off permanently. Besides, the SDP-led federal government was against separation and exclusion on principle, instead wishing, ultimately, to merge the foreigners with the German population. This had been done successfully with the Poles in the Ruhr Valley in the decades before World War I.[180]

Foreign workers had been needed in West Germany ever since Bonn concluded an agreement with Italy for an influx of Italians to work mainly in southwest German agriculture, in December 1955. The recuperation of the Federal Republic's economy was enormous in the late 1950s and 1960s; by 1960 its gross domestic product had been 296.8 billion DM, and it exceeded 400 billion by 1964.[181] The workforce was barely able to sustain this; in 1956 it had grown from 21.9 million in 1950 to 24.5 million, and it jumped to 26 million in 1957, but thereafter the increase was more gradual, as the numbers stayed just over the 26-million mark in the early 1960s, reaching 27 million only in 1963.[182] Whereas in the 1950s the workforce had steadily been enriched with refugees from the East, now in the Soviet orbit, they were reinforced by migrants from the GDR until the Berlin Wall went up in August 1961.[183] That cessation of a German influx from East Germany in part explains agreements by Bonn with other southern countries for their manpower: 1960 with Spain and Greece, 1961 with Turkey, 1963 with Morocco, 1964 with Portugal, and 1968 with Yugoslavia.[184]

A first mild recession in 1967 stopped seemingly unlimited economic growth and made West Germans face, as a problem scenario, the foreign workers who were already there. Then numbering close to 1.5 million, they were in danger of being laid off sooner than their native coworkers.[185] Increased rationalization in key sectors in which foreign workers had hitherto been employed compounded the problem – iron, steel and coal-mining, the automobile industry as in Hanover, Cologne, or Frankfurt.[186] More skilled workers were called for now, found more easily among native Germans rather than foreigners.[187] After the first energy crisis in 1973, when 2.6 million foreigners were living in West Germany, unemployment moved from 0.8 percent in that year to 6.8 percent in 1975.[188] Economic experts traced this to a vicious circle of ever-rising wages and higher inflation.[189] Because there was a second, weaker, energy crisis in 1979, foreigners, now numbering over 4 million, as well as Germans, were kept from full employment until 1980.[190] In November 1973 Bonn's politicians ended their work-immigration policy, and many understood that existing foreigners in Germany would want to stay indefinitely.[191] Now social and economic problems posed themselves – schooling for the young, establishing insurance and pension premiums.[192]

Several constituent factors were responsible for foreign workers being made to feel like an inferior species in the workplace and the, often adjacent, living quarters. One was the nature of the work itself. No matter how qualified foreign workers were originally, they were usually required to toil at a lower occupational level, not exceeding that of skilled laborers. Professional mobility on job sites in the first two decades or so was uncommon. Italian, Spanish, and particularly Turkish laborers were expected to tackle chores that Germans were loath to do, and they by and large accepted that as a work ethic for themselves.[193] Ethnic groups tended to be unjustly typecast as being especially suited for certain jobs, such as the Turks, who were credited with instinctual capabilities as pyrotechnicians – hence their supposed talents for perilous tasks involving explosives.[194]

As such, the work often occurred in hard-to-accept conditions, unsafe and perilous. At a factory in Cologne, for example, car-assembly conveyor belts in the early 1970s were running much too fast, and in a Ruhr Valley steel mill safety masks shielding against heavy metals were lacking.[195] To save costs, basic laws of hygiene were circumvented by the employers, even under supervision of the authorities, and insufficient time was allowed for washroom visits.[196] Canteen meals were low in calories, often bordering on the inedible. Communication on the job remained defective as long as Turks or Portuguese lacked opportunities to learn German well. Interpreters who were at hand usually took the employers' side; in any case, they were looked upon by the workers as cheats who by dint of their language superiority were only out to exploit the illiterate.[197]

In addition, foreign workers had reason to complain about inadequate accommodation. Well into the 1960s it was common for Italian laborers in rural areas to be quartered in stables emptied of cattle, pumps in the open serving washroom purposes.[198] Industrial workers slept in dormitories outfitted most primitively and overflowing with triple occupancy, separately for men and women. Visits by the opposite sex were strictly forbidden. Hostels, more removed from the worksites, were later not much better in appeal. When later still German landlords rented out apartments to workers' families, they were ill kept at high prices. Concentrated in great numbers in already run-down urban quarters, they usually resulted in ethnic ghettoes, such as in Berlin-Kreuzberg, where landlords became slumlords.[199]

Tension between foreign workers and their prospective hosts began even in their homelands, as discrepancies between reality and illusion were created. Workers were deceived into believing German promises that were designed to be broken. In Italy and other countries German authorities distributed a manual, which in Italian was called "Hallo Mario" ("Hallo Mustafa" in Turkish), painting paradisiac conditions for the new guest. He would be welcome in the Federal Republic, was expected to stay for the long term, and would "be known as an equal and esteemed colleague." It intimated that Germany had a tradition of democracy and self-determination even during the Third Reich, never mentioning the *Fremdarbeiter* (foreign workers), masses of whom Hitler had abused as forced labor. The Turkish version, for the benefit of the rural illiterates, published an illustration of a worker sleeping in a bed alone, in a single room, in contrast to the abysmal dwellings that awaited every newcomer.[200]

A first shock might have set in during medical examinations by German health-care workers, in Bari or Istanbul, as both men and women were examined together, standing in their underwear and having to bend down for rectal examinations. To the initiated (Italians and Yugoslavs come to mind), these were practices reminiscent of Auschwitz. As one Turkish woman recalled: "We were almost naked and went to the examination like this. They didn't have extra changing booths. We waited inside of a big room all in a queue."[201] The next horrors occurred during the days-long trip by train, before airplanes were used for transport. They were transferred in the cheapest wagons, with hardwood bench seats bereft of headrests and empty water containers; there were problems with heat, light, stopped-up toilets, and storage space. These trains were dirty and infested with fleas. After arrival at the Munich main station came unceremonious roundups in bleak collection sites and quick dispatches to Cologne or West Berlin, or anywhere in the, mostly South German, countryside.[202]

The new laborers from afar remained officially known as *Fremdarbeiter* until that term was gradually replaced with *Gastarbeiter* (guest workers) during the late 1960s.[203] But in the hosts' minds, the foreigners were often a contemptible minority deserving of manual labor and no rights, since Germany lacked a history of immigration and tolerance was not necessary.

The prevailing mood was that Turks or southern Europeans would oppress the German majority and therefore should have to leave once their economic usefulness expired. Frequently, Germans used pre-existing prejudices, many from the Third Reich, that foreign workers could not behave and were unclean, drawn to crime, and obsessed with sex.[204] The Italian worker as a sexually aggressive conqueror became one of the negative stereotypes of the 1960s (and he himself, therefore, a rival to German men); it was then complemented by the cliché of the Turk as a sexual predator hard-wired to take women by force.[205] Consequently, German families sought to resist integration, by reschooling their children or, if necessary, moving else-where.[206] Islam often turned out to be additionally divisive.[207]

German media, often lacking sympathy for migrant workers, might sensationalize abuses in weeklies such as *Der Stern*, but warnings to industry and government were disingenuous and ineffectual. The investigative journalist Günter Wallraff, born in 1942, however, tried to make a differ-ence. Messianic rather than Marxist and therefore opposed to the RAF, Wallraff proceeded to act more in the Christian tradition of suffering and sacrifice – in the ethos of Böll, whose Rhenish roots and fundamental Catholicism he shared. One of his grandmothers was a non-"Aryan," who had only just been able to hide her racial status from the Nazis. Even as a child, growing up near Cologne, Wallraff empathized with lowly manual laborers. As a journalist, he met Böll and the Expressionist painter Max Ernst, who had gone to France long before Hitler. During the 1960s, in Hamburg, he just missed Meinhof when working for *konkret*. With the proletariat in mind, he wrote a play about the dignity of man, performed, like Enzensberger's less convincing *Das Verhör von Habana* later, at the Ruhr-Festspiele in Recklinghausen. In November 1968 he received a prize for inside reports on questionable employee practices by industry, which he donated to charity.[208]

At the end of the 1960s, Wallraff began impersonating putative victims of society to publicize their ordeals. He posed as an alcoholic in a mental hospital, as a homeless person, and as a university student looking for a room. When a Frankfurt court accused him of unauthorized assumption of authority, his defense was that the public had a right to hear the truth, and that, as his transgressions were in the service of this, they were therefore excusable. He was acquitted. In May 1974, Wallraff was in Athens, chained to a lamppost in protest against the Greek military junta. He was incarcerated, tortured, and freed only in the fall. He then smuggled himself into Cologne's Gerling insurance concern, where he accused Hans Gerling of discrimination against employees. Once again he was tried, and he prevailed.[209]

In 1977 this intrepid sleuth attempted something adventurous that one newspaper later called "reinventing journalism."[210] For four months he got himself hired by *Bild-Zeitung* in Hanover under the name of Hans Esser, to expose its maleficent reportage practices. The resultant book revealed a series of journalistic abuses. Sent to a Hanoverian rubber company, he was to examine work accidents due to human failure and alcohol on the job. But foremen told him that instead of alcohol abuse there were notorious security lapses on the part of higher management, which were causing accidents. "In this department," explained a labor union delegate, "work mostly Turks, Greeks, Yugoslavs and Arabs, it is a virtual battlefield." "Fingers are cut off and arms are burned," said the union official, "half of them toil for eight-and-a-half hours without a break, and one in ten has suffered an accident. Sometimes, on the old machines, the presses come crashing down on their own." The *Bild* editor disliked Wallraff's honest report, since he could not entirely rewrite it. But a hybrid version published the next day still caused the factory directors much dismay.[211]

Thereafter, *Bild* pursued Wallraff more vigorously. He was spied upon, Springer attempted to have Wallraff's *Bild* revelations censored, and finally Springer sued. Yet the ultimate outcome of this, the so-called Lex Wallraff of 1981 cemented by the supreme court (which gave journalists the legal right to investigate undercover in Germany), allowed Wallraff to continue to expose, through publication, "serious wrongs" that were of interest to the public "to a high degree." Springer had to retreat.[212]

Years later, Wallraff landed a major coup with his investigation of the *Gastarbeiter*. Disguised as Ali Levent, a Turk, Wallraff infiltrated industrial sites for more than two years, after having undergone serious cosmetic changes especially to his head and hair. He blew the whistle on employment abuses in large conglomerates, singling out an industrial smelter and a fast-food chain. As part of this and thinking about Böll, he revealed hypocrisies among the Catholic clergy. As an Islamic Turk he was rejected for conversion by parish priests, one padre suspecting him to be a Communist and hailing what he thought was a military dictatorship in Turkey. The padre said: "There are peoples that are not ripe for parliamentarian democracy."[213]

Forthwith, and endangering his life, Wallraff endured unhygienic toilets (one primitive closet for every ten guest workers), unhealthy food, and perilous job assignments that German workers spurned. In a Ruhr machine room in the dead of winter workers could not warm themselves unless they placed their hands near heated metals, close to moving cogs.[214] At another time lethal gases escaping from heavy-industrial pipes caused loss of consciousness or death. Alerted German supervisors admitted that gas masks were available to German workers first, leaving most guest workers at risk. But "after all, the wind blows away the gas."[215]

At a social level, Wallraff detected a huge rift between German elite workers and the foreigners, with no attempts at integration on either side, intimidated Muslims always eating their lunch separately. The Turks especially were treated as subhumans, with humiliating allusions to Africa or animals. There were threatening references to the Jews and their annihilation during the Third Reich. After Alfred, a German, had announced that under Hitler things in Europe had still been fine, he affirmed that the Führer had made only one mistake: "He should have lived for another five years, so that none of them would be alive today, not one." Then Alfred continued with a joke: "'What's the difference between the Turks and the Jews?' [Said Ali in his droll Turk-German:] 'All people. No difference.' Alfred (triumphant): 'Oh yes! The Jews are done with it!'"[216]

It speaks for democracy that Wallraff's book could be published unhindered by Kiepenheuer & Witsch of Cologne, Böll's publisher, eventually selling over 2 million copies. In the late 1980s, Wallraff, whose health had suffered, was awarded six prizes; his "zeroing-in on obscured reality" was saluted.[217] Böll, who had said that Wallraff would be facing locked doors before long, was proven wrong when the journalist, as a Black waiter, persisted in looking for abuses in the restaurant sector.[218] Only one critic turned out to be unconvinced. Reich-Ranicki thought that the reality Wallraff sought to uncover was consistently prejudged as negative, hence his "reliably negative verdict."[219]

Meanwhile, what had been happening to the Jews? Had anti-Semitism disappeared from West Germany? And if it had, why did a German worker named Alfred feel called upon to excoriate Jews and demand, again, their

physical extinction? Research has determined that because of the predominance, in the media, of RAF terrorism, anti-Semitic acts were underreported
throughout the 1970s, although they continued to occur – cemetery dese-
crations, home bombings, the slandering of Jewish teachers in schools, and
the proliferation of anti-Jewish propaganda as expressed in worker Alfred's
twisted humor.[220] Compared with the 1950s, Jew-hatred in the FRG had in
fact decreased; however, it still persisted, with 20 percent of all citizens dead-
set against the Jews and only 30 percent tolerant, and about one half of the
populace harboring "vestiges of anti-Semitism."[221]

At the end of the 1970s there were fewer than 40,000 Jews in the FRG,
most concentrated in large cities such as West Berlin or Frankfurt. Of
these, under 10,000 were Israelis (many also with German citizenship), over
1,300 Iranian, and over 3,000 Soviet Jews. Relatively few were religiously
observant, even if in name they belonged to a Jewish congregation. Only
10 percent of the 1979 Jews were of German-Jewish descent, however: how
different demographically this was from January 1933, when 523,000 Jews
had lived in Germany![222]

Hence the 1970s lacked a core of *German* Jews, and the religion-bound
Central Council of Jews attracted only the older people in a Jewish population that was already much older than the national average. Younger Jews as
a rule stayed away from the Council; always sitting on their suitcases, they
were ready to move abroad. Jews seldom had social contacts with non-
Jewish Germans; those formerly persecuted were especially wary.[223]

Several factors, if not actually renewing full-fledged anti-Semitism in
West Germany, complicated the situation of Jews there. The murder of
Israeli athletes in Munich in September 1972 by Palestinians discomfited
far-sighted Jews such as Zadek. For after the entrenchment of Israel it had
become fashionable especially in leftist circles to rant against Zionism,
diatribes that often harmonized with the armchair empathy expressed
toward RAF terrorists, who were trained in Arab lands. Antipathy against
Israel, then, tended to spill over as a proxy phenomenon, affecting Jews in
Germany in the form of traditional anti-Semitism. In addition, a so-called
Hitler Wave began in the late 1970s (subject of Chapter 5), with renewed
interest by West Germans in Hitler and the Third Reich for the wrong
reasons. Erlangen historian and Wehrmacht veteran Hellmut Diwald's
book, *Geschichte der Deutschen* (*History of the Germans*), was first published in

1973, and then again in 1978–9, and was widely publicized. It glorified the course of German history, playing down National Socialism and, worse, Auschwitz.[224] And finally, although progress had been made, it was known that West Germany still had not rid itself completely of ex-Nazi personnel in major decision-making positions, as the case of Minister-President Filbinger in Stuttgart showed.[225] This added to the Jews' anxieties.

◆ ◆ ◆

The fortunes of the documenta art exhibition in Kassel did not improve after artists such as Bazon Brock and Wolf Vostell had left the mark of the 1968 student rebellion on the last staging in that very same year. A combination of adverse circumstances would also haunt the documenta 5 during its hundred summer days of 1972. Arnold Bode himself had to step down as general-secretary, to be replaced by the thirty-nine-year-old Swiss museum director Harald Szeemann, whose views were the opposite of Bode's – pro-Pop art and pro-Happening, Realismus, and mytholo-gizing. Brock was hired for the program committee, as was – a first for this event – a woman, to oversee "Play and Reality." Szeemann's avant-garde conception, next to novel photo art – portrait photographs over 2 meters high authored by Chuck Close – allowed for Trivial Realism and Consumer Realism to be featured in the exhibits, enabling items of pure kitsch such as garden gnomes or Mickey Mouse to make their appearance. As a satirical counterpoint, there was an overly didactic streak in that Brock again organ-ized a "visitors' school," obliging the digestion of up to 2,000 slides and lectures lasting for hours. A Marxist philosophy professor, Hans Heinz Holz, had a bookish, eighty-six-page disquisition, "Critical Theory of Aesthetic Drawing," printed in the visitors' catalog. And then there were the art works of mentally imbalanced patients, from the Waldau Museum of the Psychiatric Hospital in Berne, which reminded critics of the compari-sons the Nazis had forced at the 1937 exhibition of "degenerate art", likening such designs to choice examples of Expressionist painting.[226]

Documenta founder Bode himself underwrote Szeemann's program, thought to redress the negative impression of conventionalism that had, reportedly, harmed documenta 4 in 1968. Szeemann, a mercurial art historian with a doctorate in French Modernism from the Sorbonne, had headed the Berne Kunsthalle since 1961, where he had come to grief when, with an exhibition of 1968, he had over-emphasized the avant-garde. He had also, ethically questionably, experimented with the artistic output of the mentally ill taken from the Heidelberg collection of the pro-Nazi art historian and psychiatrist Hans Prinzhorn – the very source Goebbels's art minions had mined in 1937.

The iconoclast Szeemann had left stuffy Berne of his own accord. In 1972 at Kassel, it was Szeemann's renewed undoing that he reassembled most of the post-minimal and conceptual artists from his Berne show, but also added photorealism, hyperrealistic sculpture, and political propaganda, to fit in with "the era's countercultural protests and avant-garde impostures." There was an unfavorable press, with Habermas, the supreme expounder of Critical Theory, remarking that there was hardly anything he could make sense of.[227] In the end, Szeemann was accused of having caused a deficit in the vicinity of a million marks and was sued for this by Kassel's lord mayor.[228] Even though he was let off, in 1973 he was much poorer and was ruled out as a candidate to lead the next documenta in 1976.[229]

After wrangling over administrative personnel, documenta 6 started in 1977, one year late again as in previous years. Artists also canceled their shows: Georg Baselitz and Markus Lüpertz, both originally from the East, after guests from the GDR had been invited, the most prominent being Fritz Cremer, the sculptor who had memorialized Buchenwald concentration camp in accordance with Communist ideology, and Willi Sitte, the noted Socialist Realist painter. On opening day, June 24, 1977, Gerhard Richter withdrew his pictures, because there had been a picture-hanging mess-up to his disadvantage.[230]

The exhibition opened under Manfred Schneckenburger, a progressive Cologne gallery director, with Bode's conservative influence even further reduced. This happened after there had been additional misappropriations of money and the responsibility for future budgets had been questioned. The lead theme now was "Art in the Media," hackneyed and badly thought through, the main attraction being an exposition of 700 hand-drawings by 200 different artists. But painting was thought to be ill represented, even with prominent examples such as Francis Bacon's *Triptych*, showing crucifixion, or a new work by Lüpertz (who, like Baselitz, eventually did show up). Lüpertz had painted three canvases, each with the same motif – a figure reminding onlookers of a soldier, recognizable by military greatcoat,

Wehrmacht helmet, and spade, between huge menacing wheels. Stinging yellow grated next to blue-black hues on the greatcoat and the dark green of the helmet, emphasizing the martial aura.[231]

On the media side, often closely aligned with installations, was *Trans-Siberia Prospect*, the experiential simulation of a train ride from Moscow to Vladivostok by Jochen Gerz, in real space and time, having lasted eight days each way, undertaken with curtains drawn and without breaks; four chairs held sixteen tablets, and a tape recorder produced the sound of railway wheels rolling on the tracks. Anna Oppermann showed *Being an Artist*, a motley assemblage of "traces" – lime-blossom leaves and other randomly collected small things, arranged, registered, hand-drawn, photographed.[232] Although it was later said that "man as a motif of art" was missing from this exhibition, the show drew over 360,000 visitors all told, an undeniable record. The overall spectrum had been impressive – hand-drawings, photography, film and video, performances, and various installations; a cornucopia of art expressions as they dominated the market at that time.[233]

Baselitz, more than others who had been exhibited at documenta 5 in 1972, stood for the new expressions of Realism, emphasizing one's right to work as an Expressionist, protesting Nazism. He articulated his feelings not only by moving himself out of Germany as much as possible, but also by painting upside down the German Forest so beloved by hypernationalists as to be enshrined in the "Blood and Soil" images of the Nazis: *Der Wald auf dem Kopf* (*Forest on its Head*, 1969). He also delivered an upside-down eagle, yet another symbol of imperious Germandom (*Adler*, 1977).[234]

His friend Markus Lüpertz, born in 1941 in Nazi-annexed Czech lands, followed him in this, but his statements were more personal. Yet surprisingly, the individualism of Lüpertz, who had been in the French Foreign Legion as a teenager, was even wilder than Baselitz's. He had entitled his documenta 6 Wehrmacht greatcoat painting *Schwarz-Rot-Gold – dithyrambisch I* (1974). He meant to aim the dithyramb, alluding to Dionysian song, dance, and wine feasts, but by extension also to Nietzsche's philosophical canon, as a critical symbol against Nazi ideology, just as the whole of *Schwarz-Rot-Gold* was intended to be.[235]

The iconography of Jörg Immendorff, born in 1945 in Lüneburg, showed both East and West Germany (Erich Honecker and Helmut Schmidt together at a table) underneath the threatening symbol of the swastika (in the beak of an eagle), in altogether sixteen versions of his allegorical, hyper-realistic painting *Café Deutschland* of 1978. With that, this extreme left-leaning student of Beuys protested against pressures exerted by both East and West, warning of potential Nazi recurrences. As a radical Expressionist, Immendorff led a life more violent even than Baselitz's or Lüpertz's. Plagued by a terminal illness, he succumbed to cocaine and later, having become the proprietor of a bar in Hamburg's red-light district, even as a family man organized orgies with prostitutes.[236]

Sigmar Polke, born in 1941 in Silesia, had an apprenticeship with Beuys and the indulgence of drugs in common with Immendorff. Like him a radical Expressionist, he painted under the label of what he called Capitalist Realism, ironizing the Socialist Realism of the GDR – which his sometime collaborator Gerhard Richter also did later. Like Richter, Polke had studied with Karl Otto Götz, the master of Informel; as a multimedia artist he worked with drawings, paintings, collages, gouaches, photographs, video, and film. Moreover, he employed diverse techniques – brushes or spray paint, glues or cameras, crayons, fruit juices, and beeswax. In the 1960s, one of his influences had been Fluxus, and, sardonically, he borrowed from Francis Picabia's dadaistic art. The objects he figuratively reproduced were characterized by randomness, seemingly without inherent logic – tables, vases, buttons, a boy with a toothbrush, liverwurst, and potatoes: it was a caricature of modern art as modern art. On closer observation, this resembled New York Warhol's Pop art. But whereas Warhol idolized celebrities, Polke, by dwelling on ordinary consumption items, derided consumerism as brought on by the Economic Miracle, along with the comfortable bourgeois settings of its breeding grounds. And like his peers, Polke was mindful of the recent past, as he stenciled images of watchtowers and barbed-wire fences onto commercially printed fabric. He painted reverse swastikas and once uttered, in an Auschwitz twist: "Kunst macht frei."[237]

That important mentor Beuys continued in his dual role of artist and educator, turning into part philosopher and, almost, politician. Continuing from the student rebellion, he insisted that more art students should be admitted to the Düsseldorf academy even without formal qualifications – as long as they intended to attend his own classes! As a metaphysician, Beuys maintained that anybody could be an artist if so motivated, hence anyone who wished to study art should be able to. But in the eyes of academy rector

Eduard Trier and Düsseldorf culture minister Johannes Rau this would result in indefensible overflows. After the dissenting Beuys had occupied academy premises with fifty-four rejected students, Rau dismissed the untenured teacher on October 20, 1972. Rau's caustic remark that "I cannot and will not let myself be made into a possible art object" went on record. Protests signed by, among others, Böll, David Hockney, Baselitz, Walser, and Gerhard Richter remained fruitless. Allan Kaprow, the father of all performance artists, separately wrote to Rau: "Beuys is an artist of distinguished achievement, known and respected in every major art center of the world. He thus brings honor to both the Düsseldorf Academy and German art." Beuys himself sued, but it took until April 1978 for his dismissal to be declared illegal. Declining the offer of a permanent chair in Vienna, he remained a freewheeling artist known to be much in demand. In Düsseldorf, they allowed him to retain his professorial title and the use of his academy studio. In the end, Beuys had reason to consider himself as a champion of the kind of democracy he desired to prevail.[238]

As an educator with no official ties, Beuys called for the creation of a free-floating Freie Internationale Universität, initially anchored at his Düsseldorf studio but later establishing notional branches wherever he happened to create. Ideologically, it derived from the model of Soziale Plastik developed in the 1960s, but institutionally, it was bereft of structure. It sought to attract potential students disbarred at other institutions, but an academic curriculum was not discernible, nor was there research or teaching in praxis. This remained one of the many idealistic goals Beuys increasingly went about proselytizing for, with little, in the end, to show.[239]

Another ideological utopia was Beuys's allegedly novel conception of politics, with multiparty parliamentary democracy (on which, after all, good-government institutions so far had been built) to be replaced by political equality for all – in analogy to artistic equality and its entitlements. He believed that he belonged to "the avant-gardes that fight for freedom, democracy and socialism."[240] Such woolly thinking largely sprang from the esoteric Rudolf Steiner's weltanschauung, Steiner being an early-twentieth-century disciple of Nietzsche and self-professed clairvoyant, who embraced the occult. Thus, Beuys construed systems for "democracy from below" and an organization of nonvoters. Toward the end of the decade, he sympathized with the nascent Green Party, another welcome anti-establishment phenomenon in which he briefly tried to interest Dutschke while considering whether to enter the same Bundestag, even the European Parliament, he had earlier wished to negate.[241]

Any venue was right for Beuys if he had a public, and he always drove home a lesson. In November 1970 he took bones, leftovers from a fish dinner at home, to Daniel Spoerri's Eat-Art-Gallery in Düsseldorf and suspended them with string from the ceiling. After rubbing his face with ash, he wrote out certificates for the sale of fish bones. He then stood for hours in a corner of the gallery draped in a long coat, like a medicine man, and supported by a cane, with his felt hat on. It was supposed to be an appeal to live healthily by maintaining a sensible diet (eat fish!) and watching one's lifestyle, as in not smoking – urged by an artist who himself was a chain-smoker.[242]

In May 1974 a spectacular installation reflected the peak of Beuys's international renown. He flew from Europe via northern Labrador to New York and was taken, by an ambulance, to a room in SoHo, where he joined a coyote, Little John, next to a pile of straw. Armed with a long cane and a felt blanket, he engaged with the animal in a silent dialogue lasting for almost a week, sometimes poking it, sometimes lying down on the floor covered by the blanket and being sniffed at by the coyote. Little John took possession of the few things in the room, relieving himself on straw, the blanket, and a pile of *Wall Street Journal* papers. All the while, onlookers were allowed to file by. There was method in this showman's madness. Beuys wanted a discourse with the underdog – it had been the hare in Europe and now it was the coyote in America, an animal that, so he lectured, had wandered with what became America's native people across Labrador's ice caps thousands of years before. The underdog was also a scapegoat, the minority of American Indians being prone to prejudice and persecution, as had been the Jews in Europe. Beuys had isolated himself in the ambulance – on both ways to and from JFK Airport – to demonstrate his solidarity with the minority, be they Indians or Jews, and to invoke human sympathy.[243]

In 1977 at documenta 6, Beuys displayed *Honey Pump*, an installation featuring honey being forced through transparent pipes, through several rooms. The revolving honey served as symbolism for contradicting aesthetic viewpoints that should really be in unison.[244] In 1970 he produced another *Oven* installation reminiscent of the crematoria of Auschwitz-Birkenau.

Four years later he worked on *Show Your Wounds*, a fixture with biers and labeled blackboards that could have been tombstones – once more allusions to the dead as they were shoved around in Nazi concentration camps.[245] His creations *Felt Suits* and *Hearth* were further assays along those lines.[246]

Beuys's enduring interest in the Third Reich was parlayed into concern about political radicalism in the Federal Republic. Yet about his concern he appeared to be sending mixed messages. At the documenta 5 in summer 1972 – the RAF's core was arrested in June – Beuys planted himself on exhibition grounds holding two placards that read: "Dürer, I personally lead Baader + Meinhof through the documenta V J. Beuys." What did Beuys wish to convey here? Did he think that walking RAF members through the exhibition would be akin to a cleansing action? Would this restore Baader and Meinhof to the status of law-abiding citizens? Another possible reading was that Beuys was telling Albrecht Dürer that by taking the terrorists to see the exhibition, he was expressing his approval of their actions. But since it was known that Beuys condemned the terrorists, at documenta 5 he could have made that crystal clear by adding a half-sentence that had originally been on the script: "... then they will be resocialized!" Although Beuys himself had authored the full text in a, for the RAF, didactic manner, it had been transposed to the billboards without that last phrase – with Beuys either not caring or silently approving of a significant change of meaning.[247]

The ambivalence expressed here was emblematic of the artist's public statements as a persona resorting to a philosophy well intended but half-baked. Beuys was constantly mythologizing, not to say fabulating. He became the victim of his own early publicity successes that had uncritically encouraged him to utter, increasingly, a mixture of new extrasensory revelations (many based on Steiner), truisms, and commonplaces. Superficialities and half-finished touches toward the end of his career came to mark many artistic creations, conveying frequently incomprehensible meanings that detracted from his art's aesthetics, while, at another level, the showman overwhelmed the shaman, the entertainer the artist. These developments were beclouding Beuys's reputation at the time that he, after frequent bouts of ill-health, died of heart failure in January 1986.[248]

Gerhard Richter, although much impressed with Beuys as a student in Düsseldorf during the 1960s and supporting him throughout his travails, never wanted to be a shaman.[249] Born in 1932 in Dresden, he grew up in small-town Zittau. His mother Hildegard came from an upper-class family, while his father Horst was a lower-grade teacher whom Hildegard constantly humiliated. Gerhard was yet another reluctant Hitler Youth in 1942, when his father was in the war. In 1944 his mother's beloved brother Rudi Schönfelder fell in Normandy. Hildegard also had a younger sister, Marianne, diagnosed as a schizophrenic. After forced sterilization in 1938, she was consigned to the insane asylum of Grossschweidnitz nearby, where through "euthanasia" she was killed in February 1945.[250]

Richter later tried to make sense of crucial junctures in his personal history with paintings. He painted his uncle Rudi after a vacation photograph, in his full Wehrmacht regalia: Rudi is smiling proudly (*Onkel Rudi*).[251] The illustrious, flattering photograph done over in Richter's brushwork became a token of guilt, complicity in Nazi aggression and crime; the genial Rudi was, after all, dressed in a Nazi uniform. But not in an SS uniform, as at least one biographer of Richter has falsely maintained.[252] For it was Richter's aim, like Arendt's and Walser's, to demonstrate German Everyman's culpability for events between 1933 and 1945; hence his resolve in the 1960s to dedicate the painting to the Czech Lidice Memorial as part of its collection.[253] (At the village of Lidice in Bohemia on June 10, 1942, ordinary German policemen had liquidated 173 inhabitants in retaliation for the assassination of Himmler's deputy Heydrich in May; although policemen nominally came under Himmler via their commander, SS-Obergruppenführer Kurt Daluege, they were not SS.)[254] Richter's resounding message was that no matter how radiantly attractive one could be, exuding charm and kindliness, as Rudi Schönfelder had been in the photograph from which the portrait was fashioned, in the end one could not escape one's guilt. Germans should be reminded that most of them "had had a Nazi" in their family.[255]

By contrast, Richter painted his father, who returned from a POW camp in 1946, again from a photograph, as dowdy and unattractive, "a tragic clown figure," as *Der Spiegel* found. Did Gerhard think him guilty? The background story here was that even before Horst Richter was drafted, his wife had told her son that he was no good and probably not even Gerhard's biological father. Gerhard had never liked him, and as an adult continued to avoid him. After the war he learned for certain that Horst had not sired him, without ever being told the identity of his mother's lover. In 1946, Gerhard too saw Horst as a defeated person barely able to sustain himself.

"Most of our fathers," observed Richter later, "spent much time in the war and either never returned or returned as damaged persons, broken and guilty." Horst Richter also failed later in life.[256]

Gerhard Richter's narrative with his aunt Marianne Schönfelder at the center became more complex. In 1965, when he painted Rudi Schönfelder, he also painted Marianne as a fourteen-year-old girl, as she was holding him, Gerhard, in 1932, only three months old (*Tante Marianne*). Gerhard remembered later from the time he was a child that he was sometimes taunted not to be so silly, "like that foolish Marianne," already locked away. Did this disturb him? Later in the GDR, Richter married Emma Eufinger, the daughter of a Dresden gynecologist who as an SS officer had played an instrumental part in implementing "euthanasia" in Saxony. At that time, he does not seem to have known that there could have been a connection between Professor Heinrich Eufinger, Grossschweidnitz, and Marianne Schönfelder's death, but after 1961, when the Eufingers and Gerhard with his young wife had moved to the Federal Republic, things fell into place. There are no portraits of Dr. Eufinger, but in 1965 Richter painted, also from a photograph, psychiatrist Dr. Werner Heyde, one of the architects of Hitler's "euthanasia," who had been pursuing his career – under a false name like Hans Schneider/Schwerte in Erlangen and Aachen – in post-war Schleswig-Holstein, and committed suicide in 1964 while on trial for murder.[257] In the illuminating 2018 film by Florian Henckel von Donnersmarck, *Werk ohne Autor* (*Work without Author*; English release, *Never Look Away*), the impression is given that Richter married Emma knowing full well the former function of her father, who is shown to have killed Marianne personally, but Richter learned only after his wedding what role his father-in-law, who had helped him cross the German–German border, had played in the Nazi medical system.[258]

After 1945, Richter had attended a vocational school in Zittau and become interested in art only on the side. Attracted to Socialist Realist painting, he learned the ropes.[259] But when visiting documenta 2 in 1959, from the Kunstakademie in Dresden, he was introduced to Expressionist and abstract art, as practiced in the West by Pollock and Lucio Fontana, one working in random-aleatoric action-painting, the other in a monochrome fashion. Such approaches had been forbidden by the GDR's anti-Formalist regime since the late 1940s. Richter's fascination was mixed with the realization that artistic freedom was oppressed in the "totally smothering" state he lived in, later drawing parallels to the Nazis.[260] Having made the jump to Düsseldorf in March 1961, he enrolled at its academy. He was taught by Informel leader Götz and Happenings expert Beuys, and Happenings he practiced with Sigmar Polke.[261] He began painting banal objects and ordinary people on the basis of photographs, the contours of which he transposed onto canvas. While elementarily, verisimilitude between the photo original and the canvas copy was preserved, broad swishy brushstrokes derived from Informel produced the end-effect of blurred outlines. His works were monochromatic, more gray on gray.[262] The lack of clarity on canvas conveyed uncertainty; Vostell said, ironically, "to smudge, in order to see more clearly."[263] The exact likeness of a photograph was to be contrasted, caricatured, with paint on canvas, introducing doubts. Existential questions were thus posed: Was Rudi Schönfelder really a radiant young man, innocent in a military greatcoat, or did he know of war crimes, persecuted Jews? Was Marianne mentally ill at fourteen, holding him as a baby? Was her radiance not a contrast to brutality and death in an asylum?

Richter's seeming randomness in painterly makings-over of photographs was not the equivalence of happenstance but based on hundreds of carefully taken pictures. Their ordinariness suggested double meaning in the finished artwork, blurs introducing questions but no answers. For example, he showed the family of a pretty young wife next to an elderly paterfamilias, a small daughter and a son. Was the husband a Wehrmacht veteran or, worse, an SS murderer? What did he know that they did not? Had he cheated on his wife? How often would he beat her?[264]

The twin motifs of violence and death that Rudi and Marianne Schönfelder implied led Richter to themes of concentration-camp sufferers and nursing-student victims – of the 1966 Boston serial murderer Richard Speck.[265] Richter became interested in women as victims of a male-dominated society. In 1964 he painted, blurrily, a young and beautiful woman regally descending a flight of stairs, some starlet or model, but an obvious sex object in thrall to some inescapable male dominance – yet Richter left this unresolved.[266] And he painted thirty-two-year-old Helga Matura, again with a lovely face and perfect body, sitting with an adult-attired boy described as her fiancé – a ridiculous role for a possibly thirteen-year-old boy, but again in that spirit of indeterminateness. Matura had been a Düsseldorf call girl in the 1950s Rosemarie Nitribitt style, who was found stabbed to death in her apartment in January 1966; as in Nitribitt's case, her killer was never captured.[267] Richter's victim empathy is obvious, even though he publicly downplayed it. "My sole concern is the object," he once said, and he spoke of "unsentimental pity and morbid curiosity" at another time.[268]

It is likely, however, that Richter wished to uphold a much stronger moral standard than any glib interview remarks suggested. For why else would he invest so strongly in the cause of four Baader-Meinhof terrorists, mostly *after* they had killed themselves, even in 1988, more than ten years after the event? Based on photographs, he painted, in blurred fashion, the corpses of Meinhof and Ensslin, Baader and Raspe, after they had been found in their cells, and related motifs, such as arrest and burial. This constituted a fifteen-piece cycle he then called *October 18, 1977*. Although Richter himself believed the inmates had died by suicide, the blurring reinforced the possibility of murder.[269] Richter wished to remind viewers of his art that suicides of the Stammheim sort had to be questioned in an allegedly progressive society incapable of ruling out externally applied violence.[270]

By 2005, Richter had surpassed Warhol – an early idol from his Pop art phase with Polke – as one of the most highly paid painters in the world.[271] Ten years hence his younger colleague Anselm Kiefer would earn a similar distinction, surpassing Richter. Kiefer was born in 1945, sharing with Richter the antipathy against a father, an art teacher, thought a failure after the war.[272] He was an even closer pupil of Beuys's than Richter. The causes of university students also got Kiefer to thinking about German history, so that he created existentialist works of memory search, questioning identity, apportioning responsibility. During the 1970s, Kiefer complemented what Beuys and Richter had had to say about Germany's past, yet the country's terrorist present did not motivate him.

He began his artistic career in 1969 with a quest for meaning in all German history; he traveled to France, Austria, and Switzerland, and had himself photographed there, in the Wehrmacht uniform of his father in various settings with an outstretched right arm, offering the Hitler salute. He then saved this collection of images, glued into scrapbooks, along with other paraphernalia, calling it *Occupations*.[273] Much criticized for this as a crypto-Nazi, Kiefer, obviously inspired by Beuys, later said that he had had a former SS man as art teacher in school. He also said that "the 1920s, 1930s and 1940s were not being addressed in Germany" and that "at school we had two or three days for all these 30 years. It was not enough. I had no complete idea of what had happened. 'Occupations' was just a starting point."[274] About his impersonation of Hitler, he clarified, also mentioning the dictator's precursor Nero: "I do not identify with Nero or with Hitler, but I have to repeat, to a small extent, what they have done, to comprehend their insanity."[275]

As he developed, Kiefer applied various techniques in different styles, so that eventually his roots were in German Expressionism, Dadaism, Informel, and action art. He used oil paint or watercolors, and, to vary his textures, straw and sand, glass shards and lead.[276] He saw the beginnings of a complex German history at the interstice of Roman and Germanic civilizations and so became interested in Nero, with his baffling cruelties yet also culture, something he saw in would-be artist Hitler – or Hermann, who defeated the Romans in North Germany's Teutoburg Forest in AD 9. But as Baselitz had with his *Der Wald auf dem Kopf* in 1969, Kiefer critically attempted to demythologize the German forest as a symbol of national superiority. Richard J. Evans has explained that for Kiefer the forest was "a nationalist icon to be subverted." Kiefer's picture *Varus* of 1976 showed "a snowy blood-flecked path through a thick forest; above the path are written the names of German generals (Blücher, Schlieffen etc.), as well as nationalist philosophers such as Fichte and Schleiermacher: the path leads from the legendary battle of the Teutoburg Forest to the nationalism of the 19th century and the first half of the 20th."[277]

Kiefer's early works in the 1970s asked harsh questions and provided sharp comment. He painted a snow-covered field with a fringe of trees and a melancholy blue horizon (*Winterlandschaft*, or *Winter Landscape*, 1970). Superimposed upon it is a woman's severed head, the snow on the ground marked by her blood. "Evoking both destruction and rebirth, the painting conjures the devastation of Germany during World War II even as it traces the human form onto nature by juxtaposing the sky with the woman's head."[278] In 1973, Kiefer commenced painting large wooden interiors, suggesting Norse myths as well as the monumental architectural constructions of an Albert Speer, questioning late national excrescences as expressions of grandeur.[279] In 1980 he appeared at the German Pavilion of the Venice Biennale (along with Baselitz), where he introduced various wooden interiors and historical woodcuts conveying "Germanness," a depiction of Hermann's Teutoburg battle once again and *Deutschlands Geisteshelden* (*Germany's Spiritual Heroes*) of 1974 – dubious heroes: Richard Wagner, the anti-Semite; Stefan George, a sectarian of a narrow cultural nationalism; Richard Dehmel, sex-obsessed; Josef Weinheber, a Hitler-glorifying bard; and Martin Heidegger, the Führer's philosopher. He also became interested in major figures of Wagnerian opera: Gunther, Hagen, Siegfried, Brünnhilde, and Krimhild.[280]

In 2001, Kiefer stated unequivocally that "the Germans committed the immense crime of killing the Jews."[281] Already in 1980 he had reached the apotheosis of his Germano-critical œuvre. He created a work called *Dein goldenes Haar, Margarete* (*Your Golden Hair, Margarete*), as he had internalized part of a stanza from Paul Celan's famous, tragic, poem *Death Fugue*: "Your golden hair Margarete/Your ashen hair Shulamith." In the poem, Margarete is the lover of the SS officer who would shoot the young Jewish woman Shulamith, beautiful as is Margarete, into the pre-dug grave. The original Shulamith had been King Solomon's great beloved in the *Song of Songs*. On canvas, Kiefer painted golden sheaves of wheat against a bluish sky, which shows a dark streak, and his own black handwriting for the title. In all, Kiefer would paint more than thirty works with this theme over the course of his career.[282]

In November 1975 three journalists of the *FAZ* rejoiced over the success of the New German Film in London, New York, and Paris. Ahead of their West German critics, British, American, and French movie reviewers had acknowledged that the German film had awakened from its fifty-year-long "sleeping beauty's slumber." Volker Schlöndorff, Werner Herzog, Wim Wenders, and Rainer Werner Fassbinder had revealed traits of "dreamlike genius." They had attended the New York Film Festival, collected important prizes, and proved that in Europe, the New German Film currently ranked number one and could rightly be compared with the French *Nouvelle Vague* of twenty years earlier. For like much in the heyday of German film in the 1920s, the new young filmmakers were committed to reality, and with brutal honesty exposed ills in society and uncovered national angst. They produced suspenseful, interesting sequences in post-Expressionist cinematography, and with unsentimental courage they traced interhuman relations transcending national borders. Some reviewers, such as the British, had qualms about typically German images, such as "genius-obsessed and frightening" characters, having survived in a Federal Republic "not loved anywhere." And many films were depressing: "They are terribly melancholy, even monotonous, not to mention self-pitying."[283]

Significantly, Alexander Kluge was not highlighted by the journalists. He had been the virtual pioneer of the New German Film in the mid-1960s, especially with his picture *Abschied von gestern*, but his reputation fizzled out in the 1970s because of a few not so successful movies, in particular *Der Starke Ferdinand* (*Strongman Ferdinand*). Dismayed by this, but also because conditions for the new film were deteriorating progressively as the 1970s wore on, Kluge withdrew somewhat from that métier. Brilliant, he could afford to do so, with his doctorate in jurisprudence, tasks as a literary critic, and a professorship in sociology at Frankfurt.[284] Most of his younger colleagues were not so fortunate; they would be dead, like Fassbinder and Meins, or have faded from view by the mid-1980s. Some of the criticism directed at Kluge at the end of the 1960s also targeted the labors of his friends in the 1970s, contributing to their eventual demise.

In an otherwise dire situation for the movie industry during the 1970s, mitigating circumstances at first favored the New German Film makers. In 1971 the new Filmverlag der Autoren in Munich, behind which stood Wenders and Kluge, enabled the production of authorial films.[285] In 1974 coproductions between filmmakers' companies and television commenced, giving the former a head start. Thus came about Böll and Volker Schlöndorff's commercially successful movie *Die verlorene Ehre der Katharina Blum* of 1975, after the novel.[286] New publicity about the craft films abroad impressed culture mavens, notably under SPD-ruled governments, to the benefit of Schlöndorff and Fassbinder. Hamburg consented to continue funding NGF projects, as did Berlin and Bavaria, by 1979.[287]

But avant-garde German films that attracted disproportionately fewer viewers in an, absolutely speaking, declining movie landscape were ultimately doomed to fail. During the ongoing consolidation of television, from 1970 to 1979, the number of theatergoers fell from 160 million to 142 million, with a nadir of 115 million in 1976, when terrorist activities were moving to a climax and people started staying home. During this period, cinemas shrank from 3,446 to 3,196 in number, having to suffer a low point of 3,092 in 1976.[288] Flourishing commercial films needing no outside financial support were mostly soft porn, comedies, or detective stories, but they reached only segments of the population.[289] The New Filmers themselves became more ignored by the journal *Filmkritik*, once supportive, in 1974.[290] Their own Filmverlag foundered, until in 1977 a cautious Augstein helped with funds.[291] Progressive government surveillance and dependence on government funding, from television or state foundations, caused timidity in the choice of topics, with anything radically leftist thought precarious – anarchism, terrorism, angst.[292] Genre pictures likely to make it independently were a safer bet; hence Schlöndorff stuck to *Der junge Törless* and *Katharina Blum* – film scripts based on literature, as would be Grass's movie version of *Die Blechtrommel*. Fassbinder too in 1974 came out with a film version of Theodor Fontane's novel *Effi Briest*.[293] Nonetheless, over time the aging young filmmakers were becoming pessimistic. Herzog was keen to immigrate to Ireland in 1976, and Fassbinder, if not of New York, repeatedly spoke of the attraction of a street sweeper's job in Mexico.[294]

Herzog and Wenders, who did leave Germany toward the end of the 1970s for the United States, did not renounce their Germanness, however, moving to and fro. It has been said that these New German Film makers worked to rediscover the humanity Hitler had driven from German film artistry (Peter Buchka), and to avert potentially fatal sociopolitical constellations (Eric Rentschler). Herzog withdrew from any such tasks by walking out on the country.[295] Born in 1942 in Munich, he had a fatherless childhood and unhappy times in the city's film academy. His first film, *Lebenszeichen* of 1968, was an accusation of Nazi Germany, but what really counted for him were experiences in the United States. He worked there in a steel plant and studied at Duquesne University in Pittsburgh, acquiring a feel for American society and how a post-war German might fit in there. That he had doubts was shown by *Stroszek*, made in 1977. Here a down-and-out Berlin busker moves to rural Wisconsin with his sweetheart, a hooker, and with a mate, a conjurer, and fails as much in gainful employment as in relationships, let alone acculturating to American society. He ends his life with a rifle and a frozen turkey, stolen from a grocery store, hitching a ride on a ski lift at an American Native reservation, his girlfriend having returned to sex work and his companion arrested by police. The film stood for an altogether wretched warning against would-be-German immigration to the United States. Herzog's trademark in the 1970s and 1980s was adventure films mostly playing in exotic landscapes such as those of Peru – escape films, as it were, from German dilemmas.[296] With controversial actor Klaus Kinsky, Herzog established what has been called the "Herzogian archetype," an avatar of extremity – characters "whose compulsions take them beyond the limits of conventional, rational behavior toward a mania that can feel – by turns or all at once – destructive, ridiculous, and sublime."[297] The main actors in Herzog's films walk and walk, never to arrive. In 1979, Herzog, who once walked from Munich to Paris to visit iconic film writer Lotte Eisner, stated: "I am incapable of emigrating to Hollywood. I cannot leave behind my culture – my country, perhaps yes."[298] But in 1996, Herzog finally settled in Los Angeles, to make films such as *The Bad Lieutenant* with Nicolas Cage.

The 1945-born Wim Wenders made several films in Germany before trying to prove his mettle in a collaboration with Francis Ford Coppola in the United States. His trademark became road movies, originally based on the American classic *Easy Rider* of 1969, with Peter Fonda and Dennis Hopper.[299] He usually dealt with "homeless men," disengaged from reality and searching for new meaning in life – their alienation from women defines them.[300] His own understanding of what life should be had been influenced by his disappointment with society and politics in the world he grew up in, after, so he realized as a young boy early interested in movies, the Nazis had destroyed the traditional movie narrative. "We, the directors of the New Film," he said later, "experienced this loss most deeply, as it made us conscious of the lack, the absence of our own tradition, as persons without fathers."[301] In this he resembled Herzog and implicitly anticipated the analyses Buchka and Rentschler would make of the German film a few years hence. America became the country of his dreams even in his teens.[302] Then, while in his early twenties and having graduated from the Munich academy, he made short films, the earliest in 1966 with music by the Rolling Stones, his second in 1967 with an English title, *Same Player Shoots Again*. Other, American-themed, shorts followed.[303]

Two films of Wenders in the 1970s, equally indebted to Fritz Lang and Alfred Hitchcock, stand out. Based on the eponymous novel of Wenders's

Austrian friend Peter Handke, *Die Angst des Tormanns vor dem Elfmeter* (*The Goalie's Anxiety at the Penalty Kick*) was filmed in 1972.[304] Here the soccer goalie Josef Bloch, suddenly unemployed, travels aimlessly from Vienna, east to a hamlet in the Burgenland. En route, he has a one-night stand with a cinema employee but strangles her in the morning without reason. Thereupon this, obviously schizophrenic, figure believes he has found refuge in the village he has reached, but is eventually located by police. His insecure life will come to an end – in jail. It is the motion, the movement on the road, on a bus, on a bicycle, walking in the rain, that intrigues the viewer, as in a search for answers to all questions in the world, which never materialize.[305]

In *Im Lauf der Zeit* (*Kings of the Road*, 1976) Robert has left his wife and races with a Volkswagen Beetle toward the Elbe River, into which it plunges. The would-be suicide emerges through the sunroof and joins a truck driver who travels on the western side of the German–German border in order to repair – compulsively – broken movie projectors in small towns. Robert and truck driver Bruno proceed to move forward slowly and aimlessly and eventually reveal their identities to one another, both seemingly without prospects and better off alone rather than with women. Halfway through, Robert visits his father, a failing small-town newspaper editor, and scolds him for not ever having listened to him in their past lives. On a motorcycle, Bruno and Robert race from east to west, to visit the condemned house on the Rhine island Bruno grew up in, his father having fallen in World War II and his mother long dead. As the film finishes, a favorable ending for either of the two men, who now part ways, is not in sight.[306]

One genre of New Films that did not go very far in the 1970s was that of the new Heimatfilme, pursued by artists who used examples of past regional misrule to construct parallels with circumstances in the FRG. The underlying premise for such revisionism was quasi-Marxist, in that German society was viewed as divided into a small layer of exploiters at the top and masses of victims below. The fear of feudal overlordship, violence, misogyny, and rough sexuality characterize these movies. Narratives often played in preindustrial settings of the nineteenth century and mostly in the hinterland, when scores of impoverished country folk, for instance in Hesse, had to choose between starvation and emigration to America. Those movies' characters, often poachers, were always on the edge, destitute and stigmatized by criminality; they tortured and were tortured, they killed and were killed. These films were the antithesis of the classic Heimatfilme of the 1950s, which had cemented social divisions and praised patriarchy.[307] By contrast, in Reinhard Hauff's film *Mathias Kneissl* the lead character is a poacher in Bavaria who is convicted and hanged, but the director puts the blame on circumstances.[308]

The problem with these radical interpretations of socioeconomic dependencies was that as leftist critiques trying to "correct the falsifications of official German history," their depictions bore not even faint resemblance to conditions in 1970s West Germany. Hence Wolfram Schütte of the *Frankfurter Rundschau* rightly criticized that these films constituted an escapism from current reality in the Federal Republic, where the objectives of the terrorists – the total makeover of society – were failing at an alarming rate, to be fought for another day. Indeed, the images of exploitation, frustration, terror, and revenge conjured in those movies were projections of thoughts, some of them more wishful than would have been good for the nation, typically held by sympathizers of the RAF.[309]

A case in point was Schlöndorff, who after *Young Törless* produced, in 1971, *Der plötzliche Reichtum der armen Leute von Kombach* (*The Sudden Wealth of the Poor People of Kombach*). Empathy with the impoverished Kombach peasants, who conduct robbery from despair and eventually die violently, predestined Schlöndorff to collaborate with Böll during 1975 in the ballad about Katharina Blum, caught between RAF and police.[310] Thereafter, Schlöndorff, like Böll, was suspected of being an active sympathizer of the RAF, as Springer's *Welt* kept insisting. A court order prohibited him from issuing what that daily regarded as abusive statements against it. The paper's editors even demanded, and were juridically granted, that the SPD drop the filmmaker from his position as the party's official representative at the central film foundation. His exclusion from that body, which subsidized progressive directors, was forced in November 1977, at the dusk of German Autumn.[311]

Thus sensitized, Schlöndorff rejoined Böll in the making of a film codirected by Kluge, Fassbinder, and six others of the New Film group, entitled *Deutschland im Herbst* (*German Autumn*) and starting in the fall of 1977. It was produced by Filmverlag der Autoren, with Augstein behind it, questioning terrorism's putative victims, but its gaze was also on the terrorists.

The possibility of cloak-and-dagger Stammheim murders by the authorities was left open. Authentic footage showed the funeral of Schleyer, as he was eulogized by Federal President Walter Scheel, and the terrorists' interment, Ensslin's, Baader's, and Raspe's after, finally, agreement had been reached where they should lie. Böll and Schlöndorff's contribution to the film was a commentary on Ensslin's funeral. They made the Antigone of Sophocles's tragedy speak, wanting to bury her brother Polyneices, who on higher orders was to lie unburied. Many Germans at the time denied the terrorists a proper burial, and it had been Ensslin's sister Christiane (shown in the film) who with Stuttgart mayor Manfred Rommel's help had secured a final resting ground – at Stuttgart-Dornhalden, on the site of a former shooting range, not the first choice.[312]

Among the ambiguities the film eloquently addressed was that of suicide versus murder: newsreel footage of Field Marshal Erwin Rommel, Manfred Rommel's father, is shown, during his state funeral in October 1944, after that erstwhile fervent Nazi had joined the Resistance against Hitler late. In the film, a voice-over pronounces "murder by the state" – a reference to both Rommel and Schleyer, and also to the Stammheim captives.[313]

One of the criticisms of the film was that its segments were ill-fitted.[314] Indeed, Fassbinder's contribution at the beginning, well over thirty minutes long, made the film lopsided. Taking control in this fashion and, in this case, creating imbalances was not something that disturbed him. He knew that many were in awe of him, actors, cutters, and cinematographers who stood by him as a team, even if they would have much to suffer.[315]

Fassbinder was born in Munich in 1945, like so many of his contemporaries into a dysfunctional family owing to the war. His father, a military physician, after return from the front left his wife and moved to Cologne when Rainer Werner was six. The boy's early upbringing in a "semi-chaotic household" in Munich was unusual, with his father treating prostitutes and pimps, to whom the boy developed an affinity. His family was steeped in poverty, the mother frequently in sanatoriums with tuberculosis. When the child discovered movies he developed the habit of talking to the characters on the screen, blurring the lines of division between real people and film stars. As his mother became more of a comrade to him, her new husband, Wolff Eder, was regarded with hostility. When he was fourteen, Rainer Werner declared his homosexuality.[316]

After two fruitless years at Munich's film academy, Fassbinder failed the entrance examination for the Berlin school. In 1967, at the left-wing, underground Action-Theater on Munich's Müllerstrasse, he met Peer Raben, later with Peter Zadek, who had just graduated in film-music composition as well as directing and had produced *Antigone* by Sophocles. There was a posse of unsettled young artists there, one being Horst Söhnlein, frequently visited by his friend Andreas Baader, who loitered in the back. In the spring of 1968, Söhnlein and Baader departed for Frankfurt to team up with Gudrun Ensslin and Thorwald Proll, for the department-store-torching spree. Thereafter Fassbinder himself took over a new, subversive, Schwabing stage, naming it Antitheater; most of the old crew went with him.[317]

The youthful acting buff now started on his professional trajectory. Physically unattractive, Fassbinder, whom Zadek later called "an uncomfortable type, unreliable in every way, save for his art," and of whom Augstein said that he was not a person one should have to like, had charisma in spades.[318] He came to be addicted to drugs and alcohol, had sexual relationships with both men and women, tyrannized his troupe, and was financially often bankrupt. But on June 10, 1982, when he killed himself in his Munich apartment with a mixture of cocaine and medicaments, he had collaborated on stage productions in Bochum, Berlin, Frankfurt, Hamburg, Bremen, and Munich, had written several plays, and had produced no fewer than forty-three films and television dramas.[319] A few months before his death at the age of thirty-seven, the *New York Times* critic Vincent Canby compared him to legendary French filmmaker Jean-Luc Godard, calling him "the most dazzling, talented, provocative, original, puzzling, prolific and exhilarating film maker of his generation."[320]

Fassbinder's films evinced concern for the destitute, mostly at the beginning of his career, leading to an understanding of left-wing extremism and finally a condemnation of phenomena connected with Nazism and its aftermath. Fassbinder's course was therefore similar to Gerhard Richter's, who, after depicting the everyday defeats of ordinary people, problematized RAF and Nazism, although his messages were more oblique.

In Fassbinder's first feature-length film, *Liebe ist kälter als der Tod* (*Love is Colder than Death*), of 1969, a small-time gangster couple desirous of a bourgeois existence cannot escape their criminal lifestyle. In the end they escape into an uncertain future, with Fassbinder's sympathy on their side, rather than that of a treacherous gangster, murder victims, or the police.[321] His second feature, *Katzelmacher*, of 1969, brought him to public attention and made him famous early. "Katzelmacher," literally "the maker of cats," was Bavarian slang for *Gastarbeiter*, that despised lot within society, and in this black-and-white picture Fassbinder played Jorgos the Greek, subjected to ill treatment by a band of idle adolescents outside Munich. They compete for sex with their girls and develop male penis envy, as they suspect the foreigner to have the potential to steal their women. This in fact happens when Marie, played by Hanna Schygulla, leaves her boyfriend for the married stranger, who musters enough German to stammer words of love. Some of the young men have odd jobs, one of them as a rent boy, and the girl Rosy sleeps with everyone for money. Playing the Greek victim of German prejudice, the homosexual Fassbinder sides with *Gastarbeiter* as member of a despised minority himself. As in a subplot, however, he is commiserating with all these adolescents who are seen as casualties of a society where the Economic Miracle has irremovably established materialistic standards of social recognition by the turn of the 1960s.[322]

In 1971, Fassbinder filmed the pitiful life of a fruit vendor, a failed policeman who, having returned from the French Foreign Legion in the 1950s, cannot recover his moorings in an ever more affluent society. In *Der Händler der vier Jahrezeiten* (*The Merchant of Four Seasons*) Hans Epp peddles his wares aimlessly from a cart and, even after a heart attack, is henpecked at home, with his wife cheating on him. Later an old Legion comrade appears who gives him little solace. Epp takes to drink and eventually dies of over-indulgence. "Fassbinder goes about his characters carefully and tenderly," wrote *Süddeutsche Zeitung*, "he despises no one, exposes no one. The film is full of sadness but lacks self-pity, staged and acted not as a tragedy, but a virtuoso tragicomedy."[323] Tragicomedy? Yes, because there are ironic undertones and some scenes are explicitly funny, mocking reality. Nevertheless, Urs Jenny called it a "perfect melodrama."[324] Fassbinder returned to the guest-worker theme in 1973 with his film *Angst essen Seele auf* (*Ali: Fear Eats the Soul*), which documented the unlikely marriage between a dark-skinned Moroccan and an elderly Munich charwoman, showing the social marginalization not only of the foreign laborers, but also of German females of any age who entered into unions with prejudged pariahs. It became a sensation of the 1974 film festival.[325]

Fassbinder made his first film about terrorism in West Germany in 1975, after Holger Meins, whom Fassbinder had known, had died of self-starvation in November of the preceding year. How any of the key events of 1975 impacted his work at the time is not known; he may in fact have not been able to react to all of them. The Holger Meins Command broke into the German embassy in Stockholm in April of that year, with four people being killed, and in May, Meinhof, Baader, Ensslin, and Raspe were moved to the maximum-security tracts in Stammheim. Other episodes had yet to occur.

Nonetheless, Fassbinder knew where he stood on principle. He was aware that the authorities figured him to be a member of the left-radical scene ever since they knew that both Baader and Söhnlein had frequented the Action-Theater; his telephone was always tapped.[326] But no matter how much he understood them, he had lost contact with Söhnlein and Baader.[327] In 1974, a year before Fassbinder made his film *Mutter Küsters' Fahrt zum Himmel* (*Mother Kusters Goes to Heaven*), trying to comprehend left-wing terrorism, he stated that the RAF was using "crazy methods." In that film he depicted it as confused, expecting revolution overnight and failing. Although sympathetic, he could give them no advice: "I don't know what else they could have done."[328] Fassbinder introduces Mother Emma Küsters, who has just lost her husband, a factory worker. He had first shot his boss and then himself. Isolated by her grown children and seeking rehabilitation for her deceased partner, she is befriended by an elegant couple who, unbeknownst to her, wish to use her for their own DKP purposes. She meets submachine-gun-toting revolutionaries who involve her in a terrorist holdup to free hostages, and is killed by police.[329] In Berlin leftist moviegoers attacked Fassbinder, and *Der Spiegel* was not impressed because there were too many clichés, quoting him as saying: "All left-wingers are stupid."[330] Yet despite the film's stiff and artificial actions and characters more cut from cardboard than flesh and blood, its message was poignant: poverty oppressed the little people, well-off left-wing intellectuals were abusing ideologies for their own gain, and would-be revolutionaries, even if inspired, lacked true wherewithal for change.

Fassbinder began the work on his portion of *Deutschland im Herbst* a few weeks after the key events in October 1977. In the first part of this unsettling footage, Fassbinder exults in mawkish self-representation, repulsively intimate to the point of pornography, with in-the-bed scenes with his real-time lover, cameraman Armin Meier, and sequences of himself in the nude. He snorts cocaine, swills alcohol, gesticulates on the telephone, and vomits. One is confronted with the portrait of an obviously narcissist personality, a case for medical attention. But Fassbinder's consternation about the October events comes through powerfully, as he may have doubted the Stammheim suicides at this time.[331]

Then follows a tortuous conversation between Fassbinder and his mother, probably scripted beforehand. Still, contrary beliefs by Frau Eder and her son are credibly transmitted: Rainer sees the governing class winning the current crisis and sides with the terrorists whom he declares legitimate and having been wronged. They need spokespersons for their cause. His mother, disagreeing, cites incidents from when she was younger in the Third Reich and it was too dangerous to speak one's mind. As criminals, the terrorists should have been shot, certainly at Mogadishu. In a final discussion about governments, Frau Eder pronounces her ideal, "an authoritarian ruler who is quite nice and kindly and proper." This is unacceptable to Fassbinder, who wants a more radical form of workable, uncorrupted democracy.[332]

Fassbinder's third film in this genre was entitled *Die Dritte Generation* (*The Third Generation*, 1978–9). In this bitter, angry farce he ridiculed a terrorist group depicted, much as in *Mutter Küsters' Fahrt*, as clueless, except for their hunger for power. Fassbinder aimed to show the ideological vacuity of follow-up units after the demise of the original RAF – the June 2nd-movement and its empty-headed hangers-on. In this confusing scenario a greedy computer industrialist supports terrorists in order to further his business – a business they actually aim to destroy. In admirable attention to detail, Fassbinder shows a blonde young woman resembling Ensslin wearing her characteristic red leather jacket; she is in thrall to a fatuous lothario of the Baader type. In the end the industrialist becomes immured, his fate uncertain, with that of the terrorists not much brighter. Even though Fassbinder managed to parody big business, anodyne guerrilla fighters, *and* corrupt law enforcers, the convolution of storylines in this film, with the constant empty chatter by terrorists laid over nonstop media broadcasts, was too much for most viewers. West German critics rejected the movie, and in Hamburg rowdies almost destroyed the film reel. But it had defenders, such as Wolf Donner: "As shrill and provocative as this film may be, it is a work of grief. Behind the sneers and laughter, one senses Fassbinder's helplessness, his powerless rage, his desperation."[333]

Fassbinder believed, as did student rebels in line with the RAF, that the ills to be corrected in the FRG were the ultimate result of wrongdoing in the Third Reich. After 1945 there had not been sufficient atonement, and traces of Nazism obstructed democracy. It had been handed to the Germans gratuitously rather than having been "fought" for. Wolff Eder, Rainer's otherwise unloved stepfather, had had some influence on his thinking, other than Gymnasium history class, which had taught him nothing. Early on he had set himself the task of writing a script, "Just a Slice of Bread," about a filmmaker concerned with Auschwitz. Yet while this won a third prize in a local contest, it did not open the doors of the Berlin film academy for him.[334] Still, over time, his associates concurred. His wife for two years Ingrid Caven said that "the entire German culture did not prevent the catastrophe that produced murderers." Hanna Schygulla remembered that "we believed in utopias where everything can be different. We grew up on the grounds of Nazi Germany, and we wanted to do everything different. Those were the impulses for us to go into the streets and defend ourselves, to uncover everything, to open things up. Or perhaps, as Rainer has been saying, to show where the stink is."[335]

The "stink" was in situations of the Third Reich where, as Fassbinder set out to illustrate, it was used for fame and fortune while doing untold harm. In 1980, Fassbender produced *Lili Marleen*, the story of popular singer Lale Andersen who had made the Marleen song iconic among Wehrmacht (and, ironically, Allied) troops.[336] Schygulla played the German Lieselotte Bunterberg, known as nightclub singer Willie, as she falls in love with Jewish composer Robert Mendelssohn from Switzerland (based on the real-life figure of Rolf Liebermann who had conducted a long-lasting affair with Andersen). Rather than remaining with him, she decides to pursue a career in Nazi Germany. She gains stardom but compromises her integrity through friendship with an SS general and entertaining Nazis, even accepting gifts from the Führer. In the end she acquits herself by assisting her Jewish acquaintances in Switzerland, who are influential Zionists, but loses the love of Mendelssohn, now happily married in Zurich.[337]

In 1978, in *Die Ehe der Maria Braun*, Fassbinder had already demonstrated how post-war West Germans, unprincipled, carried on in the aftermath of totalitarianism.[338] In *Lola* of 1981, he continued this theme. A small-town construction-business owner who also runs a brothel is shown; the brothel's chansonette who doubles as the lead prostitute ends up marrying an aristocratic building inspector. But she grants her former boss the right of the first night. Fassbinder demonstrated how the old value system had been disturbed, men of honorable reputation had become corrupt and corrupt men even more corrupt. The Third Reich experience had deconstructed all morals and wrought further deconstruction.[339] And in a film still in 1981, Fassbinder portrayed Veronika Voss, a faded film star from the Nazi era, who runs afoul of morphine and dies.[340] When the filmmaker died a few months later, cocaine had replaced morphine as the drug of choice. But in contrast to that film star, Fassbinder had been at the pinnacle of his success.

◆ ◆ ◆

As a by-product of existing culture, the German feminist movement developed in the 1970s, in turn to react to this culture into the 1980s and beyond. Two women, the filmmaker Helke Sander and the journalist Alice Schwarzer, spurred the growth of modern feminism in West Germany in the late 1960s and early 1970s. Inspired by the student movement, Sander traveled from Berlin to Frankfurt in September 1968, in order to challenge an SDS convention over the cause of daycare for the toddlers both of single and married working women, who saw the need to work for wages in order to support themselves. Schwarzer, in conjunction with the editors of *Der Stern*, in June 1971 publicized the necessity of legal abortions, coopting prominent women, among them the film stars Romy Schneider and Senta Berger and the journalist Carola Stern, to declare publicly that they had undergone abortions. This meant they had violated paragraph 218 of the criminal code that had been in force since 1872 and needed repeal.[341]

Although Sander and Schwarzer did not start from zero, the progress of women's emancipation had been sluggish since the female-repressive regime of the Nazis. During the first post-war years, there was a temporary increase of power by women in society in the relative absence of men. Seemingly consequentially, article 3 of the Basic Law in 1949 pronounced men and women equal. However, the article remained theoretical and for years was not acted upon. In the Adenauer era, the two Christian Churches aligned with other conservative forces made certain that the nuclear-family model held sway, which favored the male as the breadwinner. As before under imperial, republican, and Third Reich regimes, the woman's main task was to look after the household and help bring up the children, over whom the father held exclusive jurisdiction. Since 1949 wives could organize themselves in women's circles or join peace movements, but their political representation was minuscule and mostly at a local level. Although women comprised at least half of the population by 1950, their proportion in the Bundestag was merely 9.2 percent in 1957, and even lower, at 5.8 percent, in 1972. Elly Heuss-Knapp, the wife of the federal president, was visible as the head of a convalescing-mothers' organization, but only one female minister served in the cabinet by 1961, the CDU's Elisabeth Schwarzhaupt, again in a caregiver position – for health.[342]

Certain emancipatory changes for women came in the wake of a larger female workforce, as an expanding economy with the aim of total reconstruction offered them more opportunities of employment. Although the conservative dictum had been that mothers should stay home with the children, by 1971 one-third of all married women with children under the age of fifteen were gainfully employed. Such opportunities increased when in the 1960s part-time work slots for women were expanded.[343] Increased well-being and wealth for West German families by the 1960s translated into greater social mobility, and this meant that more children were able to attend university, and that more of those children were female. In 1969 the percentage of female first-year university students had reached 25 again – not quite the level of 27.7 at the end of the Weimar Republic in 1932–3, but it was trending up.[344]

Helke Sander, born in 1937, had returned from Helsinki to her home town, Berlin, to commence her studies, taking her son, after divorce from her Finnish husband, with her.[345] In student circles, and especially Dutschke's SDS, she was disappointed to find that the wives and girlfriends of the males, who were setting the tone socially and politically, were relegated to secondary roles, so that they had no say in discussions about possible changes in the universities and society at large. Their tasks were to listen and applaud. Besides that, they were expected to serve as sex objects in a regimen favoring male promiscuity, for the sexual liberation that the student leaders had prescribed was chiefly to serve the men.[346] Towards the end of 1967, Sander wondered what could be done about the problem of young women and their children, for she had realized that the men were using the children as an excuse to keep women occupied and away from men's business. So she seized upon men's ultimate pre-eminence in education. She thought that if men's overall influence on education were curbed and daytime nurseries could be run exclusively by women for women, the old rules of patriarchy usually applied through home indoctrination could be neutralized. This would affect even the situation of SDS couples. But when Sander broached the question of nurseries at a private Berlin SDS get-together one evening, her male host glibly referred her to his girlfriend in the kitchen. After Sander had talked to this young woman, her quest for emancipated daycare, in order to free women, began in earnest. Like-minded friends were found, circles were formed, and the first ten emancipated nurseries, Kinderläden (literally "children's shops"), were founded in Berlin in early 1968, without men playing any part.[347]

Helke Sander's historic trip to the SDS meeting in Frankfurt occurred a few months later, in September. Here she extemporized on the theme of the Kinderläden. Women with children are particularly underprivileged, she said. Those children would consistently remind their mothers of society's failures. On the other hand, male-dominated principles of competitiveness were unacceptable, and therefore conventional schools supervised by men were unsuited for the children's further education. Those schools would have to be challenged until they were prevented from teaching children "what a capitalist society allows them to learn."[348]

In her subsequent attempts to shake off masculinist restraints, Sander founded women's groups with like-minded female SDS members and eventually connected with similar groupings already in existence. The journalist Ulrike Meinhof in Hamburg, with twin daughters and weary of her husband, linked up. With reference to Sander's Frankfurt address she wrote, in the December 1968 issue of *konkret*, that the conflict between men and women in an SDS group, in an SDS family, in any West German family, rather than being symbolic, was real, and that it was salutary that women finally had begun to analyze it, to analyze the "burden" that they carried.[349] And even though within the SDS men continued to govern and over time took control of the Kinderläden, women's groups moved forward nonetheless with their original idea of eluding male dominance and shaping their own world.[350]

Back in Berlin, having been rebuked in Frankfurt, Sander founded the Aktionsrat zur Befreiung der Frau (Action Council for the Liberation of Women), with a dedicated socialist-feminist program. Three years later, in 1971, she established another Berlin group to campaign against paragraph 218 and made a critical film, *Macht die Pille frei?* (*Does the Pill Liberate Women?*). In 1973, she and her friend Claudia von Alemann founded an autonomous women's film festival in Berlin, as well as *Frauen und Film*, the first feminist film journal in Europe. She graduated from the Berlin film academy in 1969 and then produced her own first picture – late because, as a woman, she was passed over by the New Film funding boards. But in 1977 *ReduPers* featured Edda, an unmarried photographer with a child facing the vagaries of survival, professionally and privately, in West Berlin.[351]

Meanwhile, the journalist Alice Schwarzer, born of a single mother in 1942 and with vocational-school training in Wuppertal, had set her mind to abolishing paragraph 218. She started her activities in Paris in 1970, where she had become integrated with the French women's liberation movement, which was (like the American one) much ahead of the Germans'. Here she had met Simone de Beauvoir, who had some time before published the path-breaking emancipatory book *The Second Sex* (1949), and her partner Jean-Paul Sartre.[352] Schwarzer moved with her fresh ideas to Germany to coopt prominent women for the *Stern* action and collect many thousands of signatures from other women against paragraph 218. She connected with the then existing women's groups, particularly in larger cities such as Munich, and the *Stern* declaration was published on June 6, 1971. In the end she had gathered 86,100 signatures, one of those being Sander's, whom she met in Frankfurt in July. The signatories' demand to abolish paragraph 218 from then on was discussed widely in West Germany, liberal defenders of the motion fighting it out with conservative opponents in the media, and some state attorneys laying charges. However, Schwarzer had clearly advanced the cause of progress, for in the important national Infratest poll held later in 1971, 54 percent of West German citizens were for legalizing abortion, and only 35 percent against it. In other tests pro-abortion women scored even higher.[353]

Because Schwarzer understood that she needed help from the medical community, she mobilized scores of women to lobby especially young medical professionals to assist her in her quest. After almost three years 329 of them, mostly physicians, who were up against a bulwark of conservatives in their profession, agreed to publish an appeal, which was printed in *Der Spiegel* in March 1974. It culminated in the statement for each individual signatory that "I have performed or have assisted women to have abortions without financial gain and I shall continue to do so." The doctors demanded the introduction of an abortion limit, defining the period within which abortions could safely be undertaken, the application of safe abortion methods (as was already the custom in Britain, France, and the United States), and more propaganda for birth-control usage, as the contraceptive pill had already been in use in West Germany since 1961.[354]

Such concerted efforts resulted in a modification of paragraph 218, when the social-liberal Bundestag allowed for abortions under controlled medical conditions, on April 26, 1974. After the CDU/CSU Bundesrat, led by Minister-President Filbinger, had intervened, however, the supreme court in February 1975 ruled this illegal. Yet states were allowed to go ahead with abortions in emergencies in 1976, under individual application of eugenic, ethical, or social criteria.[355] Therefore, ultimately, a woman who had long believed that "my belly belongs to me," could claim Schwarzer's original initiative as a qualified success, if not complete reform.[356]

Encouraged, Schwarzer founded *Emma*, a weekly journal for women made by women, in 1976. Eventually, with her goal of emancipating German women from the control of men, she became identified with this medium. Three others joined her in the editorial offices in Cologne, among them Gudrun Ensslin's older sister Christiane. *Emma* was not alone. There already existed *Courage*, for a left-wing readership and later came *Die Botin*, for professed lesbians. Schwarzer herself converted from initial exclusively heterosexual relationships to homosexuality.[357]

Because of her strong-willed nature, Schwarzer soon encountered opposition from editorial colleagues and in the women's groups, especially of Cologne and Berlin, which she thought she had a right to dominate. A female secretary was dismissed without due process, and Ensslin and two friends left embittered. Authors complained about distorted copy, and Schwarzer's initial promises to invest financially in women's causes were not kept. She was accused of high-handedness and her interpretation of feminism was challenged. Despite this, she kept insisting on her view of womanhood (which disregarded Marxism, for example); she could brook no divergent conceptions. She became used to fame and notoriety – an author of bestselling nonfiction in many public appearances, seemingly pre-ordained as the personification of the German women's movement. By the end of the 1970s this movement had grown exponentially, and she appeared to have as many enemies as fans. But in the 1980s it became splintered and she herself virtually powerless. In May 1979, the journalist Hannelore Schlaffer was deploring "feminist country communes and sects." And still, Schwarzer's long-term achievements were undeniable, such as the 1976 Bonn legislation establishing equal rights for both genders, now granting joint custody over children to both parents.[358]

In the late 1960s, after Paris, Alice Schwarzer volunteered with a Düsseldorf newspaper.[359] This impressed her negatively, for in such establishments chauvinism was rife.[360] Men took advantage of subordinate, younger female colleagues, their female secretaries, and subordinate staff. In journalism, such encroachments occurred through exploitation of differences in age, education, and lower standing in the hierarchy.[361] Editors as predators were always on the lookout for younger women. Hellmuth Karasek, at the arts-and-letters desk of *Der Spiegel* 1974–94, described this in a roman à clef, *Das Magazin*, mentioning the boss, Herr Kahn, as the main perpetrator. As Karasek keeps comparing Kahn to other historic figures of the publishing industry such as Bucerius, Nannen, and Augstein, it becomes clear that he based his episodes on his own experiences at *Der Spiegel*. "Power," writes Karasek unsurprisingly, "strongly exudes eroticism." He observes that "in his best years, Kahn slept with virtually all of his women editors."[362] At the *Stern* editorial offices, the handsome Henri Nannen is said to have had intimate relationships with everybody he chose to; frequently, two of his office paramours accompanied him everywhere he went.[363]

An eroticized, sexualized office culture also prevailed in publishing houses. In the enlightened left-liberal camp, Siegfried Unseld, boss at Suhrkamp in Frankfurt, was fond of sharing details of his vibrant extramarital love life with his drinking companion Martin Walser, who, like him, cherished erotica, chess, and skiing. Walser made salacious entries in his diary, now published: in June 1976, he writes, Unseld told him he was making out with a student of German literature who previously had been the girlfriend of his son Joachim. According to an entry half a year later, Unseld bragged to Walser that the two twenty-one-year-old women he was currently sleeping with even liked his pot belly, a rare situation for a man already past middle age.[364]

It is therefore not surprising to find very few women of influence in journalism and book-publishing during the 1970s, a situation that reached back to Allied-control times.[365] When Helene Rahms, a midlevel editor at *FAZ*, created a "women's page," she was regarded with suspicion and contempt by her conservative male colleagues.[366] Two exceptions were Marion Gräfin Dönhoff at *Die Zeit* and Carola Stern, who was active in radio and television. The countess, very much old-school but driving a Porsche sports car, is said to have completely acculturated to a newspaper cosmos supervised by men, and she never encouraged the recruiting of female progeny. This conservative aristocrat, whom a leading editor has characterized as "a cold, calculating woman who loved power," wielded a brilliant pen; she was treated with the greatest respect by the male *Zeit* directors and regarded as one of their own.[367] Stern, although less prominent and more congenial, was in a similar situation of respect, mainly endeavoring to maintain collegial relationships with men as equals. When employed at the Cologne WDR, she registered that female secretaries once refused to make coffee for the office boss, but soon thereafter relented.[368]

The absence of powerful females in journalism was replicated in the visual arts and music. From its beginnings, there was no woman exhibitor at the Kassel documenta until the appearance of Anna Oppermann at documenta 6 in 1977, when there was also a tiny female representation on the planning board. But Oppermann was not a name, and women artists simply did not make it to the top of the German art world, as Käthe Kollwitz had done, exceptionally, at the end of the Weimar Republic. Any development of art by women had been stifled ever since Jeanne Mammen, a Weimar fashion illustrator interested in Cubism, and Hannah Höch, a onetime Dadaist, were allowed to exhibit at the Berlin Galerie Rosen in 1947, swamped by a surfeit of men.[369] Uncannily, this situation resembled the humble presence of women artists in the reputedly progressive Bauhaus from 1919 to 1933, where talented women such as Helene Börner were restricted to weaving and could never become Masters, like Kandinsky or Klee. The mural painter Dörte Helm had fared better, but she had been rumored to be in a sexual liaison with director Walter Gropius.[370] All this was less a consequence of "the feminine mind" than of "institutional constraints," as Ruth Bernard Yeazell has pointed out in the context of European women artists since the Middle Ages.[371]

A similar situation existed in the music business, where Karajan discovered the teenage violin prodigy Anne-Sophie Mutter and then patronizingly hovered over her for years. In Darmstadt women were allowed to play some instruments such as the flute, but never reached the stage where they conducted or lectured on New Music as did Stockhausen or Kagel. Very occasionally, radio stations were moved to engage in token patronage by featuring women composers, as did Eimert with a broadcast, *Frauen komponieren*, in Cologne. Vera Brandes, a young manager, as late as 1973 was trusted with putting on stage the jazz pianist Keith Jarrett for his iconic Cologne solo recital. There was in Rhineland-Westphalia a concert series called *Frauen im Jazz*, and in the mid-1980s, Christine Stephan founded *Jazzethik*, a monthly periodical for contemporary jazz in Münster.[372] But all told, music, just like the visual arts, remained virtually sealed off to women artists, especially conductors and composers, at the top of the creative hierarchy, as both cultures were closely guarded male sanctuaries.

The situation was somewhat different for post-war literature. As in pictorial art for centuries and often centerpieces in opera such as Alban Berg's *Lulu*, women continued to be the focus of the narratives, exemplified in Heinrich Böll's 1971 novel, *Gruppenbild mit Dame*, where the heroine, the young Leni Gruyten, upholds her personal interests, including illicit love affairs, beginning in World War II. However, while not as star-crossed as Lulu, she too is a femme fatale, "no brain, but with her heart in the right spot," as the critic said, a type that had been memorialized by countless German authors before Böll.[373] It was impossible for contemporary German writers to deliver credible portraits of women not servicing the sexuality of men. In 1978, the thirty-nine-year-old author Peter Greiner published *Orpheus: Biographie eines Halbstarken* (*Orpheus: Biography of a Rowdy*), featuring four prostitutes, Heinke, Jutta, Ditte, and Anne, and their pimp Knut in their smutty daily routines.[374] As if responding to this work, "what an infinite store for provocation, those Emilys, Gretchens, Theklas," wrote Reinhard Baumgart four years later, how much false biography and how many false wishes have entered these stylized lives of women on the poets' pages, male authors all of them and hardly countable.[375]

In analogy to the Darmstadt New Music celebrations, women authors played practically no role even in the progressive establishment of literati in the Gruppe 47, well into the 1960s. Two lone women, Ingeborg Bachmann and Ilse Aichinger, who were Austrians, were received there more like special guests, both remaining outside the FRG. The men loved Bachmann chiefly because she came across as fragile, easily bursting into tears.[376] In accordance with the emancipatory trend, a few feminist women writers emerged in the 1970s with an exclusive women's agenda. Their aim was the literary establishment of a specifically feminine subjectivity.[377] Both Verena Stefan and Karin Struck published bestsellers. Stefan, born 1947, wrote *Häutungen* (*Shedding*) in 1975, for the feminist Munich publisher Frauenoffensive, a novel extolling lesbian love.[378] Even more successful was her peer Karin Struck, with the autobiographical novel *Klassenliebe* (*Class Love*). It dealt with her own life as a blue-collar worker, the daughter of proletarians, who had – untypically – risen to the status of a doctoral student in German literature. In the 1960s she had joined the DKP but, after the Soviet Union's treatment of dissident Solzhenitsyn, had departed disenchanted.[379] In the novel (as in real life until divorce in 1973), Karen has a daughter with her husband, a medical student from a similar background, but carries on an affair with Z., an established Marxist author. He becomes the father of her second child, Elias. Her problem with men results from her uncertainty as an upwardly mobile working-class member. "Between two classes" and slowly faltering in academe, Karen is losing her anchor as a woman, mother, left-winger, and aspiring intellectual.[380] Backgrounded by the student movement, the SDS, and finally the RAF, Struck constructs references from Nazi Germany to male-domination patterns in the 1970s; for her, any male of a certain age is stigmatized by a loathsome past, by Original Sin.[381]

In movies too, women remained "ghettoized and ignored by the mainstream of West Germany's paltry film culture."[382] Just as, thematically, they were treated in literature – vulnerable or as love objects – so also, in creations even of the New Film women of agency, as producers or directors, were hidden. In conceptions of New Filmmaking both in Oberhausen in 1962 and in a Hamburg declaration in 1979 the men thought only for themselves: a woman's presence was not felt and women's issues were not to be pursued.[383] Throughout the 1960s and 1970s young women even after film school were expected to become cutters and makeup artists, to help graduating male filmmakers, but not be filmmakers themselves. There were a few who dared to do so and who prevailed; next to Sander they were

Margarethe von Trotta, Helma Sanders-Brahms, and May Spils. Like Sander they were short-changed when it came to funding. Whether it be in documentaries, short films, or television (after feature films were impossible for them), men always received more. By the early 1970s, of forty-six films that were financed, merely eight were by women, and only one was a feature film. The men surrounding them realized that these women spoke a different film language, articulating issues that, in a female imagination, were not ruled by standards "patriarchal, chauvinist, and voyeuristic."[384]

Similar unspoken rulings obtained for gay male filmmakers, who were able to operate more openly after homosexuality between consenting men over eighteen had been legalized in 1969.[385] Werner Schroeter, a bisexual friend of Zadek's and Fassbinder's, was fond of stylistic and thematic excesses. In 1984 he dealt with his own sexuality in a film set in Portugal: a middle-aged woman lives on a beach with her adult son, who is interested only in roses and a young boy lover, also available to the mother, whom he keeps in a barn.[386] More well known and less bizarre was Holger Mischwitzky, whose *nom de guerre* was Rosa von Praunheim, who was sometimes financed by television. In his film of 1971 with the long-winded title *Nicht der Homosexuelle ist pervers, sondern die Situation, in der er lebt* (*It Is Not the Homosexual Who Is Perverse, But the Society in Which He Lives*), the twenty-nine-year-old filmmaker sought to draw in audiences and critics for comments on homosexuality in current society.[387]

Availing himself of an opportunity in liberal times, Fassbinder himself produced movies with homosexual motifs. In 1980 he filmed *Berlin Alexanderplatz* after Döblin's 1929 novel, a fourteen-episode television miniseries, in which the main character Franz Bieberkopf has several loves among the prostitutes he looks after as their procurer. Yet despite Fassbinder's own denial, as there was in the novel, there is more than a hint of homoerotic tension in the film between Biberkopf and his male friend Reinhold. The narrative plays during the denouement of the Weimar Republic, when the National Socialists were in the ascendance, and they punished homosexual men severely.[388] In an earlier picture, *Faustrecht der Freiheit* (*Fox and His Friends*) of 1974, Fassbinder, who always preferred men over women, himself had played the main character, a homosexual proletarian, whom he called Franz Biberkopf. He falls prey to a group of well-heeled gays who exploit him to the point of suicide.[389]

Fassbinder's films centering on women were more problematic. In some of his more mature films, women are conspicuous: *Maria Braun*, *Petra von Kant*, *Martha*, *Lola*, *Lili Marleen*, and *Veronika Voss*. Women were "dramaturgically speaking more interesting, more unpredictable and socially less conformist than men," he said.[390] But although all six women in those films are fascinating to watch, they come across with character flaws that somehow render them unsympathetic: Maria Braun is an egotistical go-getter, Petra von Kant a tyrant (in *Die bitteren Tränen der Petra von Kant*, *The Bitter Tears of Petra von Kant*), and Martha craven enough to be miserably abused by a man.[391] Lola is immoral and too opportunistic, Lili Marleen a narcissistic traitor of a noble cause, and Veronika Voss is a weak-willed drug addict.

In his work with them, Fassbinder dominated the women of his troupe, but this also meant that he typecast them over the years to an extent they became frustrated. Two of these templates were his star Hanna Schygulla, who invariably had to play the glitzy heroine and Irm Hermann, whom he cast early as a nasty shrew in *Katzelmacher* and who had to portray unattractive, grim-looking women for him, "frosty, heartless matriarchs," time and again. Significantly, Hermann remarked on this in an interview she gave after Fassbinder's death; she had finally turned his back on him in the late 1970s, after – so she said – he had laced her food with chemicals while still carrying on a sexual relationship; but it is also known about her that she had been eager to marry him early on, after they had met in the late 1960s in Munich.[392]

Opposite the spellbinding Fassbinder, the feminists Helma Sanders-Brahms and Margarethe von Trotta attempted to hold up the cause of women in New German Film. Bevor Sanders-Brahms produced *Deutschland bleiche Mutter* in 1980, which was a song of praise for women abandoned by their men during war, she made a film about a young Turkish guest worker, a prostitute and murder victim, in 1974.[393] Through this work, *Shirins Hochzeit* (*Shirin's Wedding*), Sanders-Brahms, who reportedly shared Fassbinder's need to expose strong feelings, wanted to memorialize both the exploited Turks and young women who had lost their moral compass. In the narrative, a young Anatolian woman arrives in Cologne looking for work, but secretly she searches for the man from her village she adores, who has preceded her. After employment as an unskilled laborer she is dismissed during the 1973 energy crisis and fails to put down roots. Isolated from

Germans and the Turkish men who see in her merely a sexual object, and after having been raped by a German man, she is reduced to offering sexual services to Turks in a dreadful dormitory. There she chances upon her former idol, who also uses her. From here, the road is downhill, and after she is forced to team up with a gang of petty Turkish criminals, she is shot by one of them, her pimp. Sanders-Brahms, who in 1974 was thirty-four, Gudrun Ensslin's age, and a friend of Helke Sander, reaped more criticism from Turks for this movie than from Germans, after it had run on WDR television in 1976. She, along with her lead actress, the Turkish Ayen Erten, was attacked, receiving threats of murder. It was unfortunate that *all* Turks were pictured negatively in the film, exacerbating the already existing prejudices of Germans against this large visible minority.[394]

In this era of RAF terrorism, Margarethe von Trotta emerged. She extended an earlier interest in simply solitary, disadvantaged females to women who chose to weaponize their objectives. Like Schwarzer, she was born illegitimately, in 1942 in Berlin, as the daughter of an impoverished woman with a title of nobility, and grew up in a life with no frills. In Paris in the early 1960s she became impressed with the pictures of Ingmar Bergman, Hitchcock, and the *Nouvelle Vague*. Back in Germany, she accepted parts in early films by Fassbinder and Schlöndorff. The main theme of this being the plight of the underprivileged, it seemed logical for her to cooperate with Schlöndorff, whom she had married, in the making of *Katharina Blum* four years later. This film introduced her to early motifs of young RAF members allegedly fighting for justice in the land, with women assuming an auspicious part.[395]

Although von Trotta later said that in filming *Katharina Blum* with her husband she was given a free hand and he himself substantiated this, it was clear that she felt constrained, wanting to strike out on her own.[396] Hence she wrote and directed *Das zweite Erwachen der Christa Klages* (*The Second Awakening of Christa Klages*) in 1978. This movie incorporated elements of the RAF; based on facts, it was about Christa, a kindergarten teacher in Munich, who robs a bank in order to finance the enlargement of her Kinderläden. In the course of this, her boyfriend is shot, other men's helpfulness is exposed as doubtful, and she tightly bonds with a former girlfriend. After a stretch in Portugal she resolves to face an uncertain fate back in Germany; a female teller she held hostage in the robbery refuses to betray her. Von Trotta clearly empathized with Christa as a woman who, "in order to do good, sees no other way than to become criminal," as Wolfgang Limmer wrote in *Der Spiegel*.[397]

It appears that von Trotta accepted this Faustian alternative as the least noxious of several unavoidable evils when she made her next film, about Gudrun Ensslin in prison and her sister Christiane visiting her there. Here, in *Die bleierne Zeit* (*The Leaden Time*) of 1981, it is clear that von Trotta is on the side of the woman who chooses not to break the law, as was Christiane's position. Yet the conversations she documents about the female bonding between the two sisters behind bars (as well as flashbacks of their time together as children, especially in late Nazi Germany) demonstrate sympathy for the younger RAF member Gudrun. The fact that in this film Juliane (Christiane in real life) keeps looking for ways to disprove the assumption that Marianne (Gudrun) hanged herself is testimony that the film director belonged to those who believed that a foul-play murder orchestrated from above was a real possibility.[398]

In any of her films, von Trotta did not provide a clue why women were in the majority in the RAF and its successor formations. Even in the jails of the first years, Ulrike Meinhof and Gudrun Ensslin were the strongest presence, stronger than Holger Meins, Jan-Carl Raspe, and Andreas Baader, despite the latter's macho gesticulations.[399] It was the women of the terrorism who inspired Gerhard Richter in his art: "I do think that women played the more important role in it. They impressed me much more than the men."[400] This female preponderance was a fact German law enforcement recognized early when its top-level executives instructed police to aim their guns, in confrontations, first at the women suspects.[401] Still, key members of the RAF and its extensions such as Stefan Wisniewski have stated convincingly that the women's movement was always far from their minds. After release from many years of incarceration, Monika Berberich, a leading terrorist, said that their cause had not been "the liberation of women, but the liberation of mankind."[402]

Be that as it may, reasons for the prevalence of women in the terrorist squads are hard to come by. Sociologists have adduced higher social station and, correspondingly, higher education, or disappointment in the material profusion during the Economic Miracle or authoritarian family backgrounds, but have failed to point to similar prerequisites for RAF males.[403]

Judging from her experiences as an RAF member of the first hour, Inge Viett has insisted that RAF women possessed qualities their male comrades lacked and which, when revealed, nonplussed the men. One of those was the ability to make decisions more quickly, on the spot – and shoot when the men still hesitated.[404] Berberich agreed when she said that women were, on the whole, more cool, but also that they were much more prepared to adjust to changing situations, as terrorists were faced with over time. "It was the men who shot at the ceiling in panic when banks were held up," she said. Yet another reason Berberich mentioned was that women, with an inherent charitable, curative instinct, had volunteered for the RAF because it gave them a chance to save the world.[405] Women terrorists – nurses of the universe? If this be true, it was a misdirected impulse, from the points of view of both Helke Sander and Alice Schwarzer, who had had something else in mind for the betterment of women.

New uncertainties prevailed in the 1970s. Bank robberies by RAF terrorists made German citizens more insecure, and as the state arrogated unto itself the surveillance of individuals and dented careers, many of them became more frightened. Creators in the arts and letters belonged to this latter group. Artists and intellectuals felt challenged to cope with anomalies by making them comprehensible, as Böll did in his novel about Katharina Blum and Schlöndorff did subsequently, in a film. In the 1980s such efforts would be continued by visual artists like Richter and Kiefer, and the composer Lachenmann would follow suit.

But under the conservative regime of Helmut Kohl in that decade, further atmospheric disturbances would arise. Was Hitler totally condemnable? Was there nothing positive in the nation's past? It would take reunification of the two Germanys in 1990 to create fresh political constellations and charge men and women from the culture scene with new tasks.

CHAPTER FIVE

◆ ◆ ◆

Retrenchment (1980–1990)

I N THE SPRING of 1981, as a faculty member of York University in Toronto, I was in West Berlin for research. One afternoon, I was invited by Professor Ernst Nolte for tea, in suburban Berlin. He was the leading historian of modern Europe, in particular Germany, at the Free University, and we knew each other from a panel on fascist movements we had both participated in, during 1974, at the German Historical Convention. Already at that time, Nolte was well known for a book he had published in the early 1960s, analyzing Italian Fascism, National Socialism, and the *Action Française*.[1] Born in 1923 and having avoided World War II conscription for health reasons, he had been awarded a doctorate with a dissertation on Marx, under Martin Heidegger in Freiburg, in 1952. He had been teaching in Berlin since 1973.[2]

As a matter of courtesy, I repaid him a visit a year or so later. I was struck by the reactionary tone in which Nolte talked about more recent German history and historians both in Germany and abroad. Although he did not defend the Third Reich, which had become my professional specialty, he ranted against historians who, in his opinion, distorted the more recent course of events, and especially complained about Jewish scholars. As leaders of a supposed Jewish conspiracy in North American academe, he singled out two good friends of mine who in his eyes were most guilty and who, he wanted me to know, did everything in their power to undermine his own scholarly work. He talked to me as if pleading for an ally.

I could not oblige him. The next time I was in Berlin it was 1986; he had published views downplaying the significance of Auschwitz, and I decided not to see him. He had in fact triggered the *Historikerstreit*, the War of German Historians, as Gordon A. Craig would famously explain later, to the readers of *The New York Review of Books*.[3] In this "war," mostly younger, West German left-liberal historians of modern Germany surrounding Hans-Ulrich Wehler and Hans Mommsen were aligned against a group of, mostly older, colleagues of a conservative persuasion, at the center of which was Ernst Nolte. One argued for, the other against, the significance of Adolf Hitler and the Third Reich as a watershed in modern German history. How had such a constellation, after decades of scholarly equability and consensus in German universities, come to pass?

◆ ◆ ◆

In the 1980s, the uncertainties of the 1970s, psychological and material, were largely replaced by positive achievements under a new and optimistic chancellor, Helmut Kohl, crowned at the end of the decade, as it were, by the unification of the two Germanys. Kohl had become chancellor, with the FDP's Hans-Dietrich Genscher as foreign minister, heading a Liberal-Christian Union coalition, after Helmut Schmidt's cabinet had to resign on October 1, 1982. In the preceding months, Schmidt had had to preside over deteriorating economic conditions, especially rising unemployment and welfare cuts, and increased inner-security measures that were opposed by the left wing of the SPD. While the FDP members after withdrawal from his government were preparing to ally with Kohl's CDU, a no-confidence vote by parliament sealed Schmidt's fate.[4]

Kohl had been born in 1930 in Ludwigshafen in the Rhenish Palatinate, the son of a middling tax official. Like Grass and Walser and Henze, he joined the Hitler Youth, serving in an anti-aircraft flak position at the end of the war. Despite a doctorate in history he was not an intellectual or a brilliant speaker like Schmidt, but more emotionally and instinctually gifted, impressing people with a 6 foot 4 inch frame, a stentorian voice, a firm handshake, and charming manners. He was a man who stood staunchly by the West, loved NATO, but never learned to speak English fluently. A good Catholic, he followed the Ten Commandments but later accepted illicit CDU party funding that contributed to his downfall. He was comparatively liberal in social matters when he took the reins of the CDU in 1973, but became more conservative as he got older, like the equally pious Adenauer, who was his long-time idol.[5]

At the end of 1982, as the number of unemployed had reached over 2 million in the Federal Republic for the first time, the country was technically in a recession. There were some changes in the pattern of national parties as well. The Free Democrats, standing for social liberalism and business laissez-faire, had been losing regionally, while the new ecologically minded Green Party was showing surprising strength after the general elections of March 1983, enabling it to enter the Bundestag. After those elections the SPD surprised with only 38.2 percent of the national vote – its worst showing since 1961. The Union parties, CDU and CSU combined, won 48.8 percent. This would put the SPD further on the defensive and in parliamentary opposition until its renewed ascent in the late 1990s; in the federal elections of January 1987 this party garnered only 37 percent. By contrast, the new Christian–Liberal coalition, in the words of Andreas Wirsching, the current director of the Institut für Zeitgeschichte, was driven by "progress optimism" and bent on the "strengthening of market power, individual responsibility and the return of the state."[6]

Beginning in 1983 and continuing until 1989, there was, once again, economic growth, but it was more halting than in previous decades. Unemployment, for one, stubbornly persisted, constituting the single most debilitating factor complicating progress. Much of it was owed to shifts in the economy, in particular industrial production. The traditional coal and steel industry lagged, notably in the west, and so did shipbuilding, in the north. But electronics picked up the slack, emulated by auto and machine construction, as well as the plastics industry. All those favored the southwest and south; Bavaria and Baden-Württemberg took over from the Rhineland as West Germany's economic power houses. Such shifts occasioned new imbalances in the national employment situation: because, altogether, service industries such as banking, telephony, and insurance assumed more strength, industrial manufacturing decreased. As a result, scores of workers in the latter lost their livelihoods, which they could not immediately resume as they lacked training. Thus, many older workers especially in the Ruhr Valley became permanently unemployed, while younger workers could not find trainee positions as increased automation led to ever more lay-offs.

Moreover, fast-moving advances in microelectronics laid the basis for an all-encompassing information technology industry favoring firms such as Siemens and Telefunken. These destroyed the hopes of younger, untrained children of blue-collar families of ever finding work in the conventional manual-labor industries. Instead, they forced them into service sectors of the lower orders such as office jobs, thus enhancing the ranks of the lower middle class, which grew vis-à-vis what was once the blue-collar proletariat on the one side, and educated and propertied elites on the other.[7] However, one other positive change was the growing contingent of women who were now employed outside the home – a consequence of the earlier women's movement, notwithstanding its fissures extending into the 1980s. Whereas in 1980 slightly more than 51 percent of West German women were holding down jobs, by 1990 that number had risen to more than 57 percent.

Such demographic changes must be viewed with guest workers and ethnic Germans from the European East in mind. Whereas Turks and southern European nationals had been prohibited from entering the republic since the early 1970s, the millions that were already there and showed no signs of wanting to leave had to be more lastingly accommodated. By 1970 there had been 2.6 million foreigners in West Germany, yet by 1987 there were 4.8 million and by 1990 5.2 million, altogether a jump from 4.3 percent of the total population to 8.2 percent. Especially the Turks among them continued to be perceived as a threat by native Germans. For as before, many of them refused to learn German, internalize German customs, and acculturate, and their birth rate was higher than that of German citizens, which was perceived as alarmingly negative. In July 1990 a new law was promulgated that removed some of the previous restrictions on residence in Germany from the large Turkish minority and allowed for more generous movements from Turkey, also benefiting the unification of dependents with their already resident families.[8]

Fugitives from oppressive and unstable regimes were also drifting to the Federal Republic for the first time in much stronger numbers. By the citizens and Bonn they were reluctantly received, as it was suspected that most had fled for economic reasons.[9] Such suspicion was not as strong toward ethnic Germans arriving from Poland and Russia. But there were problems here too: unfamiliarity with German language and customs and, sometimes, reluctance to integrate on the part of the newcomers compounded difficulties arising from a dearth of suitable dwellings and matching jobs. In 1970 there had been over 18,000 such resettlers; there were over 52,000 in 1980 and almost 400,000 in 1990.[10]

Helmut Kohl's government could justifiably take credit for solving most of the difficulties, economically and by social adjustments. Since 1945 the Federal Republic had come a long way; for all the world to see it had acquitted itself well after the shame of the national collapse. It had been successful developing democracy in action, rebuilding its economy, and encouraging society to grow, sanctioned by a social contract that allowed civic freedoms, accessible avenues for education, and variegated cultural expression. The Kohl cabinet's self-confidence and universal acclaim reached their pinnacle when presiding over amalgamation with what was formerly the GDR, on October 3, 1990.[11]

This altogether positive narrative was not without blemishes and risks, and some of those affected culture. They consisted of the Kiessling affair early during Kohl's reign, the danger of a recurrent neo-Nazism, persistent terrorist disruptions, and the Bitburg episode in 1985 and its successive events, which called into question West Germans' sincerity after disavowing National Socialism and the Third Reich.

The Kiessling affair demonstrated Kohl's poor political judgment and social prejudices. In the summer of 1983, Günter Kiessling, a four-star Bundeswehr general, came under suspicion of being a homosexual; in Bonn, this was considered a national security risk. Therefore, the CDU minister of defense, Manfred Wörner, suspended Kiessling in December, although he had denied allegations. In the end, Kiessling was impelled to resign and then had to be rehabilitated, because nothing against him could be found. In 1984 an embarrassed Wörner offered his resignation to the chancellor, but Kohl held on to him, because he was afraid his rival Strauss might usurp the defense portfolio. Another reason was that he wished to bind a weak minister, Wörner, in perpetual loyalty to himself, a tactic Hitler had honed to perfection.[12]

Under Kohl, who was a friend of Israel just as Adenauer had been, the specter of National Socialism was, with one or two exceptions, effectively banned. Surprisingly Werner Vogel, the senior president of the Bundestag speaking for the Green Party, in March 1983 was discovered to have concealed not only his Nazi Party membership, but also a position in the Nazi interior ministry; he immediately resigned.[13] But if, for biological reasons alone, old Nazis in the Christian Union or other traditional FRG parties ceased to be a topic in the 1980s, there were nascent groups of neo-Nazis who had to be watched. Not so nascent anymore was the far-right National Democratic Party (NPD), which had enjoyed a heyday in the late 1960s. However, it seldom received more than 5 percent of the popular vote, excluding it from most levels of government. It enjoyed success at state levels, however, and in March 1989 it was able to enter Frankfurt's city council.[14]

Historically speaking, the NPD made sense as part of growing extreme right-wing movements in all Central and western Europe. The same held true for yet another West German far-right populist party, the Republicans, which typically instrumentalized whatever aversion against incoming foreigners existed among the FRG's citizens. It was co-founded in November 1983 by Franz Schönhuber, a Munich TV journalist and onetime member of the Waffen-SS, who had risen to popularity by glorifying his former military unit in a book. In 1989, during renewed phases of economic down-cast, the Republicans managed to infiltrate city councils in Düsseldorf and other cities, and they were voted into the European Parliament. They claimed to stand for all those West Germans who were – like other Europeans, for instance in Austria – the losers in the past years of ration-alization and modernization, incipient globalization, and the government's retrenchment in social services.[15]

Besides the Republicans, more extreme but smallish groups modeled themselves ever more closely on the NSDAP. They denied the Holocaust (an action the Bundestag prosecuted after 1985 in courts of law) and spread anti-Semitic lore. One formation, the right-extremist Wehrsportgruppe Hoffmann, engaged in illegal paramilitary training with potentially terrorist consequences; there were some dynamite attacks against asylum-seekers' quarters. In September 1980 a far-right extremist blew himself up at the Munich Oktoberfest, killing and maiming bystanders. Two months later a Jewish publisher was assassinated in Erlangen. To the credit of Kohl's government, however, such miscreants were mercilessly dealt with, or they died socially ostracized, as did Michael Kühnen, a former Bundeswehr lieutenant turned neo-Nazi, in 1991.[16]

When the RAF re-emerged in late summer 1981, four years after the German Autumn, it did so after repeated tactical regrouping. A third generation of terrorists (those Fassbinder had clairvoyantly portrayed in his 1979 film) undertook a bomb attack at the U.S. Ramstein air base, with no one injured. Two weeks later a targeted American general in Heidelberg just survived. Of course, the insurrectionists of the first and second hour were either dead, in jail, or, like Inge Viett, had absconded to the GDR under new identities, only to be discovered after reunification. The hard core of this third generation consisted of around twenty men and women, supported by close to two hundred sympathizers moving about undiscovered mostly in large cities. They were sophisticated exploiters of new technologies.[17]

On February 1, 1985, Ernst Zimmermann, an industrial manager and air-space specialist deemed to be a representative of "multinational capital," became the first new murder victim. The terrorists killed Gerold von Braunmühl, a high official in Genscher's foreign office, in October 1986 in Bonn. Then Alfred Herrhausen, chairman of the board at Deutsche Bank and, like Schleyer, decision-making at Mercedes-Benz, was blown up in his armored sedan in Frankfurt in November 1989.[18]

However Kohl's cabinet may have acquitted itself during renewed terror waves, in 1985 it was jolted by the Bitburg affair, for it posed again the old question of guilt for Nazism. Rather than accepting historic accountability, Kohl comforted himself with a declaration he had made in Israel, that as a fifty-five year old he had been born too late to be charged with responsibility. Thus motivated, he invited U.S. President Ronald Reagan to a joint service commemorating fallen soldiers both of the United States and Germany at the soldiers' cemetery in Bitburg in the Eifel Mountains. A new German–American friendship was to be celebrated, as Chancellor Schmidt and President Jimmy Carter had not got along too well.[19] The fact that members of the Waffen-SS were also buried there, alongside Wehrmacht soldiers, Kohl knowingly overlooked. Despite warnings, Kohl went ahead on Sunday, May 5, 1985. Falsely, his chancellor's office claimed that Waffen-SS, merely fighting alongside regular troops, had not been responsible for any crimes. Kohl, however, should have known that all killing venues in Poland were run by Waffen-SS or police units and that the worst known offenders – to mention only Josef Mengele – wore its uniform.[20] At the wreath-laying ceremony, Reagan had just come from Bergen-Belsen, so he was somewhat more sensitized. But his statement did not exonerate the chancellor, when he said, more correctly than Kohl would have wanted to admit, "There are over 2,000 buried in Bitburg cemetery. Among them are 48 members of the SS – the crimes of the SS must rank among the most heinous in human history – but others buried there were simply soldiers in the German Army."[21] Kohl, of course, wished to honor German sufferers. Yet, as he did not make a speech, his gestures amounted to "a blatant attempt to equate German victims of war and Jewish victims of genocide" and, ultimately, "the exculpation of the Germans under Hitler." Protest resulted from within Germany and beyond, notably leftist circles and the central council of German Jews.[22]

One might think that after such tactless behavior by the federal chancellor other West German senior politicians would take the cue and at least watch their rhetoric. A few weeks after Kohl's speech, the CDU federal president Richard Freiherr von Weizsäcker, the lawyer who had defended his father at Nuremberg, proved the opposite by offering oratory of his own. By native and outside critics, it was later lauded as a model of its kind, balanced and endowed with wisdom. On May 8, 1985, forty years after Nazi capitulation to the Allies and three days after Kohl's Bitburg appearance, this aristocratic politician addressed the Bundestag in a spirit of humility and conciliation. With especial regard to Jewish victims, he appealed to memory as a force of redemption, strongly implying that Germans had no right to identify with the victors of May 8, 1945, as Kohl and Reagan had suggested at Bitburg. Then came a listing of all those who had died on account of the Third Reich and its war. Weizsäcker, already a highly popular federal president, came across as a man so liberal and humane that right-wing Union politicians such as Strauss and Alfred Dregger, then the CDU's parliamentary caucus leader, castigated him as too soft.[23]

However, as Andreas Wirsching has pointed out, in touching on criminal agency, Weizsäcker followed earlier patterns of merely acknowledging individual, not national, guilt, in a manner not significantly removed from Kohl's. He stressed that any guilt could only be conceived of as personal, not collective, and hence serviced the decades-old German-victim perspective.[24] To wit, Hitler had been the main trigger of crimes, and their execution had been in the hands of only a few. "Hitler's constant approach was to stir up prejudices, enmity and hatred," Weizsäcker said, without asking whether such sentiments had not actually existed beforehand and given Hitler the opportunity to fulfill the deep wishes of his electorate. He mentioned

"Hitler's immeasurable hatred against our Jewish compatriots," without asking if perhaps the Führer knew this would accord with a groundswell of similar feelings within Germans long before 1933. "The perpetration of such crimes was in the hands of a few people," he insisted, dismissing that those few in reality had amounted to hundreds of thousands of people – Augstein believed a million – not counting bystanders at home who knew from relatives and acquaintances what was going on.[25]

Therefore, when Bundestag president Philipp Jenninger, two years younger than Kohl and one of his confidants, delivered his own speech in memory of Kristallnacht, fifty years after the events, the idiomatic faux pas he committed was less a consequence of randomly careless phraseology than the result of a belief system similar to Weizsäcker's and Kohl's – that Jews and Germans were *both* victims of the Nazi regime and in remembrance could be treated similarly. Instead, it would have been necessary to apply different sets of nomenclature to each grouping and to mind accentuations and inflections in one's speech. Although no one among his audience had any doubt that he meant wholly well, Jenninger in his November 9, 1988 address before parliament chose descriptive and analytical turns of phrase reminiscent of National Socialist practice. In his vernacular, Jenninger used "race defilement," "vermin," and "extermination" when referring to Jews as if he were Goebbels at the Berlin Sportpalast in 1943, and asked rhetorical questions such as whether the Jews had not perhaps deserved to be put in their place.[26] Without appearing to be critical, Jenninger spoke of the years from 1933 to 1938 as a "fascinosum," mentioned Hitler's "triumphal polit- ical procession," and his "astounding series of successes" that had to be seen as a "belated slap against the Weimar system."[27] Jenninger's performance occurred after the government's neglect to invite Heinz Galinski, the chairman of Berlin's organized Jews, to a parallel Bundestag forum of his own. He was heavily criticized especially by the left-wingers in government, resigning his presidential post the next day, after apologizing for offending those he felt had misunderstood his speech. His posture was emblematic of views still held by the conservative-minded segments of German society.[28]

◆ ◆ ◆

The *Historikerstreit* of 1986–8 that changed how German historians reasoned about the past also had consequences for creators in the arts and letters. It came about because conservative historians wanted to relativize and historicize the Third Reich in comparison with other historic phenomena and thereby lift the moral stain from the country, re-constituting the FRG as a normal state in the family of nations. This meant minimalizing Nazi Germany's postulated uniqueness, which had mani-fested itself in evil. Already in 1983, Ernst Nolte had published an article in the *FAZ* in which he held that rather than Italian Fascism or National Socialism, merely Bolshevism had attained uniqueness, because it had succeeded in a "genuine revolution" of state and society. It alone had managed to murder masses of people, 20 million in fact, many more than Hitler would by May 1945. Nolte relativized Auschwitz by stating that Hitler did not just kill Jews, and that those Jews he exterminated in the "Final Solution" were, in his opinion, potential instigators of Bolshevism and capitalism, outrages understandably to be avoided.[29]

In June 1986, Nolte went on to minimize Auschwitz by using sequences precariously tied together by lumpy logic. He cited precedents to Hitler's genocide that were, arguably, worse – the Armenian massacres of 1915 by the Turks and the Bolshevik revolution two years later. During this upheaval the Communists had employed "Asiatic" torture methods, derived from the Chinese Bolshevik Cheka in the Far East. Documented was a rat in a small cage, which through hunger would be propelled to gnaw its way into a human forehead. Nolte claimed that Hitler was aware of such methods and was afraid that the Soviets would apply them to Germans; hence, equating Jews with Bolsheviks, his mental leap to Auschwitz. In Auschwitz, wrote Nolte, not just Jews but also hard-working SS guards weighed down by their heavy burden could properly be regarded as "victims." Besides, many Polish captives at Auschwitz had been fierce anti-Semites. Auschwitz's sole uniqueness consisted in the mechanization of its killing apparatus, "the technical procedure of gassing"; besides, the Russian Gulag Archipelago and its methods were another precedent. Nolte then referred to Bitburg by pointing to American pilots buried in honor graves at Arlington, Virginia, many of whom must have participated in "terror attacks" against German civilians during World War II. In analogy to Kohl–Reagan, Nolte asked whether a German federal chancellor would have been allowed *not* to visit the Arlington cemetery, as Adenauer, following protocol, did on his state visit to President Eisenhower in 1953.[30]

Also in 1986, Andreas Hillgruber published a book with the title *Zweierlei Untergang* (*Two Kinds of Downfall*), with a chapter each on Auschwitz and the demise of the Eastern Front, in 1944–5 – not only hazards for the Wehrmacht, but also civilians, who were raped, mutilated, killed, losing their homes to Soviet marauders. Hillgruber suggested that both scenarios were horrible and morally to be condemned to an equal degree, therefore cancelling each other out. Because Hitler's murder of the Jews was brought about by his idiosyncratic hatred of them, little if any blame fell on the German people. He also commended Nazi Party cadres for having assisted desperate civilians at war's end.[31]

Hillgruber, born in East Prussia in 1925, had himself fought on the Eastern Front; since 1972 he had occupied a modern-history chair in Cologne.[32] His and Nolte's findings were anathema to the conclusions younger, social-science-oriented historians had recently arrived at. Their research had transcended older methodological and conceptual limits set by their teachers – Hans Rothfels, Theodor Schieder, and Werner Conze among them, although especially the last-mentioned had provided much innovative inspiration. Yet while the main focus of those had been on traditional nation-states and their interrelations, their students now concentrated on structures of society, ideologies, and culture.[33] This led to a greater interest in the inner workings of Nazi dictatorship and its preconditions.

As the controversy opened, Jürgen Habermas, from Adorno's Critical Theory Frankfurt School, came to join this younger group, answering Nolte and Hillgruber in an article he published in *Die Zeit*. Born in 1929, he was closer in age to that younger cohort of historians born in the 1930s–1940s who, with the three notable exceptions of Hagen Schulze, Klaus Hildebrand, and Michael Stürmer, were to oppose Nolte and Hillgruber. Habermas, with a personal background typical of his generation, had been Adorno's first assistant at Frankfurt's Institut für Sozialforschung in 1956 and then studied political science with the Marxist Wolfgang Abendroth at Marburg. His early disenchantment with the Third Reich had been buttressed by what he learned during the Nuremberg Trials; later, as a graduate student, he had, incredulous, come across Heidegger's allusion to the "inner truth and greatness" of National Socialism. In the early 1980s, Habermas was a philosophy professor in Frankfurt, carrying on Adorno's social-research tradition.[34]

In his *Zeit* article of July 11, 1986, Habermas called Nolte's rat-in-the-cage example "abstruse," rejected the reduction of Nazi crimes' uniqueness merely to rationalize gassing procedures in Auschwitz, and dismissed the significance of Gulag "originality" vis-à-vis Hitler's extermination sites. He related that Nolte had recently told his visiting Israeli colleague Saul Friedländer, who had lost both parents in Auschwitz, that Chaim Weizmann, the head of the World Jewish Congress, had declared war on Germany in September 1939 and that Hitler, fearing annihilation at the hand of Jews, had had good reason to deport them. (Friedländer remembers that during this 1986 visit he had been asked by Nolte over dinner what it was like to be a Jew: was it a matter of religion or biology? Deciding for himself that it was biology, Nolte then insisted that there was something like world Jewry and that the Weimar-republican Jewish journalist Kurt Tucholsky had written he wished the German bourgeoisie would die from gas.[35])

Regarding Hillgruber, Habermas wrote that the blurb on the dust jacket for his book had expressly pointed to the interweaving of the author's two main themes. These were the murder of the Jews at Auschwitz and the demise of German civilians (and defending Wehrmacht) at Germany's eastern borders – an interrelationship Hillgruber was now at pains to deny, blaming it on a publishing error. Habermas repudiated Hillgruber's charge that the Red Army had singled out mostly Germans for punishment, for they had also been raping women of other eastern countries and committed atrocities there. Besides, there was no evidence the Western Allies had been using the Soviets to do their dirty work in demolishing the Great German Reich led by Prussia, as Hillgruber insinuated.[36]

Nolte and Hillgruber soon received assistance from two younger university historians who were still beholden to traditional historiography rather than exploring newer social-science avenues, even though they covered the Third Reich. More importantly, as they saw it, the two senior historians commendably resisted the growing trend to view the Third Reich more punitively than had been done before. Viewing unforgivingly would rob German history, as a whole, of positive content and deprive the German people, unjustly, of a legacy to recall with pride. That had, of course, been the original concern of Gerhard Ritter and Friedrich Meinecke, who after World War II had wished to reserve unsullied historical terrain for German patriots by blanking out the recent past. Such emendations were not intended by Klaus Hildebrand and Michael Stürmer; rather, they believed that a sagacious weighing of all the evidence available, and a careful parsing of written sources, would reveal Nazi phenomena to have been of lesser importance than other, positive, milestones in German history. In shifting the emphasis, as, for example, Stürmer was wont to do, from the Third Reich to "periods of great radical change in German history," new national images could be fashioned. For the nineteenth century, Stürmer was able to identify "Prussia's post-Napoleonic epoch of reforms," as he did in a talk in Munich, or Bismarck's unification of Germany, as he wrote in an essayistic book with many cartoonish illustrations. Upon such positive narratives, easy to digest even by non-academic readers, West German national pride could be securely fastened. Hence a normal historical consciousness could be restored to the German people, as other peoples had always enjoyed it and kept on enjoying. National pride, believed Stürmer, was necessary for a nation's integrity and moral health. If it had vanished, it would have to be reinstated.[37]

Stürmer, born in 1938 in Kassel as the son of musician Bruno Stürmer, had been a professor of history at Erlangen since 1973. In the early 1980s he was called to the side of Helmut Kohl, obviously sharing his visions, sometimes advising him and assisting with speechwriting.[38] Hildebrand, born in Bielefeld in 1941, as a history student was early influenced by Hillgruber. Hence he became more interested in diplomatic and military rather than social history, which the group Habermas sided with preferred. Hildebrand had, by 1986, become a respected specialist in modern German foreign policy at his history chair in Bonn. He viewed the Third Reich and in particular the Holocaust as essentially shaped by Hitler, which could suggest that ordinary Germans had less of a responsibility for any of it.[39] This attitude led him to advance the view that Nolte's attempt to "historically classify the central element of the regime's and its weltanschauung's destructive capacity" was deserving of fair consideration and further study.[40]

Defending Nolte and Hillgruber, Stürmer in the *FAZ* spread his opinion that Habermas had engaged in "fantastic invention" and insisted that it had to be allowed to create new historical identities, deviating from shop-worn leftist clichés such as eternal German guilt for the Holocaust: "German history has led to Hitler but also beyond him."[41] Hildebrand made known his opinion that Hillgruber had offered a differentiated interpretation of the German catastrophe and that Habermas had misquoted Nolte and unduly politicized against him; any historical revision was legitimate.[42]

In the ensuing exchanges left-liberal and Social Democratic members of the younger historian peer group released impressive expositions, while on the intellectual right the *FAZ* editor Joachim Fest aided especially Nolte.[43] Two aspects of these developments are significant. First, it had not been historians, but a philosopher who answered the two senior historians the first time around.[44] This could suggest that left-leaning historians were to blame for not taking their right-wing colleagues seriously enough and early enough. Second, Fest was, initially, not a conservative, but a liberal journalist critical of the Third Reich, as his early, brilliant biography of key Nazi leaders shows.[45] These two aspects combined imply that the issues under discussion were less important as routine exercises in the craft of historiography than as a weighty subtext touching on Germans' self-comprehension concerning not merely historians and even transcending the academy.

The four most vocal protagonists on the left were Hans Mommsen, Heinrich August Winkler, Jürgen Kocka, and Hans-Ulrich Wehler. Mommsen, holder of the new modern-German-history chair at Bochum since 1968, was born in 1930. He was a nephew of Wolfgang A. Mommsen, the former president of the Koblenz federal archive. His father, Wilhelm Mommsen, a historian of Germany in Marburg, had been ousted after 1945 because of too close an identification with Nazism. Hans and his twin brother Wolfgang J., an equally prolific historian, lived through a destitute teenage period because of their parents' indigence. Eventually, he obtained his doctorate, on the Habsburg Empire, under Rothfels in Tübingen, in 1959. After a spell at the Munich Institut für Zeitgeschichte he joined Conze's chair in Heidelberg as a junior scholar in 1963. There he became one of the few young historians to embark on revealing the contours of the Third Reich. Developing a social-structural interpretation opposed to the Hitlercentric views of Bracher, he stressed factors inherent in society and forces of happenstance for the development of Nazism, tending to take away responsibility from individual Nazi greats for agency. This might have suggested that he wished to absolve any humans of responsibility and therefore was apologetic, but such was never his intent. On the contrary, he held Germany and Germans accountable for the Third Reich and Holocaust, merely cautioning against the conservative historians' practice after 1945 of casting solitary blame on Nazi leaders, primarily Hitler. Because he focused on "the actual practice of the regime," observes Hitler biographer Ian Kershaw, he was able to apportion responsibility "to wide sections of German society, principally to the national conservative elites – business leaders, the aristocracy, the higher civil service, the judiciary, above all the military leadership – both for their role in allowing Hitler to take power and subsequently for their extensive collaboration with the Nazi regime."[46] It was those older historians who had been apologetic, and now Mommsen saw Nolte, Hillgruber, and their followers following in their wake.

In linking the Nolte group's revisionist remarks directly to the spirit of Bitburg, Mommsen identified them as symptoms of a broader discontent by the German right wing with the recent status quo. That had meant that, especially since Brandt's famous December 1970 genuflection in Warsaw, guilt had been acknowledged and the 1933–45 period classified as regrettable. After the return of political conservatism in Bonn under Kohl a new climate had been created, resisting penitent moods. Below the historians' controversy lay the wish, articulated by Kohl and Dregger, for a positive, "national history image," which was first on Stürmer's agenda. Specifically, Mommsen refuted Nolte's explanation of Auschwitz as the most radical manifestation of Hitler's anti-Marxism; he denied that a legal or moral justification of Hitler's deportation of European Jews could derive from an alleged declaration of war on Germany by the World Jewish Congress; and he thought that Nolte's construal of the SD-Einsatzgruppen as mere instruments of partisan control was mistaken.[47]

Heinrich August Winkler of Freiburg concurred. Eight years younger than Mommsen, he too had studied under Rothfels, as had both his parents still in Königsberg, but then his father had died as a soldier.[48] Like Mommsen (and unlike conservative historians), Winkler was, in principle, in favor of recognition of separate sovereignty for the GDR, but only after sufficient evidence that its, still oppressed, citizens were accepting of that state themselves.[49] He eschewed Nolte's "national-apologetic revision of German historical depictions"; never had the Holocaust, the greatest crime in world history, been so empathetically reconsidered by any German historian so blatantly. Nonetheless, Winkler sought to differentiate. As necessary as recognizing the exceptionalism of the Holocaust, perpetrated by fascist extremism, was, it was necessary that the perception of other crimes, including those committed on the radical left, not be occluded.[50]

Jürgen Kocka, born in 1941, was a member of the school of history that his ten-years-older colleague Hans-Ulrich Wehler had institutionalized at the new University of Bielefeld since the early 1970s. Its aim was the practice of history more like a social science than a classical discipline, in the humanities. The inspiration for this had come from the forefathers of German social science – Marx, Freud, and Max Weber – combined with impulses from pragmatists in the United States: both Wehler and Kocka had studied at American universities. The Bielefeld School's own journal, with the programmatic title *Geschichte und Gesellschaft* (*History and Society*), was a medium all younger historians of the left strove to publish in, and on its board sat progressive scholars from Germany and abroad.

Kocka started on a conciliatory note when he averred that it was neither wrong nor new to attempt comparisons in historiography – hence methodologically Nolte was following proven practice. That said, phenomena for comparisons would have to be carefully chosen. To equate a systematic killing machine conceived by educated brains of the Western world with brutal arbitrary acts such as slave-labor imposition, civil-war excesses, random mass liquidations, and arbitrary starvings as in the East was illicit. Rather, Nolte should have compared Germany with Western states such as France and England that were part of her own civilizational tradition since the Enlightenment. In those – unlike in the East – social contracts, political constitutions, the rule of law, and sophisticated systems of education had operated reliably in normative fashion. Kocka was implying that the singularity of Auschwitz, as posited by the leftists in the profession, would have become easily discernible if Nolte had chosen to research within acceptable parameters.[51]

Wehler was a one-time student of Theodor Schieder whose specialty was Kaiser Wilhelm's II Second Empire. Taking this as a point of departure, his thesis, vaunted on the left, was that Germany's trajectory since the nineteenth century had been special, a *Sonderweg*, a special path, in that it had not undergone bourgeois revolutions such as other European states and at the end of that century had politically unified and industrialized belatedly. It therefore had to go through anxieties and fears its Western neighbors France and Britain did not experience, and henceforth manifested those violently, leading, eventually, to Hitler.[52] In this, he was building on work done earlier by the Hamburg historian Fritz Fischer, somewhat older, who, solitarily, had upheld that the Second Reich was the aggressor in World War I and thus fully responsible for that conflict's bloodshed.[53]

Hence the uniqueness of the Holocaust within the German narrative, which bespoke singularity for decades, was for Wehler a given. One sprang logically from the other. Wehler referred to the *Historikerstreit's* subtext, when he charged that it was mainly "a political fight for the self-understanding of the Federal Republic, the political consciousness of its citizens," and therefore more of broader national import than merely an intellectual bone of contention for academics.[54] Wehler surmised that perhaps to provoke such a fight and reach out to a wider audience, Nolte had elected to publicize his latest views in a prominent newspaper (the *FAZ*) rather than a scholarly medium.[55] In Hillgruber's work he asked why he had defended holding the Eastern Front to the end when he knew, as he himself wrote in his second part, that such endurance would prolong the death camps.[56]

The left-wing historians were soon supported by colleagues from abroad. Richard J. Evans, then at the University of East Anglia, offered detailed criticism of the Nolte faction, charging that they were abetting "nationalist historiography" with old-fashioned historicist methodology, ultimately to bolster the current, conservative, politicians in power. It was wrong to demand that history should form the basis for an entire national consciousness, as the sentimental Kohl and his cohorts would now desire.[57] Nolte had wrongly quoted Weizmann, said Evans, for in 1939 he had not been speaking for the Jews everywhere and his Zionist World Jewish Congress was not even internationally recognized as the Jews' representative body. "So there was no justification for Hitler to 'intern' Jews," as Nolte had told an alarmed Friedländer. Nor had Hitler been afraid of the Bolshevik Gulag Archipelago when he launched the Final Solution after 1940.[58]

Against Hillgruber, Evans labeled a more fundamental charge by suggesting that this otherwise seasoned historian was not in full command of the sources, as he attempted to delineate anti-Semitism in his second chapter.[59] Evans held Michael Stürmer responsible for neglecting social and economic history, the tool of the new progressives, viewing it as irrelevant, or ignoring it altogether.[60] He further maintained that the Erlangen historian had had to resort to "hints and innuendos," because anything Stürmer had claimed as fact would not survive "intensive scholarly scrutiny." Namely: "Weimar was not destroyed by Versailles; Germany's primary responsibility for the outbreak of war in 1914 is well established; the Nuremberg Trials were not a tool of Stalinism; Bonn has never even remotely threatened to resemble Weimar; history is made not by geopolitics but by people."[61] On the whole, Evans emphasized the underlying argument regarding Germany's national sensitivities when he judged that "the whole debate ultimately has little to offer anyone with a serious scholarly interest in the German past. It brings no new facts to light; it embodies no new research; it makes no new contribution to historical understanding; it poses no new questions that might stimulate future work."[62]

Charles S. Maier of Harvard focused on historicization – however fuzzy that term – when he wrote that "Auschwitz remains incomprehensible" and therefore would not fit a taxonomy. However, he allowed for the possibility of historicization as an effort not to understand Auschwitz, but to understand a regime "in which Auschwitz and a lived normality" could coexist. This was reminiscent of Hannah Arendt.[63]

Nolte's erstwhile dinner guest Friedländer put a large question mark next to *all* historicization attempts by the Nolte group when he asked what the limits to any relativizing might be.[64] He then, too, cited Arendt – her criterion for the exceptionalism of Nazi crimes, consisting of the circumstance that never had a regime known to mankind, no matter how criminal, categorically decided "who could inhabit the world and who could not."[65] Friedländer elaborated to say that "as soon as a regime determines that groups have to be singled out, no matter for what reason, and be eliminated on the spot, and that they can never be allowed to dwell on earth, the utmost has been reached."[66] Implicitly, he charged the combative right wing for wanting not to see that.[67]

As for myself, I kept out of the battle, because as a Canadian with German roots I felt I should be silent. To be sure, I was on the leftists' side, as my publications showed. I was on good social terms both with Hillgruber and Stürmer, as they undertook a collegial visit to Toronto in 1984, but then stayed out of academically discursive, argumentative exchanges. Eventually it was clear that both Hillgruber and Nolte wanted me on their side. Still in 1986, Hillgruber mailed his book, pleading with me to see reason and signal my consent. Nolte sent me a new article of his from the *FAZ* in 1988, having written "with kind regards" in the margin, in which he sought more understanding from a still interested readership, clearly expecting me to respond. I replied to neither. As his article demonstrated, Nolte's contentions had become more modest. But at its end he showed that on the core issue he did not cede an inch: "The final result is not a moral relativization, but a historical reassessing of National Socialism."[68]

The *Historikerstreit* accelerated memory politics in the nation. That struggle had actually been prefigured by and then ran parallel to a movement, since the late 1970s, to establish memorial sites, in order to remind West Germans of their legacy.[69] But, as in the historians' feud, there was a left and a right wing clamoring for the cause. The left wished to make Germany's crimes and blunders recognizable to educate toward a better future. The right, however, rejected just that, wanting instead to conjure up a glorious past for orientation.[70]

On the drawing boards were great plans, supported by Kohl, for a German Historical Museum in West Berlin and a House of History at the government seat in Bonn, in addition to regional museums. Conservative politicians, backed by German refugee organizations, demanded a large memorial in Bonn that would also accommodate a military parade ground. This was, of course, anathema to Social Democrats and the Green Party, who had already had to witness the establishment of a series of voluptuous exhibitions – one on the Bavarian Wittelsbach dynasty in Munich in 1980 and on the Hohenzollern rulers in Prussia, in Berlin in 1981. Here the grand narrative of the past was to be resurrected, without Nazi-period abuses expressly denied; the exhibits were conceived, in one museum director's opinion, as "the modern triumphal processions of the great political gladiators." Scores of people attended.[71] But alongside those expositions, and in accord with left-wingers, memorial sites such as on former concentration camps were also expanded, as well as new ones erected, such as the former Gestapo headquarters in what used to be the Hotel Silber in Stuttgart.[72] From 1982 to 1990 the number of museums in the Federal Republic was to increase from approximately 1,500 to 2,500, and that of exhibitions from 3,000 to over 5,000.[73]

In East Berlin, there existed a Museum for German History, conceptualized as an instrument of ideological guidance by the GDR government. Kohl therefore aimed to create a counterweight, especially since he believed history professors in West German universities were teaching the wrong history, a direct reference to the new-school scholars he detested such as the Mommsen brothers. The order of the day was to re-emphasize history and bring it closer to the people, but only, in the Stürmer manner, "positive" history suited to establishing a new sense of German identity.[74] In that spirit, a commission of conservative historians and museum directors was formed, for Bonn, in 1983, among them Klaus Hildebrand from the university.[75] Martin Broszat of the Institut für Zeitgeschichte found Kohl's rationale chauvinistic and the personnel composition of the commission partisan; he preferred a concentration merely on the FRG's 1945–55 foundation decade, emphasizing democracy.[76] Nevertheless, the House of History covering a much longer historical narrative opened in 1986; two years later, judged an outside critic, it had degenerated into "a billboard space claimed by all sorts of interest groups."[77] One of its official missions was to service German martyrology; in the 1990s it staged an exhibition on the expulsion of Germans from the European East.[78]

In West Berlin, German history was to be documented from the ninth century to the present day by a Historical Museum, in a huge new complex close to the former Reichstag, still only partially refurbished. However, because of high costs and architectural squabbles, designs for the Berlin museum stalled. A major part in the blocking was played by protests from the SPD, which constituted not only the official opposition in Bonn, but also the government party in Berlin as a federal state. Further disagreements issued from complicated deliberations of committees, representing experts, not the least of them historians from both sides. Their chronic lack of consensus caused major disjunctions. Amid the scuffles, in 1988, Charles Maier, a sympathetic observer, cautioned: "The museum might well fail to encourage a sense of national identity once anticipated by the conservatives, but it could also fail to prod the active questioning of the past allegedly sought by the left." The museum as conceived did fail; it became a reality only after Germany's reunification in 1990.[79]

◆　◆　◆

Notwithstanding the arguments of the historians in the mid-1980s, historicization, that is comprehension of Hitler and the Third Reich within a traditionally acknowledged stream of history, had begun by the mid-1970s already in the public media, those arguments later abetting the developments. This happened on the right as well as on the left of the ideological spectrum. While the reasons are not entirely clear, it is noteworthy that on the left the impetus came from abroad, where different types of discourse regarding historicization prevailed, and on the right it arrived as part of the quest to seek new national meaning, provoked by left-radical terror. On the moderate left, West German audiences were persuaded to accept a television series about the Holocaust that was instigated in the United States, with British help. In moving detail, the four-part series featured the deplorable fate of a (fictional) Jewish Weiss family apposite a German Dorf family, which produced SS man Erich. Having premiered in America during April 1978, this NBC series was synchronized by WDR in Cologne and broadcast nationwide from January 1979. The film, although welcomed by center-left viewers and scores of young people, had to contend with bombings from neo-Nazis and other threats from the radical right.[80] In polite conservative society, *Die Welt* asked, preempting Andreas Hillgruber, why a depiction of the Holocaust did not take into account the mass expulsion of Germans from the east of Europe.[81]

Media historicization on the right occurred against the background of a so-called Hitler Wave, a new popular interest in things relating to Hitler, National Socialism, and the Third Reich, as the public was growing weary of the decades-long taboo that had surrounded those subjects. That the taboo was vanishing had to do with the new, younger generation of men and women without personal connection to those issues of the past, and also with the importation of images from abroad – especially in films from Hollywood where Nazis were, perhaps not heroes, but fascinating to watch or increasingly to read about in *Quick* or *Revue*, in particular if they were, defiantly, in Wehrmacht uniforms. Those movies gave pleasure, a guilty, sinful pleasure perhaps, because neither their elders nor teachers had told these younger Germans anything. In some circles this was becoming a fad and Hitler tokens were false memorabilia: it was chic to consider the imprisoned Rudolf Hess a nationalist martyr and wear swastikas on one's jeans; there was a boom in Nazi relics at flea markets; some adolescents traded recordings of Hitler speeches with their friends. Fascism became an entertainment commodity in talk and quiz shows, and it featured in mass-market novels. Obviously, in such elemental, often trivial pursuits the borderline to outright neo-Nazism was liable to be crossed, more or less mindlessly.[82]

Joachim Fest's motivation for a book he wrote and a film he codirected about Hitler from 1973 on did not stem from quite such a context, even though he shared the sentiment about worn-out taboos. He was, rather, driven by the circumstances of left-wing terrorism that dictated an increasing need for law and order and strong leadership, such as had existed in the Third Reich, ahistorically abstracting the human crimes. In his mammoth 1973 biography of Hitler, the first notable one since Alan Bullock's of 1952, the Führer appeared as ill-advised and ultimately wicked, but nevertheless as strong and a person of huge interest. Fest spoke of Hitler's "peculiar greatness" and his "guiding will," of a politician who might well have served as the model of an evil great man; evil yes, but nevertheless great and awesome, and certainly manly. About Hitler, Fest summarized, scarcely hiding admiration: "He thus altered the map of Europe, which had survived wars and changes in power, destroyed empires and helped new forces to rise up, caused revolutions and put an end to the colonial era; in the end he amplified the experiential horizon of mankind enormously."[83] Years later, Nolte judged that Fest had provided "an objective picture of the Third Reich and its Führer."[84]

As an aesthetic complement to his book, Fest codirected a film, *Hitler: Eine Karierre* (*Hitler: A Career*), screened in 1977. Archives for official Third Reich footage had been searched and films about Hitler's personal life acquired, for example about Eva Braun, from private sources. On the whole, the film serviced the current sentiment in West Germany for nostalgic trivia from thirty years ago, as film images were technically enhanced in reissues, polished, and endowed with even more vivid color and improved sound. For 150 minutes, the audiences' emotions in many movie theaters were stirred. Fest's film dwelt at great length "on mass adulation for the Führer, with shots of tearful women surging towards him in what seems partly religious and partly erotic ardor," wrote *The New York Times*.[85] Highlighting Hitler's talent for oratory, Fest had underlined his mass-democratic appeal by focusing on propagandist approaches and resultant reception from among the people – hence slyly relegitimizing Nazi rule. Hitler had been more than just a builder of autobahns, said Fest, with all those successes "that he gained beyond any doubt, after all."[86]

"The horror and the terror of Hitler's regime were not visible," was the publisher Helmut Kindler's first reaction upon viewing the picture.[87] *Der Spiegel*, while acknowledging that "this exceptional movie" had opened up new opportunities for a "filmic confrontation with the most recent German past," cautioned that Fest had engaged in a great-man portrayal that was at odds with the latest research that had gathered other evidence, such as social and institutional circumstances, to explain the phenomenon of the Hitler dictatorship.[88] Karl-Heinz Janssen went much further with his criticism. The new aural and visual enhancement technologies had re-emphasized Hitler's propagandistic appeal to influence a 1970s audience unduly in his favor, he charged, and Fest's avoidance of a moral judgment rendered the movie "dangerous." Fest had neglected a coverage of the Jews and their collective plight and had missed the opportunity for trenchant commentary on the murderous 1934 Röhm Purge. Overall, he had demonstrated an "astounding insecurity in judging all relationships, factors, and personalities, which did not belong to the more immediate area of Hitler, his existence or his actions."[89]

A most damning verdict came from Wim Wenders, who saw his educational work and that of his like-minded NGF colleagues imperiled by emotional and intellectual imbalances in the public consciousness Fest was helping to create. After taping the movie's soundtrack, he found that the commentator had been speaking demagogically in a manner much reminiscent of Nazi newsreels. Instead of explaining concentration camps, the film had conjured up sympathy with the criminal regime. Sadly, it was set to become the wrong kind of "monument" for crowds of Germans – here Wenders was anticipating the fears of progressive historians regarding the museums, ten years later.[90]

Exploiting the Hitler Wave, another young German filmmaker with right-wing leanings crafted the Führer's biography: Hans-Jürgen Syberberg. He was born in 1935 in Germany's East, as the son of a Pomeranian estate owner who displayed authoritarian traits similar to those of Bernward Vesper's father. Later, Syberberg junior expressed satisfaction over his father's sense of orderliness, authority, and obedience: this was what needed to be seen in society and its highest leaders.[91]

After learning filmmaking in the GDR and being influenced by Brecht, Syberberg continued in West Germany after 1953, where he shot a film about

Bavaria's King Ludwig II, besotted as he was with Richard Wagner.[92] He conceived it as a "declaration of war" against conventional film structures.[93] For in the movie Syberberg demonstrated an affinity with sublime kitsch as an artistic medium and loose, incoherently open forms of assemblage: these would become aesthetic trademarks of his future work. Continuing in a Wagnerian mold, he showed this again with a film portrayal of Winifred Wagner in 1975 that amounted to a frank admission of her greatness.[94] Enveloped by Richard Wagner's music, Frau Wagner ruminated for five hours about Hitler, and how he "literally smoothed the path" for her in Bayreuth: "If Hitler came through the door today, I would be as happy and pleased to see him here as always."[95] Now Syberberg became sold on Adolf Hitler also. He stressed the Bayreuth widow's importance as a "link in this chain of our historic aberrations, which we were forced to navigate."[96]

In 1977, when Syberberg made *Hitler, ein Film aus Deutschland* (*Hitler: A Film from Germany*), he appeared as a reborn, neo-Nietzschean Cultural Pessimist who abhorred the achievements of modernity, from a technological and social, political and artistic perspective. With a volatile temperament, he swung from exultation (in Wagner) to detestation (of plastic chairs or radio noise). Trendy materialist consumer attitudes toward civilization's cornucopias, as modern phenomena, were as worrisome today as had been concentration camps earlier. Syberberg professed to hate democracy, which merely produced "tired, cheap pluralism," holding that "in democracy lies our downfall." Monarchy or dictatorship was to be preferred, for only then could traditionalist values be upheld. Syberberg empathized with Hitler's early life as a rejected artist, betrayed as the current film industry was betraying him. Suffering his government then had to be accepted, because it was dictated by nature; Social Darwinism was incontrovertible: "To live, one has to kill," and, "it is bad that wars may not be waged anymore," for instance to recover his native Pomerania. About the SS guards he wrote that "one could not become soft on the Auschwitz ramps."[97]

Syberberg's film strove to be a Gesamtkunstwerk, as Hitler's Germany was supposed to have been, or Wagner's œuvre. The voices of Himmler and Goebbels sounded in overly long monologues, and Hitler was impersonated by ten different actors, played as Hamlet or Doctor Caligari. There were puppets, marionettes, ventriloquists, guiding to harrowing scenes, such as Hitler arising from Wagner's grave in a mist. The music of Wagner,

Beethoven, and Mozart – Hitler's favorites? – overflowed. Unhelpful, Syberberg expounded to receptive American reviewers: "It is not a film to entertain and to educate" and "it has no story in it, and it is no documentary." What then was its objective? "Catharsis," but for whom and of what? Syberberg did not say. He remained similarly equivocal on Hitler's key functions: "I give him a chance to express himself. I must defeat him with his own weapons."[98]

How to defeat Hitler aesthetically and exactly why? What was the moral purpose? Because Syberberg had conducted himself equally nebulously in Cannes where a short version of the film was shown in May 1977 and because of his customary arrogance, he earned a bad press from reviewers who had long been repulsed by his work. Syberberg recoiled, and instead of entering dialogue with his adversaries decided to withhold his film from the German market, especially since international prospects for it looked good. When Wolf Donner, then an executive at the Berlin film festival, entreated Syberberg to allow a showing at the upcoming Berlinade, the director, still sulking, wrote that he would withhold permission as long as the German film experts did not fully appreciate him.[99]

In the Anglo-Saxon countries just as in France, however, Syberberg's film was successful early because those countries' cultural traditions were not freighted with the problematic legacies of the Germans. Hitler and how to deal with him in retrospect was simply not their problem, but you could toss him around as in a modern video game for fun. As Anton Kaes has clarified, irrationalism in the German tradition, as in its culture, for instance Dada and early Expressionism, delighted foreigners, in particular the French. Revivified Romanticism, myth, and cosmic treatments of historic trends were therefore more than welcome, if at the expense of German would-be reformers such as Syberberg's cohorts in left-leaning NGF circles.[100]

In New York the movie was screened, with Hollywood director Coppola's help, in January 1980. Susan Sontag, who had just recently found good things to say about Leni Riefenstahl, was aglow with praise. A principled aestheticist, she called it a masterpiece and its creator a genius for "the scale and virtuosity with which he conjures up the ultimate subjects: hell, paradise lost, the apocalypse, the last days of mankind." She admired the film "as phantasmagoria," straight from Wagner, an "allegory-littered wasteland," where "carnivalesque skits alternate with arias and soliloquies, narratives, reveries," all of it "stripped-down and lush, discursive and spectacular." She liked the symbolism, the surrealist eclecticism, and the somnambulist qualities emanating from the director's young daughter Emily, a screen character. But on the moral-judgment side, Sontag admitted that the movie offered "very few ideas about Hitler." She appeared content that Syberberg echoed Friedrich Meinecke's immediate post-war judgment that Hitler had been singularly satanic, yet she also thought Hitler "the logical culmination of Western progress." She expanded on that by explaining sympathetically that Syberberg evoked "a kind of Hitler-substance that outlives Hitler, a phantom presence in modern culture, a protean principle of evil that saturates the present and remakes the past." Thus, she historicized the course of Hitler and Nazism as a parable not just in a nationalist-German, but a larger universal environment. One criticism Sontag did voice was that Syberberg's claim to "defeat" Hitler was his "grandest conceit," because he could not give anything up, trying ever new positions regarding the dictator and never finding closure. This implied a moral deficit in that the audience was at a loss how ultimately to judge Hitler and, by extension, acknowledge his guilt and their guilt. Still, this did not seem to be a great concern for her. Neither did the Jewish Sontag go so far as a Polish survivor of the Holocaust who, after seeing the film a few years later, said that "he could almost be tempted to become a Nazi himself" after "all those speeches, all that beautiful music."[101]

The German critics followed suit as the film was gradually shown in the Federal Republic from summer 1979 on. Already in July 1978, Hans C. Blumenberg, who had previewed it in Paris, had anticipated Sontag's aesthetic analysis with his impression that "in the end Hitler remains an unknown presence, the cruel god of an irrationalism that Syberberg himself internalizes."[102] Subsequent critics were harsher, especially since the attention-hungry director saw fit to resubmit many of his ideas in a companion volume.[103] Later statements of his assured that Syberberg remained an outcast from the West German film establishment. In 1980, Robert Jungk had accused him of using "the extermination of millions of Jews" merely as background against a historical spectacle, without empathy.[104] Syberberg thereafter became more vocal, saying that Hitler would never have risen to power without democracy, and the price for that had been

Auschwitz.[105] When by 1990 he insisted that "the pernicious legacy of Auschwitz" had crippled the German identity that was rooted in the German soil, he approximated Ernst Nolte.[106]

Closer to Michael Stürmer's imagining of a revival, of making visible a positive German legacy where traditional values counted, the crafts thrived, and human interrelationships were harmoniously ordered, was a more-than fifteen-hour television series with the programmatic title *Heimat*, by Edgar Reitz. Reitz was born in 1932 in Morbach in the Rhenish Palatinate, close to both Mainz and Trier. He related intimately to his birthplace's peasant population and their conventions, some still pre-industrial, medieval. In the early 1930s there was no electricity, no telephone or automobiles, and men and women did everything by hand.[107]

Reitz studied art history and theater in Munich until 1957, making short films by the end of the decade. In the mid-1960s he teamed up with Alexander Kluge as camera man for *Abschied von gestern*. He was already steeped in the new music of Cage, Kagel, and Stockhausen and familiar with the Donaueschingen festival. The Greek Modernist Niko Mamangakis became his principal film-music composer.[108]

An originator of the 1962 Oberhausen Manifesto and a pioneer of the NGF movement, Reitz made undistinguished films in the 1970s; on some, Kluge collaborated.[109] His *Heimat* series was to take place on his home ground; it was motivated by love of the animals, the country folk, the artist-craftsmen. He admired the *ordo* there; everyone had a "purpose in life."[110] Such memories of his own childhood were mixed with a lingering suspicion against everything American: Reitz sought a German counterpoint to the *Holocaust* series. His resentment against that production went deep. He linked it to a specifically American sense of aesthetics, a "terror" dictated by Hollywood and its materialistic value system, favoring commercialism. Hollywood studios ruled financially potent world-distribution systems to the disadvantage of weaker auteur producers. In content, the American treatment of the "race problem" was hypocritical, as in the *Bonanza* series, producing false emotions. In the *Holocaust* series, argued Reitz, compassion had been exploited through the treatment of the Jews, for the figures in that series were merely artificial constructions, typecast and "emotional cardboard dummies."[111]

The film, shot in the hamlet of Simmern for eighteen months, would have eleven instalments and last for almost sixteen hours. Altogether,

32 professional actors, 159 amateurs, and 3,863 extras were hired, including a local Roma woman, most of them speaking Palatian dialect. The series would follow the fate of the Simon family for three generations, starting in 1919, when Paul Simon comes walking from defeat at the Western Front to his parents' home, that of Katharina and Mathias Simon, the village smith. He eventually marries Maria Wiegand, who like him was born in 1900, the daughter of the richest farmer and mayor of the village, and they have two boys, Anton and Ernst. Paul is interested only in a radio set he is building (and the Roma Appolonia, who unaccountably vanishes). After ten uneventful years, he wanders off without explanation and resurfaces in America, where he founds an electronics empire. Meanwhile, his older brother Eduard has married a pushy Berlin brothel madam, whose shrill personality is lovingly integrated into the rural community. Schabbach, the fictional village, thrives with technological innovations, roads being built, more automobiles using them, and telephones ubiquitous. With the Third Reich this modernization boom intensifies. Maria has an affair with Otto Wohlleben, an engineer supervising road construction, from whom she gets pregnant. Men have Hitler mustaches and the prospering Eduard becomes a Nazi mayor. Maria's younger brother Wilfried, blond and movie-star handsome, joins the SS.[112]

During the war the action accelerates: Anton and Ernst are drafted but survive hostilities; Wohlleben falls victim to a field bomb. But combat spares the village; enemy planes are targeting Mainz. One day a British pilot in the meadows, his airplane crushed, is shot point-blank by Wilfried Wiegand, the darkest presence of the narrative. After May 1945, under French occupation, Paul Simon returns from Detroit in a vainglorious attempt to impress the villagers. He hopes to temporarily make out with Maria, who resists. He cannot explain why he left in 1928 without a word. The final episodes show the precarious careers of Anton and Ernst as middle-class entrepreneurs and musicians in West Germany's advancing economy. A careworn and embittered Maria, left to her own devices, withers to her death in 1982. Ultimately, the – once large – family falls apart; the technical advances brought in the wake of modernity, spurred first by the Nazi regime and then Americanization, destroy bucolic Heimat.[113]

The film was shown on ARD television in autumn 1984, to a total of 25 million viewers.[114] The German response was enthusiastic about this pictorial alternative to *Holocaust*, a corrective, a proper retrospective. The series matched Germans' renewed interest in their fatherland, in glorious Prussian history, the place of the Third Reich in an acceptable legacy, which made it part of the Hitler Wave. *Heimat* themes even correlated with the environmentalist platform of the emergent Green Party.[115] After screenings at the Venice Biennale, London, and Los Angeles the film became a cineastic milestone.[116] In New York, after its showing at the Museum of Modern Art in April 1985, Reitz was compared to Fassbinder. "'Heimat' is no 'Holocaust'," observed *The New York Times*. "It's not about guilt, but neither does it excuse anybody. One is always aware of the increasing persecution of the Jews during the 1930s."[117] As accurate as those first statements were, as misleading was the reviewer's observation about Jews.

Notwithstanding much praise, the film was, in parts, technically flawed and contained many historic falsehoods. Across the sections, the change in physical appearance of the children to adulthood, for example, was so badly done, with the use of three actors each for Anton and Ernst, that often they were not recognizable and their stories not credible. Paul Simon is refused entry to the port of Hamburg when he wishes to revisit his hometown in 1939, because he is suspected of being Jewish, but his brother Eduard is already an SA leader and the Nazi mayor of Schabbach, and there is a well-known Gauleiter in that very area called Gustav Simon – supposedly a Jewish name.[118] Schabbach's own, Hänschen Betz, is recruited to the Wehrmacht as a sniper because, having lost an eye as a child, he is believed ideally suited, when no person with his sight so challenged would have been admissible to the colors.

Because, in contradistinction to *Holocaust*, in his film Reitz wanted to show a Germany that was fundamentally intact and fitted smoothly into a larger, respectable national narrative, he presented negative influences of the Third Reich as merely peripheral to Schabbach. A concentration camp is discovered by Betz on his bicycle by chance, but it is far from the village, he is unmoved by it, and he keeps quiet. The inmates there are observed to work as any prison captives might, outside in the fresh air, adequately dressed in striped uniforms and doing useful chores. The film audience learns that they are sent there to be straightened out and re-educated, as is a Communist about to be taken from his flat after a raid by police, yet the flat is not in Schabbach but in the Ruhr Valley's Bochum, where detestable

Communism has traditionally been strong. The arrest is witnessed by the visiting Katharina Simon, but she never mentions the incident back home. On the Eastern Front, Anton films the illegal shooting of partisans, an action he abhors, but this is taking place as an aberration and far away from Schabbach. Even the murder of the British pilot on the village outskirts is understandable, for viewers will remember the "terror flyers" that bombed Bremen, Dresden, and nearby Mainz merely as criminals.[119]

Anything having to do with Hitler and his politics is rendered so as to take away any threat, as in scenes where SA mayor Eduard Simon acts silly and the newly fashionable Hitler mustaches are a comic's requisites. Hitler's takeover on January 30, 1933 comes across as operetta or like the annual carnival, and a Hitler celebration later in the village, comparing him with Columbus, is downright cartoonish. If it is correct to convey that the German countryside, especially if Catholic, was not as touched by Nazism as were urban centers, already observed in the case of Walser's Wasserburg, this does not mean it was not touched at all. After all, Reitz did subtitle his film *Eine deutsche Chronik* (*A German Chronicle*), implying that what he was showing there applied, beyond a rural isolated part, to *all* of Germany. After viewing the film it was possible to believe that, judging by Schabbach's example alone, the Nazis and their regime could not have been so bad anywhere in the land.

If there were victims of politics and war, they were always Germans; here Reitz paid homage to the long-established German martyrs' cult.[120] This leaves Reitz's discussion of the Jews in Germany, as they defined the country's history essentially before and beyond Auschwitz. What about Auschwitz? asked Timothy Garton Ash; there was an obfuscation of atrocities, claimed Saul Friedländer.[121] Although Reitz knew well that anti-Semitism was a groundswell in his region by tradition, he placed no Jews in his movie village.[122] Very briefly, a Jewish banker, obviously under pressure by the mid-1930s, is seen in Mainz, and when the naked body of a woman is found in the woods, one villager casually mentions that a Jew could have committed the murder. That the partisans Anton films could have been Jews (as they often were) is not probed, much less ascertained, and nowhere is there a mention of Jews in camps. Only SS officer Wilfried darkly alludes to "chimneys" that Jews might have to pass through as part of the Final Solution, in 1943, but it is a boast out of context made during a wedding celebration to his disbelieving sister-in-law and Wehrmacht officers, who were often informed or complicit.[123] Rendered incoherently, the comment could scarcely have made sense to a 1984 audience, and it went unmentioned by the critics.

◆ ◆ ◆

Increased popular interest in Hitleriana, floating on top of the Hitler Wave, led to developments in the German media that were hardly associable with serious debates about National Socialism in history, carried out at arcane levels. For more often than not, even if they originated at the same source of patriotic curiosity in the nation's past, they were driven by greed and a hankering for sensationalism. The most notorious of such cases involved Hitler's alleged diaries. It may have been a hoax, but it demonstrated commercial interest in Hitler myth exploitation, on the assumption that millions were still, or again, fascinated by the bygone Führer. For that reason, it deserves attention.

The main perpetrator in the story of the forged Hitler diaries that were shown publicly in a *Stern* press release on April 25, 1983, was Konrad Kujau, who was living in Stuttgart in the early 1970s as a petty forger. A devotee of Nazism from his youth, he trained himself by copying text from Hitler's *Mein Kampf* and then soaked it in tea to make it look old. At that time he came to meet Gerd Heidemann, a *Stern* journalist with a penchant for war, scandal, and the Third Reich, who had become romantically involved with Göring's thirty-four-year-old daughter Edda.[124] As Kujau turned to fabricating what he claimed were original Hitler diaries, Heidemann became interested in featuring these – a fantastic coup – in the pages of *Der Stern*.

By the early 1980s *Stern* executives, still including the retiring Henri Nannen, had allowed Heidemann to start acquiring the forgeries, putting at his disposal hundreds of thousands of marks for Kujau. At the end of 1981 eighteen so-called diary volumes had been received in the magazine's editorial offices, millions of marks had changed hands, and Heidemann himself was exhibiting a lavish lifestyle. Experts from the Bundesarchiv judged the forgeries genuine, and internationally, *Newsweek*, *Time*, *Paris Match*, and newspapers owned by Rupert Murdoch were keen to mass-publish translations.

During a *Stern* press conference in Hamburg on April 25, 1983, serialization of the diaries was announced; Murdoch's *Sunday Times* had begun publication two days before. But now the first critical voices were being heard, one of them belonging to David Irving, an amateur historian and, later, a notorious Holocaust denier. Notwithstanding those, *Stern* printed Hitler's purported views on 1938 Kristallnacht, Hess's 1941 flight to England, and the Holocaust on April 28. Later in May, as Bundesarchiv archivists reconsidered, diary samples were examined in a Zurich safe and ultimately found to be bogus. On May 26, Kujau fully confessed; both he and Heidemann were arrested for fraud, while the *Stern* executives were millions of marks out of pocket.[125]

During an August 1984 trial for both men in Hamburg, which sentenced them to prison terms, it was clear that the magazine had lost much prestige. History professors, who had first vouched for the diaries' authenticity and then recanted – they were Hugh Trevor-Roper of Cambridge, Gerhard L. Weinberg of the University of North Carolina, and Eberhard Jäckel of Stuttgart – were temporarily compromised, as they appeared to have been motivated by a craving for fame and material profit.[126]

This was the unhappy story about the most important Hitler document that never was. There was another story playing out on the mid-1980s Frankfurt stage, about a play that was not played, a play by Rainer Werner Fassbinder who had died a few years previously. Like the Hitler diary narrative, this story too originated in the 1970s.

By the middle of that decade, Fassbinder had completed a drama with a delicate topic, involving a rich post-1945 Frankfurt real-estate-owning Jew, a prostitute, and a sado-masochist pimp, among other bizarre characters such as corrupt detectives, spiteful dwarves, and gay leather fetishists. It was called *Der Müll, die Stadt und der Tod* (*Garbage, the City and Death*) and was offered in 1975 to Siegfried Unseld for print by Suhrkamp. Unseld published it early in March 1976, but after a criticism of the book by Fest in the *FAZ* a few days later withdrew it from distribution, unless an unwilling Fassbinder made changes.[127] More tamely, other critics followed Fest.[128] In 1981 the play was printed by a minor press; it remained unperformed by Fassbinder.[129] Frankfurt's Jewish community leader Ignatz Bubis was opposed: as a successful real-estate speculator he had reason to believe that Fassbinder had singled him out as a model for the Jew.

Apart from aesthetics, Unseld declined the manuscript because of the central character of the Jew and possible charges of anti-Semitism.[130] There was debate whether Fassbinder had intended the piece to be anti-Semitic or had merely attempted to depict (and censure?) anti-Semitism – not an easy question because the contrarian Fassbinder had cheekily used code in his title to keep his audience guessing. "Garbage" was associable with slum-lordship, "the city" was where most Jews traditionally thrived (at whose expense? What about Frankfurt, where most post-war Jews of West Germany had moved?), and "death" was what deep-seated popular prejudice said Jews often brought, as in ritual murder.

Fassbinder's topic was about The Rich Jew whose parents had perished in the Holocaust and who dealt risk-takingly in Frankfurt real estate, becoming very wealthy. Not without qualms: "Business is going too well, that must be punished," says the masochistic Jew, admitting a bad conscience. "I buy old houses in this town, tear them down, and build new ones, which I sell at a profit." In this business "I have to remain indifferent to the crying of children, to the suffering of the old and the infirm." In the brothel, its customer Hans von Gluck, representing the people's voice, sees in this a crime: "He is sucking us dry, the Jid. He drinks our blood and puts us in the wrong, because he is a Jid and we bear the guilt." "The Jid is at fault, because he makes us guilty, for he is here. Had he remained where he comes from, or had they gassed him, I could sleep better today. They forgot to gas him." Here von Gluck put into words the sentiment of prevailing German alt-Nazis, however few, that the Jews were at fault for having caused Auschwitz and that not enough of them had been exterminated. Auschwitz remains a theme when later the ex-SS leader Müller enters, in order to explain: "I did not care about everyone I killed, I was no individualist. I am a technocrat." And again later: "It is not a burden to be the murderer of Jews, if one possesses the convictions that I have . . . Fascism will win." At the end of the play the tubercular sex worker Roma B., Müller's daughter, who finds life unbearable, asks her beloved Rich Jew to relieve her of her suffering by killing her, and he then strangles her with his necktie but makes certain someone else is arrested for the crime.[131] According to some, Fassbinder ultimately showed that the Jew fulfilled age-old prophecies by dispensing death.

During an intense debate regarding anti-Semitism many argued that from his core Fassbinder did not hate Jews.[132] Fassbinder himself said so, and as he expounded on the issue, he maintained that in West Germany

many anti-Semites were hiding beneath a mask of philo-Semitism, which could be regarded as a new type of anti-Semitism and in the end would turn out just as lethal. This is what he had tried to show in his play, to the point where the "good" Jew who killed out of love turned into an anti-Semite himself, because in reality he hated Jews who dealt in real estate. Fassbinder pleaded honesty when he declared that it was important to acknowledge that there *were* Jewish real-estate speculators in Frankfurt, as he had himself experienced them, and that it was right to describe them. To depict anti-Semitism in a play, suggested Fassbinder, was not the same as professing anti-Semitism as a belief system.[133]

Those who thought this a specious argument maintained that Fassbinder was indeed an anti-Semite, coming from an extreme-left direction (like "leftist Fascists" within the RAF). Some thought this stemmed from his childhood immediately after the war, when his mother had told him to be nice to Jews whenever they crossed his path.[134] Zadek asserted from much personal experience that Fassbinder's anti-Semitism was "simple, brutal and existential."[135] Others pointed to the fact that Fassbinder had portrayed Jews negatively in his films – the Swiss Mendelssohn family in *Lili Marleen*, the morphine-dispensing physician Marianne Katz in *Veronika Voss*,[136] or Helmut Salomon, who torments his wife until he has her in a wheelchair in *Martha*. Before Fassbinder's death this issue could not be resolved, but the shrewdest minds agreed that even if he had not been anti-Semitic, he had created an aura in his stage drama that made it possible for anti-Semitic onlookers to feel reinforced.[137] As late as the 1980s critics likened this to the same affect that right-radicals experienced who read Nolte.[138]

By that time there had been another serious attempt to stage the play in Frankfurt. In 1985, Günther Rühle, the newly appointed director of the municipal theater, decided to put it on at its Kammerspiele, against the advice of city officials and the Jewish congregation, whose chairman was Ignatz Bubis.[139] Others, such as director Peter Palitzsch, had tried before and not been successful. One of those now in favor, despite qualitative scruples, was Zadek, who stated that Fassbinder had never concealed his "great difficulties with Jews."[140] The public premiere was set for October 31. The Rich Jew was to be portrayed as a slender, elegant Nordic type, not the caricature shown in the Nazi film *Jud Süss*. But on that day twenty-five members of the Jewish congregation occupied the stage, joined by Bubis, and unfurled a banner that read "Subsidized Anti-Semitism," so that no performance was possible, and none was attempted thereafter, except for a closed staging for the press, on November 4.[141]

Before that day, the culture critic Ulrich Greiner had a conversation with Bubis. It was known that Bubis, aged fifty-eight, had been taken, with his father, to the ghetto of Polish Deblin as a teenager in 1941, where the Judenrat appointed him postman. With everyone in his family murdered, Bubis was able to get to Soviet-occupied Saxony after the end of the war. In Dresden, he became conspicuous on the black market. Prosecuted by the KGB, he fled to West Berlin, where he dealt in gold and jewelry, and moved to Frankfurt in 1956, where his business became real estate. In conversation, Bubis found Greiner's question whether Eastern Jews had monopolized the Frankfurt real-estate scene absurd. He was against Fassbinder's piece because he thought it "weak and anti-Semitic" and well suited to support a new, hidden anti-Semitism.[142]

The Kammerspiele's aborted performance has been called West Germany's biggest theater scandal of the 1980s. There was one to match it in television that played out late in the decade. It involved TV's famous talk-show host Werner Höfer, who lost his job as a result of it in December 1987. The affair had a prehistory going back to autumn 1943. Journalist Höfer, then a thirty-year-old NSDAP member, published an article in *Das 12-Uhr Blatt*, a popular Nazi paper in Berlin. It was entitled "Artist – Example and Paragon" and warned against culture creators in the Reich who brought about "doubts instead of faith, defamation instead of trust, and desperation instead of fortitude." It referred to Ernst Robert Kreiten, a young pianist, who just previously had been hanged at Berlin-Plötzensee after listening to the BBC and then talking to his Nazi landlady, who reported him.[143] In those days, Höfer regularly roused Germans in the spirit of Nazism and demanded from them, in other articles across the Reich, a determined resistance against the enemy from without and within, especially after the loss of Stalingrad. Höfer denounced "terror attacks" by the Allies, and for cultural uplifting promoted the work of Nazi poet Josef Weinheber in the same breath as he condemned the Jewish poet Heinrich Heine. It was important for national culture to show its flag even among displays of destruction, effused Höfer, as long as concerted efforts by all Germans led to a final victory.[144]

After surviving Wehrmacht and U.S. POW camp, Höfer, like many journalists who had worked in the Third Reich – Carl Linfert, Giselher Wirsing, and Friedrich Sieburg come to mind – accommodated himself to the new post-war conditions easily because he was needed. Playing by the rules of democracy, he preferred siding with the powers that be, often conservative ones. After perfunctory denazification he was hired by the incipient NWDR in Cologne in 1946. Still under British supervision he was appointed head of the current-affairs department, and his international discussion roundtable commenced on the airwaves in 1952.[145] From there his rise was unstoppable; he became wealthy and eventually mingled with the glitterati in exclusive Kampen. Rising quickly in the WDR's hierarchy, he emerged as the Federal Republic's most popular public-affairs journalist in 1970.[146] His list of show guests was kaleidoscopic: Rudolf Augstein, Ulrike Meinhof, Joachim Fest. In 1973 he received the Great Order of Merit from Bonn.[147] His tireless efforts decidedly contributed to TV's success over film in the 1970s, and radio also benefited.[148]

Höfer was unabashedly a cultural reactionary who hated Modernist art forms such as jazz, and a staunch Cold Warrior, knowing full well that on the conservative side in the Western camp former Nazis would have little to fear. Thus, he supported the entrance of Spain into NATO even under the dictatorship of Franco in 1959.[149] Later he defended Federal President Heinrich Lübke against charges by, among others, Henri Nannen, of collaboration with concentration-camp planners.[150] Because those charges had originated in the GDR, Höfer visibly positioned himself against it. This helped him when in 1962 functionaries from East Germany were the first to raise the issue of Höfer's role after the death of Kreiten. Höfer was alerted, but he brushed accusations aside with ease, claiming that the passages in question had been written by Nazi officials. He knew that having to fend off charges from the GDR was considered an honor in West German right-wing circles, hence he prevailed.[151]

These charges resurfaced in 1987 in the editorial offices of *Der Spiegel* because of increased public interest in the Third Reich since the late 1970s – the same interest that had produced the Syberberg film, the Fest film, the Heimat TV series, the *Historikerstreit*, and the faked Hitler diaries, albeit at varying aesthetic and ideological levels. When the news magazine published its article on December 14, 1987, the tainted journalist at first went to court. Failing this, he maintained, as he had before, that the original copy of his essay had been redacted by the editors of *Das 12-Uhr Blatt*. But because he was simultaneously confronted with other published pieces of this kind, his defenses were soon down.[152] He conceded that in 1943 he should have done more to prevent the editorial manipulation, adding that during the Third Reich he had done everything possible to remain clean, in order to get through it with his family, "within a system that one could not change and with whatever you could just get away with." When the WDR directors asked him to resign, he argued that since the 1950s he had done his share to further democracy – by developing television and facilitating international understanding. In late December his show was replaced by a new one, *Presseclub*. It was staffed with younger German journalists and alternating moderators without a Nazi past.[153]

◆ ◆ ◆

As were film and drama, literature in the 1980s was thinning out. What had happened? For one, the 1970s had been exceptionally fertile in all the arts, perhaps spurred on by threats of terror. In a dialectical process the following decade could not measure up. Secondly, especially in literature the absence of even a loosely organized group such as Gruppe 47 since the late 1960s increasingly made itself felt. Left more alone, authors played less of a public role than they had in the 1960s (as had Böll) and did not mix with party politics (as did Grass). Thirdly, book sales were threatened by changes in the publishing and distribution industry, with computer electronics cutting in, shifts in bookstore sizes, and potential taxes from an anti-intellectual establishment in Bonn.[154] And fourthly, there were some personnel changes. Wolfgang Hildesheimer, a co-founder of Gruppe 47, declared the end of fiction in 1975 and wrote his last novel, *Marbot*, in 1981, before dying of a heart attack in 1991. Already in the second half of the 1980s, important authors such as Böll, Andersch, and Weiss were no longer alive. Some argue that in the 1980s ecological problems weighed on creative minds, especially after the atomic-reactor crisis of Chernobyl in 1986. There arrived a new uncertainty in the arts, with words such as "postmodern," "post-history," "post-structural" and "post-experimental" being bandied about – none of which was seen to have ushered in a newly definable era that bestowed surety. As established pillars of the literary scene such as Walser and Grass, now older, were experienced not as firebrands but, rather, more as staid traditionalists, the names of younger authors surfaced, unproven but not without chances. Unlike the Enzensbergers and Walsers, this new generation was born in the 1940s and 1950s, and some, like Peter Schneider, were veterans of the 1968 student movement. The great majority were epigonic, with names that could not withstand the test of time: Bodo Kirchhoff, Jochen Beyse, and Erwin Enzinger, who had flash successes. Christoph Ransmayr composed literature within the media imaginings Marshall McLuhan was known for, and Ingomar von Kieseritzky employed comedy in a destructive fashion – his books advanced to cult status, but he did not become an eternal. Rainald Goetz, who deliberately cut his forehead open with a razor blade during a reading at an Ingeborg Bachmann contest in Klagenfurt in 1983, in order to allow his "brain to seep out," swore by the "revolutionary potential of insanity." His entire neo-Expressionist style was labelled "postmodern."[155] The 1980s in literature? Apart from a few small gems, it was an "age of fragments," judged *Die Zeit*.[156]

There was no significant women's literature scene either, certainly not one liberating women, despite attempts in the previous decade to create it; female authors such as Karin Reschke, Saskia Vesper, and Angelika Stark did not make waves. A remarkable but isolated exception was Brigitte Kronauer, born in 1940. Having worked first as a schoolteacher, she became well known especially with her novel *Rita Münster*, which in large part told the story of her own life. She was lauded for her gift of keen observation, exact language, and realistic storytelling in the manner of Jean Paul. Fritz J. Raddatz attested her "language musicality" and "hallucinatory power." Kronauer received the Theodor Fontane Prize in 1985 and the Heinrich Böll Prize in 1989.[157]

One of the severest critics of the 1980s literary scene, not surprisingly, was Marcel Reich-Ranicki. As was his wont, he ventured a global assessment about the state of literature in the Federal Republic in an article of October 1980 in the *FAZ*. He charged that latterly the products of lyricists and novelists had become "provincial," made fun of Suhrkamp's pioneering but venal publisher Siegfried Unseld, and attacked his favorite targets Böll, Walser, and Grass for their novels, which he felt "aim to achieve a lot – and therefore achieve too little." As he had done repeatedly in the past, he lauded Wolfgang Koeppen, whose first three books in the 1950s had not been well received and who then had stopped writing. Again trying to influence the market, he singled out for praise Sarah Kirsch, originally from the GDR but residing in the Federal Republic since 1977, Günter Kunert, and Christoph Neckel, promising authors who would get stuck in the middle ground. He also praised Patrick Süskind, whose novel *Das Perfüm* indeed would outsell Grass's *Blechtrommel* in the 1990s. Yet he failed to recognize other exceptions, among them Bernhard Schlink. Therefore, with imprecise but doctrinaire analyses, this man of letters was himself contributing to the current literary malaise.[158]

He continued this course one year later, when on the occasion of the Frankfurt book fair he praised a small volume of poetry by Ulla Hahn, so that it reached a publication volume of 18,000, phenomenal for a lyricist, within a very short time. Hahn had been born in 1945 as the daughter of an unskilled worker and had achieved a doctorate in literature in straitened circumstances before marrying into one of West Germany's most illustrious families. She became the wife of Klaus von Dohnányi, whose father Hans von Dohnányi, an Austro-Hungarian aristocrat and the brother-in-law of Dietrich Bonhoeffer, had been executed by the Nazis in 1945 as a member of Bonhoeffer's Christian-motivated resistance circle. Currently, Klaus von Dohnányi was lord mayor of the state of Hamburg and a member of the German upper house in Bonn; his brother was the conductor Christoph von Dohnányi.

Hahn's *Herz über Kopf* (*Heart over Head*) poetry collection was published by Deutsche Verlags-Anstalt in Stuttgart, soon to print Reich-Ranicki's own memoirs. In the last sentence of his review, Reich-Ranicki remarked contentedly that "these days German poems are still able to reflect beauty." It was the beauty of kitsch, however, which henceforth other critics indicted, conceding that Hahn was able to compose "pretty" poems, but nothing in the range of Hölderlin or Rilke – hence she too was strictly epigonic. "Ulla Hahn is not a great lyricist," summarized Ulrich Greiner, "she is sticking to her trade and earning an honest livelihood. That is not enough."[159] Yet Reich-Ranicki insisted on defending his judgment as late as 1989.[160]

Nobel laureate Böll died in 1985, his illnesses complicated by tobacco and alcohol – legacies of World War II. In the last years of his life he hobbled around on crutches after his feet had been affected, as Walser keenly observed.[161] Turning away from the issues of the left-radical RAF (he became instead a staunch supporter of the Green Party), Böll concerned himself more with democracy behind the Iron Curtain and elsewhere. In 1982 he protested against conditions in Poland, where martial law had been imposed after General Wojciech Jaruzelski's military coup. A year later he demanded freedom for his colleague Andrei Sakharov, who was held by Soviet authorities. He also joined others in a campaign against the Americans, who were attempting to overthrow the left-of-center Sandinista government in Nicaragua. And he always opposed U.S. plans to augment nuclear missiles stationed on German soil. He did not want for honors. After the Nobel Prize of 1972 he received an American book-of-the-month citation and the Danish Jens Bjørneboe Prize; he was also offered the Order of Merit of the Federal Republic, which he rejected, because of his abiding disapproval of what he considered to be reactionary Bonn politics. But he agreed to be made an honorary citizen of Cologne and a *commandeur* in the *Ordre des Arts et des Lettres* by the French government. Böll was released from yet another hospital visit on July 15, 1985, being told that he would need more surgery. He died the next day.[162] Two obituaries from the *FAZ* three days later acknowledged him as a civic leader, but had next to nothing to say about him as a writer.[163]

Indeed, Böll's solitary work of the 1980s worthy of mention was *Frauen vor Flusslandschaft* (*Women in a River Landscape*) of 1985, which was not well received.[164] Once again he wanted to pay tribute to women whose men were despicable and were, above all, former Nazis. With this, Böll, who had left the Catholic Church in 1976, with harsh brushstrokes wanted to tarnish the Federal Republic and its establishment, forever emergent from the Third Reich and which he saw as exclusively male, in contrast to the innocent women it oppressed. The book consisted mostly of monologues and dialogues – a scenic novel, in character much like Koeppen's *Treibhaus* (1953). Böll, in a bitter, unforgiving mood, revisited the worst crimes of the Germans among whom he was living when he excoriated Auschwitz: "Where have they gone, the money and the hair and the gold from the very last gold tooth, where is it all? Who took cash for the soap they manufactured from the bodies, and for the hair, from which they fashioned mattresses?"[165] The novel received, politely, neutral mentions and some tough reviews. Reinhard Baumgart experienced it as a "mixed bag," Kaiser as the final, less than convincing, work of a dying man, and Raddatz was overawed by "this much dilettantism."[166]

However, as the last in a long line of time-critical works over decades, today the book makes eminent sense.[167]

Günter Grass was a casualty of the creativity hiatus that haunted many literati after the German Autumn of 1977. In his case, he was disabused of the notion that politics could wreak societal change, in particular SPD politics that he had previously fought for. Disappointed after Brandt's fall as chancellor in 1974, he remained removed from Helmut Schmidt. Earlier hopes were not fulfilled, for example for a national endowment to care for cultural artifacts, including relics from the German East.[168] As Reich-Ranicki mischievously told Grass later: "Willy Brandt sought your advice – and soon disappointed you bitterly. For he needed you as long as he was fighting for power – and when he became federal chancellor, he did not care to have you around anymore. Am I wrong to assume that you have never really got over this?"[169] The critic was not wrong. To the extent that Brandt complained to an aide that Grass was getting increasingly "on his nerves," Grass rued the widening estrangement, even if the ex-chancellor offered solace when critics were forsaking him.[170]

Nonetheless, Grass adhered to his left-political principles, regardless of the politics in Bonn, in a manner that evoked respect. In December 1992 he renounced his ten-year membership of the SPD on account of a change in the Basic Law that made it more difficult for foreigners to seek asylum in the FRG. The Social Democrats had approved the Kohl cabinet's judgment in this – a stance Grass could not countenance.[171] During the 1987 federal election campaign, which Kohl ultimately won, Grass had supported the SPD only reluctantly.[172]

Whatever his difficulties with that party, Grass continued to uphold two principles. As was the traditional position of most left-wingers, he believed that the two Germanys should not reunite politically. Rightly or wrongly, he argued that the GDR had developed appreciably since 1949, in the direction of a true democracy, in contrast to its western neighbor, which had clung to reactionary politics, shown through its harboring of old Nazis.[173] In 1961, Grass had protested against the fencing-in of the East German population by a Berlin Wall; by 1990, instead of unification, he advocated a sort of confederation of equal parts, as enjoyed by Swiss cantons. This friend of East German novelist Christa Wolf saw both German halves as allyable cultural nations.[174] Such conviction was tied to his second belief, namely that the FRG had to digest, had to process Auschwitz, even if this appeared insurmountable. Here he approximated the progressive position in the *Historikerstreit*. In New York during 1986 he said that it was incumbent on the intelligentsia "to grapple with the meaning of the Holocaust four decades after the fact." "Auschwitz becomes bigger and bigger, larger and larger. It grows and grows. It will never be understandable."[175] And in 1990 he unequivocally stated (contradicting Kohl) that he and his cohort colleagues belonged "to the Auschwitz generation," not as perpetrators per se, "but in the camp of perpetrators."[176] He echoed this in his Nobel Prize acceptance speech in 1999 when he said that "Auschwitz marks a rift, an unbridgeable gap in the history of civilization."[177]

As an author, Grass was trying to separate those Auschwitz images from his persona, as he had chosen to elide writing from his life in the first half of the 1980s. He concentrated instead on the first of the arts he had mastered – sculpture and drafting, learned at academies in Berlin and Düsseldorf. In 1982 he was famous enough to be the subject of a festival in New York, with "Günter Grass in Performance" staged at Manhattanville College, assisted financially by the New York Goethe House. There were exhibits depicting The Flounder from his eponymous novel of 1977 (*Der Butt*), prints of a self-portrait, heads of women – one with a moth on her forehead, another almost masked by a crayfish. Prints that, "with their implications of dazzling white light, their sinuous but firm lines and their textures that range from rich black hatching to a delicate gray stipple worthy of Aubrey Beardsley, are strange in the way that the works of Arnold Böcklin, Otto Runge and Max Klinger are strange": thus wrote Vivien Raynor in *The New York Times*.[178] Grass was always a lesser playwright, but his play *Flood* was performed in translation later in 1986, by the Project III Ensemble Theater on Broadway. Based on the Book of Genesis and starring Noah, it had been written in the 1950s. The play was "no exemplar of a well-made play; the action is sporadic, the characterization rudimentary," wrote Walter Goodman in the *Times*. The plot was such as to suggest "a timeless reality, so that the tossed off allusions to Hitler and Saigon startle us into connecting the eternal story of Noah with the catastrophes of our time."[179]

Grass's creative hiatus lasted for three years before he was able to begin work on his next novel after *Der Butt*, which curiously was called *Die Rättin* (*The She-Rat*). Again, as he had in earlier books, this gourmet cook resorted to mostly small animals for allegory, those one could eat and those one could not eat – the aquarium fish Oskar Matzerath sets free with his high-pitched scream and the eels from the dead horse's maw, not to mention the pickled fish that kill Oskar's mother Agnes, in *Die Blechtrommel*; the crafty German shepherd Wolf in *Hundejahre*; the sacrificial dachshund Max in *Örtlich betäubt*; and the imperturbable snail in *Tagebuch einer Schnecke*. According to Grass, in the animal world things could be made so much clearer than in the human cosmos, and those animals were smarter: the she-rat and her ratty cohorts survive atomic malfeasance caused by humans bent ineluctably on self-destruction.

Grass published *Die Rättin* in 1986; it was serialized, in part, in *Die Zeit*.[180] Old acquaintances from earlier works appeared, such as Oskar Matzerath, who, now fifty-nine, poses as a media mogul in a heavy Mercedes with chauffeur. There are his grandmother Anna, his mistress Maria, and their presumed son Kurtchen. In addition, implements and accoutrements of the 1950s show up – a three-wheeled Messerschmitt KR200 Kabinenroller, films such as *Die Sünderin* with Hildegard Knef, Elvis Presley's hit record "The Great Pretender," and an iconic Braun record player. A novel montage structure impeded the narrative flow; stories, essays, and lyrics were mixed; autobiographical sequences followed fictive elements – all in a "postmodern" semantic. Apart from the super-intelligent rats who survive the atomic apocalypse, Helmut Kohl (whom Grass hated) acts in it, as do men from the White House and the Kremlin, and five ecologically minded German ladies attend to their knitting and make trivial conversation. Even the Grimm brothers and their fairy-tale figures make a cameo appearance.

It was "a catastrophic book," judged Reich-Ranicki in *FAZ*, a "monstrous brainchild," found Peter Engel in *Rhein-Zeitung*. Wolfram Schütte of *Frankfurter Rundschau* now considered Grass to be "in good company, among the failures." Joachim Kaiser of *Süddeutsche Zeitung*, more cautiously, was not sure whether this was a novel or an essay, but perhaps a nightmare stuffed with too many ghouls. Even though *The New York Times* thought it "brilliant," the novel, unsurprisingly, did poorly commercially, and after its completion, Grass felt destroyed by the critics; exhausted, he considered giving up writing altogether.[181] All the same, in 1987, Günter Grass was, uncontested at home and abroad as the "most prominent author of the Federal Republic."[182]

During the 1980s, Martin Walser did not undergo an extended creative pause as did Grass, nor was his writing restricted in quantity as was Böll's. Rather, to the extent of qualitative detraction, he mirrored personal anxiety in his two most important new novels, *Brandung* (*Surf*, 1985) and *Jagd* (*Hunt*, 1987). The main motifs of both novels are resignation and restlessness. Those are the anxieties of a man getting old, Walser alias Helmut Halm in the first title, alias Gottlieb Zürn in the second, always reaching back to Anselm Kristlein of the author's confounding trilogy of decades past. Walser, going on sixty and still obsessed with bestseller lists, obviously feared decay.[183] Hence in the novels, he is jogging endlessly as Halm in *Brandung*, and as Zürn in *Jagd* he is swimming wildly against the horizon, braving the waves of Lake Constance. In *Brandung*, Halm/Walser lectures at a U.S. West Coast college and, neglecting his wife Sabine, falls in love with the student Fran, failing at a sexual relationship. Zürn/Walser in *Jagd* constantly flees his home on the lake, absconding to the city to seek futile sexual adventure. Both Halm and Zürn are frustrated in their jobs, Halm as a Gymnasium teacher in Stuttgart and Zürn as a delinquency-prone realtor.[184]

Walser, more than his two great colleagues, was always able to project his own disposition onto literary characters, but through them could also reveal his closest relationships, intimate ones or with peers. He had shown this when he portrayed Siegfried Unseld as the denture manufacturer Thiele in *Jenseits der Liebe* and resurrected him in a lesser novel of the decade, *Brief an Lord Liszt* (*Letter to Lord Liszt*) of 1982. Here Liszt again represents Uwe Johnson (as he did in *Jenseits*), to whom Walser continued to be tied in a love–hate relationship, not least because, in 1978, Johnson had refused to nominate him for a prize and always vied with him for Unseld's patronage. Johnson resurfaced, one year after his suicide, as Rainer Mersjohann, in the unreconciled Walser's book *Brandung*, where he kills himself, as Johnson killed himself with alcohol. Mersjohann is described, most unfavorably, as "fat, with bluish sagging cheeks and colorless beardlike hair hanging onto them, and a double chin," as Wieland Freund criticized in *Die Welt*.[185]

Not conducive to his stability, Walser continued to have near-paranoid relationships with colleagues and critics. He lashed out at the defenseless Böll who had beaten him to the Nobel Prize by including a passage in *Brief an Lord Liszt* in which Liszt/Johnson receives a novel by Böll. Walser writes that the book was given to Liszt by a hairdresser in Castrop-Rauxel, an ill-reputed coal-mining town in the Ruhr, and Liszt immediately handed it to his cleaning lady.[186] Such published insult was matched by the tartness with which Walser treated Enzensberger. In September 1981 the novelist had made a speech in Frankfurt about Brecht, to which the essayist reacted negatively in a letter. Walser sent that letter back to Enzensberger along with a gruffy response, "because I do not want it in my house, I cannot suffer it."[187] Walser messed again with Kaiser, whom he considered a vain man, and Jens, who had told him, facetiously, that he was "writing too well."[188] Meanwhile, the relationship with Unseld was worsening as the publisher was objecting to content in future manuscripts Walser was preparing.[189] Years later, Walser would leave Suhrkamp for Rowohlt.

Ideologically, Walser veered further to the right. In the mid-1960s he had been worried about Auschwitz, wondering how ordinary Germans, any ordinary German, could have committed Nazi crimes and to what degree they were *all* guilty. Later, he had qualified this to mean that the guilt was such as to never be atonable, hence merely academic, theoretical. Then, during a speech at the Frankfurt Paulskirche in October 1998, Walser touched on key items of his evolved catechism. For some years now, "the grim service of memory" had demanded that Auschwitz, "the burden of our history, our everlasting disgrace," be held up before us as Germans. As justified as this might be, the media and fanatical left-wingers had overstated the issue. Not least because "a routine of accusations has arisen in the media," Walser had been impelled to avert his eyes "from the worst filmed sequences of concentration camps." Something in him was rebelling "against this unceasing presentation of our disgrace." Rather than being grateful, said Walser, "I begin to look away." German disgrace was being exploited "for present purposes." He rejected the preachings of the left, which held that the division of Germany in 1945 had been punishment for Auschwitz and, the corollary, that recent reunification would cause another Auschwitz.[190] Constant media manipulation of German national shame would lead to the "ritualization" of representation and memory, which would result in mere routines; for this reason Walser opposed plans for a Holocaust Museum in Berlin, a "monumentalization of our disgrace." In all, private memory was more important than public memory. Conscience was a private, not a public thing; for this Walser adduced Hegel and Heidegger as witnesses. Contrary to Grass or Böll, Walser signally stated that he could not live in a world "in which everything had to be atoned for."[191]

Walser's remarks represented the apotheosis of his views on Auschwitz and the Third Reich, which had first crystallized in 1965. Some of what he said he had stated in 1994, namely his warning about a ritualization of Auschwitz memory.[192] His contention that a Berlin Holocaust memorial would lead to a "continuous indictment" of Germans in matters of the Holocaust coincided with the sentiment of many, from the far right to the conservative wing of the SPD, including the new chancellor Gerhard Schröder (since October 1998, oddly named like a former Adenauer minister), who pleaded for forgiveness and to let bygones be bygones.[193] The right-wing Social Democrat Klaus von Dohnányi applauded Walser when he said that Walser was correct. His speech had been "to complain, as a German, albeit a non-Jewish German, about the all-too-frequent attempt by others to take advantage of our conscience, to abuse it, to manipulate it."[194]

In November 1998, when Dohnányi wrote this, a debate between Walser and Ignatz Bubis, now the head of German Jews, was well under way. Bubis accused Walser of having supplied explosive content to right-radicals in the land. Indeed, whether he appreciated it or not, Walser was now receiving much complimentary mail from neo-Nazis on the matter, and right-extremist papers such as *Deutsche National Zeitung* were republishing parts of his Frankfurt speech out of context. This was at the core of Bubis's charge against Walser that he had committed "intellectual arson."[195] "Walser delivers ammunition to the right-extremists, as he is being taken seriously," complained Bubis to *Der Spiegel*.[196] Bubis also wondered who exactly it was that purportedly instrumentalized the Holocaust, as Walser had maintained, and for what purpose.

During this, Walser also compromised Siegfried Unseld, who was a friend of both. In his novel of 1996, *Finks Krieg* (*Fink's War*), Walser had named Bubis and characterized him in a highly unflattering manner.[197] Unseld had only reluctantly agreed to print the manuscript, and now he found himself in a situation where he had to defend his author against charges laid by Bubis, charges that, as Unseld was impelled to tell his Jewish friend, he found largely unjustified. As far as he was concerned, Bubis could not but remember that more than a decade ago Unseld had published another work of literature against him, the play by Fassbinder in which he had been caricatured as The Rich Jew.[198] In their months-long argumentation Bubis and Walser reached a compromise only sometime early in 1999, and Bubis died in August of that year, after expressing his desire to be buried in Israel.[199]

Internationally, Walser's speech had further repercussions. Anyone who had carefully parsed it would have been appalled by his mention of Hegel and Heidegger as moral supporters, when it was well known that Hegel was one of the intellectual fathers of totalitarianism and Heidegger a former professorial handmaiden of Hitler's at Freiburg University. To compound matters further, Nobel laureate Elie Wiesel, for whose famous memoir *Night* Walser had written a preface in the early 1960s, publicly announced his disconcertment. He later decided that henceforth the preface would be cut from any new editions of his book.[200]

Walser's right-wing course was further delineated as he began to service German martyrology by excoriating the Peace of Versailles of 1919, which was ultimately to blame for Hitler's rise to power, and hence, in extension, for his crimes. In this way he resurrected the image of the German Victim that had emerged after 1945. Walser judiciously acknowledged Hillgruber, who bewailed new German losses that had occurred thirty years after Versailles. The fact that he also agreed with Habermas seems to indicate that his empathy with right-wing exponents of the *Historikerstreit* was limited strictly to emotions, whereas his brain must have told him that the cerebral philosopher simply had the better arguments.[201]

Such split reaction to the national past curiously manifested itself in Walser's identification with Albert Leo Schlageter, whose documented criminal record he abstracted, while this Freikorp fighter's qualities as a German patriot and martyr he acclaimed.[202] Schlageter, born in 1894 in the Black Forest, had fought as an officer at the Western Front and then, patriotic and disillusioned, joined a soon-to-be-illegal Freikorps. Those corps fought to the east of truncated Germany in order to reclaim Upper Silesian territory ceded, by Versailles, to the Poles, and territory in the Baltic. In between, they subdued workers' rebellions in the Ruhr.[203] The valiant Schlageter, in a corps named Organisation Heinz that fought in all three theaters, in 1923 planned sabotage against French occupation troops in the Rhineland. They were pushing guns and aimed to destroy railway lines, which was against official Berlin policy and in clear contravention of the Treaty of Versailles.[204]

Schlageter may have acted heroically for what he considered his fatherland, but the criminality of his actions even then was obvious. The illegal

Organisation Heinz was known to have executed alleged spies for the French "while trying to escape," and its sabotage, such as tampering with railroad tracks, highly endangered human life.[205] Schlageter knew this when he caused a German train, destined for France with reparations goods, to derail on March 15. He was caught and tried by the French on sabotage and executed near Düsseldorf on May 26, 1923.[206]

Largely ignoring those suspicious aspects of Schlageter's later life, Walser denied that the terrorist had had associations with the fledgling Nazi Party. For Walser, Schlageter was an "idealistic nationalist," whom the Nazis appropriated for propaganda purposes after 1923.[207] That was indeed the case; Nazi commemorations culminated on April 20, 1933, when Hanns Johst had a play performed, *Schlageter*, dedicated to Hitler's birthday, celebrating its hero as the first National Socialist soldier.[208] But Walser chose to disregard that Schlageter himself had joined the Nazi Party's local chapter in Berlin in 1922, where he had intermittently conducted a business with Organisation Heinz's commander, and that he had been planning to travel to Munich to be with Hitler.[209] Overall, Walser conveniently overlooked the dark side of the Freikorps, their foundational anti-Semitism, their abject misogyny, and their deep-seated hatred of democracy, as evinced by their January 1919 murder of Spartacists Rosa Luxemburg and Karl Liebknecht.[210]

By speaking out for the unification of East and West Germany, as did the conservatives currently in government, Walser exhibited a revanchist attitude of the kind that Schlageter had maintained in his view of Germany's forlorn eastern provinces.[211] Schlageter personally could not but appeal to Walser: like him, Schlageter had been born and raised in modest circumstances in provincial southern Baden, had once wished to enter the priesthood as a pious Catholic (Walser eventually desisting), and, after World War deployment, had studied at the university.[212] And Schlageter had entered that military service as a patriot to fight for his country, as had Walser.

For Walser's old adversary Marcel Reich-Ranicki, one life was ended in the 1980s and a new one was begun. But this new one being in media, it was questionable whether his previous sway over literature could be retained. After involuntary retirement from the *FAZ* in 1988, Reich-Ranicki became moderator of a four-person panel reviewing literature on television. This, at the ZDF station, was named *Literarisches Quartett* (*Literary Quartet*) and featured two other permanent members, Hellmuth Karasek, aged fifty-four and of *Der Spiegel*, and Sigrid Löffler, aged forty-six and from Vienna. A fourth member would always join them as a guest, making, potentially, for much dissonance.[213]

The show, broadcast every two months, lasted for ninety minutes. Its first instalment was aired on March 25, 1988, and was not a success. The guest was Jürgen Busche, a not very spectacular deputy editor of the *Hamburger Morgenpost*. In the pages of *Die Zeit*, Reich-Ranicki was taken to task, understandably, for dominating the scene and for hyping, once again, his favorite author, Ulla Hahn. Karasek was given a pass and Busche was credited with having scored a few points but otherwise being far off. Sigrid Löffler, on the other hand, was dismissed as if she had never been there. Had she become a victim of misogyny in a literary world still ruled exclusively by men?[214]

However, not least because of Reich-Ranicki's personal skill as a showman and his penchant for controversy, in which he thrived even when he could be proven wrong, *Literarisches Quartett* became hugely popular. One had to learn how to interrupt the master was the unspoken rule, a serious lesson for all the younger participants. Reich-Ranicki showed his deference to forbears (but only to those) by always closing with the same quotation from Brecht, which talked of the curtain falling and leaving all questions open. Over time the show, albeit often superficial, proved to have the power to make and break new books of poetry and prose, making the difference of thousands of sales. The fact that this became a mass-medium event, not anymore limited to a chosen elite meeting clandestinely in the manner of Gruppe 47, was a plus. In the critics' opinion, more books would reach a readership, literary knowledge would rise, and authors would profit. It was well if entertainment could make Goethe and Fontane, Walser and Grass more accepted.[215]

But for all his caesaristic airs and monopolist practices, Reich-Ranicki had his comeuppance on June 30, 2000. That night the novel *Dangerous Mistress* by the Japanese novelist Haruki Murakami was under discussion, which featured sexualized language. When Reich-Ranicki provocatively asked Löffler to comment, she sensed trouble and tried to play the matter down. Thereupon the showman insisted on pronouncing the German word for "fuck" at least four times. Feeling set upon, Löffler resigned at once. There was a replacement for her, but the show silently died in 2001. Reich-Ranicki then attempted some solo performances, but without a good sparring partner he did not have success. He withdrew from television in 2002, a victim of his own overbearance.[216]

◆ ◆ ◆

In the 1980s, as installations, arrangements, and Happenings receded in West Germany, painting returned. Artists wanted to draw and paint, and they were, once again, less interested in the process of creating art – as they had been during the era of Informel since the mid-1950s – than in the finished product. How the paint found its way to the canvas did not matter and it was not to be an art per se; the canvas was a conventional one, even though certain painters, such as Anselm Kiefer, continued to use sand, lead, or other materials as a base. The paint was paint and a brush was a brush.[217]

One catchphrase in the early 1980s was "Hunger for Pictures." This hunger was satisfied by new groups known as "Die Jungen Wilden" ("Wild Youth" in English), with epicenters in Cologne-Mülheim and West Berlin, who applied the painting-for-painting's-sake philosophy, if very deftly so. As a rule, they did not want to change society, like Beuys; rather, they tended to ridicule those who did. Generally half a generation younger, they were close to the direct brushstrokes of Baselitz, Polke, and Lüpertz in painterly orientation who, for their part, in the 1980s were more removed, having gone abroad or become professors in art academies. Seemingly anachronistic, the Wild Youths' pictures, often on large formats and influenced by Italian Futurism, not to mention German Expressionism, of decades earlier, showed strong colors, which sometimes gave them a "barbaric" quality; foreign connoisseurs, especially in New York, where the Youths liked to visit and exhibit, identified them as typically German and subsumed them under "neo-Expressionism." If the much-abused term "postmodern" means returning to a more traditionalist mode of artistry after thick-and-fast inventions, this is what these painters' works exemplified.[218]

Notable members of the Cologne group, the "Mülheimer Freiheit" ("Mülheim Freedom"), were Walter Dahn and Jirí Georg Dokoupil, both born in 1954. Although a student of Beuys, Dahn did not emulate either Beuys's style or ideology, although he too valued communication. His slapdash painting manner was characterized by symbolism, punk imagery, and text, at the expense of being called naïve.[219] Six pictures Dahn showed in a 1982 West Berlin exhibition appeared to have been painted messily with intention, throwing at the audience banalities such as proverbs or caricatures of social types such as chain-smokers half in jest, but Dahn confrontationally wished to force his patrons to think hard before they formed an opinion.[220]

Dokoupil, who often collaborated with Dahn, originally came from Czechoslovakia. Like many in his cohort, he preferred giant formats. A graduate of the Cologne academy, he capriciously refused to be tied down to any style, at any one time choosing one of many, according to a premeditated formula, in order to avoid "notions of distinctive, personal expression." He was not seriously interested, the artist declared, in historic references or the establishment of continuities in his own work, instead preferring "ruptures and contradictions." To illustrate his position, he cited Picasso, Rodin, or Kandinsky, or even Nazi artists, but this he did at random and delivered tongue in cheek, provocatively satirizing earlier preceptors. Already together with Dahn, Dokoupil had created a German Forest of Nazi veneration, in which an imaginary being composed of swastikas perambulates. Was this making fun of the Third Reich? It certainly was in contradistinction to the severe images of Auschwitz objects that Beuys, Richter, and even Kiefer had designed and were still at work at, with the purpose of evoking fury against the perpetrators of Nazism and compassion with its victims.[221]

To advocate rights for gays would have been impossible some twenty years earlier, to say nothing of the Nazi period. Yet this is what the Wild Youth painters of West Berlin did. In pointing to severe deficiencies in social recognition accorded to them, they voiced a serious criticism of society. The Berliners' leader was Wolfgang Ludwig Cihlarz, born in 1954 in Karlsruhe, who called himself Salomé. Influenced by the long-deceased Ernst Ludwig Kirchner and Erich Heckel, he painted in a neo-Expressionist figurative as well as an abstract style.[222] To challenge his audience, he created homoerotic motifs – himself, for instance, in a woman's dress and with a female coiffure or, more shockingly, naked, heavily made up, and in garter-belt and hose. In an interview of the mid-1980s, Salomé claimed that sufficient remnants of National Socialism still dominated "German heads," with the result of blocking any comprehension of homosexuality in society. He then went as far as a direct comparison between German gays and "Jewish citizens" who were gassed at Auschwitz.[223]

Salomé also portrayed his queer friend Rainer Fetting, five years older. Like the work of all Wild Youths, his was marked by bold brushstrokes and vivid color.[224] Fetting's portrait of a North American Indian with bow and arrow of 1982/3 was fetishized – a sinuous figure in the process of shooting, in high-heeled ladies' booties, with a head scarf, and revealing pronounced male genitalia behind transparent loincloths. Another painting displayed a naked man in a shower, 2 phallic meters high (similar ones were 3 and 4 meters), yet another an orgy in a New York gay swingers' club, where naked bodies were shown bright red against a solitary green-clad man who, in the foreground, masochistically stabs his head.[225]

Dokoupil and Salomé were represented at documenta 7, modern art organized in Kassel for the summer of 1982.[226] In spite of all its difficulties, this event was now taking root as the pre-eminent showcase of contemporary art in the world. If it had had over 360,000 visitors in 1977, that number now rose to 387,000.[227] As its director the scholarly art historian Rudi Fuchs was chosen, a Dutchman born in 1942, in charge of the Van Abbemuseum in Eindhoven. Like Harald Szeemann in Switzerland before him, Fuchs had been something of a maverick administrator since his appointment there in 1975, very much with a mind of his own. Harking back to older conventions, Fuchs preferred painting over sculpture, photography, and other art media, and his specialty was the juxtaposition of objects, not according to chronology or style, but to inherent commonalities or opposites that spurred reaction.[228] Such thinking rejected any theory of art, notions about its impact on society, or pedagogic implications. Hence the experimentation of earlier years at Kassel was given no room in 1982, and anything but conventional painting was omitted. All that was said to matter was the individual communication between the artworks and the spectator, notwithstanding what was happening in the outside world. This was very much a view of art as narrative, which neo-Expressionist painters who preferred painting over installations, such as Dahn and Salomé, could endorse.[229] Fuchs was exclusivist in his attitude; no work was to be older than two years, and no more than 125 artists should be exhibited, as opposed to the legions invited in the past.[230]

As it turned out, compromises had to be forged. The show came to exhibit 180 artists and, again, allowed for media other than conventional paintings. There was a gate fashioned of dolomite by the German sculptor Ulrich Rückriem, a large cube of stone plates with a table made of glass by the Italian Mario Merz. There were photographs and accompanying texts by the British artists Gilbert & George. Polke exhibited images he had painted over an older picture by Goya; there was a seven-meters-high shear cutting, entitled "I Killed Anne Frank," by Felix Groese, and Jörg Immendorff displayed a fresh painting on a background of bronze.[231] There was a golden wall behind a hallstand covered by a gentleman's dark wardrobe, installed by the Greek artist Jannis Kounellis, and lines and points on darkish background, by Andy Warhol, who admitted to having first urinated on the canvas. Syberberg exhibited props from a recent Parsifal film. If Warhol and Syberberg were scandalous, Bazon Brock, the old installationist, officially not allowed in, published a counter-brochure entitled "The Ugliness of Beauty," in which he offered criticism of Kassel's jubilee, slyly peddled beyond the exhibit's gates.[232] More annoying than scandalous was the official catalog with an overload of confusing information.[233]

Gerhard Richter was represented in Kassel, as was Anselm Kiefer;[234] and so was their teacher, Joseph Beuys. No matter how many Happenings and installation events he had been responsible for, Fuchs could not help but honor Beuys, who was visibly in ill health and had only four more years to live. Beuys's large contribution to the documenta was to be the planting of trees, an act of social plasticity of the highest order. The project was done in conjunction with the mayoralty of Kassel, which had lost more than half of its 16,000 oak trees in bombardments. At a time when acid rain was killing German forests, planting new oaks was ecologically constructive, which the documenta veteran Beuys fully identified with.[235]

The action was started at the Friedrich square in front of the Fridericianum building, the main portal to the documenta, on June 19, 1982, the opening day of the exhibition. Two oak trees were planted there and 6,998 more were to follow throughout Kassel, at 500 DM each, including a basalt-stone stele for each tree. The total cost, some 4 million DM, would be financed with donations that had been initiated worldwide. A construction diploma, symbolically, came from Beuys's own Freie Internationale Universität. But as the 1.2-meter-high stelae were piled up on the Friedrich square, arranged in the form of a huge triangle, the population started protesting, as it was expecting a long period before they were carried off to planting sites. Discontented youths, in a

Happening of their own, proceeded to spray the heaps pink. Beuys immediately had the pink removed, at the sprayers' expense, so he said. Thereupon some Kassel politicians reneged on their promises; it became a public test for Beuys, the kind of which he had already endured several. His answer to the crisis again proved typically Beuystian intractable: "The stones shall remain here and if these trees do not find room in Kassel, then we shall plant them somewhere else, and the good burghers of Kassel will know, as the stones are being carted away, one by one, from Friedrich square, that the good burghers of Göttingen are receiving trees." This was a menacing remark, because the storied university town of Göttingen nearby was considered a rival by all Kasselers. But as the piles of stones diminished, tempers were calmed. In the end, Beuys had reason to be happy: the Social Democrats and his favorite, the Green Party, had collaborated, and all kinds of social groups had become committed – housewives' unions, sports-club members, citizen initiatives against nuclear power, and even inmates of a nearby prison who had volunteered for planting. If, by 1987, Beuys had wanted to see 5,000 trees planted, at the time of his death in 1986, 5,500 had actually been put in.[236]

In the summer of 1987 more than 486,000 people visited the eighth documenta, with Beuys duly being remembered.[237] His installation, the trees, was the centerpiece of the exposition, once again dedicated to social and political causes. While his widow Eva and his son Wenzel Beuys planted the last oaks for the show's opening, Beuys's final work "Lightning with Light Brilliance on Stag" was being revealed inside the Fridericianum. It was an ensemble of metal animal-like beings, crouching on the floor, over which, threateningly, a 6-meter-tall bronze wedge towered, ready to fall and crush them. As the new director, the re-employed Manfred Schneckenburger explained, Beuys had understood this as an allegory of "a conceivable catastrophe, a negative utopia."[238]

Schneckenburger was back because he favored a view of art as connected to "society and history," the issues of the past and of the day, as he had during documenta 6 in 1977, when he had tied much art to the media.[239] The American art historian Edward F. Fry, the official theoretician and a codirector of the exhibition, wrote in the catalog that art must use "aesthetics in the service of social and political awareness and action." As any, this was a postmodern application of art, clamoring for "a new modernity," one aiming for critical and emancipatory functions.[240] This fundamental message was underlined by yet another contribution to the catalog, by that philosopher of art and old friend of Beuys, Bazon Brock.[241]

The changed overall conception meant that neo-Expressionist works as executed by artists such as Baselitz and the Wild Youth, strong during the last exhibition and existing as *l'art pour l'art*, were banned.[242] Instead, the audience now was stunned by an over-abundance of exhibits somehow tied to social and political issues, to the point that *The New York Times* reviewer Michael Brenson found them "impossibly broad." Much prevalent, for instance, were artworks that could also function as furniture or architecture; hence art represented design, or design became art, all serving society.[243]

There was featured an elegant heater mounted on a slim file cabinet by the French appropriation artist Bertrand Lavier. Another room showed Bernhard Prinz's arrangement of steps, ladders, or podiums covered with cloth, blankets, and garlands, much of this in gold, to signify pathos, but also the futility of a search for pathos. Florian Borkhagen's "Chair for Peter Schlemihl" had been fashioned from three steel plates and a plate of slate, such as to suggest furniture from the 1920s, with the impression that it was freely swinging, suspended in thin air. There was a portable computer "Gridlite" by Winfried Scheuer, which was even commercially available in stores, as well as two ice pavilions made of concrete by Thomas Schütte outside, where visitors could buy real ice cream. Mercedes stood out with a precious steel-blue automobile, out of a dealership.[244]

Among the paintings, those by Richter and Kiefer dominated the scenery. Richter exhibited only abstract paintings, in a room reserved or himself.[245] The painter, who well into the late 1980s was occupied with his RAF and Auschwitz imagery, also engaged in other artistic activities, despite an alleged creative hiatus. Critics observed that he did not follow a singular theme; he painted figurative motifs such as landscapes as well as abstracts, without "a hierarchy or a possibly artistic development."[246] Richter himself revealed: "I am not following any intentions, any system, any direction. I don't have a program, a style, a mission. I am not concerned with craft problems, with work themes, with gyrations leading to mastery. I stay clear of definitions, I don't know what I want, I am neither here nor there, indifferent, passive; I prefer the indeterminate and the boundless, and continuous uncertainty."[247] A typical landscape Richter painted at that time was his *Scheune* (*Barn*) of 1983, looking like a photograph (and obviously based on one) – a plain wooden structure built into a slope, with a large tree and a meadow adjoined by a crude path in the foreground. It is neither pretty nor in any other way remarkable.[248] Richter's *Abstraktes Bild* (*Abstract Picture*) of 1986, in contradistinction, is alluring, an oil on canvas, 3 by 2.5 meters in size, and actually one of several so named in that year – bright red on the left, with a white angled form in the upper middle, and a mélange of yellow and green under red shapes.[249] (One such painting from that series was sold by Sotheby's in London for €41 million in 2015.)[250] Perhaps the fact that there were so many of similar appearance in that year alone, all titled the same (and more in other years of the 1980s), illustrates Richter's indecisiveness during that decade. This also would explain his return to earlier projects, perhaps thinking he could improve on them, by repainting *256 Colours*, for example, which he had initially created as part of a series based on color charts in 1966 (and originally called *1024 Colours*). These had resulted during 1973–4 in large-format paintings, with first enamel paint and later lacquer, on canvases sized more than 2 by 4 meters. Such shifting, renovative work was typical for Richter in the 1980s.[251]

Still, with such output, however debatable, that view of Richter's fallowness would have to be revised. Richter himself was critical of the work of his younger contemporary Kiefer, which, he noted in his 1985 diary, lacked quintessential painterly qualities. Richter thought it "macabre," not least because of the uneven surface on which Kiefer liked to apply paint. Because of the sand and lead layer, "these 'paintings' convey just what they do possess: formless, amorphous dirt as a frozen, mushy crust, nauseating filth, illusionistically creating a naturalism which – while graphically effective – has, at best, the quality of a striking stage set … Every lump of filth stands for one scrap or another, snatched from the bran chest of history." Richter was afraid, so he wrote sarcastically, that he might end up painting like this himself.[252]

But it was exactly Kiefer's idiosyncratic contemplation of history characterizing his artwork that intrigued documenta director Schneckenburger, notwithstanding controversy in the past – owing to the artist's questioning attitude regarding Nazism. Interpreting history through art was risky, cautioned Schneckenburger, for all manner of myths could be revived and nurtured and come to haunt the spectator.[253] In any event, during the early to mid-1980s, Kiefer had shifted his interest in Germanic subjects of myth somewhat to include other areas, Alexander the Great's campaigns for instance and, after a visit to Israel, Old Testament themes. In a post-Romantic tradition, they remained large and full of pathos, critics calling them irrational and seductive.[254]

Kiefer's main exhibit at documenta 8 was *Osiris und Isis*, created from 1985 to 1987 and, in two huge parts, covering an entire wall (as did other paintings of his there).[255] Typically and defiantly, it consisted of oil, acrylic emulsion applications on canvas covered with clay, porcelain, lead, and copper wire. Also encrusted with this was PCB, a highly carcinogenic organic chlorine compound once used in the manufacture of carbonless copy paper but banned in the United States since 1978. The painting was almost 4 meters high and 6 meters wide and possessed a three-dimensional quality because of the uneven elevations.[256] Depicting an Egyptian pyramid in deep brown, it was meant to signify a rebirth. In ancient Egyptian mythology, the king Osiris is murdered by his brother Set, who assumes the throne. But Osiris's wife Isis reconstitutes her husband's body so that, post-humously, their son Horus may be conceived. Eventually, after many strug-gles, Horus, displacing Set, restores order to the land, thus completing Osiris's resurrection. It was not difficult to see once more the recent history of Germany in this parable, culminating in a relative kind of progress by the mid-1980s, a progress since the Third Reich. The giant painting was sold to the San Francisco Museum of Modern Art for 400,000 dollars, an unheard-of amount at the time, and became one of Kiefer's most celebrated works.[257]

Kiefer's picture being, in part, a comment on fascist totalitarianism, veiled perhaps but a comment nevertheless, there were other allusions, some less, others more striking, that fitted Schneckenburger's overall concept. The painter Gerhard Merz showed confined spaces with perfect measurements, boxes in which individuals could feel themselves surrounded, caged, as if in a totalitarian system. Images of human skulls and smallish guillotines contrib-uted to a feeling of foreboding and threat. Schneckenburger likened such work to postmodern notions, for example Jacques Derrida's idea of decon-struction.[258] Melding architectural impressions with painting also was a specialty of Günther Förg, who, like Kiefer, painted on bronze, lead, and wood, suggesting sculpture, and who highlighted photographic structural images of Italian Fascism. When his totalitarian message became too evoca-tive, Förg was expelled from the show, because, as Edward Fry explained, he was turning "publicly neo-Fascist."[259] Another artist, the sculptor Reinhard Mucha, a friend of Förg's, did not even show up with his art, because it was thought that he was guilty by association.[260]

In the context of an engagement with the present, authoritarian and totalitarian models were not to be eulogized but forewarned against at the documenta 8. This was made clear through the installation of real guillotines, not mere pictures as in Gerhard Merz's art, and the treatment of icons of rapacious capitalism that were said to take advantage of underprivileged peoples. Four slender guillotines were positioned on a walkway against the backdrop of a small temple, flanked by trees, constructed by the Scot Ian Hamilton Finlay. They reminded onlookers of the arbitrariness of an Ancien Régime that could always be resuscitated, even if the temple signified virtue.[261] At the center of documenta was the symbol of a large German bank that had a dense history of collaboration with the Nazi regime. It and a well-known automobile manufacturer with a similar narrative were fingered as being particularly active in South Africa, whose apartheid regime was victimizing Black and brown people by the thousands. It was only ten years before that the anti-apartheid activist Steve Biko had been beaten to death by South African security police. Hence the American Leon Golub, rightly or wrongly, showed torture pictures as a protest against that regime's racial discrimination, and Hans Haacke, another American, fashioned a strong installation displaying the bank's well-known emblem and the auto company's hood ornament. Singling out the bank, it was grouped with the photograph of another Black native's funeral, that of a sixteen-year-old boy who had more recently been shot by police. It was accompanied by a sententious text, whose last strophe read, in allusion to an advertising slogan: "There exist customers who expect more from a bank than a friendly smile."[262]

It was foreign not German artists who contributed enlightenment of the humane kind. Had the *Historikerstreit* passed the German people by? This question was asked by the American painter Robert Morris, who contributed an apocalyptic three-part cycle of Bergen-Belsen concentration-camp corpses, from a single photograph already long notorious, to which, in a manner recalling Richter, he had added color. Green dominated the table to the left; yellow, a color associated with Jews for centuries, was in the middle; the right flank showed flaming red. On the left tableau the figure of a naked young woman, seemingly alive and swimming under water, was seen enlarged. Those fixtures were adjacent to a relief, of a rock embedding a prehistoric grave filled with skulls and bones. The entire montage was juxta-posed with images of bombs and firestorms – clear references to Hillgruber and Nolte, whom Morris knew about through the American press. Journalists reporting in German papers about this were oblivious to the connection.[263]

◆ ◆ ◆

In the early 1980s two prominent Berlin musicologists went on record to deplore the decline of modern music in Germany, as it had been developed on the foundations of Schoenberg and Webern in the 1950s and 1960s. Webern was totally forgotten, wrote Carl Dalhaus, and Schoenberg was remembered only through his tonal and some of his very early atonal works. Reinhold Brinkmann concurred, adding that even of Schoenberg's student Alban Berg's compositions, merely his operas *Lulu* and *Wozzeck* appeared to have purchase, never his chamber works. Younger composers, charged Brinkmann, were writing music without reference to the Second Viennese School's accomplishments, and therefore "without a confrontation with an aesthetic theory as a benchmark of critique."[264]

This paradigm change – a return to tonality from serialist and electronic sound-bite adventures – eventually became evident in the work of one of the early experimental masters of the past, Karlheinz Stockhausen. It is true that when in 1982 the Cologne music scholar Christoph von Blumröder spoke of "the aging of modern music," he still did not have Stockhausen in mind, for the composer's transition was gradual.[265] As Blumröder explained, at the beginning of the 1970s Stockhausen had further devel-oped the tradition of serial music by inventing "Formel-Komposition" (formula composition), which meant an audible melodic tone sequence (the formula) that was marked by frequency, volume, duration, timbre, and tempo, and thus constituted a self-enclosed compositional building module. Stockhausen's prototypical avatar for this was *Mantra für zwei Pianisten* (1970), whose "formula" consisted of thirteen chromatically ordered tones, beginning and ending with the note "a." This clearly recognizable formula then developed structurally into thirteen cycles, each based on one of those tones, all modulated by an electronic sound regulator – expressions of a serialist methodology. In the 1970s, Stockhausen spent much time in far-off countries, notably India and Japan. There he was influenced by non-Western philosophies such as the Sufi teachings of the Indian Hazrat Inayat Khan, who held that any and all vibrations must be subsumed under music. Now Stockhausen took these concepts further, aiming for a "world formula." By this time, the late 1970s, and now also influenced by the German nineteenth-century poet Novalis, he was paying attention to an assumed cosmic significance of music. This overlapped with other attempts in this regard, to create the genre of "world music," attempts that met up with efforts toward "new age" music and certain forms of pop and jazz – phenomena Stockhausen followed very closely.[266]

In the second half of the 1970s, Stockhausen wrote *Sirius*, now employing not one but four constantly self-transforming and eventually confluent formulas, centered on the Zodiac: Aries, Cancer, Libra, and Capricorn determined a melodic segment each. The composer expanded on this already complicated configuration by turning formula composition into "Multiformal Music," amalgamating several formula constructs, as he did in *Michaels Reise um die Erde* (*Michael's Journey around the World*) for trumpet and orchestra (1977–8); this later became the second act of the *Donnerstag aus Licht* (*Thursday from Light*) opera. He explained it by saying that all the innovations of the 1950s and 1960s, in which he himself had been a pioneer, were now synthetized – rhythms, melodies, harmony, dynamics, as well as their serial expansions, including aleatoric and improvisational elements.[267]

However, already in *Mantra*, Stockhausen was moving earlier, well-entrenched musical conventions back into the center. The most important signs of this were the return of conventional notation and increased accent on the sound of traditional instruments (as in this case the pianos) vis-à-vis artificially created soundings, by so-called ring modulators.[268] Stockhausen continued this practice in *Sirius* (1975/7), where trumpet, bass clarinet, and double bass as well as a soprano voice foregrounded an eight-channel electronics score. Then, in *Donnerstag*, the first instalment of his monumental opera cycle *Licht* of the early 1980s, a tenor, soprano, and various instruments such as trumpet and trombone carried the tunes. Here and in sequels hi-tech tape recorders were still in use, but they had vanished from the instrumentarium of *Samstag* (*Saturday*), composed in 1983 and fronted by a symphonic wind band, percussionists, and human voices. However, throughout the cycle, operas dedicated to the remaining days of the week composed up to and beyond 1990, *Saturday, Monday* (*aus Licht*), and so on, synthesizers and even tape recorders never completely disappeared.[269]

By the late 1970s, Stockhausen, who, wherever appropriate, designed his own libretti and for that reason alone, similar to Syberberg, liked to compare himself with Richard Wagner, was world-famous. His works were internationally in demand and cults formed around his personality.[270] The operatic composition *Sirius*, for instance, was performed, outside Germany, in metropoles such as Paris, Tokyo, and Washington. He prided himself on it, having attracted 6,000 concertgoers in provincial Metz alone, no fewer than on a fourteen-day conductor class that was attached to its performance in Bologna, as well as because of its usefulness for an audience of children.[271]

The premiere of his work *Donnerstag*, on March 15, 1981, in Milan's Scala, was controversial, however. The third and last act of the work had to be cut, because members of the Scala choir to be featured in it had gone on strike, having been demanding wages commensurate with those of soloists even though their solo parts were small. Stockhausen had suggested that those parts be deleted for that first performance, but the Scala demurred, allegedly for artistic reasons. Later presentations at the Scala did include the third act, after a settlement with the choristers. For the composer's devotees, it required dedication to absorb the work in its entirety during those first few weeks of spring.[272]

The opera was the history of Michael, the archangel and light angel, who grows up with his parents, quarrelling much with his father, a potential Lucifer with a threatening phallic trombone, and then travels around the world – a mythologizing of Stockhausen's own life, with an emphasis on his conflicted past, his personal, his oedipal generational conflict. His son Markus, playing a somewhat less phallic trumpet, as the character Michael personified Karlheinz; yet Michael also appeared as a singer and a dancer. The character Eva, with the seductive basset horn (it has a large womb or vulva-like opening), suggests dual functions, those of a mother and a lover. If the threefold Michael did not remind the audience of Freud, then of Wagner, there were strong elements reminiscent of Wotan, Siegmund, and Siegfried.[273]

Even though Stockhausen's "colossal" work earned much praise from later reviewers, it had to fend off strong attacks by contemporaries, not least because of that early, truncated, presentation.[274] The *FAZ* attested him "fatigue in composition" and believed the plot was marked by "a most strained naivité" and "metaphysical aplomb and banality." Overall, Stockhausen was said to have fallen prey to "messianic conceitedness." Musically, Stockhausen's daughter Majella was observed to play her piano parts as "figurative clichés."[275] The *Frankfurter Rundschau* was even more scathing. It accused Stockhausen of "giganto-maniacal contentions," "nebulous fantasies," and "substance scarcity."[276] When all was said and done, the impression left was one of gross egocentricity on the part of Stockhausen, who had already been going around telling people in all seriousness that he was not of this world but was born on the planet Sirius and completed his musical education there.[277] He succumbed further to megalomania until he came close to gambling away his credibility as a leading Modernist, when he said, six days after the catastrophe of September 11, 2001, in New York, that it was "the greatest work imaginable in the whole cosmos."[278] After that, even sympathizers had reason to doubt his sanity, to say nothing of his humanity. He became a pariah virtually until his death in 2007; his concerts at music festivals were canceled, and daughter Majella said she would no longer perform using her father's name.[279]

During the 1970s and 1980s, Stockhausen's relationship with Hans-Werner Henze, his erstwhile rival for first place in the German modern-music scene, did not improve.[280] Musically, Henze continued to pay homage both to serialism and electronic usages, as he had done in the past, but as ever, his fealty to tonality and, with it, allegiance to traditional instruments and the human voice was never in question. In *El Cimarrón* (*The Runaway Slave*, 1969–70) he employed Schoenbergian Sprechgesang, enriched with falsetto, whistling, scat, screams, chanting, and laughing. In *Voices* (1973) there was strong evidence of twelve-tone-writing, extended instrumental techniques and aleatorics. The opera *Der langwierige Weg in die Wohnung der Natascha Ungeheuer* (*The Tedious Way to Natascha Ungeheuer's Apartment*) (1971) and other compositions of this period featured electronically processed tape elements. But in works of the later 1970s and beyond such Modernist techniques were less in evidence, for instance in a Shakespearean sonata for guitar in 1979; *Orpheus behind the Wire* of 1981–3 that was built around an a cappella chorus; and the wordless *Requiem* for solo piano, concertante trumpet, and large chamber orchestra (1990–2).[281] The most advanced elements in the 1983 opera *Die englische Katze* (*The English Cat*) were sounds from instruments in the percussion section – glass bars, Chinese gongs, temple blocks, and switches.

Quite apart from how Henze's music sounded, he continued to infuse much of it with hard leftist ideology. Although far from being "a perfect Marxist," as he averred in 1971, he was writing music not for the amusement of his friends and himself, but "to help Socialism."[282] Therefore, scarcely upset by the Hamburg and Bielefeld scandals at the turn of the 1960s that had revealed him as an opportunist, he went on championing Communist causes in Cuba and deploring human inequality in general. In 1969, Henze had composed *Sinfonia Nr. 6* in Havana, which, as he admitted, was the effort of a bourgeois to direct music against the bourgeoisie, an attempt that ultimately had to fail. He had put citations from the Vietnamese Liberation Front (FLN) in it, as well as a "freedom song" by Mikis Theodorakis, who was a member of the Greek Communist Party. The work was premiered in Havana in 1969; but Henze ended up not being satisfied with the result, feeling that a specifically revolutionary message was in abeyance.[283] He rewrote it later, and a more final version was performed as late as 1994 by Ingo Metzmacher in Munich. In yet another composition of that period, *Compases para preguntas ensimismadas* (which literally means "meters for questions absorbed in self-contemplation"), for solo viola and twenty-two instrumentalists (1969–70), Henze treated each orchestral instrument as a soloist (as members in a pluralist polity) who, however, come to communal agreement, symbolizing Socialism, in the end.[284] A leftist theme was also pursued in the opera *Wir erreichen den Fluss* (*We Come to The River*, 1974–6), which related a "politically motivated morality tale" on three concert stages, each with its own orchestra. It was only in the 1980s and 1990s that Henze, turning more to classicists and romantics such as Shakespeare and Hölderlin, softened his ideological stance.[285] *Die englische Katze* was ideology-free, with no conflicts, so that the "cats" eschew killing rats and mice, and espouse harmony and peace, notwithstanding tension in a love triangle.[286]

The fact that in the 1970s and 1980s, Henze's works appeared as a regular part of a municipal repertoire, along with the old standbys such as Strauss and Beethoven, whereas compositions by Stockhausen, Kagel, and Ligeti did not, speaks volumes about the sonority of his music. In Stuttgart, for instance, the Henze œuvre comprised his second concerto for piano in

December 1977, *Wir erreichen den Fluss* in June 1977, *El Cimarrón* in April 1978, and *Die englische Katze* in June 1983, at the Staatstheater and municipal concert hall, among others.[287] At the same time, Stuttgart conceded the right of existence to works sounding much more modern than Henze's, performed in other settings.

Stuttgart ranged after Berlin and some centers in the Ruhr and Rhineland, but before Hamburg and Munich as a reliable cultivator of modern music. Under the direction of composer-conductor and Südfunk (SF) radio personality Clytus Gottwald, once a pupil of Adorno, the Swabian hub had begun a live musician series, "Music in Our Time," in the mid-1970s.[288] There were up to seven events annually, each for several days – chamber and large-orchestra concerts, often in conjunction with the conservatory and the SF. In addition, Gottwald founded an "Atelier" series, for guest performers, such as the Italian electronic-music composer Luciano Berio. During the 1980–1 season Gottwald featured the work of the German Modernist Aribert Reimann (b. 1936), and in the 1981–2 season "Atelier" played Henze's *Tristan* preludes for piano, orchestra, and tape from 1972–3. Michael Gielen, the pre-eminent New Music conductor, directed a concert by Nono in 1984. In 1985, Stockhausen's *Gruppen* (*Groups*), for three orchestras (1955–7) could be heard. In 1987 the young Wolfgang Rihm (b. 1952) came to the fore, and in 1988 it was Kagel.[289] But in 1989, collateral damage to the sliding economy since the 1970s, funds were cut for New Music programs at the radio station. Moreover, Gottwald was retiring. The ultimate consequences were, in Gottwald's words, domination by "proponents of rediscovered tonality." He writes that from then on a "postmodern program" prevailed, a patchwork quilt: "electronic music, Sufi hymns from Pakistan, lectures, string quartet, music theater, Minimal Music."[290] In 1990 there occurred a consolidation of Stuttgart's music organizers and venues, which resulted in a further "remusicalization," not so much because of a cancellation of electronics studios or emendations in New Music teaching (those did not occur), as of the inclusion of hitherto neglected music genres, such as modern jazz.[291]

West Berlin had slowly overcome its cultural doldrums after the 1945 national catastrophe that had resulted in the division between East and West. It had profited from statehood in the federal system (just like the venerated Hanse towns Hamburg and Bremen), and this meant considerable political clout and extraordinary fiscal subsidization on account of its special status. The airlift of 1948–9 had been a wake-up call concerning grave dangers to be avoided, and President John F. Kennedy's famous assertion on June 26, 1963, "Ich bin ein Berliner," had been a great catalyst, pointing to a bright future. The promise of reunification with the GDR, however indeterminate, from which cultural momentum frequently spilled over, from Brecht or Paul Dessau, added to subliminal creative tension, which much inspired some West German artists, such as Henze. Into the 1980s, the Wild Youth painters' school, who insisted on Berlin as a residence, was an expression of this.

Still, cultural activity in West Berlin was always challenged, owing to its island situation. In music, composers and musicians still may not have forgotten the fate of just-appointed conductor Leo Borchard, who, riding as the guest of a British colonel in his car toward a checkpoint in August 1945, was killed in error in Berlin-Wilmersdorf by American sentries. Borchard had been a student of the modern-music pioneer Hermann Scherchen, who spent his early professional years in the capital and whom many Berlin musicians remembered well. Old-school Modernists Helmut Roloff, Boris Blacher, and Werner Egk taught at West Berlin conservatories.

Berlin possessed several outstanding institutions to serve the modern-music connoisseur, including an electronic studio at the technical university, a Friends of Good Music society and one sponsoring "Unheard-of Music." Some of those were state-financed, others privately so. Since the 1950s and 1960s, the international avant-garde was well established there and often featured during dedicated festivals: Boulez, Stockhausen, and Ligeti. But there, too, the trend was toward more tonality. In 1986, Stockhausen's *Evas Lied* was performed, from his *Licht* series, and two years later the sacred-music specialist Dieter Schnebel's *Dahlem Mass*. *Evas Lied* was a pleasing, round-sounding concerto for children's voices, basset horns, and synthe-sizers, and the *Mass* was written for a serene church environment. The sonorous, moderately avant-garde Henze was always a constituent member of the Berlin composer community. He premiered his *Sonata da Chiesa*, reminiscent of original Baroque structures, in 1983.[292]

More advocates of a "concert-compatible melodiousness," as the Schoenberg specialist Claus-Steffen Mahnkopf has called it, made their appearance in Berlin even before the second half of the 1980s, when, as in Stuttgart, financial stringency discouraged elaborate and costly experimentation with further advanced methodologies.[293] It was a time when the relationship between tradition and progress became increasingly a subject for seminar discussion in the musicological faculties. More tonally oriented new composers such as Manfred Trojahn, originally a flautist, Hans-Jürgen von Bose, who would receive commissions from operas and philharmonic orchestras, and Wolfgang Rihm presented works, not without being criticized as regressive disciples of a "restauration." And interestingly, for West Berlin, the late 1980s saw the introduction of new East European music by Russian classic Modernists such as Nicolas Roslavets and Alfred Schnittke, which always tended to be less dissonant than in the West. Moreover, as in other West German music venues, the influence of jazz and pop on new compositions tended to divert attention from electronic contortions.[294]

Neo-Expressionism and neo-Romanticism also came to shine through in towns and cities where experimentation had been especially strong. Cologne was in the lead here but, surprisingly, so were lately some centers of the Ruhr, such as resource-rich Essen and even Duisburg, which in culture always liked to sidle up to Düsseldorf. Here the provinces had turned anti-provincial![295] In the 1980s Cologne was, visibly and audibly, losing its cachet as the Mecca of innovative Modernism, in the visual arts as well as in music, which led, for example, to an exodus of painters and sculptors. This was, unsurprisingly, because of a change in the municipal-culture administration that needed to accommodate budget restrictions. There was the electronic studio at the WDR that Kagel, for one, declared obsolescent for lack of upgrading. Several composers and musicians taught Modernism at the conservatory, which even had its own electronic studio and was where Kagel (and sometimes Henze) worked. There existed a "Feedback Studio" run by the composer Johannes Fritsch that gave room to New Music experimentalists. But the signs of regression were unmistakable. Kagel himself was increasingly composing in a more conventional mode, and the long-wave radio station Deutschlandfunk was unable to tie a new, progressive chamber group, the Ensemble Modern, to it permanently. By 1990 any New Music performances, still organized by a forward-looking WDR, were taking place in front of largely empty rows.[296]

It was in Hamburg and Munich, however, hat tonality crept back into music most noticeably. Hamburg had been a center of some gravity for Modernism, with the Swiss Rolf Liebermann at the helm, a multitalented composer who also conducted and served as a director of music, in particular opera. In the late 1930s he had been a student of the expatriate Scherchen in Vienna, returning to Switzerland after the Anschluss, where he studied dodecaphony. From 1959 to 1972 he took the reins at the Staatsoper, which he made into a respectable platform for Modernism. He commissioned new works by avant-garde composers, including Henze, and was often seen at Darmstadt and Donaueschingen. His own Modernist assays included the Concerto for Jazz Band and Symphony Orchestra that was premiered at Donauschingen in 1954, yet as a trailblazer was not convincing.[297] All the same, Hamburg's reputation as a progressive city in music was unshakeable until Liebermann left for Paris in 1973, because his influence was also felt at the NDR radio station, where he had worked two years prior to his position at the opera and which had the modern-music series titled "das neue werk." Things took a turn for the worse when Liebermann was replaced by a succession of less progressive opera directors, including August Everding, an anti-innovator at Bayreuth and soon in Munich. Until 1985, when Liebermann returned from Paris for another three years, the music scene in Hamburg was characterized by "lethargy" and "conservatism," and at the end of the 1980s and into the 1990s the fortunes of New Music, in upheaval everywhere, were irrevocably bleak in Hamburg.[298]

Liebermann had been favoring representatives of the more classical avant-garde, melodically and harmonically halfway between nineteenth-century Romanticism and late twentieth-century electronic overkill, so the fallback to tonality was not as crass in Hamburg as in other cities, such as Cologne, even if "das neue werk" had been more daring. One sign of this was that Modernists such as Rihm and Trojahn whose works were presented in Hamburg tended to return to the large *Grand opéra* format of many decades ago, rather than chamber-like formations that avant-gardists had preferred in the 1950s to 1970s. Another sign was that the NDR station relinquished its modern-music policy by the end of the 1980s, even though it had still been patronizing non-extremists such as Trojahn, Rihm, Wolfgang von Schweinitz, Aribert Reimann, and Wilhelm Killmayer. The money stream for new compositions was upended, and innovative local ensembles and New Music organizations such as L'art pour l'art were left high and dry, as the Hamburg government was demonstrating the same fiscal stinginess as the radio station. As in other towns, patrons of New Music were thinning out in the concert halls: Günter Wand, the conductor of the NDR symphony orchestra, long moved from Cologne to Hamburg, had left the Modernists behind. Disparagingly, playwright Peter Rühmkorf called him the "Bruckner conductor."[299] Another musician who, in Hamburg, returned to more conventional forms was Ligeti, who had assumed a professorship at the conservatory in 1973. "By the late 1970s the avant garde to which he had been attached, however skeptically, was no longer functioning as such: the time of shared ideals was over, and instead of being a challenge to established musical culture, the post-war generation had become the new establishment." Ligeti himself turned to evoking the Romantics of the past century by writing a horn trio in 1982 that paid homage to Brahms yet contained – vestiges of experimentation – odd tunings and syncopations that would have been alien to late nineteenth-century Romantics.[300] Significantly, a computer-music studio for the conservatory that the composer had advocated for in the 1970s remained at the planning stage.[301]

In the 1980s Munich represented the nadir in New Music development, and not just because of Everding who was the Bavarian Staatsoper's intendant since 1977, but other conservatively inclined music personalities, such as conductor Wolfgang Sawallisch, who was its Generalmusikdirektor.[302] Everding, an "unashamed traditionalist," as the British *Independent* put it, was at the head of a local clique that controlled Munich's musical life hermetically; the fact that he was a pillar of both conservatory and university only increased his power.[303] His clique was responsible for machinations obstructing progress wherever possible.[304] Progressivism in Munich after 1945 was therefore always underdeveloped, notwithstanding Hartmann's early efforts with his "Musica Viva" series. Hence avant-garde music here had even less far to fall than in Hamburg. Sergiu Celibidache, the conductor of the Munich Philharmonic since 1979, leaned toward the turn-of-the-century classics, and his aversion to record production did not lend itself to music-making that demanded the deployment of tape recorders, whistles, or synthesizers.[305]

The cronyism rooted in the conservatory had several manifestations. Here Everding was supported by its principal, Peter Jona Korn, a Berlin Jew born in 1922, who even after studies with Scherchen and, in the United States, with Schoenberg declined Modernism. Apart from composing on the side, he excelled in amassing offices.[306] Stipends designed to encourage avant-garde compositions were awarded only to confidants of Everding and Korn's coterie, while others were held back. Among the supported were Günter Bialas, Wilfried Hiller, and Peter Michael Hamel, who composed non-toxic music that was epigonic. A "Studio für Neue Musik" presented contemporary classical music that was increasingly losing Modernist characteristics. A similar fate befell the "Musica Viva" series at the radio station, now highlighting compositions of pianist Friedrich Gulda's such as *Concerto for Myself*, one of two piano concertos by him that the *Oxford Dictionary of Music* has called "derivative in style."[307] Celibidache, meanwhile, premiered Hamel's symphony *Die Lichtung*, or *The Clearing*, for conventional instruments, whose sheet music was published by Bärenreiter in Kassel, a bastion of conservatives.[308] Local composer Hiller styled operas for the little people: *Goggolori* (1985), a fairy tale, and *Die Jagd nach dem Schlarg* (*The Hunting of the Snark*, 1988), a nonsense story.[309]

The "Munich composer mafia" invited Henze to organize a Munich biennial for 1988; he then delegated younger musicians to write new works: Detlev Glanert, Gerd Kühr, Franz Josef Lechner, and Max Beckschäfer, who all used conventional instruments for conventional music. Perhaps the most daring of them was Adriana Hölszky, a German from Romania, a traditionalist who after 1990 included in some of her scores parts for accordion and electronics. All this was a far cry from Schoenberg or early Stockhausen and, not least, again showed Henze servicing the powers that be, rather than Socialism. The second such event, in 1990, approximated Broadway, as in Rodgers and Hammerstein's *The Sound of Music*, with Hans-Jürgen von Bose's opera *63 Dream Palace*. Henze himself preferred to invite his own students, such as Glanert and Kühr, or their students or friends, shunning wider competition. Hence age-old Munich traditions of stasis were safeguarded, as was unreflective high entertainment for Munich's glitterati. Initial prize juror Helmut Lachenmann, noticing this, disapproved and stayed away.[310]

Killmayer's older Munich colleague, Günter Bialas, had served in World War II. During his formative years he was much influenced by his conservative teacher (and Nazi) Max Trapp and the folksong-besotted Fritz Jöde, in studies at Berlin. He became professor of composition at the conservatory in 1959, a post he held until 1974. Thereafter – a latecomer – he continued to make his name in composition, specializing in incidental music, ballet, and opera. Although he avoided twelve-note composition per se, atonal inflections could be found in several of his works, even if Bialas's self-confessed affinity to Weill and Stravinsky was stretched. Erik Levi was able to detect the influence of Berg's *Wozzeck* in an early dramatic opus, *Hero und Leander*, for seven scenes after Franz Grillparzer, premiered in 1966.[311] Later works reprised scenic and programmatic music, some of it with fairy-tale motifs. When in the spring of 1970 the Kiel opera performed *Die Geschichte von Aucassin und Nicolette* (*The Story of Aucassin and Nicolette*), which had been premiered in Munich one year before, a critic damned it with faint praise, calling it "a piece of academically clean music."[312]

Peter Michael Hamel was active in the city through a Freies Musikzentrum München that he co-founded in 1978. This student of Orff, Celibidache, and Bialas was born in 1947. He evolved as a jack of all musical trades, including electronics (which he practiced with Cage and Morton Feldman in New York) – modern jazz, symphonic and choir music, oratoria, chamber music, organ pieces. He was a composer, pianist, organist, music professor, singer, lecturer, and electronics modulator. Apart from two symphonies, he created orchestral suites, string quartets, and electronic tape works. Within his œuvre, however, those latter ones were in the minority. In a popular book of 1976, he propagated "world music," having absorbed and processed many influences musically during international travels.[313] In the spring of 1992 in Ulm, his "song opera" *Radio Sehnsucht* (*Radio Desire*) was premiered. Melodically and harmonically traditional, it told of Andres, the son of a gas-station proprietor and a popular-song writer who loves Una, a star from the hit-parade. But no sooner has he won her than he realizes how worn out and old she is. On first impression reminiscent of Brecht and Weill, this "opera" was not Weill, judged *Die Zeit*, "for its content lacked gravity, musically as well as dramatically." And besides, the challenges for singers were modest.[314]

Wilhelm Killmayer was born in Dachau near Munich in 1927, one year older than Stockhausen. Like Hamel later, he went to study with Orff in the 1950s. Composing within the limits of modernity that were laid down by his then fashionable teacher, he won many prizes before being appointed to a composition chair at the conservatory in 1973, five years before Hamel founded his Musikzentrum. His writing was influenced by Stravinsky and

Orff, whose own music owed much to the Russian master, exemplified by rhythmic peculiarities and "motorically sustained climaxes." "The technical, stylistic and expressive spectrum of Killmayer's music is both diverse and multi-layered," writes Siegfried Mauser, his successor at the academy, "ranging from cantabile, song-like writing, through dramatic tension and depressive numbness, to comedic entertainment." Another influence was Schumann's Romanticism; chamber musics, a piano concerto, a Hölderlin poetic song cycle, and pieces for cello and piano bore witness to this and made him into a "significant figure in musical Postmodernism."[315] Moritz Eggert, who later taught in Munich, judged that even as a "modern composer" Killmayer was always intensely concerned with melody, "in contradistinction to other composers of contemporary music."[316]

Killmayer's predilection for melody and the established Romantics must have been a major reason why he was, early on, a favorite of the reactionary music critic Walter Abendroth, who had moved from Hamburg to Munich in 1955. In July 1957, Abendroth saluted Killmayer for having received one of the city's culture prizes; Killmayer had just composed his *Due canti* for orchestra.[317] When that work was presented at the Donaueschingen festival in the fall, Abendroth welcomed it as an example of time-honored musical practices amid a "plurality of all oppressing New Music works."[318] The critic was cross with Killmayer four years later after the Munich premiere of his *Tragedia de Orfeo*, which he deemed to be an Orffian plagiarism, not least because of a surfeit of percussion noise, but he applauded Killmayer again in 1964, asking why Hartmann's "Musica Viva" series had never broadcast him.[319]

Helmut Lachenmann (b. 1935), the Munich biennial jury member of 1988, was on the Stuttgart conservatory faculty when Killmayer died in 2017. He had good things to say about Killmayer, because he had been "sagacious" as a musician, and that was decisive.[320] Lachenmann himself was more inclined to Modernism, having attended the Darmstadt summer events and studied with Nono between 1957 and 1960. In the 1960s, Lachenmann's works were clearly marked by serialism, as was his String Trio of 1965. But into the 1970s he did not join others who had been experimenting with electronic sound effects. Instead, he tried to explore what sounds traditional instruments could generate once employed in a non-traditional fashion, such as bowing the body of a cello or its tail piece, generating noise. Lachenmann developed a special notational system for this music, which he called *Musique concrète instrumentale.* But in the late 1970s and into the 1980s he, too, enacted a return to older musical forms by referencing Mozart's clarinet concerto in A major or Beethoven's Ninth Symphony.[321]

In 1988, Lachenmann began composing a stage work, *Das Mädchen mit den Schwefelhölzern* (*The Little Match Girl*), after Hans Christian Andersen, which he completed in 1996. It featured 103 instrumentalists and 16 choir voices, as well as 2 sopranos and tape-recorder music, and was premiered by the Hamburg Staatsoper in 1997. There was no narrative, no libretto, only monologue in place of drama and dialogue. The two sopranos, singing not on stage but in the orchestra pit, represented the pitiable match girl with her bare feet in the snow, around New Year's Eve, fated to die of exposure. Lachenmann's new techniques had transmogrified the singers' voices to produce clicking, quaking, screaming, and the chattering of teeth, characterizing the little girl, but those sounds pervaded the entire opera, which, some critics said, did not deserve to be subsumed under that rubric. The third part consisted of an imagined vision by Leonardo da Vinci. But in the middle, there was read a letter by Gudrun Ensslin, whom the composer was comparing, was conflating, with a girl who played with matches. At the beginning of a poem, Lachenmann had Ensslin read about the "hopelessness and impotence of man within the system." His treatment of the RAF terrorist was similar to that by Gerhard Richter, who had reinforced doubts regarding the manner of her death with his artistically manipulated portraits of her corpse. Lachenmann, who was originally from Stuttgart and, like her, had a Lutheran pastor for a father, had known Ensslin personally. If the impression was conveyed that Lachenmann still believed in the murder of the terrorist by minions of the state (as might Richter), he himself did nothing to dispel it.[322]

That Hamburg premiere of an opera that in more recent times has been compared to Berg's *Wozzeck* and Zimmermann's *Soldaten*, on January 26, 1997, was not warmly received, with scores of people leaving in the middle of the performance. Among the public media, it was not just the boulevard press that scorned the music; more significantly, this press was handed an opportunity to rail against Lachenmann's suggestion of Ensslin's victim status. The establishment journals were more civil but nevertheless unforgiving. "Music theater as martyrdom ... a non-opera," cried *Der Spiegel*, pooh-poohing Ensslin and condemning what it thought was cacophony produced by noise machines.[323] *Die Zeit*, milder but still piqued, mentioned "reactionary prejudices" and noted, incredulously, that, apart from the suggestions in the opera itself, the composer, quite outré, had put Ensslin's "suicide" up for discussion in the program notes.[324]

Lachenmann may have been naïve, but he was serious. "Music is not designed to make people enslaved," he said in 1991, "but to make them prick up their ears." And he added that for his part, he had been sensitized by the Nazi period and had experienced how music could enslave people, with the *Deutschlandlied* for instance, which was always followed by the blood-curdling *Horst-Wessel-Lied*.[325] Yet while he wished to use music to remind his audience of dangers emanating from the RAF (or dangers arising from false accusations of the RAF), National Socialism and the Third Reich remained beyond his sensitivities as a musician. Who else would have ascribed analytical or curative powers to music in this period, and with particular reference to Hitlerism?

Well, there was Henze, who stated, in 1984, that "mass executions by SS thugs" characterized his opera *Wir erreichen den Fluss* of 1976.[326] Indeed, the opera dealt with an evil emperor, but not discernibly with persecuted Jews or the SS. Hamel purports to have written an opera, *Shoah: Die Endlösung der Judenfrage* (*Shoah: The Final Solution of the Jewish Question*), which appears to have been performed at an open-air theater in Koblenz in August 1996. But this seems to have been its solitary staging and no records or reviews of it have been found.[327] Stockhausen's *Donnerstag* allegorized the demise of Eva, Michael's mother in the piece, patterned on the composer's mother who died in Nazi "euthanasia" wards, but this concerned Stockhausen's own family history, not that of any Jews. Besides, as Alex Ross has cautioned, much of Stockhausen's libretto was ambivalent, because his portrayal of Eva recycled "Romantic stereotypes of the eternal feminine," and his call to produce "healthier, more beautiful, more musical human beings" smacked of "early-twentieth-century eugenics."[328] A genuine act of atonement would have been to put on the Jewish Victor Ullmann's 1944 opera *Der Kaiser von Atlantis* (*The Emperor of Atlantis*), about yet another evil emperor, which he wrote while at Terezín concentration camp (before he was killed in Auschwitz). Since the 1970s it had been produced in the United Kingdom, the Netherlands, Belgium, Italy, and the United States. But save for the Mainz and Stuttgart operas and the radio station in

Saarbrücken, neither stage nor broadcaster was interested in this in Germany into the 1990s.[329]

During one of its music festivals, in 1985, the City of Frankfurt performed the American Marc Neikrug's opera *Through Roses*, a work describing the life of a violinist who succeeds in reaching the apex of his art and, thanks to his brilliance on the violin, survives Auschwitz, entertaining the SS as a kept musician.[330] Neikrug was born in New York in 1946 of Jewish parents with ancestral roots in eastern Europe, both of whom played the cello. He studied composition at the Hochschule für Musik in Detmold and at Stony Brook University in the United States. Neikrug wrote in a chromatically tonal or an atonal mode but always paid attention to harmony. From 1966 onward he composed a piano concerto and a viola concerto, as well as chamber and solo instrumental works. His theater piece *Through Roses* was conceived for an actor and eight instruments, composed in 1979–80, the year it was premiered in London. After that it saw more than a hundred performances in five European countries. There was also a film version of it that received prizes in Besançon and New York.[331] Over time, Neikrug would collaborate with many artists, musicians Pinchas Zukerman and Zubin Mehta among them.[332]

Neikrug has explained the gestation of his work as a consequence of his Jewishness and the suffering of the Jewish people in the Holocaust. When he had been in Detmold studying with Giselher Klebe, he was shown a photograph of his conducting teacher in SS uniform, and he was told that the school's janitor had been in the Waffen-SS, with its legacy of Auschwitz and selections on the ramps. Later in London, he heard the true story of a cellist "who was ordered to play Bach in Auschwitz – while the inmates were marched to the gas chambers." In his libretto for the forty-minute-long piece, Neikrug has a cellist, who had witnessed the death of his wife in Auschwitz through a rose bush in the commandant's garden, relive the horror forty years later, in a hotel somewhere, where he has to deal with his survivor's guilt. "The piece is intentionally ambiguous; night and day, reality and illusion are blurred. The violinist is tortured by dreams, memories and hallucinations." On stage, the actor's stream-of-consciousness words are interwoven with continuous music, which includes references to the German masters: Beethoven, Berg, Haydn, and Wagner. His drama, Neikrug said, was "all about how the Nazis loved that music."[333]

Before Frankfurt, the Hamburg Staatsoper had performed *Through Roses* in a German premiere in 1984. But although Neikrug's was a powerful, moving motif and his music drama already internationally recognized many times over, West German critics found fault with it. They judged the score to be an "aggressive music collage" (Rolf Michaelis) and as such, it was a "one-hour melodrama" (Heinz Josef Herbort).[334] It could evoke neither horror nor terror, nor lament or fear. It was impossible to associate anything with its music nor call humans to action. It was not able to render visible the unimaginable, nor were there any lessons to learn.[335] The opera, so it appeared, for those critics represented a moral as well as an aesthetic failure.

◆ ◆ ◆

In the 1980s political power was again firmly in conservative hands, although Kohl's cabinet was never as far to the right as Adenauer's had been. There were even some social-minded ministers who cared greatly about growing unemployment and the state of public health. In all, those politicians failed to acknowledge, further, the gravity of, and Germans' responsibility for, if not Nazi war, then for the genocide of Jews, as the Bitburg incident showed.

In large sectors of society, the search for the root causes of Hitlerism and the Holocaust appeared to have ended; there was, instead, a resurgence of trends some thirty years old to revive the German past, by concentrating on, allegedly, redeeming aspects of Germany's past, which included more positive retrospectives of the Third Reich. Intellectually, those were highlighted in the battle of the German historians, and they found cultural expression in books such as Diwald's and Fest's, and films such as Syberberg's, about Nazi Germany and its Führer.

In the arts and letters, the dynamics of progressive change slowed as in literature, there was a return to conventional forms of articulation as in music and painting, and a standstill in filming. This occurred to the same extent that surviving Nazis were vanishing from German society. Was there a correlation? As the end of East–West confrontation drew near and there were signs of a soon-to-be-united Germany, the 1990s saw even fewer Nazis; concerns about reunification took precedence.

◆ ◆ ◆

Coda: After the West Germans

N THE EVENING of Thursday, November 9, 1989, coincidentally on the
anniversary of Hitler's Beer Hall putsch and Kristallnacht, champagne
was popped near the Berlin Wall. East Germans, some in pyjamas under
light coats, who had been fenced in by a repressive regime for twenty-eight
years, crowded the border crossings, which eventually opened, one by one.
Hundreds then poured over into West Berlin, many holding up their GDR
passports, returning only hours later. Trabant and Wartburg cars rolled
over slowly at Heinrich-Heine-Strasse, Invalidenstrasse, and Bornholmer
Strasse, their two-stroke engines roaring, with scorching fumes. The
honking was deafening. In the Bundestag in Bonn, delegates rose and broke
into song; CDU members intoned the *Deutschlandlied*. There was clapping,
singing, and speech-making when an overwhelmed Willy Brandt left the
session late in the day in tears.[1]

The two Germanys were on the verge of being reunited. Reunification
was enshrined on October 3, 1990, when the last government of the GDR
accepted that the FRG's Basic Law of 1949 be applied to its territory and
inhabitants. Henceforth it ceased to exist and several of its protagonists,
especially non-Communists, changed over to the West. One was a young
chemical physicist with a doctorate from Leipzig called Angela Merkel, to
whom Kohl, in a token gesture, entrusted first the ministry for women and
youth and then the ministry for the environment, both insignificant to

him.[2] She would form a government in 2005. The entire chain of events and procedures constituted, without question, the most important political occurrence during his reign as chancellor, even though he took more credit for this personally than was due to him. Kohl had usurped a situation where most East Germans were fed up with ineffective government, lack of personal freedom, and, some thought, economic deprivations, but had not necessarily wanted to disown Socialist governance.

Henceforth, the conservative government's political fortunes were to be tied closely to the enlarged country's economic performance; Kohl had promised "blossoming landscapes" in the East during July 1990.[3] As of 1991, West Germany was beginning to be taxed financially so that to many of its citizens the fabled Economic Miracle appeared long gone. Because the five new East German states required financial transfers to survive, West Germans were saddled with higher taxes – indirect ones, for tobacco, insurance, and gasoline, and a direct tax called the solidarity bonus. West German industrial production was beginning to falter in some sectors, such as tool manufacture, exports suffered, and as a result workers were laid off and already critical unemployment rose further. This led to strike action, as in Hamburg, where in spring 1992 postal delivery was affected; soon public services all over the FRG were in jeopardy. As social services fell off, living costs were rising; from large cities such as Munich or Frankfurt, for example, postal workers or nurses had to leave in autumn 1992 because rents became unaffordable.[4] Bonn financed virtually all the transfers to the East with credit, so that the country's total deficit rose from €538 billion (in today's money) in 1990 to €1,019 billion in 1995, reaching €1,211 billion in 2000.[5] In early 2004 it was calculated that thus far the cost of reunifying had amounted to more than €1,250 billion.[6]

Because of mounting hardships, but also much mismanagement during that process and because he seemed to be issuing ever greater promises without being able to fulfill them, Kohl was increasingly criticized not only by the electorate, but also his own cabinet members. In Bonn, for instance, he augmented the number of ministries and appointed thirty-three parliamentary state secretaries when Chancellor Kiesinger had been content with seven. More and more of the West German states changed from CDU governments to the center-left.[7] In 1998, Kohl's government fell to a coalition of SPD led by Gerhard Schröder and Greens headed by Joschka

Fischer; Kohl, who had accepted illicit financial contributions, was replaced as leader of the opposition two years later by Angela Merkel.

Already in 1990 it became apparent how desolate was the economy of the former GDR. The ongoing deindustrialization caused mounting unemployment, with scores of people leaving for the western half of united Germany, where joblessness awaited them as well. As early as fall 1992, some locales had had to lay off as much as 75 percent of their workforce. At the beginning of the twenty-first century, in all eastern Germany, 20 percent of gainfully employed persons had been fired from their jobs. As many left their hometowns, especially the young, the five new states lost populations and over the years showed serious signs of senescence, because, contrary to what Kohl had promised in 1990, rather than a land of promise, East Germany was becoming a place of despair. It did not help that cronyism and corruption, much of this in the wake of unscrupulous Western manipulators, set in chronically, compounding overall ineffectualness.[8] In 1992 a sympathetic Rolf Hochhuth cast such exploitation in prose. In his new play, *Wessis in Weimar*, he described how the historic Weimar hotel Elephant, near Goethe's house and Herderplatz, is requisitioned by cunning Westerners, who take advantage of the Easterners' lack of sophistication. This stage production was not a success in what was formerly the Bonn Republic.[9]

◆ ◆ ◆

Generally in the 1990s, when East Germans, whom the Westerners would call "Ossis," complained that they felt like second-class citizens, it was because they were mostly treated that way by the old inhabitants of the Bonn Republic, which, after the capital had moved once more to Berlin in 1999, became officially known as the Berlin Republic.[10] For years "Wessis" would travel to the former Eastern Zone and hold the new citizens in contempt, as ignoramuses whose territory had been annexed because of Communist incompetence. In their vernacular, DDR – Deutsche Demokratische Republik – became known as "Der Deutsche Rest," or The German Residual. Once former GDR residents had migrated to the western parts of the FRG, they had difficulty finding jobs and, even if they did, badly acclimatized to new customs and cultures, which caused some German observers to call them "the new Turks." In contradistinction, few Wessis moved to the East, least of all with the intent of advancing society. The main prejudices Wessis held against Ossies were that they were stupid, were merely materialistically inclined and lacked professional skills. The last criterion was applied to every occupational level, whether it be blue-collar, handicraft, or academic-professional. To a convention of surgeons in Hamburg in December 1990 East German colleagues were not invited, and in the Eastern universities in the humanities, for instance, most chairholders were replaced by Westerners, a process called *Abwicklung* that took years. A psychological rift between Westerners and Easterners that had existed before 1990, instead of being smoothed out over the years, deepened, as fixed collective mentalities refused to adjust, so that, quite apart from continuing economic and logistic chasms, a "unification" did not really occur in the residents' minds on either side. One sign of this was that right-radical politics, not Communism – although allowed – continued to grow in the five new states, and racism against all foreigners, Turks, East Asians, or Muslim asylum-seekers, was stark.[11] As late as fall 2022, 53 percent of Wessis and 44 percent of Ossies regarded unification as having failed.[12]

Such divergences played themselves out culturally on both sides as well, especially in the 1990s, after which they gradually subsided. In any of the arts, very few East German creators met with unqualified approval by colleagues in the West. With the rare exception of the odd review – the one-time Stalinist Reich-Ranicki evaluating the one-time Stalinist Stefan Hermlin – West Germans had paid little heed to East German writers before reunification.[13] Come 1990, it was said about them across the board that they should remain "where pepper grows."[14] Three musicians who were the exceptions were Götz Friedrich, Kurt Masur, and Peter Schreier. In 1972, Friedrich from East Berlin's Komische Oper shaped *Tannhäuser* under the overall direction of Wolfgang Wagner in Bayreuth, whose own attempts at stage creation were always aesthetically wanting.[15] Masur was the long-standing conductor of the Leipzig Gewandhaus Orchestra who had been touring internationally for many years. The same held true for the famous Dresden tenor and conductor Peter Schreier. However, after 1990 no East German movie star was ever featured in the West German film industry; two popular actors who made it in film and television there, Armin Müller-Stahl and Manfred Krug, had migrated already in the 1970s and 1980s, and no West German considered them outsiders. Müller-Stahl moved to the FRG permanently, in protest against the GDR's expatriation of East Berlin's dissident singer-author Wolf Biermann (b. 1936). Biermann's Jewish father, a Hamburg dock worker, had perished in Auschwitz, and he became a convinced Communist constructively critical of GDR mistakes. He had been on a concert tour of the FRG when the East German government forbade his return in 1976.[16] Müller-Stahl and Biermann were typical of several GDR artists who, more or less committed to Socialism, ended up in the western half of Germany before reunification and then acclimatized seamlessly.

Not quite into this category fell Monika Maron, a novelist born in 1941 whose stepfather had been a minister of culture in the GDR and who herself collaborated with its authorities. When she moved to West Germany a year before the Berlin Wall of August 1961 came down, she turned into a far-right critic of her former homeland; left-liberal artists in the West avoided contact with her.[17] Another writer who made that transfer in 1986 was Sascha Anderson (b. 1953), a charismatic bohemian from East Berlin's Prenzlauer Berg district with its concentration of artists. In 1991, Biermann revealed that Anderson had been an informal Stasi collaborator and been responsible for the persecution of several GDR literati who had been trying to make a creative niche for themselves. His dramatic exposure and stubborn denial were a further reason why West Germany's cultural establishment remained generally suspicious of Eastern colleagues, after 1989.[18]

Two complicated cases were those of Christa Wolf and Hermann Kant, because they were arguably the most prolific authors living in the GDR in 1989, as well as involved with the SED regime. Even before unification, Wolf counted Grass and Max Frisch as her friends in the West's enlightened circles. Two years younger than Grass, she too was born to Nazi parents on territory now incorporated into Poland. Growing up in the Soviet zone, she felt personally hurt as crimes of the Nazis were made public there, finding Communism as an antidote. In the novel *Der geteilte Himmel* (*Divided Heaven*) of 1963, which made her famous, the lovers Manfred and Rita split, he moving to the West and she choosing to remain in the GDR after the Wall has gone up. Although the work manifestly proved Wolf's fealty to her home country, she leveled criticism at what she recognized as its faults. That year, Wolf became a candidate member of the SED central committee and was set for a political career. Yet after having spoken at its eleventh plenum in 1965, her disenchantment with Socialism became more serious, and it intensified after Biermann's expulsion. She published a novella, *Was Bleibt* (*What Remains*), in the key year of 1990, telling of her surveillance by the Stasi in the 1970s. Then, in 1993, while at the Getty Research Institute in Los Angeles, Stasi files were uncovered revealing her own role in reporting on fellow writers by the end of the 1950s, under the code name "Margarete." As a defense she offered that after November 1989 she must have repressed the memory. Notwithstanding that affair, the quality of her writing over all was such that in the FRG alone, between 1963 and 1989, she received four important book prizes.[19]

Such cannot be said of Hermann Kant. Born in 1926 and originally an electrician, he served in World War II towards its end and after captivity in Poland returned to Germany to study literature at Socialist Greifswald University. In 1965 he published his internationally successful novel *Die Aula* (*The Auditorium*), largely autobiographical, which, GDR functionaries later said, had contributed to the formation of "a new, Socialist, intelligence."[20] As president of the East Berlin writers' union this undeniably gifted writer played a major part in the exclusion of Biermann, demanding, in addition, the elimination of other, sometimes critical, GDR literati such as Jurek Becker and Stefan Heym. Because of his unbending orthodoxy, Kant was tolerated merely by the staunchest Communists: he was the GDR's censor incarnate. After 1989, Kant, like Wolf, retained his residence in East Berlin but, unlike her, continued publishing novels and memoirs unrepentant. His themes in a new united Germany were that although he had, justly, served the SED regime, he had prevented much evil and caused constructive changes – boasts that his former East German colleague Günter de Bruyn exposed as unjustified.[21]

More oppressive conditions after 1989 prevailed in the visual arts. Before 1990 anti-Formalist-determined art from the GDR was anathema in the West. Saxon-born Gerhard Richter was weary of it, and Georg Baselitz, also originally from Saxony, was ever contemptuous of East German artists. There were very few shows of GDR art in the FRG; famous Socialist Realist painters such as Willi Sitte, Bernhard Heisig, and Wolfgang Mattheuer remained unrecognized. In an expert's judgment, "generally, art from the GDR was assessed negatively." Rare exceptions of personal rapport existed, such as when Jörg Immendorff visited the painter A.R. Penck (Ralf

Winkler) in East Berlin; Penck, after Stasi surveillance, was permitted to move to Cologne in 1980.[22]

In July 1990, as the assimilation of East German artists was to be expected, Baselitz, in a much-publicized interview, accused his Eastern colleagues of having reliably served as propagandists of the SED regime. They had been prone to working derivatively rather than inventively. This cemented a mood of exclusion that burdened East German visual artists until in 1997 an exhibition called "Deutschlandbilder" sought to draw two German visions of art together, but only with limited success.[23] It was not until well into the twenty-first century that art critics from the German West acknowledged that painters in the GDR were not like Nazi Realist painters, and in many instances had suffered violations of artistic freedom without risking a flight across the border.[24]

As far as a continuing culture scene in the East was concerned, West Germans saw to it that much of that came under their control. How this was done in a questionable manner was demonstrated by the new culture festival in the Goethe town of Weimar, one of four places the GDR government had cultivated since 1949 as showcases (the others being Potsdam, Dresden, and Leipzig). As part of its attempt to control the administration of Thuringia and optimally exploit all its resources in 1990, conservative bureaucrats had moved from West to East. These men, who represented economic as well as cultural stakeholders, frequently became involved in problematic schemes. In early 1990 Bonn's state secretary of inner-German relations, Walter Priesnitz, came up with the idea of an arts festival, or Kunstfest, to be established in Weimar and financed by Bonn. Priesnitz, stoutly CDU from student days, was a former functionary of Oberländer's refugees' ministry under Adenauer. The Kunstfest was to anticipate the "blossoming landscapes" Kohl forecast for the German East. The first organizer of the new event was Kari Kahl-Wolfsjäger, not a Weimar citizen but a Norwegian with the closest ties to Bonn. She was joined on the board of trustees by Johannes Gross, a right-wing journalist, and the deeply conservative Joachim Fest.[25]

The first Kunstfest, still in what was legally the GDR, occurred in July 1990. Because Kahl-Wolfsjäger knew mostly musicians, she patched together some highbrow entertainment for four weeks, consisting of Bach, Liszt, Mendelssohn, and Schumann being performed, somehow around

Goethe and Schiller. Bonn merely supplied 0.5 million DM, which was only sufficient for second-rate artists, as the better-known pianist Alexis Weissenberg neglected to show up. Local artists were not invited, and ticket prices were so high that Weimar burghers could not afford to attend. The second Kunstfest was staged one year later with scarcely more resources and hardly an improvement in musical fare. The lyric tenor Hans Peter Blochwitz, born in Bavarian Garmisch-Partenkirchen, appeared, now for the second time, and again in 1992 – he sat on the board of trustees. And even though cellist Yo-Yo Ma was a star attraction, there was a repeat of mass cancellations, organizational chaos, and lackluster programming. In a period of vanishing jobs everywhere, forty Weimar musicians wrote a letter, complaining about not having been employed.[26]

As far as one can tell, no modern, contemporary work was ever featured at the Kunstfest, perhaps by way of a premiere. During the life of those festivities and under what was perceived as an increased musical hegemony, the old arrogance was detected in Germany regarding a special place for *German music* in the world. For example, German critics suspected American composers of not being capable enough to handle the sonata form. In a Bavarian private school, there were piles of sheet music containing the compositions merely of German composers. "Musical superiority" was – again – being projected into works to be listened to with attentive and sensitive ears, works that were of *German* origin. Were these symptoms of a return of "artistic nationalism" on German soil also affecting other cultural endeavours?[27]

◆　◆　◆

Problems of unification aside, under democratic governments from Adenauer to Kohl in the early 1990s, German politicians, intellectuals, and artists were able to take credit for a long record of achievements. It was obvious that the republic, since 1949, progressed politically, relearning and improving upon practices of democracy it had once known during the Weimar era – parliamentary representation based on free elections, a two-chamber constituent assembly, governance by party majorities observing a division of legislative and executive powers, a chancellor responsible to parliament, a basic law guaranteeing fundamental freedoms. The political scientist Jan-Werner Müller has called this the most successful attempt at democracy in German history.[28] A succession of popularly elected cabinets produced a series of economic successes and conducted a foreign policy closely geared to the West, which kept it safe and, through the upholding of humanitarian principles, won international respect. Official atonement to the new state of Israel commenced. The separation from the eastern part of the country was a given, in fact a bedrock of the FRG's pro-West position, but even here politicians in Bonn did not prove intractable, as an approximation of their views with those of East Berlin's in time turned out to be possible, to the point of actual reunification in 1990. As a consequence of these developments since 1945, historian Jürgen Kocka judges that Germany became "a relatively normal country of the Western type," which meant that the theory of a "special path" for modern German history that the Bielefeld School under Hans-Ulrich Wehler's leadership had propounded could be put to rest.[29]

During this period, from 1949 to 1990 but starting as early as 1945, vestiges of National Socialism and the Third Reich had to be defeated year by year, so as to strengthen democracy. That this was possible was in great part owing to efforts made, often pioneered, in the area of culture – by its creators, whether driven by pangs of conscience or motivated by a sense of civic responsibility. If journalists, early on, had not constantly skewered former Nazis Hans Globke and Theodor Oberländer, Konrad Adenauer's initial accomplices, they would not have been comprehended as a threat to the reawakened democracy. In their early novels, both Heinrich Böll and Günter Grass called attention to patterns of malfeasance in the Third Reich and warned of their extensions in the Federal Republic. If Martin Walser had not published a disconcerting article about Auschwitz after witnessing the trial proceedings in Frankfurt, public awareness of those monstrous crimes, especially among the intelligentsia, may not have set in. If Rolf Hochhuth had not followed suit in that endeavour with his *Der Stellvertreter*, this process might have taken much longer. In the late 1970s, Hochhuth dared to expose Wehrmacht judge Hans Filbinger and thereby caused the removal of a Nazi war criminal as head of a regional government. Later, Hochhuth scoffed at West German predatory practices in newly acquired East Germany. *Spiegel* journalists unmasked the most admired West German TV host, Werner Höfer, as a former active Nazi and brought about his resignation from the Federal Republic's most popular political forum in the media. Visual artists such as Georg Baselitz and Gerhard Richter, not to mention Joseph Beuys, impressively modeled images on Auschwitz and invoked caution against human persecution. And composers such as Stockhausen, Henze, and Kagel wove themes resonating with terror, discrimination, and exclusionism into their scores, be they for opera or chamber music, even radio plays. If there were checks and balances in the West German democracy, culture was a check.

Much like the political left over time and quite consistently, the new artistic culture defined itself in antithesis to the Nazi past, even though this was not always perceivable at first. Its protagonists were, in the beginning, survivors from the war such as adherents to the Gruppe 47 and, later, survivors of postwar disorder who, largely as a function of the 1968 student movement, came to criticize their fathers for their roles in the Third Reich. The New German Film makers of the 1960s and 1970s were representative of that cohort. From Gruppe 47's beginning at the end of the 1940s, new formations of authors, painters, playwrights, theater directors, musicians, and, of course, those filmmakers espoused experimental techniques. Those moulded into artistic form their democratic convictions, their belief in basic human liberties, their willingness to once again connect internationally, as evinced by techniques borrowed especially from the United States and France. Progressive notions of sexual freedom, if not libertinage, determined their work, but for the longest time they remained oblivious to new, liberating prospects for women. This began to change, if only timidly, in the mid-1970s with the efforts of the, in her personal relations controversial, journalist Alice Schwarzer, and pioneering female filmmakers such as Margarethe von Trotta. Homosexuality also became a constituent part of the arts, as exemplified by Rosa von Praunheim's movies and the slash paintings of the Berlin "Wild Youths" in the 1980s.

Throughout the creative processes, there was disagreement and controversy, as when Reich-Ranicki criticized Grass or Walser, or the organizers of the Kassel documenta excluded Wolf Vostell, but such clashes were in character with discourses that always need to be conducted, dialectically and dispassionately, as part of human creation. Gerhard Richter's controversial probing of Gudrun Ensslin's death in his paintings in the 1980s was just as important in this context as were Helmut Lachenmann's doubts, structured into his music some ten years later. Ideally, agreement, disagreement, and discord as manifestations of democratic pluralism in society had to be reflected in the nation's culture; politics had to utilize the fruits of culture. Despite post-1970s setbacks, marked by politics and the output of artistic and ideological outliers such as Hans-Jürgen Syberberg and the, aged, Joachim Fest and Edgar Reitz, progressivism in all the arts asserted itself as the norm. This held true even if, in party-political terms, virtually all of culture's creators cautiously remained neutral, with Günter Grass even departing from the SPD.[30] Altogether, then, Adorno could be proven wrong: There was poetry after Auschwitz, even if it was as bittersweet as that of Günter Eich, Paul Celan, or Ingeborg Bachmann.

Grass personified, like no other artist encountered in these pages, the convergence of creative energy and a left-liberal disposition that appears to have been crucial in generating culture in West German society. As a model, this postulates a correlation, if not causality, between culture and good government. Did the creators of culture in Germany since 1945, as my hypothesis stated in the introduction, contribute to good government, to parliamentary democracy, up to and beyond 1990? Was culture a prerequisite for that democracy to function, having midwifed and nurtured it? A look back in history reveals flourishes of culture in phases of political disorder or decline. Renaissance art blossomed under the despotic Medicis in Florence, and one hundred and fifty years ago the culture in Fin-de-Siècle Vienna defied chaotic politics. "The growth of a new higher culture seemed to take place in Austria as in a hothouse, with political crisis providing the heat," notes Carl E. Schorske.[31] Art historian Kenneth Clark valued "despotic regimes where more great art and music got made than has ever been created under a bourgeois democracy."[32] Under what political conditions do individuals as artists thrive, then? Gustav Klimt was a luminous painter in a decomposing Habsburg empire, but he suffered for not receiving due recognition.[33] Dmitry Shostakovich composed brilliantly in Stalin's Soviet Union under duress; Richard Strauss, much freer, did not under Hitler. But what later became known as his *Vier letzte Lieder* (*Four Last Songs*) were stellar pieces, composed in 1948 in a nascent democracy.[34] Evidently there is no correlation.

Within the larger context of government–culture relations the specific question resurfaces of how culture could exist under a lingering shadow of Nazism, defined, ultimately, by the horrors of the Holocaust. If cultural dynamics lagged, as was observed for the 1980s, when old Nazis were disappearing, was there cultural progress, conversely, when they were still visible? An evaluation of the 1940s–1960s period appears to substantiate that; one might even speak of a causal relationship. In the late 1940s and 1950s, in an atmosphere of collective despondency that was gradually neutralized by acts of physical and mental reconstruction, artists were at first discouraged and confused but then began to take heart. Resignation is detected in the paintings of Karl Hofer and Wilhelm Lachnit, and in Günter Eich's poem "Inventory." Defeat is acknowledged in Böll's novels *Haus ohne Hüter* and *Und sagte kein einziges Wort*, as the 1950s were beginning. The aura of Nazism had then not been completely subdued; Nazis were still active in government posts, in the administration of regions and towns, in industry and education. But clearly, novelists such as Böll and even younger ones such as Walser and Grass thereupon set out to vanquish that aura and advance the cause of democracy with their writings, such as *Die Blechtrommel*. Painters and dramatists followed suit, and filmmakers made the public aware of old evils and new hopes with creations such as *Abschied von gestern*, even if that ended on a sad note for the protagonist. The film *Rosen für den Staatsanwalt* strongly juxtaposed a malevolent former Nazi judge (who was, like judges even later, hiding his old convictions in the service of the new democracy) with a young, putative believer in a just society. The prospective return of Nazism via some of its obstinate revenants therefore acted as a catalyst to spur the creative genius of many of the new artists and writers, even though they took longer to come to terms with the atrocities of the Holocaust. As Nazi threats faded into the background, however, so did West Germany's cultural scene begin to lose some of its former urgency, indeed quality, and the once innovative writers, artists, and musicians came to resemble pillars of society. But in having helped Germany to defeat the spirit of Nazism, to once embark on democracy and to have shared constructing that just society, therein lies those creators' historic contribution.

Notes

ONE – OUT OF RUINS

1. Langer, *Encyclopedia*, 1178–9; Jarausch, *Hitler*, 23–30.
2. Langer, *Encyclopedia*, 1179.
3. Ibid. See Menand, "Sloppy Joe," 73; Betts, *Ruin*, 33.
4. Bennett, *Bastion Berlin*, 135 (quote); Langer, *Encyclopedia*, 1179–80.
5. Robert Spencer in Schweitzer et al., *Politics*, 5; Langer, *Encyclopedia*, 1180.
6. Langer, *Encyclopedia*, 1180–1.
7. Caldwell and Hanshew, *Germany*, 27; Jarausch, *Hitler*, 53.
8. Frei, *Wir*, 29.
9. Glaser, *Kulturgeschichte*, vol. 1, 139; Buruma, *Year Zero*, 177; Jähner, *Wolfszeit*, 317; questions 41–95 in von Salomon, *Fragebogen*, 386.
10. On the French see Willis, *The French*, 147–61; Hockerts, "Stunde Null," 130; Betts, *Ruin*, 93–4.
11. Reichel, *Vergangenheitsbewältigung*, 30–1; Niethammer, *Mitläuferfabrik*, 150–6, 255; Garbe, "Abkehr," 695–7; Bessel, *Germany*, 173, 176, 194–8; Görtemaker and Safferling, *Akte*, 67–71.
12. Herbert, "NS-Eliten," 100; Bessel, *Germany*, 187.
13. Niethammer, *Mitläuferfabrik*, 255–6, 455–8; Schick, "Internierungslager," 302–14, 321–5; Bessel, *Germany*, 387–91.
14. Elkins, *Legacy*, 376–80, 511–12; Ian Cobain, "The postwar photographs that British authorities tried to keep hidden," *Guardian*, April 3, 2006.
15. *Der Prozess*, vol. 22, 466–74; Rückerl, *Strafverfolgung*, 25–7; Görtemaker and Safferling, *Akte*, 36–8.
16. Rückerl, *Strafverfolgung*, 29; Milos Vec, "Der Glaube an das Recht," *FAZ*, July 24, 2020.
17. Phillips, *Trial*, 247–61; Brown, *Beast*, 85.
18. Reichel, *Vergangenheitsbewältigung*, 32–3.
19. Kater, *Composers*, 23–30.
20. Dorn, *Inspektionsreisen*, 150–1.

21. Görtemaker and Safferling, *Akte*, 68–70; Garbe, *Abkehr*, 703; Frei, *Wir*, 30–1; Friedrich, *Amnestie*, 133–45; Biess, *Homecomings*, 63; Moses, "Die 45er," 250.
22. The quote is Ossip K. Flechtheim's in Eggebrecht, *Männer*, 38. Also see Mertz, *Theater*, 34.
23. Mertz, *Theater*, 34.
24. Merseburger, *Augstein*, 127.
25. Weiss, "Journalisten," 249.
26. Bausch, *Rundfunkpolitik*, 150.
27. The law was originally issued on November 24, 1944. Printed in German in Fischer, *Pressepolitik*, n.p.
28. *DS*, July 12, 1961.
29. Elisabeth Angermair in Prinz, *Trümmerzeit*, 194; Schnell, *Geschichte*, 104; Köllhofer, "RIAS," 103.
30. *Die Neue Zeitung*, Berlin, November 6, 1949 (quote); Martin and Porter, *Guide*, 758.
31. See Martin and Porter, *Guide*, 530.
32. Von Saldern, *Kunstnationalismus*, 412; Fehrenbach, *Cinema*, 54; Clemens, "Musik," 209–10; Bessen, *Trümmer*, 80.
33. Krauss, *Nachkriegskultur*, 166–70; Steiert, "Stuttgart," 63.
34. Poiger, *Jazz*, 39; Goedde, *GIs*, 161–2; Glaser, *Kulturgeschichte*, vol. 1, 87; von Saldern, *Kunstnationalismus*, 104, 382–5; Wachter, *Kultur*, 167–9.
35. Lt. Colonel, 8 Information Control Unit Hamburg, to Information Services Control Branch, Bünde, June 19, 1946, BAB, R9361V-143965 (quote); Klee, *Kulturlexikon*, 224.
36. D. Barring to Major Sely, Hamburg, March 6, 1947, BAB, R9361V-140407.
37. Klee, *Kulturlexikon*, 83, 133, 598; Kater, *Culture*, 133, 192–3, 228.
38. Kater, *Composers*, 118–43.
39. Andrew McCredie in Dibelius et al., *Hartmann*, 46–7.
40. Clemens, *Kulturpolitik*, 146, 248–51.
41. Eberle, "Götter," 41.
42. Krause, *Galerie*, 35; Damus, *Kunst*, 33–5; Reese, "Kunst," 10–12.
43. Schneider, *Theater*, 21; Clemens, *Kulturpolitik*, 252; Bausch, *Kulturpolitik*, 120–1.
44. Wilke, *Theater*, 153 (first quote); Clemens, *Kulturpolitik*, 257 (second quote), 259. On the authors see Klee, *Kulturlexikon*, 48, 319, 432.
45. Bausch, *Kulturpolitik*, 118–19; Clemens, *Kulturpolitik*, 258.
46. Ramthun, *Krefeld*, 55; Wachter, *Kultur*, 106.
47. *In jenen Tagen* (*In Those Days*).
48. Bessen, *Trümmer*, 82; Clemens, *Kulturpolitik*, 235–6; Dillmann-Kühn, *Brauner*, 21–5.
49. Pilgert, *Press*, 97.
50. www.deutsches-filminstitut.de/dt2tp0117b.htm; Pleyer, "Aufbau," 275; Pilgert, *Press*, 94–5; Kreimeier, *Ufa-Story*, 440–3; Fehrenbach, *Cinema*, 62–3.
51. https://www.spio-fsk.de/?seitid=16&tid=473.
52. On laxer French radio controls see Köllhofer, "RIAS," 106; Bausch, *Rundfunkpolitik*, 18–19; Glaser, *Kulturgeschichte*, vol. 1, 209–12; von Hodenberg, *Konsens*, 117.
53. Memorandum, chief editor, Radio Stuttgart, July 11, 1945, facs. in Bausch, *Kulturpolitik*, 85. Also ibid., 81–4, 86–8; von Hodenberg, *Konsens*, 103–4, 114–17. For Munich see Rüdiger Bolz in Prinz, *Trümmerzeit*, 241–51.
54. Glaser, *Kulturgeschichte*, vol. 1, 208–11; von der Grün, "Programm," 26–7; von Zahn, *Stimme*, 268.
55. Frei, "Hörfunk," 418; Glaser, *Kulturgeschichte*, vol. 1, 206.
56. Pilgert, *Press*, 30; Köllhofer, "RIAS," 98, 106.

57. Pilgert, *Press*, 30; Bausch, *Rundfunkpolitik*, 15–18, 158–9; Frei, "Hörfunk," 418.
58. U.S. Public Relations/Information Services Control Report, summer 1945, quoted in von Hodenberg, "Journalisten," 281. Also see Christian Steininger in Faulstich, *Kultur der fünfziger Jahre*, 231.
59. Von Hodenberg, "Journalisten," 282–6; idem, *Konsens*, 115–18; Schölzel, *Pressepolitik*, 83–4; Weiss, "Journalisten," 250.
60. Glaser, *Kulturgeschichte*, vol. 1, 192.
61. Frei, "Presse," 373; Jähner, *Wolfszeit*, 314–15; Glaser, *Kulturgeschichte*, vol. 2, 209.
62. Gäbler, "Zeitung," 148–9; Flottau, "Frankfurter Rundschau," 99–100.
63. Dürr, "Süddeutsche Zeitung," 64–5.
64. Heinz Friedrich in Richter, *Almanach*, 17–18; Schwab-Felisch, "Einleitung," 10–18.
65. Glaser, *Kulturgeschichte*, vol. 1, 185.
66. Demant, *Zehrer*, 149–50; Harenberg, "Die Welt," 110–11.
67. Von der Heide and Wagner, "Zeit," 165–8; Meyn, "DIE ZEIT," 275.
68. Müller, *Springer-Konzern*, 55–6; Glaser, *Kulturgeschichte*, vol. 1, 205; Brumm, "Der Spiegel," 190.
69. Döblin, *Schicksalsreise*, 410.
70. Friedrich, *Amnestie*, 192–3.
71. Glaser, *Deutsche Kultur*, 80.
72. Dorn, *Inspektionsreisen*, 76; Willenbacher, "Zerrüttung," 598; Glaser, *Kulturgeschichte*, vol. 1, 72; Jähner, *Wolfszeit*, 153.
73. Kalb, *Coming*, 24; Bude, *Karrieren*, 30; Glaser, *Kulturgeschichte*, vol. 1, 69.
74. Andersen, *Traum*, 36–7; Prinz, *Trümmerzeit*, 287–8.
75. Moeller, "Ships," 152–5; Friedrich, *Amnestie*, 199; Kaes, *Deutschlandbilder*, 22 (refugee count). Wheatcroft, "Years," 73, mentions up to 14 million refugees, which would include Sudeten Germans from the former CSR.
76. Krause, *Galerie*, 35.
77. Ramthun, *Krefeld*, 55.
78. Braun, *Theater*, 13. Examples for Cologne, 1945–6: Seifert, *Wand*, 150; Nuremberg, 1945–8: Schneider, *Theater*, 113.
79. Glaser, *Kulturgeschichte*, vol. 1, 222; Borio and Danuser, *Zenit*, vol. 1, 77.
80. Sattler, "Theater," 306–8; Daiber, *Theater*, 90–2; Monod, "Patron State," 55; Bausch, *Kulturpolitik*, 134; Ramthun, *Krefeld*, 62; Krauss, *Nachkriegskultur*, 229; Dillmann, *Hilpert*, 250; Mertz, *Theater*, 58; Wachter, *Kultur*, 65. For music (in Duisburg) see Vetter, *Kulturpolitik*, 203.
81. For Berlin see Wollenhaupt-Schmidt, *documenta 1955*, 113. Also see Wachter, *Kultur*, 185–6; Vetter, *Kulturpolitik*, 114.
82. Siedler, *Erinnerungen*, 175. Also see Jähner, *Wolfszeit*, 57–9.
83. Stern, *Doppelleben*, 36–7.
84. Henze, *Reiselieder*, 94, 100; Stockhausen interview in Cott, *Stockhausen*, 52–3.
85. Knef, *Gaul*, 160; Bessen, *Trümmer*, 229–30.
86. Böll interviewed in Eggebrecht, *Männer*, 111 (quote); Böll in *Hoffnung*, ed. Hoven, 122, 140–4; Böll, *Sagte*, esp. 8–9, 14–16, 36, 81, 102–3, 108–9, 158.
87. Glaser, *Deutsche Kultur*, 82; Biess, *Homecomings*, 71; Friedrich, *Amnestie*, 200; Bessel, *Germany*, 252.
88. Biess, "Survivors," 59–62; Biess, *Homecomings*, 87–91; Fehrenbach, *Cinema*, 95, 106; Bessel, *Germany*, 324; Jähner, *Wolfszeit*, 153–8.
89. Knight, *Frauen*, 107; Jutta Brückner in Grob et al., *Film*, 275–6; Bliersbach, *Nachkriegskino*, 198.
90. Quoted in Buruma, *Year Zero*, 40.
91. Example in Kuby, *Vaterland*, 48.

92. Engelmann, *Freunde*, 30. Also Buselmeier, "Leben," 66; von Zahn, *Stimme*, 335.
93. See Thomas Koebner in Grob et al., *Film*, 198; Waidson, *Novel*, 86.
94. See Hirsch, *Endlich*, 29.
95. Walter Uka in Faulstich, *Kultur der achtziger Jahre*, 113; Jähner, *Wolfszeit*, 151–2; Korte, *Gesellschaft*, 75; Heineman, "Hour," 36–7; Kaplan, "Search," 301.
96. Böll, *Haus*, 61.
97. See Bessen, *Trümmer*, 190; Fehrenbach, *Cinema*, 104–5.
98. Knef, *Gaul*, 148.
99. Domentat, *Fräulein*, 52–5; Hirsch, *Endlich*, 68.
100. "Germany meets the Negroe Soldier," *Ebony* 2, no. 10 (October 1946): 5–11; Poiger, *Jazz*, 35; Buruma, *Year Zero*, 46; Betts, *Ruin*, 101; Kalb, *Coming*, 37–8.
101. By June 1965, women still outnumbered men, but only by a factor of 11 to 10 (Jähner, *Wolfszeit*, 176; figures in *Statistisches Jahrbuch*, 34). Also see Korte, *Gesellschaft*, 76; Bessel, *Germany*, 273, 324; Hirsch, *Endlich*, 30–3; Fehrenbach, *Cinema*, 106–7; Willenbacher, "Zerrüttung," 699–706.
102. Enzensberger, *Jahre*, 100; Karl Ove Knausgaard, "Into the Forest With the Greatest Living Artist," *NYT*, February 12, 2020.
103. See, typically, Mathilde Wolff-Mönckeberg's sentiments of May 1945 cited in Goedde, *GIs*, 61.
104. Jaspers, *Schuldfrage*, esp. 31–4, 71 (quote), 102–6. See Wilke, "Massenmedien," 654; Reichel, *Vergangenheitsbewältigung*, 70–1; König, *Zukunft*, 23; Scholtysek, "Intellectuals," 249.
105. Bergmann, *Antisemitismus*, 66.
106. König, *Zukunft*, 25.
107. Aleida Assmann in Assmann and Frevert, *Geschichtsvergessenheit*, 141.
108. Stern, *Auschwitz*, 82; Welzer et al., *Opa*, 144; Berger, "Victims," 213; Bessel, *Germany*, 89, 167–8.
109. Spender, *Witness*, 17.
110. Kortner, *Tage*, 561.
111. Arendt, *Zur Zeit*, 46; Döblin, *Schicksalsreise*, 422; Reichel, *Vergangenheitsbewältigung*, 67–9; Biess, *Homecomings*, 52; Niven, *Nazi Past*, 95–7.
112. Example in Stern, *Saitensprünge*, 10.
113. Kuby, *Vaterland*, 49.
114. Arendt, *Zur Zeit*, 44. Also see Kuby, *Vaterland*, 49; Bessel, *Germany*, 242–3.
115. Patient case in Mitscherlich and Mitscherlich, *Unfähigkeit*, 54.
116. Kaes, *Deutschlandbilder*, 21; Wilke, "Massenmedien," 653; Frei, *Wir*, 69; Jähner, *Wolfszeit*, 392; Bessel, *Germany*, 209.
117. As quoted in Biess, *Homecomings*, 56. Also see Reichel, *Vergangenheitsbewältigung*, 70.
118. Bessel, *Germany*, 316–17.
119. Mitscherlich and Mitscherlich, *Unfähigkeit*, 40; Schildt, "Umgang," 33; Aleida Assmann in Assmann and Frevert, *Geschichtsvergessenheit*, 111, 160; Goedde, *GIs*, 62; Jähner, *Wolfszeit*, 384–5.
120. Viertel, *Kindness*, 282.
121. Betts, *Ruin*, 102; Mann, "Strauss," 4; Hamann, *Wagner*, 512–13.
122. Adorno to Mann, December 28, 1949, in Gödde and Sprecher, *Adorno Mann*, 45.
123. Wiechert quoted in Glaser, *Deutsche Kultur*, 92.
124. Meinecke, *Katastrophe*, 170–3; Ritter as quoted by Konrad H. Jarausch in Jarausch and Geyer, *Past*, 47.
125. Kästner, *Notabene*, 11 and 146 (quotes).

126. Ziebill quoted in Wachter, *Kultur*, 334.
127. Heuss quoted in Wachter, *Kultur*, 338; Mommsen, "Suche," 159 (quote).
128. Wildt, *Beginn*, 205–6.
129. Görtemaker and Safferling, *Akte*, 66; von Haselberg, *Schuldgefühle*, 53, 126.
130. Dahrendorf, *Gesellschaft*, 378; Stern, *Doppelleben*, 30–1.
131. See von Haselberg, *Schuldgefühle*, 109.
132. On Kabasta see Klee, *Kulturlexikon*, 262.
133. Text in Chapter 2 at n. 273.
134. Bachmann, *Karajan*, 180–1; Eickhoff, "Entnazifizierung," 92–3. On Knappertsbusch see Vaget, *Erbe*, 249–317.
135. Kater, *Twisted Muse*, esp. 46–56, 59–60, 63–4; Klee, *Kulturlexikon*, 303.
136. Kater, *Culture*, 100–1; Chamberlin, *Kultur*, 92–3, 97, 123–4, 177; Klee, *Kulturlexikon*, 206.
137. Monod, *Scores*, 63–5; Klee, *Kulturlexikon*, 450.
138. On the festival's foundation see Beal, "Allies," 112–13. See Kater, *Twisted Muse*, 71–2, 130, 133; Borio and Danuser, *Zenit*, vol. 2, 124; Thacker, *Music*, 52, 79; Haas, *Music*, 282, 284.
139. Kater, *Twisted Muse*, 170–1, 174; Dibelius, *Moderne Musik*, 33–41; Stephan, "Kranichstein," 24; Thacker, *Music*, 78–9; Haas, *Music*, 282.
140. Michael H. Kater, "Triumph of the Wilful," *Guardian*, August 24, 2006; Rathkolb, *Führertreu*, 96–7.
141. https://www.filmportal.de/person/heidemarie-hatheyer_15e5e003e64149e69e81 052b6346f292; Glaser, *Kulturgeschichte*, vol. 1, 250; Wilke, *Theater*, 158; von Hodenberg, *Konsens*, 123; Klee, *Kulturlexikon*, 200–1.
142. Klee, *Kulturlexikon*, 527; Fehrenbach, *Cinema*, 207.
143. Wachter, *Kultur*, 97–8; Schneider, *Theater*, 126; Söderbaum, *Nichts*, 207–22.
144. Kater, *Culture*, 193–4. Contrarily see Bessen, *Trümmer*, 130.
145. Bessen, *Trümmer*, 130; Klee, *Kulturlexikon*, 263–4.
146. Käutner, "Demontage," 33.
147. *Deutsche Filmakademie*, 4, 19–21, 89; Klee, *Kulturlexikon*, 331.
148. Blumenberg, *Leben*, 206–7; Moeller, "When," 147.
149. Goertz, *Gründgens*, 105–15; Mertz, *Theater*, 68–9; Daiber, *Theater*, 91; Glaser, *Kulturgeschichte*, vol. 1, 246–7; Klee, *Kulturlexikon*, 183–4.
150. Zadek, *Heissen Jahre*, 302.
151. Table 3, Kochenrath, "Kontinuität," 290–2.
152. Wachter, *Kultur*, 63.
153. Carl Linfert, "'Jud Süss': Der Film von Veit Harlan," *FZ*, September 26, 1940.
154. Von Hodenberg, *Konsens*, 126; Krause, *Galerie*, 38; Stern, *Doppelleben*, 191.
155. Quoted in Klee, *Kulturlexikon*, 593.
156. Ibid., 594.
157. Kortner, *Tage*, 487–9. Also see Glaser, *Kulturgeschichte*, vol. 1, 235, 248; Wilke, *Theater*, 174, 182, 190; Köpf, *Schreiben*, 155.
158. Siering, "Zeitung," 65–6.
159. Karl Korn, "Der Hofjude," *DR*, September 29, 1940.
160. Ibid. Further, see Ziesel, *Gewissen*, 163–78; Köhler, *Publizisten*, 363, 368; Payk, "Amerikakomplex," 193–9.
161. Joachim Kaiser, "Karl Korns Macht und Ruhm," *SZ*, May 20, 1983.
162. Horkenbach, *Reich*, 316, 681; Bracher, *Dictatorship*, 221.
163. Heuss, *Hitlers Weg*.
164. Köpf, *Schreiben*, 76–7.
165. Quotes ibid., 78.

166. Ibid., 76, 79–80; Klee, *Kulturlexikon*, 221.
167. Petropoulos, "Seduction," 218–19; Petsch, "Künstler," 275; Lee, "Return," 409.
168. Waidson, *Novel*, 38–85; Ketelsen, *Literatur*, 64; Kater, *Culture*, 30–2, 67–9, 222–5, 329.
169. British zone: Clemens, *Kulturpolitik*, 215–27.
170. Tauber, *Eagle*, 625–37.
171. Albrecht et al., *Lexikon*, vol. 2, 310. Also see "Das Glückwunschkind," n.d., attached to NSDAP-Ortsgruppenleiter Starnberg to NSDAP-Kreisleitung Starnberg, July 14, 1942, BAB, R9361V-10410.
172. Albrecht et al., *Lexikon*, vol. 2, 311.
173. From Agnes Miegel, "Dem Schirmer des Volkes," copy in BAB, R9361V-147907.
174. Albrecht et al., *Lexikon*, vol. 2, 97–8; Klee, *Kulturlexikon*, 369–70.
175. Tauber, *Eagle*, 500–3 (quote 500).
176. Ibid., 503–12 (quote 509); Kater, *Culture*, 310.
177. As reported by Wetzel, "Existence," 137. See Stern, *Auschwitz*, 234.
178. See Wetzel, "Existence," 136.
179. Brenner, *Holocaust*, 93; Stern, *Auschwitz*, 300.
180. Heuss's statements in Stern, *Auschwitz*, 319.
181. Stern, "Breaking," 219. See Bessel, *Germany*, 264.
182. Stern, "Breaking," 220; Nasaw, *Million*, 11; Bessel, *Germany*, 265. Richarz's figure is under 200,000 ("Juden," 17).
183. Nasaw, *Million*, 492, 547–9.
184. Stern, "Breaking," 225; Wetzel, "Mir," 349.
185. Kogon, "Erneuerung," 13; Friedrich, *Amnestie*, 191; Bessel, *Germany*, 259–62; Jacobmeyer, "Lager," 39–40.
186. Report for Aschaffenburg in Dorn, *Inspektionsreisen*, 74.
187. Bessel, *Germany*, 259; Brenner, *Holocaust*, 79; Wetzel, *Leben*, 218; Jähner, *Wolfszeit*, 79.
188. Wetzel, *Leben*, 343–4.
189. Ibid., 217, 345; Königseder and Wetzel, *Waiting*, 133; Brenner, *Holocaust*, 79–80; Jacobmeyer, "Lager," 40.
190. Wetzel, *Leben*, 268; Reichel, *Vergangenheitsbewältigung*, 79; Brenner, *Holocaust*, 83–4; Königseder and Wetzel, *Waiting*, 131; Ginzel, "Phasen," 455–6; Stern, *Auschwitz*, 102, 105, 149; Nasaw, *Million*, 450.
191. Kortner, *Tage*, 565; Bessel, *Germany*, 263, 268; Königseder and Wetzel, *Waiting*, 130–1; Jacobmeyer, "Lager," 41; Jähner, *Wolfszeit*, 78; Nasaw, *Million*, 149.
192. Stern, "Breaking," 223–5 (quote 224); Brenner, *Holocaust*, 81, 84; Grossmann, *Jews*, 173–4; Bergmann, *Antisemitismus*, 67–9; Wetzel, *Leben*, 347; Wetzel, "Mir," 356; Welzer et al., *Opa*, 61.
193. Stern, "Breaking," 224.
194. Brenner, *Holocaust*, 89.
195. Heribert Prantl, "Die vergessenen Helden der deutschen Demokratie," *SZ*, August 10, 2018.
196. Mitscherlich and Mitscherlich, *Unfähigkeit*, 68.
197. Ibid., 43; Trommler, "Nachwuchs," 11.
198. Bahr, *Weimar*, esp. 289–300; Franklin, "Salka," 86, 88–9.
199. Josef Marein, "Thomas Mann," *DZ*, June 23, 1949; Vaget, *Amerikaner*, 376–415.
200. Trommler, "Nachwuchs," 11; Krüll, *Geschichte*, 392; Schaenzler, *Mann*, 520.
201. Klee, *Kulturlexikon*, 351.
202. Döblin, *Schicksalsreise*, 403–4, 457–8; Jähner, *Wolfszeit*, 322–3 (quote 323); Klee, *Kulturlexikon*, 103.

203. https://forward.com/schmooze/163533/the-jewish-actor-who-would-not-be-intimidated/.

204. Völker, *Kortner*, 210. See Kortner's letter of 1949, ibid., 185–7.

205. Ibid., 224, 238–41; Kaiser [and Kaiser], *Mohikaner*, 118–19; Glaser, *Deutsche Kultur*, 121.

206. "Der Ruf," *DZ*, May 5, 1949; Stern, "Breaking," 224; Asper, "Fritz Kortners Rückkehr," 293–9.

207. Von Saldern, *Kunstnationalismus*, 10; Riethmüller, "Umgang," 161.

208. Schnell, *Geschichte*, 103; Glaser, *Kulturgeschichte*, vol. 1, 246.

209. Korbmacher, *Neuss*, 78. Also ibid., 88.

210. Schneider, *Theater*, 123–5; Wilke, *Theater*, 133, 156; Rischbieter, "Theater," 87; Vetter, *Kulturpolitik*, 135–6; Schultheiss and Schultheiss, *Stadttheater*, 171; Schnell, *Geschichte*, 103.

211. Petzet, *Kammerspiele*, 242.

212. Schnell, *Geschichte*, 109; Albrecht et al., *Lexikon*, vol. 2, 439–41.

213. "Carl-Zuckmayer" in *Encyclopedia Britannica*.

214. Koebner, "Dramatik," 433–45; Schnell, *Geschichte*, 107–8; Schneider, *Theater*, 83–4; Petzet, *Kammerspiele*, 437–8; Braun, *Theater*, 37, 41.

215. Borchert, *Gesamtwerk*, 109.

216. Ibid., 110.

217. Jähnert, *Wolfszeit*, 26; Moeller, "When," 141–3; Endres, *Literatur*, 67–9; Schnell, *Geschichte*, 105–7; Brockmann, *Culture*, 179–81.

218. Under the title *Liebe 47*, directed by Liebeneiner, see text at n. 148, and Becker and Schöll, *Tagen*, 72–3; Brauerhoch, *Fräuleins*, 288–95.

219. Glaser, *Kulturgeschichte*, vol. 1, 255.

220. Ibid., 247.

221. Wilke, *Theater*, 193.

222. Schneider, *Theater*, 62. On Kulturbund see Kater, *Culture*, 138–49.

223. Kahlenberg, "Film," 502; Bessen, *Trümmer*, 79.

224. Table 1, Kochenrath, "Kontinuität," 289.

225. Zimmermann, "Filmtheater," 49.

226. Clemens, *Kulturpolitik*, 140; Bessen, *Trümmer*, 84.

227. Kaes, *Deutschlandbilder*, 19; Rentschler, "Use," 157.

228. Greffrath, *Gesellschaftsbilder*, 199–200; Kater, *Culture*, 319, Heins, *Melodrama*, 199–200; Cooke, "Nation," 79–80.

229. Kater, *Culture*, 187; Raddatz quoted in Bessen, *Trümmer*, 120.

230. Pleyer, *Nachkriegsfilm*, 56–60; Bessen, *Trümmer*, 138–40; Greffrath, *Gesellschaftsbilder*, 161–5.

231. Von der Grün, "Programm," 32.

232. Rüdiger Bolz in Prinz, *Trümmerzeit*, 247; Köllhofer, "RIAS," 104.

233. Albrecht et al., *Lexikon*, vol. 1, 181; vol. 2, 276–7; Barner, *Geschichte*, 90–1; Nauck, *Risiko*, 20; Würfel, *Hörspiel*, 75.

234. Würfel, *Hörspiel*, 74.

235. Kater, *Culture*, 14–15.

236. *HörWelten*, 51; Jelavich, *Berlin Alexanderplatz*, 62–113.

237. Würfel, *Hörspiel*, 80–1; Barner, *Geschichte*, 90–2; Sauer, "Rundfunk," 449; von Saldern, *Kunstnationalismus*, 147. On the development of tape (recorders) see Taruskin, *Music*, 175–6.

238. *Hörwelten*, 26.

239. Anna Seghers, *Das siebte Kreuz* (Berlin: Aufbau, 2018; 1st edn 1942). See Albrecht et al., *Lexikon*, vol. 2, 306–10.

240. Evans, "Whiter Washing" (quote 20); Fischer, *Pressepolitik*, 421–2; Demant, *Zehrer*, 149–53.
241. Richard Tüngel, "Friede auf Erden," *DZ*, December 19, 1946.
242. Von der Heide and Wagner, "Zeit," 165–80 (Studnitz quoted 178); Köpf, *Schreiben*, 153–6.
243. Korda, "Frankfurter Allgemeine Zeitung," 84–7; Kater, *Culture*, 78–9; Evans, "Whiter Washing," 20.
244. Schreiber, *Nannen*, 49–175 (Nannen quoted 77, 80); Thomas, "STERN," 164; Klee, *Kulturlexikon*, 386–7; Christian Mayer, "Denkmalsturz," *SZ*, May 20, 2022; Kater, *Culture*, 196–9.
245. Chabbi, *Walser*, 229–32, 236; Schröder, *Augstein*, 23–9; Merseburger, *Augstein*, 8, 28–9, 34–5, 44–6, 60–1, 68–9, 82–3, 88, 106, 112–13.
246. Rudolf Diels, "Der Hofstaat um Hitler," *DS*, May 12, 1949. The final article was entitled "Die Nacht der langen Messer," July 7, 1949.
247. Wistrich, *Who's Who*, 47–8; Merseburger, *Augstein*, 118–22.
248. Fischer-Defoy, *Kunst*, 190–6.
249. Borio and Danuser, *Zenit*, vol. 1, 174; vol. 2, 19, 124. On Stürmer see text above at n. 138; for Dammert, Thacker, *Music*, 282.
250. Ramthun, *Krefeld*, 82.
251. Prinz, *Trümmerzeit*, 180.
252. Franzpeter Messmer in Prinz, *Trümmerzeit*, 173–6.
253. Quoted in Daiber, *Theater*, 143. Operetta: Ramthun, *Krefeld*, 60; Glaser, *Kulturgeschichte*, vol. 1, 213.
254. Schneider, *Theater*, 122–3; Wachter, *Kultur*, 89–91; Schultheiss and Schultheiss, *Stadttheater*, 167–70; Glaser *Kulturgeschichte*, vol. 1, 213; Eberle, "Götter," 35.
255. Schäfer, *Bühne*, 207–91.
256. "Anhang," Klein, "Realität," 145–6.
257. "Werkverzeichnis" in *Karl Amadeus Hartmann*, 357–63; Andrew McCredie in Dibelius et al., *Hartmann*, 47–8; Franzpeter Messmer in Prinz, *Trümmerzeit*, 191–2.
258. Henze, *Reiselieder*, 83; *Karl Amadeus Hartmann*, 186–203.
259. Hartmann quoted in Haas, *Music*, 281.
260. Elisabeth Hartmann in recorded interview with author, Munich, December 13, 1994, YUA, CA ON00370 F0456.
261. Dibelius, *Moderne Musik*, 78–87; Glaser, *Kulturgeschichte*, vol. 1, 215; Franzpeter Messmer in Prinz, *Trümmerzeit*, 188.
262. Thomas Mann to Adorno, July 12, 1948, in Gödde and Sprecher, *Adorno Mann*, 38–9. See Honegger and Massenkeil, *Lexikon*, vol. 2, 408.
263. Franzpeter Messmer in Prinz, *Trümmerzeit*, 189–90; Egk, *Zeit*, 543.
264. Franzpeter Messmer in Prinz, *Trümmerzeit*, 181.
265. Hindemith to Ernst Toch, September 23, 1933, UCLA, Ernst Toch Archive, Special Collections, Music Library.
266. Henze in Kolland, "Henze," 56-57; Glaser, *Kulturgeschichte*, vol. 1, 216–17; Eberle, "Götter," 39; Borio and Danuser, *Zenit*, vol. 1, 150–4.
267. *Rhein-Neckar-Zeitung*, October 3, 1946, in Borio and Danuser, *Zenit*, vol. 3, 378.
268. Ibid., vol. 1, 150; vol. 2, 22; Glaser, *Kulturgeschichte*, vol. 1, 214; Dibelius, *Moderne Musik*, 130.
269. Borio and Danuser, *Zenit*, vol. 2, 22, 30.
270. Ibid., vol. 1, 164 (first quote); *Rhein-Neckar-Zeitung*, Heidelberg, October 3, 1946 (as in n. 267), 379 (second quote). Also see Taruskin, *Music*, 449.
271. Borio and Danuser, *Zenit*, vol. 1, 161.

272. Hindemith quoted ibid., vol. 1, 195.
273. Ibid., vol. 2, 31–2.
274. Von Zahn, "Initiativen," 107; Hilberg and Vogt, *Musik*, 25-26; Kater, *Composers*, 51–2.
275. Hommel, "Frühzeit," 109. Ross, *Rest*, 350, speaks of U.S. military-transport complications.
276. Mauceri, *War*, 152. Mauceri's book is marked by inaccuracies and misjudgments, such as elevating Erich Wolfgang Korngold's operatic music to the level of his "mentor's," Richard Strauss's (69, 170–1).
277. Not 1948, as often written. See Borio and Danuser, *Zenit*, vol. 2, 48.
278. Thomas, *Kunst*, 10; Jähner, *Wolfszeit*, 345.
279. See Damus, "Kunst," 30; Glaser, *Kulturgeschichte*, vol. 1, 225; Reese, "Kunst," 12.
280. Krause, *Galerie*, 36; Korbmacher, *Neuss*, 71; Thomas, *Kunst*, 12; Glaser, *Deutsche Kultur*, 164; Glaser, *Kulturgeschichte*, vol. 1, 236; Vetter, *Kulturpolitik*, 113.
281. Döblin, *Schicksalsreise*, 453. See Jähner, *Wolfszeit*, 346; Damus, *Kunst*, 104; Betts, *Ruin*, 36; Glaser, *Kulturgeschichte*, vol. 1, 225.
282. Grohs quoted in Thomas, *Kunst*, 13.
283. Grass, *Häuten*, 423.
284. Damus, *Kunst*, 45.
285. Ibid., 44.
286. Ibid., 48.
287. Ibid., 31.
288. Thomas, *Kunst*, 31.
289. Of 1946: Heineman, "Hour," 41.
290. Gerhard Finckh in Prinz, *Trümmerzeit*, 118–21; Beate Frosch in ibid., 112; Reese, "Kunst," 29; Thomas, *Kunst*, 22.
291. Hermand, "Kalte Krieg," 590–2; Vormweg, "Literatur," 17–18; Sarkowitz and Metzner, *Literatur*, 58–64.
292. German original in Hadek, *Vergangenheitsbewältigung*, 38–9. See Albrecht et al., *Lexikon*, vol. 1, 183; Helbig, *Verlust*, 2–3; Jähner, *Wolfszeit*, 28.
293. Widmer, *Sprache*, 197–8.
294. Böll quoted in Schonauer, "Prosaliteratur," 199.
295. Reich-Ranicki, *Literatur*, 129.
296. Böll, "Zug," 24, 36.
297. Böll, *Verwundung*, 25 (quote), 62–9.
298. Richter in Neunzig, *Richter*, 59.
299. Richter, *Almanach*, 19–20; Richter in Neunzig, *Richter*, 76–87. Witness Schnurre's clipped style in *Die Tat*, 8–35, Schultz, *Autoren*, 29–32.
300. Reich-Ranicki in Neunzig, *Richter*, 36.
301. Nöhbauer, "Gruppen," 522–3.
302. See Gunter Groll, "Die Gruppe, die keine Gruppe ist," *SZ*, April 10, 1948; Kaiser [and Kaiser], *Mohikaner*, 309.
303. Richter in Neunzig, *Richter*, 81 (quote); Schonauer, "Prosaliteratur," 211.
304. Hans Werner Richter in Neunzig, *Richter*, 88; Nöhbauer, "Gruppen," 524; Glaser, *Kulturgeschichte*, vol. 1, 178.
305. Kater, *Culture*, 5, 7–8.
306. Krannhals, *Weltbild*, vol. 1, esp. 43, 46–9; vol. 2, esp. 385, 387, 389, 468, 487, 490, 493, 528, 541, 599 (quote).
307. Wollenhaupt-Schmidt, *documenta 1955*, 173; Lee, "Return," 408.
308. Sedlmayr, *Verlust*, esp. 109–64 (quotes 130, 134, 145, 148, 151); Kater, *Culture*, 45; Wollenhaupt-Schmidt, *documenta 1955*, 174–95; Damus, *Kunst*, 105-6.

309. Spotts, *Bayreuth*, 169.
310. Preetorius, *Weltbild*, esp. 22–9 (quotes 22, 24, 26–7). See Vaget, *Erbe*, 208–10, 457; Ross, *Wagnerism*, 540.
311. Scheffler, *Kunst*, esp. 33–8 (quotes 33, 34, 35, 38).
312. Quoted in Glaser, *Kulturgeschichte*, vol. 1, 240. Trommler, "Nachwuchs," 55–6; Wyss, "Baumeister," 63–6; Evers, *Darmstädter Gespräch*.
313. Glaser, *Kulturgeschichte*, vol. 1, 239; https://www.theviennasecession.com/gallery/emil-preetorius/.
314. Kater, *Twisted Muse*, 163–71.
315. Borio and Danuser, *Zenit*, vol. 1, 69–70, 152; Hans Heinz Stuckenschmidt in ibid., vol. 3, 380–3; Eberle, "Götter," 43.
316. Hamel quoted in Klee, *Kulturlexikon*, 192. Also Steiert, "Stuttgart," 66–8.
317. Kater, *Composers*, 277–9.
318. Blume quoted in Borio and Danuser, *Zenit*, vol. 1, 71. Also Potter, *Most German*, esp. 184–8.
319. Glaser, *Kulturgeschichte*, vol. 1, 250; Monod, "Patron State," 57.
320. Kater, *Culture*, 50–1, 97–8.
321. Pfitzner quoted in Kater, *Drummers*, 21.
322. Kater, *Composers*, 3–30, 111–43.
323. Exemplarily, see Scheffler, *Kunst*, 35.
324. Quotes Poiger, *Jazz*, 56.
325. Müller, *Springer-Konzern*, 59 (quotes); Franzpeter Messmer in Prinz, *Trümmerzeit*, 183; Glaser, *Kulturgeschichte*, vol. 1, 87–8.
326. *Hallo Fräulein*, soundtrack CD BCD 16162 BG, 2009; Ernst Emrich's interview with Margot Hielscher, October 22, 2001, *Bayerischer Rundfunk, BR-ONLINE*, https://www.br.de/fernsehen/ard-alpha/sendungen/alpha-forum/margot-hielscher-gespraech100~attachment.pdf?; Heldt, "Hallo Fräulein," esp. 199–208, 217–20; Greffrath, *Gesellschaftsbilder*, 356–61; Bliersbach, *Nachkriegskino*, 72–3.
327. Richter in Neunzig, *Richter*, 167; Krämer-Badoni, *Zwischen*, 145–8; Klee, *Kulturlexikon*, 240–1, 511–12; Kater, *Culture*, 77–8, 313.
328. Fehrenbach, *Cinema*, 84–5.
329. Klee, *Personenlexikon*, 401, 432.

TWO – DEFYING STASIS

1. Langer, *Encyclopedia*, 1182; Glaser, *Kulturgeschichte*, vol. 2, 19–21; Westermann, *Identität*, 41–2; Schweitzer et al., *Politics*, 320–3.
2. Glaser, *Kulturgeschichte*, vol. 2, 16–17; Biess, *Republik*, 124–9; Holub, "Guilt," 829; Caldwell and Hanshew, *Germany*, 55; Betts, *Ruin*, 323–4. Quote from Article 1,1, UNESCO Constitution, *postal.unesco.org*.
3. Améry, *Geburt*, 162; Korbmacher, *Neuss*, 40; Wildt, *Beginn*, 257; Glaser, "Leben," 155; Schildt, "Massenmedien," 635.
4. Blauhorn, "Alles," 34.
5. Moeller, "Remembering," 88; Kaes, *Deutschlandbilder*, 22; Kossert, *Heimat*, 274; Connor, "Integration," 21, 28.
6. Besson, *Aussenpolitik*, 192–5; Biess, "Survivors," 70–2; Biess, *Homecomings*, 66–7.
7. See text in Chapter 1, at notes 89, 97.
8. Walser, *Halbzeit* (e.g. 310, 336), *Einhorn*, and *Sturz*; also *Tagebücher 1951–1962*, 195–9. For yet another type, the lowly clerk Esslin memorialized in Fassbinder's film *Lola* of 1981, see Bessen, *Trümmer*, 388.

9. Jarausch, *Hitler*, 89.
10. Langer, *Encyclopedia*, 1180.
11. Wildt, *Beginn*, 10, 257; Glaser, "Leben," 161; Glaser, *Kulturgeschichte*, vol. 2, 74, 110; Demetz, *Anarchie*, 58–9; Kretschmann, *Spaltung*, 59–61; Abelshauser, *Jahre*, 91; Betts, *Authority*, 109–38.
12. Thomas Geiger, "Die wunderbarsten 75 PS der Automobilgeschichte," *DW*, August 17, 2018; Kretschmann, *Spaltung*, 60; Koetzle et al., *Fünfziger Jahre*, 34.
13. Also see text below at n. 130, and in Chapter 4 at n. 267.
14. Brunhöber, "Unterhaltungsmusik," 175.
15. Berg, *Varieté*, 236; Andersen, *Traum*, 35–48; Glaser, "Leben," 152.
16. Biess, "Survivors," 71.
17. Caldwell and Hanshew, *Germany*, 76–7 (quote 76). Glaser, *Kulturgeschichte*, vol. 2, 19; Becker, "Wirklichkeit," 68; Korte, *Gesellschaft*, 7; Jähner, *Wolfszeit*, 180.
18. *Lola*, Art Haus DVD. Bessen, *Trümmer*, 383–6; Thomsen, *Fassbinder*, 278–9.
19. *Deutschland, bleiche Mutter*, Zweitausendeins Edition DVD. Jutta Brückner in Grob et al., *Film*, 275–6.
20. See Steinbacher, *Sex*, 349–50; Betts, *Ruin*, 210–12.
21. Walser, *Tagebücher 1951–1962*, 9.
22. Succinctly: Waidson, *Novel*, 120. See Karasek, *Flucht*, 375.
23. Flemming and Ulrich, *Vor Gericht*, 58; "Die Ursache allen Übels sind die 'Frolleins'," *Allgemeine Zeitung*, Mainz, September 15, 1955.
24. Biess, *Republik*, 101, 106.
25. Gäbler, "Zeitung," 160.
26. Sascha Zoske, "Verwaltungwissenschaft," *FAZ*, September 10, 2019; Gäbler, "Zeitung," 159; Drew Middleton, "Adenauer Admits Nazis Hold Posts," *NYT*, October 17, 1951.
27. Ronen Steinke, "Im Bonner Justizministerium arbeiteten besonders viele Nazis," *SZ*, October 9, 2016.
28. Jähner, *Wolfszeit*, 301; Klee, *Personenlexikon*, 624.
29. Adenauer quoted in Weiss, "Journalisten," 276.
30. "Drittes Reich im Kleinen," *DS*, December 1, 1959; Wistrich, *Who's Who*, 93–4 (quote 94); Winkler, *Weg*, 162; Glaser, *Kulturgeschichte*, vol. 2, 22; Jähner, *Wolfszeit*, 398; Caldwell and Hanshew, *Germany*, 54; Bergmann, *Antisemitismus*, 235–6; Klee, *Personenlexikon*, 186–7, 441.
31. Klee, *Personenlexikon*, 186–7, 441.
32. Herbert, "NS-Eliten," 103.
33. Jähner, *Wolfszeit*, 401–2; Garbe, "Abkehr," 702–3; Herbert, "NS-Eliten," 104.
34. Frei, *Wir*, 32–4; Herbert, "NS-Eliten," 103–5; Reichel, *Vergangenheitsbewältigung*, 117, 122; Görtemaker and Safferling, *Akte*, 23; Kielmansegg, *Schatten*, 48–50; Schildt, "Umgang," 36; Felix Bohr, "Barmherzigkeit für Massenmörder," *DS*, October 18, 2018.
35. Zadek, *Wanderjahre*, 345.
36. Kochenrath, "Kontinuität," 290–2.
37. Ibid.; Kater, *Culture*, 301, 326–7.
38. Köpf, *Schreiben*, 69–70 (Wirsing quoted 70); Weiss, "Journalisten," 262–6; Klee, *Kulturlexikon*, 604; Kater, *Culture*, 312–13.
39. Linfert (July 1955) in Wollenhaupt-Schmidt, *documenta 1955*, 104–5.
40. "Harlan im Zwielicht," *Der Tagesspiegel*, Berlin, April 5, 1949; Bergmann, *Antisemitismus*, 87–104; Klee, *Kulturlexikon*, 196–7. See Harlan, *Schatten*, 213–18; Söderbaum, *Nichts*, 223–7.

41. "Ein überflüssiger Film," *FAZ*, November 6, 1957.
42. König, *Zukunft*, 26; Jähner, *Wolfszeit*, 399; Karasek, *Flucht*, 160; Kindler, *Abschied*, 372–84.
43. Herf, *Memory*, 201–333; Flemming and Ulrich, *Vor Gericht*, 112.
44. Wüstenberg, *Society*, 83–6; Reichel, *Vergangenheitsbewältigung*, 149.
45. Knoch, "Gedächtnis," 289.
46. Alexander Kluge, "'Ein bisschen ist er auch ein Lehrmeister'," *DZ*, November 26, 2022 (first quote); André Müller, "Interview mit Hans Magnus Enzensberger," *DZ*, January 20, 1995 (second quote).
47. See Reid, *Böll*, 100.
48. "Heimweh nach den falschen Fünfzigern," *DS*, April 3, 1978; Ute Frevert in Assmann and Frevert, *Geschichtsvergessenheit*, 202; Garbe, "Abkehr," 704; Glaser, *Kulturgeschichte*, vol. 2, 26; Viett, *Nie*, 32; Bollenbeck, "Fünfziger Jahre," 196.
49. Enzensberger, *Mittelmass*, 238.
50. Richard J. Evans, "Karl Dietrich Bracher Obituary," *Guardian*, October 18, 2016; Bracher, *Auflösung*.
51. Bracher, "Stufen," 30–42.
52. Auerbach, "Gründung," 529–54. See Norbert Frei, "Hitler-Junge, Jahrgang 1926," *DZ*, September 11, 2003; Kater, *Nazi Party*, 116; Herwig, *Flakhelfer*, 61–2, 65–6; Falter, *Mitglieder*, 26–7, 85–90.
53. APA, Professor Falter, Universität Mainz, to author, March 24, 2021; his email dated March 23, 2021.
54. See Rothfels, "Zeitgeschichte," 1–8.
55. Ulrich Greiner, "Wie schlimm ist es, ein Nazi gewesen zu sein?" *DZ*, November 1, 2013; "Theodor Eschenburg und der Nationalsozialismus," October 25, 2013, https://www.tagesspiegel.de/wissen/distanz-oder-nahe-3525004.html.
56. *The German Opposition to Hitler* (Hinsdale, IL: H. Regnery, 1948). See Osnos, *Wildland*, 173.
57. Haar, "Volksgeschichte," 187–98; Kater, *Hitler Youth*, 113–14; Winkler, *Weg*, 170–1.
58. Görtemaker and Safferling, *Akte*, 19.
59. Von Miquel, "Explanation," 51.
60. Ibid., 51–2; "Die Bestie vom Lager Buchenwald," *SZ*, June 23, 1953; "Ehe mit dem Satan," *Stern*, June 28, 1958; Gregor, *Nuremberg*, 89–90; Kater, *Weimar*, 258–61, 277.
61. Friedrich, *Amnestie*, 325–9; Görtemaker and Safferling, *Akte*, 223–5; Andreas Mix, "Als Westdeutschland aufwachte," *DS*, April 27, 2008; Klee, *Personenlexikon*, 154.
62. Reichel, *Vergangenheitsbewältigung*, 185; von Miquel, *Ahnden*, 146–85; Görtemaker and Safferling, *Akte*, 225; Kielmansegg, *Schatten*, 48–50.
63. Andreas Mix, "Nazijäger mit Vergangenheit," *DS*, November 28, 2008.
64. Wetzel, "Existence," 139.
65. Ibid.; Zipes, "Vicissitudes," 31; Brenner, *Holocaust*, 93; Abelshauser, *Jahre*, 106–9.
66. Bier, "Holocaust," 192; Krauss, *Heimkehr*, 128.
67. Bier, "Holocaust," 193; Zipes, "Vicissitudes," 29.
68. Garbe, "Abkehr," 700.
69. Höhn, *GIs and Fräuleins*, 10, 109–15.
70. "Heimstätte auf verfluchter Erde?" *DS*, July 31, 1963.
71. Figures in Bergmann, "Deutschen," 121; Stern, *Auschwitz*, 231–3; Wetzel, "Existence," 137; von Miquel, "Juristen," 233–4; Klee, *Personenlexikon*, 10; Ulrich Herbert, "Als die Nazis wieder gesellschaftsfähig wurden," *DZ*, January 10, 1997.
72. Speier, "Pubertät," 183; Reichel, *Vergangenheitsbewältigung*, 144–5.

73. Jörg Schmidt, "Ernst Moritz Arndt," *DZ*, November 5, 1998 (quote); Judith Luig and Julia Meyer, "Wie war das eigentlich bei dir in der Schule nach dem Krieg, Papa?" *DZ*, May 8, 2020.
74. Schornstheimer, *Augen*, 114–23; Stern, *Auschwitz*, 320.
75. Bergmann, *Antisemitismus*, 190, 235–7; Reichel, *Vergangenheitsbewältigung*, 147–8; Schönbach, *Reaktionen*, 22–50.
76. Reich-Ranicki, *Leben*, 409–11.
77. Elisabeth Endres in Franck, *Jahre*, 137.
78. The piece was composed for large orchestra in 1948 (Gregory S. Dubinsky on Jelinek in *Oxford Music Online;* Honegger and Massenkeil, *Lexikon*, vol. 4, 248).
79. Kurt Blaukopf in *Musical Quarterly* 37 (July 1951): 413.
80. Seifert, *Wand*, 210–11.
81. Enzensberger, *Mittelmass*, 270.
82. Schuh, "Rückblick," 640.
83. Kaiser, "Schauspiel," 333; Melchinger, "Struktur," 5. Vietta, *Katastrophe*, 15–66.
84. Ritter, "Dramatiker," 66.
85. *Theater heute* 10 (1970): 26.
86. Intendant Carl Mandelartz quoted in Vetter, *Kulturpolitik*, 152.
87. Melchinger, "Struktur," 4; Améry, *Geburt*, 169; Günther Rühle in Hoffmann and Klotz, *Die Sechziger*, 95–6; Knut Hickethier in Faulstich, *Kultur der fünfziger Jahre*, 44; Canaris, *Zadek*, 3; Glaser, *Kulturgeschichte*, vol. 2, 246.
88. Zadek, *My Way*, 264 (quote); Glaser, *Kulturgeschichte*, vol. 2, 243.
89. On Zurich 1933–45: Weber, "Dramatiker," 310; Knut Hickethier in Faulstich, *Kultur der fünfziger Jahre*, 46–7.
90. Melchinger, "Struktur," 5.
91. Schuh, "Rückblick," 461 (quote); Daiber, *Theater*, 103; Knut Hickethier in Faulstich, *Kultur der fünfziger Jahre*, 37; Henze, *Reiselieder*, 108; Luft, "Vorwort," 16.
92. Hermand, "Kalte Krieg," 602; Demetz, *Anarchie*, 126; Zadek, *My Way*, 288; Knut Hickethier in Faulstich, *Kultur der fünfziger Jahre*, 49; Rischbieter, "Theater," 101.
93. Kaiser, "Schauspiel," 343–4; Knut Hickethier in Faulstich, *Kultur der fünfziger Jahre*, 45.
94. Kaiser, "Schauspiel," 341.
95. Ibid., 335.
96. Ibid., 343.
97. Ibid., 345–6; Zadek, *My Way*, 273.
98. Mertz, *Theater*, 71.
99. Goertz, *Gründgens*, 125–33; Günther Rüle in Hoffmann and Klotz, *Die Sechziger*, 95–6; Knut Hickethier in Faulstich, *Kultur der fünfziger Jahre*, 45.
100. Kaiser, "Schauspiel," 335.
101. Melchinger, "Struktur," 6 (quote); Rischbieter, "Theater," 99–100; Knut Hickethier in Faulstich, *Kultur der fünfziger Jahre*, 49–50; Glaser, *Kulturgeschichte*, vol. 2, 245.
102. *Danton's Death*. Joachim Kaiser, "Dantons Siechtum und Tod," *SZ*, July 12, 1959; Mertz, *Theater*, 67.
103. Melchinger, "Struktur," 6; Mertz, *Theater*, 67; Knut Hickethier in Faulstich, *Kultur der fünfziger Jahre*, 49.
104. Klee, *Kulturlexikon*, 133; Koetzle et al., *Fünfziger*, 128–9; Völker, *Kortner*, 226; Siedler, *Erinnerungen*, 395.
105. Zadek, *My Way*, 265.
106. Ibid., 263, 289.
107. Zadek in 1959, quoted in Canaris, *Zadek*, 34; Zadek, *Heissen Jahre*, 147.

108. Zadek, *My Way*, 289.
109. Klee, *Kulturlexikon*, 63–4; Kater, *Culture*, 246–7.
110. https://www.imdb.com/name/nm0473228/bio?ref_=nm_ov_bio_sm.
111. Glaser, *Kulturgeschichte*, vol. 2, 235; Walter Uka in Faulstich, *Kultur der fünfziger Jahre*, 74–7.
112. Kahlenberg, "Film," 502–3.
113. https://www.filminstitut-hannover.de/junge-film-union/.
114. Bessen, *Trümmer*, 187–99; Fehrenbach, *Cinema*, 103–4.
115. Kaes, *Deutschlandbilder*, 23; Rentschler, *Film*, 108. West Germany's population was 50,808 million in 1950, 54,876 million in 1959 (*Statistisches Jahrbuch*, 27–8).
116. https://www.filmportal.de/en/movie/schwarzwaldmadel_ea43d4a6b3b55006e03 053d50b37753d. See Bessen, *Trümmer*, 240–1; Tauber, "Heimatfilm," 104–7; Kaes, *Deutschlandbilder*, 23; Höfig, *Heimatfilm*, 337–8, 360–4.
117. *Grün ist die Heide* (1951), Filmjuwelen DVD.
118. Friedemann Beyer, "Mutter Heimat," *DW*, February 19, 2020.
119. Fehrenbach, *Cinema*, 150–5 (quote 154); Bliersbach, *Nachkriegskino*, 84–7; Bliersbach, *Heide*, 37–43; Bessen, *Trümmer*, 264–70; Heins, *Melodrama*, 196–7.
120. "Neue Krawalle am Wedding," *Telegraf*, Berlin, July 13, 1956; Poiger, *Jazz*, 79–80, 100; Kalb, *Coming*, 94–102, 124–38, 148–50.
121. Biess, *Republik*, 111–13.
122. Example of Heidelberg's Michael Buselmeier, born in 1938, in Buselmeier, "Leben," 47–51. See "Die Erwachsenen sind schuld," *DZ*, January 10, 1952; Stückrath, "Überfall," 221; Willenbacher, "Zerrüttung," 613–14.
123. Mitscherlich and Mitscherlich, *Unfähigkeit*, 260.
124. Martin and Porter, *Guide*, 111, 810, 906; "Der Wilde," *Der Kurier*, Berlin, April 13, 1955; "Der Dompteur der Klasse," *Telegraf*, Berlin, December 2, 1955; Maximilian, "Saat," 28–31; Meuer, "Erziehungsprobleme," 32–3; Poiger, *Jazz*, 31, 36.
125. Taruskin, *Music*, 314 (quote); "Elvis, the Pelvis," *DS*, December 12, 1956; John Lynne, "Ausser Rand und Band," *DZ*, October 4, 1956; Faulstich, "Amerikanisierung," 156–9; Kalb, *Coming*, 109–12, 141–3.
126. "Neu in Deutschland," *DS*, October 17, 1956; Christa Rotzoll, "Gutwillige Erwachsene stören nur," *DW*, July 28, 1956; Bessen, *Trümmer*, 276–81; Poiger, *Jazz*, 102–3.
127. Kater, *Culture*, 174.
128. Hake, *Cinema*, 104.
129. https://www.imdb.com/title/tt0045980/.
130. Bliersbach, *Nachkriegskino*, 183–7. See text above at n. 13.
131. Kahlenberg, "Film," 480–1; Bessen, *Trümmer*, 286–95; Bliersbach, *Nachkriegskino*, 187–91.
132. McCormick, "Memory," 285–96; Bliersbach, *Nachkriegskino*, 197–9. See text above at notes 7 and 28.
133. "Gregor Dorfmeister ist tot," *DS*, February 6, 2018; Kaes, *Deutschlandbilder*, 24; Walter Uka in Faulstich, *Kultur der fünfziger Jahre*, 84; Grob et al., *Film*, 13; Moeller, "Victims," 55–9.
134. Schörken, *Niederlage*, 71–7; Kater, *Hitler Youth*, 215–31.
135. "Stalingrad," *DS*, April 15, 1959, 65–8.
136. Frei, "Hörfunk," 430–1; Pilgert, *Press*, 78; Glaser, *Kulturgeschichte*, vol. 2, 224–7.
137. Von Hodenberg, *Konsens*, 94–5, 297; von der Grün, "Programm," 28–30.
138. Caldwell and Hanshew, *Germany*, 103 (quote); Gerhard Schäffner in Faulstich, *Kultur der fünfziger Jahre*, 98; Schildt, "Massenmedien," 636–8.

139. Barner, *Geschichte*, 245.
140. Würfel, *Hörspiel*, 76; *HörWelten*, 26, 50–3, 67.
141. Würfel, *Hörspiel*, 109–10.
142. Barner, *Geschichte*, 247–8.
143. *Die Revolte von San Nazzaro, Oper für sizilianische Marionetten*, broadcast on May 24, 1957 (Henze, *Reiselieder*, 179).
144. Handke, *Präsenz*, 98–100; author's recorded interview with Schulz-Köhn in Baden-Baden, September 4 and 5, 1986, YUA, CA ON00370 F0456.
145. Kater, *Drummers*, 208–9.
146. Nauck, *Risiko*, 13.
147. Score, *Das Ende einer Welt*, 72 (quote); Henze, *Reiselieder*, 128.
148. Nauck, *Risiko*, 17–27, 83–8.
149. Luft, "Fernsehen," 57.
150. Geisler, "Nazis," 233; Frei, "Hörfunk," 429.
151. Frei, "Hörfunk," 429.
152. Knight, *Frauen*, 32; Müller, *Mini*, 111.
153. Luft, "Fernsehen," 54–64 (quote 56); Gerhard Schäffner in Faulstich, *Kultur der fünfziger Jahre*, 95–100; Ludes, "Programmgeschichte," 265–6; Glaser, *Kulturgeschichte*, vol. 2, 232; Gundwin, "Einflüssen," 798–801.
154. Werner Höfer in Rathke, *Die 50er Jahre*, 39–41; Geisler, "Nazis," 39–40; "Die Werner-Höfer-Schau," *DS*, December 9, 1959; Glaser, *Kulturgeschichte*, vol. 2, 229.
155. https://www.imdb.com/title/tt4379326/; Classen, *Bilder*, 38–40, 87–8, 155–6, 162–3; Fritsche, *Vergangenheitsbewältigung*, 73–5.
156. Jürgen Wilke in Faulstich, *Kultur der sechziger Jahre*, 216; von Hodenberg, *Konsens*, 88.
157. Harenberg, "Die Welt," 111.
158. Von Hodenberg, *Journalisten*, 296; Weiss, "Journalisten," 255.
159. Von Hodenberg, *Journalisten*, 296.
160. Christian Steininger in Faulstich, *Kultur der fünfziger Jahre*, 238; von Hodenberg, *Journalisten*, 293–5.
161. Hans Magnus Enzensberger quoted in Glaser, *Kulturgeschichte*, vol. 2, 211.
162. Siering, "Zeitung," 70.
163. Weiss, "Journalisten," 254–5; Siering, "Zeitung," 72–3.
164. Sethe's vita at https://www.deutsche-biographie.de/sfz121358.html. Also see Evans, "Whiter Washing," 20. Bonn political details in Winkler, *Weg*, 150–1.
165. Krause, *Frankreich*, 157–72; Reich-Ranicki, *Leben*, 429–30.
166. Müller, *Springer-Konzern*, 159.
167. Kaiser [and Kaiser], *Mohikaner*, 26; Andreas Kreye, "Langjähriger Feuilletonchef und SZ-Kritiker Joachim Kaiser ist tot," *SZ*, May 11, 2017.
168. Von Zahn, *Stimme*, 282.
169. Kuby, *Vaterland*, 261; Kater, *Drummers*, 106–7, 109, 155, 161.
170. Müller, *Springer-Konzern*, 160.
171. Ibid., 159–65; Kruip, *Journalismus*, 183; Demant, *Zehrer*, 160; Weiss, "Journalisten," 271.
172. Brumm, "BILD-Zeitung," 137.
173. Kuby's Zehrer reprint of a column from June 24, 1952, in *Vaterland*, 256.
174. Ibid., 255.
175. Frei, "Presse," 393.
176. Müller, *Springer-Konzern*, 80; Brumm, "BILD-Zeitung," 138.
177. Führer, "Bild-Zeitung," 315.

178. Améry, *Geburt*, 167; Schildt, "Massenmedien," 639; von Hodenberg, *Journalisten*, 293–4; von Hodenberg, *Konsens*, 191–3; Christian Steininger in Faulstich, *Kultur der fünfziger Jahre*, 239, 245; Frei "Presse," 395; Kindler, *Abschied*, 371–89.
179. https://www.ndr.de/geschichte/koepfe/Gerd-Bucerius-Der-Herr-ueber-die-Zeit-,gerdbucerius101.html.
180. Von Kuenheim and Sommer, *Marion*, 27–33; Wistrich, *Who's Who*, 275–7; Meyn, "DIE ZEIT," 278; Glaser, *Kulturgeschichte*, vol. 2, 213; von Hodenberg, *Journalisten*, 289–90; von der Heide and Wagner, "Zeit," 182–3; Gunter Hofmann, "Wer darf hier schreiben?" *DZ*, February 3, 2019.
181. Gunter Hofmann, "Wer darf hier schreiben?" *DZ*, February 3, 2019; Klee, *Kulturlexikon*, 381–2; Frei, *Wir*, 71–2; von der Heide and Wagner, "Zeit," 181.
182. Josef Müller-Marein, "Zum Tode von Walter Abendroth," *DZ*, October 12, 1973; Janssen et al., *Die Zeit*, 91–2; Abendroth, *Neugierige*, 253–4.
183. Brumm, "Der Spiegel," 186; Merseburger, *Augstein*, 234.
184. Jaene, *SPIEGEL*, 26, 39 (quote).
185. Merseburger, *Augstein*, 234; Kuby, *Vaterland*, 139; Hachmeister, "Spiegel," 94.
186. Hachmeister, "Spiegel," 87–9, 111.
187. "Deutschlands Schmuggler," *DS*, July 5, 1950.
188. Hachmeister, "Spiegel," 95–9 (quote is from SS "Ereignismeldung Nr. 73," September 4, 1941, ibid., 98), 101–2.
189. Hachmeister, "Spiegel," 95–6, 99–107; Klee, *Personenlexikon*, 585.
190. Damus, *Kunst*, 103–4.
191. https://www.heinrichsiepmann.de/biographie.htm.
192. http://www.artnet.com/artists/hans-werdehausen/; https://www.mutualart.com/Artist/Hans-Werdehausen/924229A9ADD5EDEC/AuctionResults?Type=Sold_Unsold&action=filter.
193. https://www.grochowiak.com/grochowiak_biografie.html.
194. Thomas, *Kunst*, 38; Korbmacher, *Neuss*, 71.
195. Thomas, *Kunst*, 28.
196. Damus, *Kunst*, 140–4, 183–4, 201; Kretschmann, *Spaltung*, 68; Jähner, *Wolfszeit*, 352; Schmidt, "Kunst," 259.
197. Schmidt, "Kunst," 282.
198. Ibid., 280–9; Damus, *Kunst*, 156.
199. Naifeh and White Smith, *Pollock*, 520, 526, 533–40, 566–7; Pells, *Not Like Us*, 77–8; Damus, *Kunst*, 154–5, 166; Damus, "Kunst," 39; Thomas, *Kunst*, 22; Jähner, *Wolfszeit*, 356–8; Faust and de Vries, *Hunger*, 11–13; Menand, *Free World*, 139, 147, 150, 152.
200. Naifeh and White Smith, *Pollock*, 662; Pells, *Not Like Us*, 66–81; Betts, *Ruin*, 241; Menand, *Free World*, 124, 219–21, 434, 519–20.
201. Damus, *Kunst*, 154–70.
202. Ibid., 168–9 (quote 169), 171.
203. Faust and De Vries, *Hunger*, 12–13; Damus, *Kunst*, 174–7.
204. Wollenhaupt-Schmidt, *documenta 1955*, 18–19; Kimpel, *documenta*, 7–23; Vowinckel, "Kunst," 8–12.
205. Vowinckel, "Kunst," 8.
206. Klee, *Kulturlexikon*, 190.
207. Kimpel, *documenta*, 17.
208. https://www.documenta.de/en/retrospective/documenta#.
209. Buttig, "Treffen," 75; https://www.documenta.de/en/retrospective/documenta#.
210. Wollenhaupt-Schmidt, *documenta 1955*, 107–8.
211. Carl Georg Heise, "Documenta," *DZ*, August 11, 1955.

212. Bachler's review of *Bremer Tageszeitung*, July 1955, cited in Wollenhaupt-Schmidt, *documenta 1955*, 107.
213. Heinz Bude and Karin Wieland, "Werner Haftmann," *DZ*, March 10, 2021; Hanno Rauterberg and Katja Nicodemus, "Hüter des falschen Friedens," *DZ*, February 6, 2020 (quote); Klee, *Kulturlexikon*, 190; Kater, *Culture*, 38–9.
214. Andreas Kilb, "Austellung zur Documenta," *FAZ*, June 18, 2021.
215. Haftmann cited in Wedekind, "Abstraktion," 174.
216. In 1957, Haftmann admitted "contradiction" (*Skizzenbuch*, 75).
217. Kimpel, *documenta*, 28–38; Damus, *Kunst*, 172; Buttig, "Treffen," 75–82; Vowinckel, "Kunst," 13–14.
218. Jill Lloyd, "Werner Haftmann," *Guardian*, August 24, 1999 (first quote); Buttig, "Treffen," 76-82 (second quote 76); Haftmann, *Skizzenbuch*, 125 (third quote).
219. Bachmann, *Karajan*, 186–9.
220. Ross, "Devil's Disciple," 72.
221. Daiber, *Theater*, 154; Klee, *Kulturlexikon*, 25, 42–3, 58, 165–6, 230–1, 272–3, 327–8, 391, 469.
222. Ibid., 120–1; Klein, "Realität," 116; corr. Wilhelm Tietjen-Alice Strauss, late 1940s, GSB, Stiftung Preussischer Kulturbesitz/I/HA/Rep119neu.
223. Glaser, *Kulturgeschichte*, vol. 2, 248–53.
224. Schäfer, *Bühne*, 107–291; Klein, "Realität," 146–9; Koegler, "Manager," 49–50.
225. On Orff: Daiber, *Theater*, 144; Thomas, *Rad*, 27; Gertrud Runge (1953) in Borio and Danuser, *Zenit*, vol. 3, 406; Monod, "Patron State," 56. On Egk: *Zeit*, 544, 547–63. On Blacher: Daiber, *Theater*, 154, 233; Dibelius, *Moderne Musik*, 57–8. On von Einem: Daiber, *Theater*, 154.
226. Dibelius, "Music," 165; Hans Werner Heister in Heister, *Geschichte*, 136.
227. Entry for October 15, 1947, in CM, Diary Gertrud Orff; Henze, *Reiselieder*, 214.
228. Fuchs, *Menschen*, 29-30; Stockhausen in "Die ausgegrenzte Avantgarde," 26 (quote).
229. Monod, "Patron State," 56.
230. Ramthun, *Krefeld*, 70.
231. Koegler, "Manager," 58–9; Martin Elste in Heister, *Geschichte*, 41; von Zahn, *Stimme*, 343.
232. Custodis, *Isolation*, 57; Gronemeyer, "Neue Musik," 57.
233. Borio and Danuser, *Zenit*, vol. 1, 171; Dibelius, "Musik," 164.
234. Borio and Danuser, *Zenit*, vol. 2, 125–7.
235. Eberle, "Götter," 44–6; Hommel, "Frühzeit," 112; Borio and Danuser, *Zenit*, vol. 1, 187–9.
236. Dibelius, *Moderne Musik*, 28–30; Eberle, "Götter," 44; Borio and Danuser, *Zenit*, vol. 1, 189; Ross, *Rest*, 83 (quotes); Malcom Gillies, "Bartók, Béla" in *Oxford Music Online*.
237. Paul Griffiths, "Serialism" in *Oxford Music Online*.
238. I follow Kathryn Bailey Puffett, "Webern, Anton" in *Oxford Music Online*. Also Ross, *Rest*, 196–7.
239. Borio and Danuser, *Zenit*, vol. 1, 213; Iddon, *New Music*, 62.
240. Borio and Danuser, *Zenit*, vol. 1, 213–17; Josef Häusler (1955) in *Zenit*, vol. 3, 413–18; Dibelius, "Musik," 136–7; Albert Rodemann (1953) in Dibelius and Schneider, *Neue Musik*, vol. 1, 149–51; Dieter Rexroth in Hoffmann and Klotz, *Die Sechziger*, 124.
241. G.W. Hopkins and Paul Griffiths, "Boulez, Pierre" in *Oxford Music Online* (quotes); Aucoin, "Sound," 18.
242. Monika Burzik in Faulstich, *Kultur der fünfziger Jahre*, 251; Ross, *Rest*, 363.

243. Christopher Fox, "Darmstadt School" in *Oxford Music Online* (quote); Honegger and Massenkeil, *Lexikon*, vol. 5, 184–5; vol. 6, 47–8; Josef Häusler in Borio and Danuser, *Zenit*, vol. 1, 214–16; vol. 3, 416; Dibelius, "Musik," 136.
244. Richard Toop, "Stockhausen, Karlheinz" in *Oxford Music Online*.
245. *Alea* is Latin for "game of dice" or "chance." See Naifeh and White Smith, *Pollock*, 663; Betty Freeman, "Cage, John" in *Oxford Music Online* (first quote); *Zwanzig Jahre Musik*, 86; Beal, *New Music*, 64–72, 92–8; Gronemeyer, "Neue Musik," 56; Ross, *Rest*, 367; Taruskin, *Music*, 65; Menand, *Free World*, 234–5, 240, 258–62, 270–1.
246. Taruskin, *Music*, 189, 191; Ross, *Rest*, 395; von Blumröder, "Stockhausen," 317–18. Donaueschingen: Karl Heinz Ruppel (1954) in Dibelius and Schneider, *Neue Musik*, vol. 1, 151–5; Kirchmeyer, "Eimert," 4–14; Custodis, *Isolation*, 58–64, Borio and Danuser, *Zenit*, vol. 2, 91–3; Monika Burzik in Faulstich, *Kultur der fünfziger Jahre*, 252.
247. Geitel, *Henze*, 11–17 (quote 15); Henze, *Musik*, 306.
248. Virginia Palmer-Füchsel, "Henze, Hans Werner" in *Oxford Music Online* (quote); Henze in Lindlar, *Fortner*, 86–7; Henze, *Musik*, 128, 312, 321, 368; Henze, *Reiselieder*, 90, 115; Borio and Danuser, *Zenit*, vol. 2, 18–24.
249. Henze, *Musik*, 134, 136, 149, 301, 306, 313, 322; Henze, *Reiselieder*, 142–3, 181–2. Strobel: Prieberg, *Musik*, 314–17; Custodis, "Wirken," 158–9; Custodis and Geiger, *Netzwerke*, 31–72.
250. Henze in Henze, *Musik*, 136 (quote), 323; Henze, *Reiselieder*, 151; Henze in Kolland, "Henze," 70; Borio and Danuser, *Zenit*, vol. 2, 17; Flammer, *Musik*, 110.
251. Stockhausen in Cott, *Stockhausen*, 52 (quotes); Kurtz, *Stockhausen*, 30–8.
252. Obituary, "Karlheinz Stockhausen," *The Times*, London, December 8, 2007.
253. "Karlheinz Stockhausen" in *Encyclopedia Britannica*; Morgan, "Stockhausen's Writing," 6–7; Dibelius, *Moderne Musik*, 95–103; Taruskin, *Music*, 45–9, 190; Kurtz, *Stockhausen*, 71; Frisius, *Stockhausen*, 15–17; von Blumröder, "Stockhausen," 310–16.
254. Henze in Kolland, "Henze," 58.
255. Pascal Decroupet in Heister, *Geschichte*, 149 (quote); Dibelius, *Moderne Musik*, 30; Albert Rodemann (1953) in Dibelius and Schneider, *Neue Musik*, vol. 1, 149–51; Dieter Rexroth in Hoffmann and Klotz, *Die Sechziger*, 124; Christopher Fox, "Darmstadt School" in *Oxford Music Online*.
256. Adorno, "Musik" (quotes 178, 179). Also Borio and Danuser, *Zenit*, vol. 1, 189; Josef Häusler (1955) in Borio and Danuser, *Zenit*, vol. 3, 414–15; Heinz Joachim in Borio and Danuser, *Zenit*, vol. 3, 424–5; Henze, *Reiselieder*, 87; Eberle, "Götter," 44–6.
257. Henze, *Musik*, 311 (first quote), 315–17; Henze, *Reiselieder*, 167, 182; Borio and Danuser, *Zenit*, vol. 2, 17, 34; Stockhausen in Custodis, *Isolation*, 64 (second quote), also 102–3; Ross, *Rest*, 394; Menand, *Free World*, 274–7.
258. Taruskin, *Music*, 54; Borio and Danuser, *Zenith*, vol. 1, 62; Dieter Rexroth in Hoffmann and Klotz, *Die Sechziger*, 125; Pascal Decroupet in Heister, *Geschichte*, 149; Christopher Fox, "Darmstadt School" in *Oxford Music Online*.
259. Bermbach, *Entnazifizierung*, 5.
260. Spotts, *Bayreuth*, 171.
261. Ibid., 185–6, 189–99; Wagner, *Wagner Theater*, 167.
262. Hamann, *Wagner*, 482–4; Wagner, *Wagner Theater*, 324.
263. Hamann, *Wagner*, 509, 527; Spotts, *Bayreuth*, 199–202.
264. Hamann, *Wagner*, 547, 554, 558–9, 564, 566; Wagner, *Wagner Theater*, 260; Kolland, "Kleider," 157; Wagner, *Lebensakte*, 138–41, 159.

265. Vaget, "Entnazifizierung," 88.
266. Johannes Jacobi, "Orchester contra Bühne," *DZ*, August 16, 1951 (quote); Ruppel, "Bayreuth 1951," 364; Oehlmann, "Bayreuth," 636–8; Bachmann, *Karajan*, 182; Kolland, "Kleider," 165–6; Daiber, *Theater*, 156.
267. Oehlmann, "Bayreuth," 636 (first quote); Wagner, *Wagner Theater*, 346 (second quote); Ruppel, "Bayreuth 1951," 362–3.
268. Spotts, *Bayreuth*, 217, 221–3, 230; Wagner, *Wagner Theater*, 21, 173, 176, 178, 333.
269. Wagner, *Wagner Theater*, 331.
270. Ross, *Wagnerism*, 613; Wagner, *Wagner Theater*, 332.
271. Johannes Jacobi, "Orchester contra Bühne," *DZ*, August 16, 1951.
272. Ruppel, "Bayreuth 1951," 364 (quote); Wagner, *Wagner Theater*, 174, 333.
273. Kolland, "Kleider," 165 (quote); Bachmann, *Karajan*, 182.
274. Bermbach, *Entnazifizierung*, 4; Vaget, "Entnazifizierung," 90–1.
275. Kolland, "Kleider," 150; Wagner, *Wagner Theater*, 332.
276. Johannes Jacobi, "Neue Weichenstellung in Bayreuth," *DZ*, July 31, 1959.
277. Ruppel, "Bayreuth 1951," 362; Oehlmann, "Bayreuth," 635–9; Wagner, *Wagner Theater*, 173; Kolland, "Kleider," 153, 166.
278. Hamann, *Wagner*, 559; https://www.dw.com/en/nike-wagner-opens-up-on-her-fathers-nazi-ties-and-a-childhood-overshadowed-by-the-bayreuth-festival/a-39805826.
279. Wagner, *Wagner Theater*, 241, 357.
280. Johannes Jacobi, "Neue Weichenstellung in Bayreuth," *DZ*, July 31, 1959; and "Wieland und Wolfgang," *DZ*, August 12, 1960; Wagner, *Wagner Theater*, 346, 357; Kolland, "Kleider," 168; Spotts, *Bayreuth*, 233.
281. Kater, *Drummers*, 48–9.
282. Kater, *Drummers*, 130–5.
283. Fuchs, *Menschen*, 36–7; Wachter, *Kultur*, 170; Kater, *Drummers*, 204–5.
284. https://www.cbc.ca/news/entertainment/Jazz-musician-peter-appleyard-dies-at-84-1.1312337.
285. Monika Schlecht, "Jazzmusikanten als Werbetrommler," *SZ*, February 17, 1960; https://www.Jazzmessengers.com/en/68650/ira-kriss/Jazzanova; https://passages.winnipegfreepress.com/passage-details/id-174820/Haugsoen_Knut: https://digitalcollections.lib.uct.ac.za/islandora/object/islandora%3A12862.
286. Hassenkamp, *Sieg*, 32; Willett, *Americanization*, 96–7; Berendt, *Fenster*, 167, 186–7; Kotschenreuther, "Glanz," 204–5; Holzt-Edelhagen, *Jazz-Geschichte(n)*, 108–9.
287. Berendt, *Fenster*, 164, 167; Kater, *Drummers*, 204.
288. Berendt, *Fenster*, 183–7; Jost, *Europas Jazz*, 201–2; Kater, *Drummers*, 207.
289. "Musikergespräch mit Michael Naura," 161–2.
290. McClure, *Thing*, 137.
291. https://www.eclassical.com/shop/17115/art97/4917097-cae70e-IPPNWCD18_Booklet.pdf.
292. https://de.wikipedia.org/wiki/Datei:Muefeilitzschstr131974c99.jpg.
293. Hassenkamp, *Sieg*, 31; Domentat, *Coca Cola*, 112–27; Berendt, *Fenster*, 174, 177; Lange, *Jazz*, 157; Kater, *Drummers*, 208–9; Zahn, *Jazz*, 84–93; Knauer, "Emanzipation," 144.
294. Lange, *Jazz*, 155; Strack, "Kulturbeziehungen," 290–8; Willett, *Americanization*, 91; Höhn, *GIs and Fräuleins*, 61; Kurth, "Jazz," 121; Berendt, *Fenster*, 176, 179–80, 184.
295. Werner Höfer, "Bebop – eine Revolution des Jazz?" *DZ*, August 5, 1948.
296. "Der älteste Hahn ist tot," *DS*, October 13, 1949.

297. Adorno in *Musik* 21 (1929): 625; Adorno, "Kleiner Zitatenschatz," *Musik*, 24 (1932): 738.
298. Adorno, "Zeitlose Mode," esp. 537 (quote), 538–9, 545–6.
299. Berendt, "Thema Jazz," esp. 768–72, 774–6, 778.
300. See Kaestner, "Jazz," esp. 43.
301. Poiger, *Jazz*, 173; Maase, *BRAVO Amerika*, 18, 28–31, 100, 103, 178; Kleinsteuber, "Hörfunk," 522; Schildt, "Not," 345–6.
302. Lange, *Jazz*, 119; Willett, *Americanization*, 91–2, 97; Höhn, *GIs and Fräuleins*, 79; *DS*, March 31, 2003, 143; Kaiser, *Jugend*, 176–7; Eberhard, *Rundfunkhörer*, 132–3; Kupffer, *Swingtime*, 112; Zinnecker, *Jugendkultur*, 161, 163–4; Maase, *BRAVO Amerika*, 179.
303. Nazi anti-Black propaganda: "Negersoldaten gesucht! Onkel Toms Urenkel als Kanonenfutter für das Sternenbanner," *Koralle* (August 20, 1944): 228–9. Racist stereotype/Black GIs: Goedde, *GIs*, 65–6.
304. Bollenbeck, "Jahre," 195–6.
305. Kimmig, *Atlantik*, 24 (quote); Frederik, *Amerika*, 40–1, 44–5; Ingensand, *Amerikaner*, 135–7; *Der Neger*, [23–4], [31–2].
306. Kaiser, *Süden*, 71.
307. Frederik, *Amerika*, 46.
308. Ben Ratcliff, "Jutta Hipp, 78, Jazz Pianist With a Lean, Percussive Style," *NYT*, April 11, 2003; "Jutta Hipp," *Daily Telegraph*, London, April 22, 2003; author's recorded interview with Emil Mangelsdorff, Munich, May 30, 1987, YUA, CA ON00370 F0456; https://www.Jazzwax.com/2013/05/jutta-hipp-the-inside-story.html. Author's 1989 corr. with Hipp in YUA, CA ON00370 F0456.
309. Kiesel, "Gedächtnis," 51. Also Weniger, "Trümmerliteratur," 7.
310. Jens, *Literatur*, 150–2.
311. Joachim Kaiser in Kaiser [and Kaiser], *Mohikaner*, 193. Also see Schonauer, "Prosaliteratur," 239; Ute Frevert in Assmann and Frevert, *Geschichtsvergessenheit*, 224.
312. Reich-Ranicki, *Literatur*, 41-44.
313. Koeppen, *Tauben*, 63; Wettberg, *Amerika-Bild*, 64-66.
314. 1948 in Reinhardt, "Politik," 41; 1949 in Trommler, "Realismus," 201; 1950 in Wettberg, *Amerika-Bild*, 58; 1951 in Schnell, *Geschichte*, 287.
315. Reinhardt, "Politik," 42–5.
316. Koeppen, *Tauben*, 11–14; Demetz, *Anarchie*, 220.
317. Knapp, *Roman*, 53.
318. See Ute Frevert in Assmann and Frevert, *Geschichtsvergessenheit*, 225.
319. Reich-Ranicki, *Literatur*, 51–2; Schnell, *Geschichte*, 288; Horst, *Literatur*, 135–6.
320. See Endres, *Literatur*, 163–4.
321. Linder, *Böll*, 373.
322. See Koch, "Roman," 213; Waidson, *Novel*, 106; Endres, *Literatur*, 147; Brockmann, *Culture*, 81.
323. Jens, *Nein*, 106.
324. Ibid., 163.
325. Knapp, *Roman*, 83.
326. Ibid., 84.
327. Andersch, *Sansibar*, 206–7; Angress, "Judenproblem," 26; Reich-Ranicki, *Literatur*, 107; Lehnert, "Gruppe 47," 58.
328. Ryan, *Past*, 73; Knapp, *Roman*, 83,
329. Andersch, *Sansibar*, 23; Reich-Ranicki, *Literatur*, 107; Lehnert, "Gruppe 47," 57; Trommler, "Cocoon," 315; Hartmann, "Romane," 294.

330. Angress [=Klüger], "Judenproblem," 25.
331. Reich-Ranicki, *Literatur*, 113.
332. Böll, "Adam," 207, 235-39; Améry, *Geburt*, 190; Horst, *Literatur*, 136-37; Waidson, *Novel*, 111.
333. Reich-Ranicki, *Literatur*, 137.
334. See Böll, *Sagte*, 8. See text in Chapter 1 at n. 86.
335. Böll, *Haus*, 38, 52, 61, 158, 222-4, 228-9; Reid, *Böll*, 101.
336. Böll, *Haus*, 284; Reid, *Böll*, 100, 105.
337. Paul Hühnerfeld, "Wir sind nicht verloren," *DZ*, September 23, 1954; Reid, *Böll*, 73.
338. Böll interviewed in Eggebrecht, *Männer*, 120; Marcel Reich-Ranicki, "Dichter, Narr, Prediger," *FAZ*, July 18, 1985.
339. Böll, *Billard*, 176.
340. Paul Hühnerfeld, "Heinrich Böll," *DZ*, October 9, 1959; Reich-Ranicki, *Literatur*, 137-8; Ryan, *Past*, 81-90; Knapp, *Roman*, 25-37.
341. Joachim Kaiser, "Was ist ein Mensch ohne Trauer?" *SZ*, December 12/13, 1959.
342. Marcel Reich-Ranicki, "Der wackere Provokateur Martin Walser," *DZ*, September 27, 1963.
343. Walser, *Flugzeug*, 19-20.
344. Boris vom Berg, "Ehen in Philippsburg by Martin Walser," literaturzeitschrift.de, June 30, 2017, https://literaturzeitschrift.de/book-review/ehen-in-philippsburg/.
345. Walser, *Ehen*, 219-27.
346. Walser, *Tagebücher 1951–1962*, 265-76, 300-1, 312, 466-7.
347. Few World War II exceptions: Walser, *Ehen*, 82, 187, 196-7.
348. Martin Walser in Walser and Augstein, *Leben*, 121. See Florian Illies, "Der vergessene grosse Roman," *DZ*, April 9, 2008.
349. Grass, *Blechtrommel*, 63-4.
350. "Zunge heraus," *DS*, September 3, 1963; Koch, "Roman," 228; 1959 play reviews in Luft, *Stimme*, 299-302; Hensel, *Zeitgenossen*, 148-9.
351. Enzensberger, "Meister," 835.
352. Günter Grass, "Rückblick auf die Blechtrommel," *SZ*, January 12/13, 1974.
353. Caldwell and Hanshew, *Germany*, 97; Knapp, *Roman*, 95-101.
354. Knapp, *Roman*, 105.
355. Quote Reich-Ranicki, *Literatur*, 222.
356. Marcel Reich-Ranicki, "Auf gut Glück getrommelt," *DZ*, January 1, 1960.
357. Joachim Kaiser, "Die Gruppe 47 lebt auf," *SZ*, November 5, 1958.
358. Marcel Reich-Ranicki, "Auf gut Glück getrommelt," *DZ*, January 1, 1960.
359. Reich-Ranicki, *Leben*, 384-7 (quote 386-7). Wittstock, *Reich-Ranicki*, 269-70.
360. Reich-Ranicki, *Leben*, 11 (quotes), 387. Wittstock, *Reich-Ranicki*, 270-1.
361. Endres, *Literatur*, 135.
362. Magenau, *Walser*, 111.
363. *Guardian*, December 21, 2016; https://www.jewishvirtuallibrary.org/ilse-aichinger; Hans Werner Richter in Neunzig, *Richter*, 111.
364. Glaser, *Kulturgeschichte*, vol. 2, 179.
365. Grass, *Häuten*, 462 (quote). See also Henze, *Reiselieder*, 132; Hans Daiber in Nonnenmann, *Schriftsteller*, 28-32.
366. Emre, "Meticulous," 24-6; "Ingeborg Bachmann," *Encyclopedia Britannica*.
367. Hans Werner Richter in Neunzig, *Richter*, 107-8, 130-2, 139-40; Endres, *Literatur*, 134; Glaser, *Kulturgeschichte*, vol. 2, 183-4.
368. Hans Werner Richter in Neunzig, *Richter*, 100-1, 140; Joachim Kaiser in Kaiser [and Kaiser], *Mohikaner*, 310; Demetz, *Anarchie*, 60 (quote).

369. Magenau, *Walser*, 111.
370. Schroers, "Gruppe 47," 453.
371. Hans Schwab-Felisch, "Dichter auf dem 'elektrischen Stuhl'," *FAZ*, November 1, 1956.
372. Journal *Die Gegenwart* quoted in Glaser, *Kulturgeschichte*, vol. 2, 184.
373. Rudolf Walter Leonhardt, "Die Gruppe 47 und ihre Kritiker," *DZ*, October 30, 1959.
374. Franklin, "Word," 71–4; Richter, *Almanach*, 154–5.
375. Hans Werner Richter in Neunzig, *Richter*, 111–12; Lettau, *Gruppe 47*, 384; Hirsch, *Endlich*, 209; Frank Schirrmacher, "Warum ich nach sechzig Jahren mein Schweigen breche," *FAZ*, August 12, 2006 (Grass's quote).
376. Helmut Böttiger, "In der Todesmühle," *DZ*, January 27, 2015; "Briefwechsel Max Frisch-Paul Celan," *FAZ*, July 27, 2001; Hans Werner Richter in Neunzig, *Richter*, 111–12; Lettau, *Gruppe 47*, 384; Hirsch, *Endlich*, 209; Emre, "Meticulous," 25–6.
377. Klee, *Kulturlexikon*, 156; Hohoff, *Geist*, 193–4.
378. Quotes Gaiser, *Reiter*, 34, 42, 58, also poem "Reiter am Himmel," *Reiter*, 64–5.
379. Reich-Ranicki, "Fall Gerd Gaiser," 78.
380. Gaiser, *Stimme*, 297, 299.
381. Reich-Ranicki, "Fall Gerd Gaiser," 83.
382. Gaiser, *Schlussball*, 214–15.
383. Reich-Ranicki, "Fall Gerd Gaiser," 79: Walter Jens, "Gegen die Überschätzung Gerd Gaisers," *DZ*, November 25, 1960.
384. Sieburg (1955) in Raddatz, *Sieburg, 1924–1956*, 456–8; Reich-Ranicki, "Fall Gerd Gaiser," 69; Knapp, *Roman*, 46; Koch, "Roman," 217; Kater, *Culture*, 313; Hohoff, *Geist*, 190–7; Blöcker, *Lesebuch*, 331–6.
385. Friedrich Sieburg, "Kriechende Literatur," *DZ*, August 14, 1952; Helmut Böttiger, "In der Todesmühle," *DZ*, January 27, 2015; "Briefwechsel Max Frisch-Paul Celan," *FAZ*, July 27, 2001; Franklin, "Word," 74; Lettau, *Gruppe 47*, 342, 344; Nöhbauer, "Gruppen," 524–5; Kröll, *Gruppe 47*, 5; Glaser, *Kulturgeschichte*, vol. 2, 184; Schildt, *Medien-Intellektuelle*, 416.
386. Sieburg, *Lust*, 250–4.
387. Karl Korn, "Der Ruf nach dem Sittenzensor," *FAZ*, September 8, 1952.
388. Bessen, *Trümmer*, 193–4.
389. Karl Korn, "Filme, die ankommen," *FAZ*, January 24, 1951; Glaser, *Kulturgeschichte*, vol. 2, 100-1; Fehrenbach, *Cinema*, 92–102; Walter Uka in Faulstich, *Kultur der fünfziger Jahre*, 78; Payk, "Amerikakomplex," 202–6; Payk, *Geist*, 237–41.
390. See Twittenhoff, "Rückblick," 141.
391. Kater, *Twisted Muse*, 146–50; Klee, *Kulturlexikon*, 257.
392. Prieberg, *Musik*, 325; Kater, *Composers*, 121–2; Kater, *Twisted Muse*, 137.
393. Klee, *Kulturlexikon*, 397; Kater, *Twisted Muse*, 151; https://www.musiklexikon.ac.at/ml/musik_O/Oberborbeck_Felix.xml.
394. Klee, *Kulturlexikon*, 604, 609.
395. Ibid., 542.
396. Jöde, "Jugendmusik," 170. See Kater, "Jugendbewegung," 127–74.
397. Jöde, "Jugendmusik," 171–2 (quotes 171).
398. Kolland, "Ideale," 89.
399. Ibid., 90.
400. Sass, "Sinn," 173–5 (first quote 173); Wolschke, "Musikfest," 94–5; Oberborbeck, "Historische Stunde," 96–7 (second quote 96). Knab and Spitta: Kater, *Twisted Muse*, 167–70.
401. Twittenhoff, "Festliche Tage," 148–51 (quote 149); Kolland, "Ideale," 91.

402. Kolland, "Ideale," 94–5.
403. Twittenhoff, "Wanne-Eickel," 132.
404. Hammer, "Student," 191; *Junge Musik* (1957): 192; Kolland, "Ideale," 95.
405. Twittenhoff, "Bilanz," 198–9.
406. Wiese, "Junge Musik," 15–16.
407. Custodis, *Isolation*, 100 (quote); Kater, *Twisted Muse*, 140; Kater, *Hitler Youth*, 32–3.
408. Prieberg, *Musik*, 22–4; biography in https://www.bach-cantatas.com/Bio/Melichar-Alois.htm.
409. Melichar, *Schönberg*, 6–46 (quote 6). Also see Melichar, *Musik*, e.g. 58–80.
410. Melichar, *Überwindung*, 47 (quote), 119.
411. Henze, *Musik*, 318; Geiger, "Abendroth," 141–2 (quotes are Melichar's).
412. Blume, *Rasseproblem*, esp. 3, 82–3; Potter, *Most German*, 186–7; Pamela M. Potter, "Blume, Friedrich," in *Oxford Music Online;* Custodis, "Entnazifizierungsverfahren," 5, 18.
413. Kirchmeyer, "Eimert," 11; Gottwald, "Musikwissenschaft," 76–7.
414. Blume, *Was ist Musik*, 16–17.
415. Kurtz, *Stockhausen*, 143; Gottwald, "Musikwissenschaft," 71.
416. Walter Abendroth, "Das grosse Kopfschütteln über die Jugend," *DZ*, September 27, 1956 (first quote); Abendroth, "Der Reichtum des Westens," *DZ*, June 12, 1952 (last two quotes).
417. Abendroth quoted in Bernhard Woerdehoff, "National nach Noten," *DZ*, July 5, 1996.
418. Walter Abendroth, "Ausverkauft!" *DZ*, May 24, 1951.
419. Wagner, *Wagner Theater*, 187.
420. Walter Abendroth, "Der Reichtum des Westens," *DZ*, June 12, 1952.
421. Ibid.
422. Walter Abendroth, "Kein Dogmatiker," *DZ*, May 27, 1954 (quotes); and "Musikalische Psychoanalyse," *DZ*, October 7, 1954.
423. Walter Abendroth, "Die Krise der Neuen Musik," *DZ*, November 14, 1958.
424. Abendroth, *Geschichte*, 168.

THREE – THE CLASH OF GENERATIONS (1960–1970)

1. Haar, "Friedrich Valjavec," 104–6.
2. Corr. Estland-Lettland, 1939–1941, NAW, T-580, 174/320–323; BAB, file "Generaltreuhänder Ost: Baltische Staaten," Ahnenerbe-Sievers; Klee, *Kulturlexikon*, 375.
3. Diary entry quoted in Lehr, *Osteinsatz*, 161.
4. Klee, *Kulturlexikon*, 375.
5. Bauer, *Wurzeln*, 109–15, quote 110.
6. Werner Renz, "Fritz Bauer," *DZ*, June 27, 2018; Görtemaker and Safferling, *Akte*, 245–6; Reichel, *Vergangenheitsbewältigung*, 177–8.
7. Görtemaker and Safferling, *Akte*, 233–9; Wilke, "Massenmedien," 656–7.
8. Görtemaker and Safferling, *Akte*, 244–6; Reichel, *Vergangenheitsbewältigung*, 159–78; Flemming and Ulrich, *Vor Gericht*, 121; Frei, "Auschwitz-Prozess," 123–30.
9. Reichel, *Vergangenheitsbewältigung*, 158; Flemming and Ulrich, *Vor Gericht*, 111, 120–1; Pendas, *Auschwitz Trial*, 265.
10. Arendt, *Eichmann*, 53.
11. Entry for February 27–9, 1964, in Walser, *Tagebücher, 1963–1973*, 101.
12. Von Miquel, "Juristen," 222; Reichel, *Vergangenheitsbewältigung*, 163.

13. Boger quoted in Dietrich Strothmann, "Im Schatten des Galgens," *DZ*, April 24, 1964.
14. Reichel, *Vergangenheitsbewältigung*, 168–9.
15. https://collections.ushmm.org/search/catalog/irn1004810; Kater, *Drummers*, 180–1.
16. *Oxford Music Online*; Reichel, *Vergangenheitsbewältigung*, 174–5.
17. Pendas, *Auschwitz Trial*, 251 (quote). Also see Ute Frevert in Assmann and Frevert, *Geschichtsvergessenheit*, 219; Jähner, *Wolfszeit*, 13.
18. Von Miquel, "Explanation," 54–5; Pendas, *Auschwitz Trial*, 250.
19. Ute Frevert in Assmann and Frevert, *Geschichtsvergessenheit*, 215–16.
20. Mitscherlich and Mitscherlich, *Unfähigkeit*, 123; Pendas, *Auschwitz Trial*, 253–4.
21. Biess, *Republik*, 217; Pendas, *Auschwitz Trial*, 262.
22. Pendas, *Auschwitz Trial*, 266–8.
23. Flemming and Ulrich, *Vor Gericht*, 121; Biess, *Republik*, 218.
24. Reichel, *Vergangenheitsbewältigung*, 181.
25. Werner Renz, "Sang- und klanglos und verheerend milde," *FR*, August 18, 2020; Harald Wiederschein, "Hans Hofmeyer," *FocusOnline*, December 5, 2019, https://www.focus.de/wissen/mensch/geschichte/nationalsozialismus/vorsitzender-im-auschwitzprozess-forscher-enthuellt-vorzeige-richter-liess-in-der-nazizeit-jugendliche-unfruchtbar-machen_id_10591605.html.
26. D. St. [Dietrich Strothmann], "Bewältiger der Vergangenheit," *DZ*, August 20, 1965.
27. Langer, *Encyclopedia*, 1183; Caldwell and Hanshew, *Germany*, 105; Schildt, "Wohlstand," 46–7; Schnell, *Geschichte*, 311; Jarausch, *Hitler*, 147–8; Winkler, *Weg*, 199–201.
28. Schildt, "Wohlstand," 25–49; Kurt Hickethier in Faulstich, *Kultur der sechziger Jahre*, 14–16; O'Dochartaigh, *Germany*, 92–4; Kater, "NPD," 8–10.
29. Caldwell and Hanshew, *Germany*, 104–5 (Adenauer quoted 104); Brumm, "Der Spiegel," 191–3; Hachmeister, "Spiegel," 97; Knut Hickethier in Faulstich, *Kultur der sechziger Jahre*, 17–18; Jarausch, *Hitler*, 160.
30. Lettau, *Gruppe 47*, 515; Magenau, *Walser*, 220.
31. McCormick, *Politics*, 37, 41; Biess, *Republik*, 227–38.
32. Schweitzer et al., *Politics*, 133–5.
33. Meinhof, "Notstand – Klassenkampf" (1968) in Meinhof, *Würde*, 145.
34. Rusinek, "Entdeckung," 123; Glaser, *Kulturgeschichte*, vol. 3, 27. Lübke: Rühmkorf, *Tabu II*, 246–7. Minister Gerhard Schröder must not be confused with Chancellor Gerhard Schröder, who was born in 1944.
35. Reichel, *Vergangenheitsbewältigung*, 183–6.
36. Ibid., 186–93; von Miquel, "Juristen," 226–9.
37. Reichel, *Vergangenheitsbewältigung*, 193–4.
38. Rusinek, "Entdeckung," 138–9.
39. Redekop later became a professor of American literature at Western University in London, Ontario.
40. Haar, *Historiker*, 283–6.
41. Hohls and Jarausch, *Fragen*, 446; Klee, *Personenlexikon*, 96; Wehler, "National-sozialismus," 322–3; Kindt, *Jugendbewegung*, 1371–87; Dunkhase, *Conze*, 66, 68–71.
42. Hans-Ulrich Wehler in Hohls and Jarausch, *Fragen*, 254–5; Wolfgang J. Mommsen, in ibid., 200–1; Dunkhase, *Conze*, 62–3; Aly, "Schieder," 172–3; Wehler, "Nationalsozialismus," 322–3 (Conze quoted 322).
43. Beer, "Spannungsfeld," 345–84.
44. Dunkhase, *Conze*, 116 (quote); Etzemüller, *Sozialgeschichte*, 54–64.

45. Conze, "Pöbel," 333–64. See Wolfgang Schieder and Heinrich August Winkler in Hohls and Jarausch, *Fragen*, 284, 379; Etzemüller, *Sozialgeschichte*, 160–70.

46. Wolfram Fischer, Reinhard Rürup, Wolfgang Schieder in Hohls and Jarausch, *Fragen*, 103, 116, 275, 285; Dieter Groh in Dunkhase, *Conze*, 83; Etzemüller, *Sozialgeschichte*, 154–5.

47. The first was Reinhard Bollmus's, *Das Amt Rosenberg*.

48. See Imanuel Geiss and Wolfgang Schieder in Hohls and Jarausch, *Fragen*, 227, 286; Dunkhase, *Conze*, 219–23.

49. Hans-Urich Wehler in Hohls and Jarausch, *Fragen*, 259; Etzemüller, *Sozialgeschichte*, 44–7.

50. E.g. Streit, *Keine Kameraden*.

51. Conze quoted in Weisbrod, "Moratorium," 261–2.

52. Dunkhase, *Conze*, 95–7.

53. Klee, *Personenlexikon*, 419; Seeliger, *Braune Universität*, vol. 1, 47–8 (Mühlmann quoted 47).

54. Klee, *Personenlexikon*, 66; Seeliger, *Braune Universität*, vol. 2, 17–19 (Bornkamm quoted 17).

55. Klee, *Personenlexikon*, 350; Seeliger, *Braune Universität*, vol. 6, 46–56 (Kuhn quotes from *Tübinger Chronik* [April 3, 1933]: 47, 48, 50).

56. Klee, *Personenlexikon*, 159; Seeliger, *Braune Universität*, vol. 6, 21–6 (Forsthoff quoted 23). See Biess, *Republik*, 201–2.

57. Müller, "Freie Universität" (first quote 26); Müller, *Country* (second quote 263).

58. Buselmeier, "Leben," 60–8 (quotes 61).

59. "Berlin," *DS*, June 5, 1967 (quote); Knut Nevermann, "Nachruf auf Ekkehart Krippendorf," *Der Tagesspiegel*, Berlin, February 28, 2018; Hopf, "Faschismusthema," 76; Karl, *Dutschke*, 58; Menand, "Sloppy Joe," 71–5; Schrecker, *Promise*, esp. 84–114.

60. Diehm, "Nachwort," 237–40; Schmidtke, "New Left," 177–8.

61. Walter Boehlich, "Der neue Bonner Rektor" *DZ*, October 23, 1964; "Noch einmal," *DZ*, November 6, 1964; "Walter Boehlich," https://frankfurter-personenlexikon. de/node/3275; Rusinek, "Entdeckung," 132–3.

62. Schmidtke, "New Left," 178.

63. Kraushaar, *Mythos*, 8–10.

64. Winkler, *Weg*, 281–2.

65. Hermann Lübbe in Broszat, *Weg*, 331.

66. Jarausch, "Memory," 21. Also Stern, *Doppelleben*, 194–5, 256–8; Thamer, "NS-Vergangenheit," esp. 39, 53.

67. König, *Zukunft*, 34. See Zipes, "Vicissitudes," 36; Schnell, *Geschichte*, 313; Ute Frevert in Assmann and Frevert, *Geschichtsvergessenheit*, 227–8; Kraushaar, *Mythos*, 37; Rusinek, "Endeckung," 114–16, 120; Schmidtke, "New Left," 182–3.

68. Kretschmann, *Spaltung*, 112–13, 115.

69. See Habermas, *Schriften*, esp. 250–9; Wilcox, "Negative Identity," 169–87; Glaser, *Kulturgeschichte*, vol. 2, 205–8; Kaiser [and Kaiser], *Mohikaner*, 194; Müller, *Mini*, 74.

70. Schneider, *Lenz*, esp. 21–3, 57, 67, 69; Timm, *Sommer*, esp. 24–5, 89, 92, 96, 110, 139, 172–3, 181, 187, 217, 299. Critically: Schnell, *Geschichte*, 423; Buselmeier, "Leben," 165–77; Gerlach, *Abschied*, 54–9.

71. Böll, "Jungen," 17; Linder, *Böll*, 276; Reid, *Böll*, 25.

72. Reid, *Böll*, 28.

73. Böll, *Briefe*, vol. 1, 65.

74. Böll to family, July 10, 1940, *Briefe*, vol. 1, 73 (first quote); July 16, 1940, 78 (second quote).

75. Böll quoted in Linder, *Böll*, 159.
76. Böll quoted ibid., 158.
77. Böll to Annemarie, September 2, 1942, in Böll, *Briefe*, vol. 1, 457.
78. Böll quoted in Linder, *Böll*, 157. Also Böll, *Briefe*, e.g. vol. 1, 543, 616–17, 672, and vol. 2, 890.
79. See Böll, *Man*, 28–80.
80. Martin Walser in Walser and Augstein, *Leben*, 54–5, 58, 61–2, 64–6, 75–6, 85; Magenau, *Walser*, 42–3.
81. Martin Walser in Walser and Augstein, *Leben*, 71, 107.
82. Martin Walser in Chabbi, *Walser*, 233.
83. Kater, *Hitler Youth*, 23–6.
84. Fest, "Jahre," 188–91.
85. Joachim Kaiser in Kaiser [and Kaiser], *Mohikaner*, 61.
86. See text in Chapter 2 at n. 52.
87. Herwig, *Flakhelfer*, 66–7.
88. "Zunge heraus," *DS*, September 4, 1963, 64–78, esp. 69; Grass, *Die Blechtrommel*; *Hundejahre*; *Katz und Maus*.
89. Grass, *Häuten*, 26–7, 43, 126–71; Frank Schirrmacher's interview with Grass, "Warum ich nach sechzig Jahren mein Schweigen breche," *FAZ*, August 12, 2006.
90. Günter Grass, "Rückblick auf die Blechtrommel," *SZ*, Munich, January 12/13, 1974.
91. Baldur von Schirach on May 24, 1946, in *Der Prozess*, vol. 14, 476–7.
92. Joachim Kaiser in Kaiser [and Kaiser], *Mohikaner*, 193; Kaiser interviewed by Georg Diez and Dominik Wichmann in *SZ Magazin* 50 (2008), https://sz-magazin.sueddeutsche.de/gesellschaft-leben/ich-weiss-dass-ich-sterben-muss-und-zwar-relativ-bald-82007.
93. Kater, *Hitler Youth*, 207–14; Röhl, *Finger*, 36–40.
94. Dey quoted in Melissa Eddy, "Former Nazi Guard is Convicted in One of Germany's Last Holocaust Trials," *NYT*, July 23, 2020.
95. Böll interviewed in Eggebrecht, *Männer*, 132; Reid, *Böll*, 111; Böll, *Vorlesungen*, 26 (quote).
96. Böll interviewed in Eggebrecht, *Männer*, 133–4; Reid, *Böll*, 143–4.
97. Example of Schnurre in Böll, "Angst," 780.
98. Reid, *Böll*, 111, 141, 142 (Böll quoted).
99. Böll, *Krieg*, 21–2.
100. Böll in "Brot und Boden," *DS*, December 6, 1961; Böll, *Vorlesungen*, 78.
101. "Kanonisches Auge," *DS*, August 3, 1969; Linder, *Böll*, 479–80; Vormweg, *Deutsche*, 303–6 (Böll quoted 304).
102. Böll, *Ende* (1969), 16, 50–7, 98–101, 116–18.
103. Böll, *Ansichten*, esp. 23, 33, 108, 123, 138, 170, 187–93, 214.
104. Böll interviewed in Eggebrecht, *Männer*, 136. Also Reich-Ranicki, *Literatur*, 139–41; Waidson, *Novel*, 113–14; Schnell, *Geschichte*, 344–5; Barner, *Geschichte*, 377; Ute Frevert in Assmann and Frevert, *Geschichtsvergessenheit*, 224–5.
105. Moses, "Die 45er," 235. Cf. Bude, *Karrieren*, 9–19, 24–9, 65–71; von Hodenberg, *Konsens*, 248–73, 283, 299–308.
106. Magenau, *Walser*, 171, 178, 207, 220–1, 251, 256; Hadek, *Vergangenheitsbewältigung*, 42–4; Walser in Siblewski, *Walser*, 239; Walser, *Tagebücher, 1963–1973*, 159.
107. Dahrendorf, *Gesellschaft*, 318 (quote); Walser in Chabbi, *Walser*, 75–6; Magenau, *Walser*, 273–4.
108. "Unser Auschwitz," in Walser, *Ansichten*, 158–72 (quotes 162, 166). Also see Walser, *Tagebücher, 1963–1973*, 99–104, 133–6; Walser in Walser and Augstein, *Leben*, 265–7; Magenau, *Walser*, 209–13.

109. Walser, *Halbzeit*, 156, 363, 525, 545, 570, 595 (first quote), 601, 613; *Einhorn*, 19, 182–3, 191, 199, 210–11 (second quote). See Endres, *Literatur*, 240; Glaser, *Kulturgeschichte*, vol. 2, 182; Frank Hertweck, "Unsere Romanhelden," *FAZ*, August 31, 2012.
110. Walser, *Halbzeit*, 85, 173–4, 187–8, 198–201, 334–5, 414–15, 420–1, 446, 571, 607–8, 787, 811–13; *Einhorn*, 40–1, 56, 72, 91, 204, 228; Doane, *Aspekte*, 40, 43.
111. Walser, *Halbzeit*, 335, 440, 571, 573, 748; *Einhorn*, 107, 260–7. Hans Georg Rauch, "Martin Walser," *DZ*, March 13, 1981; "Halbzeit," *DS*, December 14, 1960; Karasek, *Flucht*, 174; Magenau, *Walser*, 237–8.
112. "Halbzeit," *DS*, December 14, 1960; Rolf Becker, "Wortwörtliche Streichlerei," *DS*, September 5, 1966. See Schnell, *Geschichte*, 348–9.
113. Sieburg (1960) in Raddatz, *Sieburg, 1957–1963*, 199; Blöcker, *Lesebuch*, 187–91.
114. Reich-Ranicki, *Literatur*, 208–15.
115. Walser's diary entry of November 9, 1969, *Tagebücher, 1963–1973*, 335.
116. Walser, *Tagebücher, 1963–1973*, 198 (quote), 209, 214, 216, 221, 226.
117. Reinhard Baumgart, "Die Tragödie der Vernunft des Günter Grass," *SZ*, June 8/9, 1968; Neuhaus, *Grass*, 196, 217–24; Mayer-Iswandy, *Grass*, 93, 107–12, 116–17, 122; Preece, *Life*, 93; Caldwell and Hanshew, *Germany*, 105; Schnell, *Geschichte*, 311 (Grass's quote).
118. Reinhard Baumgart, "Die Tragödie der Vernunft des Günter Grass," *SZ*, June 8/9, 1968; Neuhaus, *Grass*, 225; Mayer-Iswandy, *Grass*, 119–21; Preece, *Life*, 94–6; Enzensberger, *Jahre*, 156–9, 184–5.
119. Grass, *Örtlich betäubt*, 173.
120. Ibid., 184.
121. Ibid., 75–8, 190, 220.
122. Preece, *Life*, 107–17.
123. Grass, *Katz und Maus*, 126, 138. See Ryan, *Past*, 95–113; Reich-Ranicki, *Literatur*, 228–30.
124. Grass, *Hundejahre*, 182, 192, 225–6, 392, 472; Koch, "Roman," 229 (quote); Waidson, *Novel*, 123; "Zunge heraus," *DS*, September 4, 1963.
125. Joachim Kaiser, "Drei Tage und ein Tag," *SZ*, April 30/May 1, 1966.
126. Friedrich Sieburg, "Freiheit in der Literaturkritik," *FAZ*, December 1, 1962; Sieburg cited in Leonhardt, "Aufstieg," 69 and Siedler, *Erinnerungen*, 389–90; Hans Werner Richter in Neunzig, *Richter*, 167; Walter Boehlich, "Friedrich Sieburgs Unmut," *DZ*, December 7, 1962.
127. Günter Blöcker, "Die Gruppe 47 und ich," *DZ*, October 26, 1962.
128. Glaser, *Kulturgeschichte*, vol. 2, 185 (quote); Lettau, *Gruppe 47*, 516–17.
129. Habe quoted in Martin Walser, "Sozialisieren wir die Gruppe 47!" *DZ*, July 3, 1964.
130. Nöhbauer, "Gruppen," 527–8.
131. Hans Werner Richter in Neunzig, *Richter*, 142; Magenau, *Walser*, 203–4.
132. Rudolf Walter Leonhardt, "Was gilt die deutsche Literatur im Inland?" *DZ*, October 26, 1962.
133. Dieter E. Zimmer, "Gruppe 47 in Princeton," *DZ*, May 6, 1966; Böll, "Angst," 778 (first quote); Hans Werner Richter in Neunzig, *Richter*, 164–6 (second quote 165); Schnell, *Geschichte*, 315–16.
134. Karasek, *Flucht*, 486–7.
135. Hans Werner Richter in Neunzig, *Richter*, 168–71; Reich-Ranicki, *Leben*, 463–5; Magenau, *Walser*, 248 (quote).
136. Martin Walser interviewed in Siblewski, *Walser*, 240.
137. Magenau, *Walser*, 204–6.

138. Martin Walser, "Brief an einen ganz jungen Autor," *DZ*, April 13, 1962.
139. Martin Walser, "Sozialisieren wir die Gruppe 47!" *DZ*, July 3, 1964.
140. See Reich-Ranicki's criticisms in "Neue Gedichte von Günter Grass," *DZ*, May 19, 1967; "Martin Walsers 'Zimmerschlacht' in München inszeniert von Fritz Kortner," *DZ*, December 15, 1967.
141. Typical reaction: Uwe Nettelbeck, "Es war in jeder Weise ein gemischtes Vergnügen," *DZ*, December 3, 1965.
142. Friedrich Sieburg quoted in Payk, *Geist*, 349.
143. Richter to Lenz, September 26, 1961, in Uwe Neumann, "Freund und Feind in der Gruppe 47," *literaturkritik.de*, May 4, 2020, https://literaturkritik.de/freund-und-feind-in-der-gruppe-47-reich-ranicki-als-literarische-figur,26730.html; Wittstock, *Reich-Ranicki*, 174–8.
144. See Günther Rühle in Hoffmann and Klotz, *Die Sechziger*, 95–102; Nehring, "Bühne," 69–71.
145. "Biographische Angaben aus dem Handbuch 'Wer war wer in der DDR?'", https://www.bundesstiftung-aufarbeitung.de/de/recherche/kataloge-daten-banken/biographische-datenbanken/peter-palitzsch?ID=2593; "Prozess in Ulm," September 12, 1961; Hugh Rorrison, "Peter Palitzsch," *Guardian*, December 28, 2004; Rischbieter, *Schreiben*, 209–10.
146. "Biographische Angaben . . .," (as in n. 145); Hugh Rorrison, "Peter Palitzsch," *Guardian*, December 28, 2004 (quote); Canaris, *Zadek*, 39; Rischbieter, *Schreiben*, 210–11.
147. Canaris, *Zadek*, 39–41; Schäfer, *Bühne*, 142–3; Rischbieter, "Theater," 107.
148. Zadek, *My Way*, 399 (quote), 438.
149. Canaris, *Zadek*, 52–4, 71, 106; Petzet, *Kammerspiele*, 546; Rühle, *Theater*, 196–8.
150. Canaris, *Zadek*, 71; Zadek, *My Way*, 391–2.
151. Zadek, *Wanderjahre*, 259.
152. Idem, *My Way*, 317; Canaris, *Zadek*, 51 (quote).
153. Zadek, *My Way*, 362.
154. Both under the nonsense-title *Ich bin ein Elephant, Madame* (*I am an Elephant, Madame*), Canaris, *Zadek*, 72; Zadek, *My Way*, 400, 407–8, 468–9.
155. Zadek, *My Way*, 439, 443–4, 457, 458 (quote).
156. Mitscherlich and Mielke, *Medizin*, 7–17.
157. Walser, *Eiche*, 18–19, 26–7, 54, 82, 102–4; Walser, *Tagebücher 1951–62*, 564–9, 575–6; Walter Uka in Faulstich, *Kultur der sechziger Jahre*, 52; Magenau, *Walser*, 181; Barner, *Geschichte*, 468; Hadek, *Vergangenheitsbewältigung*, 63–73; Rühle, *Theater*, 127; Brändle, *Stücke*, 43–52.
158. Walser, *Tagebücher 1951–1962*, 636; Johannes Jacobi, "Walsers erster grosser Versuch," *DZ*, October 5, 1962; Karasek, *Kulturkritik*, 194–7.
159. Hints in Walser, *Schwan*, 41, 44–5, 47–8, 64–7.
160. Hadek, *Vergangenheitsbewältigung*, 73–85; Rühle, *Theater*, 129–30; Barner, *Geschichte*, 469; Magenau, *Walser*, 215–17.
161. Hellmuth Karasek, "Martin Walser als Dramatiker," *DZ*, October 23, 1964; Marel Reich-Ranicki, "War es ein Mord?" *DZ*, December 15, 1967 (quote); Magenau, *Walser*, 217–18.
162. https://www.frankfurt1933-1945.de/beitraege/einzelschicksale-1/beitrag/rose-schloesinger-mutige-widerstandskaempferin; Michael Coveney, "Rolf Hochhuth Obituary," *Guardian*, May 5, 1920.
163. Nehring, "Bühne," 75.
164. Erwin Piscator in Kreuzer, *Dramaturgie*, 34; Nehring, "Bühne," 75.

165. Hochhuth quoted in Rühle, *Theater*, 134.
166. Menand, *Free World*, 90.
167. Hochhuth quoted in Barner, *Geschichte*, 470.
168. Peter Maxwill, "Attacke des Papst-Lästerers," *DS*, February 20, 2013.
169. From Catholics: "'Hochhuth ist Vergangenheit'," *deutschlandfunk.de*, February 22, 2019, https://www.deutschlandfunk.de/hochhuth-ist-vergangenheit-100.html. Also Hellmuth Karasek (1963), *Kulturkritik*, 209–13.
170. Berg, *Stellvertreter*, n.p., text near n. 50.
171. Maxwill, "Attacke des Papst-Lästerers" (as in n. 168).
172. Friedländer, *Pius XII.*, esp. 93, and Grosser, cited ibid., 165–6.
173. Expressed in the autobiographical *Fluchtpunkte* and *Abschied*. See "Gesang von der Schaukel," *DS*, October 20, 1965; Fritz J. Raddatz, "Wen spreche ich eigentlich beim Schreiben an?" *DZ*, November 6, 1981.
174. "Gesang von der Schaukel," *DS*, October 20, 1965; Koch, "Todesnähe," 262–3; Nehring, "Bühne," 82–3; Schnell, *Geschichte*, 340.
175. Weiss, *Ermittlung*, 9.
176. Ibid., 53.
177. Ibid., 160.
178. Ibid., 92, 93 (quote).
179. Fritz J. Raddatz, "Wen spreche ich eigentlich beim Schreiben an?" *DZ*, November 6, 1981; Nehring, "Bühne," 84–5; Trommler, "Nachwuchs," 80.
180. Demetz, *Anarchie*, 158; Rühle, *Theater*, 138.
181. Müller, *Mini*, 90.
182. Kipphardt, *Joel Brand*, 11.
183. Ibid., 92–3, 118–20.
184. Nehring, "Bühne," 81.
185. https://encyclopedia.com/arts/encyclopedias-almanacs-transcripts-and-maps/kipphardt-heinar; Ritter, "Dramatiker," 72.
186. Kipphardt in "Wäre ich Eichmann geworden?" *DS*, May 15, 1967.
187. Kipphardt quoted ibid.
188. Grass quoted in "Jagd auf Dra-Dra," *DS*, May 23, 1971.
189. Hellmuth Karasek, "Alle für Kipphardt," *DZ*, May 28, 1971.
190. Kahlenberg, "Film," 483–4, 503, 507; Barthel, *Kino*, 70–1, 82–5; Walter Uka in Faulstich, *Kultur der sechziger Jahre*, 201–2.
191. "Flucht nach Teneriffa," *DS*, November 18, 1964; Müller, *Mini*, 106–8; Jenny, "Jahr," 478; sex-film industry parodied in *Teuflische Jahre* (1970), 26–8.
192. "Oberhausener Manifest," quoted in Bessen, *Trümmer*, 358. Last quote in Kaes, *Deutschlandbilder*, 16. Also Fehrenbach, *Cinema*, 224–6.
193. "'Wir wollen den neuen deutschen Film machen'," *SZ*, March 10/11, 1962; Kaes, *Deutschlandbilder*, 16–17, 26-27, 32; Kahlenberg, "Film," 483–4; Rentschler, *Film*, 33–5.
194. Kahlenberg, "Film," 485–8, 508; Knight, *Frauen*, 32–3; Fehrenbach, *Cinema*, 231–3; Lewandowski, *Kluge*, 6–8.
195. *Lebenszeichen*, Zweitausendeins Edition DVD; Rost, "Kinostunden," 377–83.
196. "Ach, der Papili," *DS*, December 25, 1967 (quote); Dörrlamm, "Film," 33.
197. Walter Uka in Faulstich, *Kultur der sechziger Jahre*, 204–5; Rauh, *Reitz*, 72; Kreimeier, "RAF," 1159.
198. *Schonzeit für Füchse*, DVD remake by Ascot Elite.
199. https://musilmuseum.at/robert-musil/biographie.html; Albrecht et al., *Lexikon*, vol. 2, 121–3.

200. *Der junge Törless*, Arthaus DVD; Rentschler, "Specularity," 177–87; Hilmar Hoffmann in Hoffmann and Klotz, *Die Sechziger*, 196; Lewandowski, *Schlöndorff*, 11–56; Moeller and Lellis, *Cinema*, 26–39.

201. Kluge, *Lebensläufe*, 11–25, 142–5.

202. Kluge, *Schlachtbeschreibung*, e.g. 10, 21, 27–31, 46–7, 68–9, 112–13, 130, 137–40. See Andreas Kilb, "Neue Kameraden," *DZ*, January 22, 1993.

203. Kluge, *Lebensläufe*, 7.

204. *Abschied von gestern*, DVD Edition Filmmuseum München; Lewandowski, *Kluge*, 71–88; Wenzel, *Film*, 78–111.

205. But see Elsaesser, *Cinema*, 97.

206. Reich-Ranicki, *Literatur*, 284–7 (quote 285); Andreas Kilb, "Neue Kameraden," *DZ*, January 22, 1993; Reichmann, "Baustelle Stalingrad," 471.

207. Kluge called his approach "associational theory" (Lewandowski, *Kluge*, 10–13, 33–9, Kluge quoted 36).

208. Rentschler, *Film*, 42.

209. Dörrlamm, "Film," 32.

210. Wolfram Schütte, "Für eine rationale Phantasie im Kino," *FR*, November 18, 1967.

211. Meyer, "Zeitung," 104–12; Korda, "Frankfurter Zeitung," 81-96; Dürr, "Süddeutsche Zeitung," 63–79; Gäbler, "Zeitung," 146–64; Flottau, "Frankfurter Rundschau," 97–107.

212. Meyn, "DIE ZEIT," 275–91.

213. Von Hodenberg, "Journalisten," 311.

214. "Drittes Reich im Kleinen," *DS*, December 1, 1959; "Vollstrecker des Weltgewissens," *DS*, June 2, 1997, 108–17; Walter, "SPIEGEL," 797–805 (quote 801); Brumm, "Der Spiegel," 192–5; Enzensberger, *Einzelheiten*, 74–92; Engelmann, *Freunde*, 206–7; Merseburger, *Augstein*, 234.

215. Enzensberger, *Einzelheiten*, 92.

216. Brumm, "BILD-Zeitung," 139; Müller, *Springer-Konzern*, 80, 108, 118–19; "Presseportal: Journalist," July 4, 2018, https://www.presseportal.de/pm/20126/3988616.

217. Kruip, *"Welt"-Bild*, 111; Diller, "Rundfunk," 158.

218. Frei, "Hörfunk," 435–7; Diller, "Rundfunk," 150–8; Glaser, *Kulturgechichte*, vol. 2, 227; Gerhard Schäffner in Faulstich, *Kultur der sechziger Jahre*, 101–2.

219. Ludes, "Programmgeschichte," 257.

220. Grob et al., *Film*, 12; Andersen, *Traum*, 119.

221. Lehmann, *Sechziger*, 146–7.

222. Ludes, "Programmgeschichte," 265; Müller, *Mini*, 111–15; Fabian Baar in Faulstich, *Kultur der sechziger Jahre*, 231–5.

223. Von Hodenberg, *Konsens*, 327.

224. Ibid., 249–50; von Hodenberg, "Journalisten," 306, 309; Karasek, *Flucht*, 383–4; Stern, *Doppelleben*, 190–3.

225. Von Hodenberg, *Konsens*, 308; "Das Kreuzfeuer als Marken- und Qualitätszeichen," *SZ*, May 21, 1985 (quote).

226. Von Hodenberg, *Konsens*, 308; https://heritage-images.com/preview/2611864; Bennett Center for Judaic Studies, https://jta.org/archive/rajakovic-arrested-in-vienna-his-role-in-deporting-jews-investigated; Klee, *Personenlexikon*, 228, 477.

227. Von Hodenberg, *Konsens*, 308; "Vorführung empfiehlt sich," *DS*, July 10, 1962; Klee, *Personenlexikon*, 159.

228. Von Hodenberg, *Konsens*, 93; Handke, *Präsenz*, 62–3; Gerhard Schäffner in Faulstich, *Kultur der fünfziger Jahre*, 101, 232–3.

229. Zahn, *Jazz*, 133; Gerhard Schäffner in Faulstich, *Kultur der fünfziger Jahre*, 236–7; Handke, *Präsenz*, 98–102; von der Grün, "Programm," 31.

230. Sauer, "Rundfunk," 451; Würfel, *Hörspiel*, 148–50, 156–7; 171; Barner, *Geschichte*, 459–60; Custodis, *Isolation*, 154–6; Schöning, "Konturen," 80–5 (Kagel quoted 82).

231. Franz Mon, *das gras wies wächst* (Würfel, *Hörspiel*, 158–9).

232. Würfel, *Hörspiel*, 159–61.

233. Damus, *Kunst*, 191.

234. Müller, *Mini*, 61.

235. Ibid., 59–60; Ingrid Severin, "Klapheck, Konrad (Peter Cornelius)," *Oxford Art Online*; Dominik Bartmann, "Antes, Horst," *Oxford Art Online* (quote); Damus, *Kunst*, 193, 211.

236. Stephan von Wiese, "Zero," *Oxford Art Online*; idem in Joachimides et al., *Kunst*, 463–4; Damus, *Kunst*, 203–7; Karl Ruhrberg in Hoffmann and Klotz, *Die Sechziger*, 155.

237. https://bundestag.de/besuche/kunst/kuenstler/uecker/; http://eugeniodavenezia.eu/en/amici_pittori.php?id=130; Müller, *Mini*, 58.

238. Stephan von Wiese, "Mack, Heinz," *Oxford Art Online* (quote).

239. Stephan von Wiese, "Piene, Otto," *Oxford Art Online*.

240. See Karl Ruhrberg in Hoffmann and Klotz, *Die Sechziger*, 152.

241. Andreas Franzke, "Baselitz [Kern], Georg," *Oxford Art Online* (quote); https://guggenheim.org/artwork/artist/georg-baselitz.

242. Reproductions in Belting, *Kunst*, 59; Faust and de Vries, *Hunger*, 34.

243. Sarah Wessel, "Skandal um jeden Preis? (I)," (January 2017), https://kstreit.hypotheses.org/34.

244. Damus, *Kunst*, 211–13, 335; Müller, *Mini*, 60; Manske, "Lachen," 793; Günther Gercken in Joachimides et al., *Kunst*, 468–9.

245. Baselitz quoted in Belting, *Kunst*, 63.

246. See his *Der Mann am Baum* (*The Man at the Tree*) of 1969, in Faust and de Vries, *Hunger*, 36.

247. Holland Cotter, "Allan Kaprow, Creator of Artistic 'Happenings,' Dies at 78," *NYT*, April 10, 2006.

248. "Wolf Vostell – Pioneer of Happening and Video Art," *Exposition Art Blog*, January 19, 2018, https://milenaolesinska77.medium.com/wolf-vostell-pioneer-of-happening-and-video-art-cfaa1a94ed85.

249. Damus, *Kunst*, 225–6; Gisela Stelly, "Go-in, Love-in, Sit-in, usw.," *DZ*, November 3, 1967.

250. Julia Robinson, "Maciunas, George," *Oxford Art Online*; Sabine Ehrmann-Herfort in Heister, *Geschichte*, 260.

251. "Manifesto," n.d., facsimile in Heister, *Geschichte*, 259.

252. Müller, *Mini*, 56; Damus, *Kunst*, 223; Dillon, "Chaos," 14.

253. Schmidt, "Kunst," 284; Rühle, *Theater*, 182.

254. Werner Faulstich in Faulstich, *Kultur der sechziger Jahre*, 70–1.

255. Beuys quoted in Adriani et al., *Beuys*, 91–2.

256. Beuys, *Beuys*, 283–4; Andres Veiel, "Die Ursache liegt in der Zukunft," *DZ*, May 12, 2021.

257. Chametzky, *Objects*, 180–1.

258. Stachelhaus, *Beuys*, 27.

259. See examples of Beuys's pre-1950 work in Tisdall, *Beuys*, 18-19; van der Grinten, "Beuys," 17, 25; Adriani et al., *Beuys*, 17–18, 24, 29.

260. Stachelhaus, *Beuys*, 56–7, 68–9.

261. Ibid., 86.
262. Adriani et al., *Beuys*, 36 (quote).
263. Stachelhaus, *Beuys*, 94–5.
264. Ibid., 164–6; Chametzky, *Objects*, 183–4.
265. Adriani et al., *Beuys*, 12–13.
266. Beuys, *Beuys*, 279.
267. Beuys to parents, December 12, 1942, *Beuys*, 259.
268. Beuys in Jappe, "Interview," 190–1; Stachelhaus, *Beuys*, 14.
269. Adriani et al., *Beuys*, 16; Stachelhaus, *Beuys*, 49.
270. Stachelhaus, *Beuys*, 35.
271. Ray, "Beuys," 62–4, 70; van der Grinten, "Beuys," 25–6; Chametzky, *Objects*, 171, 186–9; Hadek, *Vergangenheitsbewältigung*, 71.
272. Ray, "Beuys," 59–60.
273. Reproduction in Chametzky, *Objects*, 177.
274. Obituary for Joseph Beuys in *NYT*, January 25, 1986.
275. Stachelhaus, *Beuys*, 114.
276. Adriani et al., *Beuys*, 114–15; Manske, "Lachen," 798.
277. Stachelhaus, *Beuys*, 225–6; Manske, "Lachen," 797.
278. Vischer, "Kunstbegriff," 41.
279. Adriani, "Hinweise," 100.
280. Eduard Trier, "Die Akademie ist keine Kirche," *DZ*, December 20, 1968 (quote); Norbert Kricke, "Kein Fall für mich," *DZ*, December 20, 1968; "In Sachen Beuys," *DZ*, December 20, 1968; Stachelhaus, *Beuys*, 117–21.
281. Vowinckel, "Kunst," 18.
282. Kimpel, *documenta*, 39–42.
283. Ibid., 42. Also Damus, *Kunst*, 188–93.
284. Kimpel, *documenta*, 48 (quote); Müller, *Mini*, 58.
285. Kimpel, *documenta*, 43–5, 48.
286. Ibid., 48.
287. Damus, *Kunst*, 197.
288. Kimpel, *documenta*, 52–64 (quotes 53, 56); Damus, *Kunst*, 241–3; Vowinckel, "Kunst," 25; Manske, "Lachen," 782–4.
289. Gottfried Sello, "Gruselkabinette und Primary Structures auf der documenta IV," *DZ*, July 5, 1968.
290. Damus, *Kunst*, 188–90.
291. Steinkamp, "Schöpfung," 298; Fulda and Soyka, "Nolde," 187–8, 190–2; Paret, *Artist*, 69; Evans, *The Coming*, 414; Stefan Koldehoff, "Noldes Bekenntnis," *DZ*, October 10, 2013.
292. Nolde, *Leben*, 393–4; Nolde in https://www.dhm.de/lemo/biografie/emil-nolde.html.
293. Petropoulos, *Artists*, 174–5 (quote 175); Kater, *Culture*, 320.
294. Kater, *Culture*, 320, 389, n. 86.
295. Petropoulos, *Artists*, 175; Fulda, *Nolde*, 240.
296. Haftmann, *Nolde*, 15–16 (quotes 15).
297. Fulda, *Nolde*, 239.
298. *Ausstellungskatalog Deutsche Kunst*, n.p. (items 116 and 117).
299. Werner Weber, "Rugbüll zum Beispiel," *DZ*, September 20, 1968.
300. Fulda, *Nolde*, 237. See Lenz interviewed in "Vom Erfolg überrascht," *DZ*, July 4, 1969; "Die Siggi-Lenz-Show," *DZ*, February 5, 1971; John F. O'Connor, "TV: As a Boy Saw Nazis," *NYT*, September 10, 1979; Peter Demetz, "More German Lessons," *NYT*, November 26, 1989.

301. Raddatz, *Unruhestifter*, 227.
302. Helmut Schmidt's speech, February 10, 1982, "Nolde-Ausstellung im Bundeskanzleramt: Ansprache des Bundeskanzlers," *Bulletin: Presse- und Informationsdienst der Bundesregierung* (March 4, 1982): 150–1.
303. Ulrich Greiner, "Emil Nolde und Siegfried Lenz," *DZ*, April 30, 2014.
304. Maletzke, *Lenz*, 17–21, 30.
305. "Dieter Hildebrandt soll in der NSDAP gewesen sein," *DW*, June 30, 2007; Fulda, *Nolde*, 237; William Yardley, "Siegfried Lenz, Novelist of Germany's Past, Dies at 88," *NYT*, October 10, 2014.
306. Fulda, *Nolde*, 237. Haftmann: Rolf Wedewer, "Notwendigkeit der Diskussion," *DZ*, September 15, 1967; Hanno Rauterberg and Katja Nicodemus, "Hüter des falschen Friedens," *DZ*, February 6, 2020.
307. See Fulda, *Nolde*, 236; Maletzke, *Lenz*, 63.
308. Maletzke, *Lenz*, 149; Fulda, *Nolde*, 238.
309. https://prabook.com/web/martin.urban/1036979; Fulda, *Nolde*, 238.
310. Tobias Timm, "Dunkelbraune Idyllen," *DZ*, April 3, 2019 (quotes); Catherine Hickley, "Stripping Away Lies to Expose a Nazi Painter's Past," *NYT*, April 10, 2019; Florian Illies, "Die falsche Deutschstunde," *DZ*, April 10, 2019.
311. Schultheiss and Schultheiss, *Stadttheater*, 182 (quote); Christoph von Dohnányi in Hoffmann and Klotz, *Die Sechziger*, 116–17.
312. Werner Faulstich in Faulstich, *Kultur der sechziger Jahre*, 61.
313. Hellmuth Steger in Dibelius and Schneider, *Neue Musik*, vol. 2, 295; Joachim Klaiber in ibid., 296–7; Lehnert, *Musiktheater*, 33; Schultze, *Theater*, 600–1, 606–7, 614–15, 626, 635; Kretschmann, *Spaltung*, 45.
314. Seifert, *Wand*, 280–96, quote 283; Gielen quoted in Mark Berry, "A Composer of Dark Explosions Turns 100," *NYT*, March 16, 2018.
315. Wagner, *Wagner Theater*, 180–9, 231; Spotts, *Bayreuth*, 224–47 (quote 225); Hamann, *Wagner*, 582; Wieland Wagner quoted in Kolland, "Kleider," 169. Knappertsbusch: Kater, *Twisted Muse*, 40–6.
316. Joachim Kaiser, "Des Meisters Worte und der Enkel Sinn (V)" *DZ*, August 21, 1964.
317. Spotts, *Bayreuth*, 255–8 (quotes 256, 257).
318. Obituary for August Everding in *Chicago Tribune*, January 30, 1999; Heinz Josef Herbort, "Die Neuen scheiterten kläglich," *DZ*, August 1, 1969.
319. Taruskin, *Music*, 54.
320. Wolf-Eberhard von Lewinski in Borio and Danuser, *Zenit*, vol. 3, 450; Brigitte Schiffer in ibid., 454; ibid., vol. 2, 127–8.
321. Honegger and Massenkeil, *Lexikon*, vol. 4, 192; Rudolf Heinemann in Borio and Danuser, *Zenit*, vol. 3, 445.
322. Wolf-Eberhard von Lewinski in Dibelius and Schneider, *Neue Musik*, vol. 2, 294; Pascal Decroupet in Borio and Danuser, *Zenit*, vol. 2, 116–18.
323. Borio and Danuser, *Zenit*, vol. 2, 350.
324. Wolf-Eberhard von Lewinski in ibid., vol. 3, 448–9.
325. György Ligeti quoted in Ross, *Rest*, 467.
326. Adorno quoted in Dibelius, *Moderne Musik*, 227.
327. Rudolf Heinemann in Borio and Danuser, *Zenit*, vol. 3, 443–4 (Stockhausen quoted 444).
328. Matthias Knauer in Borio and Danuser, *Zenit*, vol. 3, 459; Heinz Josef Herbort, "Profane Wallfahrten," *DZ*, September 6, 1996.
329. Heinz Josef Herbort, "Gehört, beklatscht, vergessen," *DZ*, September 23, 1966 (quote); "Nicht jedes Jahr eine Handvoll Genies und Meisterwerke," *DZ*, October 30, 1964.

330. Rudolf Heinemann in Borio and Danuser, *Zenit*, vol. 3, 444 (quote); Wolf-Eberhard von Lewinski in ibid, 447–50; Brigitte Schiffer ibid, 452–3; Matthias Knauer in Borio and Danuser, *Zenit*, vol. 3, 460–1; Wolf-Eberhard von Lewinski in Dibelius and Schneider, *Neue Musik*, vol. 2, 294; Pascal Decroupet in Heister, *Geschichte*, 149; Heinz Josef Herbort, "Musikalische Avantgarde als Establishment," *DZ*, September 16, 1966.
331. Rudolf Heinemann in Borio and Danuser, *Zenit*, vol. 3, 444; Mary Bauermeister in Gronemeyer, "Neue Musik," 57.
332. Custodis, *Isolation*, 120–1 (Paik quoted 120).
333. Ibid., 118; Gronemeyer, "Neue Musik," 58; Dibelius, "Musik," 165; Ross, *Rest*, 475–6, 492–5.
334. Heinz-Klaus Metzger, "Das Contre-Festival," *Kölner Stadtanzeiger*, June 25/26, 1960.
335. Custodis, *Isolation*, 122 (Paik quoted ibid.).
336. Karl Heinz Ruppel in Dibelius and Schneider, *Neue Musik*, vol. 2, 163–5; Gronemeyer, "Neue Musik," 59; Kurtz, *Stockhausen*, 156–8.
337. Dibelius, "Leier," 123.
338. Schnebel, "Musik," 14.
339. Aucoin, *Art*, 78; Stockhausen, *Texte*, 473.
340. "'Sprengt die Opernhäuser in die Luft!'," *DS*, September 25, 1967; Dibelius, "Leier," 120; Hakemi and Hecken, "Warenhausbrandstifter," 318; Daiber, *Theater*, 257; Taruskin, *Music*, 223.
341. Aucoin, "Sound," 20.
342. *DS*, August 17, 2020.
343. Müller, *Mini*, 94–6.
344. Eimert, *Grundlagen*, 9–14 (quotes 12, 13).
345. Dieter Rexroth in Hoffmann and Klotz, *Die Sechziger*, 123–8.
346. Morgan, "Stockhausen's Writings," 3–9.
347. Frisius, *Stockhausen*, 21 (quote); "Karlheinz Stockhausen" in *Encyclopedia Britannica*; Stockhausen obituary in *The Times*, London, December 8, 2007.
348. Karlheinz Stockhausen in Dibelius and Schneider, *Neue Musik*, vol. 2, 243–5; Kurtz, *Stockhausen*, 184.
349. Ritzel, *Musik*, 22–8.
350. Claus Spahn, "Der Klang der Sterne," *DZ*, December 13, 2007 (quote); Baird, *To Die*, 73–107).
351. Custodis, *Isolation*, 134; Andrew D. McCredie and Marion Rothärmel, "Zimmermann, Bernd Alois," *Oxford Music Online*; Mark Berry, "A Composer of Dark Explosions Turns 100," *NYT*, March 16, 2018; Ross, *Rest*, 463–4.
352. Daiber, *Theater*, 236; Wolfram Schwinger, "Zum Tod von Bernd Alois Zimmermann," *DZ*, August 21, 1970.
353. Unitel Classica DVD, *Die Soldaten* (Ingo Metzmacher, Wiener Philharmoniker, Salzburg Festival, August 2012); Eimert (1965) in Dibelius and Schneider, *Neue Musik*, vol. 2, 236–8 (quote 238); Andrew D. McCredie and Marion Rothärmel, "Zimmermann, Bernd Alois," *Oxford Music Online*; Edward Rothstein, "Review/City Opera," *NYT*, October 10, 1991; Wolfram Schwinger, "Zum Tod von Bernd Alois Zimmermann," *DZ*, August 21, 1970; Daibert, *Theater*, 235–6; Dieter Rexroth in Hoffmann and Klotz, *Die Sechziger*, 131.
354. Edward Rothstein, "Review/City Opera," *NYT*, October 10, 1991; Andrew D. McCredie and Marion Rothärmel, "Zimmermann, Bernd Alois," *Oxford Music Online*; Wolfram Schwinger, "Zum Tod von Bernd Alois Zimmermann," *DZ*, August 21, 1970 (Zimmermann's "death" quote); Ross, *Rest*, 464 (Hitler quoted).

355. Custodis, *Isolation*, 135.
356. Paul Attinello, "Kagel, Mauricio (Raúl)," *Oxford Music Online*; Wulf Herzogenrath in Herzogenrath and Lueg, *60er Jahre*, 17–18.
357. Paul Attinello, "Kagel, Mauricio (Raúl)," *Oxford Music Online*.
358. Ibid.
359. Ibid.
360. David Sawer, "Kagel, Mauricio (opera) [Maurizio] (Raúl)," *Oxford Music Online* (quote); Dibelius, "Musik," 145; Dibelius and Schneider, *Neue Musik*, vol. 2, 167–8.
361. Henze, *Reiselieder*, 201; Paul Attinello, "Kagel, Mauricio (Raúl)," *Oxford Music Online*; Riethmüller, "Gedanken," 217–19.
362. Paul Attinello, "Kagel, Mauricio (Raúl)," *Oxford Music Online* (quote); Schnebel, "Musik," 14–16; Dieter Rexroth in Hoffmann and Klotz, *Die Sechziger*, 129–30; Scharberth, *Musiktheater*, 144–61; Heinz Josef Herbort, "Das eitle Drum und Dran der Oper," *DZ*, April 30, 1971.
363. Kagel quoted in Stockhausen, *Texte*, 481. Also see Hilberg and Vogt, *Musik*, 42.
364. The John Tusa Interviews (July 16, 2006), BBC Radio 3.
365. Paul Griffiths, "Ligeti, György (Sándor)," *Oxford Music Online* (quote); Ross, *Rest*, 465–9; Taruskin, *Music*, 49.
366. Paul Griffiths, "Ligeti, György (Sándor)," *Oxford Music Online*.
367. Paul Griffiths, "Ligeti, György (Sándor)," *Oxford Music Online*; Taruskin, *Music*, 214–15 (Ligeti quoted 214).
368. Paul Griffiths, "Ligeti, György (Sándor)," *Oxford Music Online*.
369. Kretschmann, *Spaltung*, 134.
370. Hans Werner Henze in Hoffmann and Klotz, *Die Sechziger Jahre*, 119–21.
371. Henze, *Reiselieder*, 206.
372. Ibid., 207.
373. Ibid., 208.
374. "'Sprengt die Opernhäuser in die Luft!'" *DS*, September 25, 1967.
375. Henze, *Reiselieder*, 198–9 (quote 198); Scharbeth, *Musiktheater*, 52–7.
376. Josef Müller-Marein, "Hut ab, eine Oper!" *DZ*, May 27, 1960.
377. Walter Abendroth, "Ein Pfiff löste den Erfolg aus," *DZ*, May 26, 1961.
378. Heinz Josef Herbort, "Dionysisches in epischer Breite," *DZ*, August 12, 1966; Petersen, *Henze*, 245–6.
379. Christoph von Dohnányi in Hoffmann and Klotz, *Die Sechziger Jahre*, 119.
380. Fritz Hennenberg, "Dessau, Paul," *Oxford Music Online*; Honegger and Massenkeil, *Lexikon*, vol. 2, 293–4.
381. Paul Hofmann, "Feltrinelli Case Takes New Turn," *NYT*, April 18, 1972; https://palazzoesposizioni.it/pagine/1955-la-tartaruga-titina-maselli-eng.
382. Henze, *Reiselieder*, 250.
383. Ibid., 248; Neuhaus, *Grass*, 219.
384. Speech reprinted in Henze, *Reiselieder*, 249–50.
385. Ibid., 287–94.
386. Henze, *Musik*, 139–43, 151.
387. Quote from Jens Brockmeier ibid., 15.
388. "Ho-Ho-Ho-Tschi-Minh in Schönklang," *DZ*, December 13, 1968; Klaus Geitel in Dibelius and Schneider, *Neue Musik*, vol. 2, 374–6.
389. Heinz Josef Herbort, "Rot vor den Augen," *DZ*, December 13, 1968 (quotes); Ruth Herrmann, "Klimmzüge am Hals," *DZ*, January 23, 1970.
390. Wolfram Schwinger in Dibelius and Schneider, *Neue Musik*, vol. 2, 377 (quotes); "Ho-Ho-Ho-Tschi-Minh in Schönklang," *DZ*, December 13, 1968; Glaser, *Deutsche Kultur*, 290.

391. See Kater, "Himmler's Circle," 76–93; "Nazi-forged Fortune Creates Hidden German Billionaire," *Irish Times*, February 3, 2014, https://www.irishtimes.com/business/nazi-forged-fortune-creates-hidden-german-billionaire-1.1677631.
392. Haug von Kuenheim, "Ohne Oetker keine Feier," *DZ*, October 4, 1968 (quote); Rudolf Walter Leonhardt, "Musik oder Revolution?" *DZ*, October 11, 1968.

FOUR – NEW UNCERTAINTIES (1970–1980)

1. "'Natürlich kann geschossen werden'," *DS*, June 15, 1970.
2. Bohrer, *Jetzt*, 136–9, 406.
3. Reich-Ranicki, *Leben*, 459–60 (quote 459); Meinhof, *Würde*, 52–8.
4. "Vollstrecker des Weltgewissens," *DS*, June 2, 1997.
5. Meinhof, *Würde*, 85; Meinhof in Brückner, *Meinhof*, 12–14, 90–1.
6. Aust, *Komplex*, 24–8; Seifert, "Meinhof," 350–6; Röhl, *Marsch*, 66–7.
7. Aust, *Komplex*, 29–31; Seifert, "Meinhof," 356–64; Röhl, *Marsch*, 73–92.
8. Aust, *Komplex*, 47–9; Wieland, "Baader," 342; Wittstock, *Reich-Ranicki*, 171.
9. Vesper, *Reise*, 18, 39, 59, 66, 471; Koenen, *Vesper*, 19; Tauber, *Eagle*, 668–9.
10. Seghers in Vesper and Ensslin, *Stimmen*, 39–41; Baumann in ibid., 42; Brecht in ibid., 134.
11. Koenen, *Vesper*, 26–36.
12. Eberhard Lämmert in Lämmert et al., *Germanistik*, esp. 32–5; Kater, *Weimar*, 278.
13. Vesper, *Reise*, 500; Koenen, *Vesper*, 39, 82–90, 101–5; Bentz et al., *Protest*, 20–6, 30–5; Bressan and Jander, "Ensslin," 404–5; Aust, *Komplex*, 35–6.
14. Preece, *Novel*, xix; Pflieger, *Rote Armee Fraktion*, 187; Kraushaar et al., *Dutschke*, 69–71, 80; Flemming and Ulrich, *Vor Gericht*, 152–5.
15. Ulrike Meinhof, "Warenhausbrandstiftung," *konkret* (no. 14, 1968), reprinted Meinhof, *Würde*, 153–6 (quote 156).
16. Preece, *Novel*, xx; Pflieger, *Rote Armee Fraktion*, 187; Aust, *Komplex*, 15–16; Kraushaar et al., *Dutschke*, 71–82; Flemming and Ulrich, *Vor Gericht*, 154–5.
17. Pflieger, *Rote Armee Fraktion*, 183–5.
18. "'Natürlich kann geschossen werden'," *DS*, June 15, 1970.
19. Pflieger, *Rote Armee Fraktion*, 187–8.
20. "Baader-Meinhof," *DS*, December 2, 1974; Preece, *Novel*, xxii.
21. Preece, *Novel*, xxiii–xxiv; Brückner, *Meinhof*, 106; Flemming and Ulrich, *Vor Gericht*, 160.
22. Wunschik, "Aufstieg," 487.
23. "Stark genug, den Krieg zu erklären?" *DS*, September 12, 1977; "Fall Schleyer: Der zweite Schlag," *DS*, October 17, 1977; Preece, *Novel*, xxiv; Pflieger, *Rote Armee Fraktion*, 190–1.
24. Walser, *Tagebücher, 1974–1978*, 45, 430, 439 (quote).
25. Jürgen Habermas to Kurt Sontheimer, September 19, 1977, in Habermas, *Schriften*, 374.
26. See, e.g., Dutschke's diary entries of November 10, 25 and 26, 1974, in Dutschke, *Jeder*, 224–5, 229–30; Kurt Sontheimer (1977) in Habermas, *Schriften*, 388.
27. Kraushaar et al., *Dutschke*, 46–7, 71.
28. See Dutschke's diary, *Jeder*. Meinhof: *Würde*. Ensslin: *Briefe*, e.g. 50, 56–62, 78–81, 85–90. Baader: Wieland, "Baader," 348.
29. Kraushaar et al., *Dutschke*, 67–8 (quote 67), 79; Aust, *Komplex*, 33–4; Bressan and Jander, "Ensslin," 404; Flemming and Ulrich, *Vor Gericht*, 150–1.
30. Kraushaar et al., *Dutschke*, 66–95; Wieland, "Baader," 332–46; Enzensberger, *Jahre*, 187; Aust, *Komplex*, 16–17; Scribner, *Gender*, 43.

31. Aust, *Komplex*, 33; Bressan and Jander, "Ensslin," 400.
32. Jarausch, "Memory," 22.
33. Gudrun Ensslin quoted in Aust, *Komplex*, 54. Also Bressan and Jander, "Ensslin," 401.
34. *Rote Armee Fraktion*, 55, 167–8; Röhl, *Marsch*, 95.
35. Preece, *Novel*, 9.
36. König, "Ikonen," 434–5.
37. Hachmeister, *Schleyer*, 345.
38. Horst-Eberhard Richter, "Was bedeutet es, die RAF zu verstehen?" *Die Tageszeitung (taz)*, Berlin, October 27, 2004; Kraushaar et al., *Dutschke*, 101–2. Also Wunschik, "Aufstieg," 478–9.
39. Ensslin, *Briefe*, 79, 87 (quote).
40. Meinhof quoted in Hanshew, *Terror*, 155.
41. Viett, *Nie*, 124–5.
42. Ibid., 21.
43. Ibid., 18.
44. *Rote Armee Fraktion*, 187–9.
45. Meinhof, *Würde*, 41–2, 136; Meinhof in Brückner, *Meinhof*, 76.
46. Kraushaar, *Flecken*, 352.
47. Viett, *Nie*, 100.
48. Boock in Jürgen Leffers, "Der Tag, als Jürgen Ponto starb," *DS*, July 29, 2017.
49. Thomas Schmid, "Hanns Martin Schleyer, das unbekannte Opfer," *DW*, October 19, 2007.
50. Hachmeister, *Schleyer*, 384.
51. Ibid., 12, 52, 64, 73–4, 80, 95, 181, 223, 229, 232, 235, 318.
52. Walter Boehlich in Botzat et al., *Herbst*, 73–5; Friedrich Christian Delius, "Die Dialektik des Deutschen Herbstes," *DZ*, July 25, 1997.
53. Jessen, "Vergangenheit," 182; König, "Siebziger Jahre," 87, 91–2; Jarausch, "Strukturwandel," 9, 23.
54. Soell, "Schmidt," 279; Lehmann, *Sechziger*, 52–3.
55. "Bittere Wahrheit, kein Konzept," *DS,* September 5, 1977.
56. Ibid.
57. Winkler, *Weg*, 321–3.
58. Stern, *Doppelleben*, 206.
59. Winkler, *Weg*, 313–14.
60. "'Finster schaut's aus'," *DS*, December 2, 1974, 28; Klaus Hartung, "Pathetiker der Distanz," *DZ*, November 23, 2000; Enzensberger, *Brosamen*, 84–6.
61. Stern, *Doppelleben*, 207–8; Karasek, *Flucht*, 428.
62. Bressan and Jander, "Ensslin," 422; Winkler, *Weg*, 349; Flemming and Ulrich, *Vor Gericht*, 156–7.
63. "Fall Schleyer," *DS*, September 19, 1977; Biess, *Republik*, 348, 351; Stern, *Doppelleben*, 206; Habermas, *Schriften*, 369.
64. "Fall Schleyer," *DS*, September 19, 1977; Habermas, *Schriften*, 379.
65. Winkler, *Weg*, 348. Case of musician Manfred Ritter in "'Wen suchen wir denn eigentlich?'" *DS*, November 7, 1977.
66. Rudolf Augstein, "Schuldige gesucht," *DS*, September 19, 1977.
67. "'Wen suchen wir denn eigentlich?'" *DS*, November 7, 1977.
68. Winkler, *Weg*, 301–2; Werner Faulstich in Faulstich, *Kultur der Siebziger Jahre*, 10–11; McCormick, *Politics*, 42; O'Dochartaigh, *Germany*, 148.
69. *Der Tagesspiegel*, Berlin, February 28, 2018.
70. Enzensberger in *Brosamen*, 84.

71. Wunschik, "Aufstieg," 487; "'Wir wollten alles und gleichzeitig nichts'," *DS*, August 11, 1980.
72. Wunschik, "Aufstieg," 473.
73. Ibid., 473–4; Rutschky, *Erfahrungshunger*, 161; Hachmeister, *Schleyer*, 373; Stern, *Doppelleben*, 206; Röhl, *Marsch*, 225.
74. Preece, *Novel*, xxii; Elsaesser, *Cinema*, 122–3.
75. Hachmeister, *Schleyer*, 370–3.
76. Flemming and Ulrich, *Vor Gericht*, 160.
77. Böll, *Gruppenbild*, 74, 130, 182, 196, 287.
78. Böll, "'Will Ulrike Gnade oder Freies Geleit?'" *DS*, January 9, 1972.
79. Diether Posser, "'Diese Praxis ist verheerend'," *DS*, January 23, 1972.
80. Dolf Sternberger, "Böll, der Staat und die Gnade," *FAZ*, February 2, 1972.
81. Linder, *Böll*, 187.
82. Joachim Kaiser in preface to Heinrich Böll, "'Man muss zu weit gehen'," *SZ*, January 29/30, 1972.
83. Böll, *Ehre*, 182.
84. "Fall Schleyer: 'Die Dramatik muss raus'," *DS*, September 19, 1977; Sölle, "Böll," 885–7; Wolf Donner, "Der lüsterne Meinungsterror," *DZ*, October 10, 1975; Reid, *Böll*, 182–3; Vormweg, *Deutsche*, 365–7.
85. Böll, *Berichte*, 23, 43, 58; Böll interviewed in Eggebrecht, *Männer*, 133 (quote).
86. Böll, *Berichte*, 59; Böll interviewed in Eggebrecht, *Männer*, 130–1 (quote 131).
87. Böll (1977) in Böll, *bange*, 165.
88. Marcel Reich-Ranicki, "'Nette Kapitalisten und nette Terroristen'," *FAZ*, August 4, 1979. Also Vormweg, *Deutsche*, 375–6.
89. See Böll, *Belagerung*, 48–9, 79, 134–5, 138, 173–5, 237, 322–6.
90. Linder, *Böll*, 180; Vormweg, *Deutsche*, 328.
91. Walser, *Sturz*, 192.
92. Walser, *Tagebücher, 1974–1978*, 37; *Tagebücher, 1979–81*, 303–5.
93. Marcel Reich-Ranicki, "Jenseits der Literatur," *FAZ*, March 27, 1976; Walser, *Tagebücher, 1963–1973*, 368–9, 558; Walser, *Tagebücher, 1974–1978*, 204, 451–2; Magenau, *Walser*, 299–300, 351.
94. Walser, *Tagebücher, 1979–1981*, 251–4; *Ansichten*, 611, 631–6; Magenau, *Walser*, 372–3.
95. Walser, *Sturz*, 111, 118, 130–2; Auerbach, "Einheit Dirlewanger," 150–63.
96. Walser, *Sturz*, 29, 31, 77, 95–7, 100, 145, 147, 151, 223.
97. Walser, *Liebe*, 48, 256; "Ich war ihm ausgeliefert," *DZ*, April 16, 2015; Jens, *Vatermord*, 181–4; Franz Schonauer in Nonnenmann, *Schriftsteller*, 182–8.
98. Marcel Reich-Ranicki, "Jenseits der Literatur," *FAZ*, March 27, 1976.
99. Joachim Kaiser, "Isoliertes Ich, dem Abgrund nahe," *SZ*, April 7, 1976.
100. Rolf Michaelis, "Leben aus zweiter Hand'," *DZ*, March 26, 1976; Rolf Becker, "Der Sturz des Franz Horn," *DS*, April 5, 1976; Wolfram Schütte, "'Von den Alltagsfreundlichkeiten'," *FR*, April 10, 1976.
101. Walser, *Pferd*, 93, 138–9.
102. Marcel Reich-Ranicki, "Martin Walsers Rückkehr zu sich selbst," *FAZ*, March 24, 1978.
103. Walser, *Tagebücher, 1974–1978*, 464.
104. Ibid., 169–70, 208–16, 220–5, 228, 245 (quote entry for March 27, 1976, 214).
105. Walser in Walser and Augstein, *Leben*, 247–9; Walser, *Tagebücher, 1974–1978*, 110, 217–19, 296–7.
106. Walser, *Tagebücher, 1974–1978*, 277, 294–6, 301–3; *Tagebücher, 1979–81*, 220, 380.

107. "Hinweis auf einen alten Hut," *DS*, February 11, 1974. Also Walser, *Tagebücher, 1974–1978*, 12–15; "Ich war ihm ausgeliefert," *DZ*, April 16, 2015.
108. Mayer-Iswandy, *Grass*, 122–3.
109. Grass to Brandt, May 17, 1974, in *Willy Brandt*, 622. See Baier and Claussen, "Intellektuellen," 131.
110. Günter Grass, "Wiederholter Versuch," *SZ*, February 5/6, 1972.
111. Preece, *Novel*, 79–80 (quotes 80).
112. "Hausmitteilung," *DS*, August 20, 1995.
113. Reich-Ranicki, *Leben*, 468–9; 490–1. Also Walser, *Tagebücher, 1974–78*, 414.
114. Walser, diary entry for March 27, 1976, *Tagebücher, 1974–1978*, 212.
115. Ibid., for November 5, 1978, 523.
116. Michalzik, *Unseld*, 301.
117. Walser, *Tod*, 39, 49, 72.
118. " 'Ich habe manipuliert, selbstverständlich!'," *DS*, January 2, 1989.
119. Reich-Ranicki, "Anmerkungen," 176–7.
120. Marcel Reich-Ranicki, "Martin Walser's Rückkehr zu sich selbst," *FAZ*, March 24, 1978.
121. Reich-Ranicki, "Deutsche Literatur 1977," *FAZ*, October 13, 1977; "Anmerkungen," 169, 179.
122. Text in Chapter 3 at n. 114.
123. Reich-Ranicki, "Jenseits der Literatur," *FAZ*, March 27, 1976.
124. Reich-Ranicki, "Nette Kapitalisten und nette Terroristen," *FAZ*, August 4, 1979.
125. Walser, entry for April 7, 1976, *Tagebücher, 1974–1978*, 248 (quote), 251.
126. Ibid., 526.
127. Walser, entry for September 12, 1979, *Tagebücher, 1979–1981*, 285.
128. Lau, *Enzensberger*, 13–19; Philip Oltermann, "A Life in Writing," *Guardian*, May 15, 2010 (quote); Enzensberger, *Jahre*, 38.
129. Lau, *Enzensberger*, 28–9; Winkler, *Netz*, 226–7; "Beinahe harmlos," *DS*, November 26, 1963.
130. Lau, *Enzensberger*, 29.
131. Ibid., 67, 144; Philip Oltermann, "A Life in Writing," *Guardian*, May 15, 2010 (quote); Enzensberger in André Müller, "Ich will nicht der Lappen sein, mit dem man die Welt putzt," *DZ*, January 20, 1995; Jörg Lau, "Windhund mit Ohren," *DZ*, November 11, 1999.
132. Benno Reifenberg, "Hans Magnus, ein böswilliger Leser," *FAZ*, July 7, 1962.
133. Lau, *Enzensberger*, 145–217; Enzensberger in Müller, "Ich will nicht der Lappen sein", (as in n. 131) Glaser, *Kulturgeschichte*, vol. 2, 172–3; Schnell, *Geschichte*, 315–16; Demetz, *Anarchie*, 112; Reid, *Böll*, 145; Stern, *Doppelleben*, 194 (quote).
134. Lau, *Enzensberger*, 242.
135. Hans Magnus Enzensberger, "On Leaving America," *NYRB*, February 29, 1968, https://www.nybooks.com/articles/1968/02/29/on-leaving-america/?printpage= true.
136. "German Poet Hails 'Joy' of Life in Cuba," *NYT*, February 17, 1968.
137. Roberts, "Tendenzwenden," 293. Sarcastically: Reich-Ranicki, "Anmerkungen," 172.
138. Lau, *Enzensberger*, 284.
139. Enzensberger, *Verhör*, 166–7, 207.
140. Trnka, *Subjects*, 112; Werner Dolph, "Die Szene – kein Tribunal," *DZ*, June 12, 1970; Karoll Stein, "Verhör in Ostberlin," *DZ*, June 16, 1970.
141. See Blumer, *Theater*, 346–50.

142. Hugo Loetscher, "Die Invasoren der Schweinebucht," *DZ*, June 12, 1970; Blumer, *Theater*, 342–3, 351; *FAZ* quoted in Lau, *Enzensberger*, 288.

143. Lau, *Enzensberger*, 289; Blumer, *Theater*, 344; Hugo Loetscher, "Die Invasoren der Schweinebucht," *DZ*, June 12, 1970.

144. Enzensberger quoted in Philip Oltermann, "A Life in Writing," *Guardian*, May 15, 2010; Enzensberger in Müller, "Ich will nicht der Lappen sein"; Bentz et al., *Protest*, 508–9.

145. Selectively: Stuttgart's repertory of the 1970s in Doll, *Theaterarbeit*, 134–8.

146. Knut Hickethier in Faulstich, *Kultur der fünfziger Jahre*, 50; Walter Uka in ibid., 56; Rischbieter, "Theater," 109–12.

147. Iden, *Palitzsch*, 77–80 (Palitzsch quoted 77); Mennicken, *Palitzsch*, 26–32; Rischbieter, "Theater," 106–7; Hugh Rorrison, "Peter Zadek," *Guardian*, August 3, 2009.

148. Schroeter, *Tage*, 131–69; Zadek, *Heissen Jahre*, 206–7.

149. Zadek, *Heissen Jahre*, 215.

150. Canaris, *Zadek*, 44 (quote), 113–15, 126–28, 147–51.

151. Hugh Rorrison, "Peter Palitzsch," *Guardian*, December 28, 2004.

152. Zadek, *My Way*, 317–18; Canaris, *Zadek*, 174–77.

153. Zadek, *Wanderjahre*, 55.

154. Ibid., 56.

155. Ibid., 57.

156. Ibid., 58, 311 (quote).

157. Koberg, *Peymann*, 29–100.

158. Ibid., 173–90.

159. Ilse Ensslin's missive, Stuttgart, June 5, 1977, facs. ibid., 191.

160. "Neue Zähne für Terroristen," *Bild-Zeitung*, August 29, 1977.

161. Koberg, *Peymann*, 193–9; Heinrich Böll, "Wo leben wir eigentlich," *FAZ*, September 18, 1977; Ferbers et al., *Peymann*, 108–15; 118–19; Walser, *Tagebücher, 1974–1978*, 427.

162. Bernhard, *Ruhestand*, 35, 72, 89, 115; Benjamin Henrichs, "Herr Bernhard und die Deutschen," *DZ*, July 6, 1979; Koberg, *Peymann*, 108–9.

163. Bernhard, *Ruhestand*, 117; Ferbers et al., *Peymann*, 122–34.

164. Theo Sommer, "Die Bürde der Vergangenheit," *DZ*, May 5, 1978; Hochhuth, *Juristen*, 100–1, 174; Karasek, *Kulturkritik*, 224–7; Habermas, *Schriften*, 377; Riewoldt, "Drama," 161.

165. Hochhuth, *Liebe*, 62. Rowohlt published the novel in 1978.

166. Hochhuth, "Schwierigkeiten, die wahre Geschichte zu erzählen," *DZ*, February 17, 1978.

167. Theo Sommer et al., "Dokumentation," *DZ*, May 5, 1978; Nina Grunenberg, "'Mein Gott, Herr Ministerpräsident ...'," *DZ*, August 11, 1978; Kurt Becker, "Der Sturz von Stuttgart," *DZ*, August 11, 1978; Theo Sommer, "Fünf vor acht/ Rolf Hochhuth," *DZ*, May 19, 2020 (quotes); Koberg, *Peymann*, 206; Filbinger in Grützbach, *Böll*, 47–8; Knesebeck, *Filbinger*, 19–37, 84; Dürr, "Süddeutsche Zeitung," 64.

168. Von Miquel, *Juristen*, 231–2; Klee, *Personenlexikon*, 484; Gerhard Mauz, "Richter – Instrument für jeden Machthaber?" *DS*, December 23, 1968.

169. Meinhof, *Würde*, 163.

170. "'Der Kerl gehört gehängt!'" *DS*, July 9, 1978; von Miquel, *Juristen*, 232–5; Friedrich, *Amnestie*, 358–64.

171. Kater, "*Ahnenerbe*", 525–6.

172. Klee, *Personenlexikon*, 577; Gert Heidenreich, "Freiheit im Freistaat," *DZ*, October 20, 1978.

173. Ibid.; "Wunderbare Wegbegleiter," *DS*, December 5, 1993.

174. Kater, *Hitler Youth*, 128.

175. Klee, *Personenlexikon*, 688–9.

176. Kater, *"Ahnenerbe"*, 170–90; "Stich ins Wespennest," *DS*, September 14, 1998; Ulrich Greiner, "Mein Name sei Schwerte," *DZ*, May 12, 1995; Frank Gerstenberg, "Der 'Braun-Schweiger'," *SZ*, December 30, 1999; Eric Pace, "Hans Schwerte, 90, Ex-SS Man Who Hid Identity," *NYT*, January 10, 2000.

177. Bauer to Kater, February 26, 1968, IfZ, Archiv, ZS/A-25.

178. Brigitte Zander, "Kein Schlösschen für die Heimatlosen," *DZ*, August 11, 1978; Caldwell and Hanshew, *Germany*, 182–3.

179. "Gastarbeiter," *DZ*, February 20, 1976; Karl-Heinz Meier-Braun, "Ausländerpolitik," *DZ*, October 22, 1982; Herbert and Hunn, "Guest Workers," 208–9.

180. Pagenstecher, *Ausländerpolitik*, 56, 58.

181. *Statistisches Jahrbuch*, 544.

182. Ibid., 148.

183. Herbert and Hunn, "Guest Workers," 192.

184. Caldwell and Hanshew, *Germany*, 108.

185. Rolf Weber, "Auch Gastarbeiter sind kein Freiwild," *DW*, December 17, 1966.

186. Jarausch, "Strukturwandel," 20; Schäfer, "Germanisierung," 29; Werner Faulstich in Faulstich, *Kultur der siebziger Jahre*, 12.

187. Herbert and Hunn, "Guest Workers," 205.

188. Pagenstecher, *Ausländerpolitik*, 49.

189. Rudolf Herlt, "Was die Wissenschaft vorschlägt," *DZ*, February 25, 1977.

190. Jarausch, "Strukturwandel," 9.

191. Wolfgang Hoffmann, "Draussen vor der Tür," *DZ*, August 27, 1976; Herbert and Hunn, "Guest Workers," 211; Pagenstecher, *Ausländerpolitik*, 48, 52.

192. Pagenstecher, *Ausländerpolitik*, 53–60.

193. "IG Metall – ein angeschlagener Dinosaurier," *DS*, July 3, 1973; Schäfer, "Germanisierung," 25–6, 29–30; Hunn, *Jahr*, 116–17; Herbert and Hunn, "Guest Workers," 199.

194. Hunn, *Jahr*, 104–5.

195. "IG Metall – ein angeschlagener Dinosaurier," *DS*, July 3, 1973; Wallraff, *Ganz unten*, 141–2.

196. "IG Metall – ein angeschlagener Dinosaurier," *DS*, July 3, 1973.

197. Hunn, *Jahr*, 118; "IG Metall – ein angeschlagener Dinosaurier," *DS*, July 3, 1973; Töteberg, *Fassbinder*, 49–50.

198. Gerhard Mauz, "Ein Raum, in dem zehn Männer auf Strohsäcken liegen können," *DW*, August 22, 1960.

199. "Die Türken kommen – rette sich, wer kann," *DS*, July 30, 1973; Hunn, *Jahr*, 141, 409; Herbert and Hunn, "Guest Workers," 199; Miller, *Guest Workers*, 85, 140.

200. Miller, *Guest Workers*, 40–1, 86 (quote 40).

201. Ibid., 50–1 (quote 50).

202. Ibid., 67–70.

203. Pagenstecher, *Ausländerpolitik*, 57; Herbert and Hunn, "Guest Workers," 191–2; Miller, *Guest Workers*, 210, n. 102.

204. "Die Türken kommen – rette sich, wer kann," *DS*, July 30, 1973; Dahrendorf, *Gesellschaft*, 377; Hunn, *Jahr*, 141; Pagenstecher, *Ausländerpolitik*, 45, 59, 62; Herbert and Hunn, "Guest Workers," 188, 202–3; *Teuflische Jahre* (1966), 13; *Teuflische Jahre 1970*, 46, 74, 76; Miller, *Guest Workers*, 123; Winifred Wagner cited in Hamann, *Wagner*, 607.

205. Hunn, *Jahr*, 143–5; *Teuflische Jahre 1966*, 42, 174.
206. Hunn, *Jahr*, 409–10.
207. Ibid., 442–4.
208. Günter Wallraff: Biographie, http://www.guenter-wallraff.com/biographie.html; Barbara Stühlmeyer, "Wegschauen geht nicht," *Die Tagespost*, Würzburg, September 29, 2017.
209. Günter Wallraff: Biographie (as in n. 208).
210. Barbara Stühlmeyer, "Wegschauen geht nicht," *Die Tagespost*, Würzburg, September 29, 2017.
211. Wallraff, *Aufmacher*, 67–72 (quotes 68).
212. Günter Wallraff: Biographie (as in n. 208).
213. Wallraff, *Ganz unten*, 65.
214. Ibid., 94.
215. Ibid., 95.
216. Ibid., 108–11.
217. Günter Wallraff: Biographie (as in n. 208); Gerhard Sport, "Ali, der gute Deutsche," *DZ*, February 7, 1986; Schnell, *Geschichte*, 367–72 (quote 368); Bohn, "Hinscheiden," 354–65; Frei, "Presse," 405.
218. Barbara Stühlmeyer, "Wegschauen geht nicht," *Die Tagespost*, Würzburg, September 29, 2017; https://www.tagesschau.de/inland/rassismusinterview100.html; Wolfgang Büscher and Annabel Wahba, "Günter Wallraff'," *DZ*, December 17, 2009.
219. Reich-Ranicki, "Anmerkungen," 172.
220. Bergmann, *Antisemitismus*, 313; Zipes, "Vicissitudes," 38.
221. Bergmann, "Deutschen," 114.
222. Zipes, "Vicissitudes," 29–30; https://encyclopedia.ushmm.org/content/en/article/germany-jewish-population-in-1933.
223. Zipes, "Vicissitudes," 30; Kuschner, "Minderheit," 143–4, 158, 164–8.
224. Hellmut Diwald, *Geschichte der Deutschen* (Frankfurt am Main: Propyläen, 1973). See Wand, "German History Backwards," 154–80.
225. Zipes, "Vicissitudes," 36–7.
226. Petra Kipphoff, "Heiss und kalt in Kassel," *DZ*, July 7, 1972; Kimpel, *documenta*, 65–78.
227. Petra Kipphoff, "Über Kunst kann man nicht abstimmen," *DZ*, May 1, 1970.
228. Kimpel, *documenta*, 78; Jason Farago, "Curation as Creation," *NYRB*, October 24, 2019, https://www.nybooks.com/articles/2019/10/24/harald-szeemann-curation-creation/; Peter Schjedahl, "Harald Szeemann's Revolutionary Curating," *TNY*, July 15, 2019, https://www.newyorker.com/magazine/2019/07/22/harald-szeemanns-revolutionary-curating.
229. Petra Kipphoff, "Blick zurück fast ohne Zorn," *DZ*, October 27, 1972.
230. Petra Kipphoff, "Im Dunst," *DZ*, May 31, 1974; Karl Ruhrberg, "Fünf Minuten vor zwölf," *DZ*, June 21, 1974; Kimpel, *documenta*, 79–90; Kater, *Weimar*, 281.
231. Petra Kipphoff, "documenta VI als Mediengespenst," *DZ*, March 26, 1976; "Ein ruhiges Chaos," *DZ*, July 1, 1977; Damus, *Kunst*, 337–8.
232. "Ein ruhiges Chaos," *DZ*, July 1, 1977; Damus, *Kunst*, 312–13 (quote 312); Kimpel, *documenta*, 87.
233. "Ein ruhiges Chaos," *DZ*, July 1, 1977 (quote); Petra Kipphoff, "Debakel mit Erfolg," *DZ*, October 7, 1977; Alfred Nemeczek, "Der Kasseler Weltmoment," *DZ*, July 7, 1995.
234. See Georg Baselitz, https://www.guggenheim.org/artwork/artist/georg-baselitz; Faust and De Vries, *Hunger*, 37–8; Damus, *Kunst*, 337, 341; Günther Gercken in Joachimides et al., *Kunst*, 468.

235. Dominik Bartmann, "Lüpertz, Markus," *Oxford Art Online*; Faust and De Vries, *Hunger*, 38–42; Damus, *Kunst*, 337–41; Günther Gercken in Joachimides et al., *Kunst*, 468; Markus Lüpertz in Klotz, *Neuen Wilden*, 32–4, and in *DZ*, January 5, 2011; Michael Slackman, "Artist Puts Hercules, and Himself, on Pedestals," *NYT*, October 29, 2010.

236. Andreas Franzke, "Immendorff, Jörg," *Oxford Art Online*; A. Fichter, "Geld – Macht – Hass," *SZ*, January 16, 2011; Holland Cotter, "Art in Review," *NYT*, February 23, 2001; Barbara Smith, "Jörg Immendorff, 61, Painter With Provocative Themes, Dies," *NYT*, May 31, 2007; Faust and De Vries, *Hunger*, 70–3; Damus, *Kunst*, 273; Belting, *Kunst*, 64–7.

237. Hal Foster, "Sigmar Polke," *London Review of Books* (June 19, 2014), https://www.lrb.co.uk/the-paper/v36/n12/hal-foster/at-moma (quote); Beatrice von Bismarck, "Polke, Sigmar," *Oxford Art Online*; Roberta Smith, "Sigmar Polke, Whose Sly Works Shaped Contemporary Painting, Dies at 69," *NYT*, June 11, 2010; Christopher Masters, "Sigmar Polke Obituary," *Guardian*, June 14, 2010; Faust and De Vries, *Hunger*, 80–6; Müller, *Mini*, 62; Damus, *Kunst*, 231, 233, 235; Glaser, *Kulturgeschichte*, vol. 3, 241–2.

238. Adriani et al., *Beuys*, 236–58, 284 (quotes 252, 258); Stachelhaus, *Beuys*, 111–13, 121–33; Oman, *Kunst*, 114, 125–6; "Joseph Beuys – ein Grüner im Museum," *DS*, November 5, 1979.

239. Joseph Beuys, "Aufruf zur Alternative," *FR*, December 23, 1978; Oman, *Kunst*, 151–4.

240. Deposition (1971–6) in Beuys, *Beuys*, 417.

241. Joseph Beuys, "Aufruf zur Alternative," *FR*, December 23, 1978; Oman, *Kunst*, 145–50; Adriani, "Hinweise," 102–7; Karl, *Dutschke*, 388–9.

242. Stachelhaus, *Beuys*, 180–1.

243. Tisdall, *Beuys*, 6–15; "Joseph Beuys – ein Grüner im Museum," *DS*, November 5, 1979.

244. Kimpel, *documenta*, 87; "Joseph Beuys – ein Grüner im Museum," *DS*, November 5, 1979.

245. Glaser, *Kulturgeschichte*, vol. 3, 347–8; Chametzky, *Objects*, 163.

246. Ray, "Beuys," 67.

247. "Dürer, ich führe persönlich Baader + Meinhof durch die Dokumenta [*sic*] V" ["dann sind sie resozialisiert!"]. Hemken, *Richter*, 7, 97–100, 103; Hans-Joachim Müller, "Die RAF und die Kunst," *DZ*, November 5, 2007.

248. Horst Janssen in Günther Uecker, "Zum Tod von Joseph Beuys," *DZ*, January 31, 1986.

249. Richter in Obrist, *Richter*, 127, 137; Chametzky, *Objects*, 203; Elger, *Richter*, 102.

250. Elger, *Richter*, 4–7; Heidi Stecker, "Opfer und Täter," *Deutsches Ärzteblatt* (July 17, 2006), https://www.aerzteblatt.de.

251. Elger *Richter*, 136–40.

252. Scribner, *Gender*, 168.

253. Chametzky, *Objects*, 205–6; Elger, *Richter*, 143–4.

254. Sven Felix Kellerhoff, "Nicht die SS, Polizisten mordeten in Lidice," *DW*, June 8, 2012; Památník Lidice, https://www.lidice-memorial.cz/en/.

255. Müller, *Mini*, 62.

256. Both quotes (last quote Richter's) in Susanne Beyer and Ulrike Knöfel, "'Mich interessiert der Wahn'," DS, August 14, 2005. Also Michael Kimmelman, "Art Review," *NYT*, February 15, 2002; Elger, *Richter*, 140.

257. *Herr Heyde, 1965*, in Wagstaff and Buchloh, *Richter*, 113; Elger, *Richter*, 129–35; Heidi Stecker, "Opfer und Täter," *Deutsches Ärzteblatt*, July 17, 2006, https://www.

aerzteblatt.de/archiv/52165/Opfer-und-Taeter-Tante-Marianne-und-so-weiter (Richter's quote); Kater, *Doctors*, 137, 224; Wistrich, *Who's Who*, 133–4.

258. *Never Look Away*, DVD, Sony Pictures Classics 55612; A. O. Scott, "Never Look Away Review," *NYT*, January 24, 2919.

259. Chametzky, *Objects*, 200; Obrist, *Richter*, 274; Elger, *Richter*, 7.

260. Hemken, *Richter*, 14–16; Obrist, *Richter*, 69, 132, 274; Chametzky, *Objects*, 203; Richter quoted in Susanne Beyer and Ulrike Knöfel, "'Mich interessiert der Wahn'," *DS*, August 14, 2005.

261. Hemken, *Richter*, 15; Obrist, *Richter*, 133–4; Chametzky, *Objects*, 203; Müller, *Mini*, 62.

262. Lucius Grisebach, "Richter, Gerhard," *Oxford Art Online*; Obrist, *Richter*, 70–5, 130.

263. Vostell quoted in Eckhart Gillen, "Gerhard Richter," *DZ*, March 30, 2015.

264. See Schjeldahl, "Painting History," 94; Faust and De Vries, *Hunger*, 43–8; Friedel, "Gerhard Richter," 5–12; Butin, *Oktober-Bildern*, 21–4; Hemken, *Richter*, 17–21, 42–6; Obrist, *Richter*, 33, 96, 143; Elger, *Richter*, 83–5; Fer, "Chronotechniken," 56–66; *Familie am Meer, 1964*, in Wagstaff and Buchloh, *Richter*, 106.

265. Elger, *Richter*, 102, 129–31; Obrist, *Richter*, 57, 185; *Acht Lernschwestern, 1966*, in Wagstaff and Buchloh, *Richter*, 114–15.

266. Elger, *Richter*, 86–7, 126.

267. Kai Hermann, "Nachwort zum Fall Matura," *DZ*, February 18, 1966; Florian Welle, "'Tod der schönen Sünderin'," *DZ*, March 22, 2019. On Nitribitt see Chapter 2 near n. 13.

268. Elger, *Richter*, 127; Richter's first quote is in Obrist, *Richter*, 37, his second paraphrased in Michael Kimmelman, "Art Review," *NYT*, February 15, 2002.

269. Kligerman, "Hauntings," 44–61; Scribner, *Gender*, 45–7, 139–40, 166–9; Hemken, *Richter*, 62–91; Butin, *Oktober-Bildern*, 13–20.

270. Richter in Hemken, *Richter*, 94–5; Richter in Obrist, *Richter*, 173–5, 190–5, 200–10; Elger, *Richter*, 281–4, 300–9.

271. Susanne Beyer and Ulrike Knöfel, "'Mich interessiert der Wahn'," DS, August 14, 2005.

272. See text in Chapter 1 near n. 102.

273. Damus, *Kunst*, 341; Biro, *Kiefer*, 9; Helmut Schneider, "Ausstellung in München," *DZ*, January 26, 1991; Karl Ove Knausgaard, "Into the Forest with the Greatest Living Artist," *NYT*, February 12, 2020.

274. Kiefer quoted in Alan Riding, "Unseen as He Stares Down History," *NYT*, April 3, 2001; Adam Soboczynski, "Anselm Kiefer," *DZ*, September 11, 2019; Roger Cohen, "A Master Still Conjures History's Ghosts," *NYT*, November 20, 2022.

275. Kiefer quoted in Petra Kipphoff, "Das bleierne Land," *DZ*, July 28, 1989.

276. Ibid.; Damus, *Kunst*, 342.

277. Richard J. Evans, "'Equality Exists in Valhalla'," *London Review of Books* (December 4, 2014), https://www.lrb.co.uk/the-paper/v36/n23/richard-j.-evans/equality-exists-in-valhalla.

278. https://www.artsy.net/artwork/anselm-kiefer-winter-landscape-winterlandschaft; Biro, *Kiefer*, 10 (quote).

279. Stephan Mann, "Kiefer, Anselm," *Oxford Art Online*; Biro, *Kiefer*, 11; Damus, *Kunst*, 343; Petra Kipphoff, "Ausstellungen in Düsseldorf und Basel," *DZ*, April 13, 1984.

280. Ross, *Wagnerism*, 628–9; Biro, *Kiefer*, 43 (quote); Faust and De Vries, *Hunger*, 73–80; Glaser, *Kulturgeschichte*, vol. 3, 242–3; Petra Kipphoff, "Ausstellungen in Düsseldorf und Basel," *DZ*, April 13, 1984.

281. Anselm Kiefer quoted in Alan Riding, "Unseen as He Stares Down History," *NYT*, April 3, 2001.

282. https://www.metmuseum.org/art/collection/search/490046; Faust and De Vries, *Hunger*, 78.

283. Karl Heinz Bohrer, Peter Figlestahler, and Werner Bökenkamp, "Bilder einer gigantischen Selbstentblössung," *FAZ*, November 15, 1975 (quotes). See also "Lorbeer für Wunderkinder," *DS*, November 16, 1975; Vincent Canby, "The German Renaissance'," *NYT*, December 11, 1977.

284. Lewandowski, *Kluge*, 9–10; Rentschler, *Film*, 55; Peter Buchka, "Wir leben in einem toten Land," *SZ*, August 20/21, 1977.

285. Kahlenberg, "Film," 508; Lewandowski, *Kluge*, 8.

286. *Die verlorene Ehre der Katharina Blum*, ArtHaus DVD. See Kahlenberg, "Film," 490, 509; Lewandowski, *Kluge*, 8; Walter Uka in Faulstich, *Kultur der siebziger Jahre*, 198.

287. "Deutscher Film – ein neuer Optimismus," *DS*, June 18, 1979; "'Wir sind nicht mehr der Jungfilm'," ibid.; Kahlenberg, "Film," 510; Walter Uka in Faulstich, *Kultur der siebziger Jahre*, 199; Rentschler, *Film*, 56–7; Neumann, "Erstarrung," 256; Knight, *Frauen*, 37.

288. Table in Kahlenberg, "Film," 503; Barthel, *Kino*, 86.

289. Rentschler, *Film*, 49–50; Henryk M. Broder, "Unterm Dirndl wird gekurbelt" *DZ*, January 17, 1975.

290. Rentschler, *Film*, 50.

291. Ibid., 54.

292. Ibid., 51–2, 54.

293. Walter Uka in Faulstich, *Kultur der siebziger Jahre*, 193–4; Moeller and Lellis, *Cinema*, 8.

294. Rentschler, *Film*, 50, 54–5; Rost, "Kinostunden," 407; Knight, *Frauen*, 40.

295. Buchka, *Augen*, 12; Eric Rentschler in Grob et al., *Film*, 246.

296. "Werner Herzog: The Extreme is his Normal," https://www.dw.com/en/werner-herzog-the-extreme-is-his-normal/a-51527351; [Herzog] Long Biography, https://www.wernerherzog.com/long-biography.html.

297. Scott, "Strangeness," 89.

298. Herzog quoted in "'Wir sind nicht mehr der Jungfilm'," *DS*, June 18, 1979.

299. Wenders, *Emotion Pictures*, 40–5.

300. Grob, *Wenders*, 16 (quote); Roman Mauer in Grob et al., *Film*, 209–12.

301. Wenders quoted in Buchka, *Augen*, 11. Also see Roman Mauer in Grob et al., *Film*, 208.

302. "Wim Wenders: Show, Don't Tell," *Daily Telegraph*, April 4, 2011. See Gerald Clarke, "Seeking Planets That Do Not Exist," *Time*, March 20, 1978, 53.

303. Grob, *Wenders*, 289; Buchka, *Augen*, 7–8.

304. See Demetz, *Anarchie*, 202–4; Mixner, *Handke*, 125–39.

305. *Die Angst des Tormanns beim Elfmeter*, ArtHaus DVD.

306. *Im Lauf der Zeit*, ArtHaus DVD.

307. Schacht, *Fluchtpunkt*, 180–289.

308. Ibid., 96–121. See, for example, dialogue in Sperr, *Räuber*, 41–6.

309. Rentschler, *Film*, 104–23 (quote 104); Wolfram Schütte, "Linke Flucht in die rechte Vergangenheit," *FR*, May 19, 1971; Karl Korn, "Der Kneissl," *FAZ*, April 22, 1971.

310. *Der plötzliche Reichtum der armen Leute von Kombach*, Zweitausendeins Edition DVD. See Schacht, *Fluchtpunkt*, 64–93; Wolf Donner, "Wenig Lärm um viel," *DZ*, February 5, 1971; Ruf, "Leute," 14–19; Wolf Donner, "Der lüsterne Meinungsterror,"

DZ, October 10, 1975; Brigitte Jeremias, "Eine neue Art von Heimatfilm," *FAZ*, January 27, 1971; "Lorbeer für die Wunderkinder," *DS*, November 16, 1975; Lewandowski, *Schlöndorff*, 194–206; Moeller and Lellis, *Cinema*, 128–9.

311. Hembus, *Film*, 328; Moeller and Lellis, *Cinema*, 131.
312. *Deutschland im Herbst*, ArtHaus DVD 506324; Hans C. Blumenberg, "Deutschland im Herbst," *DZ*, March 10, 1978; Wenzel, *Film*, 244–63; Blumenberg, "Lage der Nation," *DZ*, March 24, 1978; Wolfgang Knorr, "'Wer die Wahrheit weiss, lügt'," *Die Weltwoche*, Zurich, May 3, 1978; Preece, "German Autumn," 218; Kaes, *Deutschlandbilder*, 32–4.
313. Wenzel, *Film*, 251 (quote).
314. Kreimeier, "RAF," 1164.
315. Lorenz, *Chaos*, esp. 434.
316. Liselotte Eder in André Müller, "Der tote Sohn," *DZ*, April 24, 1992; Lorenz, *Chaos*, 429–31; Töteberg, *Fassbinder*, 175; Thomsen, *Fassbinder*, 3–7 (Fassbinder quoted 3).
317. Lorenz, *Chaos*, 430–1; Ursula Strätz, ibid., 53–8; Töteberg, *Fassbinder*, 15–16; Thomsen, *Fassbinder*, 14–15; Limmer, *Fassbinder*, 12–13, 16–18; Bessen, *Trümmer*, 380.
318. Zadek, *My Way*, 376; Augstein in Lorenz, *Chaos*, 281.
319. Kaes, *Deutschlandbilder*, 77; Limmer, *Fassbinder*, 146–9.
320. Vincent Canby, "Fassbinder on Terrorism," *NYT*, September 9, 1980.
321. Limmer, *Fassbinder*, 177.
322. *Katzelmacher*, ArtHaus DVD; Thomsen, *Fassbinder*, 78–83; Norbert Grob in Grob et al., *Film*, 168; Limmer, *Fassbinder*, 14, 178; Wolfram Schütte, "Momentaufnahmen aus den Vorstädten," *FR*, December 3, 1969; Greif, *Drama*, 56–64; Fassbinder in Töteberg, *Fassbinder*, 48–9.
323. Hans Günther Pflaum, "Der Händler der vier Jahreszeiten," *SZ*, March 10, 1972; Wolfram Schütte, "Ein Mann, Opfer der Frauen," *FR*, May 27, 1972; Limmer, *Fassbinder*, 186–7; Norbert Grob in Grob et al., *Film*, 171–4.
324. Jenny, "Der Händler," 270.
325. *Angst essen Seele auf*, ArtHaus DVD. See Limmer, *Fassbinder*, 32–3, 191; Thomsen, *Fassbinder*, 138–44; Hembus, *Film*, 300; Wolfram Schütte, "Lakonische Parabel," *FR*, June 27, 1974.
326. Fassbinder in Töteberg, *Fassbinder*, 92.
327. Ingrid Caven in Lorenz, *Chaos*, 89.
328. Fassbinder in Thomsen, *Fassbinder*, 90.
329. *Mutter Küsters' Fahrt zum Himmel*, ArtHaus DVD; Peter Buchka, "Kopf hoch, wenn die Sicherung durchbrennt," *SZ*, January 5/6, 1976; Limmer, *Fassbinder*, 28, 197–8; Thomsen, *Fassbinder*, 16; Preece, "German Autumn," 217; Kreimeier, "RAF," 1161–2.
330. Thomsen, *Fassbinder*, 16; Fritz Rumler, "Rote Hilfe," *DS*, July 13, 1975.
331. Eric Rentschler in Grob et al., *Film*, 244; Wolfgang Limmer, "Bilder aus der Wirklichkeit," *DS*, March 5, 1978; Hans C. Blumenberg, "Lage der Nation," *DZ*, March 24, 1978.
332. Liselotte Eder quoted in Kaes, *Deutschlandbilder*, 81. Also Grob et al., *Film*, 44; Eric Rentschler in Grob et al., *Film*, 243–4; Eder in Lorenz, *Chaos*, 264–5; Thomsen, *Fassbinder*, 251–4.
333. *Die dritte Generation*, ArtHaus DVD. Donner quoted in Limmer, *Fassbinder*, 217. Also Hans C. Blumenberg, "Land der Lemminge," *DZ*, September 28, 1979; Peter Buchka, "Terror als Komödie," *SZ*, September 15/16, 1979; Thomsen, *Fassbinder*, 263–72; Elsaesser, *Cinema*, 208–9.

334. Fassbinder in Töteberg, *Fassbinder*, 15, 146, 168, and quoted in Pott, *Film*, 16–17.

335. Fassbinder quoted in Limmer, *Fassbinder*, 89; Caven quoted in Lorenz, *Chaos*, 88; Schygulla quoted in Lorenz, *Chaos*, 42. Also Fassbinder in Bessen, *Trümmer*, 390.

336. Kater, *Drummers*, 186–7; Studdert, *Jazz War*, 132–3.

337. Limmer, *Fassbinder*, 38–9, 90–1, 218–19; Thomsen, *Fassbinder*, 294–6; Töteberg, *Fassbinder*, 163–54; Hellmuth Karasek, "Berlinale," *DS*, February 18, 1979.

338. Wolfram Knorr, "Mutter Courage der Wunderjahre," *Die Weltwoche*, Zurich, April 11, 1979; Limmer, *Fassbinder*, 11, 36, 209–11; Thomsen, *Fassbinder*, 274–9; Andreas Kilb in Grob et al., *Film*, 248–54; Kaes, "History," 277–85, and text in Chapter 2 at n. 18.

339. Rost, "Kinostunden," 398–400; Norbert Grob, "Lola in Rosa," *DZ*, August 28, 1981, and text in Chapter 2 at n. 18.

340. *Die Sehnsucht der Veronika Voss*: Lorenz, *Chaos*, 434. See text at n. 390.

341. Gebhardt, *ALICE*, 63; Kretschmann, *Spaltung*, 120; Schwarzer, *Alice*, 31.

342. Figures in *Statistisches Jahrbuch*, 28; Gebhardt, *ALICE*, 127–30.

343. Mattes, "Aufbrüche," 223; Schildt, "Wohlstand," 25–6.

344. Mattes, "Aufbrüche," 219; figures in *Deutsche Hochschulstatistik*, 4.

345. Helke Sander (1937–), https://hist259.web.unc.edu/helke-sander-1937/.

346. Biess, *Republik*, 251–2; 275–6; Baumann, *Wie*, 95–6; Müller, *Mini*, 76–7; Glaser, *Kulturgeschichte*, vol. 3, 56–7.

347. Gebhardt, *ALICE*, 144–6; Mika, *Schwarzer*, 95–9.

348. Sander as quoted in Glaser, *Kulturgeschichte*, vol. 3, 56. Also Gebhardt, *ALICE*, 149–50.

349. Meinhof quoted in Mika, *Schwarzer*, 104–5.

350. Mika, *Schwarzer*, 106–7.

351. Helke Sander, https://hist259.web.unc.edu/helke-sander-1937/; Gebhardt, *ALICE*, 149. ReduPers was short for "Die allseitig reduzierte Persönlichkeit" (The All-Around Reduced Personality).

352. Mika, *Schwarzer*, 84–5; Menand, *Free World*, 69.

353. Mika, *Schwarzer*, 110–14; Wiebke Eden, "Alice Schwarzer", https://www.fembio. org/english/biography.php/woman/biography/alice-schwarzer/.

354. "'Hiermit erkläre ich . . .'," *DS*, March 10, 1974 (quote); Mika, *Schwarzer*, 124; Kater, *Doctors*, 1–11.

355. Winkler, *Weg*, 335–6. Gebhardt, *ALICE*, 219–23, confuses the sequence of events.

356. Quotation https://www.deutschlandfunk.de/mein-bauch-gehoert-mir-100.html.

357. Eva Marie von Münch, "Neu an der Frauenfront," *DZ*, January 28, 1977; Mika, *Schwarzer*, 176–9, 190, 193; Gebhardt, *ALICE*, 260–1; Glaser, *Deutsche Kultur*, 392–3.

358. Hannelore Schlaffer, "Der Aufzug der neuen Romantiker," *FAZ*, May 29, 1979; Eva Marie von Münch, "Neu an der Frauenfront," *DZ*, January 28, 1977; Mika, *Schwarzer*, 157–61, 179–82, 211–19, 228–32; Gebhardt, *ALICE*, 266–8; O'Dochartaigh, *Germany*, 131; Beck-Gernsheim, "Liebe," 48; Frankfurter Frauen, October 1977, "Aufruf an alle Frauen zur Erfindung des Glücks," in Botzat et al., *Herbst*, 86–7.

359. Eden, "Alice Schwarzer."

360. For *Bild* Götz Hamann, "'Es wurde gevögelt, dass es rauchte'," *DZ*, June 21, 2017. For *SZ*, "Friedmann war kein Opfer," *DZ*, July 1, 1960.

361. Von Hodenberg, *Konsens*, 243–4.

362. Karasek, *Magazin*, 71 (quote). Also ibid., 66, Raddatz, *Unruhestifter*, 255, 259, 264–5; Merseburger, *Augstein*, 340, writing more ad hominem.

363. Schreiber, *Nannen*, 225, 232–3, 355–6, 359–60. Also Suhr, *Schreib*, 20, 25.
364. Walser, *Tagebücher, 1974–1978*, 296, 362; Henscheid, *Fälle*, 138–45.
365. Frei, "Presse," 376.
366. Rahms, *Clique*, 109–11.
367. Von Hodenberg, *Konsens*, 243; Raddatz, *Unruhestifter*, 356–7 (quote), 360.
368. Stern, *Doppelleben*, 192; von Zahn, *Stimme*, 295.
369. Krause, *Galerie*, 74–5; Reese, "Kunst," 14.
370. Kater, *Weimar*, 159–61.
371. Yeazell, "Painting Herself" (quotes 4).
372. Gronemeyer, "Music," 56; Weyer, "Jazz," 99.
373. Reich-Ranicki, "Nachdenken über Leni G.," *DZ*, August 6, 1971.
374. Benjamin Heinrichs, "Prolet und Orpheus in der Unterwelt," *DZ*, September 29, 1978.
375. Reinhard Baumgart, "Spiel-Räume der Erotik," *DZ*, June 11, 1982.
376. Iris Radisch, "Frauen im Schatten," *DZ*, June 8, 2022.
377. Biess, *Republik*, 320–1.
378. Verena Stefan in *The Literary Encyclopedia*, https://www.litencyc.com/php/speople.php?rec=true&UID=12460.
379. Waltraud Schwab, "Die in jeder Hinsicht radikal Suchende," *Die Tageszeitung* (*taz*), Berlin, February 9, 2006.
380. Bentz et al., *Protest*, 451–3 (Struck quoted 451); Richard Baumgart, "Ein Buch wie eine Person," *DS*, April 29, 1973; McCormick, *Politics*, 68, 97–117; Gerlach, *Abschied*, 46–53.
381. Struck, *Klassenliebe*, 40, 72, 115, 123–4, 132, 159, 169, 219, 253.
382. Rentschler, *Film*, 50.
383. Fehrenbach, *Cinema*, 224; Knight, *Frauen*, 42–4.
384. Grob et al., *Film*, 46 (quote); Möhrmann, *Frau*, 156–7; Knight, *Frauen*, 42–8.
385. Schwartz, "Homosexuelle," 378.
386. Dave Kehr, "Werner Schroeter, German Film and Stage Director, Dies at 65," *NYT*, April 22, 2010; Ronald Bergan, "Werner Schroeter Obituary," *Guardian*, April 22, 2010; Harvard Film Archive, September 28, 2012, https://harvardfilmarchive.org/calendar/the-rose-king-2012-09.
387. *It Is Not the Homosexual Who Is Perverse, But the Society in Which He Lives.* See Randall Halle in Grob et al., *Film*, 160–5.
388. Limmer, *Fassbinder*, 171–6; Ulrich Greiner, "Die Schrecken der Liebe," *DZ*, October 10, 1980; Jim's Reviews/Fassbinder, November 13, 2007, https://jclark-media.com/fassbinder36/; Jelavich, *Berlin Alexanderplatz*, 10, 17–18, 213.
389. Limmer, *Fassbinder*, 196; Hans C. Blumenberg, "Der Rest sind Tränen," *DZ*, June 13, 1975.
390. Fassbinder quoted in Kaes, *Deutschlandbilder*, 83.
391. On *Martha* (1974) see *Martha*, ArtHaus DVD; and Hans C. Blumenberg, "Lüstern und sadistisch," *DZ*, May 31, 1974. On *Petra von Kant* see the ArtHaus DVD and Reinhard Baumgart, "Gefühle, Gefühle – ganz unnatürlich echt," *SZ*, December 8, 1972.
392. Quote in Catherine Shoard, "Irm Hermann, star of 20 Fassbinder films, dies at 77," *Guardian*, May 28, 2020; interview with Irm Hermann, *Katzelmacher*, ArtHaus DVD; David Hudson, "Irm Hermann, from Torture to Triumph," *The Daily*, May 28, 2020, https://www.criterion.com/current/posts/6965-irm-hermann-from-torture-to-triumph.
393. On *Deutschland bleiche Mutter*, see Kaplan, "Search," 290–302, and text in Chapter 1 at notes 89, 95.

394. *Shirins Hochzeit*, Zweitausendeins Edition DVD; Hunn, "Jahr," 329–31; Möhrmann, *Frau*, 146–56; Cooke, "Nation," 85–6; Knight, *Frauen*, 104–9.

395. Margarethe von Trotta in GermanFlicks.com, https://web.archive.org/web/20081208001650/http://www.germanflicks.com/trotta.html; Möhrmann, *Frau*, 195-97 Wolf Donner, "Sieben Fragen an Volker Schlöndorff und Margarethe von Trotta," *DZ*, October 10, 1975

396. Contradictory statements by von Trotta and Schlöndorff in Raimund Hoghe, "Balanceversuch einer Rebellin," *DZ*, May 8, 1981. Also Möhrmann, *Frau*, 198–9, 203–5; Lewandowski, *Schlöndorff*, 31.

397. German title: *Das zweite Erwachen der Christa Klages*. See Wolfgang Limmer, "Bilder aus der Wirklichkeit," *DS*, March 5, 1978 (quote); Hans C. Blumenberg, "Akte des Widerstands," *DZ*, March 3, 1978; Blumenberg, "Edle Räuberin," *DZ*, April 21, 1978; Möhrmann, *Frau*, 199–200.

398. German original available on https://www.alleskino.de/en/movies/812a6191-0503-4fe4-9b84-ffd5095f5746. English titles: *The German Sisters* or *Marianne and Juliane*. See Weber, *Zeit*, 26–69; Scribner, *Gender*, 99–113; Cooke, "Nation," 87–8; Möhrmann, *Frau*, 201–2, 206–7; Knight, *Frauen*, 115–19.

399. Kraushaar et al., *Dutschke*, 93; Preece, *Novel*, 26; Biess, *Republik*, 349.

400. Gerhard Richter quoted in Obrist, *Richter*, 190.

401. Tanja Stelzer, "RAF," *DZ*, October 1, 2007.

402. Wisniewski in Mika, *Schwarzer*, 192; Monika Berberich quoted in Tanja Stelzer, "RAF: Die Waffen der Frauen," *DZ*, October 1, 2007.

403. See, for example, Kraushaar, *Flecken*, 169–70.

404. Viett, *Nie*, 176.

405. Monika Berberich in Tanja Stelzer, "RAF," *DZ*, October 1, 2007.

FIVE – RETRENCHMENT (1980–1990)

1. Ernst Nolte, *Der Faschismus in seiner Epoche: Die Action française, der italienische Faschismus, der Nationalsozialismus* (Munich: R. Piper, 1963). See: Ernst Nolte, "Nolte über Nolte," *FAZ*, April 13, 1988.

2. Ernst Nolte, "Nolte über Nolte," *FAZ*, April 13, 1988; Sam Roberts, "Ernst Nolte, Historian Whose Views on Hitler Caused an Uproar, Dies at 93," *NYT*, August 19, 2016; Richard J. Evans, "Ernst Nolte Obituary," *Guardian*, August 29, 2016.

3. Gordon A. Craig, "The War of the German Historians," *NYRB*, January 15, 1987, https://www.nybooks.com/articles/1987/01/15/the-war-of-the-german-historians/.

4. Caldwell and Hanshew, *Germany*, 223–7.

5. "Helmut Kohl: Chancellor of Germany" in *Encyclopedia Britannica*; Dan van der Vat, "Helmut Kohl Obituary," *Guardian*, June 16, 2017; Winkler, *Weg*, 403.

6. Wirsching, *Abschied*, 18–46 (quote 46).

7. Ibid., 225–400.

8. Gesetz zur Neuregelung des Ausländerrechts vom 9. Juli 1990, https://www.bgbl.de/xaver/bgbl/text.xav?SID=&tf=xaver.component.Text_0&tocf=&qmf=&hlf=xaver.component.Hitlist_0&bk=bgbl&start=%2F%2F*%5B%40node_id%3D%27964050%27%5D&skin=pdf&tlevel=-2&nohist=1&sinst=B2CB0E73; Wirsching, *Abschied*, 290–303.

9. Wirsching, *Abschied*, 303–6.

10. Ibid., 306–7.

11. Ibid., 614–55; Kater, *Weimar*, 321–8.

12. Horst Bacia, "Günter Kiessling gestorben," *FAZ*, July 28, 2011; Wirsching, *Abschied*, 59–65; Manfred Wörner, https://www.nato.int/cps/en/natohq/who_is_who_7306.htm.

13. https://second.wiki/wiki/werner_vogel_politiker; Wirsching, *Abschied*, 123.
14. "National Democratic Party of Germany" in *Encyclopedia Britannica*; Wirsching, *Abschied*, 415.
15. Wirsching, *Abschied*, 414–16; O'Dochartaigh, *Germany*, 160–1.
16. Wirsching, *Abschied*, 417–18.
17. Karl-Heinz Janssen et al., "Deutschland im Herbst," *DZ*, September 25, 1981; Strassner, "Generation," 490–5; Wirsching, *Abschied*, 404–5. Fugitives to GDR: Schlöndorff's 2000 film *Die Stille nach dem Schuss*, DVD, Zweitausendeins Edition (*The Legend of Rita*).
18. Strassner, "Generation," 496–7 (quote 496), 501–4; Wirsching, *Abschied*, 405–13; Pflieger, *Rote Armee Fraktion*, 193–8; Henscheid, *Fälle*, 131–7.
19. Wüstenberg, *Society*, 64; Niven, *Nazi Past*, 105.
20. Wirsching, *Abschied*, 477–80.
21. Ronald Reagan, Remarks at a Joint German-American Military Ceremony at Bitburg Air Base in the Federal Republic of Germany, May 5, 1985, http://www.vlib.us/amdocs/texts/reagan051985.html. Also George Skelton, "Reagan to Honor German War Dead on V-E Day Trip," *Los Angeles Times*, April 12, 1985.
22. Hanshew, *Terror*, 256 (first quote); Niven, *Nazi Past*, 105–6 (second quote 105). Also Diner, "Aporie," 63–4.
23. Gunter Hofmann, "Das lästige Leitbild," *DZ*, December 5, 1986. See Niven, *Nazi Past*, 107–8; Ute Frevert in Assmann and Frevert, *Geschichtsvergessenheit*, 269–71; Felix Steiner, "The Speech about History that Made History," https://www.dw.com/en/opinion-the-speech-about-history-that-made-history/a-18250339.
24. Wirsching, *Abschied*, 482–3. Also Winkler, *Weg*, 441–2.
25. Speech by von Weizsäcker, May 8, 1985, at the Bundestag, Bonn, https://www.bundespraesident.de/SharedDocs/Downloads/DE/Reden/2015/02/150202-RvW-Rede-8-Mai-1985-englisch.pdf?__blob=publicationFile. See Rudolf Augstein, "Die neue Auschwitz-Lüge," *DS*, October 6, 1986, 63.
26. Wirsching, *Abschied*, 481–5.
27. Wolfgang Benz, "Unglücklicher Staatsakt," *Deutschland Archiv Online*, November 4, 2013, http://www.bpb.de/171555.
28. Ibid.; Gunter Hofmann, "Der Alleingang ins Abseits," *DZ*, November 18, 1988; "Früherer Bundestagspräsident Jenninger gestorben," *FAZ*, January 5, 2018; Michael J. Bonin, "Bearers of Bad News," *The Harvard Crimson*, November 16, 1988, https://www.thecrimson.com/article/1988/11/16/bearers-of-bad-news-pbibts-said/.
29. Ernst Nolte, "Revolution im zwanzigsten Jahrhundert," *FAZ*, January 29, 1983.
30. Ernst Nolte, "Vergangenheit, die nicht vergehen will," *FAZ*, June 6, 1986.
31. Hillgruber, *Untergang*, 15–99.
32. Eric Pace, "Andreas Hillgruber, 64, Historian in West German Dispute, is Dead," *NYT*, May 25, 1989.
33. Etzemüller, *Sozialgeschichte*, 344–54; Caldwell and Hanshew, *Germany*, 231–2.
34. "Jürgen Habermas," *Stanford Encyclopedia of Philosophy*, https://plato.stanford.edu/entries/habermas/ (quote); "Jürgen Habermas" in *Encyclopedia Britannica*.
35. Friedländer, *Memory*, 215–18.
36. Jürgen Habermas, "Eine Art Schadensabwicklung," *DZ*, July 11, 1986.
37. Stürmer quoted in Hans Schwab-Felisch, "Eine entscheidende Frage," *FAZ*, April 11, 1984; Stürmer, *Reich*, esp. 143–71.
38. Biographical Sketch Michael Stürmer, Future of European Foreign Policy Seminar, https://web.archive.org/web/20110717141250/http://www.jhubc.it/future_of_european_foreign_policy/biosturmer.pdf.
39. Klaus Hildebrand, https://prabook.com/web/klaus.hildebrand/134222.

40. Hildebrand in *Historische Zeitschrift* 242 (1986): 466.
41. Stürmer quoted in Jarausch, "Removing," 288, 296, also 289.
42. Ibid., 288–9, 291.
43. Reich-Ranicki, *Leben*, 543–4.
44. Ibid., 543; Friedländer, *Memory*, 222.
45. Synopsis in Fest, *Gesicht*, 391–411.
46. Ian Kershaw, "Hans Mommsen Obituary," *Guardian*, November 12, 2015. Also Stefan Wagstyl, "German Historian Hans Mommsen Dies Aged 85," *Financial Times*, November 6, 2015; Margalit Fox, "Hans Mommsen, 85, Dies," *NYT*, November 17, 2015.
47. Mommsen, "Aufarbeitung," 74–87 (quote 82).
48. Heinrich August Winkler, https://eu.boell.org/en/person/heinrich-august-winkler.
49. Winkler, *Weg*, 435–8.
50. Ibid., 446; Winkler, "Schatten," 259–61.
51. Kocka, "Hitler," 134–6.
52. Richard J. Evans, "Hans-Ulrich Wehler Obituary," *Guardian*, July 18, 2014.
53. Müller, *Country*, 51; Winkler, *Weg*, 247; Hartmut Pogge von Strandmann, "Obituary: Professor Fritz Fischer," *Independent*, December 13, 1999; Wolfgang Saxon, "Fritz Fischer, 91, German Historian Blamed Germany for First War," *NYT*, December 10, 1999.
54. Wehler, *Entsorgung*, 10.
55. Ibid., 46.
56. Ibid., 56.
57. Evans, "New Nationalism," 786.
58. Ibid., 767–8 (quote 767).
59. Ibid., 773–4.
60. Ibid., 786.
61. Ibid., 785.
62. Ibid.
63. Maier, *Past*, 92–3 (quote 93).
64. Friedländer, "Überlegungen," 42–6.
65. Ibid., 49–50.
66. Ibid., 50.
67. Friedländer, *Memory*, 221–3.
68. Ernst Nolte, "Nolte über Nolte," *FAZ*, April 13, 1988.
69. Maier, *Past*, 126.
70. Nolte, *Vergehen*, 13; Wirsching, *Abschied*, 487.
71. Wüstenberg, *Society*, 89; Lenz Kriss-Rettenbeck quoted in Glaser, *Deutsche Kultur*, 408.
72. Wüstenberg, *Society*, 91–101.
73. Table in Wirsching, *Abschied*, 423.
74. Ibid., 485–6 (quote 485).
75. Ibid., 487–8.
76. Broszat, "Errichtung," 304–6, 308.
77. Maier, *Past*, 132.
78. Kater, *Weimar*, 365.
79. Mommsen, "Suche," 171–3; Maier, *Past*, 127.
80. Zielinski and Custance, "History," 86–94; Ute Frevert in Assmann and Frevert, *Geschichtsvergessenheit*, 267–8; Herf, "'Holocaust' Reception," 213–18; Biess, *Republik*, 336–42; Zipes, "Vicissitudes," 37–8; Knilli and Zielinski, *Holocaust*, 219–39; Tim Darmstädter, "Die Verwandlung der Barbarei in Kultur," http://www.martinblumentritt.de/agr206s.htm.

81. After previews: *DW*, July 10, 1978.
82. Rolf Henkel, "Anfällige Jugend," *DZ*, April 21, 1978; Paepcke, *Ich*, 128; Kreuzer, "Neue Subjektivität," 92; Kaes, *Deutschlandbilder*, 67; Weiss, "Journalisten," 286; Zielinski and Custance, "History," 85–6. On Hess: Reichel, *Vergangenheitsbewältigung*, 122–3.
83. Fest, *Hitler*, 17, 1029.
84. Ernst Nolte, "Vergangenheit, die nicht vergehen will," *FAZ*, June 6, 1986.
85. Paul Hofmann, "Germans Are Flocking to a Movie Showing Rise and Fall of Hitler," *NYT*, July 31, 1977.
86. Fest in Heinz Höhne, "Faszination des Demagogen," *DS*, June 26, 1977.
87. Kindler, *Abschied*, 552
88. Höhne, "Faszination des Demagogen," *DS*, June 26, 1977.
89. Karl-Heinz Janssen, "High durch Hitler," *DZ*, July 8, 1977. Corroborative: Bier, "Holocaust," 199–200; Tim Darmstädter, "Die Verwandlung der Barbarei in Kultur," http://www.martinblumentritt.de/agr206s.htm.
90. Wenders, *Emotion Pictures*, 113–20.
91. Syberberg in André Müller, "Man will mich töten," *DZ*, September 30, 1988; Syberberg in Lawrence van Geldern, "A German View of Hitler," *NYT*, January 13, 1980.
92. Bernd Kiefer in Grob et al., *Film*, 224–5; "Syberberg," *DS*, March 15, 1970.
93. Kaes, *Deutschlandbilder*, 139.
94. *Winifred Wagner und die Geschichte des Hauses Wahnfried, 1914–1975* (*The Confessions of Winifred Wagner*).
95. Winifred Wagner quoted in Wolf Donner, "Der gute Onkel von Bayreuth," *DZ*, July 18, 1975; also "Syberbergs Film über Winifred Wagner und seine Folgen," *DZ*, August 1, 1975.
96. Hans-Jürgen Syberberg, "Winifred Wagner," *DZ*, March 14, 1980.
97. Syberberg in interview with André Müller, "Man will mich töten," *DZ*, September 30, 1988.
98. Lawrence van Geldern, "A German View of Hitler," *NYT*, January 13, 1980, Syberberg quoted ibid; Vincent Canby, "Screen," *DZ*, January 15, 1980; Bernd Kiefer in Grob et al., *Film*, 226–7.
99. Wolf Donner, "Ein offener Brief von 'Berlinale'-Direktor Wolf Donner an Hans-Jürgen Syberberg," *DZ*, December 23, 1977; Hans-Jürgen Syberberg, "'Hitler' noch nicht für Deutschland," *DZ*, January 13, 1978.
100. Kaes, *Deutschlandbilder*, 169.
101. Susan Sontag, "Eye of the Storm," *NYRB*, February 21, 1980, https://www.nybooks.com/articles/1980/02/21/eye-of-the-storm/?printpage=true; Ian Buruma, "There's No Place Like Heimat," *NYRB*, December 20, 1990, https://www.nybooks.com/articles/1990/12/20/theres-no-place-like-heimat/.
102. Hans C. Blumenberg, "Träume in Trümmern," *DZ*, July 7, 1978.
103. "Klaus Jeziorkowski über H. J. Syberberg," *DS*, June 21, 1981; Syberberg, *Gesellschaft*.
104. Robert Jungk in "Zeitmosaik," *DZ*, March 28, 1980.
105. Hellmuth Karasek, "Frühling für Hitler?" *DS*, September 2, 1990.
106. Syberberg quoted in Buruma, "There's No Place Like Heimat"; John Rockwell, "The Re-Emergence of an Elusive Director," *NYT*, September 2, 1992.
107. Rauh, *Reitz*, 20–3.
108. Ibid., 23–47; Manuela Reichart in Grob et al., *Film*, 338–9; Reitz, *Liebe*, 216.
109. Reitz, *Liebe*, 217–19.
110. Ibid., 136, 142–69 (quote 167).

111. Ibid., 98–104, 141–2.
112. Ibid., 219–20; Manuela Reichart in Grob et al., *Film*, 340–2; Rentschler, "Homeland," 936–9; Kaes, *Deutschlandbilder*, 178;
113. Kaes, *Deutschlandbilder*, 178–94; Manuela Reichart in Grob et al., *Film*, 342–5; Kaes, *Deutschlandbilder*, 177; Rentschler, "Homeland," 938–9, 941.
114. Rentschler, "Homeland," 937.
115. "'Geh über die Dörfer!'," DS, September 30, 1984; Urs Jenny, "Lebenszeit, neue Zeit, Mitte der Welt," *DZ*, September 9, 1984; Hansen, *Dossier*, 3–4; Wirsching, *Abschied*, 468.
116. "Schweigen gebrochen," *DS*, March 17, 1985
117. Vincent Canby, "New Directors/New Films," *NYT*, April 6, 1985.
118. Gustav Simon was from 1931 Gauleiter for the Koblenz-Trier-Birkenfeld area where Schabbach would have been situated (Klee, *Personenlexikon*, 584).
119. Reitz and Steinbach, *Heimat*, 268.
120. See Kaes, *Deutschlandbilder*, 195–6, 202.
121. Timothy Garton Ash, "The Life of Death," *NYRB*, December 19, 1985, https://www.nybooks.com/articles/1985/12/19/the-life-of-death/; Saul Friedländer, "Bewältigung – oder nur Verdrängung?" *DZ*, February 8, 1985. Also Elsaesser, *German Cinema*, 96; Maier, *Past*, 118–19.
122. Reitz, *Liebe*, 149.
123. Reitz and Steinbach, *Heimat*, 298–9.
124. Suhr, *Schreib*, 99–100.
125. Harris, *Selling Hitler*, 9–356; Hamilton, *Hitler Diaries*, 8–58; Seufert, *Skandal*, 248–9; "Hitler-Tagebücher," *DS*, May 2, 1983; "Hitler-Tagebücher," *DS*, May 9, 1983; Hannes Laipold, "Fälschungen oder Das Grosse im Kleinen," *DZ*, May 13, 1983; Karl-Heinz Janssen, "Unternehmen 'Grünes Gewölbe'," *DZ*, June 1, 1984.
126. "'Plump? – Das hat mich gekränkt'," *DS*, March 12, 1984; Frei, "Presse," 395.
127. Bergmann, *Antisemitismus*, 317–18.
128. Rentschler, *West German Film*, 147–8; Herz, "Fassbinderstreit," 173–4, 176, 181.
129. Limmer, *Fassbinder*, 144; Ingrid Caven in Lorenz, *Chaos*, 91.
130. Siegfried Unseld, "In dieser Form nicht mehr," *DZ*, April 9, 1976. See Michalzik, *Unseld*, 301–2; Bergmann, *Antisemitismus*, 326. Conciliatory: Joachim Kaiser, "Gerechtigkeit für Fassbinders Ungerechtigkeit," *SZ*, March 31, 1976.
131. Fassbinder, *Müll*, 17, 20, 35, 42, 47–50.
132. Dieter E. Zimmer, "Fassbinder, die kaputte Stadt und der Jude," *DZ*, April 9, 1976; Jean Améry, "Shylock, der Kitsch und die Gefahr," *DZ*, April 9, 1976; Hans C. Blumenberg, "Müllhaufen mit Zuckerguss," *DZ*, August 13, 1976; Günther Grack cited in Bergmann, *Antisemitismus*, 320, n. 19.
133. Fassbinder in Töteberg, *Fassbinder*, 83–4, 88; Hellmuth Karasek, "Shylock in Frankfurt," DS, April 4, 1976; Thomsen, *Fassbinder*, 206; Kaes, *Deutschlandbilder*, 97; Rentschler, *West German Film*, 148; Bergmann, *Antisemitismus*, 316, 322–3.
134. Fassbinder in Töteberg, *Fassbinder*, 82; Ingrid Caven in Lorenz, *Chaos*, 91.
135. Zadek, *My Way*, 378; also *Heissen Jahre*, 199–200.
136. Koch, "Torments," 36–7; Angress, "Judenproblem," 35–8.
137. Benjamin Henrichs, "Fassbinder, ein linker Faschist?" *DZ*, March 26, 1976; Jean Améry, "Shylock, der Kitsch und die Gefahr," *DZ*, April 9, 1976; Kaes, *Deutschlandbilder*, 94, 97.
138. Reich-Ranicki, *Leben*, 541–2.
139. Ulrich Greiner, "Der Jude von Frankfurt," *DZ*, November 1, 1985.

140. Peter Zadek, "Aufführen!" *DZ*, September 13, 1985.
141. Benjamin Henrichs, "Hass im Kopf, Liebe im Bauch," *DZ*, November 8, 1985; Thomsen, *Fassbinder*, 203; Hensel, *Achtziger Jahre*, 40–3.
142. Bubis quoted in Ulrich Greiner, "Der Jude von Frankfurt," *DZ*, November 1, 1985.
143. Werner Höfer, "Künstler – Beispiel und Vorbild," *Das 12-Uhr Blatt*, Berlin, September 20, 1943. Also Harald Wieser, "Tod eines Pianisten," *DS*, December 14, 1987, 157–8; Kater, *Twisted Muse*, 221–2.
144. Examples reprinted in *DS*, December 14, 1987 (Höfer quoted ibid.); Köpf, *Schreiben*, 123.
145. Harald Wieser, "Tod eines Pianisten," *DS*, December 14, 1987; Alan Cowell, "Werner Hofer [*sic*], 84, a Fallen Idol of TV Journalism in Germany," *NYT*, November 27, 1997; Schildt, *Medien-Intellektuelle*, 615.
146. Otto Köhler, "Schreibmaschinentäter," *DZ*, January 15, 1988; Höfer, "Mein Radio," 56–8; Jens, *Demenz*, 17, 40; Hickethier, *Geschichte*, 339, 381; Geisler, "Nazis," 247.
147. Kraushaar et al., *Dutschke*, 79; Schildt, *Medien-Intellektuelle*, 483, 615, 683; Harald Wieser, "Tod eines Pianisten," *DS*, December 14, 1987.
148. Frei, "Hörfunk," 439, 444–5; Sauer, "Rundfunk," 456; Klippert, *Elemente*, 3; Widlok, "Hörfunkanbieter," 138–45; Faulstich, "Weg," 124–8; Krüger, "Fernsehanbieter," 104–47; Jutta Röser and Corinna Peil in Faulstich, *Kultur der achtziger Jahre*, 155–62; Werner Höfer and Hans Janke in Hoffmann and Klotz, *Die Sechziger*, 213–15.
149. "Die Werner-Höfer-Schau," *DS*, December 9, 1959.
150. Schreiber, *Nannen*, 290–4.
151. Geisler, "Nazis," 249; Harald Wieser, "Tod eines Pianisten," *DS*, December 14, 1987; Robert Leicht, "Der Fall Höfer," *DZ*, December 25, 1987; Alan Cowell, "Werner Hofer [*sic*], 84, a Fallen Idol of TV Journalism in Germany," *NYT*, November 27, 1997.
152. Harald Wieser, "Tod eines Pianisten," *DS*, December 14, 1987; Alan Cowell, "Werner Hofer [*sic*], 84, a Fallen Idol of TV Journalism in Germany," *NYT*, November 27, 1997.
153. Kammann, "Höfer," 232–3 (Höfer quoted 232); Weiss, "Journalisten," 293–4; Geisler, "Nazis," 248–50; Helmut Schödel, "Gespensterrepublik Deutschland," *DZ*, November 13, 1987; Robert Leicht, "Der Fall Höfer," *DZ*, December 25, 1987; Barbara Sichtermann, "Spätes Tribunal," *DZ*, January 22, 1988.
154. Schuckert, "Buchmarkt," 642–8.
155. See Frank Schirrmacher, "Idyllen in der Wüste oder Das Versagen vor der Metropole," *FAZ*, October 10, 1989; Rath, "Romane," 318–25 (quotes); Riha, "Quergelesen," 175–86; Lützeler, "Einleitung," 350–3.
156. "Zeitalter der Bruchstücke," *DZ*, November 10, 1989.
157. Language samples: Kronauer, *Rita Münster*, 7–12, 55–6, 268–71. Fritz J. Raddatz, "Glück," *DZ*, December 23, 1983 (quotes); Reinhart Baumgart, "Das Licht, das keine Schatten wirft," *DZ*, December 15, 1989; Rath, "Romane," 324.
158. Marcel Reich-Ranicki, "Der Kaiser ist nackt oder," *FAZ*, October 7, 1980; Volker Hage, "Die Enkel kommen," *DS*, October 10, 1999. See Henscheid, "Lautester," 178–9.
159. Wittstock, *Reich-Ranicki*, 232–4; Munzinger Archiv (Hahn), https://www.munzinger.de/search/go/document.jsp?id=00000017976. Ulrich Greiner, "Ulla Hahn und ihre Gedichte," *DZ*, September 23, 1983 (quotes, including Reich-Ranicki's from the *FAZ*). Similarly cutting: Andreas Kilb, "Gesang von Amsel und alten Meistern," *DZ*, March 25, 1988.

160. Reich-Ranicki quoted in "'Ich habe manipuliert, selbstverständlich!'" *DS*, January 2, 1989.
161. Walser, *Tagebücher, 1979–1981*, 603–4.
162. Böll vita in Heinrich Böll Stiftung, https://us.boell.org/en/2017/12/01/timeline-heinrich-bolls-life; Wirsching, *Abschied*, 101.
163. Mathias Schreiber, "Bürger Böll," *FAZ*, July 18, 1985; Franz Josef Görtz, "Der redliche Erzähler," ibid. Also "Internationale Pressestimmen zur Preisverleihung," *DZ*, October 27, 1972.
164. Böll's short story, "Brief an meine Söhne," an unremarkable and maudlin rehash, appeared in *DZ*, March 15, 1985.
165. Böll, *Frauen*, 73, 87, 128–9.
166. Reinhard Baumgart, "Götzendämmerung mit Nornen," *DS*, September 1, 1985; Joachim Kaiser, "Bitter absurdes Theater mit Bonn," *SZ*, September 21/22, 1985; Fritz J. Raddatz, "Seelen nur aufgemalt," *DZ*, October 11, 1985.
167. Rina, "Quergelesen," 182; Schnell, *Geschichte*, 495–6; Linder, *Böll*, 341–5.
168. Günter Grass, "'Kopfgeburten'," *DZ*, May 16, 1980.
169. Marcel Reich-Ranicki, ". . . und es muss gesagt werden," *DS*, August 20, 1995.
170. Alexander Cammann, "Briefe an den Kanzler," *DZ*, May 8, 2013.
171. "Der Asylkompromiss von 1992," *Deutschlandfunk*, May 9, 2022, https://www.deutschlandfunk.de/der-asylkompromiss-von-1992-kampf-um-artikel-100.html; Neuhaus, *Grass*, 306.
172. Hadek, *Vergangenheitsbewältigung*, 74.
173. Rolf Michaelis, "Grosses JA mit kleinem nein" *DZ*, December 4, 1987; Günter Grass, "Kurze Rede eines vaterlandslosen Gesellen," *DZ*, February 9, 1990; Esther B. Fein, "Gunter [*sic*] Grass Considers the Inescapable," *NYT*, December 29, 1992; Jürgs, *Bürger Grass*, 378; Müller, *Country*, 261.
174. Müller, *Country*, 67–74; Raddatz, *Unruhestifter*, 335–42.
175. Grass quoted in Lloyd Grove, "Gunter [*sic*] Grass," *Washington Post*, February 23, 1986.
176. Günter Grass, "Schreiben nach Auschwitz," *DZ*, February 23, 1990.
177. Günter Grass, Nobel Lecture, 1999, https://www.nobelprize.org/prizes/literature/1999/grass/199760-nobel-lecture-german/.
178. Vivien Raynor, "A Festival Devoted to Gunter [*sic*] Grass," *NYT*, March 28, 1982.
179. Walter Goodman, "The Stage: Gunter [*sic*] Grass's 'Flood'," *NYT*, June 2, 1986.
180. [Fritz J. Raddatz and Günter Grass], "Die Rättin: In Zukunft nur Ratten noch," *DZ*, November 29, 1985.
181. Görtz, "Apokalypse," 462–9 (Reich-Ranicki quoted 469); Gunter E. Grimm in Faulstich, *Kultur achtziger Jahre*, 101–2 (Engel, Schütte, and Kaiser quoted); Janette Turner, "Post Futurum Blues," *NYT*, July 5, 1987; Mayer-Iswandy, *Grass*, 85; Raddatz, *Unruhestifter*, 218, 330–4.
182. Rolf Michaelis, "Grosses JA mit kleinem nein" *DZ*, December 4, 1987.
183. Entry for November 13, 1980, in Walser, *Tagebücher, 1979–1981*, 484.
184. Hellmuth Karasek, "Malvolio in Kalifornien," *DS*, August 25, 1985; Ulrich Greiner, "Der Selbstverhinderungskünstler," *DZ*, August 30, 1985; Volker Hage, "Fliehender Romeo," *DZ*, September 16, 1988; Hellmuth Karasek, "Hasenherz am Bodensee," *DS*, August 28, 1988.
185. Wieland Freund, "Der Wiederholungstäter," *DW*, June 1, 2002; Walser, *Tagebücher, 1979–1981*, 560–1.
186. Walser, *Brief*, 83.
187. Entry for September 23, 1981, in Walser, *Tagebücher, 1979–1981*, 605; also 867.

188. Entry for September 9, 1980, in Walser, *Tagebücher, 1979–1981*, 458 (quote), and for November 10, 1981, 633.
189. Magenau, *Walser*, 457; Walser, *Tagebücher, 1979–1981*, 486.
190. On that point, see Aleida Assmann in Assmann and Frevert, *Geschichtsvergessenheit*, 62.
191. Quotes from Walser in Kovach and Walser, *Burden*, 86, 89–92. See Heinrich August Winkler, "Lesarten der Sühne," *DS*, August 23, 1998.
192. Schödel, *Gedächtnis*, 91; Hadek, *Vergangenheitsbewältigung*, 145.
193. Hadek, *Vergangenheitsbewältigung*, 146 (quote); Müller, *Country*, 245.
194. Klaus von Dohnányi, "Eine Friedensrede," *FAZ*, November 1998; Tjark Kunstreich, "Eine Kriegserklärung" (1998), https://www.jungle.world/print/pdf/node/33000.
195. Hadek, *Vergangenheitsbewältigung*, 150, 155; Kliche-Behnke, *Nationalsozialismus*, 63; Hans-Joachim Hahn, "Auschwitz ohne Folgen," *Literaturkritik.de*, March 3, 2015, https://literaturkritik.de/id/20407.
196. Bubis in Jürgen Hogrefe and Henryk M. Broder, "'Moral verjährt nicht'," *DS*, November 29, 1998.
197. Walser, *Krieg*, 106–7, 118, 209, 215.
198. Michalzik, *Unseld*, 301–2, 305–6.
199. Müller, *Country*, 246-53; Edmund L. Andrews, "Ignatz Bubis, Jewish Leader in Germany, Is Dead at 72," *NYT*, August 14, 1999.
200. "Ohne Schande," *DZ*, December 10, 1998; Wiesel in Werner A. Perger, "Von Walser enttäuscht," *DZ*, December 28, 2013.
201. Martin Walser, "Über Deutschland reden," *DZ*, November 4, 1988. Also see Magenau, *Walser*, 404.
202. Walser in Chabbi, *Walser*, 96; Magenau, *Walser*, 404; Walser, *Ansichten*, 668–80.
203. Waite, *Vanguard*, 1–238.
204. Baird, *To Die*, 17–20.
205. Karl-Heinz Janssen, "'Der erste Soldat des Dritten Reiches'," *DZ*, December 2, 1999.
206. Baird, *To Die*, 21–5; Karl-Heinz Janssen, "'Der erste Soldat des Dritten Reiches'," *DZ*, December 2, 1999.
207. Walser, *Ansichten*, 668–74, 677–9 (quote 673).
208. Kater, *Culture*, 40–1, 94.
209. Baird, *To Die*, 20, 32, 253, n. 28; von Salomon, *Fragebogen*, 347–8.
210. Waite, *Vanguard*, 62.
211. Martin Walser, "Über Deutschland reden," *DZ*, November 4, 1988; Walser in Kovach and Walser, *Burden*, 62.
212. Baird, *To Die*, 14–15. See Martin Walser, "'Ich bin schuldunfähig'," *DZ*, March 23, 2017.
213. Schildt, *Medien-Intellektuelle*, 613; Wittstock, *Reich-Ranicki*, 289–93; Reich-Ranicki, *Leben*, 535–6.
214. Ulrich Greiner, "Punkt Punkt Komma Sieg," *DZ*, April 1, 1988.
215. Reich-Ranicki, *Leben*, 537–9; Wittstock, *Reich-Ranicki*, 293–8; Barbara Sichtermann, "Heisser Hickhack," *DZ*, March 17, 1989; Fokke Joel, "Mehr als bloss Kritikertheater," *DZ*, December 14, 2011; Ulrich Greiner and Iris Radisch, "Ich bin nicht glücklich," *DZ*, May 27, 2010. Superficiality: Rühmkorf, *Tabu I*, 216.
216. Joerg Albrecht, "'Kinder, was soll diese Prüderie?'" *DZ*, July 27, 2000; Wittstock, *Reich-Ranicki*, 298–9.
217. Faust and de Vries, *Hunger*, 8–9.
218. Schmidt, "Kunst," 264–5 ("barbaric" quote 264); Faust and de Vries, *Hunger*, 87–145; Günther Gercken in Joachimidis et al., *Kunst*, 468; Damus, *Kunst*,

327–52; "Sturmflut der Bilder," *DS*, May 30, 1982. New York: John Russell, "Art," *NYT*, December 11, 1981; John Russell, "Art," *NYT*, October 3, 1986; "Artist Asks the Guggenheim To Withdraw His Painting," *NYT*, February 11, 1989.

219. Walter Dahn, artnet, http://www.artnet.com/artists/walter-dahn/.

220. Damus, *Kunst*, 328–9, 376; Faust and de Vries, *Hunger*, 145–6; Schmidt, "Kunst," 287.

221. Jiri Georg Dokoupil, artnet, http://www.artnet.com/artists/jiri-georg-dokoupil/ (first quote); Faust and de Vries, *Hunger*, 146–51 (second quote 149).

222. Salomé, artnet, http://www.artnet.com/artists/salom%C3%A9-wolfgang-ludwig-cihlarz/; Faust and de Vries, *Hunger*, 90–1.

223. Self-portrait of Salomé (1976) in Klotz, *Neuen Wilden*, 154, and 1978 in Damus, *Kunst*, 321. Also interviewed (1984) in Klotz, *Neuen Wilden*, 158–9 (quotes).

224. Klotz, *Neuen Wilden*, 154; Fetting, artnet, http://www.artnet.com/artists/rainer-fetting/.

225. Klotz, *Neuen Wilden*, 82–3, 99; gay-club painting: https://www.ngv.vic.gov.au/explore/collection/work/3954/. Also Faust and de Vries, *Hunger*, 91–3.

226. Salomé, artnet, http://www.artnet.com/artists/salom%C3%A9-wolfgang-ludwig-cihlarz/.

227. Damus, *Kunst*, 375; Kimpel, *documenta*, 91.

228. 1975–87: Rudi Fuchs, https://vanabbemuseum.nl/en/about-the-museum/building-and-history/1975-1987-rudi-fuchs/; Rudi Fuchs, artnet, http://www.artnet.com/magazine/features/esman/esman5-12-03.asp.

229. Kimpel, *documenta*, 93–5.

230. Petra Kipphoff, "Eine Erzählung aus dem Wald der Künste," *DZ*, October 9, 1981; Peter Sager, "Kostbarmacher von Kunst," *DZ*, June 11, 1987.

231. "In die Wälder hinunter," *DS*, June 20, 1982.

232. "Es hat gebrannt," *DS*, August 29, 1982; "Momentaufnahmen von zwei Mythen," *DZ*, June 225, 1982; "Zeitmosaik," *DZ*, August 13, 1982; Kimpel, *documenta*, 99–103.

233. Petra Kipphoff, "Begegnungen im Wald der Künste," *DZ*, June 25, 1982; "Kunst wie ist sie?" *DZ*, November 7, 1986 (quote).

234. Petra Kipphoff, "Begegnungen im Wald der Künste," *DZ*, June 25, 1982.

235. Norbert Scholz in Kimpel, *Aversion*, 83–4.

236. Scholz in Kimpel, *Aversion*, 84–93 (Beuys's quote 87); Petra Kipphoff, "Begegnungen im Wald der Künste," *DZ*, June 25, 1982; Oman, *Kunst*, 156–61; Stachelhaus, *Beuys*, 182–3; Tilman Spreckelsen, "Wie Kassel '7000' Eichen bekam," *FAZ*, May 10, 2021.

237. Kimpel, *documenta*, 104.

238. Petra Kipphoff, "Kunst ist, was uns umtreibt," *DZ*, March 20, 1987 (Schneckenburger quoted); Petra Kipphoff, "Das hohe Fest der Beliebigkeit," *DZ*, June 19, 1987; Kimpel, *documenta*, 109, 111; Laszlo Glozer, "Bedeutungsschwanger bis unterhaltsam," *SZ*, June 13/14, 1987; Michael Brenson, "Art," *NYT*, June 15, 1987; Eduard Beaucamp, "Daphne und Holocaust," *FAZ*, June 13, 1987.

239. Kimpel, *documenta*, 106.

240. Fry in Michael Brenson, "Art," *NYT*, June 15, 1987. See Roberta Smith, "Edward F. Fry, 56, A Historian Devoted to 20th-Century Art," *NYT*, April 21, 1992.

241. Petra Kipphoff, "Das hohe Fest der Beliebigkeit," *DZ*, June 19, 1987.

242. Eduard Beaucamp, "Daphne und Holocaust," *FAZ*, June 13, 1987.

243. Michael Brenson, "Art," *NYT*, June 15, 1987.

244. Damus, *Kunst*, 379, 389–91, 401–4.

245. Michael Brenson, "Art," *NYT*, June 15, 1987; Petra Kipphoff, "Das hohe Fest der Beliebigkeit," *DZ*, June 19, 1987.

246. Schreier, "Krise," 288.

247. Richter quoted ibid., 289.

248. Ibid.; https://www.google.com/search?client=firefox-b-d&q=richter+scheune+1983.

249. https://www.gettyimages.ie/photos/abstraktes-bild; Schreier, "Krise," 290.

250. Eckhart Gillen, "Gerhard Richter," *DZ*, March 30, 2015.

251. https://www.gerhard-richter.com/en/art/paintings/abstracts/colour-charts-12/256-colours-6066; Lucius Grisebach, "Richter, Gerhard," *Oxford Art Online*.

252. Richter (diary entry of March 25, 1985) in Obrist, *Richter*, 120.

253. Schneckenburger in Petra Kipphoff, "Kunst ist, was uns umtreibt," *DZ*, March 20, 1987. Also Eduard Beaucamp, "Verdrängte Geschichte?" *FAZ*, June 29, 1985.

254. Stephan Mann, "Kiefer, Anselm," *Oxford Art Online*; Eduard Beaucamp, "Die verbrannte Geschichte," *FAZ*, April 11, 1984.

255. Petra Kipphoff, "Das hohe Fest der Beliebigkeit," *DZ*, June 19, 1987; Michael Brenson, "Art," *NYT*, June 15, 1987.

256. http://www.artnet.com/magazineus/features/polsky/polsky8-15-05_detail.asp?picnum=2.

257. https://sfmoma.tumblr.com/post/24009099271/anselm-kiefer-osiris-und-isis-osiris-and-isis.

258. Schneckenburger in Petra Kipphoff, "Kunst ist, was uns umtreibt," *DZ*, March 20, 1987; Damus, *Kunst*, 382–3, 394–5, 400–1; https://schellmannart.com/Gerhard_Merz.

259. Fry quoted in Michael Brenson, "Art," *NYT*, June 15, 1987. See Hans-Joachim Müller, "Und hinter tausend Farbbahnen keine Geschichte," *DW*, December 5, 2013; Bruce Weber, "Günther Förg, German Artist Who Made Modernism His Theme, Dies at 61," *NYT*, December 18, 2013.

260. Michael Brenson, "Art," *NYT*, June 15, 1987; Mika Ross-Southall, "Reinhard Mucha's Unsettling Precision," https://hyperallergic.com/490770/reinhard-mucha.

261. Kimpel, *documenta*, 108, 111; Petra Kipphoff, "Kunst ist, was uns umtreibt," *DZ*, March 20, 1987; Petra Kipphoff, "Das hohe Fest der Beliebigkeit," *DZ*, June 19, 1987; Ian Hamilton Finlay in *Ingleby*, https://www.inglebygallery.com/artists/37-ian-hamilton-finlay/overview/.

262. Leon Golub, artnet, http://www.artnet.com/artists/leon-golub/; Hans Haacke, artnet, http://www.artnet.com/artists/hans-haacke; "Bedeutungsschwanger bis unterhaltsam," *SZ*, June 13/14, 1987 (quote); Petra Kipphoff, "Das hohe Fest der Beliebigkeit," *DZ*, June 19, 1987; Eduard Beaucamp, "Daphne und Holocaust," *FAZ*, June 13, 1987; Damus, *Kunst*, 383-84. See https://de-de.facebook.com/DeutscheBankAG/photos/a.122552351111302/2151717964861387/?type=3.

263. Werckmeister, *Zitadellenkultur*, 140–4; Derrick R. Cartwright, "Morris, Robert," *Oxford Art Online*; Petra Kipphoff, "Kunst ist, was uns umtreibt," *DZ*, March 20, 1987; Eduard Beaucamp, "Daphne und Holocaust," *FAZ*, June 13, 1987. See Michael Brenson, "Art," *NYT*, January 15, 1988.

264. Dalhaus, "Vorwort," in Dalhaus, *Wiener Schule*, 7; idem, "Krise," 80; Brinkmann, "Einleitung," 11, 17 (quote).

265. Von Blumröder, "Konzeptionen," 183.

266. Stockhausen in Felder, "Interview," 86; von Blumröder, "Konzeptionen," 183–9; Cott, *Stockhausen*, 15, 179–81; Glaser, *Kulturgeschichte*, vol. 3, 254.

267. Von Blumröder, "Konzeptionen," 190–1; Stockhausen in Felder, "Interview," 87–8, 92–3, 98.

268. Frisius, *Stockhausen*, 21; Conen, *Formel-Komposition*, 17; Misch, *Stockhausen*, vii–viii; Stockhausen obituary, "Karlheinz Stockhausen," *The Times*, London, December 8, 2007.

269. "Karlheinz Stockhausen" in *Encyclopedia Britannica*; Tannenbaum, *Conversations*, 97; von Blumröder, "Stockhausen," 323; Richard Toop, "Stockhausen, Karlheinz," *Oxford Music Online*. See Frieder Reininghaus in de la Motte and Barthelmes, *Geschichte*, 124–5; Claus Spahn, "Nachruf," *DZ*, December 13, 2007.

270. See Gerhard R. Koch, "Das Neue und die Heilsherrschaft," *FAZ*, August 22, 1988.

271. Stockhausen in "Das Volk ist die einzige tragende Kraft," *Neue Musikzeitung*, no. 3 (June/July 1977).

272. Hans-Klaus Jungheinrich, "Globaltheater; verwackelt," *FR*, March 17, 1981; APA, Professor Albrecht Riethmüller, emails to the author, Berlin, May 13, 28, June 5, 2022.

273. Kurtz, *Stockhausen*, 277–86; Riethmüller, "Michael," 120, 128.

274. Ross, "Infinity Opera," 76–7 (quote 76).

275. Gerhard R. Koch, "Streik verhindert Welterlösung," *FAZ*, March 18, 1981.

276. Hans-Klaus Jungheinrich, "Globaltheater; verwackelt," *FR*, March 17, 1981; Stockhausen in Tannenbaum, *Conversations*, 35.

277. Stockhausen in Felder, "Interview," 99, and in Tannenbaum, *Conversations*, 35.

278. Stockhausen quoted in Terry Castle, "Stockhausen, Karlheinz," *New York Magazine*, August 27, 2011, https://nymag.com/news/9-11/10th-anniversary/karlheinz-stockhausen/; Taruskin, *Questions*, 70.

279. Castle, "Stockhausen, Karlheinz" (as in n. 278).

280. See Cott, *Stockhausen*, 119; Henze, *Musik*, 317.

281. Virginia Palmer-Füchsel, "Henze, Hans Werner," *Oxford Music Online*; Thaler, "Komponisten," 143; Glaser, *Deutsche Kultur*, 420.

282. Henze, *Musik*, 151–2.

283. Ibid., 153, 170–1.

284. Virginia Palmer-Füchsel, "Henze, Hans Werner," *Oxford Music Online*.

285. Ibid. (quote); Glaser, *Kulturgeschichte*, vol. 3, 256–7. Also see Hans Otto Spingel, "Fragwürdige Schönheit," *DZ*, June 6, 1975; "Mahnen, erinnern, Hoffnung machen," *DZ*, July 9, 1976.

286. Tim Page, "Opera," *NYT*, March 21, 1986.

287. Doll, *Theaterarbeit*, 29, 31, 43, 62.

288. Gottwald in Honegger and Massenkeil, *Lexikon*, vol. 3, 339.

289. Gottwald, "Neue Musik," 171–3.

290. Ibid., 173–4.

291. Ibid., 174–5; Wolfgang von Schweinitz in Faulstich, *Kultur der siebziger Jahre*, 120 (quote).

292. Barthelmes, "Neue Musik," 121–3.

293. Quote is from Mahnkopf, "Neue Musik," 866.

294. Barthelmes, "Neue Musik," 123–7 (quote 123).

295. Quote is from Hans-Werner Heister in Heister, *Geschichte*, 361. See Stenger, "Wege," 132–7; Bolín, "Neue Musik," 25–7.

296. Struck-Schloen, "Hauptstadt-Ruhm," 155–60.

297. Tom Sutcliffe, "Rolf Liebermann Obituary," *Guardian*, January 14, 1999; Peter Ross, "Liebermann, Rolf," *Oxford Music Online*.

298. Wilson, "Null," 147–8 (quotes 147).

299. Ibid., 148–51; entry for May 20, 1971, in Rühmkorf, *Tabu II*, 53 (quote).

300. Paul Griffiths, "Ligeti, György (Sandor)," *Oxford Music Online*.

301. Wilson, "Null," 152.

302. Alan Blyth, "Everding, August," and Noël Goodwin, "Sawallisch, Wolfgang," *Oxford Music Online*.

303. Elizabeth Forbes, "Obituary: August Everding," *Independent*, February 15, 1999.

304. Kater, *Composers*, 114–17, 222; Reissinger, "Neue Musik," 161–3.
305. Charles Barber and Irina Boga, "Celibidache, Sergiu," *Oxford Music Online*.
306. Harald Müller, "Korn, Peter Jona," *Oxford Music Online*.
307. Gerhard Brunner and Martin Elste, "Gulda, Friedrich," *Oxford Music Online*.
308. https://www.baerenreiter.com/en/shop/product/details/BA7305/.
309. Reissinger, "Neue Musik," 163–7.
310. Ibid., 167–9 (quote 167); Heinz Josef Herbort, "Utopie von einer anderen Oper," *DZ*, June 10, 1988.
311. Erik Levy, "Bialas, Günter," *Oxford Music Online*.
312. Heinz Josef Herbort, "Rattengift und Halleluja," *DZ*, April 10, 1970.
313. Stefan Fricke, "Hamel, Peter Michael," *Oxford Music Online*; Peter Michael Hamel, *celestial harmonies*, https://www.harmonies.com/biographies/hamel.htm; Carola Schormann in Faulstich, *Kultur der achtziger Jahre*, 172.
314. Eckhard Roelcke, "Vorsicht! Verführung!," *DZ*, April 10, 1992.
315. Siegfried Mauser, "Killmayer, Wilhelm," *Oxford Music Online* (quotes); Dibelius, "Musik," 158; "Wilhelm Killmayer, 1927–2017," *Schott Music*, August 21, 2017, https://www.schott-music.com/en/person/wilhelm-killmayer; Kater, *Composers*, 115–16, 123, 128.
316. Moritz Eggert, "Zum Tod von Wilhelm Killmayer," *Deutschlandfunk*, August 21, 2017, https://www.deutschlandfunk.de/zum-tod-von-wilhelm-killmayer-vielleicht-der-eigenwilligste-100.html (quotes). Also Marcus Stäbler, "Von der Stille zum Melos," *Neue Zürcher Zeitung*, September 7, 2012.
317. Walter Abendroth, "Nach alter Methode," *DZ*, July 18, 1957.
318. Walter Abendroth, "Moderne Musik und Jazz," *DZ*, October 24, 1957.
319. Walter Abendroth, "Ein Orfeo zuviel," *DZ*, June 30, 1961; "Musica Viva," *DZ*, May 15, 1964; Ulrich Dibelius, "Die Musica Viva," *DZ*, June 5, 1964.
320. Lachenmann quoted in BR Klassic, https://www.pcmsconcerts.org/artist/marc-neikrug-piano/.
321. Frank Hilberg in de la Motte and Berthelmes, *Geschichte*, 178–83; Ulrich Mosch, "Lachenmann, Helmut," *Oxford Music Online*.
322. Ulrich Mosch, "Lachenmann, Helmut," *Oxford Music Online*; Frank Hilberg in de la Motte and Berthelmes, *Geschichte*, 183–7; Claus Spahn, "Pochen unterm Eis," *DZ*, October 4, 2001 (quote).
323. Klaus Umbach, "Qualm vom Quälgeist," *DS*, January 26, 1997 (quote); Volker Hagedorn, "Zwischen Romantik und Heavy Metal, *DZ*, September 19, 2013.
324. Eleonore Buening, "Ritsch!" *DZ*, January 31, 1997.
325. Lachenmann in de la Motte and Berthelmes, *Geschichte*, 183.
326. Henze, *Musik*, 266.
327. Griffel, *Operas*, 443.
328. Ross, "Infinity Opera," 77.
329. Kater, *Twisted Muse*, 104–5.
330. Thaler, "Komponisten," 142.
331. Severine Neff, "Neikrug, Marc (Edward)," *Oxford Music Online*; Alvin Klein, "Theater; Music is Subtext in 'Through Roses'," *NYT*, May 10, 1987.
332. "Marc Neikrug, piano," PCMS, https://www.pcmsconcerts.org/artist/marc-neikrug-piano/.
333. Alvin Klein, "Theater; Music is Subtext in 'Through Roses'," *NYT*, May 10, 1987 (Neikrug's first two quotes); Frank J. Oteri and Marc Neikrug, *NEWMUSIC USA*, March 1, 2014, https://newmusicusa.org/nmbx/marc-neikrug-an-outlet-for-emotional-experience/ (Neikrug's last quote).

334. Rolf Michaelis, "Mords-Musical," *DZ*, July 20,1984; Heinz Josef Herbort, "Für alles und nichts," *DZ*, October 14, 1988.

335. Heinz Josef Herbort, "Für alles und nichts," *DZ*, October 14, 1988.

CODA: AFTER THE WEST GERMANS

1. See "'Eine friedliche Revolution'," *DS*, November 12, 1989.
2. Caldwell and Hanshew, *Germany*, 276–308.
3. Ibid., 270.
4. "Notgemeinschaft in Bonn," *DS*, April 14, 1991; "'Ein mühsamer Hürdenlauf'," *DS*, April 26, 1992; "'Dieses Land wird unregierbar'," *DS*, September 13, 1992; "'Es kommt noch schlimmer'," *DS*, January 24, 1993; "'Baggern statt denken'," *DS*, February 12, 1995; "'Avanti Dilettanti'," *DS*, June 8, 1997.
5. "Staatsverschuldung von Deutschland von 1950 bis 2021," https://de.statista.com/statistik/daten/studie/154798/umfrage/deutsche-staatsverschuldung-seit-2003/.
6. "'Tabuzone Ost'," *DS*, April 4, 2004.
7. "'Dieses Land wird unregierbar'," *DS*, September 13, 1992; Rolf Michaelis, "Grüss Gott, Provinz!" *DZ*, October 29, 1993.
8. "Notgemeinschaft in Bonn," *DS*, April 14, 1991; "'Dieses Land wird unregierbar'," *DS*, September 13, 1992; "'Baggern statt denken'," *DS*, February 12, 1995; "Der Osten wird bunt," *DS*, October 6, 1996; "Tabuzone Ost," *DS*, April 4, 2004; Kater, *Weimar*, 328–33.
9. "Hochhuth ist ein Feigling," *DZ*, February 19, 1993.
10. Staud, "Immigranten," 267–73.
11. "'Es ist ein anderes Leben'," *DS*, September 23,1990; "'Ein mühsamer Hürdenlauf'," *DS*, April 26, 1992; "Ossis sind Türken," *DZ*, October 1, 2003; "Vereint in der Entfremdung," *DZ*, October 2, 2010.
12. "Viele halten Wiedervereinigung für wenig geglückt," *DW*, October 2, 2022; "Ministerpräsidenten sehen Ergebnisse von Aufbau Ost in Gefahr," *DZ*, October 3, 2022.
13. Reich-Ranicki, *Literatur*, 392, 399–400, 404–5; Jan Philipp Engelmann, "Krieg und Frieden oder deutsch-deutscher Literaturaustausch," July 1, 2015, https://zeitgeschichte-online.de/themen/literaturaustausch.
14. "'Es ist ein anderes Leben'," *DS*, September 23, 1990.
15. Spotts, *Bayreuth*, 273, 276–80.
16. Burns, *Cultural Studies*, 187.
17. "'Distanz, Enttäuschung, Hass'," *DS*, August 16, 1992; "Monika Maron" [2021], *Deutsche Welle*, https://www.dw.com/en/monika-maron-chronicler-of-the-gdr-turns-80/a-57758191.
18. Hell, "Dissidents," 102; "Anderson, Sascha" (b. 1953), Bundesstiftung Aufarbeitung, https://www.bundesstiftung-aufarbeitung.de/de/recherche/kataloge-datenbanken/biographische-datenbanken/sascha-anderson?ID=51.
19. Sally McGrane, "Remembering Christa Wolf," *NY*, December 13, 2011, https://www.newyorker.com/books/page-turner/remembering-christa-wolf; Kate Webb, "Christa Wolf Obituary," *Guardian*, December 1, 2011.
20. Albrecht et al., *Lexikon*, vol. 1, 441.
21. Günter de Bruyn, "Scharfmaul und Prahlhans," *DZ*, September 19, 1991; Hans Hütt, "Immer so haarscharf an der Wahrheit vorbei," *DZ*, August 15, 2016; Jens Jessen, "Mit Super-Ironie," *DZ*, September 13, 2016; "Hermann Kant 80," *DW*, June 14, 2006.

22. Karin Thomas, "Die Rezeption der Kunst aus der DDR in der Bundesrepublik bis 1989," https://karinthomas.eu/?p=321 (quote); "A.R. Penck," *Encyclopedia Britannica*; "Deutsche Einheit," *DZ*, September 23, 2010.

23. Karin Thomas, "Die Rezeption der Kunst aus der DDR in der Bundesrepublik bis 1989," https://karinthomas.eu/?p=321.

24. Kunst aus der DDR, Magazin Goethe-Institut, https://www.goethe.de/ins/cz/de/kul/mag/23010819.html; Lenore Lötsch, "Die 'Ost-Künstler' und die Einheit," October 2, 2020, *NDR.de*, https://www.goethe.de/ins/cz/de/kul/mag/23010819.html.

25. Kater, *Weimar*, 341.

26. Ibid., 341–50.

27. Riethmüller, *Lost*, 77–8, 84–5 (first quote 84); von Saldern, *Kunstnationalismus*, 422–4 (second quote 422).

28. Müller, *Country*, 55, 63.

29. Jürgen Kocka, "Nur keinen neuen Sonderweg," *DZ*, October 19, 1990.

30. Barner, *Geschichte*, 956.

31. Schorske, *Vienna*, xxvii. Also Pim, *Flight*, 60–4.

32. Gopnik, "System Upgrade," 64.

33. Schorske, *Vienna*, 208–78.

34. Kater, *Culture*, 338; Kater, *Composers*, 263.

Archival Sources

Author's private archive (APA)
Miscellanea

Bundesarchiv Berlin (BAB)
File Generaltreuhänder Ost; R93615

Carl-Orff-Zentrum München (CM)
Diary Gertrud Orff

Geheimes Staatsarchiv Berlin (GSB)
Stiftung Preussischer Kulturbesitz/I/HA/Rep119neu

Institut für Zeitgeschichte München (IfZ)
Archiv, ZS/A-25

National Archives Washington (NAW)
T-580/174, SS-Ahnenerbe

University of California at Los Angeles (UCLA)
Music Library, Special Collections, Ernst Toch Archive

York University Archives and Special Collections, Toronto (YUA)
CA ON00370 F0456

Bibliography

Abelshauser, Werner, *Die langen fünfziger Jahre: Wirtschaft und Gesellschaft der Bundesrepublik Deutschland, 1949–1966* (Düsseldorf: Schwann, 1987)

Abendroth, Walter, *Ich warne Neugierige: Erinnerungen eines kritischen Zeitbetrachters* (Munich: List, 1966)

Abendroth, Walter, *Kleine Geschichte der Musik* (Frankfurt am Main: Heinrich Scheffler, 1959)

Adorno, Theodor W., "Die gegängelte Musik," *Der Monat* 5 (May 1953): 178–83

Adorno, Theodor W., "Zeitlose Mode: Zum Jazz," *Merkur* 7 (1953): 537–48

Adriani, Götz, "Biographische Hinweise," in Heiner Bastian, ed., *Joseph Beuys: Skulpturen und Objekte* (Munich: Schirmer/Mosel, 1988), 89–110

Adriani, Götz, Winfried Konnertz, and Karin Thomas, *Joseph Beuys: Life and Works* (New York: Barron's, 1979)

Albrecht, Günter, Kurt Böttcher, Herbert Greiner-Mai, and Paul Günther Krohn, eds, *Lexikon deutschsprachiger Schriftsteller von den Anfängen bis zur Gegenwart*, 2nd edn (Leipzig: VEB Bibliographisches Institut, vol. 1, 1972; vol. 2, 1974)

Aly, Götz, "Theodor Schieder, Werner Conze oder die Vorstufen der physischen Vernichtung," in Winfried Schulze and Otto Gerhard Oexle, eds, *Deutsche Historiker im Nationalsozialismus* (Frankfurt am Main: Fischer Taschenbuch, 1999), 163–82

Améry, Jean, *Geburt der Gegenwart: Gestalten und Gestaltungen der westlichen Zivilisation seit Kriegsende* (Olten: Walter, 1961)

Andersch, Alfred, *Sansibar oder der letzte Grund: Roman* (Olten: Walter-Verlag, 1957)

Andersen, Arne, *Der Traum vom guten Leben: Alltags- und Konsumgeschichte vom Wirtschaftswunder bis heute* (Frankfurt am Main: Campus, 1997)

Angress, Ruth K., "Gibt es ein 'Judenproblem' in der deutschen Nachkriegsliteratur?" *Die Neue Sammlung* 26 (January–March 1986): 22–40

Applegate, Celia, *The Necessity of Music: Variations on a German Theme* (Toronto: University of Toronto Press, 2017)

Arani, Miriam Y., "'Und an den Fotos entzündete sich die Kritik': Die 'Wehrmachtsaustellung', deren Kritiker und die Neukonzeption: Ein Beitrag aus fotohistorisch-quellenkritischer Sicht," *Fotogeschichte* 85/6 (2002): 97–124

448

Arendt, Hannah, *Eichmann in Jerusalem: Ein Bericht von der Banalität des Bösen* (Munich: R. Piper, 1964)

Arendt, Hannah, *Zur Zeit: Politische Essays*, ed. Marie Luise Knott (Munich: DTV, 1989)

Asper, Helmut, "Fritz Kortners Rückkehr und sein Film Der Ruf," in Helmut Asper, ed., *Wenn wir von gestern reden, sprechen wir über heute und morgen: Festschrift für Marta Mierendorff zum 90. Geburtstag* (Berlin: Edition Sigma, 1991), 287–300

Assmann, Aleida, and Ute Frevert, *Geschichtsvergessenheit, Geschichtsversessenheit: Vom Umgang mit deutschen Vergangenheiten nach 1945* (Stuttgart: Deutsche Verlags-Anstalt, 1999)

Aucoin, Matthew, "Sound and Fury," *New York Review of Books* (November 5, 2020): 18–20

Aucoin, Matthew, *The Impossible Art: Adventures in Opera* (New York: Farrar, Straus and Giroux, 2021)

Auerbach, Hellmuth, "Die Einheit Dirlewanger," *Vierteljahrshefte für Zeitgeschichte* 10 (1962): 250–63

Auerbach, Hellmuth, "Die Gründung des Instituts für Zeitgeschichte," *Vierteljahrshefte für Zeitgeschichte* 18 (1970): 529–54

Ausstellungskatalog "Deutsche Kunst im 20. Jahrhundert": Malerei und Plastik aus Privatbesitz (Aachen: Verlag des Aachener Museumsvereins, 1964)

Aust, Stefan, *Der Baader Meinhof Komplex* (Hamburg: Hoffmann und Campe, 1986)

Bachmann, Robert C., *Karajan: Anmerkungen zu einer Karriere*, 2nd edn (Düsseldorf: Econ, 1983)

Bahr, Ehrhard, *Weimar on the Pacific: German Exile Culture in Los Angeles and the Crisis of Modernism* (Berkeley: University of California Press, 2007)

Baier, Lothar, and Detlev Claussen, "Die Intellektuellen nach der Revolte: Ein Gespräch," in W. Martin Lüdke, ed., *Nach dem Protest: Literatur im Umbruch* (Frankfurt am Main: edition suhrkamp, 1979), 125–39

Baird, Jay W., *To Die for Germany: Heroes in the Nazi Pantheon* (Bloomington: Indiana University Press, 1990)

Barner, Wilfried, ed., *Geschichte der deutschen Literatur von 1945 bis zur Gegenwart*, 2nd edn (Munich: C.H. Beck, 2006)

Barthel, Manfred, *Als Opas Kino jung war: Der deutsche Nachkriegsfilm* (Frankfurt am Main: Ullstein, 1991)

Barthelmes, Barbara, "Neue Musik im Berlin der achtziger Jahre: Das letzte Jahrzehnt einer Insel-Stadt," in Martin Thrun, ed., *Neue Musik seit den achtziger Jahren: Eine Dokumentation zum deutschen Musikleben*, vol. 2 (Regensburg: ConBrio Verlagsgesellschaft, 1994), 119–29

Basker, David, "'Deutschland lebt an der Nahtstelle, an der Bruchstelle': Literature and Politics in Germany, 1933–1950," in William Niven and James Jordan, eds, *Politics and Culture in Twentieth-Century Germany* (Rochester, NY: Camden House, 2003), 89–106

Bauer, Fritz, *Die Wurzeln faschistischen und nationalsozialistischen Handelns*, 4th edn (Hamburg: Europäische Verlagsanstalt, 2020; 1st edn 1965)

Bauer, Oswald Georg, *Die Geschichte der Bayreuther Festspiele: Band II, 1951–2000* (Berlin: Deutscher Kunstverlag, 2016)

Baumann, Bommi [Michael], *Wie alles anfing* ([Berlin]: Rotbuch, 1991)

Bausch, Hans, *Rundfunkpolitik nach 1945: Erster Teil: 1945–1962* (Munich: DTV, 1980)

Bausch, Ulrich M., *Die Kulturpolitik der US-amerikanischen Information Control Division in Württemberg-Baden von 1945 bis 1949: Zwischen militärischem Funktionalismus und schwäbischem Obrigkeitsdenken* (Stuttgart: Klett-Cotta, 1992)

Beal, Amy, "Negotiating Cultural Allies: American Music in Darmstadt, 1946–1956," *Journal of the American Musicological Society* 53 (2000): 105–39

Beal, Amy C., *New Music, New Allies: American Experimental Music in West Germany from Zero Hour to Reunification* (Berkeley: University of California Press, 2006)

Beck-Gernsheim, Elisabeth, "Liebe, Ehe, Scheidung," in Christian W. Thomsen, ed., *Aufbruch in die Neunziger: Ideen, Entwicklungen, Perspektiven der achtziger Jahre* (Cologne: DuMont, 1991), 42–63

Becker, Franz, "Wirklichkeit oder Phantasma? Die 'Amerikanisierung' von Politik und Gesellschaft in der Bundesrepublik," in Alexander Stephan and Jochen Vogt, eds, *America on my Mind: Zur Amerikanisierung der deutschen Kultur seit 1945* (Munich: Wilhelm Fink, 2006), 51–73

Becker, Wolfgang, and Norbert Schöll, *In jenen Tagen . . . Wie der deutsche Nachkriegsfilm die Vergangenheit bewältigte* (Opladen: Leske + Budrich, 1995)

Beer, Mathias, "Im Spannungsfeld von Politik und Zeitgeschichte: Das Grossforschungsprojekt 'Dokumentation der Vertreibung der Deutschen aus Ost-Mitteleuropa'," *Vierteljahrshefte für Zeitgeschichte* 46 (1998): 345–89

Belting, Hans, *Die Deutschen und ihre Kunst: Ein schwieriges Erbe* (Munich: C.H. Beck, 1992)

Bennett, Lowell, *Bastion Berlin: Das Epos eines Freiheitskampfes* (Frankfurt am Main: Friedrich Rudl/Verleger-Union, 1951)

Bentz, Ralf, Sabine Brtnik, Christoph König, Roman Luckscheiter, Ulrich Ott, and Brigitte Raitz, *Protest! Literatur um 1968: Eine Ausstellung des Deutschen Literaturarchivs in Verbindung mit dem Germanistischen Seminar der Universität Heidelberg und dem Deutschen Rundfunkarchiv im Schiller-Nationalmuseum Marbach am Neckar* (Marbach am Neckar: Deutsche Schillergesellschaft, 1998)

Berendt, Joachim Ernst, *Ein Fenster aus Jazz: Essays, Portraits, Reflexionen* (Frankfurt am Main: S. Fischer, 1977)

Berendt, Joachim Ernst, "Zum Thema Jazz," *Frankfurter Hefte* 7 (1952): 768–79

Berg, Jan, *Hochhuths "Stellvertreter" und die "Stellvertreter-Debatte": "Vergangenheitsbewältigung" in Theater und Presse der sechziger Jahre* (Kronberg: Scriptor-Verlag, 1977)

Berg, Rainer, *Varieté: Gutgelaunt durchs Wirtschaftswunder* (Hanover: Fackelträger, 1988)

Berger, Stefan, "On Tabus, Traumas and Other Myths: Why the Debate about German Victims of the Second World War is not a Historians' Controversy," in Bill Niven, ed., *Germans as Victims: Remembering the Past in Contemporary Germany* (Houndmills: Palgrave Macmillan, 2006), 210–24

Bergmann, Werner, *Antisemitismus in öffentlichen Konflikten: Kollektives Lernen in der politischen Kultur der Bundesrepublik, 1949–1989* (Frankfurt am Main: Campus, 1997)

Bergmann, Werner, "Sind die Deutschen antisemitisch? Meinungsumfragen von 1946–1987 in der Bundesrepublik Deutschland," in Werner Bergmann and Rainer Erb, eds, *Antisemitismus in der politischen Kultur nach 1945* (Opladen: Westdeutscher Verlag, 1990), 108–30

Bermbach, Udo, *Die Entnazifizierung Richard Wagners: Die Programmhefte der Bayreuther Festspiele, 1951–1976* (Stuttgart: J.B. Metzler, 2020)

Bernhard, Thomas, *Vor dem Ruhestand: Eine Komödie von deutscher Seele* (Frankfurt am Main: Suhrkamp, 1979)

Bessel, Richard, *Germany 1945: From War to Peace* (New York: HarperCollins, 2009)

Bessen, Ursula, *Trümmer und Träume: Nachkriegszeit und fünfziger Jahre auf Zelluloid: Deutsche Spielfilme als Zeugnisse ihrer Zeit: Eine Dokumentation* (Bochum: Studienverlag Dr. N. Brockmeyer, 1989)

Besson, Waldemar, *Die Aussenpolitik der Bundesrepublik: Erfahrungen und Massstäbe* (Munich: R. Piper, 1970)

Betts, Paul, *Ruin and Renewal: Civilizing Europe after World War II* (New York: Basic Books, 2020)

Betts, Paul, *The Authority of Everyday Objects: A Cultural History of West German Industrial Design* (Berkeley: University of California Press, 2004)

Beuys, Eva, ed., *Joseph Beuys: Das Geheimnis der Knospe zarter Hülle: Texte, 1941–1986* (Munich: Schirmer/Mosel, 2000)

Bier, Jean-Paul, "The Holocaust, West Germany, and Strategies of Oblivion, 1947–1979," in Anson Rabinbach and Jack Zipes, eds, *Germans and Jews since the Holocaust: The Changing Situation in West Germany* (New York: Holmes & Meier, 1986), 185–207

Biess, Frank, *Homecomings: Returning POWs and the Legacies of Defeat in Postwar Germany* (Princeton: Princeton University Press, 2006)

Biess, Frank, *Republik der Angst: Eine andere Geschichte der Bundesrepublik*, 2nd edn (Reinbek: Rowohlt, 2019)

Biess, Frank, "Survivors of Totalitarianism: Returning POWS and the Reconstruction of Masculine Citizenship in West Germany, 1945–1955," in Hanna Schissler, ed., *The Miracle Years: A Cultural History of West Germany, 1949–1968* (Princeton: Princeton University Press, 2001), 57–82

Biro, Matthew, *Anselm Kiefer* (London: Phaidon, 2013)

Blauhorn, Kurt, "Alles soll jetzt besser werden," in Dieter Franck, ed., *Die fünfziger Jahre: Als das Leben wieder anfing* (Munich: R. Piper, 1981), 34–59

Bliersbach, Gerhard, *Nachkriegskino: Eine Psychohistorie des deutschen Nachkriegsfilms* (Giessen: Psychosozial-Verlag, 2014)

Bliersbach, Gerhard, *So grün war die Heide: Der deutsche Nachkriegsfilm in neuer Sicht* (Weinheim: Beltz Verlag, 1985)

Blöcker, Günter, *Kritisches Lesebuch: Literatur unserer Zeit in Probe und Bericht* (Hamburg: Leibnitz, 1962)

Blume, Friedrich, *Das Rasseproblem in der Musik: Entwurf zu einer Methodologie musikwissenschaftlicher Rasseforschung* (Wolfenbüttel: Georg Kallmeyer, 1939)

Blume, Friedrich, *Was ist Musik? Ein Vortrag* (Kassel: Bärenreiter, 1960)

Blumenberg, Hans-Christoph, *Das Leben geht weiter: Der letzte Film des Dritten Reiches* (Berlin: Rowohlt, 1993)

Blumer, Arnold, *Das dokumentarische Theater der sechziger Jahre in der Bundesrepublik Deutschland* (Meisenheim am Glan: Anton Hain, 1977)

Blumröder, Christoph von, "Karlheinz Stockhausen – 40 Jahre Elektronische Musik," *Archiv für Musikwissenschaft* 50 (1993): 309–23

Blumröder, Christoph von, "Musikalische Konzeptionen der siebziger Jahre," *Neuland/Ansätze zur Musik der Gegenwart Jahrbuch* 2 (1981/2): 183–205

Bohn, Volker, "Zum Hinscheiden der These vom Tod der Literatur," in W. Martin Lüdke, ed., *Nach dem Protest: Literatur im Umbruch* (Frankfurt am Main: edition suhrkamp, 1979), 241–68

Bohrer, Karl Heinz, *Jetzt: Geschichte meines Abenteuers mit der Phantasie* (Frankfurt am Main: Suhrkamp, 2017)

Bolín, N., "Neue Musik für Orchester nach 1945 in Nordrhein-Westfalen," in *Zeitklänge: Zur Neuen Musik in Nordrhein-Westfalen, 1946–1996* (Cologne: Gisela Schewe, [1996]), 21–33

Böll, Heinrich, *Als der Krieg ausbrach, Als der Krieg zu Ende war: Zwei Erzählungen* (Frankfurt am Main: Insel, 1962)

Böll, Heinrich, "Angst vor der Gruppe 47?" *Merkur* 19 (1965): 775–83

Böll, Heinrich, *Ansichten eines Clowns: Roman*, 3rd edn (Munich: DTV, 1967)

Böll, Heinrich, *Berichte zur Gesinnungslage der Nation* (Cologne: Kiepenheuer & Witsch, 1975)

Böll, Heinrich, *Briefe aus dem Krieg, 1939–1945*, 2 vols, ed. Jochen Schubert (Cologne: Kiepenheuer & Witsch, 2001)

Böll, Heinrich, "Der Zug war pünktlich" (1949), in Heinrich Böll, *1947 bis 1951*, (Cologne: Friedrich Middelhauve Verlag, 1964), 7–126

Böll, Heinrich, *Die Hoffnung ist wie ein wildes Tier: Der Briefwechsel mit Ernst-Adolf Kunz, 1945–1953*, ed. Herbert Hoven (Munich: DTV, 1997)

Böll, Heinrich, *Die verlorene Ehre der Katharina Blum, oder: Wie Gewalt entstehen und wohin sie führen kann: Eine Erzählung* (Cologne: Kiepenheuer & Witsch, 1974)

Böll, Heinrich, *Die Verwundung und andere frühe Erzählungen* (Bornheim: Lamuv, 1983)

Böll, Heinrich, *Ende einer Dienstfahrt* (Munich: DTV, 1969)

Böll, Heinrich, *Es kann einem bange werden: Schriften und Reden, 1976–1977* (Munich: DTV, 1985)

Böll, Heinrich, *Frankfurter Vorlesungen* (Cologne: Kiepenheuer & Witsch, 1966)

Böll, Heinrich, *Frauen vor Flusslandschaft: Roman in Dialogen und Selbstgesprächen* (Deutsche Buch-Gemeinschaft: Berlin, 1985)

Böll, Heinrich, *Fürsorgliche Belagerung: Roman* (Cologne: Kiepenheuer & Witsch, 1979)

Böll, Heinrich, *Gruppenbild mit Dame: Roman*, 3rd edn (Munich: DTV, 1974)

Böll, Heinrich, *Haus ohne Hüter: Roman* (Cologne: Kiepenheuer & Witsch, 1954)

Böll, Heinrich, *Man möchte manchmal wimmern wie ein Kind: Die Kriegstagebücher, 1943 bis 1945*, ed. René Böll (Cologne: Kiepenheuer & Witsch, 2017)

Böll, Heinrich, *Romane: Billard um halb zehn* [1959]; *Ansichten eines Clowns* [1963]; *Ende einer Dienstfahrt* [1966] (Stuttgart: Europäische Bildungsgemeinschaft Verlag, n.d.)

Böll, Heinrich, *Und sagte kein einziges Wort: Roman* (Cologne: Kiepenheuer & Witsch, 1953)

Böll, Heinrich, "Was soll aus dem Jungen bloss werden?" in Marcel Reich-Ranicki, ed., *Meine Schulzeit im Dritten Reich: Erinnerungen deutscher Schriftsteller* (Munich: DTV, 1984), 7–30

Böll, Heinrich, "Wo warst du, Adam?" (1951), in Heinrich Böll, *1947 bis 1951* (Cologne: Friedrich Middelhauve Verlag, 1964), 129–294

Bollenbeck, Georg, "Die fünfziger Jahre und die Künste: Kontinuität und Diskontinuität," in Georg Bollenbeck and Gerhard Kaiser, eds, *Die janusköpfigen 50er Jahre: Kulturelle Moderne und bildungsbürgerliche Semantik III* (Wiesbaden: Westdeutscher Verlag, 2000), 190–213

Bollmus, Reinhard, *Das Amt Rosenberg und seine Gegner: Zum Machtkampf im national-sozialistischen Herrschaftssystem* (Stuttgart: Deutsche Verlags-Anstalt, 1970)

Borchert, Wolfgang, *Das Gesamtwerk* (Hamburg: Rowohlt, 1949)

Borio, Gianmario, and Hermann Danuser, eds, *Im Zenit der Moderne: Die Internationalen Ferienkurse für Neue Musik Darmstadt, 1946–1966*, 4 vols (Freiburg im Breisgau: Rombach, 1997)

Bösch, Frank, "Die Krise als Chance: Die Neuformierung der Christdemokraten in den siebziger Jahren," in Konrad H. Jarausch, ed., *Das Ende der Zuversicht? Die siebziger Jahre als Geschichte* (Göttingen: Vandenhoeck & Ruprecht, 2008), 296–309

Botzat, Tatjana, Elisabeth Kiderlen, Frank Wolff, and Wolfgang Kraushaar, *Ein deutscher Herbst: Zustände 1977* (Frankfurt am Main: Verlag Neue Kritik, 1997)

Bracher, Karl Dietrich, *Die Auflösung der Weimarer Republik: Eine Studie zum Problem des Machtverfalls in der Demokratie*, 5th edn (Villingen: Ring-Verlag, 1971; 1st edn 1955)

Bracher, Karl Dietrich, "Stufen totalitärer Gleichschaltung: Die Befestigung der national-sozialistischen Herrschaft 1933/34," *Vierteljahrshefte für Zeitgeschichte* 4 (1956): 30–42

Bracher, Karl Dietrich, *The German Dictatorship: The Origins, Structure and Effects of National Socialism* (New York: Praeger, 1972)

Brändle, Werner, *Die dramatischen Stücke Martin Walsers: Variationen über das Elend des bürgerlichen Subjekts* (Stuttgart: Akademischer Verlag Hans Dieter Heinz, 1978)

Brauerhoch, Annette, *"Fräuleins" und GIs: Geschichte und Filmgeschichte* (Frankfurt am Main: Stroemfeld, 2006)

Braun, Hanns, *Theater in Deutschland* (Munich: Bruckmann, 1952)

Brenner, Michael, *Nach dem Holocaust: Juden in Deutschland, 1945–1950* (Munich: C.H. Beck, 1995)

Bressan, Susanne, and Martin Jander, "Gudrun Ensslin," in Wolfgang Kraushaar, ed., *Die RAF und der linke Terrorismus*, vol. 1 (Hamburg: Hamburger Edition, 2006), 398–429

Brinkmann, Reinhold, "Einleitung am Rande," in Carl Dalhaus, ed., *Die Wiener Schule heute* (Mainz: Schott, 1983), 9–18

Brockmann, Stephen, "Die Politik deutschen Leidens: Günter Grass' *Im Krebsgang*," in Bill Niven, ed., *Die Wilhelm Gustloff: Geschichte und Erinnerung eines Untergangs* (Halle: Mitteldeutscher Verlag, 2011), 285–304

Brockmann, Stephen, *German Literary Culture at the Zero Hour* (Rochester, NY: Camden House, 2004)

Broszat, Martin, ed., *Deutschlands Weg in die Diktatur: Internationale Konferenz zur Nationalsozialistischen Machtübernahme im Reichstagsgebäude zu Berlin: Referate und Diskussionen: Ein Protokoll* (Berlin: Siedler, 1983)

Broszat, Martin, "Zur Errichtung eines 'Hauses der Geschichte der Bundesrepublik Deutschland' in Bonn," in Hermann Graml and Klaus-Dietmar Henke, eds, *Nach Hitler: Der schwierige Umgang mit unserer Geschichte: Beiträge von Martin Broszat* (Munich: R. Oldenbourg, 1987), 304–9

Brown, Daniel Patrick, *The Beautiful Beast: The Life and Crimes of SS-Aufseherin Irma Grese* (Venture: Golden West Historical Publications, 1996)

Brückner, Peter, *Ulrike Meinhof und die deutschen Verhältnisse* (Berlin: Verlag Klaus Wagenbach, 1977)

Brumm, Dieter, "Sprachrohr der Volksseele? Die BILD-Zeitung," in Michael Wolf Thomas, ed., *Porträts der deutschen Presse: Politik und Profit* (Berlin: Verlag Volker Spiess, 1980), 127–43

Brumm, Dieter, "Sturmgeschütz der Demokratie? 'Der Spiegel'," in Michael Wolf Thomas, ed., *Porträts der deutschen Presse: Politik und Profit* (Berlin: Verlag Volker Spiess, 1980), 183–200

Brunhöber, Hanna, "Unterhaltungsmusik," in Wolfgang Benz, ed., *Die Geschichte der Bundesrepublik Deutschland, Band 4: Kultur* (Frankfurt am Main: Fischer Taschenbuch, 1989), 169–99

Buchka, Peter, *Augen kann man nicht kaufen: Wim Wenders und seine Filme* (Munich: Carl Hanser, 1983)

Bude, Heinz, *Deutsche Karrieren: Lebenskonstruktionen sozialer Aufsteiger aus der Flakhelfer-Generation* (Frankfurt am Main: Suhrkamp, 1987)

Burns, Rob, ed., *German Cultural Studies: An Introduction* (Oxford: Oxford University Press, 1996)

Buruma, Ian, *Year Zero: A History of 1945* (New York: Penguin, 2014)

Busch, Stefan, *"Und gestern, da hörte uns Deutschland": NS-Autoren in der Bundesrepublik: Kontinuität und Diskontinuität bei Friedrich Griese, Werner Beumelburg, Eberhard Wolfgang Möller und Kurt Ziesel* (Würzburg: Königshausen & Neumann, 1998)

Buselmeier, Michael, "Leben in Heidelberg," in W. Martin Lüdke, ed., *Nach dem Protest: Literatur im Umbruch* (Frankfurt am Main: edition suhrkamp, 1979), 42–84

Butin, Hubertus, *Zu Richters Oktober-Bildern* (Cologne: Verlag der Buchhandlung Walther König, 1991)

Buttig, Martin G., "Das grosse Treffen der Abstrakten: Zur 'documenta II' in Kassel," *Der Monat* 11 (August 1959): 75–82

Caldwell, Peter C. and Karrin Hanshew, *Germany Since 1945: Politics, Culture, and Society* (London: Bloomsbury, 2018)

Canaris, Volker, *Peter Zadek: Der Theatermann und Filmemacher* (Munich: Hanser, 1979)

Chabbi, Thekla, ed., *Martin Walser: "Ich würde heute ungern sterben": Interviews von 1978 bis 2016* (Reinbek: Rowohlt Taschenbuch-Verlag, 2018)

Chamberlin, Brewster S., ed., *Kultur auf Trümmern: Berliner Berichte der amerikanischen Information Control Section, Juli–Dezember 1945* (Stuttgart: Deutsche Verlags-Anstalt, 1979)

Chametzky, Peter, *Objects as History in Twentieth-Century German Art: Beckmann to Beuys* (Berkeley: University of California Press, 2010)

Classen, Christoph, *Bilder der Vergangenheit: Die Zeit des Nationalsozialismus im Fernsehen der Bundesrepublik Deutschland, 1955–1965* (Cologne: Böhlau, 1999)

Clemens, Gabriele, *Britische Kulturpolitik in Deutschland, 1945–1949: Literatur, Film, Musik und Theater* (Stuttgart: Franz Steiner, 1997)

Clemens, Gabriele, "Die britische Kulturpolitik in Deutschland: Musik, Theater, Film und Literatur," in Gabriele Clemens, ed., *Kulturpolitik im besetzten Deutschland, 1945–1949* (Stuttgart: Franz Steiner, 1994), 200–18

Cobler, Sebastian, "Das Gesetz gegen die 'Auschwitz-Lüge': Anmerkungen zu einem rechtspolitischen Ablasshandel," *Kritische Justiz* 18 (1985): 159–70

Collenberg, Carrie, "Dead Holger," in Gerrit-Jan Berendse and Ingo Cornils, eds, *Baader-Meinhof Returns: History and Cultural Memory of German Left-Wing Terrorism* (Amsterdam: Rodopi, 2008), 65–81

Conen, Hermann, *Formel-Komposition: Zu Karlheinz Stockhausens Musik der siebziger Jahre* (Mainz: Schott, 1991)

Connor, Ian, "The Integration of Refugees and Foreign Workers in the Federal Republic of Germany since the Second World War," *German Historical Institute London Bulletin* 22 (May 2000): 18–30

Conze, Werner, "Vom 'Pöbel' zum 'Proletariat': Sozialgeschichtliche Voraussetzungen für den Sozialismus in Deutschland," *Vierteljahrshefte für Sozial- und Wirtschaftsgeschichte* 41 (1954): 333–64

Cooke, Paul, "The Continually Suffering Nation? Cinematic Representations of German Victimhood," in Bill Niven, ed., *Germans as Victims: Remembering the Past in Contemporary Germany* (Houndmills: Palgrave Macmillan, 2006), 76–92

Cott, Jonathan, *Stockhausen: Conversations with the Composer* (New York: Simon and Schuster, 1973)

Custodis, Michael, *Die soziale Isolation der neuen Musik: Zum Kölner Musikleben nach 1945* (Stuttgart: Franz Steiner Verlag, 2004)

Custodis, Michael, "Friedrich Blumes Entnazifizierungsverfahren," *Die Musikforschung* 65 (2012): 1–24

Custodis, Michael, "'Unter Auswertung meiner Erfahrungen aktiv mitgestaltend': Zum Wirken von Wolfgang Steinecke bis 1950," in Albrecht Riethmüller, ed., *Deutsche Leitkultur Musik? Zur Musikgeschichte nach dem Holocaust* (Stuttgart: Franz Steiner, 2006), 145–62

Custodis, Michael and Friedrich Geiger, *Netzwerke der Entnazifizierung: Kontinuitäten im deutschen Musikleben am Beispiel von Werner Egk, Hilde und Heinrich Strobel* (Münster: Waxmann, 2013)

Dalhaus, Carl, "Die Krise des Experiments," in Ekkehard Jost, ed., *Komponieren heute: Ästhetische, soziologische und pädagogische Fragen* (Mainz: Schott, 1983), 80–94

Dahlhaus, Carl, ed., *Die Wiener Schule heute* (Mainz: Schott, 1983)

Dahrendorf, Ralf, *Gesellschaft und Demokratie in Deutschland* (Munich: Piper, 1968)

Daiber, Hans, *Deutsches Theater seit 1945: Bundesrepublik Deutschland, Deutsche Demokratische Republik, Österreich, Schweiz* (Stuttgart: Philipp Reclam jun., 1976)

Damus, Martin, *Kunst in der BRD, 1945–1990: Funktionen der Kunst in einer demokratisch verfassten Gesellschaft* (Reinbek: Rowohlt Taschenbuch Verlag, 1995)

Damus, Martin, "Moderne Kunst in Westdeutschland, 1945–1959: Versuche Vergangenheit und Gegenwart rückwärtsgewandt to bewältigen und die Moderne in Harmonie zu vollenden," in Gerda Breuer, ed., *Die Zähmung der Avantgarde: Zur Rezeption der Moderne in den 50er Jahren* (Basel: Stroemfeld Verlag, 1997), 25–41

Das Ende einer Welt: The End of a World: Oper in einem Akt von Wolfgang Hildesheimer: Opera in one act by Wolfgang Hildesheimer: Musik: Hans Werner Henze: Bühnenfassung/ Stage Version 1964/English Translation by Wesley Balk: Klavierauszug/Vocal Score von Heinz Moehn: Edition Schott 5673 (Mainz: B. Schott's Söhne, [1964])

De la Motte, Helga, and Barbara Barthelmes, eds, *Geschichte der Musik im 20. Jahrhundert: 1975–2000* (Laaber: Laaber, 2000)

Demant, Ebbo, *Von Schleicher zu Springer: Hans Zehrer als politischer Publizist* (Mainz: v. Hase & Koehler, 1971)

Demetz, Peter, *Die süsse Anarchie: Skizzen zur deutschen Literatur seit 1945* (Frankfurt am Main: Ullstein, 1973)

Der Neger im amerikanischen Leben (Frankfurt am Main: U.S.-Archivdienst, 1950)

Der Prozess gegen die Hauptkriegsverbrecher vor dem Internationalen Militärgerichtshof Nürnberg, 14. November 1945 – 1. Oktober 1946 (Nuremberg: Internationaler Militärgerichtshof, 1947; rp Munich: Delphin, 1984), 23 vols.

Deutsche Filmakademie mit dem Arbeitsinstitut für Kulturfilmschaffen (Berlin-Babelsberg: Max Hesses Verlag, [1938])

Deutsche Hochschulstatistik: Wintersemester 1932/33 (Berlin: von Struppe und Windler, 1933)

Dibelius, Ulrich, *Moderne Musik, 1945–1965: Voraussetzungen, Verlauf, Material*, 2nd edn (Munich: R. Piper, 1972; 1st edn 1966)

Dibelius, Ulrich, "Musik," in Wolfgang Benz, ed., *Die Geschichte der Bundesrepublik Deutschland, Band 4: Kultur* (Frankfurt am Main: Fischer Taschenbuch, 1989), 131–68

Dibelius, Ulrich, "Die zerschlagene Leier des Orpheus," in Ulrich Dibelius, ed., *Musik auf der Flucht vor sich selbst* (Munich: Carl Hanser, 1969), 116–32

Dibelius, Ulrich, A. Krause, A.D. McCredie, and H.M. Palm-Beulich, *Karl Amadeus Hartmann* (Tutzing: Hans Schneider, 1995)

Dibelius, Ulrich, and Frank Schneider, eds, *Neue Musik im geteilten Deutschland: [Band 1:] Dokumente aus den fünfziger Jahren* (Berlin: Henschel-Verlag, 1993)

Dibelius, Ulrich, and Frank Schneider, eds, *Neue Musik im geteilten Deutschland: Band 2: Dokumente aus den sechziger Jahren* (Berlin: Henschel-Verlag, 1995)

"Die ausgegrenzte Avantgarde: Karlheinz Stockhausen im Gespräch über '40 Jahre Bundesrepublik'," mit Gisela Gronemeyer, *Zeitschrift für Neue Musik* 33/4 (April 1990): 21–9

Diehm, Hermann, "Nachwort," in Andreas Flitner, ed., *Deutsches Geistesleben und Nationalsozialismus: Eine Vortragsreihe der Universität Tübingen* (Tübingen: Rainer Wunderlich/Hermann Leins, 1965), 237–40

Dietz, Gabriele, ed., *Klamm, Heimlich & Freunde: Die Siebziger Jahre* (Berlin: Elefanten Press, 1987)

Diller, Ansgar, "Öffentlich-rechtlicher Rundfunk," in Jürgen Wilke, ed., *Mediengeschichte der Bundesrepublik Deutschland* (Cologne: Böhlau, 1999), 146–66

Dillmann, Michael, *Heinz Hilpert: Leben und Werk* (Berlin: Edition Hentrich: 1990)

Dillmann-Kühn, Claudia, *Artur Brauner und die CCC: Filmgeschäft, Produktionsalltag, Studiogeschichte, 1946–1990* (Frankfurt am Main: Deutsches Filmmuseum, 1990)

Dillon, Brian, "Chaos and Cathode Rays," *New York Review of Books* (October 22, 2020): 14–16

Diner, Dan, "Zwischen Aporie und Apologie: Über Grenzen der Historisierbarkeit des Nationalsozialismus," in Dan Diner, ed., *Ist der Nationalsozialismus Geschichte? Zu Historisierung und Historikerstreit* (Frankfurt am Main: Fischer Taschenbuch, 1987), 62–73

Doane, Heike, *Gesellschaftspolitische Aspekte in Martin Walsers Kristlein-Trilogie: Halbzeit, Das Einhorn, Der Sturz* (Bonn: Bouvier Verlag Herbert Grundmann, 1978)

Döblin, Alfred, *Schicksalsreise: Bericht und Bekenntnis* (Frankfurt am Main: Josef Knecht, 1949)

Doll, Hans Peter, ed., *Stuttgarter Theaterarbeit, 1972–1985* (Stuttgart: Württ. Staatstheater, 1985)

Domentat, Tamara, *Coca Cola, Jazz & AFN: Berlin und die Amerikaner* (Berlin: Schwarzkopf und Schwarzkopf, 1995)

Domentat, Tamara, *"Hallo Fräulein": Deutsche Frauen und amerikanische Soldaten* (Berlin: Aufbau, 1998)

Dorn, Walter L., *Inspektionsreisen in der US-Zone: Notizen, Denkschriften und Erinnerungen*, ed. Lutz Niethammer (Stuttgart: Deutsche Verlags-Anstalt, 1975)

Dörrlamm, Rolf, "Junger Film – alte Filmhilfe," *Der Monat* 22 (July 1967): 49–56

Drüner, Ulrich, and Georg Günther, *Musik und "Drittes Reich": Fallbeispiele 1910 bis 1960 zu Herkunft, Höhepunkt und Nachwirkungen des Nationalsozialismus in der Musik* (Vienna: Böhlau, 2012)

Dunkhase, Jan Eike, *Werner Conze: Ein deutscher Historiker im 20. Jahrhundert* (Göttingen: Vandenhoeck und Ruprecht, 2010)

Dürr, Alfred, "Weltblatt und Heimatzeitung: Die 'Süddeutsche Zeitung'," in Michael Wolf Thomas, ed., *Porträts der deutschen Presse: Politik und Profit* (Berlin: Verlag Volker Spiess, 1980), 63–79

Dutschke, Rudi, *Jeder hat sein Leben ganz zu leben: Die Tagebücher, 1963–1979*, ed. Gretchen Dutschke (Cologne: Kiepenheuer & Witsch, 2003)

Eberhard, Fritz, *Der Rundfunkhörer und sein Programm: Ein Beitrag zur empirischen Sozialforschung* (Berlin: Colloquium, 1962)

Eberle, Gottfried, "Die Götter wechseln, die Religion bleibt die gleiche: Neue Musik in Westdeutschland nach 1945," in Hans-Werner Heister and Dietrich Stern, eds, *Musik 50er Jahre* (Berlin: Argument-Verlag, 1980), 34–49

Eggebrecht, Axel, ed., *Die zornigen alten Männer: Gedanken über Deutschland seit 1945* (Reinbek: Rowohlt, 1979)

Egk, Werner, *Die Zeit wartet nicht: Künstlerisches, Zeitgeschichtliches, Privates aus meinem Leben* (Mainz: Schott, 2001)

Eickhoff, Thomas, "'Mit Sozialismus und Sachertorte ...' – Entnazifizierung und musikpolitische Verhaltensmuster nach 1945 in Österreich," in Albrecht Riethmüller, ed., *Deutsche Leitkultur Musik? Zur Musikgeschichte nach dem Holocaust* (Stuttgart: Franz Steiner, 2006), 85–99

Eimert, Herbert, *Grundlagen der musikalischen Reihentechnik* (Vienna: Universal Edition, 1964)

Elger, Dietmar, *Gerhard Richter: A Life in Painting* (Chicago: Chicago University Press, 2002)

Elkins, Caroline, *Legacy of Violence: A History of the British Empire* (New York: Alfred A. Knopf, 2022)

Elsaesser, Thomas, *German Cinema – Terror and Trauma: Cultural Memory since 1945* (New York: Routledge, 2014)

Emre, Merve, "The Meticulous One," *New York Review of Books* (October 22, 2020): 24–6

Endres, Elisabeth, *Die Literatur der Adenauerzeit* (Munich: Verlag Steinhausen, 1980)

Engelmann, Bernt, *Meine Freunde – die Millionäre: Ein Beitrag zur Wohlstandsgesellschaft nach eigenen Erlebnissen*, 4th edn (Darmstadt: Franz Schneekluth, 1964)

Ensslin, Gudrun, *"Zieht den Trennungsstrich, jede Minute": Briefe an ihre Schwester Christiane und ihren Bruder Gottfried aus dem Gefängnis, 1972–1973*, ed. Christiane Ensslin and Gottfried Ensslin (Hamburg: Konkret Literatur Verlag, 2005)

Enzensberger, Hans Magnus, *Das Verhör von Habana* (Frankfurt am Main: Suhrkamp, 1970)

Enzensberger, Hans Magnus, *Einzelheiten I: Bewusstseins-Industrie* (Frankfurt am Main: Suhrkamp, 1969)

Enzensberger, Hans Magnus, *Mittelmass und Wahn: Gesammelte Zerstreuungen* (Frankfurt: Suhrkamp, 1988)

Enzensberger, Hans Magnus, *Politische Brosamen*, 2nd edn (Frankfurt am Main: Suhrkamp, 1984; 1st edn 1982)

Enzensberger, Hans Magnus, "Wilhelm Meister auf Blech getrommelt," *Frankfurter Hefte* 14 (1959): 833–6

Enzensberger, Ulrich, *Die Jahre der Kommune I: Berlin, 1967–1969* (Cologne: Kiepenheuer und Witsch, 2004)

Etzemüller, Thomas, *Sozialgeschichte als politische Geschichte: Werner Conze und die Neuorientierung der westdeutschen Geschichtswissenschaft nach 1945* (Munich: R. Oldenbourg, 2001)

Evans, Richard J., *The Coming of the Third Reich* (New York: Penguin, 2004)

Evans, Richard J., "The New Nationalism and the Old History: Perspectives on the West German Historikerstreit," *Journal of Modern History* 59 (1987): 761–97

Evans, Richard J., "Whiter Washing," *London Review of Books* (June 6, 2019): 19–20

Evers, Hans Gerhard, ed., *Darmstädter Gespräch 1950: "Das Menschenbild in unserer Zeit"*, 2nd edn (Darmstadt: Neue Darmstädter Verlagsanstalt, [1951])

Falter, Jürgen W., *Hitlers Parteigenossen: Die Mitglieder der NSDAP, 1919–1945* (Frankfurt am Main: Campus: 2020)

Fassbinder, Rainer Werner, *Der Müll, die Stadt und der Tod* (Frankfurt am Main: Verlag der Autoren, 1981)

Fassbinder, Rainer Werner, "Imitation of Life: Über die Filme von Douglas Sirk," *Fernsehen + Film*, 9 (February 1971): 8–13

Faulstich, Werner, "'Amerikanisierung' als kultureller Mehrwert: Amerikanische Rocksongs, Bestseller und Kinofilme in der Bundesrepublik der fünfziger, sechziger und siebziger Jahre," in Alexander Stephan and Jochen Vogt, eds, *America on my Mind: Zur Amerikanisierung der deutschen Kultur seit 1945* (Munich: Wilhelm Fink, 2006), 153–71

Faulstich, Werner, "Auf dem Weg zur totalen Mediengesellschaf: Kleiner Überblick über Daten, Zahlen, Trends der 80er Jahre," in Christian W. Thomsen, ed., *Aufbruch in die Neunziger: Ideen, Entwicklungen, Perspektiven der achtziger Jahre* (Cologne: DuMont, 1991), 97–141

Faulstich, Werner, ed., *Die Kultur der achtziger Jahre* (Munich: Wilhelm Fink, 2005)

Faulstich, Werner, ed., *Die Kultur der fünfziger Jahre* (Munich: Wilhelm Fink, 2002)

Faulstich, Werner, ed., *Die Kultur der sechziger Jahre* (Munich: Wilhelm Fink, 2003)

Faulstich, Werner, ed., *Die Kultur der siebziger Jahre* (Munich: Wilhelm Fink, 2004)

Faust, Wolfgang Max, and Gerd de Vries, *Hunger nach Bildern: Deutsche Malerei der Gegenwart*, 4th edn (Cologne: DuMont Buchverlag, 1987)

Fehrenbach, Heide, *Cinema in Democratizing Germany: Reconstructing National Identity after Hitler* (Chapel Hill: University of North Carolina Press, 1995)

Felder, David, "An Interview with Karlheinz Stockhausen," *Perspectives of New Music* 16, no. 1 (Autumn–Winter 1977): 85–101

Fer, Briony, "Chronotechniken: Richters Familienbilder," in Sheena Wagstaff and Benjamin H. D. Buchloh, eds, *Gerhard Richter: Malerei* (Cologne: Walther König, 2020), 54–67

Ferbers, Julia, Anke Geidel, Miriam Lüttgemann, and Sören Schultz, eds, *Claus Peymann: Mord und Totschlag: Theater/Leben*, 2nd edn (Berlin: Alexander Verlag, 2017)

Fest, Joachim C., *Das Gesicht des Dritten Reiches: Profile eine totalitären Herrschaft* (Munich: R. Piper, 1964)

Fest, Joachim, "Glückliche Jahre," in Marcel Reich-Ranicki, ed., *Meine Schulzeit im Dritten Reich: Erinnerungen deutscher Schriftsteller* (Munich: DTV, 1984), 183–96

Fest, Joachim C., *Hitler: Eine Biographie* (Frankfurt am Main: Propyläen, 1973)

Fischer, Heinz-Dietrich, *Reeducations- und Pressepolitik unter britischem Besatzungsstatus: Die Zonenzeitung "Die Welt," 1946–1950: Konzeption, Artikulation und Rezeption* (Düsseldorf: Droste, 1978)

Fischer-Defoy, Christine, *Kunst, Macht, Politik: Die Nazifizierung der Kunst- und Musikhochschulen in Berlin* (Berlin: Elefanten Press, [1988])

Flammer, Ernst H., *Politisch engagierte Musik als kompositorisches Problem, dargestellt am Beispiel von Luigi Nono und Hans Werner Henze* (Baden-Baden: Valentin Koerner, 1981)

Flemming, Thomas, and Bernd Ulrich, *Vor Gericht: Deutsche Prozesse in Ost und West nach 1945* (Berlin: be.bra, 2005)

Flottau, Heiko, "Liberal auf schwankendem Boden: Die 'Frankfurter Rundschau'," in Michael Wolf Thomas, ed., *Porträts der deutschen Presse: Politik und Profit* (Berlin: Verlag Volker Spiess, 1980), 97–107

Franck, Dieter, ed., *Die fünfziger Jahre: Als das Leben wieder anfing* (Munich: R. Piper, 1981)

Franklin, Ruth, "A Word, A Corpse: How Paul Celan Reconceived Language for a Post-Holocaust World," *New Yorker* (November 3, 2020): 71–5

Franklin, Ruth, "Salka the Salonière: On the Queen of Hollywood's Émigrés," *Harper's* (January 2020): 86–90

Frederik, Hans, *Lebendiges Amerika: Amerika, wie es wirklich ist* (Bühl: Konkordia, 1959)

Frei, Norbert, "Der Frankfurter Auschwitz-Prozess und die deutsche Zeitgeschichtsforschung," in *Auschwitz: Gechichte, Rezeption und Wirkung*, 2nd edn (Frankfurt am Main: 1997), 123–38

Frei, Norbert, "Die Presse," in Wolfgang Benz, ed., *Die Geschichte der Bundesrepublik Deutschland, Band 4: Kultur* (Frankfurt am Main: Fischer Taschenbuch, 1989), 370–416

Frei, Norbert, "Hörfunk und Fernsehen," in Wolfgang Benz, ed., *Die Geschichte der Bundesrepublik Deutschland, Band 4: Kultur* (Frankfurt am Main: Fischer Taschenbuch, 1989), 417–63

Frei, Norbert, *1945 und Wir: Das Dritte Reich im Bewusstsein der Deutschen* (Munich: C.H. Beck, 2005)

Friedländer, Saul, "Überlegungen zur Historisierung des Nationalsozialismus," in Dan Diner, ed., *Ist der Nationalsozialismus Geschichte? Zu Historisierung und Historikerstreit* (Frankfurt am Main: Fischer Taschenbuch, 1987), 34–50

Friedländer, Saul, *Pius XII. Und das Dritte Reich: Eine Dokumentation* (Reinbek: Rowohlt, 1965)

Friedländer, Saul, *Where Memory Leads: My Life* (New York: Other Press, 2016)

Friedrich, Jörg, *Die kalte Amnestie: NS-Täter in der Bundesrepublik* (Frankfurt am Main: Fischer Taschenbuch, 1984)

Frisius, Rudolf, *Karlheinz Stockhausen: Einführung in das Gesamtwerk: Gespräche mit Karlheinz Stockhausen* (Mainz: Schott, 1996)

Fritsche, Christiane, *Vergangenheitsbewältigung im Fernsehen: Westdeutsche Filme über den Nationalsozialismus in den 1950er und 1960er Jahren* (Munich: Martin Meidenbauer Verlagsbuchhandlung, 2003)

Fuchs, Ralf-Peter, "Neue Menschen und Kultur der Moderne: Der Jazz und sein Publikum in der deutschen Nachkriegspresse, 1945–1953," in Wolfram Knauer, ed., *Jazz und Gesellschaft: Sozialgeschichtliche Aspekte des Jazz* (Hofheim: Wolke Verlag, 2002), 17–40

Führer, Karl Christian, "Erfolg und Macht von Axel Springers 'Bild'-Zeitung in den 1950er Jahren," *Zeithistorische Studien/Studies in Contemporary History* 4 (2007): 311–36

Fulda, Bernhard, *Emil Nolde: The Artist during the Third Reich* (Munich: Prestel, 2019)

Fulda, Bernhard, "Myth-making in Hitler's Shadow: The Transfiguration of Emil Nolde after 1945," in Jan Rüger and Nikolaus Wachsmann, eds, *Rewriting German History: New Perspectives on Modern Germany* (Houndmills: Palgrave Macmillan, 2015), 177–94

Fulda, Bernhard, and Aya Soika, "Emil Nolde and the National Socialist Dictatorship," in Olaf Peters, ed., *Degenerate Art: The Attack on Modern Art in Nazi Germany, 1937* (Munich: Prestel, 2014), 186–95

Gäbler, Bernd, "Die andere Zeitung: Die Sonderstellung der 'Frankfurter Rundschau' in der deutschen Nachkriegspublizistik," in Lutz Hachmeister and Friedemann Siering, eds, *Die Herren Journalisten: Die Elite der deutschen Presse nach 1945* (Munich: C.H. Beck, 2002), 146–64

Gaiser, Gerd, *Eine Stimme hebt an: Roman* (Munich: Carl Hanser, 1950)

Gaiser, Gerd, *Reiter am Himmel: Gedichte* (Munich: Albert Langen/Georg Müller, 1941)

Gaiser, Gerd, *Schlussball: Aus den schönen Tagen der Stadt Neu-Spuhl*, 6th edn (Munich: Carl Hanser, 1958)

Garbe, Detlef, "Äusserliche Abkehr, Erinnerungsverweigerung und 'Vergangenheits-bewältigung': Der Umgang mit dem Nationalsozialismus in der frühen Bundesrepublik," in Axel Schildt and Arnold Sywottek, eds, *Modernisierung im Wiederaufbau: Die westdeutsche Gesellschaft der 50er Jahre* (Bonn: J.H.W. Dietz Nachf., 1993), 693–716

Gebhardt, Miriam, *ALICE im Niemandsland: Wie die deutsche Frauenbewegung die Frauen verlor* (Munich: Deutsche Verlags-Anstalt, 2012)

Gehlen, Arnold, "Soziologischer Kommentar zur modernen Malerei," *Merkur* 12 (1958): 301–15

Geiger, Friedrich, "'Can Be Employed': Walter Abendroth im Musikleben der Bundesrepublik," in Albrecht Riethmüller, ed., *Deutsche Leitkultur Musik? Zur Musikgeschichte nach dem Holocaust* (Stuttgart: Franz Steiner, 2006), 131–42

Geisler, Michael E., "Nazis into Democrats? The *Internationale Frühschoppen* and the Case of Werner Höfer," *Tel Aviver Jahrbuch für deutsche Geschichte* 31 (2003): 231–52

Geitel, Klaus, *Hans Werner Henze* (Berlin: Rembrandt, 1968)

Gerlach, Ingeborg, *Abschied von der Revolte: Studien zur deutschsprachigen Literatur der siebziger Jahre* (Würzburg: Königshausen & Neumann, 1994)

Ginzel, Günther Bernd, "Phasen der Etablierung einer Jüdischen Gemeinde in der Kölner Trümmerlandschaft, 1945–1949," in Jutta Bohnke-Kollwitz, Willehad Paul Eckert, Franz Golczewski, and Hermann Greive, eds, *Köln und das rheinische Judentum: Festschrift Germania Judaica, 1959–1984* (Cologne: J.P. Bachem, 1984), 445–61

Glaser, Hermann, *Deutsche Kultur, 1945–2000* (Munich: Carl Hanser, 1997)

Glaser, Hermann, *Die Kulturgeschichte der Bundesrepublik Deutschland, vol 1: Zwischen Kapitulation und Währungsreform, 1945–1948* (Frankfurt am Main: Fischer Taschenbuch, 1990)

Glaser, Hermann, *Die Kulturgeschichte der Bundesrepublik Deutschland, vol 2: Zwischen Grundgesetz und Grosser Koalition, 1949–1967* (Fischer Taschenbuch, 1990)

Glaser, Hermann, *Die Kulturgeschichte der Bundesrepublik Deutschland, vol 3: Zwischen Protest und Anpassung, 1968–1989* (Frankfurt am Main: Fischer Taschenbuch, 1990)

Glaser, Hermann, "Schöner Leben: Die Kultur der 50er Jahre," in Gerda Breuer, ed., *Die Zähmung der Avantgarde: Zur Rezeption der Moderne in den 50er Jahren* (Basel: Stroemfeld Verlag, 1997), 147–71

Gödde, Christoph, and Thomas Sprecher, eds, *Theodor W. Adorno Thomas Mann: Briefwechsel, 1943–1955* (Frankfurt am Main: Fischer Taschenbuch, 2003)

Goedde, Petra, *GIs and Germans: Culture, Gender, and Foreign Relations, 1945–1949* (New Haven and London: Yale University Press, 2003)

Goertz, Heinrich, *Gustaf Gründgens in Selbstzeugnissen und Bilddokumenten* (Reinbek: Rowohlt Taschenbuch, 1982)

Gopnik, Adam, "System Upgrade: Can We Find a Better Model of Government than Liberal Democracy?" *New Yorker* (September 12, 2022): 64–9

Görtemaker, Manfred, and Christoph Safferling, *Die Akte Rosenburg: Das Bundesjustizministerium und die NS-Zeit* (Munich: C.H. Beck, 2016)

Görtz, Franz Josef, "Apokalypse im Roman: Günter Grass' Die Rättin," *The German Quarterly* 63 (Summer–Autumn 1990): 462–70

Gottwald, Clytus, "Deutsche Musikwissenschaft: Ein Bericht," in Ulrich Dibelius, ed., *Verwaltete Musik: Analyse und Kritik eines Zustands* (Munich: Carl Hanser, 1971), 68–81

Gottwald, Clytus, "Neue Musik in Stuttgart, 1980–1990," in Martin Thrun, ed., *Neue Musik seit den achtziger Jahren: Eine Dokumentation zum deutschen Musikleben*, vol. 2 (Regensburg: ConBrio Verlagsgesellschaft, 1994), 171–6

Grass, Günter, *Beim Häuten der Zwiebel* (Göttingen: Steidl, 2006)

Grass, Günter, *Die Blechtrommel: Roman*, 13th edn (Neuwied: Luchterhand, 1968)

Grass, Günter, *Hundejahre: Roman* (Neuwied: Hermann Luchterhand, 1963)

Grass, Günter, *Im Krebsgang: Eine Novelle* (Göttingen: Steidl, 2002)

Grass, Günter, *Katz und Maus: Eine Novelle* (Reinbek: rororo Taschenbuch, 1964)

Grass, Günter, *Örtlich betäubt: Roman* (Neuwied: Hermann Luchterhand, 1969)

Greffrath, Bettina, *Gesellschaftsbilder der Nachkriegszeit: Deutsche Spielfilme, 1945–1949* (Pfaffenweiler: Centaurus-Verlagsgesellschaft, 1995)

Gregor, Neil, *Haunted City: Nuremberg and the Nazi Past* (New Haven and London: Yale University Press, 2008)

Greif, Hans-Jürgen, *Zum modernen Drama: Martin Walser, Wolfgang Bauer, Rainer Werner Fassbinder, Siegfried Lenz, Wolfgang Hildesheimer* (Bonn: Bouvier Verlag Herbert Grundmann, 1973)

Griffel, Margaret Ross, *Operas in German: A Dictionary* (Lanham: Rowman & Littlefield, 2018)

Grob, Norbert, *Wenders* (Berlin: Wissenschaftsverlag Volker Spiess, 1991)

Grob, Norbert, Hans Helmut Prinzler, and Eric Rentschler, eds, *Neuer deutscher Film* (Stuttgart: Philipp Reclam jun. GmbH, 2012)

Gronemeyer, Gisela, "Neue Musik gegen den Strich: Experiment und Alternative," in *Zeitklänge: Zur Neuen Musik in Nordrhein-Westfalen, 1946–1996* (Cologne: Gisela Schewe, [1996]), 55–67

Grossmann, Atina, *Jews, Germans, and Allies: Close Encounters in Occupied Germany* (Princeton: Princeton University Press, 2007)

Grün, Rita von der, "'Wer macht das Programm': Rundfunkentwicklung nach 1945," in Hans-Werner Heister and Dietrich Stern, eds, *Musik 50er Jahre* (Berlin: Argument-Verlag, 1980), 25–33

Grützbach, Frank, ed., *Heinrich Böll: Freies Geleit für Ulrike Meinhof: Ein Artikel und seine Folgen* (Cologne: Kiepenheuer & Witsch, 1972)

Gundwin, Peter, "Und wieder unterliegen wir neuen Einflüssen," *Frankfurter Hefte* 11 (1956): 798–801

Haar, Ingo, "Friedrich Valjavec: Ein Historikerleben zwischen den Wiener Schiedssprüchen und der Dokumentation der Vertreibung," in Lucia Scherzberg, ed., *Theologie und Vergangenheitsbewältigung: Eine kritische Bestandsaufnahme im interdisziplinären Vergleich* (Paderborn: Ferdinand Schöningh, 2005), 103–19

Haar, Ingo, *Historiker im Nationalsozialismus: Deutsche Geschichtswissenschaft und der "Volkstumskampf" im Osten*, 2nd edn (Göttingen: Vandenhoeck & Ruprecht, 2002)

Haar, Ingo, "'Volksgeschichte' und Königsberger Milieu: Forchungsprogramme zwischen Weimarer Revisionspolitik und nationalsozialistischer Vernichtungsplanung," in Hartmut Lehmann and Otto Gerhard Oexle, eds, *Nationalsozialismus in den Kulturwissenschaften*, vol. 1 (Göttingen: Vandenhoeck & Ruprecht, 2004), 169–209

Haas, Michael, *Forbidden Music: The Jewish Composers Banned by the Nazis* (New Haven and London: Yale University Press, 2013)

Habe, Hans, *Im Jahre Null: Ein Beitrag zur Geschichte der deutschen Presse* (Munich: Kurt Desch, 1966)

Habermas, Jürgen, *Kleine Politische Schriften (I–IV)* (Frankfurt am Main: Suhrkamp, 1981)

Hachmeister, Lutz, "Ein deutsches Nachrichtenmagazin: Der frühe 'Spiegel' und sein NS-Personal," in Lutz Hachmeister and Friedemann Siering, eds, *Die Herren Journalisten: Die Elite der deutschen Presse nach 1945* (Munich: C.H. Beck, 2002), 87–120

Hachmeister, Lutz, *Schleyer: Eine deutsche Geschichte* (Munich: C.H. Beck, 2004)

Hadek, Nadja, *Vergangenheitsbewältigung im Werk Martin Walsers* (Augsburg: Wissner-Verlag, 2006)

Haftmann, Werner, *Emil Nolde: Ungemalte Bilder* (Cologne: M. DuMont Schauberg, 1963)

Haftmann, Werner, *Skizzenbuch: Zur Kultur der Gegenwart: Reden und Aufsätze* (Munich: Prestel, 1960)

Hake, Sabine, *German National Cinema*, 2nd edn (London: Routledge, 2008)

Hakemi, Sara, and Thomas Hecken, "Die Warenhausbrandstifter," in Wolfgang Kraushaar, ed., *Die RAF und der linke Terrorismus*, vol. 1 (Hamburg: Hamburger Edition, 2006), 316–31

Hamann, Brigitte, *Winifred Wagner oder Hitlers Bayreuth* (Munich: Piper, 2002)

Hamilton, Charles, *The Hitler Diaries: Fakes that Fooled the World* (Lexington: The University Press of Kentucky, 1991)

Hammer, Jörg, "Ein Student berichtet," *Junge Musik* 8 (1957): 190–2

Handke, Silvia, *Präsenz und Dynamik regionaler Musikkulturen in den Sendekonzepten des WDR-Hörfunks* (Berlin: Merseburger, 1997)

Hansen, Miriam, "Dossier on *Heimat*," *New German Critique* 36 (October 1986): 3–6

Hanshew, Karrin, *Terror and Democracy in West Germany* (New York: Cambridge University Press, 2012)

Harenberg, Karl-Heinz, "Aus Bonn für 'Deutschland': 'Die Welt'," in Michael Wolf Thomas, ed., *Porträts der deutschen Presse: Politik und Profit* (Berlin: Verlag Volker Spiess, 1980), 109–26

Harlan, Veit, *Unter dem Schatten meiner Filme: Selbstbiographie*, ed. H.C. Oppermann (Gütersloh: Sigbert Mohn, 1966)

Harris, Robert, *Selling Hitler: The Story of the Hitler Diaries* (London: Faber and Faber, 1986)

Hartmann, Karl-Heinz, "Romane und Erzählungen der fünfziger und sechziger Jahre (BRD)," in Horst Albert Glaser, ed., *Deutsche Literatur zwischen 1945 und 1995* (Berne: Paul Haupt, 1997), 287–308

Haselberg, Peter von, *Schuldgefühle: Postnazistische Mentalitäten in der frühen Bundesrepublik* (Frankfurt am Main: Campus, 2020)

Hassenkamp, Oliver, *Der Sieg nach dem Krieg: Die gute schlechte Zeit* (Munich: Herbig, [1983])

Heide, Mathias von der, and Christian Wagner, "'Weiter rechts als die CDU': Das erste Jahrzehnt der 'Zeit'," in Lutz Hachmeister and Friedemann Siering, eds, *Die Herren Journalisten: Die Elite der deutschen Presse nach 1945* (Munich: C.H. Beck, 2002), 165–84

Heineman, Elizabeth, "The Hour of the Woman: Memories of Germany's 'Crisis Years' and West German National Identity," in Hanna Schissler, ed., *The Miracle Years: A Cultural History of West Germany, 1949–1968* (Princeton: Princeton University Press, 2001), 21–56

Heins, Laura, *Nazi Film Melodrama* (Urbana: University of Illinois Press, 2013)

Heister, Hans-Werner, ed., *Geschichte der Musik im 20. Jahrhundert: 1945–1975* (Laaber: Laaber 2005)

Helbig, Louis Ferdinand, *Der ungeheure Verlust: Flucht und Vertreibung in der deutschsprachigen Belletristik der Nachkriegszeit* (Wiesbaden: Otto Harrassowitz, 1988)

Heldt, Guido, "'Hallo Fräulein!' – Amerikanische Popularmusik im westdeutschen Nachkriegsfilm," in Albrecht Riethmüller, ed., *Deutsche Leitkultur Musik? Zur Musikgeschichte nach dem Holocaust* (Stuttgart: Franz Steiner, 2006), 199–220

Hell, Julia, "Loyal Dissidents and Stasi Poets: Sascha Anderson, Christa Wolf, and the Incomplete Project of GDR Research," *German Politics & Society* 20 (Winter 2002): 82–118

Hembus, Joe, *Der deutsche Film kann gar nicht besser sein: Ein Pamphlet von gestern, eine Abrechnung von heute* (Munich: Rogner & Bernhard, 1981)

Hemken, Kai-Uwe, *Gerhard Richter, 18. Oktober 1977: Eine Kunstmonographie* (Frankfurt am Main: Insel Taschenbuch, 1998)

Hennig, Albert, "Das Judentum in der Malerei," in Theodor Fritsch, ed., *Handbuch der Judenfrage: Die wichtigsten Tatsachen zur Beurteilung des jüdischen Volkes*, 38th edn (Leipzig: Hammer-Verlag, 1935), 352–5

Henscheid, Eckhard, *Erledigte Fälle: Bilder deutscher Menschen* (Frankfurt am Main: Zweitausendeins, 1986)

Henscheid, Eckhard, "Unser Lautester demissioniert: Marcel Reich-Ranicki – auf diesen Fels baute Gott seine Literaturabteilung," in Hermannus Pfeiffer, ed., *Die FAZ: Nachforschungen über ein Zentralorgan* (Cologne: Pahl-Rugenstein, 1988), 174–82

Henscheid, Eckhard, Joachim Kaiser, Moritz Schwarz, Heimo Schwilk, Thorsten Thaler, Martin Walser, and Günter Zehm, *Der Streit um Martin Walser* (Berlin: Junge Freiheit Verlag, 2002)

Hensel, Georg, *Spiel's noch einmal: Das Theater der achtziger Jahre*, 2nd edn (Frankfurt am Main: Suhrkamp, 1991)

Hensel, Georg, *Theater der Zeitgenossen: Stücke und Autoren* (Frankfurt am Main: Ullstein, 1972)

Henze, Hans Werner, *Musik und Politik: Schriften und Gespräche, 1955–1984*, ed. Jens Brockmeier (Munich: DTV, 1984)

Henze, Hans Werner, *Reiselieder mit böhmischen Quinten: Autobiographische Mitteilungen, 1926–1995* (Frankfurt am Main: S. Fischer, 1996)

Herbert, Ulrich, "NS-Eliten in der Bundesrepublik," in Wilfried Loth and Bernd A. Rusinek, eds, *Verwandlungspolitik: NS-Eliten in der westdeutschen Nachkriegsgesellschaft* (Frankfurt am Main: Campus, 1998), 93–115

Herbert, Ulrich, and Karin Hunn, "Guest Workers and Policy on Guest Workers in the Federal Republic," in Hanna Schissler, ed., *The Miracle Years: A Cultural History of West Germany, 1949–1968* (Princeton: Princeton University Press, 2001), 187–218

Herf, Jeffrey, *Divided Memory: The Nazi Past in the Two Germanys* (Cambridge, MA: Harvard University Press, 1997)

Herf, Jeffrey, "The 'Holocaust' Reception in West Germany: Right, Center, and Left," in Anson Rabinbach and Jack Zipes, eds, *Germans and Jews since the Holocaust: The Changing Situation in West Germany* (New York: Holmes & Meier, 1986), 208–33

Hermand, Jost, "Der Kalte Krieg in der Literatur: Über die Schwierigkeiten bei der Rückeingliederung deutscher Exilautoren und autorinnen nach 1945," in Hans-Erich Volkmann, ed., *Ende des Dritten Reiches – Ende des Zweiten Weltkriegs: Eine perspektivische Rückschau* (Munich: Piper, 1995), 581–605

Hermand, Jost, *Die Kultur der Bundesrepublik Deutschland, 1965–85* (Munich: Nymphenburger Verlagsanstalt, 1988)

Hermand, Jost, *Kultur im Wiederaufbau: Die Bundesrepublik Deutschland, 1945–1965* (Munich: Nymphenburger Verlagsanstalt, 1986)

Herwig, Malte, *Die Flakhelfer: Eine gebrochene Generation* (Munich: Pantheon, 2014)

Herz, Thomas A., "Der Fassbinderstreit – ein Beitrag zur politischen Kultur(-forschung) der Bundesrepublik," in Thomas A. Herz and Michael Schwab-Trapp, eds, *Umkämpfte Vergangenheit: Diskurse über den Nationalsozialismus seit 1945* (Opladen: Westdeutscher Verlag, 1997), 167–92

Herzogenrath, Wulf, and Gabriele Lueg, eds, *Die 60er Jahre: Kölns Weg zur Kunstmetropole: Vom Happening zum Kunstmarkt* (Cologne: Kölnischer Kunstverein, 1986)

Heuss, Theodor, *Hitlers Weg: Eine Schrift aus dem Jahre 1932*, ed. Eberhard Jäckel (Tübingen: Wunderlich 1968; 1st pub. 1932)

Hickethier, Kurt, *Geschichte des deutschen Fernsehens* (Stuttgart: J.B. Metzler, 1998)

Hilberg, Frank, and Harry Vogt, eds, *Musik in der Zeit 1951–2001: 50 Jahre Neue Musik im WDR: Essays – Erinnerungen – Dokumentation* (Hofheim: Wolke Verlag, 2002)

Hillgruber, Andreas, *Zweierlei Untergang: die Zerschlagung des Deutschen Reiches und das Ende des europäischen Judentums* (Berlin: Siedler, 1986)

Hirsch, Helga, *Endlich wieder leben: Die fünfziger Jahre im Rückblick von Frauen* (Munich: Siedler, 2012)

Hochhuth, Rolf, *Der Stellvertreter: Ein christliches Trauerspiel* (Reinbek: Rowohlt, 1998; 1st edn 1963)

Hochhuth, Rolf, *Eine Liebe in Deutschland* (Reinbek: Rowohlt, 1978)

Hochhuth, Rolf, *Juristen: Drei Akte für sieben Spieler* (Reinbek: Rowohlt, 1979)

Hochhuth, Rolf, *Wessis in Weimar: Szenen aus einem besetzten Land*, 3rd edn (Berlin: Volk & Welt, 1993)

Hockerts, Hans Günter, "Gab es eine Stunde Null? Die politische, gesellschaftliche und wirtschaftliche Situation in Deutschland nach der bedingungslosen Kapitulation," in Stefan Krimm and Wieland Zirbs, eds, *Nachkriegszeiten – Die Stunde Null als Realität und Mythos in der deutschen Geschichte* (Munich: Bayerischer Schulbuch-Verlag, 1996), 119–56

Hodenberg, Christina von, "Die Journalisten und der Aufbruch zur kritischen Öffentlichkeit," in Ulrich Herbert, ed., *Wandlungsprozesse in Westdeutschland: Belastung, Integration, Liberalisierung, 1945–1980* (Göttingen: Wallstein, 2002), 278–311

Hodenberg, Christina von, *Konsens und Krise: Eine Geschichte der westdeutschen Medienöffentlichkeit, 1945–1973* (Göttingen: Wallstein, 2006)

Höfer, Werner, "Mein Radio: Erinnerungen – Erfahrungen – Erwartungen," *Der Monat* 23 (March 1971): 56–9

Hoffmann, Hilmar, and Heinrich Klotz, eds, *Die Sechziger: Die Kultur unseres Jahrhunderts* (Düsseldorf: Econ, 1987)

Höfig, Willi, *Der deutsche Heimatfilm, 1947–1960* (Stuttgart: Ferdinand Enke, 1973)

Hohls, Rüdiger, and Konrad H. Jarausch, eds, *Versäumte Fragen: Deutsche Historiker im Schatten des Nationalsozialismus* (Stuttgart: Deutsche Verlags-Anstalt, 2000)

Höhn, Maria, *GIs and Fräuleins: The German–American Encounter in 1950s West Germany* (Chapel Hill: The University of North Carolina Press, 2002)

Hohoff, Curt, *Geist und Ursprung: Zur modernen Literatur* (Munich: Ehrenwirth, [1954])

Holst, Niels von, *Moderne Kunst und sichtbare Welt* (Berlin: Springer-Verlag, 1957)

Holub, Robert C., "Guilt and Atonement," in David E. Wellbery, ed., *A New History of German Literature* (Cambridge, MA: Belknap/Harvard University Press, 2004), 824–30

Holzt-Edelhagen, Joachim, *Jazz-Geschichte(n)* (Frankfurt am Main: Buchhandlung & Antiquariat Heinz A. Eisenbletter & Bernhard S.M. Naumann, 1989)

Hommel, Friedrich, "Aus der Frühzeit der Kranichsteiner Ferienkurse – Fragestellungen, Überlegungen, Folgerungen zur Situation der Musik: Ein Exkurs," in Carl Dalhaus, ed., *Die Wiener Schule heute* (Mainz: Schott, 1983), 105–15

Honegger, Marc, and Günther Massenkeil, eds, *Das Grosse Lexikon der Musik: In acht Bänden*, 8 vols (Freiburg im Breisgau: Herder, 1978–82)

Hopf, Christel, "Das Faschismusthema in der Studentenbewegung und in der Soziologie," in Heinz Bude and Martin Kohli, eds, *Radikalisierte Aufklärung: Studentenbewegung und Soziologie in Berlin, 1965 bis 1970* (Weinheim: Juventa, 1989), 71–86

Horkenbach, Cuno, ed., *Das Deutsche Reich von 1918 bis Heute* (Berlin: Verlag für Presse, Wirtschaft und Politik, 1930)

Horst, Karl August, *Die deutsche Literatur der Gegenwart* (Munich: Nymphenburger Verlagshandlung, 1957)

HörWelten: 50 Jahre Hörspielpreis der Kriegsblinden, 1952–2001 (Berlin: Aufbau, 2001)

Hunn, Karin, *"Nächstes Jahr kehren wir zurück …" Die Geschichte der türkischen Gastarbeiter in der Bundesrepublik* (Göttingen: Wallstein, 2005)

Iddon, Martin, *New Music at Darmstadt: Nono, Stockhausen, Cage and Boulez* (Cambridge: Cambridge University Press, 2013)

Iden, Peter, *Peter Palitzsch: "Theater muss die Welt verändern"* (Berlin: Henschel, 2005)

Ingensand, Harald, *Amerikaner sind auch Menschen* (Stuttgart: Steingruben, 1956)

Jacobmeyer, Wolfgang, "Die Lager der jüdischen Displaced Persons in den deutschen Westzonen 1946/47 als Ort jüdischer Selbstvergewisserung," in Micha Brumlik, Doron Kiesel, Cilly Kugelmann, and H. Schoeps, eds, *Jüdisches Leben in Deutschland seit 1945* (Frankfurt am Main: Jüdischer Verlag bei Altenäum, 1986), 31–48

Jaene, Hans Dieter, *DER SPIEGEL: Ein deutsches Nachrichten-Magazin* (Frankfurt am Main: Fischer Bücherei, 1968)

Jähner, Harald, *Wolfszeit: Deutschland und die Deutschen, 1945–1955* (Berlin: Rowohlt, 2019)

Janssen, Karl-Heinz, Haug von Kuenheim, Theo Sommer, *Die Zeit: Geschichte einer Wochenzeitung, 1946 bis heute* (Munich: Siedler, 2006)

Jappe, Georg, "Interview with Beuys about Key Experiences, September 27, 1976," in Gene Ray, ed., *Joseph Beuys: Mapping the Legacy* (New York: Distributed Art Publishers, Inc., 2001), 185–98

Jarausch, Konrad H., *After Hitler: Recivilizing Germans, 1945–1995* (New York: Oxford University Press, 2006)

Jarausch, Konrad H., "Critical Memory and Civil Society: The Impact of the 1960s on German Debates about the Past," in Philipp Gassert and Alan E. Steinweis, eds, *Coping with the Nazi Past: West German Debates on Nazism and Generational Conflict, 1955–1975* (New York: Berghahn Books, 2007), 11–30

Jarausch, Konrad H., "Removing the Nazi Stain? The Quarrel of the German Historians," *German Studies Review* 11 (May 1988): 285–301

Jarausch, Konrad H., "Verkannter Strukturwandel: Die siebziger Jahre als Vorgeschichte der Probleme der Gegenwart," in Konrad H. Jarausch, ed., *Das Ende der Zuversicht? Die siebziger Jahre als Geschichte* (Göttingen: Vandenhoeck & Ruprecht, 2008), 9–26

Jarausch, Konrad H., and Michael Geyer, *Shattered Past: Reconstructing German Histories* (Princeton: Princeton University Press, 2003)

Jaspers, Karl, *Die Schuldfrage* (Heidelberg: Lambert Schneider, 1946)

Jelavich, Peter, *Berlin Alexanderplatz: Radio, Film and the Death of Weimar Culture* (Berkeley: University of California Press, 2006)

Jenny, Urs, "Der Händler der vier Jahreszeiten," *Filmkritik* 185 (May 1972): 270–1

Jenny, Urs, "Nach einem Jahr: Der junge deutsche Film," *Merkur* 21 (1967): 474–85

Jens, Inge, *Unvollständige Erinnerungen* (Reinbek: Rowohlt, 2009)

Jens, Tilman, *Demenz: Abschied von meinem Vater*, 2nd edn (Gütersloh: Gütersloher Verlagshaus, 2009)

Jens, Tilman, *Vatermord: Wider einen Generalverdacht* (Gütersloh: Gütersloher Verlagshaus, 2010)

Jens, Walter, *Deutsche Literatur der Gegenwart: Themen, Stil, Tendenzen* (Munich: Piper, 1961)

Jens, Walter, *Nein: Die Welt der Angeklagten: Roman* (Hamburg: Rowohlt, 1950)

Jessen, Ralph, "Bewältigte Vergangenheit – blockierte Zukunft? Ein prospektiver Blick auf die bundesrepublikanische Gesellschaft am Ende der Nachkriegszeit," in Konrad H. Jarausch, ed., *Das Ende der Zuversicht? Die siebziger Jahre als Geschichte* (Göttingen: Vandenhoeck & Ruprecht, 2008), 177–95

Joachimides, Christos M., Norman Rosenthal, and Wieland Schmidt, eds, *Deutsche Kunst im 20. Jahrhundert: Malerei und Plastik, 1905–1985* (Munich: Prestel, 1995)

Jöde, Fritz, "Die Jugendmusik in dieser Zeist," *Junge Musik* 2 (1951): 169–72

Jost, Ekkehart, *Europas Jazz, 1960–80* (Frankfurt am Main: Fischer, 1987)

Jürgs, Michael, *Bürger Grass: Biografie eines deutschen Dichters* (Munich: Bertelsmann, 2002)

Kaes, Anton, "History, Fiction, Memory: Fassbinder's *The Marriage of Maria Braun* (1979)," in Eric Rentschler, ed., *German Film & Literature: Adaptations and Transformations* (New York: Methuen, 1986), 276–88

Kaes, Anton, *Deutschlandbilder: Die Wiederkehr der Geschichte als Film* (Munich: edition text + kritik, 1987)

Kaestner, Heinz, "Der Jazz und die abendländische Kultur: Eine kritische Studie," *Junge Musik* 2 (1951): 42–4

Kahlenberg, Friedrich P., "Film," in Wolfgang Benz, ed., *Die Geschichte der Bundesrepublik Deutschland, Band 4: Kultur* (Frankfurt am Main: Fischer Taschenbuch, 1989), 464–512

Kaiser, Elisabeth, *Tief im Süden Dixies: Eindrücke und Begegnungen im anderen Amerika* (Bremen: Carl Schünemann, 1960)

Kaiser, Günther, *Randalierende Jugend: Eine soziologische und kriminologische Studie über die sogenannten "Halbstarken"* (Heidelberg: Quelle und Meyer, 1959)

Kaiser, Joachim, "Schauspiel in der Bundesrepublik," *Frankfurter Hefte* 5 (1952): 333–46

Kaiser, Joachim, [and Henriette Kaiser], *"Ich bin der letzte Mohikaner"* (Berlin: Ullstein, 2008)

Kalb, Martin, *Coming of Age: Constructing and Controlling Youth in Munich, 1942–1973* (New York: Berghahn, 2020)

Kammann, Uwe, "Spätschoppen: Der Fall Werner Höfer," in Lutz Hachmeister and Friedemann Siering, eds, *Die Herren Journalisten: Die Elite der deutschen Presse nach 1945* (Munich: C.H. Beck, 2002), 213–37

Kaplan, E. Ann, "The Search for the Mother/Land in Sanders-Brahms's *Germany, Pale Mother* (1980)," in Eric Rentschler, ed., *German Film & Literature: Adaptations and Transformations* (New York: Methuen, 1986), 289–304

Karasek, Hellmuth, *Auf der Flucht: Erinnerungen* (Berlin: Ullstein Taschenbuch, 2006)

Karasek, Hellmuth, *Das Magazin: Roman* (Reinbek: Rowohlt, 1998)

Karasek, Hellmuth, *Karaseks Kulturkritik: Literatur, Film, Theater* (Hamburg: Rasch und Röhring, 1988)

Karl Amadeus Hartmann und die Musica Viva (Munich: R. Piper, 1980)

Karl, Michaela, *Rudi Dutschke: Revolutionär ohne Revolution* (Frankfurt am Main: Verlag Neue Kritik, 2003)

Kästner, Erich, *Notabene 45: Ein Tagebuch* (Berlin: Cecilie Dressler Verlag, 1961)

Kater, Michael H., "Bürgerliche Jugendbewegung und Hitlerjugend in Deutschland von 1926 bis 1939," *Archiv für Sozialgeschichte* 17 (1977): 127–74

Kater, Michael H., *Composers of the Nazi Era: Eight Portraits* (New York: Oxford University Press, 2000)

Kater, Michael H., *Culture in Nazi Germany* (New Haven and London: Yale University Press, 2019)

Kater, Michael H., *Das "Ahnenerbe" der SS: Ein Beitrag zur Kulturpolitik des Dritten Reiches, 1935–1945*, 4th edn (Munich: Oldenbourg, 2006; 1st pub. 1974)

Kater, Michael H., *Different Drummers: Jazz in the Culture of Nazi Germany* (New York: Oxford Univerity Press, 1992)

Kater, Michael H., *Doctors under Hitler* (Chapel Hill: University of North Carolina Press, 1989)

Kater, Michael H., "Heinrich Himmler's Circle of Friends, 1931–1945," *MARAB: A Review* 2, no. 1 (Winter 1965–6): 74–93

Kater, Michael H., *Hitler Youth* (Cambridge, MA: Harvard University Press, 2004)

Kater, Michael H., "How Dangerous is the NPD?" *The Canadian Forum* 46 (April 1967): 8–11

Kater, Michael H., *The Nazi Party: A Social Profile of Members and Leaders, 1919–1945* (Cambridge, MA: Harvard University Press, 1983)

Kater, Michael H., *The Twisted Muse: Musicians and their Music in the Third Reich* (New York: Oxford University Press, 1997)

Kater, Michael H., *Weimar: From Enlightenment to the Present* (New Haven and London: Yale University Press, 2014)

Käutner, Helmut, "Demontage der Traumfabrik," *Film-Echo* 1, no. 5 (June 1947): 33

Ketelsen, Uwe-Karsten, *Literatur und Drittes Reich* (Schernfeld: SH-Verlag, 1992)

Kielmansegg, Peter Graf, *Lange Schatten: Vom Umgang der Deutschen mit der national-sozialistischen Vergangenheit* (Berlin: Siedler, 1989)

Kiesel, Helmuth, "'So ist unser Gedächtnis jetzt angefüllt mit Furchtbarem': Literaturgeschichtliche Anmerkungen zum 'Historikerstreit' und zu der von Martin Broszat beklagten 'Beziehungslosigkeit zwischen Literatur und Geschichte bei der Verarbeitung der Nazizeit'," in Klaus Oesterle and Siegfried Schiele, eds, *Historikerstreit und politische Bildung* (Stuttgart: J.B. Metzlersche Verlagsbuchhandlung, 1989), 42–94

Kimmig, Adolf, *Zwischen Atlantik und Pazifik: Aus meinem amerikanischen Tagebuch* (Bad Godesberg: US-Informationsdienst, 1954)

Kimpel, Harald, ed., *Aversion/Akzeptanz: Öffentliche Kunst und öffentliche Meinung: Ausseninstallationen aus documenta-Vergangenheit* (Marburg: Jonas, 1992)

Kimpel, Harald, *documenta: Die Überschau: Fünf Jahrzehnte Weltkunstausstellung in Stichwörtern* (Cologne: Dumont Literatur und Kunst Verlag, 2002)

Kindler, Helmut, *Zum Abschied ein Fest: Die Autobiographie eines deutschen Verlegers* (Munich: Kindler, 1991)

Kindt, Werner, ed., *Die deutsche Jugendbewegung, 1920 bis 1933: Die Bündische Zeit* (Düsseldorf: Eugen Diederichs, 1974)

Kipphardt, Heinar, *Joel Brand: Die Geschichte eines Geschäfts: Schauspiel* (Frankfurt am Main: Suhrkamp, 1965)

Kirchmeyer, Helmut, "Kleine Monographie über Herbert Eimert," *Abhandlungen der Sächsischen Akademie der Wissenschaften zu Leipzig: Philologisch-historische Klasse* 75, no. 6 (1998): 4–50

Klee, Ernst, *Kulturlexikon zum Dritten Reich: Wer war was vor und nach 1945* (Frankfurt am Main: Fischer Taschenbuch, 2009)

Klee, Ernst, *Personenlexikon zum Dritten Reich: Wer war was vor und nach 1945*, 2nd edn (Hamburg: Nikol, 2016)

Klein, Hans-Günther, "Aktuelle Realität in Opern der 50er Jahre," in Hans-Werner Heister and Dietrich Stern, eds, *Musik 50er Jahre* (Berlin: Argument-Verlag, 1980), 123–49

Kleinsteuber, Hans J., "Hörfunk und Populärkultur in den USA der 50er Jahre," in Axel Schildt and Arnold Sywottek, eds, *Modernisierung im Wiederaufbau: Die westdeutsche Gesellschaft der 50er Jahre* (Bonn: J.H.W. Dietz Nachf., 1993), 513–29

Kliche-Behnke, Dorothea, *Nationalsozialismus und Shoah im autobiographischen Roman: Poetologie des Erinnerns bei Ruth Klüger, Martin Walser, Georg Heller und Günter Grass* (Berlin: De Gruyter, 2016)

Kligerman, Eric, "Transgenerational Hauntings: Screening the Holocaust in Gerhard Richter's *October 18, 1977* Paintings," in Gerrit-Jan Berendse and Ingo Cornils, eds, *Baader-Meinhof Returns: History and Cultural Memory of German Left-Wing Terrorism* (Amsterdam: Rodopi, 2008), 41–63

Klippert, Werner, *Elemente des Hörspiels* (Stuttgart: Philipp Reclam jun., 1977)

Klotz, Heinrich, *Die Neuen Wilden in Berlin* (Stuttgart: Klett-Cotta, 1984)

Kluge, Alexander, *Lebensläufe* (Frankfurt am Main: Suhrkamp, 1986; 1st pub. 1962))

Kluge, Alexander, *Schlachtbeschreibung* (Olten: Walter-Verlag, 1964)

Knapp, Ursula, *Der Roman der fünfziger Jahre: Zur Entwicklung der Romanästhetik in Westdeutschland* (Würzburg: Königshausen & Neumann, 2002)

Knauer, Wolfram, "Emanzipation wovon? Zum Verhalten des amerikanischen und des deutschen Jazz in den 50er und 60er Jahren," in Wolfram Knauer, ed., *Jazz in Deutschland: Darmstädter Beiträge zur Jazzforschung Band 4* (Hofheim: Wolke Verlag, 1996), 141–57

Knef, Hildegard, *Der geschenkte Gaul: Bericht aus einem Leben* (Vienna: Fritz Molden, 1970)

Knesebeck, Rosemarie von dem, ed., *In Sachen Filbinger gegen Hochhuth: Die Geschichte einer Vergangenheitsbewältigung* (Reinbek: Rowohlt Taschenbuch, 1980)

Knight, Julia, *Frauen und der Neue Deutsche Film* (Marburg: Hitzeroth, 1995)

Knilli, Friedrich, and Siegfried Zielinski, eds, *Holocaust zur Unterhaltung: Anatomie eines internationalen Bestsellers: Fakten – Fotos – Forschungsreportagen* (Berlin: Elefanten Press, 1982)

Knoch, Habbo, "Das mediale Gedächtnis der Heimat: Krieg und Verbrechen in den Erinnerungsräumen der Bundesrepublik," in Habbo Knoch, ed., *Das Erbe der Provinz: Heimatkultur und Geschichtspolitik nach 1945* (Göttingen: Wallstein, 2001), 275–300.

Koberg, Roland, *Claus Peymann: Aller Tage Abenteuer: Biografie* (Berlin: Henschel, 1999)

Koch, Gertrud, "Todesnähe und Todeswünsche: Geschichtsprozesse mit tödlichem Ausgang: Zu einigen jüdischen Figuren im deutschen Nachkriegsfilm," in Micha Brumlik, Doron Kiesel, Cilly Kugelmann, and Julius H. Schoeps, eds, *Jüdisches Leben in Deutschland seit 1945* (Frankfurt am Main: Jüdischer Verlag bei Altenäum, 1986), 258–74

Koch, Gertrud, "Torments of the Flesh, Coldness of the Spirit: Jewish Figures in the Films of Rainer Werner Fassbinder," *New German Critique* 38 (Spring–Summer 1986): 28–38

Koch, Manfred, "Der westdeutsche Roman der fünfziger und frühen sechziger Jahre," in Manfred Durzak, ed., *Deutsche Gegenwartsliteratur: Ausgangspositionen und aktuelle Entwicklungen* (Stuttgart: Philipp Reclam jun., 1981), 204–33

Kochenrath, Hans-Peter, "Kontinuität im deutschen Film," in Wilfried von Bredow and Rolf Zurek, eds, *Film und Gesellschaft in Deutschland: Dokumente und Materialien* (Hamburg: Hoffmann und Campe, 1975), 286–92

Kocka, Jürgen, "Hitler sollte nicht durch Stalin und Pol Pot verdrängt werden: Über Versuche deutscher Historiker, die Ungeheuerlichkeit von NS-Verbrechen zu relativieren," in *"Historikerstreit": Die Dokumentation der Kontroverse über die Einzigartigkeit der nationalsozialistischen Judenvernichtung*, 5th edn (Munich: R. Piper, 1987), 132–42

Koebner, Thomas, "Dramatik und Dramaturgie seit 1945," in Thomas Koebner, ed., *Tendenzen der deutschen Literatur seit 1945* (Stuttgart: Alfred Kröner, 1971), 348–469

Koegler, Horst, "Manager der Musik: Eine Reise durch das deutsche Konzertleben," *Der Monat* 9 (May 1957): 44–59

Koenen, Gerd, *Vesper, Ensslin, Baader: Urszenen des deutschen Terrorismus*, 4th edn (Cologne: Kiepenheuer & Witsch, 2004)

Koeppen, Wolfgang, *Das Treibhaus: Roman*, 3rd edn (Stuttgart: Scherz & Goverts, 1953)

Koeppen, Wolfgang, *Der Tod in Rom: Roman* (Stuttgart: Scherz & Goverts, 1954)

Koeppen, Wolfgang, *Tauben im Gras: Roman* (Stuttgart: Scherz & Goverts, 1951)

Koetzle, Michael, Klaus-Jürgen Sembach, and Klaus Schölzel, *Die fünfziger Jahre: Heimat– Glaube – Glanz: Der Stil eines Jahrzehnts* (Munich: Callwey, 1998)

Kogon, Eugen, *Die unvollendete Erneuerung: Deutschland im Kräftefeld, 1945–1963: Politische und gesellschaftliche Aufsätze aus zwei Jahrzehnten* (Frankfurt am Main: Europäische Verlagsanstalt, 1964)

Kohl, Jerome, *Karlheinz Stockhausen: Zeitmasse* (London: Routledge, 2017)

Köhler, Otto, *Unheimliche Publizisten: Die verdrängte Vergangenheit der Medienmacher* (Munich: Knaur, 1995)

Kolland, Dorothea, "Musikalische Ideale aus Krähwinkel: Die 'Junge Musik' der 50er Jahre," in Hans-Werner Heister and Dietrich Stern, eds, *Musik 50er Jahre* (Berlin: Argument-Verlag, 1980), 84–103

Kolland, Hubert, "Bayreuths neue Kleider: Wagner 'abstrakt'," in Hans-Werner Heister and Dietrich Stern, eds, *Musik 50er Jahre* (Berlin: Argument-Verlag, 1980), 150–71

Kolland, Hubert, "Die Schwierigkeit, ein bundesdeutscher Komponist zu sein: Neue Musik zwischen Isolierung und Engagement: Gespräch mit Hans Werner Henze," in Hans-Werner Heister and Dietrich Stern, eds, *Musik 50er Jahre* (Berlin: Argument-Verlag, 1980), 50–77

Köllhofer, Hanna, "RIAS – Stimme der Freien Welt? Zu den Anfängen des *Rundfunks im amerikanischen Sektor* von Berlin," in Alexander Stephan and Jochen Vogt, eds, *America on my Mind: Zur Amerikanisierung der deutschen Kultur seit 1945* (Munich: Wilhelm Fink, 2006), 93–108

König, Helmut, *Die Zukunft der Vergangenheit: Der Nationalsozialismus im politischen Bewusstsein der Bundesrepublik* (Frankfurt am Main: Fischer Taschenbuch, 2003)

König, Karin, "Zwei Ikonen des bewaffnete Kampfes: Leben und Tod Georg von Rauchs und Thomas Weisbeckers," in Wolfgang Kraushaar, ed., *Die RAF und der linke Terrorismus*, vol. 1 (Hamburg: Hamburger Edition, 2006), 430–71

König, Wolfgang, "Die siebziger Jahre als konsumgeschichtliche Wende in der Bundesrepubik," in Konrad H. Jarausch, ed., *Das Ende der Zuversicht? Die siebziger Jahre als Geschichte* (Göttingen: Vandenhoeck & Ruprecht, 2008), 84–99

Königseder, Angelika, and Juliane Wetzel, *Waiting for Hope: Jewish Displaced Persons in Post-World War II Germany* (Evanston: Northwestern University Press, 2001)

Köpf, Peter, *Schreiben nach jeder Richtung: Goebbels-Propagandisten in der deutschen Nachkriegspresse* (Berlin: Ch. Links Verlag, 1995)

Korbmacher, [Christel], *Kulturszene Neuss, 1945–1960* (Neuss: Galerie Küppers, [1988])

Korda, Rolf Martin, "Für Bürgertum und Business: Die 'Frankfurter Allgemeine Zeitung'," in Michael Wolf Thomas, ed., *Porträts der deutschen Presse: Politik und Profit* (Berlin: Verlag Volker Spiess, 1980), 81–96

Korte, Hermann, *Eine Gesellschaft im Aufbruch: Die Bundesrepublik Deutschland in den sechziger Jahren* (Wiesbaden: VS Verlag, 2009)

Kortner, Fritz, *Aller Tage Abend* (Munich: Kindler, 1959)

Kossert, Andreas, *Kalte Heimat: Die Geschichte der deutschen Vertriebenen nach 1945*, 3rd edn (Munich: Siedler, 2008)

Kotschenreuther, Hellmut, "Glanz und Elend des Jazz: Anmerkungen zu einem musikalischen Phänomen," in Harald Kunz, ed., *Musikstadt Berlin zwischen Krieg und Frieden: Musikalische Bilanz einer Viermächtestadt* (Wiesbaden: Bote & G. Bock, 1956), 198–210

Kovach, Thomas A., and Martin Walser, *The Burden of the Past: Martin Walser on Modern German Identity: Texts, Contexts, Commentary* (Rochester, NY: Camden House, 2008)

Kramer, Sven, "Wiederkehr und Verwandlung der Vergangenheit im deutschen Film," in Peter Reichel, Harald Schmid, and Peter Steinbach, eds, *Der Nationalsozialismus – Die Zweite Geschichte: Überwindung – Deutung – Erinnerung* (Munich: C.H. Beck, 2009), 283–99

Krämer-Badoni, Rudolf, *Zwischen allen Stühlen: Erinnerungen eines Literaten* (Munich: F. A. Herbig Verlagsbuchhandlung, 1985)

Krannhals, Paul, *Das organische Weltbild: Grundlagen einer Neuentstehung deutscher Kultur*, 2 vols. (Munich: F. Bruckmann, 1936; 1st edn 1928)

Krause, Markus, *Galerie Gerd Rosen: Die Avantgarde in Berlin, 1945–1950* (Berlin: Ars Nicolai, 1995)

Krause, Tilman, *Mit Frankreich gegen das deutsche Sonderbewusstsein: Friedrich Sieburgs Wege und Wandlungen in diesem Jahrhundert* (Berlin: Akademie, 1993)

Kraushaar, Wolfgang, *Die blinden Flecken der RAF* ([Stuttgart]: Klett-Cotta, 2017)

Kraushaar, Wolfgang, *1968 als Mythos, Chiffre und Zäsur* (Hamburg: Hamburger Edition HIS, 2000)

Kraushaar, Wolfgang, Karin Wieland, and Jan Philipp Reemtsma, *Rudi Dutschke, Andreas Baader und die RAF* (Hamburg: Hamburger Edition, 2005)

Krauss, Marita, *Nachkriegskultur in München: Münchner städtische Kulturpolitik, 1945–1954* (Munich: R. Oldenbourg, 1985)

Kreimeier, Klaus, "Die RAF und der deutsche Film," in Wolfgang Kraushaar, ed., *Die RAF und der linke Terrorismus*, vol. 2 (Hamburg: Hamburger Edition, 2006), 1155–84

Kreimeier, Klaus, *Die Ufa-Story: Geschichte eines Filmkonzerns* (Munich: Carl Hanser, 1992)

Kretschmann, Carsten, *Zwischen Spaltung und Gemeinsamkeit: Kultur im geteilten Deutschland* (Berlin-Brandenburg: be.bra verlag, 2012)

Kreuzer, Helmut, ed., *Deutsche Dramaturgie der Sechziger Jahre: Ausgewählte Texte* (Tübingen: Max Niemeyer, 1974)

Kreuzer, Helmut, "Neue Subjektivität: Zur Literatur der siebziger Jahre in der Bundesrepublik Deutschland," in Manfred Durzak, ed., *Deutsche Gegenwartsliteratur: Ausgangspositionen und aktuelle Entwicklungen*(Stuttgart: Philipp Reclam jun., 1981), 77–106

Kröll, Friedhelm, *Gruppe 47* (Stuttgart: J.B. Metzler, 1979)

Kronauer, Brigitte, *Rita Münster: Roman* (Stuttgart: Klett-Cotta, 1983)

Krüger, Udo Michael, "Fernsehanbieter und Fernsehangebote im dualen System," in Otfried Jarren, ed., *Politische Kommunikation in Hörfunk und Fernsehen* (Opladen: Leske + Budrich, 1994), 97–110

Kruip, Gudrun, *Das "Welt"-"Bild" des Axel Springer Verlags: Journalismus zwischen westlichen Werten und deutschen Denktraditionen* (Munich: R. Oldenbourg, 1999)

Krüll, Marianne, *Im Netz der Zauberer: Eine andere Geschichte der Familie Mann* (Frankfurt am Main: Fischer Taschenbuch, 1995)

Kuby, Erich, *Das ist des Deutschen Vaterland: 70 Millionen in zwei Wartesälen* (Stuttgart: Henry Goverts, 1957)

Kuenheim, Haug von, and Theo Sommer, eds, *Ein wenig betrübt, Ihre Marion: Marion Gräfin Dönhoff und Gerd Bucerius: Ein Briefwechsel aus fünf Jahrzehnten* (Berlin: Siedler, 2003)

Kunst in Deutschland, 1898–1973 ([Hamburg: n. pub., 1973])

Kupffer, Heinrich, *Swingtime: Chronik einer Jugend in Deutschland, 1937–1951* (Berlin: Frieling, 1987)

Kurth, Ulrich, "Als der Jazz 'cool' wurde," in Hans-Werner Heister and Dietrich Stern, eds, *Musik 50er Jahre* (Berlin: Argument-Verlag, 1980), 110–23

Kurtz, Michael, *Stockhausen: Eine Biographie* (Kassel: Bärenreiter, 1988)

Kuschner, Doris, "Die jüdische Minderheit in der Bundesrepublik Deutschland: Eine Analyse" (diss. phil. Universität Köln, 1977)

Lämmert, Eberhard, Walther Killy, Karl Otto Conrady, and Peter V. Polenz., *Germanistik – eine deutsche Wissenschaft: Beiträge* (Frankfurt am Main: Suhrkamp, 1967)

Lange, Horst H., *Jazz in Deutschland: Die deutsche Jazz-Chronik, 1900–1960* (Berlin: Colloquium, 1966)

Langer, William L., ed., *An Encyclopedia of World History* (Boston: Houghton Mifflin, 1968)

Lau, Jörg, *Hans Magnus Enzensberger: Ein öffentliches Leben* (Berlin: Alexander Fest Verlag, 1999)

Lee, Mia, "The Return of the Avant-Garde in Post-War West Germany,"*Australian Journal of Politics and History* 60 (2014): 405–15

Lehmann, Johannes, ed., *Die unruhigen Sechziger: Ein Jahrzehnt in Rückblenden* (Ismaning: Max Hueber, 1986)

Lehnert, Herbert, "Die Gruppe 47: Ihre Anfänge und ihre Gründungsmitglieder," in Manfred Durzak, ed., *Deutsche Gegenwartsliteratur: Ausgangspositionen und aktuelle Entwicklungen* (Stuttgart: Philipp Reclam jun., 1981), 32–60

Lehnert, Walter, ed., *Ein Vierteljahrhundert Musiktheater Nürnberg: Hans Gierster, 1964 bis 1988* (Nuremberg: Stadt Nürnberg, 1988)

Lehr, Stefan, *Ein fast vergessener "Osteinsatz": Deutsche Archivare im Generalgouvernement und im Reichskommissariat Ukraine* (Düsseldorf: Droste, 2007)

Lenz, Siegfried, *Es waren Habichte in der Luft: Roman*, 3rd edn (Hamburg: Hoffmann und Campe, 1970; 1st edn 1951)

Lenz, Siegfried, *Zeit der Schuldlosen* [1961], ed. P. Prager (London: Harrap, 1981)

Leonhardt, Rudolf Walter, "Aufstieg und Niedergang der Gruppe 47," in Manfred Durzak, ed., *Deutsche Gegenwartsliteratur: Ausgangspositionen und aktuelle Entwicklungen* (Stuttgart: Philipp Reclam jun., 1981), 61–76

Lettau, Reinhard, ed., *Die Gruppe 47: Bericht, Kritik, Polemik: Ein Handbuch* (Neuwied: Luchterhand, 1967)

Lewandowski, Rainer, *Die Filme von Alexander Kluge* (Hildesheim: Olms Presse, 1980)

Lewandowski, Rainer, *Die Filme von Volker Schlöndorff* (Hildesheim: Olms Presse, 1981)

Limmer, Wolfgang, *Rainer Werner Fassbinder, Filmemacher* (Hamburg: SPIEGEL-Verlag, 1981)

Linder, Christian, *Das Schwirren des heranfliegenden Pfeils: Heinrich Böll: Eine Biographie* (Berlin: Matthes & Seitz, 2009)

Lindlar, Heinrich, ed., *Wolfgang Fortner: Eine Monographie: Werkanalysen, Aufsätze, Reden, Offene Briefe, 1950–1959* (Rodenkirchen/Rhein: P.J. Tonger, 1960)

Lorenz, Juliane, ed., *Das ganz normale Chaos: Gespräche über Rainer Werner Fassbinder* (Berlin: Henschel, 1995)

Ludes, Peter, "Programmgeschichte des Fernsehens," in Jürgen Wilke, ed., *Mediengeschichte der Bundesrepublik Deutschland* (Cologne: Böhlau, 1999), 255–76

Luft, Friedrich, "Ich lerne Fernsehen," *Der Monat* 8 (November 1955): 54–64

Luft, Friedrich, *Stimme der Kritik: Berliner Theater seit 1945*, 3rd edn (Velber: Friedrich, 1965)

Luft, Friedrich, "Vorwort," in *25 Jahre Theater in Berlin: Theaterpremieren, 1945–1970* (Berlin: Heinz Spitzing Verlag, 1972), 7–20

Lützeler, Paul Michael, "Einleitung: Von der Spätmoderne zur Postmoderne – Die deutschsprachige Literatur der achtziger Jahre," *German Quarterly* 63 (Summer–Autumn 1990): 350–8

Maase, Kaspar, *BRAVO Amerika: Erkundungen zur Jugendkultur der Bundesrepublik in den fünfziger Jahren* (Hamburg: Junius, 1992)

Magenau, Jörg, *Martin Walser: Eine Biographie* (Reinbek: Rowohlt, 2005)

Mahnkopf, Claus-Steffen, "Neue Musik am Beginn der Zweiten Moderne," *Merkur* 52 (1998): 864–75

Maier, Charles S., *The Unmasterable Past: History, Holocaust, and German National Identity* (Cambridge, MA: Harvard University Press, 1988)

Maletzke, Erich, *Siegfried Lenz: Eine biographische Annäherung* (Springe: Zu Klampen, 2006)

Mann, Klaus, "Strauss Still Unabashed About Ties with Nazis," *Stars and Stripes* (May 29, 1945): 4

Manske, Hans-Joachim, "'Das Lachen der Beatles gilt mehr als die Anerkennung von Marcel Duchamp' – Zur Bildenden Kunst der 60er Jahre in Deutschland," in Axel Schildt, Detlef Siegfried, and Karl Christian Lammers, eds, *Dynamische Zeiten: Die 60er Jahre in den beiden deutschen Gesellschaften* (Hamburg: Christians, 2000), 768–807

Martin, Mick, and Marsha Porter, *DVD and Video Guide 2004* (New York: Ballantine, 2003)

Mattes, Monika, "Ambivalente Aufbrüche: Frauen, Familie und Arbeitsmarkt zwischen Konjunktur und Krise," in Konrad H. Jarausch, ed., *Das Ende der Zuversicht? Die siebziger Jahre als Geschichte* (Göttingen: Vandenhoeck & Ruprecht, 2008), 215–28

Mauceri, John, *The War on Music: Reclaiming the Twentieth Century* (New Haven and London: Yale University Press, 2022)

Maximilian, Fried, "Die Saat der Gewalt," *Film, Bild, Ton* 5, no. 11 (February 1956): 28–31

Mayer-Iswandy, Claudia, *Günter Grass* (Munich: DTV, 2002)

McClure, Barney, *There is No Such Thing As A Mistake: A No-Stress Approach to Bandstand Theory* (Ukiah, CA: BMP Publications, 1997)

McCormick, Richard, "Memory and Commerce, Gender and Restoration: Wolfgang Staudte's Roses for the State Prosecutor (1959) and West German Film in the 1950s," in Hanna Schissler, ed., *The Miracle Years: A Cultural History of West Germany, 1949–1968* (Princeton: Princeton University Press, 2001), 281–300

McCormick, Richard W., *Politics of the Self: Feminism and the Postmodern in West German Literature and Film* (Princeton: Princeton University Press, 1991)

McGuinness, Patrick, "Outside in the Bar," *London Review of Books* (October 21, 2021): 11–14

Meinecke, Friedrich, *Die deutsche Katastrophe: Betrachtungen und Erinnerungen* (Wiesbaden: Brockhaus, 1946)

Meinhof, Ulrike, *Die Würde des Menschen ist antastbar: Aufsätze und Polemiken* (Berlin: Verlag Klaus Wagenbach, 1981)

Melchinger, Siegfried, "Struktur, Klima, Personen: Deutsches Theater seit 1945: Ein Überblick," *Theater heute* 10 (1970): 3–7

Melichar, Alois, *Musik in der Zwangsjacke: Die deutsche Musik zwischen Orff und Schönberg*, 2nd edn (Vienna: Eduard Wancura, 1959)

Melichar, Alois, *Schönberg und die Fogen: Eine notwendige kulturpolitische Auseinandersetzung* ([Stuttgart]: Wels, [1960])

Melichar, Alois, *Überwindung des Modernismus: Konkrete Antwort an einen abstrakten Kritiker* (Vienna: Josef Weinberger, 1954)

Menand, Louis, "Sloppy Joe: Senator Joseph McCarthy and the Force of Political Falsehoods," *New Yorker* (August 3 and 10, 2020): 71–5

Menand, Louis, *The Free World: Art and Thought in the Cold War* (New York: Farrar, Straus and Giroux, 2021)

Mennicken, Rainer, *Peter Palitzsch* (Frankfurt am Main: Fischer Taschenbuch, 1993)

Merseburger, Peter, *Rudolf Augstein: Biographie* (Munich: Deutsche Verlags-Anstalt, 2007)

Mertz, Peter, *Das gerettete Theater: Die deutsche Bühne im Wiederaufbau* (Weinheim: Quadriga, 1990)

Meuer, Adolph, "Verfälschte Erziehungsprobleme," *Film, Bild, Ton* 5, no. 11 (February 1956): 32–3

Meyer, Claus Heinrich, "Zeitung für Deutschland," *Der Monat* 21 (September 1969): 104–12

Meyn, Hermann, "'Liberaler Kaufmannsgeist': 'DIE ZEIT'," in Michael Wolf Thomas, ed., *Porträts der deutschen Presse: Politik und Profit* (Berlin: Verlag Volker Spiess, 1980), 275–91

Michalzik, Peter, *Unseld: Eine Biographie* (Munich: btb, 2003)

Michels, Eckard, *Von der Deutschen Akademie zum Goethe-Institut: Sprach- und auswärtige Kulturpolitik, 1923–1960* (Munich: Oldenbourg, 2005)

Mika, Bascha, *Alice Schwarzer: Eine kritische Biographie* (Reinbek: Rowohlt, 1998)

Miller, Jennifer A., *Turkish Guest Workers in Germany: Hidden Lives and Contested Borders, 1960s to 1980s* (Toronto: University of Toronto Press, 2018)

Miquel, Marc von, *Ahnden oder amnestieren? Westdeutsche Justiz und Vergangenheitspolitik in den sechziger Jahren* (Göttingen: Wallstein, 2004)

Miquel, Marc von, "Explanation, Dissociation, Apologia: The Debate over the Criminal Prosecution of Nazi Crimes in the 1960s," in Philipp Gassert and Alan E. Steinweis, eds, *Coping with the Nazi Past: West German Debates on Nazism and Generational Conflict, 1955–1975* (New York: Berghahn Books, 2007), 50–63

Miquel, Marc von, "Juristen: Richter in eigener Sache," in Norbert Frei, ed., *Karrieren im Zwielicht: Hitlers Eliten nach 1945* (Frankfurt am Main: Campus, 2001), 181–237

Misch, Imke, ed., *Karlheinz Stockhausen: Kompositorische Grundlagen Neuer Musik: Sechs Seminare für die Darmstädter Ferienkurse 1970* (Kürten: Stockhausen-Stiftung für Musik, 2009)

Mitscherlich, Alexander, and Fred Mielke, eds, *Medizin ohne Menschlichkeit: Dokumente des Nürnberg Ärzteprozesses* (Frankfurt am Main: Fischer Bücherei, 1962)

Mitscherlich, Alexander' and Margarete Mitscherlich, *Die Unfähigkeit zu trauern: Grundlagen kollektiven Verhaltens* (Munich: Piper, 1967)

Mixner, Manfred, *Peter Handke* (Kronberg: Athenäum, 1977)

Moeller, Hans-Bernhard, and George Lellis, *Volker Schlöndorff's Cinema: Adaptation, Politics, and the "Movie-Appropriate"* (Carbondale: Southern Illinois University Press, 2002)

Moeller, Robert G., "Remembering the War in a Nation of Victims: West German Pasts in the 1950s," in Hanna Schissler, ed., *The Miracle Years: A Cultural History of West Germany, 1949–1968* (Princeton: Princeton University Press, 2001), 83–109

Moeller, Robert G., "Sinking Ships, the Lost Heimat and Broken Taboos: Günter Grass and the Politics of Memory in Contemporary Germany," *Contemporary German History* 12 (2003): 147–81

Moeller, Robert G., "Victims in Uniform: West German Combat Movies from the 1950s," in Bill Niven, ed., *Germans as Victims: Remembering the Past in Contemporary Germany* (Houndmills: Palgrave Macmillan, 2006), 43–61

Moeller, Robert G., "When *Liebe* was just a Five-Letter Word: Wolfgang Liebeneiner's *Love 47*," in Wilfried Wilms and William Rasch, eds, *German Postwar Films: Life and Love in the Ruins* (Houndmills: Palgrave Macmillan, 2008), 141–56

Möhrmann, Renate, *Die Frau mit der Kamera: Filmemacherinnen in der Bundesrepubik Deutschland: Situation, Perspektiven, 10 exemplarische Lebensläufe* (Munich: Carl Hanser, 1980)

Mommsen, Hans, "Aufarbeitung und Verdrängung: Das Dritte Reich im westdeutschen Geschichtsbewusstsein," in Dan Diner, ed., *Ist der Nationalsozialismus Geschichte? Zu Historisierung und Historikerstreit* (Frankfurt am Main: Fischer Taschenbuch, 1987), 74–88

Mommsen, Hans, "Suche nach der verlorenen Geschichte?" in *"Historikerstreit": Die Dokumentation der Kontroverse über die Einzigartigkeit der nationalsozialistischen Judenvernichtung*, 5th edn (Munich: R. Piper, 1987), 156–73

Monod, David, "Americanizing the Patron State? Government and Music under American Occupation, 1945–1953," in Albrecht Riethmüller, ed., *Deutsche Leitkultur Musik? Zur Musikgeschichte nach dem Holocaust* (Stuttgart: Franz Steiner, 2006), 47–59

Monod, David, *Settling Scores: German Music, Denazification and the Americans, 1945–1953* (Chapel Hill: University of North Carolina Press, 2005)

Morgan, Robert P., "Stockhausen's Writings on Music," *The Musical Quarterly* 61 (January 1975): 1–18

Moses, Dirk, "Die 45er: Eine Generation zwischen Faschismus und Demokratie?" *Die Neue Sammlung* 40 (2000): 233–63

Müller, Hans Dieter, *Der Springer-Konzern: Eine kritische Studie* (Munich: Piper, 1968)

Müller, Jan-Werner, *Another Country: German Intellectuals, Unification and National Identity* (New Haven and London: Yale University Press, 2000)

Müller, Peter, "Wie frei ist die Freie Universität Berlin?" in Rolf Seeliger, ed., *Braune Universität: Deutsche Hochschullehrer gestern und heute*, vol. 4 (Munich: Selbstverlag Rolf Seeliger, 1966), 6–26

Müller, Siegfried, ed., *Mini, Mofa, Maobibel: Die sechziger Jahre in der Bundesrepublik* (Kerber Verlag, Bielefeld, 2013)

"Musikergespräch mit Michael Naura: Es war ein lustiges Völkchen," in Wolfram Knauer, ed., *Jazz in Deutschland: Darmstädter Beiträge zur Jazzforschung Band 4* (Hofheim: Wolke Verlag, 1996), 159–73

Naifeh, Steven, and Gregory White Smith, *Jackson Pollock: An American Saga* (New York: HarperPerennial, 1991)

Nasaw, David, *The Last Million: Europe's Displaced Persons from World War to Cold War* (New York: Penguin, 2020)

Nauck, Gisela, *Risiko des kühnen Experiments: Der Rundfunk als Impulsgeber und Mäzen* (Saarbrücken: PFAU-Verlag, 2004)

Nehring, Wolfgang, "Die Bühne als Tribunal: Das Dritte Reich und der Zweite Weltkrieg im Spiegel des dokumentarischen Theaters," in Hans Wagener, ed., *Gegenwartsliteratur und Drittes Reich: Deutsche Autoren in der Auseinandersetzung mit der Vergangenheit* (Stuttgart: Philipp Reclam jun., 1977), 69–94

Neuhaus, Volker, *Günter Grass: Schriftsteller – Künstler – Zeitgenosse: Eine Biographie* ([Göttingen]: Steidl, n.d.)

Neumann, Hans-Joachim, "Ästhetische und organisatorische Erstarrung: Der deutsche Film in den achtziger Jahren," in Uli Jung, ed., *Der deutsche Film: Aspekte seiner Geschichte von den Anfängen bis zur Gegenwart* (Trier: WVT Wissenschaftlicher Verlag Trier, 1993), 247–66

Neunzig, Hans A., ed., *Hans Werner Richter und die Gruppe 47: Mit Beiträgen von Walter Jens, Marcel Reich-Ranicki, Peter Wapnewski u.a.* (Munich: Nymphenburger Verlagshandlung, 1979)

Niethammer, Lutz, *Die Mitläuferfabrik: Die Entnazifizierung am Beispiel Bayerns* (Bonn: J.H.W. Dietz Nachf., 1988)

Niven, Bill, *Facing the Nazi Past: United Germany and the Legacy of the Third Reich* (London: Routledge, 2002)

Nöhbauer, Hans F., "Literarische Gruppen," in Thomas Koebner, ed., *Tendenzen der deutschen Literatur seit 1945* (Stuttgart: Alfred Kröner, 1971), 520–34

Nolde, Emil, *Mein Leben* (Cologne: DuMont, 1976)

Nolte, Ernst, *Das Vergehen der Vergangenheit: Antwort an meine Kritiker im sogenannten Historikerstreit*, 2nd edn (Berlin: Ullstein, 1988)

Nolte, Ernst, *Three Faces of Fascism: Action Française, Italian Fascism, National Socialism* (New York: Holt, Rinehart and Winston, 1966)

Nonnenmann, Klaus, ed., *Schriftsteller der Gegenwart: Deutsche Literatur* (Olten: Walter, 1963)

O'Dochartaigh, Pól, *Germany since 1945* (Houndmills: Palgrave Macmillan, 2004)

Oberborbeck, Felix, "Historische Stunde der Jungen Musik," *Junge Musik* 3 (1952): 96–8

Obrist, Hans-Ulrich, ed., *Gerhard Richter: The Daily Practice of Painting: Writings and Interviews, 1962–1993* (Cambridge, MA: MIT Press, 1995)

Oehlmann, Werner, "Das neue Bayreuth: Ein Rückblick auf die Festspiele 1951 und 1952," *Der Monat* 4 (September 1952): 635–40

Oman, Hiltrud, *Die Kunst auf dem Weg zum Leben: Joseph Beuys* (Weinheim: Quadriga, 1988)

Osnos, Evan, *Wildland: The Making of America's Fury* (New York: Farrar, Straus and Giroux, 2021)

Paepcke, Lotte, *Ich wurde vergessen: Bericht einer Jüdin, die das Dritte Reich überlebte* (Freiburg im Breisgau: Herder, 1979; 1st pub. 1952)

Pagenstecher, Cord, *Ausländerpolitik und Immigrantenidentität: Zur Geschichte der "Gastarbeit" in der Bundesrepublik* (Berlin: Dieter Bertz Verlag, 1994)

Paret, Peter, *An Artist against the Third Reich: Ernst Barlach, 1933–1938* (Cambridge: Cambridge University Press, 2003)

Payk, Marcus M., "Der 'Amerikakomplex': 'Massendemokratie' und Kulturkritik am Beispiel von Karl Korn und dem Feuilleton der 'Frankfurter Allgemeinen Zeitung' in den fünfziger Jahren," in Arnd Bauerkämper, Konrad H. Jarausch, and Marcus M. Payk, eds, *Demokratiewunder: Transatlantische Mittler und die kulturelle Öffnung Westdeutschlands, 1945–1970* (Göttingen: Vandenhoeck & Ruprecht, 2005), 190–217

Payk, Marcus M., *Der Geist der Demokratie: Intellektuelle Orientierungsversuche im Feuilleton der frühen Bundesrepublik: Karl Korn und Peter de Mendelssohn* (Munich: Oldenbourg, 2008)

Pells, Richard, *Not Like Us: How Europeans Have Loved, Hated, and Transformed American Culture Since World War II* (New York: Basic Books, 1997)

Pendas, Devin O., *The Frankfurt Auschwitz Trial, 1963–1965: Genocide, History, and the Limits of the Law* (Cambridge: Cambridge University Press, 2006)

Petersen, Peter, *Hans Werner Henze: Ein politischer Musiker: Zwölf Vorlesungen* (Hamburg: Argument, 1988)

Petropoulos, Jonathan, *Artists under Hitler: Collaboration and Survival in Nazi Germany* (New Haven and London: Yale University Press, 2014)

Petropoulos, Jonathan, "From Seduction to Denial: Arno Breker's Engagement with National Socialism," in Richard A. Etlin, ed., *Art, Culture and Media under the Third Reich* (Chicago: University of Chicago Press, 2002), 205–29

Petsch, Joachim, "'Unersetzliche Künstler': Malerei und Plastik im 'Dritten Reich'," in Hans Sarkowicz, ed., *Hitlers Künstler: Die Kultur im Dienst des Nationalsozialismus* (Frankfurt am Main: Insel, 2004), 245–77

Petzet, Wolfgang, *Theater: Die Münchner Kammerspiele, 1911–1972* (Munich: Kurt Desch, 1973)

Pflieger, Klaus, *Die Rote Armee Fraktion – RAF, 14.5.1970 bis 20.4.1998* (Baden-Baden: Nomos, 2004)

Phillips, Raymond, ed., *Trial of Josef Kramer and Forty-four Others (The Belsen Trial)* (London: Hodge, 1949)

Pilgert, Henry P., *Press, Radio and Film in West Germany, 1945–1953* (n.pl.: Office of the U.S. High Commission for Germany, 1953)

Pim, Keiron, *Endless Flight: The Life of Joseph Roth* (London: Granta, 2022)

Pleyer, Peter, "Aufbau und Entwicklung der deutschen Filmproduktion nach 1945," in Wilfried von Bredow and Rolf Zurek, eds, *Film und Gesellschaft in Deutschland: Dokumente und Materialien* (Hamburg: Hoffmann und Campe, 1975), 266–85

Pleyer, Peter, *Deutscher Nachkriegsfilm, 1946–1948* (Münster: C. J. Fahle, 1965)

Poiger, Uta G., *Jazz, Rock and Rebels: Cold War Politics and American Culture in a Divided Country* (Berkeley: University of California Press, 2000)

Pott, Sabine, *Film als Geschichtsschreibung bei Rainer Werner Fassbinder: Fassbinders Darstellung der Bundesrepublik Deutschland anhand ausgewählter Frauenfiguren in seiner "BRD-Trilogie": Die Ehe der Maria Braun (1978), Lola (1981) und die Sehnsucht der Veronika Voss (1982)* (Frankfurt am Main: Peter Lang, 2002)

Potter, Pamela M., *Art of Suppression: Confronting the Nazi Past in Histories of the Visual and Performing Arts* (Oakland: University of California Press, 2016)

Potter, Pamela M., *Most German of the Arts: Musicology and Society from the Weimar Republic to the End of Hitler's Reich* (New Haven and London: Yale University Press, 1998)

Preece, Julian, *Baader-Meinhof and the Novel: Narratives of the Nation/Fantasies of the Revolution, 1970–2010* (New York: Palgrave Macmillan, 2012)

Preece, Julian, "Reinscribing the German Autumn: Heinrich Breloer's *Todesspiel* and the Two Clusters of German 'Terrorist' Films," in Gerrit-Jan Berendse and Ingo Cornils, eds, *Baader-Meinhof Returns: History and Cultural Memory of German Left-Wing Terrorism* (Amsterdam: Rodopi, 2008), 213–29

Preece, Julian, *The Life and Work of Günter Grass: Literature, History, Politics* (Houndmills: Palgrave Macmillan, 2004)

Preetorius, Emil, *Weltbild und Weltgehalt: Zur Krise künstlerischen Schaffens* (Frankfurt am Main: Vittorio Klostermann, 1947)

Prieberg, Fred K., *Musik im NS-Staat* (Frankfurt am Main: Fischer Taschenbuch, 1982)

Prinz, Friedrich, ed., *Trümmerzeit in München: Kultur und Gesellschaft einer deutschen Grossstadt im Aufbau, 1945–1949* (Munich: C.H. Beck, 1984)

Pross, Harry, ed., *Deutsche Presse seit 1945* (Berne: Scherz, 1965)

Rabinbach, Anson, "Introduction: Reflections on Germans and Jews since Auschwitz," in Anson Rabinbach and Jack Zipes, eds, *Germans and Jews since the Holocaust: The Changing Situation in West Germany* (New York: Holmes & Meier, 1986), 3–24

Raddatz, Fritz J., ed., *Friedrich Sieburg: Zur Literatur, 1924–1956* (Stuttgart: Deutsche Verlags-Anstalt, 1981)

Raddatz, Fritz J., ed., *Friedrich Sieburg: Zur Literatur, 1957–1963* (Stuttgart: Deutsche Verlags-Anstalt, 1981)

Raddatz, Fritz J., "Tradition und Kommerz," *Der Monat* 18 (September 1966): 13–28

Raddatz, Fritz J., *Unruhestifter: Erinnerungen* (Munich: Propyläen, 2003)

Rahms, Helene, *Die Clique: Journalistenleben in der Nazizeit* (Berne: Scherz, 1999)

Ramthun, Gudrun, *Kulturpolitik in Krefeld nach dem 2. Weltkrieg* (Frankfurt am Main: Peter Lang, 1982)

Rath, Wolfgang, "Romane und Erzählungen der siebziger bis neunziger Jahre," in Horst Albert Glaser, ed., *Deutsche Literatur zwischen 1945 und 1995* (Berne: Paul Haupt, 1997), 309–28

Rathke, Christian, ed., *Die 50er Jahre: Aspekte und Tendenzen: Katalog zur Ausstellung des Kunst- und Museumsvereins Wuppertal, 23.9.–13.11.77* (Wuppertal: Kunst- und Museumsverein Wuppertal, 1977)

Rathkolb, Oliver, *Führertreu und gottbegnadet: Künstlereliten im Dritten Reich* (Vienna: Österreichischer Bundesverlag, 1991)

Rauh, Reinhold, *Edgar Reitz: Film als Heimat* (Munich: Heyne, 1993)

Ray, Gene, "Joseph Beuys and the After-Auschwitz Sublime," in Gene Ray, ed., *Joseph Beuys: Mapping the Legacy* (New York: Distributed Art Publishers, Inc., 2001), 55–74

Reese, Beate, "Kunst im Zeichen wiedergewonnener Freiheit," in Beate Reese, ed., *Befreite Moderne: Kunst in Deutschland, 1945 bis 1949* (Munich: Deutscher Kunstverlag, 2015), 9–33

Reich-Ranicki, Marcel, "Anmerkungen zur Literatur der siebziger Jahre," *Merkur* 33 (1979): 169–79

Reich-Ranicki, Marcel, "Der Fall Gerd Gaiser," *Der Monat* 15 (September 1963): 68–84

Reich-Ranicki, Marcel, *Deutsche Literatur in West und Ost: Prosa seit 1945* (Munich: Piper, 1966)

Reich-Ranicki, Marcel, *Mein Leben* (Munich: DTV, 2003; 1st pub. 1999)

Reichel, Peter, *Vergangenheitsbewältigung in Deutschland: Die Auseinandersetzung mit der NS-Diktatur von 1945 bis heute* (München: C.H. Beck, 2001)

Reichmann, Wolfgang, "Baustelle Stalingrad: Alexander Kluges 'Schlachtbeschreibung'," *Zeitgeschichtliche Forschungen/Studies in Contemporary History* 6 (2009): 470–6

Reid, J. Hamish, *Heinrich Böll: A German for His Time* (Oxford: Berg, 1988)

Reinhardt, Stephan, "Politik und Resignation: Anmerkungen zu Koeppens Romanen," *Text + Kritik* 34 (April 1972): 38–45

Reissinger, Marianne, "Neue Musik in München, 1980–1990," in Martin Thrun, ed., *Neue Musik seit den achtziger Jahren: Eine Dokumentation zum deutschen Musikleben*, vol. 2 (Regensburg: ConBrio Verlagsgesellschaft, 1994), 161–9

Reitz, Edgar, *Liebe zum Kino: Utopien und Gedanken zum Autorenfilm, 1962–1983* (Cologne: KÖLN 78, [1984])

Reitz, Edgar, and Peter Steinbach, *Heimat: Eine deutsche Chronik* (Nördlingen: GRENO, 1985)

Rentschler, Eric, "Homeland and Holocaust," in David E. Wellbery, ed., *A New History of German Literature* (Cambridge, MA: Belknap/Harvard University Press, 2004), 936–42

Rentschler, Eric, "Specularity and Spectacle in Schlöndorff's *Young Törless* (1966)," in Eric Rentschler, ed., *German Film & Literature: Adaptations and Transformations* (New York: Methuen, 1986), 176–92

Rentschler, Eric, "The Use and Abuse of Memory: New German Film and the Discourse of Bitburg," *New German Critique* 36 (Autumn 1985): 67–90

Rentschler, Eric, *West German Film in the Course of Time: Reflections on Twenty Years since Oberhausen* (Bedford Hills, NY: Redgrave, 1984)

Richarz, Monika, "Juden in der Bundesrepublik Deutschland und in der Deutschen Demokratischen Republik seit 1945," in Micha Brumlik, Doron Kiesel, Cilly Kugelmann, and Julius H. Schoeps, eds, *Jüdisches Leben in Deutschland seit 1945* (Frankfurt am Main: Jüdischer Verlag bei Altenäum, 1986), 14–30

Richter, Hans Werner, ed., *Almanach der Gruppe 47, 1947–1962* (Reinbek: Rowohlt, 1962)

Richter, Hans Werner, *Die Geschlagenen* (Munich: Kurt Desch, n.d.)

Riethmüller, Albrecht, "Einige Gedanken bei Gelegenheit von Mauricio Kagels *Ludwig van* (1970)," in Albrecht Riethmüller, ed., *Beethoven im Film: Titan auf Tonspur und Leinwand* (Munich: Richard Boorberg Verlag, 2022), 209–19

Riethmüller, Albrecht, *Lost in Music: Essays zur Perspektivierung von Urteil und Erfahrung* (Stuttgart: Franz Steiner, 2015)

Riethmüller, Albrecht, "Michael im Himmel wie auf Erden," in Otto Kolleritsch, ed., *Oper heute: Formen der Wirklichkeit im zeitgenössischen Musiktheater* (Vienna: Universal Edition, 1985), 117–35

Riethmüller, Albrecht, "Vom jüngeren Umgang mit einer Musikerikone," in Albrecht Riethmüller and Gregor Herzfeld, eds, *Furtwänglers Sendung: Essays zum Ethos des deutschen Kapellmeisters* (Stuttgart: Franz Steiner, 2020): 161–77

Riewoldt, Otto F., "Zum Drama und Theater der siebziger Jahre in der Bundesrepublik Deutschland," in Manfred Durzak, ed., *Deutsche Gegenwartsliteratur: Ausgangspositionen und aktuelle Entwicklungen* (Stuttgart: Philipp Reclam jun., 1981), 137–65

Riha, Karl, "Quergelesen – quergeschnitten: Zur Literatur der 80er – ein Situationsbericht," in Christian W. Thomsen, ed., *Aufbruch in die Neunziger: Ideen, Entwicklungen, Perspektiven der achtziger Jahre* (Cologne: DuMont, 1991), 171–90

Rischbieter, Henning, *Schreiben, Knappwurst, abends Gäste: Erinnerungen* (Springe: zu Klampen, 2009)

Rischbieter, Henning, "Theater," in Wolfgang Benz, ed., *Die Geschichte der Bundesrepublik Deutschland, Band 4: Kultur* (Frankfurt am Main: Fischer Taschenbuch, 1989), 86–130

Ritter, Heinz, "Was treiben die deutschen Dramatiker?" *Der Monat* 13 (September 1961): 63–72

Ritzel, Fred, *Musik für ein Haus: Kompositionsstudie Karlheinz Stockhausen, Internationale Ferienkurse für Neue Musik, Darmstadt 1968* (Mainz: B. Schott's Söhne, 1970)

Roberts, David, "Tendenzwenden: Die sechziger und siebziger Jahre in literaturhistorischer Perspektive," *Deutsche Vierteljahrsschrift für Literaturwissenschaft und Geistesgeschichte* 56 (1982): 290–313

Rogers, Thomas, "Welcome to Germany," *New York Review of Books* (April 29, 2021): 29–31

Röhl, Klaus Rainer, *Fünf Finger sind keine Faust* (Cologne: Kiepenheuer & Witsch, 1975)

Röhl, Klaus Rainer, *Mein langer Marsch durch die Illusionen: Leben mit Hitler, der DKP, den 68ern, der RAF und Ulrike Meinhof* (Vienna: Universitas, 2009)

Ross, Alex, "Infinity Opera: A Sampler of Stockhausen's Massive 'Licht,' in Amsterdam," *New Yorker* (June 24, 2019): 76–7

Ross, Alex, "The Devil's Disciple: A Composer Who Embraced the Third Reich Gets a New Hearing," *New Yorker* (July 21, 1997): 72–7

Ross, Alex, *The Rest is Noise: Listening to the Twentieth Century* (New York: Farrar, Straus and Giroux, 2007)

Ross, Alex, *Wagnerism: Art and Politics in the Shadow of Music* (New York: Farrar, Straus and Giroux, 2020)

Rost, Andreas, "Kinostunden der wahren Empfindung: Herzog, Wenders, Fassbinder und der Neue Deutsche Film," in Michael Schaudig, ed., *Positionen deutscher Filmgeschichte: 100 Jahre Kinematographie: Strukturen, Diskurse, Kontexte* (Munich: diskurs film, 1996), 367–408

Rote Armee Fraktion: Texte ud Materialien zur Geschichte der RAF (Berlin: ID-Verlag, 1997)

Rothfels, Hans, "Zeitgeschichte als Aufgabe," *Vierteljahrshefte für Zeitgeschichte* 1 (1953): 1–8

Rückerl, Adalbert, *Die Strafverfolgung von NS-Verbrechen, 1945–1978: Eine Dokumentation* (Heidelberg: C. F. Müller Juristischer Verlag, 1979)

Ruf, Wolfgang, "Die armen Leute von Kombach und anderswo oder: Gibt es einen Neuen Deutschen Heimatfilm?" *Fernsehen und Film*, no. 4 (April 1971): 14–19

Rühle, Günther, *Theater in unserer Zeit* (Frankfurt am Main: suhrkamp taschenbuch, 1976)

Rühmkorf, Peter, *Tabu I: Tagebücher, 1989–91* (Reinbek: Rowohlt, 1995)

Rühmkorf, Peter, *Tabu II: Tagebücher, 1971–1972* (Reinbek: Rowohlt, 2004)

Ruppel, Karl Heinz, "Bayreuth 1951," *Merkur* 5 (September 1951): 362–4

Rusinek, Bernd-A., "Von der Entdeckung der NS-Vergangenheit zum generellen Faschismusverdacht – akademische Diskurse in der Bundesrepublik der 60er Jahre," in Axel Schildt, Detlef Siegfried, and Karl Christian Lammers, eds, *Dynamische Zeiten: Die 60er Jahre in den beiden deutschen Gesellschaften* (Hamburg: Christians, 2000), 114–47

Rutschky, Michael, *Erfahrungshunger: Ein Essay über die siebziger Jahre* (Cologne: Kiepenheuer & Witsch, 1980)

Ryan, Judith, *The Uncompleted Past: Postwar German Novels and the Third Reich* (Detroit: Wayne State University Press, 1983)

Saldern, Adelheid von, *Kunstnationalismus: Die USA und Deutschland in transkultureller Perspektive, 1900–1945* (Göttingen: Wallstein, 2021)

Salomon, Ernst von, *Der Fragebogen* (Hamburg: Rowohlt, 1951)

Sarkowicz, Hans, and Alf Mentzer, *Literatur in Nazi-Deutschland: Ein biografisches Lexikon: Erweiterte Neuausgabe* (Hamburg: Europa, 2002)

Sass, Herbert, "Sinn und Aufgabe unseres Jahrestreffens 1951," *Junge Musik* 2 (1951): 172–5

Sattler, Dieter, "Subventioniertes Theater?" *Frankfurter Hefte* 5 (1950): 306–10

Sauer, Klaus, "Rundfunk und deutsche Gegenwartsliteratur," in Manfred Durzak, ed., *Deutsche Gegenwartsliteratur: Ausgangspositionen und aktuelle Entwicklungen* (Stuttgart: Philipp Reclam jun., 1981), 444–59

Schacht, Daniel Alexander, *Fluchtpunkt Provinz: Der Neue Heimatfilm zwischen 1968 und 1972* (Münster: MAkS Publikationen, 1991)

Schaenzler, Nicole, *Klaus Mann: Eine Biographie* (Berlin: Aufbau-Taschenbuch, 2001)

Schäfer, Hermann, "Zwischen Germanisierung und Verdrängung – Zur Lage der Arbeitsemigranten in der Bundesrepublik," in Hans-Günter Thien and Hanns Wienold, eds, *Herrschaft, Krise, Überleben: Gesellschaft der Bundesrepublik in den achtziger Jahren* (Münster: Westfälisches Dampfboot, 1986), 25–43

Schäfer, Walter Erich, *Bühne eines Lebens: Erinnerungen* (Stuttgart: Deutsche Verlags-Anstalt, 1975)

Scharberth, Irmgard, *Musiktheater mit Rolf Liebermann. Der Komponist als Intendant. 14 Jahre Hamburgische Staatsoper: Ein Bericht* (Hamburg: Hans Christians, 1975)

Scheffler, Karl, *Kunst ohne Stoff* (Überlingen: Otto Dirkreiter, 1950)

Schelsky, Helmut, *Die skeptische Generation: Eine Soziologie der deutschen Jugend* (Düsseldorf: E. Diederichs, 1963)

Schick, Christa, "Die Internierungslager," in Martin Broszat, Klaus-Dietmar Henke, and Hans Woller, eds, *Von Stalingrad zur Währungsreform: Zur Sozialgeschichte des Umbruchs in Deutschland* (Munich: Oldenbourg, 1988), 301–25

Schildt, Axel, "Der Umgang mit der NS-Vergangenheit in der Öffentlichkeit der Nachkriegszeit," in Wilfried Loth and Bernd A. Rusinek, eds, *Verwandlungspolitik: NS-Eliten in der westdeutschen Nachkriegsgesellschaft* (Frankfurt am Main: Campus, 1998), 19–54

Schildt, Axel, "Massenmedien im Umbruch der fünfziger Jahre," in Jürgen Wilke, ed., *Mediengeschichte der Bundesrepublik Deutschland* (Cologne: Böhlau, 1999), 633–48

Schildt, Axel, "Materieller Wohlstand – pragmatische Politik – kulturelle Umbrüche: Die 60er Jahre in der Bundesrepublik," in Axel Schildt, Detlef Siegfried, Karl

Christian Lammers, eds, *Dynamische Zeiten: Die 60er Jahre in den beiden deutschen Gesellschaften* (Hamburg: Christians, 2000), 21–53

Schildt, Axel, *Medien-Intellektuelle in der Bundesrepublik*, ed. Gabriele Kandzora and Detlef Siegfried (Göttingen: Wallstein, 2020)

Schildt, Axel, "Von der Not der Jugend zur Teenager-Kultur: Aufwachsen in den 50er Jahren," in Axel Schildt and Arnold Sywottek, eds, *Modernisierung im Wiederaufbau: Die westdeutsche Gesellschaft der 50er Jahre* (Bonn: J.H.W. Dietz Nachf., 1993), 335–48

Schmidt, Doris, "Bildende Kunst," in Wolfgang Benz, ed., *Die Geschichte der Bundesrepublik Deutschland, Band 4: Kultur* (Frankfurt am Main: Fischer Taschenbuch, 1989), 243–89

Schmidtke, Michael, "The German New Left and National Socialism," in Philipp Gassert and Alan E. Steinweis, eds, *Coping with the Nazi Past: West German Debates on Nazism and Generational Conflict, 1955–1975* (New York: Berghahn Books, 2007), 176–93

Schjeldahl, Peter, "Painting History: The Dense Layers of Gerhard Richter's Work," *New Yorker* (March 16, 2020): 94-95

Schnebel, Dieter, "Sichtbare Musik," in Ulrich Dibelius, ed., *Musik auf der Flucht vor sich selbst* (Munich: Carl Hanser, 1969), 11–28

Schneider, Peter, *Lenz: Eine Erzählung* (Berlin: Rotbuch Verlag, 1974)

Schneider, Rolf, *Theater in einem besiegten Land: Dramaturgie der deutschen Nachkriegszeit, 1945–1949* (Frankfurt am Main: Ullstein Sachbuch, 1984)

Schnell, Ralf, *Geschichte der deutschsprachigen Literatur seit 1945* (Stuttgart: J.B. Metzler, 1993)

Schnurre, Wolfdietrich, *Die Tat: Ein Fall für Herrn Schmidt: Zwei Kurzgeschichten* (Copenhagen: Grafisk Forlag A/S, 1972)

Schödel, Kathrin, *Literarisches versus politisches Gedächtnis? Martin Walsers Friedenspreisrede und sein Roman Ein springender Brunnen* (Würzburg: Königshausen & Neumann, 2010)

Scholtysek, Joachim, "Conservative Intellectuals and the Debate over National Socialism and the Holocaust in the 1960s," in Philipp Gassert and Alan E. Steinweis, eds, *Coping with the Nazi Past: West German Debates on Nazism and Generational Conflict, 1955–1975* (New York: Berghahn Books, 2007), 238–57

Schölzel, Stephan, *Die Pressepolitik in der französischen Besatzungszone, 1945–1949* (Mainz: v. Hase & Koehler, 1986)

Schonauer, Franz, "Die Prosaliteratur der Bundesrepublik," in Jost Hermand, ed., *Literatur nach 1945 I: Politische und regionale Aspekte* (Wiesbaden: Akademische Verlagsgesellschaft Athenaion, 1979), 195–272

Schönbach, Peter, *Reaktionen auf die antisemitische Welle im Winter 1959/1960* (Frankfurt am Main: Europäische Verlagsanstalt, 1961)

Schöning, Klaus, "Konturen der Akustischen Kunst," in Heinz Ludwig Arnold, ed., *Bestandsaufnahme Gegenwartsliteratur: Bundesrepublik Deutschland, Deutsche Demokratische Republik, Österreich, Schweiz* (Munich: edition text + kritik, 1988), 67–86

Schörken, Rolf, *Die Niederlage als Generationserfahrung: Jugendliche nach dem Zusammenbruch der NS-Herrschaft* (Weinheim: Juventa, 2004)

Schornstheimer, Michael, *Die leuchtenden Augen der Frontsolaten: Nationalsozialismus und Krieg in den Illustriertenromanen der fünfziger Jahre* (Berlin: Metropol, 1995)

Schorske, Carl E., *Fin-de-Siècle Vienna: Politics and Culture* (New York: Vintage Books, 1981)

Schrecker, Ellen, *The Lost Promise: American Universities in the 1960s* (Chicago: University of Chicago Press, 2021)

Schreiber, Hermann, *Henri Nannen: Drei Leben*, 3rd edn (Munich: C. Bertelsmann, 1999)

Schreier, Christoph, "Krise oder Agonie der Avantgarde? Thesen zur Malerei und Plastik der späten 80er Jahre," in Christian W. Thomsen, ed., *Aufbruch in die Neunziger: Ideen, Entwicklungen, Perspektiven der achtziger Jahre* (Cologne: DuMont, 1991), 280–302

Schröder, Dieter, *Augstein* (Munich: Siedler, 2004)

Schroers, Rolf, "'Gruppe 47' und die deutsche Nachkriegsliteratur," *Merkur* 19 (1965): 448–62

Schroeter, Werner, *Tage im Dämmer, Nächte im Rausch: Autobiographie* (Berlin: Aufbau, 2011)

Schuckert, Christine, "Der bundesdeutsche Buchmarkt 1986/87: Aktuelle Entwicklungen und Probleme," *Media Perspektiven* 10 (1987): 642–9

Schuh, Oscar Fritz, "Rückblick und Ausblick," *Der Monat* 5 (September 1953): 640–7

Schultheiss, Gisela, and Ernst-Friedrich Schultheiss, *Vom Stadttheater zum Opernhaus: 500 Jahre Musiktheater in Nürnberg* (Nuremberg: A. Hofmann, 1990)

Schultz, Uwe, ed., *Fünfzehn Autoren suchen sich selbst: Modell und Provokation* (Munich: List, 1967)

Schultze, Friedrich, ed., *Theater im Gespräch: Ein Forum der Dramaturgie* (Munich: Albert Langen Georg Müller, 1963)

Schwab-Felisch, Hans, "Einleitung," in Hans Schwab-Felisch, ed., *Der Ruf: Eine deutsche Nachkriegszeitschrift* (München: DTV, 1962), 10–18

Schwartz, Michael, "Homosexuelle im modernen Deutschland: Eine Langzeitperspektive auf historische Transformationen," *Vierteljahrshefte für Zeitgeschichte* 69 (2021): 377–414

Schwarzer, Alice, *Alice im Männerland: Eine Zwischenbilanz* (Cologne: Kiepenheuer & Witsch, 2002)

Schweitzer, Carl-Christoph, Detlev Karsten, Robert Spencer, R. Taylor Cole, Donald Kommers, and Anthony Nicholls, eds, *Politics and Government in the Federal Republic of Germany: Basic Documents* (Leamington Spa: Berg, 1984)

Scott, Anthony Oliver, "The Defiant Strangeness of Werner Herzog," *The Atlantic* (June 2022): 87–9

Scribner, Chastity, *After the Red Army Faction: Gender, Culture and Militancy* (New York: Columbia University Press, 2015)

Sedlmayr, Hans, *Verlust der Mitte: Die bildende Kunst des 19. und 20. Jahrhunderts als Symptom und Symbol der Zeit* (Salzburg: Otto Müller Verlag, 1948)

Seeliger, Rolf, ed., *Braune Universität: Deutsche Hochschullehrer gestern und heute*, 6 vols. (Munich: Selbstverlag Rolf Seeliger, 1964–8)

Seifert, Jürgen, "Ulrike Meinhof," in Wolfgang Kraushaar, ed., *Die RAF und der linke Terrorismus*, vol. 1 (Hamburg: Hamburger Edition, 2006), 350–71

Seifert, Wolfgang, *Günter Wand: So und nicht anders: Gedanken und Erinnerungen* (Hamburg: Hoffmann und Campe, 1998)

Seufert, Michael, *Der Skandal um die Hitler-Tagebücher* (Frankfurt am Main: S. Fischer, 2008)

Siblewski, Klaus, ed., *Martin Walser Auskunft: 22 Gespräche aus 28 Jahren* (Frankfurt am Main: suhrkamp taschenbuch, 1991)

Sieburg, Friedrich, *Die Lust am Untergang: Selbstgespräche auf Bundesebene* (Hamburg: Rowohlt, 1954)

Siedler, Wolf Jobst, *Wir waren noch einmal davongekommen: Erinnerungen* (Munich: Siedler, 2004)

Siering, Friedemann, "Zeitung für Deutschland: Die Gründergeneration der 'Frankfurter Allgemeinen'," in Lutz Hachmeister and Friedemann Siering, eds, *Die Herren Journalisten: Die Elite der deutschen Presse nach 1945* (Munich: C.H. Beck, 2002), 35–86

Söderbaum, Kristina, *Nichts bleibt immer so: Rückblenden auf ein Leben vor und hinter der Kamera*, 3rd ed. (Bayreuth: Hestia, 1984)

Soell, Hartmut, "Helmut Schmidt: Zwischen reaktivem and konzeptionellem Handeln," in Konrad H. Jarausch, ed., *Das Ende der Zuversicht? Die siebziger Jahre als Geschichte* (Göttingen: Vandenhoeck & Ruprecht, 2008), 279–95

Sölle, Dorothee, "Heinrich Böll und die Eskalation der Gewalt," *Merkur* 28 (1974): 885–7

Speier, Sammy, "Von der Pubertät zum Erwachsenendasein: Bericht einer Bewusstwerdung," in Micha Brumlik, Doron Kiesel, Cilly Kugelmann, and Julius H. Schoeps, eds, *Jüdisches Leben in Deutschland seit 1945* (Frankfurt am Main: Jüdischer Verlag bei Altenäum, 1986), 182–93

Spender, Stephen, *European Witness* (London: Hamish Hamilton, 1946)

Sperr, Martin, *Der Räuber Mathias Kneissl: Textbuch zum Fernsehfilm* (Munich: Piper, 1970)

Spotts, Frederic, *Bayreuth: A History of the Wagner Festival* (New Haven and London: Yale University Press, 1994)

Stachelhaus, Heiner, *Joseph Beuys*, 2nd edn (Düsseldorf: Claassen, 1988)

Stange, Alfred, *Über die Einsamkeit der modernen Kunst* (Bonn: Ludwig Rohrscheid, 1951)

Statistisches Jahrbuch für die Bundesrepublik Deutschland 1966 (Stuttgart: W. Kohlhammer, 1966)

Staud, Toralf, "Die ostdeutschen Immigranten," in Tanja Busse and Tobias Dürr, eds, *Das neue Deutschland: Die Zukunft als Chance* (Berlin: Aufbau, 2003), 266–81

Steiert, Thomas, "Zur Musik- und Theaterpolitik in Stuttgart während der amerikanischen Besatzungszeit," in Gabriele Clemens, ed., *Kulturpolitik im besetzten Deutschland, 1945–1949* (Stuttgart: Franz Steiner, 1994), 55–68

Steinbacher, Sybille, *Als der Sex nach Deutschland kam: Der Kampf um Sittlichkeit und Anstand in der frühen Bundesrepublik* (Munich: Siedler, 2011)

Steinkamp, Maike, "Eine wahrhaft deutsche Schöpfung: Der Kampf um Emil Noldes 'Abendmahl' vom Kaiserreich zur frühen DDR," in Uwe Fleckner, ed., *Das verfemte Meisterwerk: Schicksalswege moderner Kunst im "Dritten Reich"* (Berlin: Akademie-Verlag, 2009), 283–306

Stenger, Michael, "Neue Wege durch Aktive Musik," in Martin Thrun, ed., *Neue Musik seit den achtziger Jahren: Eine Dokumentation zum deutschen Musikleben*, vol. 2 (Regensburg: ConBrio Verlagsgesellschaft, 1994), 131–7

Stephan, Rudolf, "Kranichstein: Vom Anfang und über einige Voraussetzungen," in Rudolf Stephan, Lothar Knessl, Otto Tomek, Klaus Trapp, and Christopher Fox, eds, *Von Kranichstein zur Gegenwart: 50 Jahre Darmstädter Ferienkurse zur Neuen Musik* (Stuttgart: DACO, 1996), 21–7

Stern, Carola, *Doppelleben: Eine Autobiographie*, 7th edn (Cologne: Kiepenheuer & Witsch, 2001)

Stern, Frank, "Breaking the 'Cordon Sanitaire' of Memory: The Jewish Encounter with German Society," in Alvin H. Rosenfeld, ed., *Thinking about the Holocaust: After Half a Century* (Bloomington: Indiana University Press, 1997), 213–32

Stern, Frank, *Im Anfang war Auschwitz: Antisemitismus und Philosemitismus im deutschen Nachkrieg* (Gerlingen: Bleicher, 1991)

Stern, Hellmut, *Saitensprünge* (Berlin: Transit, 1991)

Stockhausen, Karlheinz, *Texte zur Musik: Band 6: Interpretation* (Cologne: DuMont Buchverlag, n.d.)

Strack, Manfred, "Amerikanische Kulturbeziehungen zu (West-)Deutschland, 1945–1955," *Zeitschrift für Kulturaustausch* 37 (1987): 283–300

Strassner, Alexander, "Die dritte Generation der RAF," in Wolfgang Kraushaar, ed., *Die RAF und der linke Terrorismus*, vol. 1 (Hamburg: Hamburger Edition, 2006), 489–510

Streit, Christian, *Keine Kameraden: Die Wehrmacht und die sowjetischen Kriegsgefangenen, 1941–1945* (Stuttgart: Deutsche Verlags-Anstalt, 1978)

Struck, Karin, *Klassenliebe: Roman*, 9th edn (Frankfurt am Main: Suhrkamp, 1974; 1st edn 1973)

Struck-Schloen, Michael, "Hauptstadt-Ruhm mit Rissen: Neue Musik in Köln, 1980–1990," in Martin Thrun, ed., *Neue Musik seit den achtziger Jahren: Eine Dokumentation zum deutschen Musikleben*, vol. 2 (Regensburg: ConBrio Verlagsgesellschaft, 1994), 155–60

Stückrath, Fritz, "Der Überfall der Ogalalla auf die Jugend," *Westermanns Pädagogische Beiträge* 4 (April 1952): 220–2

Studdert, Will, *The Jazz War: Radio, Nazism and the Struggle for the Airwaves in World War II* (London: I.B. Tauris, 1918)

Stürmer, Michael, *Das ruhelose Reich: Deutschland, 1866–1918* (Berlin: Severin und Siedler, 1983)

Suhr, Herbert, *Schreib das auf, Herbert! 40 Jahre beim Stern* (Hamburg: Rasch und Röhring, 1996)

Syberberg, Hans-Jürgen, *Die freudlose Gesellschaft: Notizen aus dem letzten Jahr* (Munich: C. Hanser, 1980)

Tannenbaum, Mya, *Conversations with Stockhausen* (Oxford: Clarendon Press, 1987)

Taruskin, Richard, *Cursed Questions: On Music and Its Social Practices* (Berkeley: University of California Press, 2020)

Taruskin, Richard, *Music in the Late Twentieth Century* (Oxford: Oxford University Press, 2010)

Tauber, Fritz, "Heimatfilm: Systematising a Phenomenon," in Claudia Dillmann and Olaf Möller, eds, *Beloved and Rejected: Cinema in the Young Federal Republic of Germany from 1949 to 1963* (Frankfurt am Main: Deutsches Filminstitut, 2016), 103–7

Tauber, Kurt P., *Beyond Eagle and Swastika: German Nationalism Since 1945*, vol. 1 (Middletown: Wesleyan University Press, 1967)

Teuflische Jahre: Das Beste aus Pardon (Frankfurt am Main: Bärmeier & Nikel, 1966)

Teuflische Jahre: Das Beste aus Pardon (Frankfurt am Main: Bärmeier & Nikel, 1970)

Thacker, Toby, *Music after Hitler, 1945–1955* (Aldershot: Ashgate, 2007)

Thaler, Lotte, "Komponisten die Treue halten: Neue Musik in Frankfurt," in Martin Thrun, ed., *Neue Musik seit den achtziger Jahren: Eine Dokumentation zum deutschen Musikleben*, vol. 2 (Regensburg: ConBrio Verlagsgesellschaft, 1994), 139–46

Thamer, Hans-Ulrich, "Die NS-Vergangenheit im politischen Diskurs der 68er-Bewegung," *Westfälische Forschungen* 48 (1998): 39–53

Thomas, Karin, *Zweimal deutsche Kunst nach 1945: 40 Jahre Nähe und Ferne* (Cologne: DuMont Buchverlag, 1985)

Thomas, Michael Wolf, "Tendenzwende: 'Der STERN'," in Michael Wolf Thomas, ed., *Porträts der deutschen Presse: Politik und Profit* (Berlin: Verlag Volker Spiess, 1980), 163–82

Thomas, Werner, *Das Rad der Fortuna: Ausgewählte Aufsätze zu Werk und Wirkung Carl Orffs* (Mainz: Schott, 1990)

Thomsen, Christian Braad, *Fassbinder: The Life and Work of a Provocative Genius* (London: Faber and Faber, 1997)

Timm, Uwe, *Heisser Sommer: Roman* (Munich: Bertelsmann, 1974)

Tisdall, Caroline, *Joseph Beuys: Coyote* (Munich: Schirmer/Mosel, 2008)

Töteberg, Michael, ed., *Rainer Werner Fassbinder: Die Anarchie der Phantasie: Gespräche und Interviews* (Frankfurt am Main: Fischer Taschenbuch, 1986)

Trnka, Jamie H., *Revolutionary Subjects: German Literatures and the Limits of Aesthetic Solidarity with Latin America* (Berlin: De Gruyter, 2015)

Trommler, Frank, "Creating a Cocoon of Public Acquiescence: The Author–Reader Relationship in Postwar German Literature," in Hanna Schissler, ed., *The Miracle Years: A Cultural History of West Germany, 1949–1968* (Princeton: Princeton University Press, 2001), 301–25

Trommler, Frank, "Der zögernde Nachwuchs: Entwicklungsprobleme der Nachkriegsliteratur in Ost und West," in Thomas Koebner, ed., *Tendenzen der deutschen Literatur seit 1945* (Stuttgart: Alfred Kröner, 1971), 1–116

Trommler, Frank, "Realismus in der Prosa," in Thomas Koebner, ed., *Tendenzen der deutschen Literatur seit 1945* (Stuttgart: Alfred Kröner, 1971), 179–275

Twittenhoff, Wilhelm, "Bilanz von Münster," *Junge Musik* 8 (1957): 197–9

Twittenhoff, Wilhelm, "Festliche Tage – Junge Musik Passau 1954: Ein Rückblick," *Junge Musik* 5 (1954): 148–52

Twittenhoff, Wilhelm, "Rückblick," *Junge Musik* 3 (1952): 140–1

Twittenhoff, Wilhelm, "Wanne-Eickel – Passau – Münster: (Zur Kritik der 'Festlichen Tage')," *Junge Musik* 8 (1957): 131–5

Vaget, Hans Rudolf, "Entnazifizierung? Udo Bermbach untersucht den Neu-Bayreuther Gründungsmythos," *Musik & Ästhetik* 25, no. 1 (2021): 87–96

Vaget, Hans Rudolf, "Knappertsbusch in Bayreuth," *Wagner Journal* 13, no. 3 (November 2019): 3–19

Vaget, Hans Rudolf, *Thomas Mann, der Amerikaner: Leben und Werk im amerikanischen Exil, 1938–1952* (Frankfurt am Main: S. Fischer, 2011)

Vaget, Hans Rudolf, *"Wehvolles Erbe": Richard Wagner in Deutschland: Hitler, Knappertsbusch, Mann* (Frankfurt am Main: S. Fischer, 2017)

Valentin, Thomas, *Die Unberatenen: Roman* (Oldenburg: Igel Verlag, 1999; 1st pr. 1963)

Van der Grinten, Franz Joseph, "Joseph Beuys: Die frühen Jahre," in Heiner Bastian, ed., *Joseph Beuys: Skulpturen und Objekte* (Munich: Schirmer/Mosel, 1988), 14–17

Vesper, Bernward, *Die Reise: Romanessay: Ausgabe letzter Hand*, ed. Jörg Schröder and Klaus Behnken, 16th edn (Jossa: März bei Zweitausendeins, 1979)

Vesper, Bernward, and Gudrun Ensslin, eds, *Gegen den Tod: Stimmen deutscher Schriftsteller gegen die Atombombe* (Stuttgart-Cannstadt: studio neue literatur gudrun ensslin, [1964])

Vetter, Rose, *Kulturpolitik in Düsseldorf nach dem Zweiten Weltkrieg* (diss. phil. Universität Düsseldorf, 1984)

Viertel, Salka, *The Kindness of Strangers* (New York: Holt, Rinehart, and Winston, 1969)

Viett, Inge, *Nie war ich furchtloser: Autobiographie*, 4th edn (Hamburg: Edition Nautilus, 2007; 1st edn 1997)

Vietta, Egon, *Katastrophe oder Wende des deutschen Theaters* (Düsseldorf: Droste, 1955)

Vischer, Theodora, "Zm Kunstbegriff von Joseph Beuys," in Heiner Bastian, ed., *Joseph Beuys: Skulpturen und Objekte* (Munich: Schirmer/Mosel, 1988), 37–44

Völker, Klaus, *Fritz Kortner, Schauspieler und Regisseur* (Berlin: Edition Hentrich, [1987])

Vormweg, Heinrich, "Deutsche Literatur 1945–1960: Keine Stunde Null," in Manfred Durzak, ed., *Deutsche Gegenwartsliteratur: Ausgangspositionen und aktuelle Entwicklungen* (Stuttgart: Philipp Reclam jun., 1981), 14–31

Vormweg, Heinrich, *Der andere Deutsche: Heinrich Böll: Eine Biographie* (Cologne: Kiepenheuer & Witsch, 2000)

Vormweg, Heinrich, *Günter Grass* (Reinbek: Rowohlt Taschenbuch Verlag, 2002)

Vowinckel, Andreas, "Ist Kunst das, was bedeutende Künstler machen? Fragen zur Geschichte und Tätigkeit der documenta-Foundation 1964–1977 sowie zum Selbstverständnis der documenta," in Harald Kimpel, ed., *Die documenta-Foundation: Ein Modell der Kulturfinanzierung* (Marburg: Jonas Verlag für Kunst und Literatur GmbH, 2002), 7–34

Wachter, Clemens, *Kultur in Nürnberg, 1945–1950: Kulturpolitik, kulturelles Leben und Bild der Stadt zwischen dem Ende der NS-Diktatur und der Prosperität der fünfziger Jahre* (Nuremberg: Stadtarchiv Nürnberg, 1999)

Wagner, Nike, *Wagner Theater* (Frankfurt am Main: Insel, 1998)

Wagner, Wolfgang, *Lebensakte: Autobiographie* (Munich: Albrecht Knaus, 1994)

Wagstaff, Sheena, and Benjamin H.D. Buchloh, eds, *Gerhard Richter: Malerei* (Cologne: Walther König, 2020)

Waidson, Herbert Morgan, *The Modern German Novel, 1945–1965*, 2nd edn (London: Oxford University Press, 1971)

Waite, Robert G. L., *Vanguard of Nazism: The Free Corps Movement in Postwar Germany, 1918–1923* (New York: W.W. Norton, 1969)

Wallraff, Günter, *Der Aufmacher: Der Mann, der bei Bild Hans Esser war* (Cologne: Kiepenheuer & Witsch, 1977)

Wallraff, Günter, *Ganz unten: Mit einer Dokumentation der Folgen* (Cologne: Kiepenheuer & Witsch, 1988)

Walser, Martin, *Ansichten, Einsichten: Aufsätze zur Zeitgeschichte* (=*Werke in zwölf Bänden*, vol. 11) (Frankfurt am Main: Suhrkamp, 1997)

Walser, Martin, *Brandung: Roman* (Frankfurt am Main: Suhrkamp, 1985)

Walser, Martin, *Brief an Lord Liszt: Roman* (Frankfurt am Main: Suhrkamp, 1982)

Walser, Martin, *Das Einhorn: Roman* (Frankfurt am Main: Fischer Bücherei, 1970; 1st edn 1966)

Walser, Martin, *Der schwarze Schwan* (Frankfurt am Main: Suhrkamp, 1965; 1st edn 1964)

Walser, Martin, *Der Sturz: Roman* (Frankfurt am Main: Suhrkamp, 1973)

Walser, Martin, *Die Verteidigung der Kindheit: Roman* (Frankfurt am Main: Suhrkamp, 1991)

Walser, Martin, *Dorle und Wolf: Eine Novelle* (Frankfurt am Main: Suhrkamp, 1987)

Walser, Martin, *Ehen in Philippsburg: Roman* (Reinbek: Rowohlt Taschenbuch, 1963; 1st edn 1957)

Walser, Martin, *Eiche und Angora: Eine deutsche Chronik* (Frankfurt am Main: Suhrkamp, 1962)

Walser, Martin, *Ein fliehendes Pferd: Novelle* (Frankfurt am Main: Suhrkamp, 1978)

Walser, Martin, *Ein Flugzeug über dem Haus und andere Geschichten* (Frankfurt am Main: Suhrkamp, 1955)

Walser, Martin, *Ein springender Brunnen: Roman* (Frankfurt am Main, Suhrkamp, 1998)

Walser, Martin, *Finks Krieg: Roman* (Frankfurt am Main: Suhrkamp, 1995)

Walser, Martin, *Halbzeit: Roman* (Frankfurt am Main: Suhrkamp, 1960)

Walser, Martin, *Jagd: Roman* (Frankfurt am Main: Suhrkamp, 1988)

Walser, Martin, *Jenseits der Liebe: Roman* (Frankfurt am Main, Suhrkamp, 1976)

Walser, Martin, *Leben und Schreiben: Tagebücher, 1951–1962* (Reinbek: Rowohlt, 2005)

Walser, Martin, *Leben und Schreiben: Tagebücher, 1963–1973* (Reinbek: Rowohlt, 2007)

Walser, Martin, *Leben und Schreiben: Tagebücher, 1974–1978* (Reinbek: Rowohlt, 2010)

Walser, Martin, *Schreiben und Leben: Tagebücher, 1979–1981* (Reinbek: Rowohlt, 2014)

Walser, Martin, *Tod eines Kritikers: Roman* (Frankfurt am Main: Suhrkamp, 2002)

Walser, Martin, *Überlebensgross Herr Krott : Requiem für einen Unsterblichen*, 2nd edn (Frankfurt am Main: Suhrkamp, 1969; 1st edn 1964)

Walser, Martin, and Jakob Augstein, *Das Leben wortwörtlich: Ein Gespräch* (Reinbek: Rowohlt, 2017)

Walter, Hans-Albert, "DER SPIEGEL Oder: Politische Aufklärung im Massenzeitalter," *Frankfurter Hefte* 12 (1962): 797–805

Wand, James, "German History Backwards," *New German Critique* 21 (Autumn 1980): 154–80

Weber, Hans Jürgen, ed., *Die bleierne Zeit: Ein Film von Margarethe von Trotta* (Frankfurt am Main: Fischer Taschenbuch, 1981)

Weber, Richard, "Neue Dramatiker in der Bundesrepublik," in Horst Albert Glaser, ed., *Deutsche Literatur zwischen 1945 und 1995* (Berne: Paul Haupt, 1997), 407–24

Wedekind, Gregor, "Abstraktion und Abendland: Die Erfindung der *documenta* als Antwort auf 'unsere deutsche Lage'," in Nikola Doll, Ruth Heftrig, Olaf Peters, and Ulrich Rehm, eds, *Kunstgeschichte nach 1945: Kontinuität und Neubeginn in Deutschland* (Cologne: Böhlau, 2006), 165–81

Wehler, Hans-Ulrich, *Entsorgung der deutschen Vergangenheit? Ein polemischer Essay zum "Historikerstreit"* (Munich: C.H. Beck, 1988)

Wehler, Hans-Ulrich, "Nationalsozialismus und Historiker," in Winfried Schulze and Otto Gerhard Oexle, eds, *Deutsche Historiker im Nationalsozialismus* (Frankfurt am Main: Fischer Taschenbuch, 1999), 306–39

Weisbrod, Bernd, "Das Moratorium der Mandarine: Zur Selbstentnazifizierung der Wissenschaften in der Nachkriegszeit," in Hartmut Lehmann and Otto Gerhard Oexle, eds, *Nationalsozialismus in den Kulturwissenschaften*, vol. 2 (Göttingen: Vandenhoeck & Ruprecht, 2004), 259–79

Weiss, Matthias, "Journalisten: Worte als Taten," in Norbert Frei, ed., *Karrieren im Zwielicht: Hitlers Eliten nach 1945* (Frankfurt am Main: Campus, 2001), 241–301

Weiss, Peter, *Abschied von den Eltern: Erzählung* (Frankfurt am Main: Suhrkamp, 1964)

Weiss, Peter, *Die Ermittlung: Oratorium in 11 Gesängen* (Reinbek: Rowohlt, 1970; 1st pub. 1965)

Weiss, Peter, *Fluchtpunkt: Roman* (Frankfurt am Main: Suhrkamp, 1967)

Weiss, Rainer, ed., *Ich habe ein Wunschpotential: Gespräche mit Martin Walser* (Frankfurt am Main: suhrkamp taschenbuch, 1998)

Wellershoff, Dieter, *Der lange Weg zum Anfang: Zeitgeschichte, Lebensgeschichte, Literatur* (Cologne: Kiepenheuer & Witsch, 2007)

Wellershoff, Dieter, *Die Arbeit des Lebens: Autobiographische Texte* (Cologne: Kiepenheuer & Witsch, 1985)

Welzer, Harald, Sabine Moller, and Karoline Tschuggnall, *"Opa war kein Nazi": Nationalsozialismus und Holocaust im Familiengedächtnis*, 5th edn (Frankfurt am Main: Fischer Taschenbuch, 2005)

Wenders, Wim, *Emotion Pictures: Essays und Filmkritik, 1968–1984* (Frankfurt am Main: Verlag der Autoren, 1986)

Weniger, Heinz, "Warum denn immer noch Trümmerliteratur?" *Die Literatur* (August 15, 1952): 7

Wenzel, Eike, *Gedächtnisraum Film: Die Arbeit an der deutschen Geschichte in Filmen seit den 60er Jahren* (Stuttgart: J.B. Metzler, 2000)

Werckmeister, Otto Karl, *Zitadellenkultur: Die Schöne Kunst des Untergangs in der Kultur der achtziger Jahre* (Munich: Carl Hanser, 1989)

Westermann, Bärbel, *Nationale Identität im Spielfilm der fünfziger Jahre* (Frankfurt am Main: Peter Lang, 1990)

Wettberg, Gabriela, *Das Amerika-Bild und seine negativen Konstanten in der deutschen Nachkriegsliteratur* (Heidelberg: Carl Winter Universitätsverlag, 1987)

Wetzel, Juliane, "An Uneasy Existence: Jewish Survivors in Germany after 1945," in Hanna Schissler, ed., *The Miracle Years: A Cultural History of West Germany, 1949–1968* (Princeton: Princeton University Press, 2001), 131–44

Wetzel, Juliane, *Jüdisches Leben in München, 1945–1951: Durchgangsstation oder Wiederaufbau?* (Munich: Stadtarchiv München, 1987)

Wetzel, Juliane, "'Mir szeinen doh': München und Umgebung als Zuflucht von Überlebenden des Holocaust, 1945–1948," in Martin Broszat, Klaus-Dietmar Henke, and Hans Woller, eds, *Von Stalingrad zur Währungsreform: Zur Sozialgeschichte des Umbruchs in Deutschland* (Munich: Oldenbourg, 1988), 327–64

Weyer, Rolf-Dieter, "Fünfzig Jahre Jazz in Nordrhein-Westfalen," in Heike Stumpf and Matthias Pannes, eds, *Zeitklänge: Zur Neuen Musik in Nordrhein-Westfalen, 1946–1996* (Cologne: Gisela Schewe, [1996]), 95–103

Wheatcroft, Geoffrey, "Europe's Most Terrible Years," *New York Review of Books* (December 17, 2020): 72–3

Widlok, Peter, "Hörfunkanbieter und Hörfunkprogramme in Deutschland," in Otfried Jarren, ed., *Politische Kommunikation in Hörfunk und Fernsehen* (Opladen: Leske + Budrich, 1994), 135–48

Widmer, Urs, *1945 oder die "Neue Sprache": Studien zur Prosa der "Jungen Generation"* (Düsseldorf: Schwann, 1966)

Wieland, Karin, "Andreas Baader," in Wolfgang Kraushaar, ed., *Die RAF und der linke Terrorismus*, vol. 1 (Hamburg: Hamburger Edition, 2006), 332–49

Wiese, Klaus M., "'Junge Musik' – eine Dritte Kraft? Gespräch in der Akademie Loccum: Was blieb von der 'Singbewegung'?" *Kontakte* (February 1, 1958): 14–16

Wilcox, Evelyn, "Negative Identity: Mixed German Jewish Descent as a Factor in the Reception of Theodor Adorno," *New German Critique* 81 (Autumn 2000): 169–87

Wildt, Michael, *Am Beginn der "Konsumgesellschaft": Mangelerfahrung, Lebenshaltung, Wohlstandshoffnung in Westdeutschland in den fünfziger Jahren*, 2nd edn (Hamburg: Ergebnisse Verlag, 1995)

Wilke, Christiane, *Das Theater der grossen Erwartungen: Wiederaufbau des Theaters, 1945–1948, am Beispiel des Bayerischen Staatstheaters* (Frankfurt am Main: Peter Lang, 1989)

Wilke, Jürgen, "Massenmedien und Vergangenheitsbewältigung," in Jürgen Wilke, ed., *Mediengeschichte der Bundesrepublik Deutschland* (Cologne: Böhlau, 1999), 649–71

Willenbacher, Barbara, "Zerrüttung und Bewährung der Nachkriegsfamilie," in Martin Broszat, Klaus-Dietmar Henke, Hans Woller, eds, *Von Stalingrad zur Währungsreform: Zur Sozialgeschichte des Umbruchs in Deutschland* (Munich: Oldenbourg, 1988), 595–618

Willett, Ralph, *The Americanization of Germany, 1945–1949* (London: Routledge, 1989)

Willy Brandt und Günter Grass: Der Briefwechsel, ed. Martin Kölbel (Göttingen: Steidl, 2013)

Willis, F. Roy, *The French in Germany, 1945–1949* (Stanford: Stanford University Press, 1962)

Willrich, Wolfgang, *Säuberung des Kunsttempels: Eine kunstpolitische Kampfschrift zur Gesundung deutscher Kunst im Geiste nordischer Art* (Munich: J.F. Lehmanns, 1937)

Wilms, Wilfried, "Rubble without a Cause: The Air War in Postwar Film," in Wilfried Wilms and William Rasch, eds, *German Postwar Films: Life and Love in the Ruins* (Houndmills: Palgrave Macmillan, 2008), 27–44

Wilson, Peter Niklas, "Die Null im Norden: Neue Musik in Hamburg, 1980–1990: Ein Jahrzehnt der Sterbehilfe," in Martin Thrun, ed., *Neue Musik seit den achtziger Jahren: Eine Dokumentation zum deutschen Musikleben*, vol. 2 (Regensburg: ConBrio Verlagsgesellschaft, 1994), 147–54

Winkler, Heinrich August, "Auf ewig in Hitlers Schatten? Zum Streit über das Geschichtsbild der Deutschen," in *"Historikerstreit": Die Dokumentation der Kontroverse über die Einzigartigkeit der nationalsozialistischen Judenvernichtung*, 5th edn (Munich: R. Piper, 1987), 256–63

Winkler, Heinrich August, *Der lange Weg nach Westen: Deutsche Geschichte vom "Dritten Reich" bis zur Wiedervereinigung*, 3rd edn (Munich, C.H. Beck, 2001)

Winkler, Willi, *Das braune Netz: Wie die Bundesrepublik von früheren Nazis zum Erfolg geführt wurde* (Berlin: Rowohlt, 2019)

Wirsching, Andreas, *Abschied vom Provisorium, 1982–1990* (Stuttgart: Deutsche Verlags-Anstalt, 2006)

Wistrich, Robert, *Who's Who in Nazi Germany* (New York: Macmillan, 1982)

Wittstock, Uwe, *Marcel Reich-Ranicki: Die Biographie* (Munich: Piper, 2020)

Wollenhaupt-Schmidt, Ulrike, *documenta 1955: Eine Ausstellung im Spannungsfeld der Auseinandersetzungen um die Kunst der Avantgarde, 1945–1960* (Frankfurt am Main, Peter Lang, 1994)

Wolschke, Martin, "Musikfest im Alltag," *Junge Musik* 3 (1952): 94–6

Wood, Michael, "Probably Quite Coincidental," *London Review of Books* (January 6, 2022): 29–30

Wunschik, Tobias, "Aufstieg und Zerfall: Die Zweite Generation der RAF," in Wolfgang Kraushaar, ed., *Die RAF und der linke Terrorismus*, vol. 1 (Hamburg: Hamburger Edition, 2006), 472–88

Würfel, Stefan Bodo, *Das deutsche Hörspiel* (Stuttgart: J.B. Metzlerische Verlagsbuchhandlung, 1978)

Wüstenberg, Jenny, *Civil Society and Memory in Postwar Germany* (New York: Cambridge University Press, 2018)

Wydra, Thilo, *Volker Schlöndorff und seine Filme* (Munich: Wilhelm Heyne, 1998)

Wyss, Beat, "Willi Baumeister und die Kunsttheorie der Nachkriegszeit," in Gerda Breuer, ed., *Die Zähmung der Avantgarde: Zur Rezeption der Moderne in den 50er Jahren* (Basel: Stroemfeld Verlag, 1997), 55–71

Yeazell, Ruth Bernard, "Painting Herself," *New York Review of Books* (May 12, 2022): 4–8

Zadek, Peter, *Die heissen Jahre, 1970–1980* (Cologne: Kiepenheuer & Witsch, 2006)

Zadek, Peter, *Die Wanderjahre, 1980–2009*, ed. Elisabeth Plessen (Cologne: Kiepenheuer & Witsch, 2010)

Zadek, Peter, *My Way: Eine Autobiographie, 1926–1969* (Cologne: Kiepenheuer & Witsch, 1998)

Zahn, Peter von, *Stimme der ersten Stunde: Einnerungen, 1913–1951* (Stuttgart: Deutsche Verlags-Anstalt, 1991)

Zahn, Robert von, "Freie Initiativen und Ensembles für Neue Musik in Nordrhein-Westfalen seit 1946," in Heike Stumpf and Matthias Pannes, eds, *Zeitklänge: Zur Neuen Musik in Nordrhein-Westfalen, 1946–1996* (Cologne: Gisela Schewe, [1996]), 105–14

Zahn, Robert von, *Jazz in Köln seit 1945: Konzertkultur und Kellerkunst* (Cologne: Emons Verlag, 1997)

Zielinski, Siegfried, and Gloria Custance, "History as Entertainment and Provocation: The TV Series 'Holocaust' in West Germany," *New German Critique* 19 (January 1980): 81–96

Ziesel, Kurt, *Das verlorene Gewissen: Hinter den Kulissen der Presse, der Literatur und ihren Machtträgern von heute*, 6th edn (Munich: J.F. Lehmanns, 1960)

Zimmermann, Gustav, "Filmtheater kein Forum Academicum," *Film-Echo* 1, no. 7 (July 1947): 49

Zinnecker, Jürgen, *Jugendkultur, 1940–1985* (Opladen: Leske + Budrich, 1987)

Zipes, Jack, "The Vicissitudes of Being Jewish in West Germany," in Anson Rabinbach and Jack Zipes, eds, *Germans and Jews since the Holocaust: The Changing Situation in West Germany* (New York: Holmes & Meier, 1986), 27–49

Zitelmann, Rainer, *Wohin treibt unsere Republik? Wie Deutschland links und grün wurde*, 2nd edn (Berlin: Ullstein, 2021)

Zwanzig Jahre Musik im Westdeutschen Rundfunk: Eine Dokumentation aus der Hauptabteilung Musik, 1948–1968 (Cologne: Westdeutscher Rundfunk, [1969])

Index